BURYING the LEAD

The Media and the JFK Assassination

MAL HYMAN

Published by:
Trine Day LLC
PO Box 577
Walterville, OR 97489
1-800-556-2012
www.TrineDay.com
trineday@icloud.com

Library of Congress Control Number: 2018962608

Hyman, Mal
 — 1st ed.
p. cm.
Includes references
Epub (ISBN-13) 978-1-63424-188-5
Mobi (ISBN-13) 978-1-63424-189-2
Print (ISBN-13) 978-1-63424-187-8
1. Kennedy, John F. -- (John Fitzgerald), -- 1917-1963 -- In mass media. 2. Kennedy, John F. -- (John Fitzgerald), -- 1917-1963 -- Assassination. 3. Conspiracies -- United States -- History -- 20th century. 4. United States -- History -- 1961-1969. 5. HISTORY -- United States -- 20th Century. 6. Kennedy, John F. -- (John Fitzgerald), -- 1917-1963. 7. Mass media I. Hyman, Mal. II. Title

First Edition
10 9 8 7 6 5 4 3 2 1

Printed in the USA

Distribution to the Trade by:
Independent Publishers Group (IPG)
814 North Franklin Street
Chicago, Illinois 60610
312.337.0747
www.ipgbook.com

Publisher's Foreword

Congress shall make no law respecting an establishment of religion, or prohibiting the free exercise thereof; or abridging the freedom of speech, or of the press; or the right of the people peaceably to assemble, and to petition the Government for a redress of grievances.
　　　　　　　　　　– Constitution of United States of America, 1789

The events of recent weeks may have helped to illuminate that challenge for some; but the dimensions of its threat have loomed large on the horizon for many years. Whatever our hopes may be for the future – for reducing this threat or living with it – there is no escaping either the gravity or the totality of its challenge to our survival and to our security – a challenge that confronts us in unaccustomed ways in every sphere of human activity

This deadly challenge imposes upon our society two requirements of direct concern both to the press and to the President – two requirements that may seem almost contradictory in tone, but which must be reconciled and fulfilled if we are to meet this national peril. I refer, first, to the need for a far greater public information; and, second, to the need for far greater official secrecy.

The very word "secrecy" is repugnant in a free and open society; and we are as a people inherently and historically opposed to secret societies, to secret oaths and to secret proceedings. We decided long ago that the dangers of excessive and unwarranted concealment of pertinent facts far outweighed the dangers which are cited to justify it.
　　　　　　　　　　– JFK, Address before the American Newspaper
　　　　　　　　　　　　　　Publishers Association, April 1961

Well, here we are, over half-a-century after the fact, and we are still writing and fretting about the nation-numbing murder of our 35th president, John F. Kennedy.

Mal Hyman has done our country a great service with his book, *Burying the Lead: The Media and the JFK Assassination*. Professor Hyman spent over twenty years gathering materials that show how our vaunted "free" press was complicit in the cover-up and subsequent coup d'état. They blessed the "junta" by spreading the Warren Commission's lies and led the charge against citizens that questioned the stilted findings.

I was in the ninth grade and had recently turned fourteen when President Kennedy was killed. Our class named itself the "Fun-lovin' Frosh," and was proud of it's partying and dancing prowesses. We had grown-up in the world of our grandfatherly President Eisenhower and now were traveling into President Kennedy's "New Frontier." He was charismatic with a blossoming family. We were going to the moon! It was a great time to be young. The future appeared boundless ... then *it* happened.

Then *it* happened again and again. Our lives changed: war, division, drugs and despair. Where was our country going?

Our Founders in their wisdom gave us a tool to help with our grand experiment of freedom and liberty: a free press. A fourth estate to act as watchdog alongside the three branches of government: legislative, executive and judicial. A role that is important to a functioning republic, allowing for political advocacy, the ability to frame political issues, and hopefully informing the public with honest reporting so that citizens may uphold their civic responsibilities with integrity.

Sadly, during one of our darkest times, America was very ill-served by its media, leaving us to twist in the winds of uncertain facts and fancies.

Only by understanding where we have been, can we get to where we are going. My hope is that by publishing Professor Hyman's book and others, we can help bridge the divide that separates us from our more perfect union. But it will take more than books, it will take actions. Please inform your friends, relations and acquaintances, for much needs to be done – for our country and for our children.

As President Kennedy so eloquently stated:

> And so, my fellow Americans: ask not what your country can do for you — ask what you can do for your country. My fellow citizens of the world: ask not what America will do for you, but what together we can do for the freedom of man.

Onward to the Utmosts of Futures

Peace,
Kris Millegan
Publisher
TrineDay
January 24, 2019

This book is dedicated to my parents Nick and Ginger Hyman.

When the people lead, the leaders sometimes follow--

I have sworn on the altar of God, eternal hostility against every form of tyranny over the mind of man."

– Thomas Jefferson

Political truth can be the biggest damnedest lie ever, but if motivated toward a pragmatic political goal, preferably for reasons of national interest, and stated with total belief and fervor, it becomes true.

– Harry Truman, *Esquire* 8/71)

There comes a time when silence is betrayal.

– Martin Luther King Jr., 4/4/67

CONTENTS

INTRODUCTION

President John Kennedy declared at a press conference on NBC in December of 1962 that the press is "an invaluable arm of the presidency, as a check on what is going on in the administration… so I would say that Mr. Khrushchev operating in a totalitarian system, which has many of the advantages of moving in secret…that there is a terrific disadvantage of not having the abrasive quality of the press applied to you daily… even though you never like it, and even though we disapprove, there isn't any doubt that we could not do the job at all in a free society without a very, very active press." Contrast this with President Donald Trump declaring that "the media is the enemy" of the people, and that news critical of him or his administration is "fake news" from the "lying media; that "doesn't love America."

President Kennedy's call to clarify the power of the press to protect our security was generally betrayed by the mainstream media after his assassination. We will explore the Cold War context, the media ties to intelligence agencies, some strategies and tactics of "fake news" (propaganda) the evolution of the media, the role of the public and the alternative media as well as the impact of this case on our democracy.

Washington Post investigative reporter Carl Bernstein of Watergate fame lamented,

> The failures of the press have contributed immensely to a talk show nation in which public discourse is reduced to ranting and raving … For, next to race, the story of contemporary America media is the great uncovered story in America today. We need to start asking the same fundamental questions about the press that we do about other powerful institutions. … For the reality is that the media are probably the most powerful of all institutions today; and they are squandering their power and ignoring their obligation … (*The New Republic* 6/8/92)

Few Americans had the political background in 1963 to analyze the assassination of President Kennedy and its implications. Not many scholars or journalists accused the CIA of overthrowing foreign governments and manipulating foreign elections, unions, the media and church movements. Fewer still realized the extensive CIA role in psychological warfare, assassination teams, alliances with the mafia, cooperation with corporations, the autonomous nature of the CIA's foreign and domestic policies, the extensive co-opting of American academics, or the scale and scope of the CIA's domestic operations (Chapters 2, 5, 9, and 15). Only after the 9/11 tragedy did we learn of "Operation Northwoods", approved by the Joint Chiefs of Staff in 1962, which proposed launching a secret and bloody war of terrorism against America, which could plausibly be seen as originating in Cuba, in order to develop public support for a war they intended to launch against Cuba. Although FBI Director J. Edgar Hoover was generally viewed as an oppressive, racist anti-communist who often used sexual blackmail, few knew that Hoover regularly vacationed at mafia-owned hotels and was possibly vulnerable to sexual blackmail.

Polls show that public confidence in government institutions has plummeted since 1963. Consistently a large majority of Americans think that there has been an official cover-up and a conspiracy in the JFK assassination, despite decades of reluctance by much of the mass media to critique the Warren Report. The assassination of the president and the mass media coverage of the event serve as a Rosetta Stone, revealing some of the mysteries of post World War II American power.

From 1940 through the 1960s most of the funding for research in social psychology and communication studies came from the Defense Department with the primary intent of developing weapons of psychological warfare, which become a major strategy during the Cold War. Few could imagine that these new tactics would be used domestically, especially after the assassination of a president.

By 1963 CIA media assets were extensive and could be quickly employed to protect national security or misperceptions of it. Cooperation between the mass media and elements of government endured well beyond any initial crisis after the assassination, and appears to be an integrated facet of our National Security state. Political sociologist C. Wright Mills warned of the predominance of a military-industrial complex supported by an elite corporate-owned media in 1956, a critique made famous by Dwight Eisenhower in his farewell address. Sociologists G. William Domhoff and Ralph Miliband clarified elite-media-government connections by exploring schooling, social clubs, businesses, and government concerns. This overview of the coverage of the mass and alternative media will incorporate these perspectives. A chronological approach affords a sense of the unfolding fragmentary, confusing, sometimes misleading and often contradictory coverage, which confronted the public. Had the media functioned as a vigorous fourth estate on this case our country would be very different today. I will explore to what extent the media have been witting and unwitting accomplices.

After the assassination, cold war media elite cooperation mixed with selected disinformation, memories of McCarthyism, as well as concerted Justice Department and FBI efforts "to convince the public that Oswald was the lone assassin" The complexity of the case, the collective trauma, the caution regarding national security, political naiveté, and the disinformation from some government agencies and elements of the press, confounded most of the American media for a while. The mass media meekly acquiesced to their exclusion from the Warren Commission, yet provided vigilant support for the Warren Report, even prior to the release of the hearings and evidence on which it was based. Though some intrepid reporters raised questions regarding the Warren Report, the mass media chose not to explore most of these leads. After a few years, an uncoordinated citizens' inquest along with a handful of alternative and mass media outlets, had revealed enough mistakes and ambiguity in the Warren Report that much of the mass media slowly responded. However CBS, NBC, *Time, Newsweek, New York Times, L.A. Times, Saturday Evening Post, Life,* AP and UPI, generally remained resistant to the rising chorus of critics.

In late 1966, amid widespread race riots and anti-war protests, the D.A. from New Orleans, Jim Garrison, opened an investigation of the assassination. The CIA and FBI generated a psychological war against Garrison using their media assets to protect themselves, as well as the waning legitimacy of government.

The media rush to New Orleans saw an outspoken but out-manned D.A., who received no governmental cooperation, whose team was infiltrated by "volunteers" from the defense team, who endured media attacks by covert intelligence-media assets, and who had his case weakened by the strange deaths of witnesses before they could testify. Garrison knew much more than he could prove. His concern and frustration sometimes caused him to misperceive the media responses to his public speculation. He needed a P.R. team, as well as government cooperation.

The media vitality of Watergate was short-lived, and coverage of the assassination remained limited and erratic, even after the House Select

Committee on Assassinations was formed. Although their final report in 1979 concluded that President Kennedy was "probably assassinated due to a conspiracy", most of the mass media denigrated the conclusions, and ignored the new leads. The sphere of legitimate controversy had been briefly widened, but the gatekeepers seemed to resist the questioning of political legitimacy as threatening national security. Most of the alternative media seemingly shifted to movement building. A decade later the Justice Department quietly concluded in March 1988 that "no further investigation appears to be warranted…unless new information…became available…"

By 1991 the political crime of the century, in the world's most powerful empire, was drifting from memory into history. The mass and alternative media, as well as government and academe, had become co-opted, confused and weary. Filmmaker Oliver Stone stunned the country and catalyzed a reinvestigation with his highly controversial movie, *JFK*. The public response pushed Congress to create the President John F. Kennedy Assassination Records Collection Act of 1992, which led to the declassification of more than five million pages of documents. Yet a number of agencies have not fully complied with the law. Prior to October 2017, the legal date for full release of all of the files, the CIA did not declassify about 50,000 pages of documents. The National Declassification Center, without reasoning or justification, took the position that the JFK records will not be part of the declassification until further CIA evaluation in 2017. However, most of the classified files were not declassified even in 2017.

The National Archives 2, in College Park Maryland, which houses the JFK collection, is a modern, handsome, glass and steel structure with a friendly and efficient staff. Yet the access to the collection is often convoluted, and HSCA counsel notes on the CIA are filed with FBI Administrative files. The computer database is incomplete. The research file numbers sometimes don't correlate with storage boxes. Some documents are removed, some misfiled, some unclear from government recopying, some are just listed as miscellaneous. Others have restricted access, or a withdrawn notice, or delayed release which could only be released by filing a Freedom of Information Act release request. Some declassified files are being reclassified in the Interagency Reclassification Project. The CIA segregated file, released through the Assassination Records Review Board (ARRB) and HSCA, contains deletions, redactions and inscrutable acronyms. So with the assassination finally ready for re-examination, most of the mass media as well as the alternative media did not critically pursue the case even during their 50 year retrospectives. How long can they bury this lead before they cripple democracy?

In the wake of the Warren Commission Report, thousands of citizen patriots substantially broadened, and deepened the investigation into the assassination of President Kennedy. These researchers like colonial Committees of Correspondence in the wake of British oppression, frankly debated justice and treason. They embodied the Jeffersonian notion that "the price of liberty is eternal vigilance." I am indebted in this media analysis to Vincent Salandria, Jerry Policoff, Mark Lane, Bud Fensterwald, Jim Lesar, Jim Garrison, Roger Feinman, Jim DiEugenio, Dick Russell, Jerry Rose, David Starks, Rex Bradford, Cyril Wecht, John Judge, Mae Brussell, Lisa Pease, Jefferson Morley, John Newman, Andrew Kreig, Walt Brown, Jerel Rosati, and Bill Davy.

Ironically, in relenting to the public release of the twenty-six volumes of the Warren Commission Hearings and Exhibits, former CIA Director Allen Dulles noted, "Don't believe people read in this country. There will be a few professors that will read the record … the public will read very little". Fortunately he was wrong. In part because of the media's role in the cover-up, discovering the full truth regarding the assassination is probably not possible, yet by continuing the investigation and by exploring the failure of our institutions we can strengthen democracy.

Although Kennedy was still a Cold Warrior in 1963, he was moderating many aspects of his foreign policy; he was speaking of and formulating policy to withdraw combat troops from Vietnam, he publicly proposed a joint space shot with the Soviets, he was exploring a complete ban on nuclear testing, and using the Pope as an intermediary, he was also exploring diplomacy with Cuba while building the Alliance for Progress. Kennedy was attempting to control the CIA by his unprecedented firing of the Director of the CIA, Allen Dulles, and two of Dulles' top aides, tasking oversight to his brother Robert, and then developing National Security Action Memorandums 55 and 57, which limited war power to the Joint Chiefs. Kennedy was the first president to influence the conditions on World Bank loans and to promote nation-to-nation soft loans. Domestically he was significantly limiting the powers of the FBI, and was the first president in decades to effectively prosecute the Mafia. He was also pushing to end the lucrative 27.5% oil depletion allowance. He pressed to close 52 domestic military bases, 25 overseas bases, and significantly cut military spending. After his death President Johnson rapidly reversed or modified all of these policies.

Eight official investigations and numerous researchers have developed oceans of information leading to widely divergent conclusions. The military destroyed many of their files on the assassination. The DOD, the CIA, the FBI and the Secret Service have still not declassified all of their files of the assassination. Some autopsy information has been misinterpreted, omitted, burned, forged and lost. Some of the major witnesses died mysterious deaths; others were intimidated or never questioned. In 1975, the Senate Intelligence Subcommittee chaired by Senators Gary Hart and Richard Schweiker examined the roles of the FBI and CIA in their inquiry into the assassination and concluded "The FBI and CIA did all the wrong things if they wanted to find out who killed John Kennedy." Schweiker declared that the Warren Commission "fed pabulum to the American public." The Chief Counsel for the House Select Committee on Assassinations, Robert Blakey, declared years later that "My position about the agency [CIA] is they didn't cooperate with us, they made an effort to not cooperate with us, and therefore everything that they told us was a lie.... We were had." (AARC Conference, 2014)

The Chair of the HSCA, Congressman Richardson Preyer, told me in 1989 that he was deeply frustrated that the military had destroyed many of their files, and that his committee needed more cooperation, time, and money to do their job.

Less than a month before he was assassinated, President Kennedy declared in a speech at Amherst College: "The men who create power make an indispensable contribution to a nation's greatness, but the men who question power make a contribution just as indispensable, especially when they are disinterested, for they determine whether we use power or power uses us."

1

Crisis Coverage:
Confusion, Cooperation & Cover-ups

Popular government, without popular means of acquiring information, is but a prologue to a tragedy, a farce, or both.

– James Madison

Public sentiment is everything.... He who molds public opinion is greater than the law.

– Abraham Lincoln

I look with commiseration over the body of my fellow citizens who, reading newspapers, live and die in the belief that they have known something of what has been passing in the world in their time.

– Harry Truman

NBC reporter Robert MacNeil was the only reporter in a press bus headed toward Dealey Plaza who scrambled out to explore immediately after the assassination.

On both sides of the roadway people were throwing themselves down and covering their children with their bodies. The air was filled with screaming, a high unison soprano wail. I saw several people running up the grassy hill beside the road.... I ran after them.... It did not enter my head at that moment that Kennedy was hit.... I was thinking what an incredible story. How do I cover this? Where should I be...? Actually I think I was so stunned by the improbability of what happened that I was emotionally anaesthetized. Part of my brain went to sleep in disbelief. My thoughts came in slow motion...[1]

Some tearful veteran reporters spoke of the eeriness amid the chaos. They struggled between traumatic emotions and the responsibilities of reporting during a crisis. What constitutes evidence? When does a report have enough support to justify passing it along? Most journalists in the presidential entourage were not accustomed to reporting murder cases, and most were in press buses headed to the Dallas Trade Mart – a distance from Dealey Plaza. Curiously, a press pool station wagon that was assigned to follow JFK's Secret Service car was somehow shifted further back to seventh in the motorcade. This prevented the media photographers from witnessing the assassination or getting it on film.[2]

Then, more so than now, journalistic norms conferred trust to official sources. For a while cooperation rather than competition existed between news organizations, particularly between the local and out of town press. Most news outlets and reporters relied on official sources soon after the President was shot rather than clarifying contradictions or developing new leads. White House reporters of this era perceived their role as political reporters, not gumshoes.[3] The lingering legacy of the McCarthy era raised concerns regarding even the misperception of unpatriotic reporting in both the mainstream and alternative media. At first, some reporters viewed Oswald as the sole assassin and a lone nut, while some touted his Cuban and Marxist connections.

NBC news correspondent David Brinkley lamented the journalistic pressures: "There is seldom any time to think anymore, and today there was none … what happened has just been too much, too ugly, and too fast."[4]

Commercial programming on the networks quickly halted following the early reports of the president being shot, as the most massive and concentrated coverage in television history got underway. NBC-TV devoted more than 71 hours of airtime, NBC radio 68 hours, CBS-TV 55 hours; CBS radio 58 hours, ABC-TV 60 hours, ABC radio 80 hours and Mutual 64 hours. Elmer Lower, President of ABC News, observed that this was "the toughest job I have ever had in 30 years of journalism." Lower mobilized 500 ABC employees but noted "with no opportunity to plan, and with news breaking so fast, we could not always get in touch with people who had to make decisions..." Ernest Leiser, General Manager and Vice-President of CBS News noted, "Never did we do so much programming for so intensive a period of time, without enough people."[5]

America's first reports came from television news departments much smaller and more Spartan than today. Just two months earlier CBS and NBC had extended their evening news time slot to one half hour, up from fifteen minutes. Reporters often had greater access than today but their equipment was limited. Television cameras needed to warm up and were linked to electrical systems. TV news relied mostly on film, not live broadcasts, and most people got breaking news from radio. Print and broadcast newsrooms were still dependent on the wire service Teletype for breaking news. By the end of 1963, a Roper survey showed that Americans relied as much on television news as on the printed press. Many journalists think that this assassination coverage changed America to a TV nation.

The State Department quickly briefed certain news outlets on the national security implications of Oswald's past. The FBI edited some very early reports from the *Dallas Times Herald* and possibly some reports from the Associated Press. The combined influence of the AP, UPI, *New York Times*, Time-Life, *Los Angeles Times, New York Herald Tribune* and television networks the first days after the assassination contributed to the convergence of coverage. The alternative press was constrained by limited resources as well as clear memories of the McCarthy-era investigations of the press.

Some of the coverage seemed spun from the outset. The rapid news release of a biography and picture of Oswald wearing a tie (he was arrested wearing a t-shirt) occurred while he was still being questioned by the Dallas Police Department. This could indicate that someone was waiting to feed information on Oswald to the media. Years later, journalist Seth Kantor of the *Dallas Morning News* and the Scripps-Howard representative in the President's press corps, checked why the Warren Commission and the FBI had classified for 12 years the telephone calls he had made during the afternoon of the assassination. He found that FBI Document 1133, about his calls, "might reveal the identity of confidential sources of information." One of his calls was to the Scripps-Howard news service bureau in Washington, where the managing editor told Kantor to call Hal Hendrix, a Scripps-Howard journalist, for background information on Oswald. Kantor called Hendrix at his Coral Gables home and was given extensive information. According to CIA officials, Hendrix, the Pulitzer Prize winner from the *Miami News*, was one of the most valuable CIA assets in the 1960s. Hendrix's source regarding the Russian missiles in Cuba, which led to his Pulitzer Prize, was CIA agent Ted Shackley, Chief of JM/WAVE in Miami.[6]

Years later, in the CIA-engineered coup in Chile (1973), Hendrix was positively identified as a CIA operative working under journalistic cover. Former CIA agent Colonel John Stockwell viewed the Warren Commission's decision to classify these phone calls as proof of an intelligence connection with Hendrix and an early involvement in the cover-up.[7] According to CIA agent Frank Terpil, CIA Chief of Western Hemisphere

Division, David Phillips (a propaganda expert), had been friendly with Hendrix in the early 1960s. Phillips has been referred to by two CIA operatives as running Guy Banister's operation in New Orleans in 1963 which included anti-Castro Cubans and Lee Harvey Oswald. Remarkably, on 9/24/63, Hendrix described and justified the coup that ousted the pro-Kennedy President Juan Bosch of the Dominican Republic – the day before he was actually overthrown. The CIA station chief in the Dominican Republic was David Phillips.

The CIA considered Hendrix "extremely helpful to the Agency in providing information about individuals in Miami's Cuban exile community."[7] In 1976 Hendrix pleaded guilty to withholding information from a Senate Committee investigating links between multinational corporations and the CIA. The Senate Subcommittee on Multinational Corporations also received information that Hendrix had used "black propaganda" (lies) during the late 1950s and early 1960s.[8]

Although Oswald had not yet been charged with killing a police officer, Lt. Col. Robert Jones of the 112th Military Intelligence Group, Fort Sam Houston, sent a file on Oswald to FBI's Gordon Shanklin, Special Agent in Charge (SAIC) Dallas, sometime between 2:00 and 2:30 PM, less than an hour after Oswald's arrest.[9] The FBI also had some files on Oswald, though the Dallas police did not. An FBI document from the San Antonio office indicates that they received information about Oswald from the 112th Military Group at 3:15 CST. By 3:23 the television networks were using Oswald's name, and by 3:26 they mentioned Oswald's application for Russian citizenship.

Curiously, the plane carrying a number of cabinet members, returning to Washington from Hawaii a few hours after the assassination, heard government reports about Oswald and his past which implied that Oswald was the assassin before he was charged in Dallas. The information was coming from the White House Situation Room. Portions of those conversations are also apparently missing from the tape collection at the LBJ Library.[10] This, along with the background spinning by Hal Hendrix, raises questions regarding intelligence manipulation in the reporting immediately after the assassination.

Although many people in Dealey Plaza reported hearing four, five or six shots, the early national reporting stated that three shots were fired. NBC at 1:21 CST ran WBAP's report by Tom Whalen with witness Jean Hill, who stood about 15 feet from the Presidential limousine at the time of the fatal shot. Hill said, "... just as the President looked up and these three shots rang out and he grabbed his chest ... after that more shots rang out and the car sped away." Whalen asked, "Where did the shots come from?" Hill stated," the shots come from the hill – it was just east of the underpass. We were on the south side..." Whalen, "Could you see anyone?" Hill said, I thought I saw this man running (up there on the hill). Hill changed her story somewhat in an NBC interview at 3:16, when she said that two shots rang out and he grabbed his chest ... Jackie said, "my God, he's shot. And there was an interval and then three or four more shots rang out..." Later that afternoon ABC's Bill Lord interviewed Jean Hill and Mary Moorman, her companion at the time of the assassination. Moorman recalled 'three or four shots close together ... and then more shots were fired." Hill repeated her version of two shots at first, followed by three or four more.

Initial reports from both UPI reporter Merriman Smith, and AP reporter Jack Bell, from the press pool car in the motorcade, stated that three shots had been heard. Smith had grabbed the portable phone in his media pool car, and fought off other correspondents to be the first to report. He stalled on the phone by giving four takes, in order to keep Jack Bell from reporting to AP, until Bell grabbed the phone. Smith thought he heard the sounds of an automatic weapon. About six minutes later, Don Gardiner broke into ABC programming and announced, using UPI wording, that "in Dallas Texas, three shots were fired at President Kennedy's motorcade. The first reports say that the President was seriously wounded." In Robert MacNeil's first report to NBC radio he surmised three shots, though he wrote of only hearing two distinctly. "People screamed and lay down on the grass as three shots rang out. Police chased an unknown gunman up a grassy hill. It is not known if the shots were directed at the president."[11] Pierce Allman, Program manager at Dallas WFAA-TV and Radio, reported that there were three shots. They were very distinct. "Later on, in trying to recreate the time sequence, my timing on it was six and a half seconds."[12] Bob Clark, ABC news reporter in the press pool car with Merriman Smith and Jack Bell, also reported "three shots were fired'. These early versions also can be partly attributed to the reliance on the Dallas Police reports as well as "groupthink" among the reporters based in Dallas.

Remarkably, when Oswald was arrested in the Texas Theater, somehow more than a dozen Dallas policemen were accompanied by a bevy of reporters. Critics have long contended that factions of the media were unwittingly influenced to create an illusion of Oswald's guilt from the outset.

Dallas KLIF Radio read their first bulletin alert at 12:39 PM CST. "Three shots reportedly were fired at the motorcade of President Kennedy today near the downtown section…" While their early report could have been in good faith, KLIF was owned by Jack Ruby's good friend Gordon McLendon, a Dallas broadcast millionaire. McLendon, a former Office of Naval Intelligence (ONI) officer had invested with oil magnate Clint Murchison. Years later, McLendon worked with CIA officer David Phillips. Ruby called McLendon's unlisted phone number later that day.[13]

Dallas ABC television affiliate WFAA news director Jay Watson broke into programming at 12:45 PM. "…you'll excuse me if I am out of breath. A bulletin from the United Press in Dallas: president Kennedy and Governor Connally have been cut down by assassins' bullets in Downtown Dallas," ABC radio network at 12:46 PM reported three shots were fired at President Kennedy's motorcade today in downtown Dallas…. We are going to stand by for more details…" The first Associated Press dispatch stated that "the shots apparently came from a grassy knoll in the area." This location soon shifted to the Texas School Book Depository.

About an hour after the assassination CBS anchor Walter Cronkite reported that, "regarding the probable assassin, the sheriff's office have taken into police custody a twenty-five-year-old man." A number of journalists huddled in groups outside Parkland Hospital, and many listened to wire service reports on the radio, further generating a convergence of perspectives.[14]

Perhaps it was a still-stunned Robert MacNeil who stated in a lengthy live report to NBC an hour and seven minutes after the president was shot, "that he left from the press bus to go to the building Texas School Book Depository (TSBD) from which the shots reportedly came." MacNeil though has subsequently both written and stated that he first ran up the grassy knoll area up to the top of the picket fence before running to the TSBD. The witnesses MacNeil interviewed for his NBC report included two citizens and a policeman, who claimed that shots came from the second or fourth floor of the TSBD.

When NBC anchor Frank McGee asked MacNeil if it would be possible to hit the president in the right temple from that location (the TSBD) MacNeil replied: "Well … um I believe that if the assailant was using a high power rifle with a telescopic sight, and the one policeman reported it was a high power rifle, I don't know about a telescopic sight, then I assume that it could be." Although a shot from the grassy knoll, the location where MacNeil had initially run, would have been a more likely location for a shot hitting the right temple, this possibility was not mentioned.

An hour and fifteen minutes after the president was shot, an impromptu press conference at Parkland Hospital, held by Acting Press Secretary Malcolm Kilduff, confirmed that the president "died of a gunshot wound in the brain" and he pointed to the right portion of his forehead. In an atmosphere of bedlam at the subsequent medical briefing, surgeon Malcolm Perry was asked if it were possible that one bullet could have struck the president from the front. Perry said yes. *Time* reporter Hugh Sidney curiously cried out, "Doctor, do you realize what you are doing? You're confusing us."[15] Did Hugh Sidey realize the implications of Dr. Perry's statement? By the next morning many Americans read stories of a rifleman who had fired from the top of the underpass.

The emotional impact of the assassination on the media was daunting. Bill Rivers, managing editor of the *Dallas Morning News* described his city room an hour after the announcement of Kennedy's death, just a frozen look of futility on every face, and then, back to work as silently as possible, grimly, swiftly, effectively."[16]

Some reporters tried to examine the hole in the windshield of the Presidential limousine and they were shoved away by the Secret Service. Richard Dudman, a reporter for the *St. Louis Post-Dispatch* later wrote, "A few of us noticed the hole in the windshield when the limousine was standing at the emergency entrance after the President had been carried inside. I could not approach close enough to see which side was the cup-shaped spot that indicates a bullet had pierced the glass from the opposite side "[17]

Rumors flew in the chaos like the "fog of war." By 2:18 PM, AP reported incorrectly "Vice President Johnson had been wounded slightly." At 2:28, UPI quoted Senator Ralph Yarborough as saying that he saw the President's lips moving "at a normal rate of speed while the presidential limousine was racing to Parkland hospital." By 3:50 PM, CBS reporter Charles Collingswood reported, "We still don't know who the assassin was ... They refer to him as the man in a brown shirt.... He shot and killed a police officer before he was subdued." A CBS columnist on KRLD stated " we are told that the fatal wound inflicted on the president of the United States entered at the base of the throat and came out at the base of the neck on the back side." Dan Rather reported that "The police immediately ringed the Texas School Book Depository. It is believed that the assassin was in the building on the 4th or 5th floor ... witnesses believed 3 or 4 shots were fired from there." Footage of the "prime suspect" Oswald, had already been shown, and Oswald's name was used on the air in another two hours. Some early reports raised questions regarding shots from the grassy knoll area.

Photographers William Allen (*Dallas Times Herald*), George Smith (*Fort Worth Star-Telegram*), and Jack Beers (*Dallas Morning News*) all took a series of pictures of Sergeant D.V. Harkness arresting three men from a railroad car in the railroad yard behind the picket fence. Harkness turned the men (so-called "tramps") over to policemen Martin Wine and Billy Bass, who walked them to the Sheriff's office. Remarkably, there is no record that these men were booked – and the pictures were never shown to the Warren Commission.

The first reports of a suspect in the Oak Cliff area were given by WFAA-TV newsman Bert Shipp, who hurriedly noted that "the police may have the assassin" at about the same time as a "policeman may have been shot in the theater." A trenchant WFAA-TV background segment featured President Eisenhower's press secretary who asserted that the assassination must have been a conspiracy due to poor presidential security arrangements. He recounted that when Ike visited Tehran "every single window was guarded" on the parade route. This observation seemingly evaporated in the pandemonium.

By 3 PM CBS President Frank Stanton announced, "In respect for the feelings of a shocked nation, the CBS Television Network and CBS Radio Network will carry no commercial announcements and no entertainment programs until after the president's funeral."

Rapid UPI and AP reports, which ran in "EXTRA" editions of the Friday 11/22 *L.A. Times*, already referred to an assassin, rather than possibly more than one. The AP report, which ran after the president was pronounced dead, already appeared to set the outline for the Warren Report. "President John F. Kennedy ... was shot to death Friday by a hidden assassin armed with a high-powered rifle."

According to Peter Noyes, a CBS news producer, "Our State Department, immediately after Oswald was captured and identified, contacted the major news services, TV networks etc., requesting them to play down the possibility that Oswald was or is a communist."[18] It remains unclear who conceived this crisis admonition, what was said, and how widely this was disseminated. Professor and Author Peter Dale Scott views the lone nut scenario as a "phase 2" story, to cover the "phase 1" story regarding Oswald's apparent communist ties. Otherwise the public would demand revenge for a "communist plot," and such a demand could lead to world war.[19]

An early version of a "phase 1 story" may have come from CIA asset/reporter Hal Hendrix who was able to publish a Scripps-Howard story linking Oswald to the Fair Play for Cuba Committee, and thus ostensibly part of a pro-Castro communist conspiracy. The varying stories of Oswald with Communist ties or Oswald as a "lone nut" (phase 1 & 2) might also indicate competing factions within government promoting different agendas. Perhaps "phase 1" supporters, including many in the CIA wanted a national response against Cuba. We will explore this possibility later.

Files from the Dallas Police Department show that FBI Agent James Hosty was asserting that Oswald, the communist, had killed President Kennedy – just hours after the assassination. He was sharing this "information" with the police and reporters in the Dallas Police Department. Remarkably, years later Hosty declared that he was ordered by Bill Sullivan, the head of FBI Counterintelligence and liaison to the National Security Council, not to cooperate further with the investigation. This order came at 4:05 PM.

The evening edition of the *Dallas Times Herald* ran a piece "Candid Snapshot: Picture of Death" featuring reporter James Featherstone's interviews with witnesses Jean Hill and Mary Moorman. "They glanced up to see a man run up the hill across the street from them, the grassy knoll, and another (near the motorcade) pepper bullets at the running figure." The next day The *Dallas Times Herald* shifted perspective regarding the location of the shots to the Texas School Book Depository (TSBD).

By the evening, journalists were descending on Dallas and increasingly pressuring Dallas officials to bring Oswald to the press. Ike Pappas, WNEW Radio, recalls:

> The agreement was that we would ask no questions… [When] they put him on the platform, and were all screaming [questions]… People yelled, "did you shoot the President?" He said, "That's what I'm accused of. I want to see a lawyer" … He disappears and everyone is running for telephones to file their stories … I'm dying for a phone to file … suddenly this guy comes up to me … he looked like a vice cop. He said, "I'm not a detective. My name is Jack Ruby …" I told him I need a telephone. He walks over and interrupts Henry Wade, the district attorney and says, "There's a reporter here from New York and he needs a telephone and wants to do an interview with you." Wade says take him to my office.[20]

Journalists in the early 1960s were accustomed to getting their information from official sources, and they reported, rather than challenged, the Dallas D.A.'s statements. Decades later, Bill Moyers, then one of President Johnson's top advisors, told the *Village Voice* that "when it came to this [reporting on the assassination], the working press was a lobster in a trap.... Back then what government said was the news ... the official view of reality was the agenda for the Washington press corps...[21] Moyers was right, but this alone cannot account for lack of investigative coverage of the early contradictions within the official reports. As the FBI and Dallas Police reports coalesced, mass media reporting rapidly shifted to support the guilt of a lone gunman.

At first there was considerable contention over the murder weapon and its caliber. Initially the AP identified it as a .30-.30 rifle, but this soon changed to a .25 caliber, and then by 11/23 to a .50 caliber Enfield. UPI referred to it as a "German-made" rifle, "a 7.65 Mauser" and noted that the police reported that no fingerprints were found on the rifle. The ABC affiliate in Dallas, Station WFAA-TV, initially reported it was a "high powered Army or Japanese rifle of .25 calibers fired from the second floor window." Later in the afternoon the rifle was referred to as "An Argentine-made Mauser." According to WFAA-TV's Bob Clark, 1:00 AM, 11/23/63 the murder weapon was an "Argentine rifle" Further, "the word was either there were no prints on the gun, or they (Dallas police) would not care to comment." NBC initially reported the rifle as a British .305. The *N.Y. World-Telegram & Sun* reported the rifle as a German Mauser 7.65 as did a UPI dispatch. As late as 11/24 The *N.Y. Post* was still referring to the rifle as a 7.65 Mauser.

Somehow by the morning of the 24th, the FBI said it "discovered" that Oswald purchased an Italian 6.5 mm. rifle. At that point most of the mass media accepted the Dallas Police reports of a Mannlicher-Carcano rather than resolving the varying accounts.

On the day of the assassination, reporter/intelligence asset Priscilla Johnson portrayed Oswald as "That Stuff of Which Fanatics are Made," bolstering the lone nut thesis (phase 2) in the *Boston Globe*. Similar articles by Johnson later appeared in the *Dallas Morning News* and *L.A. Times* (11/24/63), the *Philadelphia Bulletin* as well as in *Time*, *Life*, the *New York Times*, the *Christian Science Monitor*, and later in *Harper's* (4/64). These articles were widely quoted in other journals. Nothing suggests that the *Boston Globe*, the *Philadelphia Bulletin*, the *Christian Science Monitor*, and *Harper's* were anything more than unwitting accomplices.

As a "prospective agent" or a "source" the CIA set up a "201 file" on Priscilla Johnson in the 1950s, where she was listed as a "witting collaborator." After the assassination, reporter/intelligence asset Priscilla Johnson (now Priscilla McMillan) wrote a number of articles about her alleged "interviews" with Oswald in Moscow in 1959. FBI document #105-82555 shows that Johnson was working for the State Department at the U.S. Embassy and her contact with Oswald was official business.[22] She was a friend and neighbor of CIA officer Cord Meyer. At the Embassy she worked with CIA asset Richard Snyder and wrote for the North American Newspaper Alliance (NANA), a CIA and British intelligence asset which was set up by former Office of Strategic Service (OSS) operative Ernest Cuneo. The CIA Soviet Branch Chief, Donald Jameson noted in a memo (12/11/62) "... I think that Miss Johnson can be encouraged to write pretty much the articles we want."[23] Johnson's House Select Committee on Assassination (HSCA) Executive Session interview, 4/20/78, still has 40 pages withdrawn by the CIA.[24]

Later, in the afternoon, 11/23/63, Assistant District Attorney Bill Alexander had informed the press that he was "prepared to charge Oswald with murdering the president as part of an international Communist conspiracy." NBC News at 5 aired the video portion of Oswald's interview with WDSU-TV in New Orleans August 21, 1963, where Oswald stated "I would definitely say that I am a Marxist." He then spoke about the goals of the Fair Play for Cuba Committee. The Coordinator for the interview was CIA asset Ed Butler. These connections will be explored later.

Dallas officials, under intense pressure to appear competent, shipped off evidence to the FBI on the night of 11/22, and were told by the FBI that the evidence pointed to Oswald. They jumped to conclusions about Oswald and were later criticized for this by the Warren Commission and ACLU. Later that night Dallas D.A Henry Wade went to Chief Jesse Curry in order to deal with press rumors but Curry refused to give him the police case. Wade nonetheless recounted to reporters what he remembered. The Warren Report would assert that Wade's lack of thorough knowledge of the case "provided much of the basis for the myths and rumors that came into being after the president's death." We may come to view this assessment as scapegoating. Chief Curry after the first day emphasized the open nature of the investigation on the question of accomplices. However, when Dallas D.A. Henry Wade, a former FBI agent and a staunch, longtime supporter of LBJ, held a press conference at 12:30 AM on 11/23 he categorically stated, "There is no one else but him [Oswald]. Later when asked if they were looking for other suspects, Wade responded, "We're always looking for suspects but we have none at the present." He later noted, contrary to many mass media reports, that Oswald was not a "nut."[25]

Jack Ruby returned to the Dallas Police Station with corned beef sandwiches for his police friends and stayed there after midnight, when Oswald was brought briefly into a mob of reporters. A few minutes later when D.A. Henry Wade mistakenly told the press that Oswald belonged to the Free Cuba Committee, Ruby unexpectedly pointed out that the D.A. had meant the Fair Play for Cuba Committee, a pro-Castro group. The Free Cuba Committee was an anti-Castro Group.[26] Stop for a minute, how did Ruby know the difference or anything about Oswald's background? Ruby was somehow conveniently positioned to significantly influence mass media reports that reached large portions of the nation with a "phase 1" version.

Following the comments of Chief Curry and Captain Will Fritz, by early morning the day after the assassination a mass media consensus appears to have emerged regarding the origin of the shots, Oswald's lone role, the murder weapon, and the location of the President's wounds.

Although the Dallas authorities rushed to the conclusion that Oswald was guilty, by 11/24 they moved tentatively and unevenly from their early judgment of Oswald acting alone, to openness on the question of accomplices. Dallas Police Chief Jesse Curry and District Attorney Henry Wade did most of the talking to the press the first few days, while Captain Will Fritz, who directed the investigation, made fewer statements. Curry's statements on 11/22 noted that they probably had "sufficient evidence" to convict Oswald; however, he also stated "there are many things we have to work on." By 11/23 Curry sounded slightly less certain. He stated that he thought they had the "right man" but that "we don't have proof positive." When asked about the possibility of accomplices, Curry replied, "We don't believe so at this time."

1. During the day of the assassination the FBI focused on Oswald. However, J. Edgar Hoover continued to qualify his observations about Oswald the next morning as seen in his phone conversation with President Johnson. At 10:01 AM Hoover inaccurately informed Johnson:

2. A gun used by Oswald had been shipped to a Dallas PO Box belonging to a woman named A. Heidel.

3. Officials were in possession of a bullet that fell out of the President when his heart was being massaged.

4. There were latent fingerprints on the gun.

5. Oswald lived with his mother.

6. The rifle had been wrapped in a blanket in his mother's house.

7. Shots were fired from the fifth floor of the TSBD.

8. Oswald engaged in a gun battle with police at the theater.

He was wrong on all counts. Hoover indicated to Johnson that the evidence against Oswald "was not very strong," and that "the case as it stands now is not strong enough to get a conviction." And this is when Hoover tells LBJ that the pictures of Oswald supposedly visiting the Cuban and Russian Embassies in Mexico City are not pictures of Oswald. Further, the audio tapes of Oswald supposedly calling those embassies is not Oswald's voice.

There was exhaustion on the faces of reporters Saturday as the stress took its toll. Chief Curry was moving toward a 4:00 PM transfer of Oswald, although Captain Fritz wanted more time for questioning. According to reporter Seth Kantor only a few trusted people around the police station knew of the proposed transfer, yet somehow Jack Ruby did. Ruby offered a "scoop" about Oswald's transfer to reporter Wesley Wise, a sports reporter from KRLD radio and TV Dallas, who was pressed into news responsibilities. Ruby then called KLIF radio, Gordon McLendon's station, on a private phone line to DJ Ken Dowe. "I understand they are moving over to the county jail. Would you like me to cover it, because I am a pretty good friend of Henry Wade's and I believe I can get some news stories?" Although the transfer was postponed, Ruby continued to court the press. In November 1965, Gordon McLendon was approved as a CIA asset. His ties to the intelligence community will be explored later.

Later that day Ruby poked around the WBAP in Fort Worth TV van where Frederic Rheinstein, an NBC producer-director, was working. At one point Ruby brushed aside the curtain in the van to view activities up in the third floor corridor on a closed-circuit monitor. Rheinstein was annoyed and got a good look at Ruby, who later that day was seen on the monitor visiting Wade's third floor office, an office which was barred to reporters by the police. Still later, Ruby told a cameraman and a stage manager at WBAP that he knew Wade personally and could furnish NBC information.

The lone nut thesis was already strongly endorsed by most mainstream media outlets. The *New York Herald Tribune* 11/23/63, run by millionaire publisher and editor-in-chief Jock Whitney acting as a copy reader, ran an editorial that claimed that all assassins in America were loners. "Shame of a Nation – History of Assassinations" asserted:

Historically, assassination has been a weapon in the struggle for political power in countries around the world, but attempts on American presidents have not followed this pattern. In a book on Presidential assassinations, *The Assassins* Robert J. Donovan, former Washington bureau chief of the *New York Herald Tribune* and then of the *L.A. Times*, similarly asserted: They involved neither organized attempts to shift political power from one group to another, nor to perpetuate a particular man or party in office, nor to alter the policy of government, nor to resolve ideological disputes. With one exception (Truman) no terrorist or secret society planned these assaults on our presidents or was in any way involved.

A pillar of the Establishment, Jock was a member of the Council on Foreign Relations and was friends with the Rockefellers as well as CIA officer Frank Wisner. According to *Fortune* (10/64), Whitney "is willing to use the power of the *Tribune* to push energetically the editorial views he holds in local and national politics." A friendly biography of Whitney, *Jock: the Life and Times of John Hay Whitney,* stated "on November 22, President Kennedy was killed; Whitney … was pressed into emergency service that tumultuous night as a copy reader." Was the very wealthy owner really "pressed" into emergency service as a "copy reader"?

The *Tribune* then trumpeted this position in its editorial.

Americans take consolation from the fact that the assassins of their presidents have, in nearly every case, been crazed individuals, representing nothing but their own imaginings. There is, however, a climate that encourages the growth of homicidal fantasies…. The heat of normal politics has its reflex on the lunatic fringe. And the 'hate sheets,' rumor mongering, the unbalanced charges of the lunatic fringe affects the real lunatics, the killers.

The most basic evidence remained muddled in their story, "Lee Harvey Oswald was arrested after a gun battle in a Dallas theater in which he shot and killed one policeman and slashed another." Oswald neither shot nor slashed a policeman.

The *Herald Tribune* also misreported the statements of Dr. Malcolm Perry at the medical press conference the previous day.

Dr. Malcolm Perry, 34, attendant surgeon at Parkland Hospital who attended the President, said he saw two wounds – one below the Adams's apple, the other at the back of the head. He said he did not know if two bullets were involved. It is possible he said that the neck wound was the entrance and the other the exit of the missile.

Later the Warren Commission would ironically utilize the misrepresentation of Perry's remarks as accurate reporting. Perry, under Secret Service pressure, changed his position on the nature of the neck wound from one of entrance – to being uncertain. (Warren Report) It seems apt to note that Secret Service Chief James Rowley claimed that he could not locate a tape or transcript of the medical press conference where Dr. Perry spoke, yet Joe Long, Dallas KLIF news director, told Marvin Garson (editor of the alternative *S.F. Express Times*) that the Secret Service confiscated the original recordings.[27]

An AP article briefly raised vital, but unfollowed, leads from a doctor at Parkland Hospital. "Asked if the wounds could have been made by two bullets, he said he did not know, but that a bullet had entered the front of his head ..." The *N.Y. World-Telegram & Sun* reporter Ed Wallace observed, 11/23, that "He used a strange gun; there is no evidence he had done any practicing; he was an unstable figure on a mission that would shake the nerves... of a much cooler man."

Lengthy excerpts from *The Assassins* ran in the 11/23/63 *L.A. Times* as well. So the *Tribune* and the *L.A. Times* almost immediately had strongly asserted the position later taken by Dulles and John McCloy at the outset of the Warren Commission.

The *L.A. Times* had already ruled out a conspiracy by running Robert Donovan's piece on the front page, "Sniper's Bullet Kills President in Dallas" In the "EXTRA" edition, later on 11/23/63, Donovan led his story "A 24-year-old ex-Marine and admitted pro-Communist fanatic was charged by police late Friday night with the murder of President Kennedy," while the headline blared "Assassin Named."

Donovan somehow claimed that "the President (was shot) facing the warehouse. In all probability he was hit just once, though doctors don't discount the possibility that two bullets struck him." This would mean that the President turned completely around to face the TSBD and then was shot, since the shots came from the front. "It appeared that a bullet hit him below the Adam's apple and was deflected up through the brain and then passed out through the back of his head." The *L.A. Times* also ran a picture of the 6th floor of the TSBD already labeled "Assassin's Nook."

A possible Cuban communist role in the assassination was bolstered by the AP report carried in the *Washington Post* 11/23/63, "Castro foe details infiltration effort." Carlos Bringuier, "reporting" as a New Orleans delegate for the Cuban Student Directorate (DRE) asserted that Oswald tried to infiltrate his organization and that "at first he thought Oswald was FBI or CIA." Bringuier described Oswald as "a very, very cold blooded one." Today we know DRE was a CIA-funded organization run by George Joannides, chief of the CIA's anti-Castro "psychological warfare" operations in Miami. DRE activists called the *New York Times* and other news organizations recounting Oswald's pro-Castro attitudes.

The "Extra" edition of the *Washington Post*, based on reports from Merriman Smith, stated, "A Dallas reporter said he saw a rifle being withdrawn from a window on the fifth or sixth floor of an office building shortly after the gunfire." The article reported that the Dallas Sheriff's Department found a German Mauser 7.65 in the TSBD; however, the Mauser would be re-identified as a Mannlicher-Carcano in a few days.

By 11/23 the *Dallas Morning News* seemingly received noteworthy editorial guidance. Reporter Mary Woodward, an eyewitness in Dealey Plaza, wrote her account in the November 23rd morning edition. "There was a horrible ear shattering noise, coming from behind us and a little to the right... which would have been in the direction of the grassy knoll, and the railroad overpass." Woodward speculated to fellow reporter Connie Kritzberg that this account was omitted from subsequent coverage because "civic leaders are responsible people, whether it be the mayor or managing editor of the paper, almost felt it a responsibility to kind of not 'rock the boat,' perhaps." Dallas Mayor Earle Cabell, (whose brother CIA Deputy Director General Charles Cabell had been fired by President Kennedy after the Bay of Pigs), was quoted in two articles later that day. He had somehow already determined that it was "the irrational act of a single man," and that "it could only be the act of a deranged mind," although this contradicted the assessment of Oswald by the Dallas Police Chief.

The *New York Times* and the *Washington Post*, 11/23/63, reported the nature of the wounds similarly. They left no doubt as to the origin of the shots. "The bullets have come from a 45 degree angle from the 6th floor of the building." No source, however, was credited for this assertion. Curiously, Senator Yarborough was purported to have said that three shots came from the rear – though this contradicts all of Yarborough's subsequent written and verbal statements.

The *New York Times* headlines, 11/23/63, also already declared a lone assassin "Kennedy is Killed by Sniper As He Rides in Car in Dallas: Johnson Sworn In On Plane," "Evidence Against Oswald Described as Conclusive," "Marxism Called Oswald's Religion," "Fatal Shot Struck Base of Skull Causing Immediate Unconsciousness." The sub-heading for Tom Wicker's front page story, "President is Struck Down by a Rifle Shot from Building on Motorcade Route," also definitively asserted a lone assassin.

Tom Wicker began his story, "an assassin ... fired from a building just off the motorcade route." He opaquely wrote that Parkland Memorial Hospital doctors, Malcolm Perry and Kemp Clark, described the president's wounds: "Mr. Kennedy was hit by a bullet to the throat.... This wound had the appearance of a bullet entry. Mr. Kennedy also had a massive gaping wound on the right side of his head." While a wound on the right side of the head could be consistent with shots from behind, Dr. Perry clearly pointed to the right temple area as the place where the President was hit. Since Wicker was at the press briefing immediately following the assassination either he got confused or ignored it. Few mass media accounts attempted to reconcile a wound in the president's throat and one in his right temple with shots from the Texas School Book Depository.

Wicker's boss, James Reston, in his story "Why America Weeps," had already not only determined a lone gunman, but also divined that the cause of the assassination was "some strain of madness and violence" which plagued the country. Notably though, those in the Dallas Police close to the investigation repeatedly stated that Oswald seemed sane. Reston was soon promoted to associate editor in 1964.

The AP report, in the *Charleston News and Courier* 11/23 asserted that "2 shots hit (the) President" from a "45° angle." They reported that three shots were fired from the Texas School Book Depository, while those in Dealey Plaza who rushed the grassy park [area] were confused and "terrified ... and dived forward for protection fearing more shots." The AP quoted Dallas Police Captain Will Fritz as charging Oswald with the murder, and the gun found was listed as "an old 30-caliber Enfield."

The *Chicago Tribune* headline read "Assassin Kills Kennedy," and they characterized the difficulty of the marksmanship in their sub-headline as "Easy Shot." The Chicago Tribune Press Service report mistakenly alleged that Treasury agents in the Secret Service bodyguard fired submachine guns at the (TSBD) building. They characterized the wounds to the President with "The surgeons would not state positively that the President was shot once or twice." Oswald "having left the book depository building entered an automobile and drove three quarters of a mile into the Oak Cliff residential area of Dallas..." This was an uncorroborated report about a suspect, and Oswald supposedly did not drive.

Reporter Gladwin Hill, in his *New York Times* piece exploring the evidence against Oswald quoted Dallas police captain Will Fritz, "We're convinced beyond any doubt that he killed the President.... I think the case is clinched." Hill raised no questions.

Physician Howard Rusk's *New York Times* piece did not attempt to reconcile the report by Parkland Surgeon Malcolm Perry, who located the entrance to the head wound in the right temple, nor did he attempt to address the throat wound, which had also been discussed at the press conference the day before in Dallas.

The *New York Times* reporter Richard J.H. Johnston in "Movie Amateur Filmed Attack" noted that, "*Life* editors bought the Zapruder film but they were unable to give precise details as to what the film showed." This was the apparent rationale used by those news organizations that saw and bid for the film, yet elected to avoid reporting any observation about it.

The *Fort Worth Star-Telegram* ran a front-page headline "Paraffin Tests of Oswald Show He Had Fired Gun." This was contradicted in a subsequent article where Dallas Police Chief Curry stated: "...he could not at this time state whether paraffin tests on Oswald's face also were positive."

The *Houston Post* headline, 11/23/63, "How Oswald Spilled out U.S. Hate, Love of Reds," featured UPI reporter Aline Mosby's 1959 interview with Oswald in Moscow. The other major front-page headline, "New Oswald Evidence" by UPI reporter John Young, highlighted Marina Oswald's supposed statement that Oswald had a rifle of the type used in the assassination. Young wrote that a German Mauser 7.65 was found on the sixth floor. This contradiction regarding the rifle remained unexplained.

The day after the assassination the *Washington Post* and the *Miami Herald* ran stories which portrayed Oswald as a pro-Castro operative. The source of the stories was Jose Antonio Lanusa an anti-Castro DRE operative. This press release claimed that DRE operative Carlos Bringuier's account of Oswald's' visit to his New Orleans clothing store, was where supposedly Oswald tried to infiltrate his anti-Castro group. Lanusa cleared the story after approval from his CIA controller George Joannides. The *Miami Herald* titled their story "Oswald tried to Spy on Anti-Castro Exile Group;" the *Washington Post* titled theirs "Castro Foe Details Infiltration Effort." Ironically, the first conspiracy theories printed were paid for by CIA psychological warfare specialist George Joannides.[28] CIA asset John Martino told *Miami Newsday* reporter John Cummings that he spread false stories implicating Oswald in the assassination of President Kennedy.[29]

Confusion regarding forensic evidence also emerged from FBI editing. *Dallas Times Herald* reporter Connie Kritzberg noted early evidence of FBI "editing regarding the location of the wounds." Reports on the location of the wounds in the *Dallas Times Herald* 11/22 and 11/23, indicated Dr. Kemp Clark and Dr. Malcolm Perry thought that at least one of the wounds was one of entrance. Kritzberg recalled in her book, *Secrets from the Sixth Floor Window*, that an editor added a sentence to her first story on the assassination: "A doctor admitted that it was possible there was only one wound." When Kritzberg questioned the editor as to where the sentence had come from, he "matter of fact[ly]" said "The FBI." Kritzberg asked what physician made the statement. And why was the FBI at the newspaper so soon? The rest of her story remained as she had written it.[30]

> Wounds in the lower front portion of the neck and the right rear side of the head ended the life of President John F. Kennedy say doctors at Parkland Hospital. Whether there were one or two wounds was not decided. The front neck hole was described as an entrance wound. The wound at the back of the head was either an exit or tangential entrance wound. A doctor admitted that it was possible there was only one wound.
>
> Dr. Kemp Clark, 38, Chief of Neurosurgery and Dr. Malcolm Perry, 34, described the President's wounds.... Dr. Clark said the President's principle wound was on the right rear of his head.... Dr. Perry was busy with the wound in the President's neck. "It was at midline in the lower portion of his neck in front." Asked if it was just below the Adam's apple, he said, "Yes below the Adam's Apple." "There were two wounds. I do not know if they were directly related or not,. It was an entrance wound in the neck."
>
> The doctors were asked whether one bullet could have made both wounds and whether there were two bullets. Dr. Clark replied, "The head wound could have been an exit or tangential entrance wound."
>
> The neurosurgeon described the back of the head wound as "A large gaping wound with considerable loss of tissue." Dr. Perry added, "It is conceivable it was one wound, but there is no way for me to tell. It did however appear to be the entrance wound at the front of the throat..." There were at least eight or ten physicians in attendance at the time the President succumbed...

An AP article of 11/23/63, without byline, quoted Homicide Captain Will Fritz: "We are convinced beyond any doubt that Oswald is our man.... Without going into the evidence I can tell you this – this case is a cinch. This man killed the president." He added, "we are going to work on this until we have a perfect case." D.A. Henry Wade stated that he was "confident of getting the death penalty for Oswald."

According to the *N.Y. Times*, 11/23, the Dallas police gave the Secret Service agents "a list of known agitators who might cause trouble" and "buildings along the route were checked." However, The *N.Y. Post*, 11/25, contended that, "there is still no indication of what, if any, advance security arrangements were made about the textbook warehouse."

The *Dallas Morning News* of Sunday, November 24, 1963, revealed a stunning assertion in its banner story – "Oswald met with the FBI November 16, 1963." This assertion was quickly addressed by the Dallas Police Chief but was not pursued by mass media outlets, or initially by the alternative media.

Police Chief Jesse Curry's original statement regarding the FBI in a late morning interview on 11/24 had changed markedly by that afternoon. At first Curry noted that the FBI knew of Oswald's presence in Dallas and that, speaking for his department, "we were not informed of this man." Later in the afternoon, a visibly shaken Curry repeated several times that the FBI was "under no obligation" to give them any information whatsoever, but that they have "always cooperated 100% with us." Hoover told Johnson's aide to tell Curry to "shut up" regarding the press. Johnson's aide Cliff Carter called Curry and Dallas D.A. Wade and directed them to avoid any discussion of conspiracy.[31]

The wire services chose not to pursue this or other significant discrepancies. The AP story by Arthur Everett on 11/24 seems to be sensitive to the position of a lone assassin. No questions were raised regarding any of the contradictory evidence, such as the change in rifle description or location of where the shots were fired, and the location of the wounds, this connection to the FBI or any other contradictions. Dallas Captain Will Fritz and District Attorney Henry Wade already seemed certain that Oswald was the lone assassin. Captain Fritz claimed:

> We don't know of anyone else who was involved in it, and as far as we are concerned the case is closed. There is no question in my mind that Oswald was the man who shot President Kennedy.... I don't want to get into the basis. I don't want to get into the evidence. I just want to tell you that we are convinced beyond any doubt that he did the killing.

The AP, 11/24, ran a radio "debate" from New Orleans between Oswald and Ed Butler of the Information Council of the America's (INCA) in 1963 sent to them by INCA. Years later researchers would determine that Butler was a CIA asset along with DRE's Carlos Bringuier; Oswald left the impression that he was a clever communist sympathizer who had defected to the Soviet Union. Oswald claimed his support for Cuba with FPCC as well as affirming his Marxist rather than communist perspectives. A close reading shows an otherwise poised Oswald curiously stumbling only on his response regarding his status while in the Soviet Union.

> ...I worked in Russia er, it was under the protection, er, of the, er, that is to say I was not under the protection of the American government but as I was at all times, er, considered an American citizen. I did not lose my American citizenship ... at no time did I renounce my citizenship ... or at no time was I out of contact with the American embassy...

Fingerprints of intelligence seem clear in the event leading to the "debate," at the "debate," as well as distributing the tape of the "debate." Ed Butler, in testimony to Senator Eastland's Senate Internal Security Committee, at an unusual Sunday meeting, painted Oswald as a "rational, wholly indoctrinated procommunist" and placed the "blame for Oswald's actions on the authors or disseminators of that material [FPCC leaflets.]

Ironically the FPCC leaflets were stamped 544 Camp St. New Orleans, which was the corner of the building which was also the location of Guy Banister's office (though Banister used a different street address). Banister, ostensibly a New Orleans private eye, was formerly FBI SAIC in Chicago, and had earlier worked with the Office of Naval Intelligence (ONI). In the unedited "debate" Butler and INCA appear to have created a legend of Oswald as being part of a communist plot.

On 11/24/63, prior to Oswald's murder, Chief Curry continued his commitment to cooperate with the media and held yet another press conference. Several of the questions focused on Oswald's accomplices.

> **Curry:** This is the man we are sure, that murdered the patrolman and murdered ... and assassinated the president. But to say that there was no other person who had any knowledge of what this man might do, I wouldn't make that statement, because there is a possibility of other people who might have known this man's thoughts and what he might could do, or what he might do.

27

Years later, in Curry's book, *JFK Assassination File*, he criticized the media for distorting eyewitness testimony about who was in the Book Depository window at the time of the shooting. He argued that the Dallas police immediately began to look for accomplices and continued to do so, while the press focused on Oswald alone.[32] In the turmoil of that weekend, Curry may not have noticed the seemingly more conclusive statements made by Captain Fritz and District Attorney Wade, which contributed to mass media generalizations about Oswald as the lone assassin.

To establish credibility there was a decision by the Dallas city manager and the police chief to let the press into the police station. To confirm their competence and control, they wanted the world to see that they had the accused assassin. Reporters now formed a "mob" in the Dallas Police Station. Adding to the confusion, the commitment to television coverage caused TV cameras to be placed in the police station hallways. Television reporters, for the first time, took over coverage of a major event, causing print reporters to search for angles.[33]

The UPI story of 11/24 by Michael Rabun quoted D.A. Wade, "As far as we are concerned the case is closed ... the case was a 'cinch.'" The case of Oswald as the lone assassin was developed by reporting new evidence from an unmentioned source. A map of Dealey Plaza with lines from the TSBD was purported to have been found in Oswald's room according to the *Dallas Morning News*, which oddly quoted an unmentioned source.

According to the UPI, this much was known:

> Paraffin tests for gunpowder on both hands were "positive" indicating he had recently fired a rifle [But there was no mention of a lack of powder residue on Oswald's face after supposedly firing a bolt action rifle.]
>
> His wife said he owned a rifle like the one used to slay President Kennedy.
>
> He bought it for $12.78 from a mail-order house. The order was in his handwriting. [No mention about the quality of the rifle or the sight on it.]
>
> He was an expert marksman in the Marine Corps from 1956-59. [No mention that he was not a sharpshooter.]
>
> He was employed in the building from which the assassin used an upper window to shoot the President and Governor. [No mention of other possible assassins.]
>
> He was seen in the building immediately after the President was assassinated. [No mention was made that he was seen on the second floor in a calm state just 90 seconds after the assassination.]

Finally, the *New York Daily News*, (11/24/63), voiced some journalistic doubts about the Dallas Police rendition by implying that a shot came from the front of the presidential limousine. They reported that the two motorcycle officers trailing the presidential limousine to the left rear were splattered with blood and brain matter. Motorcycle officer Bobby Hargis was struck so hard by a piece of skull bone that he said, "I thought at first I might have been hit."

Later that Sunday, two days after the assassination, Jack Ruby, after somehow slipping into the Dallas Police and Courts building, bolted forward from the journalists with whom he was clustered and shot Oswald in front of rolling TV cameras. This was the first time in the history of television that a homicide was carried live nationally.

Reporter Ike Pappas moved forward while Oswald was being transferred to ask "Do you have anything to say in your defense?" Just as he said defense he felt the explosion of the gun – and reported "Oswald has been shot." The story ran live on NBC; CBS recorded the event on a local camera, while the ABC cameraman had already moved to the county jail.

Reporter Seth Kantor asserted that Ruby entered the Dallas police basement by ostensibly helping two cameramen from WBAP Channel 5 TV Fort Worth, John Tankersly and Dave Timmons, maneuver a large camera set on a dolly. Two Dallas policemen admitted to seeing a man with a dark suit (like the one Ruby wore that day) bent low and assisting the struggling cameramen. The Warren Report later claimed that by viewing a reel of videotape, they thought that only two men pushed the camera. In 1977 Kantor and friends from KRDL reviewed reel 13 and could not determine how many people were pushing that camera because a number of detectives were blocking the view.[34]

Meanwhile, extensive photo essays and video footage paying homage to the fallen President, along with the pictures of Ruby shooting Oswald commanded the public's attention. Coverage of the funeral Monday was viewed by 93% of household with televisions. Media coverage offered consolation and a mood of continuity rather than upheaval. The *New York Times* declared that television coverage as a "chapter of honor." *Broadcasting Magazine* saw the coverage as "mature, dignified, expert and professional."

Since no trial now was possible, an elite consensus emerged; one which J. Edgar Hoover and Assistant Attorney General Nicholas Katzenbach claimed was necessary. By 4:00 PM the same day, Hoover's views could already be seen in a memo to LBJ aide Walter Jenkins, which formed the basis of a memo from Deputy Attorney General Katzenbach to LBJ aide

Bill Moyers. Have "something issued so we can convince the public that Oswald is the real assassin and that he does not have confederates that are still at large" and that the "evidence was such that he would have been convicted at trial." It continued:

> Speculation about Oswald's motivation ought to be cut off, and we should have some basis for rebutting thought that this was a Communists conspiracy or (as the Iron Curtain press is saying) a right wing conspiracy to blame it on the communists. Unfortunately the facts on Oswald seem too pat – too obvious. (Marxist, Cuba, Russian wife, etc.) the Dallas police put out statements on the Communist conspiracy theory, and it was they who were in charge when he was shot and thus silenced. The matter has been handled thus far with neither dignity nor conviction. Facts have been mixed with rumor and speculation. We can scarcely let the world see us totally in the image of the Dallas police when the President is murdered …

Alan Belmont, the number three man at the FBI, Director of Domestic Intelligence, led the FBI investigation. He concluded at 4:15 PM Sunday that Oswald was the man who killed the president. Instead of investigating major leads, Belmont closed the case.

Several newsmen covering the case in Dallas heard allegations of Oswald-Ferrie-Marcello mafia connections.

> CBS producer Peter Noyes recalls a conversation he once had with … a former member of the NBC television camera team that had covered the murders of the President and Oswald. Sometime toward the middle of the week of November 25, as interest in Ferrie was reaching a crescendo in New Orleans and Dallas, the NBC man had a discussion about Ferrie's links to Oswald and Marcello with a group of FBI agents and newsmen that he remembered everyone found provocative. However, the FBI soon put a damper on his interest in the subject. For immediately after the discussion broke up, one of the agents took him aside and told him that he should never discuss what they had just been talking about with anyone, "for the good of the country." [35]

By the next day the L.A. Times editorial, (11/25/63), "Epilogue to Tragedy" would have impressed George Orwell.

> President Kennedy died because of one man's violent hate, victim of the complete renunciation of law and order. His martyrdom will

be cruelly diminished if his death does not inspire in all Americans a greater sense of common purpose and a stronger belief in the democratic process and in justice.… Nor can we permit blame for the assassination to be extended from one man to whole segments of American life.

This may well have been a time when the "Standby Voluntary Censorship Code" was implemented. This national security propaganda mechanism will be described more later, but essentially it consisted of a few top journalists, PR experts, businessmen, government employees and college presidents, who could have been dispatched to monitor key communications – ranging from phone calls to mass media reports.

Dan Rather, the CBS southern bureau chief in 1963, who was reporting from Dallas on President Kennedy's November trip, claims to have been the first reporter to contact Abraham Zapruder, who had filmed the assassination with his 8mm camera. According to David Belin, Counsel to the Warren Commission and Executive Director of the 1975 Rockefeller Commission, Rather "took the film and was able to have the processing expedited."[36]

A day later, Rather, who was apparently the only journalist who reported his viewing of the Zapruder film prior to 1973, curiously reported on 11/25/63 that Kennedy's head "snapped *forward* with considerable violence" upon receiving the fatal shot. Rather's version for the *CBS Evening News* thus supported the Katzenbach and Hoover memos, as well as the subsequent Warren Commission findings of Oswald firing alone and from behind. Time-Life Inc. West Coast editor Richard Stolley, on a tip from intern Patsy Swank, flew back to Dallas and purchased the picture and film rights to use the Zapruder's film for $150,000. Representatives from AP, UPI and several national magazines also viewed the film, some with an intention to buy, but they were vastly outbid. The purchase agreement stated that Time-Life would agree to "…present the film to the public in a manner consistent with good taste and dignity…" They then suppressed it for over a decade; however, by 1969 bootleg copies were distributed by Penn Jones, publisher of the *Midlothian Mirror*.[37]

Several things remain unclear. How was Rather able to find Zapruder so quickly? How did the film get to the CIA and the Defense Intelligence Agency (DIA) controlled National Photo Interpretation Center, possibly as soon as the night of November 22nd? What happened to the Zapruder film frames which are missing on the FBI and Zapruder copies but remain in the Secret Service copies? According to Rather:

We started a search for anybody and everybody who might have been there carrying an 8mm camera.... And slowly we picked up a trail. Someone had seen a man standing at a certain spot. Someone else thought he was in the retail clothing business. We ran our leads through the FBI and the Dallas police. Finally we had a name: Abraham Zapruder.[38]

Since Zapruder has stated that he traveled directly to his office after the assassination, it seems possible that someone followed him. Rather was promoted to the CBS White House correspondent in less than a year. Years later (1976), in his book *The Camera Never Blinks*, Rather maintained that he had made an "honest mistake" regarding the motion of the President's head.[39]

The Warren Commission argued that the film went from Zapruder to Kodak in Dallas; then back to Jamison Film Co. in Dallas, where three prints were made; then back to Zapruder; and then to a vault at Time-Life, Inc. in New York. Through the Freedom of Information Act, author Paul Hoch found CIA item 450, a document indicating that the 8mm Zapruder film was at the National Photo Interpretation Center, one of the most sophisticated labs in the world. Years later, Doug Horne, who served on the Assassination Records and Review Board (ARRB), explored the chain of custody and alterations to the Z-film. The NPIC was run by Arthur Lundahl who had been recruited into the CIA in 1953. Lundahl's chief Information Officer, Dino Brugioni, recalls that when the Zapruder film was brought over by two Secret Service agents late Saturday evening "we went white glove" on the analysis. Brugioni's NPIC team was watched by the two Secret Service agents and "What grabbed us all were his [JFK] brains and part of his skull flying through the air."[40]

Sunday night, 11/23/63, after Brugioni and his team finished their analysis; a lone Secret Service agent came to NPIC with a different version of the Zapruder film. He identified himself as "Bill Smith" and was met by NPIC deputy director Captain Pierre Sands, USN. NPIC employees Ben Hunter and Homer McMahon were sworn to secrecy as they examined a 16 mm film version, which had been altered at the CIA/military state of the art facility, referred to as the Hawkeye Works lab, run by Eastman Kodak in Rochester, NY. Hawkeye Works was used to examine U-2 film footage as well as satellite spy footage. Dino Brugioni is convinced that there are two versions of the Zapruder film and that what he saw on Saturday night was not the same as the version NPIC worked on Sunday night.

The *Washington Post* 11/25/63, unearthed a bit more of Oswald's intriguing background, yet raised no questions.

> Oswald told the Embassy (Soviet) that he planned to tell Soviet officials everything he learned while he was a radar operator during his three years enlistment in the Marines. Embassy officials said Russia never granted Oswald's request for citizenship. In February 1962 he apparently had a change of heart ... and since he had not been granted Soviet citizenship, it was decided to give him a passport to the United States ... and $435 to defray costs.

Meanwhile, on Monday J. Edgar Hoover was directed by President Johnson to communicate a general agreement on investigation strategies to the *Washington Post*, on 11/25/63, because the paper intended to run an editorial calling for a Presidential Commission. An FBI memo showed that Assistant Attorney General Katzenbach called *Washington Post* editor, Russell Wiggins, and told him that "the Department of Justice seriously hoped that the *Washington Post* would not encourage any special means" by which the facts should be made available to the public. The memo also noted that an FBI agent had a similar conversation with Al Friendly, the *Washington Post's* managing editor. The editorial never appeared.

The rush to judgment to convict Oswald in the public mind was accelerated by some mass media outlets after Oswald was shot. The *New York Times* 11/25/63 headlines declared: "President's Assassin Shot to Death" – not the "Alleged Assassin," as they later admitted would have been more accurate. Other stories that day strongly supported a lone nut thesis: "Doctors Question Oswald's Sanity" and "Lone Assassin the Rule in the U.S." Life profiled the "Assassin: The Man Held – And Killed for Murder." *Time's* story was entitled "The Man Who Killed Kennedy." The *Fort Worth Star-Telegram* morning headline "JFK Assassin Slain," though, was revised by the afternoon to "Suspect Oswald Slain in Dallas." In recapping the case against Oswald the *New York Times* reported:

> Gordon Shanklin, FBI agent in charge at Dallas said today that ... a paraffin test used to determine whether a person has fired a weapon recently was administered to Oswald shortly after he was apprehended Friday, one hour after the assassination. It showed that particles of gunpowder from a weapon probably a rifle, remained on Oswald's cheek and hands.

This report is misleading in two respects. First, the paraffin test does not test for gunpowder, but rather for nitrates, which are found in gunpowder. This test can never substantiate that someone fired a weapon, because nitrates are found in other substances such as cigarettes, lighted matches, soap, newspaper ink, or toothpaste. Police departments have since abandoned the paraffin test since it was not reliable.

The second problem was that nitrates were not found on Oswald's right cheek, according to the Warren Commission. Since Oswald was right-handed, nitrate deposits would have been found there. The paraffin test did not establish Oswald's innocence, but the Dallas Police and reporters could have reported that it was consistent with Oswald's innocence. The FBI, through Shanklin, overrode the original report from Dallas Police that the paraffin tests on Oswald's cheek were negative.

Peter Kihss of the *New York Times* reported on Oswald's background, psychologizing about Oswald's "queer" youth in which he played with toy guns and felt his teachers did not understand him. Based on unmentioned sources:

> Oswald had gotten out of the Marine Corps on a hardship claim to support his mother; he had immediately headed for the Soviet Union and sought Soviet citizenship; only then had he wound up in Minsk, where he married a Minsk girl; he got a $435.71 U.S. government loan to pay for his family trip.

One source of Kihss' information for another story, "Oswald told an untrue story of his Soviet stay, says man who aided him on return" was Spas Raikin of the philanthropic Traveler's Aid Society. The Warren Commission did not divulge Raikin's other affiliation but we now know that Raikin was then a member of the CIA-funded American Friends of Anti-Bolshevik Bloc Nations and that he had met numerous times with the CIA before and after 1963. Since Kihss later boldly wrote articles critical of the Warren Report, in this instance apparently he reported unwittingly.

Reporter Foster Hailey underscored a rapidly emerging consensus for the *New York Times* 11/25/63 asserting "Lone Assassin the Rule in U.S., Plotting More Prevalent Abroad."

> ...In the U.S., in all except two cases [Lincoln and Truman] the attempts were made by a single person.... That seems to have been the case with Lee Harvey Oswald, the killer of President Kennedy who was himself slain yesterday.

Jack Ruby's motives also were clear for the *Times* as seen in their headline "Kennedy Admirer Fired One Bullet." Thus, while on 11/24, while the Dallas officials, particularly Chief Curry, were more open to the possibility of Oswald accomplices than on 11/22, the day after Oswald's murder, the *Times* was closing down the discussion.

Unlike the *New York Times*, the *Washington Post* indirectly raised some questions regarding the lone gunman thesis in a piece, "Other Countries Hear Quickly about Shooting." Tass (the Soviet Union's news service): 1) noted that Jack Ruby was well known by the Dallas police; 2) wondered why an assassin would have a picture taken of himself with a murder weapon and give it to his wife; 3) questioned why Oswald's wife and mother were reportedly completely isolated by the FBI; and 4) speculated that "the murderers of John F. Kennedy are trying to cover up their traces." Reports in newspapers from Rome to Johannesburg to Cuba to Vietnam raised questions about Ruby's motives as something besides impulsive patriotism, but not in the American mass media.

The *Post* was less curious about their own reporting. They ran a story based on dispatches "Palm Print Links Oswald to Rifle" and quoted Dallas D.A. Henry Wade "As far as Oswald is concerned the case is closed." No questions were raised about why no palm prints had been detected on the rifle for the last two days by the Dallas Police before handing it over to the FBI.

The *Washington Post* quoted a statement Ruby made to an unnamed policeman, "I did it to spare Mrs. Kennedy the agony of going to Dallas." Ruby was portrayed as an emotional, patriotic, fair, honest, congenial, nightclub owner, and even as a "king except when someone crosses him." *Dallas Morning News* nightclub columnist Toni Zoppi claimed: "Dallas doesn't have a syndicate." Ruby's ties to organized crime went unreported. Years later the HSCA determined that Zoppi worked with the syndicate in Las Vegas.

The *Washington Post* was prepared to dispatch reporter Brad Nossiter to Dallas but after Ruby killed Oswald they supposedly lost interest. Editors informed Nossiter "We'll just let the wire services handle it."

Severe stress and sleeplessness in newsrooms contributed to inconsistent coverage. Some reporters, years later, admitted to breaking down and crying or just drinking themselves to sleep during the early crisis period. This contributed to Oswald being tried and convicted many times in the media.

The *Wall Street Journal* editorial of 11/25/63 seemingly followed the Katzenbach memo and bellowed a lone nut scenario.

…Idiots we have always amongst us, and if they have coloration at all it is more likely to be the black might of the individual than the political shades of red or white. His [Kennedy's] sense of history would have told him that all such murders were the work of individual hysteria, just as was the murder of the assassin, not the working of the historical process.…So, we believe, he would not have made the occasion of his own tragic death the opportunity for a new witch-hunt of either the left or the right without ascertaining the facts.… All the more shame on those who were so ready to attribute his assassination to some organized diabolical plot of the so-called radical right.

The *Wall Street Journal* relied on the Dallas law enforcement officials, as had the AP and UPI, who asserted that "they had an air tight case against Oswald" and that after his death the case was "closed." They added that the FBI would continue its investigation.

Other stories in the *New York Times* reinforced the idea that conspiracies were not common in American politics – "Doctors Question Oswald's Sanity" and "Lone Assassin the Rule in the U.S.: Plotting More Prevalent Abroad" (11/25/63). Assassins "Charles J. Guiteau, Leon Czolosz, John Schrank, Giuseppe Zangara were all men who acted alone." John Wilkes Booth's cohorts were conveniently forgotten.

The *N.Y. World-Telegram & Sun*, 11/25, carried a Scripps-Howard story "FBI Disputes DA on a Rifle Palm Print" which stated that… there is a behind the scenes rift today between the FBI and the Dallas DA Henry Wade… Wade said Oswald's palm print was found on the metal of the rifle which killed the President. Federal authorities have confided that no reliable print was found on the murder weapon when it was flown to Washington for the laboratory study."

Scripps-Howard columnist, Richard Starnes (11/26) posed a poignant admonition. "Our credentials as a civilized people stand suspect before the world, of course, but the real depth of the disaster that has befallen us cannot yet be measured. In its 188th year, the republic has fallen upon unspeakably evil days and great mischief is abroad in the land, it remains to be seen whether more convulsions will rock us."

The *N.Y. Herald Tribune* shifted to some skepticism by 11/26. "Just two hours before Jack Ruby gunned Lee Harvey Oswald to death in a basement garage in Dallas Police Headquarters, the FBI warned both the police and the sheriff in Dallas of an anonymous threat to the life of the man charged with the assassination of President Kennedy.… We don't know what happened after that." The *N.Y. Herald Tribune* questioned Oswald's passport process, "the passport was issued one day later. It still isn't clear how it was processed so rapidly." Further, while Americans were not required to check in with American immigration officials when crossing the border to Mexico, "Immigration has a folder on Oswald's trip."

The *Washington Post* 11/26/63 again indirectly questioned officialdom in their piece "Dallas Police are Target Abroad" by quoting French political commentators on privately owned TV station *Europe Number One*:

> The investigation carried out by the Dallas Police flaunts every honest man's conception of justice and the right of the people to know the truth.... Shifty politicians ... and slick talking policemen are doing everything to prevent the truth from coming out.

The well-respected *Le Monde* observed, "Serious doubts soil the behavior of the Dallas Police." In response to these concerns, American journalists should have raised questions about the role of the police.

Finally, by November 27 a print journalist, John Herbers of the *New York Times*, commented on the Zapruder film. He creatively reconciled the frontal wounds with the supposed position of the assassin in the TSBD by suggesting that the gunman could have fired as the presidential limousine was approaching the TSBD on Houston Street, then could have swung the rifle almost 180° and fired twice more. This account not only ignores all of the accounts from the eyewitnesses in Dealey Plaza, but also fails to note the obvious backward motion of the president's head after he was shot on Elm Street. Herbers neglected to cite any source for this interpretation.

The *Times* then recounted tests, which had been conducted by "a firearms expert from the National Rifle Association." The expert used a "Model 1938 6.4 mm bolt-action rifle." His target had been 50 feet away. He was able to get off three shots in 11 seconds and they struck within a one-inch circle. On a second try, the expert was able to get off three shots in eight seconds with comparable accuracy. Therefore, the "expert" reasoned that a well-practiced person could have done as well or better during the assassination. The story did not address: hitting a moving target; accuracy at about 90 yards; the quality of the Mannlicher-Carcano; the scope being poor and misaligned; or Oswald's lack of riflery skills.

In Herbers' other story that day he avowed, "Three shots are known to be fired. Two hit the President. One did not emerge [according to Dr. Clark]." Yet, this account does not square with a *New York Times* report two days earlier wherein Fred Powledge noted, "A bullet that Secret Servicemen removed from a stretcher at Parkland Hospital after the shooting, and two bullet fragments removed from the presidential automobile matched bullets fired from the rifle by FBI agents." Thus we now have a stretcher bullet, the fragmented bullet, and the bullet that remained in the president. Also unmentioned was a report from other newspapers that one bullet missed the President and hit the sidewalk past the motorcade with a chip hitting bystander James Tague. These conflicting reports were not reconciled.

The *New York Post* (11/27) at least questioned Dallas D.A. Henry Wade's assertion three days earlier that Oswald's palm print was found on the rifle in the warehouse.

> Edward Bennet Williams, one of the nation's leading defense lawyers … said the police's purported discovery of Oswald's palm prints in the room where the assassin lay was not necessarily conclusive. Palm prints are not nearly as conclusive as fingerprints.

The powerful pundit Walter Lippmann imaginatively pronounced on 11/27/63 that "Oswald was an extremist, outsider … addicted to the fascination of violence in his futile and lonely and brooding existence. The salient fact about him was his alienation from humanity … there is no limit to his hatred … and America should follow the mayor of Dallas in prayerful reflection." Four days later President Johnson called him and Lippmann observed, "I'm very satisfied with you." Johnson then proceeded to invite himself over for a drink. Lippmann condoned "managed news" as inevitable, the cardinal sin was not to do it but rather to admit doing it. Noted reporter Heywood Bruhn once wrote that Lippmann "espouses the comforting idea that we are safe in the arms of J. P. Morgan."

The *Washington Post* on 11/27/63, raised concerns in a piece "Dozens of Questions Remain Unanswered." "Could Oswald have done the shooting? Does Oswald's map exist? Did the Dallas police do their part in protecting the President? What did Oswald actually do in Mexico City? Was there a connection between Oswald and Ruby? How did Ruby get into the Dallas police garage? What are Ruby's ties to the underworld? Until these questions are answered the mystery may grow."

Rather than pursue the questions it had just raised, the *Washington Post* ran a piece by Lawrence Stern, which, by psychologizing, bolstered the lone nut thesis. He quoted Michael Paine, Oswald's acquaintance in Dallas, and the husband of Marina's friend Ruth:

> After the assassination there were reports that the killer took his time and aimed his rifle deliberately. That would be characteristic of Lee Oswald…. He had little respect for people…. He saw them as pawns.

Although we now know of the CIA's connections to the Paine family, Stern was not likely to have known this then.

The *N.Y. Herald Tribune*, 11/27, questioned Oswald's whereabouts during the assassination by interviewing the head of the TSBD, Ray S. Truly. "I rushed into the building with a policeman. He thought the shooting came from the roof and we ran up the stairway. On the second floor he stuck his head into a snack bar we have and saw Oswald sitting at one of the tables."

One of the leading alternative weeklys, *The Nation*, on 11/28/63 editorialized about the need to resist speculation, regardless of the "obvious discrepancies and inconsistencies," until the report is released. The public was admonished to stay "alert and skeptical" since the Warren Commission "is heavily weighted in favor of the 'official' or Establishment view."

Life, then the most popular magazine in America, was even more influential than TV or radio news. After purchasing the Zapruder film, they selectively edited and creatively described it before asserting the case against the "strange" and "fanatic" Oswald (11/29/63). Life chose to print only 31 frames. The frame when the president was struck in the head (Z-313) was not shown. The only description of injuries was of a "clutching towards his throat" – no mention was even made of the shot to the head. Jackie Kennedy, who crawled on the trunk of the limousine to retrieve a portion of the president's head, which she held in her hands at Parkland Hospital, was instead described as "in a pathetic search for help" – presumably to pull aboard a leaping Secret Service man. This was the largest picture in the whole unnumbered sequence, covering 4/5 of a page. If Jackie Kennedy was described as reaching for a portion of the president's brain, it would have indicated that a shot most likely came from the front of the limousine.

Life claimed that the assassin's shots came solely from the sixth floor of the TSBD, in their story "Death found him from this window." Another piece "Assassin: The Man Held – And Killed – for Murder" by Thomas Thompson portrays a "strange" misfit, which is as perplexing regarding its sources as its content. Thompson reportedly determined where Oswald lived by "deftly extracting it from a chatty sheriff." He learned from Oswald's landlady that he frequently phoned the town of Irving. Thompson then ostensibly spoke with a sheriff's dispatcher and learned "that feds had been nosing around town earlier in connection with the assassination – looking for some women a few streets south." By knocking on doors he was able to find the Paine household where Marguerite and Marina Oswald were located. He was the only reporter to interview these people before the Secret Service interview began, but his intuition and instinct quickly evaporated.

Thompson portrayed Oswald as a confused, withdrawn loser, despite the pleas of his wife and mother that he was decent and innocent. The other main source Thompson used was Priscilla Johnson, although he may have been unaware that she was a "witting asset" for the CIA. Johnson's article had already appeared in numerous newspapers, and she again portrayed Oswald as a confused ideologue, "maybe … a fanatic."

Although the case against Oswald was quite fragmentary when Thompson finished his story on Saturday evening, 11/23/63, he nonetheless had already characterized the police as "methodically building the case" (Actually the FBI built much of their case for them).

> …Connecting Oswald with the mail order purchase of a rifle like the one that fired the fatal bullet, placing him on the scene of the shooting with a long parcel the size and shape of a rifle, comparing his palm marks with one found on the murder weapon, finding traces of burned powder on his hands. Then the police turned up the most damning evidence of all. It was a snapshot of Oswald showing him holding a rifle that apparently was identical with the one that killed the president…

Since the palm prints did not become part of the official record until after Oswald was shot, almost two days later, Thompson was either clairvoyant, deceptive, or given a version of the "facts."

Throughout the summer of 1963, *Life* laboriously worked on a critical story concerning LBJ's corrupt relationship with his top aide Bobby Baker. Much of the material was coming from RFK. *Life* chief assistant to the Publishing Projects Directors, James Wagenvoord thought that the story which was supposed to run after JFK's trip to Dallas would "Blow Johnson out of the water. He was done." After the assassination the research files were shredded and the story never ran.[41]

Wagenvoord recalled that the CIA's Operation Mockingbird was influencing *Life*. On November 24th, before Ruby shot Oswald, Wagenvoord was unexpectedly handed a manila envelope by a man in a gray suit who showed FBI credentials. "This is Oswald material" he stated before quickly leaving. Wagenvoord remembered taking out a short 16 mm film taken by a New Orleans television news cameraman of Oswald passing out pro-Castro flyers on Canal St. in New Orleans. An hour later Ruby shot Oswald.

In the week after the assassination the European press was more skeptical and analytical than the American press. In France, *Paris-Jour* ran an article "Oswald cannot have acted alone" (11/27). *Paris Press* asserted that a Dallas patrolman J.D. Tippit was shot to allow a getaway." Liberation wrote, "There is no doubt that President Kennedy fell into a trap.... The Dallas police, protectors of gangsters like Ruby ... created a defendant then allowed one of their stool pigeons to kill him." The conservative *Le Monde* declared 11/25 its "serious doubts" about the role of the Dallas police.

In Great Britain, the conservative *London Daily Telegraph* reported "world opinion as much as American is not fully satisfied about this terrible affair. This has resulted in an elephantine attempt on the part of local authorities concerned to cover it up for one another." (11/26) The *London Daily Mail* (11/27) said that "facts can be produced that a far right wing plot against the president caused his death.' In Germany the *Hamburger Echo* (11/26) declared that Oswald's murder raised suspicions that "would make the assassination a gang plot." The *Frankfurter Abendpost* viewed Dallas Police captain Will Fritz's declaration that the case was closed as "pitiful."

The *Berliner Morgenpost* of West Berlin, 11/26, speculated that "it is possible that Ruby silenced Oswald to cover the men behind the plot." *Pravda*, 11/24, asserted that the murder of the President and the arrest of Oswald were being deliberately used to "stir up anti-Soviet and anti-Cuban hysteria. " *Izvestia* asked "Were there two men linked in a plot? And were not people from the Dallas police linked in one plot?" *Trybuna Judu* in Poland charged that the arrest of Oswald and his identification as a Communist was similar to the conviction of Vander Lubbe on charges of starting the Reichstag fire in Berlin in 1933. (11/26) Some Arab papers noted that Jack Ruby was Jewish and they hinted that Zionism was involved.[42]

Suspicions of a plot against President Kennedy echoed in India as well. The *Patriot* from New Delhi said, "it looks as though Oswald was only an agent ... the ease with which a night club owner with a criminal record could get access to a prisoner in police custody and shoot him suggests collusion.… The effort of the Dallas authorities … was to insinuate that Oswald was connected with Communism and the Soviet Union. This, taken together with the Dallas police chief's haste in declaring that "the case has been closed" with the killing of Oswald, points to the existence of influences bent on changing Mr. Kennedy's policies at all costs.

Back in the U.S., *N.Y. Journal-American* investigative reporter and columnist Dorothy Kilgallen raised a loud call of caution in her column. "The Oswald File must not close." If Johnson "could walk invisibly on the streets of the nation and listen to ordinary people talking, he would realize that he must be sure that the mystery of Lee Harvey Oswald is solved and laid before the nation down to the smallest shred of evidence. Well I'd like to know how, in a big, smart town like Dallas, a man like Jack Ruby – owner of a strip tease honkey tonk – can stroll in and out of police headquarters as if it was a health club at a time when a small army of law enforcers' is keeping a 'tight security guard' on Oswald. Security! What a word for it."

The *New York Journal-American* and the *N.Y. Herald Tribune* also raised questions about the FBI. On 11/29, John Harris in a Hearst Headline Service report to the *N.Y. Journal-American* reported, "The FBI interviewed Lee Harvey Oswald, accused slayer of President John F. Kennedy, as late as September of this year … in the nearby community of Irving. The other two sessions were in Fort Worth in 1962 after Oswald's return from defection to the Soviet Union, and in New Orleans last summer.… The FBI denied comment on these reports." David Wise, Washington Bureau Chief of the *N.Y. Herald Tribune* confirmed this in his 12/3 piece.

The *N.Y. Journal-American*, 11/29, editorial attempted to tie Fidel Castro to the assassination "even if he were not involved in the foul deed in Dallas, he is demonstrating every day, through the behavior of his agents in Caracas, that he is perfectly capable of political assassination."

The *L.A. Times*, 11/30/63 ran a UPI photo essay, "Final Seconds of the Assassination Detailed in Photos" which, courtesy of *Life* magazine showed only six frames of the Zapruder film. The grainy reprints neither showed nor described the president's head snapping backward. The one enlarged photo showed Jacqueline Kennedy scrambling on the trunk of the limousine to retrieve portions of the president's brain (as she later recalled), yet this was described as Time-Life had described it, as a "scramble for help" to "help a Secret Service man into the car." While UPI did not own or have access to the Zapruder film, they had seen it prior to Time-Life purchasing it. Thus they had some idea of the editing and inaccurate descriptions which were used. Whether the *L.A. Times* knew of the editing by UPI and Time-Life remains unclear.

Perhaps the most probing piece during this crisis period was written by the renowned reporter Richard Dudman in the *St. Louis Post-Dispatch*, 12/1/63. The headline declared "Uncertainties Remain Despite Police View of Kennedy Death." Dudman wrote:

> The strangest circumstance of the shooting, in this reporter's opinion, is the position of the throat wound, thought to have been caused by the first of two shots that struck Mr. Kennedy. Surgeons who attended him at Parkland Hospital described it as an entrance wound.... The question that suggests itself is: How could the President have been shot in the front from the back? Dr. Perry described the bullet hole as an entrance wound. Dr. McClelland told the *Post-Dispatch*: "It certainly did look like an entrance wound." He explained that a bullet from a low velocity rifle like the one thought to have been used characteristically makes a small entrance wound, sets up shock waves inside the body and tears a big opening when it passes out the other side. Dr. McClelland conceded that it was possible that the throat wound marked the exit of a bullet fired into the back of the President's neck ... "but we are familiar with wounds" he said "we see them every day – sometimes several a day. This did appear to be an entrance wound."

Legal authorities were among the first to criticize the treatment of Oswald by the Dallas police and the media. The *New York Times* ran a statement from the S.F. Bar Association 11/28/63, "We believe that television, radio and the press must bear a portion of the responsibility which falls primarily on law enforcement officials. Both press media and law enforcement officials must seek to protect the rights of accused persons against the damage to them, and consequently to our system of justice." The *New York Times* expanded that concern 12/1/63 by printing a critical letter issued by seven law professors at Harvard Law School.

> The law enforcement agencies, in permitting virtually unlimited access to the news media made the [vindication of the law] impossible.... Justice is incompatible with the notion that police, prosecutors, attorneys, reporters and cameramen should have unlimited right to conduct separate trials in the press and television ... the lamentable behavior of the Dallas law enforcement agencies and the communications media reflect a flaw in ourselves as a society.

U.S. News & World Report, 12/2/63, faithfully followed the official story. Their lengthy articles on the new president's background and ideas dwarfed the terse and sketchy overview of "The Capture of a Killer." Their commentary by David Lawrence sympathized with the Secret Service and the problems of protection from the "insane impulse" of a "despicable individual."

The popular columnist Drew Pearson, however, revealed serious Secret Service lapses in his "Merry-Go-Round" piece, 12/2/63.

> Six Secret Service men were drinking late in the Fort Worth Press Club [the night] before Kennedy was killed: Lee Oswald was not on the list of dangerous suspects: rivalry between FBI and Secret Service endangers life of President.
>
> There are three agencies of government which are sacrosanct as far as Congressional investigation or criticism is concerned – the FBI, the Secret Service and the Central Intelligence Agency.... It is my belief that a serious investigation should be undertaken regarding the first two.
>
> Some of them [Secret Service] were drinking until nearly 3 AM. One was reported to have been inebriated ... three were reported en route to an all-night beatnik rendezvous "The Cellar".... Obviously men who have been drinking are in no condition ... to protect anyone.
>
> It has been stated that it was an impossibility for the Secret Service to check the occupancy of every building along the route. While that is true, it is also true that warehouse type buildings, such as that in which the assassin hid, should be searched, and the extra time spent by Secret Service men at the Fort Worth Press Club could have been spent in so doing.

Newsweek's article "The Marxist Marine" 12/2/63, commented on Oswald's statement that he had not killed anyone by already stating "This is a lie." By 12/16/63 they ran a story "Portrait of a Psychopath."

The next day the UPI wire carried a story leaked by the FBI with the following lead: "An exhaustive FBI report now nearly ready for the White House will indicate that Lee Harvey Oswald was the lone and unaided assassin of President Kennedy, Government sources said today." According to Assistant FBI Director William Sullivan, Hoover himself ordered the report leaked to the press, in an attempt to "blunt the drive for an independent investigation of the assassination."[43]

Independent journalist Fred Cook, who wrote for a number of journals including *The Nation*, learned in early December 1963 that a number of veteran newsmen were concerned about the lightning fast wrap-up of the case. One of Cook's contacts said that a CBS news executive was frustrated because a research team in Dallas had uncovered leads, which appeared to require further investigation, but had encountered network indifference.

Cook's efforts to report on the Mannlicher-Carcano and its ammunition as well as the origins of the almost instantaneous and precise Dallas news reports of Oswald were discouraged by the editor of *The Nation*, Carey McWilliams. McWilliams respected Warren Commission senior counsel Joseph Ball, whom he had known in law school, as well as counsel Norman Redlich who had been active in civil rights cases, as had Chief Justice Earl Warren. McWilliams expressed faith in a Commission headed by Chief Justice Earl Warren, "Nothing is going to be covered up. Let's wait until the Commission has time to make its investigation and file its report."

For historical precedent, during the trial after President Lincoln's assassination the military tribunal afforded defendants some rights that Oswald was denied. The national press was allowed to attend the proceedings, and additionally a defense by counsel was permitted. The Warren Commission heard its testimony in closed hearings, while a compliant press raised no objection.

As the above account of crisis coverage depicts, the mainstream and alternative media were heavily influenced by the historical context of a Cold War consensus. Initially political reporters found themselves covering a series of complicated homicides and relied heavily on establishment sources. Amid the collective trauma some reporters aggressively questioned Oswald about his cries of innocence; however, statements from Dallas law enforcement officials soon prevailed. The press assignment of reporting the President's trip to Dallas was called "Covering the Body," and it quickly necessitated behavior beyond the bounds of journalistic standards. The immediate penetration of some elements of the mass media by CIA assets, FBI "editing" and State Department pressure contributed to the quickly coalesced consensus of Oswald as a lone nut assassin. Perhaps collective trauma also pressed some reporters toward a psychological regression – leading to further deference to government authorities.

The suppression and disinformation regarding the Zapruder film by Time-Life contributed significantly to framing the early reporting. In addition, mass media reliance on the wire services as well as government sources was the norm. Most of the powerful mass media organizations promoted the lone-nut scenario before Oswald was shot, including the *New York Times*, the *New York Herald Tribune*, the *Los Angeles Times*, the *Dallas Morning News*, AP, UPI, CBS and Time-Life.

After Ruby killed Oswald, the mass media came under increased government pressure, particularly after the memos from Hoover and Katzenbach that "the public must be convinced that Oswald was the assassin and that he did not have confederates." Critic Mark Lane spoke with some executives at the Associated Press convention in 1966 who claimed that they "were powerless to act since the government had only wanted one side presented." The handful of mainstream reporters and editors who raised critical question's however, remained marginalized. Some reporters have told me that they had heard that the prevailing attitude of the mainstream media was "Let's get this behind us – let's not look like a banana republic."

Probably Tom Wicker and most other reporters did not pursue the contradictory evidence for reasons he confessed in a *Harper's* magazine interview years later. Reporters who challenged the official story regarding matters of importance to powerful people: "lost access, [endured] complaints to editors and publishers, social penalties, leaks to competitors, a variety of responses no one wants." Walter Karp of *Harper's* conceded, "It is bitter irony of source journalism that the most esteemed reporters are precisely the most servile. For it is by making themselves useful to the powerful that they gain access to the "best" sources."

Remnants of the McCarthy era intimidation of the mass media still resonated with most of the mainstream mass media. The "Cold War Consensus" that American divisions on national security matters aided our enemies, again confronted a potential threat, but media-elite perception that patriotism was needed to keep the peace and calm in the country prevailed. This self-censorship strengthened the mass media support for the secretive Warren Commission process, which was shielded from the press. Leaks from the FBI Report were reported as facts, which acclimated the public to the lone nut thesis. It seems fair to suggest that the "Standby Voluntary Censorship Code" could have been placed into effect during this national emergency. The alternative media were weak and divided in late 1963. After initial caution, however, the *New Republic*, the independent socialist journal *The National Guardian*, *New Times*, and *Saga* did print critical coverage.

The tiny, pro-Soviet *New Times* blamed reactionary rightist elements in the U.S. whose goal was to deepen the Cold War; however, only a handful of critical articles explored contradictions between the evidence and government assertions. *The Nation* remained more cautious, generally supportive of the official process, as well as of the integrity of Chief Justice Earl Warren. The frightening foreign policy implications, combined with a weak progressive movement, vivid recent memories of McCarthyism, limited resources, and a lack of access to evidence contributed to this caution. Just five years earlier, *The Nation* had printed an article by Fred Cook critical of the FBI. The FBI memos referred to the article as a "smear campaign" and characterized Cook as a Communist. FBI agents interrogated Cook's friends and neighbors. J. Edgar Hoover was then "untouchable" by Congress. Years later, "William Sullivan, head of the FBI's Domestic Intelligence Division, admitted to congressional investigators that those who presented findings contrary to Hoover's prejudices could find themselves transferred or fired."[44] The mainstream media generally followed the traditional national security consensus and waited for the Warren Report. If only the Internet was around in 1963, the critics could have already had some traction. Let's briefly explore some aspects of the mass media's participation in developing a Cold War Consensus.

2

COLD WAR COOPERATION

The least initial deviation from the truth is multiplied later a thousand fold.
— Aristotle

Man may be governed by reason and truth. Our first objective should therefore be to leave open to him all avenues of truth. The most effective hitherto found is freedom of the press.
— Thomas Jefferson

Reporters are puppets... They simply respond to the pull of the most powerful strings.
— Lyndon B. Johnson

In the turmoil following the assassination, the press were misled by a number of government agencies as well as subjected to pressure by the President, the FBI Director, the State Department, the CIA, the Assistant Attorney General, and some Dallas authorities. These influences virtually constituted a coordinated policy of voluntary prior restraint based on national security needs. This restraint was followed by almost all the major mass media outlets for well over a year. Journalists confronted the usual challenges of limited time and money. More fundamentally they confronted professional risks in developing a vital, complicated, and controversial story within a traditional context of elite-media-government cooperation on national security issues.

The news media of the 1950s and 1960s had close links to both the CIA and the Ivy League alumni who ran it. They frequently had gone to the same prep schools and colleges, joined the same country clubs, attended the same dinner parties, and shared the Cold War Consensus about the role of the CIA. Most in the field of journalism appear to have long accepted the sentiment Richard Helms (later the Director of the CIA) shared in a 1971 speech to newspaper editors that "the nation must, to a degree, take it on faith that we ... are honorable men devoted to her service."[1]

All major industrial powers tightly controlled their mass media on national security matters throughout the early 20th century. American correspondents reporting on World War I were far more successful in covering and publishing events than their British or French counterparts, until America entered the war. American foreign correspondents were then given officer rank, housed with officers, had their access to battlefields restricted, were required to swear an oath to "convey the truth," and refrain from any writing which would aid the enemy; and then their stories had to pass through military censors. [2]

During WWI, mass media leaders coordinated and supervised numerous psychological warfare operations with government agencies through the U.S. Committee on Public Information, directed by George Creel. To its practitioners this was a necessary progressive management of public opinion, or as Walter Lippmann called it, "The manufacture of consent." By 1919, the muckraking journals had been either driven out of business or bought out by corporations. The U.S. Government utilized some of the new strategies in exacerbating the "Red Scares" of the 1920's, contributing to national and journalistic confusion. A competing journalistic notion, advocated by John Dewey, viewed public information as necessary to strengthen the democracy, although it failed to resonate as widely as popular columnist Lippmann's ideas.

This cooperation intensified during World War II, when national security concerns again often justified hiding the truth. Formal and informal elite-mass media-national security connections strengthened this cooperation, which evolved into a Cold War Consensus. The norm then for the press and the public was to trust government sources.

In May 1940 Winston Churchill quickly moved to protect his vulnerable country by setting up the British Security Coordination, an intelligence and propaganda service, to persuade the American public to overcome its widespread isolationism and enter the war against the Nazis and Fascists. Canadian industrialist William Stephenson coordinated the connections which were quickly embraced by FDR. Roosevelt assigned William Donovan to spearhead the U.S. actions, which soon coalesced a wide range of reporters and publishers in propaganda efforts. The major organizations, "Fight for Freedom'" led by Ernest Cuneo, and the "Council for Democracy" led by C.D. Jackson (Time-Life) had members including: Allen Dulles, Walter Winchell, Walter Lippmann, Ed Murrow, Eric Severeid, Helen Kirkpatrick, Elmer Davis (CBS), Geoffrey Parsons (*N.Y. Herald Tribune*) Herbert Agar (*Louisville Courier-Journal*), Arthur Sulz-

berger (*N.Y. Post*), Barry Bingham (*Louisville Courier-Journal*), Paul Patterson (*Baltimore Sun*), Dorothy Schiff (*New York Post*) Ralph Ingersoll
(*Picture Magazine*).

At the outset of WWII there were two schools of thought regarding
news and national security. The Office of War Information, headed by the
noted journalist Elmer Davis, thought that America would do best in the
long run by reporting the truth. Another school of thought, instituted at
the Office of Strategic Services (OSS), directed by Bill Donovan, believed
that propaganda ("patriotic reporting") would maintain morale and better win the war. The OSS perspective prevailed.

In 1940, President Roosevelt sent his trusted friend, corporate lawyer
Bill Donovan, to assess the war in Europe. Donovan proposed the creation
of the OSS, to gather intelligence as well as to create propaganda to counter the "insidious" Nazi strategy of "psychological attacks on the moral and
spirited defenses of a nation." The majority of "Wild Bill" Donovan's assets
at the OSS were journalists. Psychological warfare included "*propaganda,
sabotage, guerilla activities, bribing, blackmail, assassination...*"[3]

During World War ll Supreme Commander General Dwight Eisenhower told a meeting of newspaper editors, "Public opinion wins wars ...
I have always considered as quasi staff officers, correspondents accredited
to my headquarters." When CBS President Bill Paley began working at
the Office of War information (OWI) along with C.D. Jackson, an executive at Time-Life, he was given the rank of colonel. Paley's first major assignment was to establish a radio network in Italy through Armed Forces
Radio "to lure Italian listeners with entertainment programs interspersed
with propaganda – just the sort of arrangement CBS had used for its
South American network." Paley's value was enhanced by his ability to
work with both "black" and "white" (truthful) propaganda. [4]

Jackson became the deputy chief of the Psychological Warfare Branch
in North Africa by the spring of 1963, under General Robert A. McClure.
The "psy-ops" included public relations, censorships, behavior modifica-
tion, false identity, deep deception, fictional event staging, false defectors
and legends. [5] Coverage of the impact of nuclear attacks on Japanese civil-
ians was suppressed in part by the military briefings. According to *New
York Times* reporter William Laurence, thirty journalists were given a pro-
paganda-laden military junket which would dispute Japanese assertions
that "radiation was responsible for deaths even after the attacks." [6]

After WWII ended, the OSS offices of propaganda, covert action and
psychological operations were combined into the Office of Policy Coor-

dination (OPC) housed at the State Department, while the Office of War Information was dissolved.

After the war McClure wrote to Jackson about his power as military director of the Psychological Warfare Division: "We now control 37 newspapers, 6 radio stations, 314 theaters, 642 movies, 101 magazines, 237 book publishers, 7,384 book dealers and printers, conduct 15 public opinion surveys a month, publish a newspaper with 15 million circulation, run the Associated Press of Germany and operate 20 library centers...[7]

During most of the Cold War, journalists faithfully deferred to the dictates of national security. The real and perceived threat due to the Soviet expansion into Eastern Europe after WWII caused both the State and Defense Departments to pressure Congress for the National Security Act of 1947, which established the CIA. A major function of the agency was to counter the appeal of communism, and Radio Free Europe (RFE) and Radio Liberty were quickly planned as part of this psychological warfare. The OPC, led by Frank Wisner, became the fastest growing section of the CIA. Its budget swelled from $4.7 million in 1949 to $82 million in 1952. The CIA paid for this propaganda by skimming from the Marshall Plan funds. One CIA agent, Gilbert Greenway recalled, "We couldn't spend it all..."[8]

The CIA propaganda efforts in the 1948 Italian election led to an expansion of psychological warfare in National Security Council directive 10/2. Essentially this approved covert actions against foreign countries "which are so planned and executed that any U.S. Government responsibility for them is not evident to unauthorized persons, and that if uncovered the U.S Government can plausibly disclaim any responsibility for them." By 1949, CIA-financed radio propaganda was quietly set in motion to complement the State Department program, Voice of America.

Many of the psychological warfare operations remained unknown to most of Congress. Fewer than 20 members of Congress knew of the overarching Free Europe Committee, which coordinated Radio Free Europe and Radio Liberty. Some representatives of America's most powerful media leaders were involved in the committee, including Henry Luce of *Time-Life-Fortune* and DeWitt Wallace, founder of *Reader's Digest*; however, the press never revealed any government involvement. These efforts were significantly strengthened in April 1950 by National Security Council directive #68, which called for "hard-hitting psychological warfare." It argued that America needed a "long distance CBS to compete on equal terms against a local NBC."[9] At the spring 1950 meeting of the State Department foreign policy investment banker Robert Lovett, advocated that "we have a much vaster propaganda machine to tell our story at home and abroad."

RFE was publicly described in 1951 as "a citizen's adventure in the field of psychological warfare... its mission is to keep hope alive among our friends behind the Iron Curtain and to sow dissension among our enemies.... We are unhampered by the niceties of intercourse. We enter the fight with bare fists."[10]

Numerous media experts were recruited to sit on the American Committee for Liberation including: C.D. Jackson of *Fortune Magazine* (Time-Life) to be the first RFE president; reporters Eugene Lyons (*Reader's Digest*) and William Chamberlain, correspondents in the Soviet Union along with publisher William White. Allen Grover, vice-president of Time, Inc., was appointed as the vice president. By the mid-1960s Frank Stanton, corporate president of CBS, was the chairman of the executive committee of the Radio Free Europe Fund. When the CIA cover was blown in the early 1970's, the stations were merged, and Sig Mickelson, former CBS news service president and vice president of Time-Life, was appointed as the new chief.

In response to a loose propaganda network called the International Organization of Journalists, which had been taken over by Communists by 1950, the CIA developed "Operation Mockingbird," conceived by Frank Wisner, (the covert operations director of the CIA, and a major organizer of Radio Liberty and Radio Free Europe,) his assistant Richard Helms, and Phil Graham, publisher and then part owner·of the *Washington Post*. This program formalized the recruitment of journalists. By the early 1950s, Mockingbird was operational; each journalist had a code name, a field supervisor and a field office.[11] Phil Graham would recommend reporters for jobs with other newspapers especially those with overseas bureaus, and Wisner reciprocated by paying for *Post* reporters' trips.

After 1951, the CIA, following the policies of its Eberstadt task force, set in motion by then High Commissioner of Germany, John McCloy, published about twenty "generally highbrow" magazines in Europe. They included the *Encounter* in London, *Socialist Commentary* and *Der Monat* in Germany, *Preves* in France, *Forum* in Vienna, *Tempo Presente* in Rome, *Hiwar* in Lebanon, *Candernos* in Latin America, and *Chinese Quarterly* in China among others.[12] *Der Monat* was strongly supported by John Mc-Cloy because of its left-of-center intellectual stance.

In 1952 the CIA launched the American Newspaper Guild (ANG) as a founding member of the anti-communist International Federation of

Journalists. The ANG attempted to influence trade unionism and "professional journalism" in Europe, Asia, Africa, and Latin America through technical assistance and educational and training seminars.[13] The Eisenhower Administration embraced psychological warfare more fully than the Truman Administration and it attained the status of a scientific doctrine. The efforts of Henry Kissinger in the 1950s at the Psychological Strategy Board expanded psywar targets to include indigenous populations and to focus on youth.

At home the CIA worked with *The New Leader, The Reporter*, and *Time*, accessing a range of political perspectives. *The New Leader*, led by anti-Stalinist social democrat Al Levitas, was given financial support and consulted frequently with George Kennan, Allen Dulles and C.D. Jackson. *The Reporter*, launched in 1949 by liberal anticommunist Max Ascoli, worked with Nelson Rockefeller, John Hay Whitney and C.D. Jackson.

Two former OSS members, Philip Horton and Douglas Carter, served on the CIA magazine staff and maintained their intelligence contacts with Allen Dulles (Director of Central Intelligence) and James Angleton, (CIA Director of Counter Intelligence.) Carter, an expert in psychological warfare, helped found the National Students Association for the CIA, and would later serve as a special assistant to President Johnson.[14] During the Korean War military censorship severely impacted U.S. reporters, yet perceptions of this as a pragmatic patriotism were common. United Press reporter Robert Miller noted in 1952 that:

> We are not giving them the true facts about Korea, we haven't been for the last sixteen months and there will be little improvement in the war coverage unless radical changes are made in the military censorship... There are certain facts and stories from Korea that editors and publishers have printed which were pure fabrications. You didn't know that when you printed them. Many of us who sent the stories knew they were false, but we had to write them because they were official releases from responsible military headquarters, and were released for publication even though the people responsible knew they were untrue.

> General Douglas MacArthur responded to critical reports of the war by expelling reporters or pressuring news organizations to recall correspondents who offended him. The top brass of CBS killed a report by Edward R. Murrow challenging the military's assessment of the war. Bill Paley warned correspondents to be careful of what they said in these difficult times. Paley's directive clarified

that CBS had diversified and was responsible to shareholders and vulnerable to politicians. (P103-4)

In 1953 Eisenhower's Cold War Psychological Operation's Chief; C. D. Jackson worked with the State Dept., the NSC, the CIA and the White House. By March 1953 Jackson became the White Houses' ad hoc director of national psychological warfare, which put him in the small group of Eisenhower's advisors John and Allen Dulles.

Censorship of the press throughout the Korean War became virtually complete during the peace negotiations in 1953. According to journalist James Aronson:

> Correspondents assigned to the U.N. Command were not permit-
> ted to speak with U.N. negotiators; they were briefed, several hours
> after each session by a U.S. Army officer who had not even been
> at the talks. They were refused permission to inspect documents
> presented at the discussions and were dependent entirely on U.S.
> armed forces public relations officers in Korea and at Supreme
> headquarters in Tokyo... [15]

When the truce talks opened in July, North Korea proposed a cease-fire at the 38th Parallel; however, the U.S. proposed a line 32 miles north of the 38th Parallel, which would have meant surrender by the North Koreans and Chinese of the impregnably fortified mountains under their control. The U.N. Chief, U.S. Admiral Turner Joy, told the Western press that the North Koreans had refused to discuss a cease-fire at the 38th Parallel. This disinformation was printed in American newspapers for weeks before the fact emerged that it was the U.S. which was refusing to discuss the 38th Parallel. [16]

The informal journalistic notions of patriotism can be seen in the statements of *Newsweek's* foreign editor, Harry Kern, as well as syndicated columnist and CIA asset Joseph Alsop. Kern noted, "...What we knew we told them (CIA) and the State Department... We thought it was admirable at the time." Alsop traveled to the Philippines when asked to by the CIA. "I'm proud they asked me and proud to have done it... The notion that a newspaperman doesn't have a duty to his country is perfect balls." [17]

The rare dissent was revealing, as with the *New York Times* Chief of Staff, John Swinton, at a toast before the New York Press Club in 1953.

> There is no such thing, at this date in history, as an independent
> press. You know it and I know it. There is not one of you who dare

to write your honest opinions, and if you did, you know before-hand that it would never appear in print … any of you who would be so foolish as to write honest opinions would be out on the streets looking for another job.

By 1954, the CIA Special Study Group for Covert Actions, the Doo-little Committee (chaired by General James Doolittle) recommended ex-panding the role and methods of psywar:

> It is now clear that we are facing an implacable enemy whose avowed objective is world domination by whatever means and whatever cost. There are no rules in such a game. Hitherto accept-able norms of human conduct do not apply. If the United States is to survive, longstanding American concepts of "fair play" must be reconsidered. We must develop espionage and counterespionage services and must learn to subvert, sabotage, and destroy our en-emies by cleverer, more sophisticated and more effective methods than used against us. It may become necessary that the American people be made acquainted with, understand, and support this fundamentally repugnant philosophy.

During this time even CIA covert operations to overthrow elected foreign presidents, such as agrarian reformer Jacob Arbenz in Guatemala, could be shielded from American reporters. CIA Director Allen Dulles claimed to Arthur Hays Sulzberger that *New York Times* reporter Sydney Grusom was unable to be "objective." So Grusom was kept in Mexico City during the CIA-directed coup d'état.[18]

Radio Free Europe actually contributed to the failed Hungarian revolt of students and workers in 1956 by hinting that there would be U.S. aid. The CIA was blamed, and psywar efforts were temporarily diminished. C.D. Jackson, furious with the temporary constraints, resigned from the Board of RFE in 1958.[19]

By the mid-1950's, the prominent American news and feature service, North American Newspaper Alliance (NANA), was bought by former British Intelligence Officer Ivor Bryce and his American partner former BSC and OSS officer Ernest Cuneo.

Bryce and Cuneo were friends of legendary British spy Ian Fleming, (the creator of James Bond) and hired him as the NANA European Editor and Vice-President. During WWII Cuneo was a liaison between FDR, William "Bill" Donovan, Chief of the OSS, and William Stephenson, the representative of British Intelligence in the U.S. Victor Lasky, a public relations executive for Radio Liberty (one of the CIA's largest propaganda operations) had his conservative column run by NANA from 1962-1980.

In the 1964 Chilean election, the CIA spent more per vote than was spent by the Johnson and Goldwater presidential campaigns combined. [20] They extensively used the press, radio, films, pamphlets, posters, leaflets, direct mailings, and wall paintings. "Disinformation" and "black propaganda" material which purported to originate from another source, such as the Chilean Communist Party, were used as well.[21]

Globally, at its peak in 1967, the CIA communications empire embraced more than 800 news and public information organizations and individuals. It was known inside the CIA as "Wisner's Wurlitzer." Frank Wisner, also a member of the elite and powerful Council on Foreign Relations, liked to think that he could orchestrate any political tune anywhere.[22] At the height of the Cold War "the CIA made 70 to 80 insertions into various media outlets each day ... flowing secretly from Agency headquarters into hundreds of different channels around the globe."[23] More information regarding this relationship was sought by the Senate Intelligence Committee in 1976, but the investigation was restricted by then CIA Director George H.W. Bush.[24] The number of U.S. reporters working in some relationship with the CIA has been estimated at more than 400, based on information from Senate Intelligence Committee staffers.

Even according to the *New York Times*, "the CIA has at times owned or subsidized more than 50 newspapers, news services, radio stations, periodicals, and other communications entities, sometimes in the country, but mostly overseas.... At least 22 American news organizations had employed, though sometimes only on a casual basis, American journalists who were also working for the CIA."[25] The organizations included ABC, CBS, *Time, Life, Newsweek,* the *New York Times,* Associated Press and United Press International, the Scripps-Howard chain of newspapers, the Hearst newspaper chain, the *Christian Science Monitor,* the *Wall Street Journal,* the *Louisville Courier-Journal, Forbes,* a publisher of travel guides, College Press Service, *Business International,* the McLendon Broadcasting Organization, and the Copley News Services, among others. When former CIA Director William Colby was asked if he ever told journalists what to write, he answered, "Oh sure, all of the time."[26]

In 1975 the Senate Intelligence committee found that the CIA owned "more than 200 wire services, newspapers, magazines, and book publishing complexes" and subsidized many more. The CIA covertly commissioned more than 1200 books, many of which were reviewed by CIA agents in various U.S. media, including (the *New York Times*).[27] Colby was hated by many CIA officers for his revelations. A few years later he was found floating in the Potomac River, the victim of an alleged boating accident.

A partial list of foreign beneficiaries of CIA funding, in addition to the aforementioned European magazines, includes: *Africa Forum, Africa Report, Berliner Verein, Center of Studies and Documentation* (Mexico), Foreign News Service, Inc., Interamerican Federation of Newspapermen's Organizations, International Federation of Free Journalists, International Journalists, International Student Conference, Public Services International and the World Confederation of Organizations of Teaching Professors as well as hundreds of foreign journalists. Conduits for CIA funding to American and foreign organizations included corporate and elite philanthropic foundations such as: the Borden Trust; Dodge Foundation, Edsel Foundation, Monroe Fund, Charitable Trust, and the Tower Fund just to name a few.[28]

Carl Bernstein's revelations in *Rolling Stone* 10/20/77, "The CIA and the Media," clarified some of the shades of gray.

> Some of these journalists' relationships with the Agency were taut; some were explicit. There was cooperation, accommodation, and overlap. Journalists provided a full range of clandestine services— from simple intelligence gathering to serving as go-between with spies in Communist countries. Reporters shared their notebooks with the CIA. Editors shared their staffs. Some of the journalists were Pulitzer prize winners, distinguished reporters who considered themselves ambassadors-without-portfolio for their country. Most were less exalted: foreign correspondents who found that their association with the Agency helped their work; stringers and freelancers who were as interested in the derrying-do of the spy business as in filing articles; and the smallest category, full-time CIA employee's masquerading as journalists abroad. In many instances, CIA documents show journalists were engaged to perform tasks for the CIA with the consent of the managements of America's leading news organizations.
>
> The peculiar nature of the job of the foreign correspondent is ideal for such work; he was accorded unusual access by his host country, and permitted to travel in areas often off-limits to other Americans, spends much of his time cultivating sources in governments, academics institutions, the military establishment and scientific communities. He has the opportunity to form long-term personal relationships…

"After a foreigner is recruited, a case officer often has to stay in the background," explained a CIA official. "So you use a journalist to carry messages to and from both parties."

The tasks they performed sometimes consisted of little more than serving as "eyes and ears" ... On other occasions their assignments were more complex: planting subtly concocted pieces of misinformation; hosting parties or receptions designed to bring together American agents and foreign spies, serving up "black" propaganda to leading foreign journalists at lunch or dinner; providing their hotel rooms as "drops" for highly sensitive information moving to and from foreign agents; conveying instruction and dollars to CIA controlled members of foreign governments."

In the 1950's and 1960's journalists were used as intermediaries – spotting, paying, passing instructions – to the Christian Democratic party in Italy and the Social Democrats in Germany ... reporters were used extensively against Salvador Allende in Chile, supporting his opponents who wrote anti-Allende propaganda for CIA proprietary publications that were distributed in Chile.

In the field, journalists were used to help recruit and handle foreigners as agents; to acquire and evaluate information, and to plant false information with officials of foreign governments...

Within the CIA, journalist operatives were accorded elite status, a consequence of the common experience journalists shared with high level CIA officials. Many had gone to the same schools as their CIA handlers, moved in the same circles ... and were part of the same "old boy" network that constituted something of establishment elite in the media, politics and academia of postwar America. [29]

Congressman Otis Pike's opening comments to the Congressional hearings on the "CIA and the Media" in 1978 raised concerns:

Simply stated, we know that in the past the CIA has had contractual relationships, paid and unpaid, with individual journalists in both American and foreign news organizations.... In some cases, officials of these organizations were witting of these relationships; in others not.... Some of the journalists did positive intelligence gathering for the CIA; others merely exchanged information or offered information on their own.... Some journalists went further; they published stories both true and false for the CIA or they helped recruit agents. Sometimes the journalists weren't really journalists at all, but rather CIA agents under cover.... No doubt the motives behind the relationships were varied. There are a number of questions, which arise from what they know of these CIA-press relations. They reach the very heart of a free press, its impartiality, and credibility, and they raise the possibility that Americans at home can be victims of disinformation sown by their own government.[30]

The Church Committee report explored the impact of "blowback" or "black propaganda fallout" – lies which are unwittingly picked up by the American press. They admonished: "Because the source of black propaganda is so fully concealed, the CIA recognizes that it risks seriously misleading U.S. policymaking."[31]

Former Chief of Counterintelligence James Angleton "ran a completely independent group of journalist operatives who performed sensitive and frequently dangerous assignments; little is known about the group." The CIA even ran a formal training program to teach agents to be journalists.

The scope of the approved operations for the Forty Committee covert actions for media and propaganda operations was larger than those approved for Election Support, about 29% of the covert actions budget. The 1978 annual budget for CIA propaganda was $250-265 million – larger than the combined budgets of Reuters, AP and UPI.[32]

In 1983 former CIA executive Tom Braden revealed on CNN's *Cross Fire* that the CIA funded the *Communist Worker* newspaper in the 1950's. Braden maintained that "The CIA licked Joseph Stalin's last great offensive in Western Europe, and it did it by helping liberals, intellectuals and socialists, which is to say conservatives, because socialism in France and Belgium is nothing but a sort of moderate Republicanism."[33]

The FBI under J. Edgar Hoover also developed strong relationships with the media, most notably *Time, Life, Fortune, Newsweek, Business Week, Reader's Digest, U.S. News & World Report* and *Look*. The sources regularly forwarded notes from editorial conferences about forthcoming or proposed articles. Hoover was close friends with *Reader's Digest's* publisher and editor, DeWitt Wallace and Fulton Ousler, as well as the Cowles brothers who published *Look. Reader's Digest* ran more than a dozen of Hoover's ghost-written articles, the *U.S. News & World Report* printed twenty-five.[34]

Informal, social, and business relationships between the press, the intelligence community, State Department, and corporate elites had existed long before WWII. The Whitney family, one of America's wealthiest families, for example, was accustomed to wielding power in government and the mass media.

The best example of this alliance of Wall Street and left-wing publication was the *New Republic*, a magazine founded by Willard
Straight using Payne Whitney money. The original purpose for establishing the paper was to provide an outlet for the progressive
left and to guide it quietly in an Anglophile direction.... The first
editor of the *New Republic*, the well-known "liberal" Herbert Croly,
was aware of the situation.... Croly's biography of Straight, published in 1914, makes perfectly clear that Straight was in no sense
a liberal or progressive, but was, indeed, a typical international
banker, and that the *New Republic* was simply a medium for certain
designs of such international bankers, notably to blunt the isolationism and anti-British sentiments so prevalent among American
progressives...

In the 1930s major stockholders controlling *Newsweek* included Paul
Mellon (Mellon Bank), the Harrimans, and the Whitneys. The Whitneys
were related through marriage to the Harrimans and the Vanderbilts as
well as to William Paley of CBS. The Whitneys were also close to Nelson
Rockefeller, Joseph Alsop, and high-level CIA officers Frank Wisner, William H. Jackson, and Allen Dulles. Jock Whitney's grandfather had served
under President Grover Cleveland as Secretary of War and Jock served
in World War II coordinating propaganda in Latin America with Nelson
Rockefeller in the Office of the Coordinator of Inter-American Affairs.
Whitney also worked for a stint with corporate lawyer William "Wild
Bill" Donovan, the Director of the OSS. By 1956 Whitney was the Chair-
man of Freeport Sulphur as well as Chairman of the United Republican
Finance Committee. High-level CIA officer Tracy Barnes was the son of
Jock Whitney's second cousin, and they became friends while attending
the Army Air Corps intelligence school in Harrisburg, Pennsylvania.[35]

Jock Whitney's close friend and business associate Walter Thayer was
a director of the Morgan affiliated Bankers Trust Fund and had spent four
years in William Donovan's law firm. In 1961, Thayer was president of
the *New York Herald Tribune* when Jock Whitney was its editor-in-chief
and publisher, a far cry from the independent *Tribune* founded by Horace
Greeley. The Whitney trust was financed in part with money from the
Granary Fund, a CIA conduit. Jock Whitney along with Richard Mellon
Scaife cooperated with a range of CIA media sources. In 1958 they helped
fund a CIA front company which dispersed six articles weekly from the
Forum World Features in 50 countries to 120 foreign and 30 domestic clients; including the *Washington Post*. Jock Whitney was also closely asso-

ciated with Katherine Graham of the *Washington Post*, and Graham held a 45% share of the *New York Herald Tribune* stock, with an option for 5% more upon Whitney's death.

In 1948 and 1949, CIA director Allen Dulles assisted his friends, John Hayes and Phil Graham, in their purchase of WTOP-CBS radio from another friend, Colonel William Paley, previously a prominent staffer at the Army's Psychological Warfare Division. CBS and the *Washington Post* then began to share news staffs. Phil Graham's experience with army intelligence created an affinity with CIA men and he staffed the *Post* with men who had intelligence backgrounds. This included Alfred Friendly and Russell Wiggins from Army Intelligence, Alan Barth from the Office of War Information, and John Hayes from the Armed Forces Network of the OSS. Graham also arranged in 1951 for *Post* reporter Ben Bradlee to be hired as a press attaché in the American Embassy in Paris, where for a year Bradlee worked on the staff of the Office of U.S. Information and Educational Exchange (USIE), the parent of Voice of America and U.S. Information Agency (USIA). In 1953 Bradlee was under orders from the "head of the CIA in Paris" to write an "Operations Memorandum," which asserted that Julius and Ethyl Rosenberg deserved the death sentence for their alleged sharing of nuclear secrets with the Soviet Union. This story was disseminated to forty different countries.[36]

These elite connections could also be seen in the informal lengthy brunches, or "salons," at the home of Phil and Katherine Graham, owners of the *Washington Post*, and later *Newsweek*, which were attended by the press, top foreign policy officials, the intelligence community, and politicians. Phil built on the connections of his father-in-law, Eugene Graham, who had chaired the Federal Reserve Band as well as the World Bank. One party held in 1960 for the powerful nationally syndicated columnist and CIA asset Joseph Alsop, a cousin of FDR, featured a guest list which included former Secretary of State Dean Acheson, Allen Dulles, Desmond FitzGerald, Tracy Barnes and Alsop's lifelong friend Richard Bissell of the CIA; diplomats Chip Bowen and David Bruce; Justice Felix Frankfurter; and reporters Arthur Krock, Walter Lippmann, Cy Sulzberger and candidate John Kennedy among others. Joe Alsop's brother, Stewart, his journalistic partner for years, had been in the OSS, and was an old friend of Allen Dulles and Frank Wisner. The Alsops also hosted legendary dinner parties with similar guest lists, which have been called "the Georgetown set."[37]

By 1960 the increasingly powerful Phil Graham was strongly backing Lyndon Johnson for the presidency, until the first day of the Democratic Convention. After reassessing Kennedy's power, Graham and his close friend Joe Alsop worked to reconcile the often-antagonistic Kennedy with Johnson and helped broker the vice-presidential position for Johnson. FBI director J. Edgar Hoover was also a significant force promoting Johnson, though his cooperation with Graham and Alsop is unclear.

When Phil Graham bought *Newsweek* in 1961 from the Astor Foundation, Gates White McGarrah, president of the Bank for International Settlements in the 1930s, was on its board. McGarrah's grandson, Richard McGarrah Helms (the former Director of the CIA), was Ben Bradlee's childhood friend. Bradlee was a *Newsweek* editor in 1963, a close friend of President Kennedy, brother-in-law to CIA covert operations chief Cord Meyer, and former senior editor of the *Washington Post*. In 1963 the chairman of *Newsweek* and the *Washington Post* was Frederick S. Beebe, a father figure to Katherine Graham, and a member of the Council on Foreign Relations. He was a close friend of Allen Dulles (Director of the CIA and later Warren Commission member) and had practiced law at Cravath, Swaine and Moore with another Warren Commission member, John McCloy, also both members of the Council on Foreign Relations.[38] Katherine Graham was also close to Henry Luce's wife, Clare Booth Luce and viewed her as a role model.

Similar elite-corporate-government-media connections can be seen with the Luce media empire of *Time*, *Life*, and *Fortune*, which had been financed with the Morgan and Rockefeller banking conglomerates from its outset in the 1920s. In the 1930's Time Inc. was owned by an "inner circle of American finance and its policies reflected its ownership." Henry Luce, or Harry as his friends called him, was the major force behind Republican Wendell Willkie's presidential campaign. Luce's crusade-like anti-communism included notions of free trade and anti-isolationism that were expounded by Willkie. In the 1930s he supported the military expansion of Hitler and Mussolini through the Rhineland, Ethiopia, and Spain. In the early 1940s Luce advocated an "American Century" consisting of free enterprise, free trade, vigilant anti-communism, all bolstered by a strong military. *Time*, the most influential U.S. periodical in 1963, promoted Luce's agenda: "I don't pretend that this is an objective magazine. It's an editorial magazine from the first page to the last and whatever comes out has to reflect my view...." Luce wrote that it is "the crowds [that] will destroy civilization" and implored the press "to assist people in governing themselves." He closely controlled a process of group writing in *Time* which "blended (the news) with opinion and editorializing so that the reader got not mere news but a proper understanding of it."[39]

As a Skull & Bones member at Yale, Luce had long been friends with Winston Churchill, John D. Rockefeller III, the Duke and Duchess of Windsor, and John and Allen Dulles. He had readily allowed members of his staff to work for the CIA, and Dulles regularly hosted dinners for *Time* foreign correspondents. *Time's* senior vice-president, C. D. Jackson, had worked closely with President Eisenhower, Allen Dulles, and John McCloy on a number of psychological warfare projects, and had married into the Astor family. Luce's sister was married to *Time* director Maurice Moore, a man who had worked with Warren Commissioner John McCloy at the law firm of Cravath, Swaine and Moore.[40] Six of Time's fourteen directors were members of the Council on Foreign Relations, as was C. D. Jackson. *Time* supported *The Partisan Review* and *The New Leader*, considered worthy causes by the CIA. *Time* collaboration with the CIA was so extensive that it "was difficult to tell precisely where the Luce Empire's overseas intelligence network ended and the CIA's began. "You don't need to manipulate *Time* magazine because there are CIA people at the management level." (William Bader CIA officer).

The Luces were so frustrated with JFK's foreign policy after the Cuban Missile Crisis that a White House luncheon was arranged to mend fences. The Luces pressed Kennedy hard about the need to go to war with Cuba, "for American prestige and survival." Kennedy suggested that Henry Luce was a "warmonger," and the Luces left before dessert.[41]

Another dimension of the elite media government connections is seen in the rise of political pundits. Walter Lippmann was the most influential of the early nationally syndicated columnists. Soon after he started with the *New Republic* he was invited to President Woodrow Wilson's summer home in New Jersey to clarify the U.S. foray into Mexico. The Harvard-educated journalist lamented the dangers of a populace becoming "inevitable victims of agitation and propaganda" and through his books and columns he envisioned himself performing an essential service "to find out what is going on under the surface ... and what it could mean..." Theologian Reinhold Niebuhr suggested that later in Lippmann's career he condoned "managed news" as inevitable and saw the solution for the ills of democracy lying in more executive power by an elitist government. Lippmann benefited from the patronage of the powerful, such that columnist Michael Kinsley referred to him as "the American sycophancy." Lippmann's friend, *NYT* editor James Reston, saw him "more attached to politicians than any other columnist, a man who loved going to embassies, (a standard diplomatic cover for intelligence agents) philosophizing after dinner and he liked to be asked to the White House. It's true that people talk about money as corruptive, but the social life is much more so than money."

Similar mass media-government-elite connections existed outside of the so-called Eastern Establishment. The Copley News Service was inspired by a meeting between the late James S. Copley, publisher and sole owner of Copley Press, and President Eisenhower to supplement the CIA. Captain E. Robert Anderson, who headed the Copley Press San Diego operations, drew on his background in Naval Intelligence and coordinated intelligence gathering. Copley's father, Colonel Ira Copley, had hired OSS officer Robert Richards to run their Washington Office before the end of WWII. General Victor Krulak, onetime head of liaison between the Joint Chiefs of Staff and the intelligence services, succeeded Anderson as editorial director of Copley Press in 1968. From well-placed CIA sources, reporter Joe Trento has determined that no fewer than twenty-three Copley News Service employees had worked for the CIA simultaneously.[42] CNS's first Latin American editor was CIA man, David Hellyer, who held the position until he returned to the CIA in 1960.

James Copley also cooperated closely with the FBI, particularly by 1964, when the former FBI director of the San Diego office, Frank Price, became his "security consultant." According to photographers and reporters at Copley Press, Price and Krulak ran a system of intelligence gathering for the FBI. Further, the FBI used the Copley Press to release "raw" and unverified data about individuals of whom it didn't approve.

Sociologist Herbert Gans observed that during the 1960s both CIA and FBI agents obtained press passes from local news organizations, presumably with executive compliance, to spy on anti-war protesters. This was confirmed by Senate Intelligence Committee hearings in the mid-1970s. Local television stations often voluntarily supplied outtakes of films made at anti-war demonstrations to help the CIA, FBI or local police "red squads" identify individual demonstrators.[43]

Whereas a number of intelligence officers started their careers with the press, quite a few CIA officers made the reverse trip to the mass media. Richard Helms, Henry Pleasants, Wallace Deuel, Jake Goodwin and Angus Thuermer moved from the mass media to intelligence services. Those relocating from Langley to the mass media include: Tom Braden, international organizations director for the CIA 1950-1954, moved to writing nationally syndicated columns; Bonner Day worked for the Foreign Broadcast Information Service, then moved to U.S. News & World Report; Pentagon correspondent Robert Myers shifted from the CIA Asia desk to publish *The New Republic*; George Packard, CIA Far East, moved to *Newsweek,* then to executive editor of the *Philadelphia Bulletin*; Bruce von Voorst, former CIA Africa, became a *Newsweek* diplomatic correspondent; Philip Geyelin cycled from the *Wall St. Journal* to the CIA and then returned to the *Wall St. Journal,* and in 1967 became the editorial page editor of the *Washington Post.*[44]

The relationship between the *New York Times* and the CIA was considered the most valuable among newspaper assets, according to CIA officials. A few executives, such as Arthur Hayes Sulzberger of the *New York Times* and his son Cy, signed a secrecy oath. From 1950-1966 some CIA employees were provided cover with approval from Sulzberger, who socialized with former Director of the CIA, Allen Dulles, as well as subsequent Directors of Central Intelligence John McCone and Richard Helms.

Former *New York Times* editor Harrison Salisbury has observed that most of them came from the same social circles and had married into each other's families.

> They were Yale and Harvard and Princeton ... they were lawyers, and bankers and businessmen and journalists. They were General Alder and Allen Dulles; Ben Welles and Walter Sullivan and James Angleton; they were John Oakes and his brother ... they were Kim Roosevelt, the CIA men who pulled off the Mossedegh coup [Iran-1953] and Pope Brewer and Kenneth Love; they were James Reston and his deputy in the Washington bureau ... Wallace Carroll and Carroll's intimate friend, Richard Helms, with whom he worked in prewar UPI days in Europe; they were all the correspondents who had been wined and dined and flattered by Allen Dulles and Frank Wisner and Des FitzGerald ... and Tracy Barnes – Reston, Daniel, Frankel, Drew Middleton and myself; they were Cy Sulzberger and Frank Wisner and Bob Joyner and Allen Dulles and Colby's and station chiefs all over the world.... They knew each other, they stayed at each other's houses, and they drank together and dined together ... and knew each other's secrets...[45]

In 1966, when Secretary of State Dean Rusk protested to the *New York Times* that an upcoming news series on the CIA was not in the national interest, the *Times* responded by sending the completed series to John McCone, a former director of the CIA, for editing. Turner Catledge, the managing editor, wrote a memo to *Times* publisher "Punch" Sulzberger: "I don't know of any other series in my time which has been prepared with greater care and with such remarkable attention to the views of the agency involved as this one."[46]

Harrison Salisbury noted in his book, *Without Fear or Favor* that James Angleton, Director of Counterintelligence at the CIA, had boasted of how his assets within the *Times* had alerted him to an upcoming series on the CIA. Angleton used his contacts to tone down the story.

> Angleton said privately that he had his own men on the *Times*; men whom he could meet on street corners, men who weren't on his payroll but to whom he provided expense money. Never, he said, had he gone to *Times'* management about this. He just took the people he wanted and got what he wanted…[47]

Angleton had worked in the X-2 group of OSS with *NYT* editorial page chief John Oakes, and diplomatic correspondent Ben Welles, who thought of Angleton as a "good friend." Welles was thought by many of his colleagues to be remarkably intimate with the CIA.

> Arthur Sulzberger designated John Oakes liaison to the CIA when it was still known as CIG. One of Angleton's top deputies, Jim Hunt, designated Alfred Corning Clark to serve as case officer to *New York Times* writers.[48]

Reporter Carl Bernstein wrote that, "CBS was unquestionably the CIA's most valuable broadcasting asset." CBS president Colonel William Paley and Allen Dulles had a social as well as a working relationship, which some authors argue set the standard for future cooperation between the CIA and the major broadcast companies. William Paley had also become an integral part of foreign policy planning on the Council on Foreign Relations even before he was tapped in 1951 by President Truman to chair a presidential commission on raw materials. The Paley Commission, which consisted of numerous corporate leaders, clarified foreign policy options.[49] CBS executive Frank Stanton had also long worked with the CIA on psychological warfare with Radio Free Europe, Free Europe Fund and the National Committee for a Free Europe.[50] Stanton, a longtime friend and advisor of Lyndon Johnson, later became a trustee for the Rockefeller Foundation and for a decade a chairman of the RAND Corporation, a "think tank" funded almost entirely with Air Force money. Stanton also served as the Chairman of the United States Advisory Commission on Information, which assessed the operations of the United States Information Agency, (USIA), and the propaganda arm of the American government overseas. Over the years CBS provided cover for CIA employees and annually from 1950 through 1960, CBS correspondents joined the CIA hierarchy for a private New Year's Day dinner at the exclusive Alibi Club, paid for by Dulles.[51]

In 1964, Richard Salant, later CBS News president, served on a super-secret CIA task force which explored methods of beaming American propaganda to the People's Republic of China.

> The other members of the study team were Zbigniew Brzezinski, then a professor of political science at MIT; and John Hayes, then vice-president of the Washington Post Company for radio-TV. The principle government officials associated with the project was Cord Meyer of the CIA; McGeorge Bundy, then special assistant to the president for national security; Leonard Marks, the director of USIA; and Bill Moyers, the special assistant to President Lyndon Johnson.

In May of 1977 the President of CBS News, Richard Salant, confirmed that CBS had connections with the CIA that had been formed back in the 1950s. CBS Chairman William Paley and Sig Mickelson, Paley's predecessor, had forged these ties. Salant stated that any CBS foreign correspondent returning to the U.S. after assignment was traditionally "debriefed" by CIA Director Allen Dulles. CIA operatives were allowed to screen CBS news film, and to eavesdrop on conversations between CBS news officials in New York and the field. Paley also permitted his own Paley Foundation to funnel money to CIA-sponsored projects abroad.[52] In February 1976, prior to the formation of the House Select Committee on Assassinations (HSCA), CIA Director George H.W. Bush called a meeting with Paley and Salant to gain support for the CIA's policy of "burying the past." One of the CBS executives told Bush, "we protect ours, you protect yours" when dealing with CIA contacts within the CBS news organization, as well as with stringers working for other national publications.[53]

Other facets of CBS policy demonstrated the depth of Cold War cooperation as well. Reports and editorials criticizing the Truman Doctrine, the Korean War and the early McCarthy era were aggressively discouraged. The former president of CBS News, Fred Friendly, has written about the pressure he received from Frank Stanton regarding dove positions on the Vietnam War, "… his [Stanton's] concern was that too much 'dove-hawk' talk unsteadied the hand of the Commander-In-Chief." Friendly admitted that "… in my almost two years as head of CBS news I tempered my news judgment and tailored my conscience more than once."[54] All CBS employees signed loyalty oaths and all news guests were checked in advance for their political background. CBS also shared information with NBC for cross-checking, according to Frank Stanton.[55]

In testimony before the Pike Committee former CBS and ABC foreign correspondent Sam Jaffe revealed that he had been an FBI agent. He asserted that leading anchorman Walter Cronkite (CBS) and John Chancellor (NBC) had worked for the CIA when they were foreign correspondents in Moscow, though Cronkite and Chancellor denied this.[56]

NBC was owned by RCA in 1963 when the RCA Chairman of the Board was "General" David Sarnoff. During WWII Sarnoff worked in the Signal Corps and restored the destroyed Radio France, which was renamed Radio Free Europe. RFE become a major project of Allen Dulles. RCA became the technological base of the National Security Agency (NSA), and Sarnoff helped staff the NSA in the 1950's. Sarnoff's son Robert worked in broadcasting for the OSS. David Sarnoff was also a member of the Citizen's Committee on Communications for International Cooperation and a former president as well as a permanent director of the Armed Forces Communication and Electronics Association (AFCEA). Sarnoff claimed that AFCEA "serves the industry military team."In an address to the organization Sarnoff observed, "AFCEA has fashioned a community of interest so closely interwoven that whatever affects the progress of one partner is reflected in the progress of the other." Among the directors of AFCEA were: Lt. General Gordon Blake, formerly Director of the National Security Agency; James McNitt, President of IT&T; Lowell Wingert, VP of AT&T; Lt. General Harold Grant, USAF, Director of Telecommunications Policy in the Department of Defense; and Lt. General R. P. Klocko, Director of the Defense Communications Agency.[57]

In 1986 NBC was bought by GE, a major defense contractor. Just the year before ABC was bought by Cap Cities, a conglomerate with strong ties to the American intelligence community. William Casey, the recently resigned Director of the CIA, was a founder and former director of Cap Cities. Thomas Murphy, the executive at Cap Cities, also had voting control of Resorts Intertel, the largest private security and spy organization in America. (*Networks of Power: Corporate TV's Threat to Democracy* by Dennis Mazzocco, Boston: South End Press 1994, page 4).

Texas broadcast millionaire Gordon McLendon had interesting CIA and business connections in addition to his regular contact with Jack

Ruby. After Yale, McLendon served as an intelligence officer in ONI before making his fortune in radio. In 1967, McLendon worked with CIA officer David Phillips, an expert in psychological warfare, to develop a CBS series on the exploits of the CIA. He invested with oil baron Clint Murchison, one of LBJ's major supporters, and he was friendly with Bobby Baker, LBJ's aide; yet most notably McLendon was the first person Jack Ruby asked to see in prison. However, many of McLendon's records remain classified. [58]

DCI William Colby began his remarks to the American Society of Newspaper Publishers in 1975, "The press and the CIA have much in common. After all, aren't we all in the information business?" Colby pleaded that the CIA needed a good deal less public attention as well as the keeping of "good secrets."

Forty percent of CIA secret operations were propaganda programs, according to Dr. Loch Johnson, top aide to Senator Frank Church, a former Chairman of the Senate Intelligence Committee.[59] According to the final report of the Senate Select Committee on Intelligence activities:

> The FBI attempted to influence public opinion by supplying information or articles to "confidential sources" in the news media. The FBI's Crime Records Division was responsible for covert liaison with the media to advance two main domestic intelligence objectives: 1) providing derogatory information to the media intended to generally discredit the activities or ideas of targeted groups or individuals; and 2) disseminating unfavorable articles, news releases and background information in order to disrupt particular activities. Typically a local FBI agent would provide information to a "friendly news source" on the condition "that the bureau's interest ... be kept in the strictest confidence." Thomas E. Bishop a former director of the Crime Records Division testified that he kept a list of the bureau's "press friends" in his desk ...
>
> After a public meeting in New York City, where the "handling of the (JFK assassination) investigation was criticized" the FBI prepared a news item for placement "with a cooperative media source to discredit the meeting on the grounds that "a reliable FBI source" had reported a "convicted perjurer and identified espionage agent was present in the audience ..." [60]

Another aspect of the cooperation between the government and the mass media, which originated from WWII, was the Censorship Code. Bryan Price, a former executive of the Associated Press, who issued a

Code of Wartime Practices to guide editors, headed this wartime oper-ation. It was not required that news copy be submitted to the director of censorship prior to publication but generally editors and broadcasters complied with the code. After WWII, Price's deputy, Theodore Koop, the Director of CBS News in Washington, served as standby director of cen-sorship. Two-dozen persons, including a few active and former newsmen, served on this rarely activated committee. Major revisions in the Censor-ship Code occurred from 1958 to 1963 so that, if activated by a President, the government would ask AP and UPI to move the code on their wires and would leave it in the hands of the news media "within forty-five to sixty minutes."

After the Bay of Pigs invasion, the Kennedy Administration called Koop and Price to the White House to explore aspects of voluntary cen-sorship. President Kennedy was distressed over the published stories pri-or to the Bay of Pigs, but Koop and Price resisted voluntary censorship in this case. [61]

Prescott Courier, *NYT* 10/1/70, quoted Sam Archibald, director of the Freedom of Information Center:

> The government has set up a "Standby Voluntary Censorship Code" and has planned all the bureaucratic trappings necessary to enforce the code. The plan would "become effective either in war-time or some undefined national emergency." The plans are ready to be applied in "all kinds of less than war situations." ...Only 5 of the 26 board members are working newsmen, "the rest are public relations men; businessman; government employees; college pro-fessors or listed merely as retired. In the event of a crisis, members of the standby censorship office would be dispatched throughout the country to monitor and censor all channels of communication, from private letters to telephone calls to public television and radio broadcasts.

The genteel collegiality of media elites and the top people in national security remained steadfast during the Cold War, strengthening a consen-sus of policy. According to award winning journalist David Halberstam, an unspoken assumption was that debate would help the enemy. The great heads of the media were anxious to be good loyal citizens, and working reporters themselves had almost without question accepted the word of the White House on foreign policy. The height of this credulousness had come during the Kennedy years. Kennedy had shrewdly made the most verbal and articulate members of his administration available to the press, their information made more pure and less political by the fact that many of them came from academe or seemed to come from academe.[62]

Cold War cooperation was extensive during the Bay of Pigs operation. Before the Bay of Pigs fiasco in 1961 reporters and editors at both the *New York Times* and *Washington Post* knew of the invasion and wanted to print stories and editorials critical of it. The hierarchy at the *Washington Post*, including Phil Graham, Fred Friendly, Chalmers Roberts, and Al Wiggens found no fault with the CIA operation and hoped it would succeed. Critical articles and editorials were crushed. According to Halberstam "... the *Post* at the time of the Bay of Pigs, did not criticize the most important issue of that disaster, the fact that the machinery (of government) was out of control; ... the editors of the *Post* were simply too close to that machinery."[63]

The *New York Times* was also planning to run a story prior to the invasion, by reporter Tad Szulc. But when word leaked out, President Kennedy called *Times* Washington Bureau Chief, James "Scotty" Reston to kill the story. A heated debate among *Times* editors and publisher Orvil Dryfoos ensued which led to a gutting of the story. Miami newspapers were submitting copy to the CIA for "clearance" and the *Miami Herald* admitted withholding a story on the Guatemalan airlift for two months until the news appeared elsewhere. The *Miami News* published a cover story denying the projected invasion of Cuba, contradicting its own earlier predictions – though certain that this story was untrue. Copley News Service, and particularly William Gandoni, later the Latin American editor, knew of the invasion in late 1960 and both suppressed the news and wrote stories downplaying the invasion possibility. It also appears that the Associated Press and United Press International suppressed the story as well. *The Nation* editor Jesse Gordon dispatched material to AP and UPI three times revealing the Guatemalan training, yet it failed to reach the Latin American desks of those particular wire services.[64]

As with all presidents, Kennedy tried surreptitiously to manage aspects of the news. Close friend *Washington Post* Editor, Ben Bradlee would serve as a confidant as well as a source of information. Kennedy the witty raconteur would critique news coverage, and suggest leads, topics, and perspectives, the epitome of a respectful and friendly government-media symbiosis.[65]

Failures in Vietnam led again to an effort to stifle dissident reporters. Just 18 years after WWII, reporters were again not supposed to question senior military commanders, yet David Halberstam was doing just that.

Kennedy asked the *New York Times* publisher Arthur Sulzberger to reassign Halberstam but Sulzberger refused.[66]

In Vietnam from 1961-1964 the U.S. reporters in Saigon knew how poorly the war was going yet visiting journalists with strong military and CIA connections, like Joe Alsop and Marguerite Higgins, traveled there to strengthen existing policy rather than to report facts. Halberstam recalled a time when Alsop lectured a group of resident reporters about the poor progress of the war: Alsop said, "Who cares about that? That had nothing to do with it. You are naive to report so pessimistically. It was unpatriotic on the part of the local men, and it would, of course, cost them their careers. You'll be like the fools that lost their jobs in China..." Alsop proceeded to write many columns saying that their negative reporting was undermining the war effort. *Newsweek* Bureau Chief in Saigon, Everett Martin noted that Alsop had open use of a military jet and that "he doesn't get briefed by the Colonels, he briefs them." Alsop printed stories for the CIA whether they were true or not. He never denied his ties to the CIA, stating "I'm proud they asked me and proud to have done it." Later, Alsop would be one of the early voices pressuring President Johnson to create what became the Warren Commission.[67]

Time magazine was notably aggressive in creating a successful war effort in Vietnam. Veteran reporters Charles Mohr and Mert Perry had their extensive analysis of an American failed policy immediately rewritten into an optimistic assessment. U.S. reporters in Vietnam were characterized as forming a "club" which focused on negative stories.[68]

Veteran reporter Arthur Krock who had worked with JFK on his college thesis, wrote in the *New York Times*, 2/25/63 that "news management not only exists, but in the form of direct and deliberate action has been enforced more cynically and boldly than by any previous administration in a period when the U.S. was not at war."

The Kennedy White House, unaccustomed to dissenting reporters, began a publicity campaign to sell Saigon through Washington-based reporters to the American people. President Johnson, who liked to do his own briefings for reporters headed to Vietnam, continued these efforts. Johnson once admonished, "Don't be like those boys Halberstam and Sheehan. ... They're traitors to their country."[69]

Sometimes, however, elements of the elite-media-CIA network had other connections and independent agendas. Apparently without the knowledge of the State Department or the President, in September of 1963, an anti-Castro raid alternately known as the "Bayo-Pawley mission"; "Operation Red Cross"; and in the CIA as "Operation Tilt," was coordinated among elements of the CIA, mafia and Time-Life. Anti-Castro Cuban activist Eduado Perez "Eddie Bayo," a decorated Cuban revolutionary now a veteran of the anti-Castro Cuban exile group Alpha 66, coalesced right-wing industrialist and former U.S. Ambassador William Pawley, along with the hierarchy at *Life* magazine, by showing them a letter, purportedly smuggled out of Cuba, which claimed that two Soviet colonels stationed there had knowledge of hidden Soviet missiles and wanted to defect. The plan was to bring the Soviet colonels to the U.S., but rather than turn them over to the government, a press conference would be held. This would serve to embarrass President Kennedy and pressure him to get tough in Cuba.[70]

The mission also included John Martino, an associate of Mafioso Santos Trafficante, who later claimed to be a CIA contract agent; Loran Hall, also an associate of Trafficante and California Chairman for James Milteer's racist Constitution Party; Eddie Bayo; Rolando Martinez, an activist Cuban exile and contract CIA employee (who would later be convicted in the Watergate burglary); William "Rip" Robertson, a CIA veteran who may or may not have still been with the CIA, and a close friend of John Roselli; former *Life* photographer Terrance Spencer; and Richard Billings, editor of *Life* magazine, later a reporter of the JFK assassination and chosen to be the editorial editor for the House Select Committee on Assassinations (HSCA). William Pawley, who in pre-Castro Cuba owned the Havana bus system as well as sugar mills, was a close friend of Richard Nixon, Henry Luce, and Allen Dulles.[71] He had used his business cover to cooperate on clandestine operations with the CIA including the Guatemalan coup as well as lobbying President Eisenhower to approve the Bay of Pigs plan. Back in 1954, Pawley had served on the Eisenhower Doolittle Commission, which cleared the CIA director to fight the Cold War without rules. A member of the old boys CIA network, the dapper tycoon provided his yacht the Flying Tiger II, and coordinated security for the mission. Others involved in the planning included Gerry Patrick Hemming, Frank Sturgis (born Frank Fiorino) both military assets, and the powerful Senator James O. Eastland.

Much later the House Select Committee on Assassinations learned that Julian Sourwine, counsel to the Senate Internal Security Committee, "was involved in financing the operation" and that it "saw evidence that the CIA knew of Sourwine's involvement."[72] *Life* Managing Editor George P. Hunt contributed $15,000. According to former *Life* staff writer Miguel

Acoca, "A deal was made between *Life* and the CIA, that for providing the operational funds, *Life* would receive an exclusive if the operation was successful. If it were not, *Life* agreed not to publish anything concerning the operation."[73] If the plot/operation succeeded, Kennedy's credibility would be weakened, and it would strengthen the case for an invasion of Cuba. The reasons for this failed mission remain a mystery.

This provocative plan was modest compared to Operation North-woods.

> Approved by every member of the Joint Chiefs of Staff, Operation Northwoods called for terrorism against Americans to be blamed on Cubans including: innocent people to be shot on American streets; for boats carrying refugees fleeing Cuba to be sunk on the high seas; for a wave of violent terrorism to be launched in Washington D.C, Miami and elsewhere. People would be framed for bombings they did not commit; planes would be hijacked. Using phony evidence, all of it would be blamed on Castro, thus giving General Lemnitzer and his cabal the excuse, as well as the public and international backing to launch their war.[74]

This extensive elite-CIA-mass media cooperation has many unexplored dimensions since the government and the mass media avoid discussing these relationships. The Senate Intelligence Committee examined CIA-mass-media connections in 1977, in what is referred to as the Congressional Bader Report, yet it remains classified. Imagine this massive network set in motion domestically to protect misperceptions of national security, after President Kennedy was assassinated, which was concocted by a dissident elite-CIA faction. Or worse, imagine that this massive network was engaged to create misperceptions of national security, concocted by a dissident elite-CIA faction, after the assassination.

3

LBJ's Damage Control

Every government degenerates when trusted to the rulers of the people alone... The people themselves are its only safe depositories.

– Thomas Jefferson

He who controls the past controls the present. Those who control the present control the future.

– George Orwell

The Soviet Union, Cuba, American intelligence agencies, and even President Johnson were possible suspects in the assassination of President Kennedy. Transcripts of President Lyndon Johnson's phone calls made immediately after the assassination of JFK reveal his aggressive courtship of the mass media, which may have exceeded that of his predecessors. Johnson quickly understood he would have to contend with competing and murky investigations with ominous implications.

Almost immediately after he assumed the presidency, the CIA sent Johnson unclear and misleading information regarding Oswald. The source of the information on Oswald's actions in Mexico City was the CIA. According to historian Michael Bechloss, CIA Director John McCone briefed Johnson on the morning of 11/23/63, regarding foreign connections to Lee Harvey Oswald. This version of events supposedly suggested to LBJ that Kennedy might have been murdered by an international conspiracy.

Soon afterward however, FBI Director J. Edgar Hoover called to update President Johnson, his longtime friend and neighbor. A perplexed Hoover frankly admitted, "The evidence at the present time is not very strong."

> **Johnson:** Have you established any more about the Oswald visit to the Soviet Embassy in Mexico in September?
>
> **Hoover:** No, that's one angle that's very confusing for this reason. We have up here the tape and photograph of the man who was at the Soviet Embassy, using Oswald's name. That picture and tape do

not correspond to this man's voice or appearance. In other words, it appears that there is a second person that was at the Soviet Embassy.

The CIA had claimed that the surveillance tapes of the Soviet Embassy in Mexico were routinely destroyed prior to the assassination, leaving only transcripts as evidence. Documents released in the 1990s, however, corroborate Hoover's statement. The House Select Committee on Assassinations (1977-1979) staff report on Oswald's trip to Mexico City, "The Lopez Report," revealed an FBI memo from Alan Belmont to Clyde Tolson 11/23/63:

> ...Inasmuch as the Dallas agents who listened to the tape of the conversation allegedly of Oswald from the Cuban Embassy in Mexico and examined the photographs of the visitor to the embassy in Mexico and were of the opinion that neither the tape nor the photograph pertained to Oswald.

Also in the Lopez Report is an excerpt of a memo from Hoover to Secret Service Chief Rowley:

> The CIA advised that on October 1, 1963 an extremely sensitive source [wire tap] had reported that an individual identified himself as Lee Oswald, who contacted the Soviet Embassy in Mexico City inquiring as to any messages. Special Agents of this Bureau who have conversed with Oswald in Dallas, Texas, have observed photographs of the individual referred to above and have listened to his voice. These Special Agents are of the opinion that the above referred- to- individual was not Lee Harvey Oswald.

On one of these "Oswald" tapes the caller identifies himself as "Lee Harvey Oswald" and then refers to a previous meeting with a man named Kostikov. Varerij Kostikov was a known KGB agent supposedly working in the Soviet Embassy, and a member of KGB's "Department 13," which dealt with sabotage and assassinations.

Hoover was aware of the CIA double dealing on Oswald's trip to Mexico City, and he continued to talk to Johnson. When researcher Rex Bradford bought a copy of this tape of LBJ talking to Hoover from the LBJ library in 2000 he found that the next critical fourteen minutes were silent – yet the tape, both before and after, sounded clear! Curiously, just the transcript of the fourteen minutes remains.

Whatever Hoover and Johnson actually thought may have been lost to history (though as with the eighteen-minute gap on the Nixon Watergate tapes, an audio engineer might be able to determine when and how the erasure occurred). They surely surmised that the CIA rather than the Cubans or Soviets was concealing evidence or setting up Oswald. Either way, this information would not see the light of day. A thorough investigation could reveal CIA complicity, or incredible incompetence. Based on early FBI reports it strains credibility that Oswald was part of a communist plot … a scenario which could have led to public sentiment for retaliation – war with Cuba and probably escalating to war with the Soviet Union.

Johnson also became concerned that the Dallas prosecutors were threatening to charge Oswald with killing Kennedy as part of "an international Communist conspiracy," so he directed his aides to cajole the Dallas D.A. Henry Wade to support a Texas Court of Inquiry. On Monday, November 25th, an hour before President Kennedy's funeral ceremonies, Johnson called J. Edgar Hoover.

> **LBJ**: Apparently some lawyer in Justice is lobbying the *Washington Post* because that's where the suggestion came from for this presidential commission, which we think would be very bad and put it right in the White House … the *Post* is calling up saying they are going to run an editorial if we don't do things. Now we're going to do two things I wanted you to know about it. One – we believe that the way to handle this, as we said yesterday – your suggestion – that we put every facility at your command making a full report to the Attorney General and then make it available to the country in any form that seem desirable. Second – it's a state matter too and the State Attorney General is young and able and prudent and very cooperative with you.
>
> **Hoover**: Exactly. I don't have much influence with the *Post* because I frankly don't read it. I view it like the *Daily Worker* [an old American Communist newspaper].
>
> **LBJ**: [laughs] You told me that once before. I just want your people to know the facts, and your people can say that. And that kind of negates it you see.[1]

Initially Johnson wanted to have the FBI and the state of Texas carry out the investigation until *Washington Post* syndicated columnist (and CIA asset) Joseph Alsop, confidant to *Washington Post* owner Katherine Graham, gently pressured him to call for a "Blue Ribbon" commission.

The hawkish Alsop was also concerned about the "Bold Easterners" at the CIA being forced out by the intelligence technocrats whom he saw as "dead wrong" in thinking Vietnam could not be won.[2] At 10:40 AM November 25th Alsop called Johnson, and after Johnson outlined his strategy, Alsop asserted:

> **J. Alsop**: Let me make one suggestion because I think this bridges the gap which I believe and Dean Acheson [Secretary of State under Truman and the architect of the U.S. East Asian policy] believes still exists ... and [Al] Friendly [*Washington Post* managing editor] is going to come out tomorrow morning with a big thing about a blue ribbon commission which he thought of independently ... I suggest that you announce that as you do not want the Attorney General to have the painful responsibility of reporting on his own brother's assassination, that you have authorized the three jurists and I would suggest the Texas jurists and two non-Texas jurists to review all of the evidence by the FBI and produce a report to the nation for the nation ... you've been simply marvelous in the most painful circumstances, but I do feel that there is that much of gap, and I'm sure that if Moyers [Bill Moyers, White House press adviser] calls Friendly, you have a terrific support from the Washington Post and from the whole of the rest of the press instantly...

> **LBJ**: I'll ruin both procedures we've got though...

> **J. Alsop**: No you won't ... no you won't ... just use the procedures you've got and add to those procedures a statement saying that "when the FBI has completed its work, when it has completed its work...you have asked two or three, including I would include the best judge on the Texas bench ... American jurists beyond, or individuals, Dean Acheson, for example, two or three individuals beyond any possible suspicion as to their independence and impartiality, to draw up a written report giving to the public everything of the FBI that is relevant and then you will have this written report ... which is not Texas which tells the whole story which is based on FBI evidence ... it doesn't need to use the things that the FBI says can't be used.

> (later)

> **Alsop**: "...ask Dean Acheson ... he's the man to ask."

> (later)

> **LBJ**: "Well, let me talk to Acheson..."

> (Later in the conversation.)

Alsop: If you make this decision and have Moyers call Friendly or Kay [Graham] instead of being ... well you know ... this is what we ought to do ... this is what ought to be done and then [rather than] what you do being denounced as inadequate, they'll be put so hard and will do you a tremendous piece and I'm sure you'll have the strongest possible support...

(Later)

Alsop: ... what I'm really honestly giving you is public relation advice not legal advice...

Alsop appears to be calling on behalf of Dean Acheson, and although Johnson agrees to call him, there is no recording of such a call in the LBJ Library archives. (not all calls were recorded, though).

FBI Director Hoover was then instructed by Johnson to communicate a general agreement on investigation strategies to the *Washington Post* that day. An FBI memo shows that Assistant Attorney General Nicholas Katzenbach called *Washington Post* editor Russell Wiggins and told him that "the Department of Justice seriously hoped that the *Washington Post* would not encourage any special means by which the facts should be made available to the public." The memo also notes that an FBI agent had a similar conversation with Al Friendly, the *Washington Post's* managing editor. The editorial never appeared. Johnson accepted this "advice" and soon jested that the "Kay Graham" commission had been formed. The FBI actually was the sole source of information for the commission. Thus Alsop, along with the hawkish Dean Acheson, gave legal as well as P.R. "advice."

LBJ's intimate relationship with CBS, NBC, the *L.A. Times* and *U.S. News & World Report* was seen in short calls made on November 27th. One was to Dr. Frank Stanton, President of CBS, an old friend and business mentor of Johnson since 1938 and an expert on CIA psychological warfare programs in Europe:

Dr. Stanton: How are you Mr. President?

LBJ: I have never felt better and never needed you more ... I just wanted to thank you for how good all of your people have been to me ... tell you how proud I was I knew you and you'd better get ready cause I'm liable to work your little tail off.

Dr. Stanton: (Laughter) ... well it is ready to be worked, sir.

LBJ: Well, I want you ... it is going to take all we've got to hold this country together in the next few months and the world together and I want your suggestions and advice … get over that reticent modesty of yours … act like you've lived in Texas…

An excerpt of the telephone conversation between President Johnson and Otis Chandler, owner of the *L.A. Times*, 11/27/63 demonstrates a deepening cooperation.

> **LBJ**: I want to thank you very much for your little note … and I'm so grateful for your coming down and have a chance to be together and I'm looking to you for all the help that you can give me in the next few days.
>
> **Chandler**: Yes sir. We'll do everything we can and congratulations on what I thought were a magnificent performance this morning.

An excerpt from the conversation between President Johnson and General David Sarnoff, President of NBC underscored the media-government cooperation.

> **LBJ**: … as usual I've been mighty grateful … and I'm mighty grateful. Max Lair had supplied me with some stuff … Anna Rosenberg called me to be helpful and you're always there, and I just wanted you to know that I appreciate it.
>
> **General Sarnoff**: Well, you're mighty kind to call. I want you to know that I'm praying for you and will be glad to help in any way that I can … at any time.
>
> **LBJ**: Well I never needed you more than I need you now … and we'll be in touch.

Portions of a conversation between the President and David Lawrence, Managing Editor Of *U.S. News & World Report* reinforces creative cooperation prior to a formal request.

> **LBJ**: … I want to tell you what I've told you a good many times before … but I just want to repeat it. I think first, you've got the best magazine in the business and I think you were extremely imaginative and quite partial and generous to me during this trial I went through the last two or three days … as they always have been … and second, to tell you how much I appreciated your personal confidence and how hard I'll try to be worthy of it.
>
> **D. Lawrence**: Well thank you very much and all of us have been thinking about you…

One wonders what LBJ meant by "extremely imaginative."

A conversation with powerful Senator James Eastland, 11/28, reveals Johnson's political skills to consolidate the investigation under his control as well as his fears. Senator Eastland, Chairman of the Senate Internal Security Subcommittee, shared a national security mindset and perhaps even had prior knowledge about Oswald from the Louisiana Un-American Activities Committee.

> **LBJ**: Jim … on this investigation … this Dallas thing … what does your Committee plan to do on it? I didn't ask you that and I intended to and had it on my mind and I got to talking and didn't do it.
>
> **Senator Eastland**: Well … we plan to hold hearings and just make a record of what the proof is … that is all. Show that this man was the assassin. To begin with we've had a great number of Senators that have come to me to us to request to … beginning with Morse… that it be done…now if you want it dropped … we'll drop it…
>
> (Later in the conversation.)
>
> **LBJ**: …if we could have two Congressman and two Senators … and maybe a justice of the Supreme Court to take the FBI report and review it and write a report … and do anything they felt needed to be done … this is a very explosive thing and it could be a very dangerous thing for the country … and a little publicity could just fan the flames…

The conversation 11/29 with Senator Richard Russell, Johnson's mentor in the Senate, raises more questions than it answers:

> **LBJ**: …it concerns Hoover and the Secretary of State and some others. We're trying to avoid all the House Committee, Hale Boggs and a bunch has got things started over there and Jim Eastland and Ev Dirksen and a bunch has got them started in the Senate … and Bobby Kennedy has his ideas … Hoover has got his report and they want Dewey in … so I've about concluded that I can get people pretty well together and I talked to the leadership on trying to have the three branches … have two Congressman and two Senators … and maybe two or three outsiders and maybe somebody from the Court … or at least some person of a judicial background … that are absolutely top flight folks … on about a 7 men board to evaluate Hoover's report and it would be largely done by staff … but they can work on it … and I want to get your reaction to it. I think it would be better than the Judiciary running one investiga-

tion, the House running another investigation ... and having four or five going opposite directions...

Senator Russell: I agree with that ... but I don't think that Hoover ought to make his report too soon.

LBJ: He's ready with it now and he wants it off just as quickly as he can.

Senator Russell: Oh ... Oh ... but he ain't going to publish the damned thing ... is he?

LBJ: He's going to turn it over to this group and there's some things about it I can't talk about ... going to try to get Allen Dulles ... going to try Senator Russell and Senator Cooper from the Senate.

Senator Russell: Oh no ... no ... no ... get someone else, now...

LBJ: Well wait a minute, now ... I want to try to get...

Senator Russell: I haven't got time.

LBJ: All you've got to do is evaluate a Hoover report that he has already made. The Secretary Of state came over this afternoon; He is deeply concerned about the idea spreading through the communist world that Khrushchev killed Kennedy. Now he didn't have a damn thing to do with it.... It's not going to take much time...but we've got to get states rights in there and somebody that the country has confidence in ... and I'm going to have Boggs ... he has entered a resolution over there and I haven't talked to anybody about the membership but you...

(Later in the conversation.)

LBJ: Hoover tells me all three of these shots were aimed for the President ... and that this telescopic sight will bring this thing up where you could shoot a man as easy as you can a man talking with you ... he said he looked through the telescopic himself and he said, Mr. President, I could hit a man on the street going 20 mph ... as easy as I could hit you, talking to you.

LBJ: I know you don't want to do anything but I want you to and I think that this is important enough and you'll see why and now the next thing ... I know how you feel about this CIA ... but they're worried about having to go into a lot of this stuff ... with foreign relations committee ... how much of a problem would it give you to just quietly let [Senator] Fulbright and [Senator] Hickenlooper come into your CIA committee.

Senator Russell: As long as it is confined to those two ... it wouldn't be any problem at all.

LBJ: That's all we make it now.

Senator Russell: See if you can get someone else.

LBJ: Well if I can I wil … But I'm not going … this country has a lot of confidence in you and if I have my way, you'd be in my place and I'd trade with you…

Conversation 11/29 with Congressman Les Arends:

LBJ: …why we just don't want to leave any doubt that any foreign nation had anything to do with this, you see, and we want the facts … and Hoover is going to have the facts … and this Commission can go over them…. He said he'd protect this Commission … I mean the flanks … go all the way and back Gerry Ford.

Conversation between President Johnson and Congressman Gerry Ford, 11/29:

LBJ: I've got to have a top blue ribbon Presidential Commission to investigate this assassination. I'm going to ask the Chief Justice to head it and then I'm going to ask John McCloy and Allen Dulles … and I want it non partisan … I've got 5 Republicans and 2 Democrats … you forget what party you belong to and just serve as an American and I want Dick Russell and Sherman Cooper … Dick is on the Armed Services over there and I want somebody who knows CIA over in your shop … I'm covering armed services with Russell … going to ask Hale Boggs and you to serve in the House…

Gerald Ford: Well you know very well I will be honored to do it…

Excerpts of the conversation between President Johnson and Senator Russell, 11/29:

LBJ: (Reviews blue ribbon commission membership.)

Senator Russell: Well now Mr. President, I know I don't have to tell you of my devotion to you … but I just can't serve on that Commission … I'm honored you'd think about me in connection with it … but I couldn't serve on it … with Chief Justice Warren … I don't like the man … I don't have any confidence in him at all … I realize he is a much greater man in the U.S. … than anyone … and so you get John Stennis.

LBJ: Dick...it has already been announced and you can serve with anybody for the good of America and this is a question that has a good many more ramifications than on the surface and we've got to take this out of the arena where they're testifying that Khrushchev and Castro did this and did that and kick us into a war that can kill 40 million Americans in an hour and you'd put on your uniform in a minute and the reason I've asked Warren is because he is the Chief Justice of this country and we've got to have the highest Judicial people we can have. The reason I ask you is because you have the same kind of temperament ... and you can do anything for your country and don't go giving me that kind of stuff about you can't serve with anybody ... you'll do anything.

(Later in the conversation.)

LBJ: ...you're going to lend your name to this thing because you're head of the CIA Committee and the Senate and you're to have Fulbright and Hickenlooper on it *because this thing is breaking faster than you think*... [Author's emphasis]

(Later in the conversation.)

LBJ: Well you want me to tell you the truth? You know what happened? Bobby then went to see him [Justice Warren] and he turned them down cold and said no. Two hours later I called him and ordered him down here and he didn't want to come. I insisted he come ... came down here and told me no twice and I just pulled out what Hoover told me about a little incident in Mexico City and I say now, I don't want Mr. Khrushchev to be told tomorrow and be testifying before a camera that he killed this fellow ... and that Castro killed him and all I want you to do is look at the facts and bring in any other facts you want in here and determine who killed the President and I think you can put on your uniform of WWI ... fat as you are ... and do anything you could to save one American life ... and I'm surprised that you the Chief Justice of the U.S. would turn me down.... And he started crying and said, well I won't turn you down ... I'll just do whatever you say...but he turned the general down.

Greek philosopher Plato admonished Greek leaders that a "Noble Lie" was necessary from mythmakers to maintain elite power for societal security. Lyndon Johnson was similarly inclined. Former President Harry Truman would later assess the difference between real truth and political truth; "Political truth can be the biggest damnedest lie ever, but if motivated toward a pragmatic goal, preferably for reasons of national security, and stated with total belief and fervor, it becomes true."

What President Johnson believed when he spoke to senators, congressmen, Earl Warren and the mass media, remains uncertain? If he did believe most of it, then the CIA manipulated the new president, and provided a national security rationale to facilitate a cover-up. Johnson was possibly protecting himself as well, and knew the value of a compelling cover story.

The immediate promotion of a presidential commission from powerful government-corporate elites Joseph Alsop and Dean Acheson raises questions. Their relationships with militant cold warriors may take on new meaning when we later explore the volatile dissent to President Kennedy's foreign policy.

4

WHILE WAITING FOR THE WARREN REPORT

I hold it therefore certain that to open the doors of truth and to fortify the habit of testing everything by reason, are the most difficult manacles we can rivet on the hands of our successors to prevent their manacling the people with their own consent.

— Thomas Jefferson, 1804.

In framing a government ... the great difficulty lies in this: you must first enable the government to control the governed; and in the next place oblige it to control itself.

— James Madison, Federalist #51.

In wartime, truth is so precious that she should always be attended by a bodyguard of lies.

— Sir Winston Churchill

*L*ife's version of the Zapruder film strengthened the lone shooter scenario. Then following the rapid release of the five volume FBI Report on the assassination, most of the mainstream media appeared content to wait for the Warren Commission findings rather than pursue investigations. *Life* vigorously supported the lone nut scenario, while the *New York Times* and the Associated Press steadily printed FBI leaks. A few mainstream journalists raised critical questions, notably Lonnie Hudkins of the *Houston Post*, Eric Norden a freelance reporter, and Dorothy Kilgallen of the *New York Journal-American*. Some media outlets and press organizations criticized the press for failing to protect Oswald's legal rights, while most commended the crisis coverage as comprehensive. The alternative media, though faint, was finding a critical voice.

Now that Time-Life had time to analyze the Zapruder film, let's review their interpretation in their 12/6/63 *Life* issue. In "End of Nagging Rumors: The Six Critical Seconds," reporter Paul Mandel simply stated that Oswald shot President Kennedy in the throat, from the rear, and that Oswald's rifle could fire three shots fast enough. In describing the Zapruder film, Mandel asserted that the first shot hit the President in the throat; 4.1 seconds later, a shot hit Governor Connally; and 2.7 seconds after that the final bullet struck the President's head. This description placed the first shot to hit Kennedy at a point just under one second before he temporarily disappeared from the film as a road sign came between Zapruder and the limousine. The film, however, actually showed the President smiling and waving to the crowd before he disappeared behind the sign. Similarly, the film contradicts Mandel's description of when Connally was hit. Nearly two seconds before Mandel claimed Connally was hit, Connally's shoulder collapses, his hair flies up and his face contorts in pain – leaving no doubt when he was shot. Public airing of the Zapruder film could have allowed the country to witness the assassination, yet *Life* magazine not only withheld the film, it consistently misreported what the film showed.

Mandel asserted that the Zapruder film "shows the President turning his body far around to the right as he waves to someone in the crowd. His throat is exposed to the sniper's nest just before he clutches it." A simple viewing of the Zapruder film reveals this statement to be a fabrication. The rest of the one-page piece read like a synopsis of the soon to be released FBI report. This suggests that Mandel was assured that the Zapruder film would stay suppressed.

Time, 12/6/63, printed just four frames of the Zapruder film, which purportedly show Jackie Kennedy crawling on the trunk to help a Secret Agent aboard. Although *Time* asserted that the film "made what happened horrifyingly clear," they chose to describe a three-shot scenario, with "the third shot, all too literally, exploding in Kennedy's head." No mention was made regarding 1) Jackie Kennedy picking up part of the president's brain on the trunk; or 2) the president's head snapping backward violently. Again, no mention of Dallas citizens and police running bravely toward the grassy knoll after the shots were fired.

Oswald they referred to as "The Man Who Killed Kennedy," and as a hateful Marxist nut that frequently beat his wife. The evidence was viewed as "overwhelming." Astoundingly they also claimed that a "lonely psychopath" killed President Lincoln, apparently to strengthen the impression of Oswald as a lone nut. Jack Ruby was described as an emotional, anti-communist patriot, "a real guy," "Sparky" to his friends, and as a man who acted alone.

Time-Life, Inc. also denied access to the Zapruder film for use in either a motion picture or a TV documentary. *Life* even failed to grant one of its consultants, author Josiah Thompson, the reproduction rights to the film's frames for a book. When Thompson's publisher offered *Life* all of the profits from the book in exchange for publication rights to the frames, *Life* still balked. When the book was published in 1966 with sketches replacing the missing frames, *Life* sued to stop the sale of the book. They lost and from these sketches America first saw President Kennedy's head snap backward, not forward, after being hit.

It seems possible that his past service in national intelligence affected the journalistic judgment of *Time's* Senior Vice-President C. D. Jackson. He was General Eisenhower's expert on psychological warfare when he was CBS president Colonel William Paley's boss at the Office of War Information during WWII. By 1953, Jackson was appointed chief of the Psychological Strategy Board, a White House agency to promote covert operations. He subsequently directed Radio Free Europe and later served as a CIA analyst. Recall that prior to the position at *Life*, Jackson headed the board of directors of the National Committee for a Free Europe (NCFE) along with Henry Luce of Time-Life, Eugene Lyons of *Reader's Digest*, Allen Dulles of the CIA and former OSS chief William Donovan. (The OSS, Office of Strategic Services, was the precursor to the CIA.) The NCFE channeled CIA funds to neo-Nazi émigré groups intent on "liberating" Eastern Europe. While a *Time* executive, Jackson coauthored a CIA-sponsored study to reorganize American intelligence services.

Jackson also worked with Warren Commissioner John McCloy on a number of CIA projects, including Task Force C of Project Solarium dealing with psychological warfare in covert operations. Notably, Jackson's philosophy called for 1) ample money; 2) no holds barred; and 3) no questions asked.

Time-Life ownership of the Zapruder film strengthened their already considerable credibility and helped shape public opinion as well as opinion within the mass media itself. Time-Life editorial decisions seem to be a contemporary version of Plato's "Noble Lie," used to enhance national security.

U.S. News & World Report asserted three times that Oswald acted alone. Then with shameless historical revisionism they implied that just one person assassinated Lincoln. *Newsweek* concluded that Oswald acted alone, and that apparently he had "cancer of the psyche."

The *New York Times* coverage avoided the contradictions in the forensic evidence as creatively as Time-Life. Reporter Joseph Loftus noted,

12/6/63, that FBI agents wondered "How the President could have received a bullet in the front of the throat from a rifle in the Texas School Book Depository building, after his car had passed the building? ... One explanation from a competent source was that the President had turned to his right to wave, and was struck at that moment."

Eleven days after the assassination the FBI leaked an overview of its assassination report to the *Dallas Times Herald*. The overview was run with its conclusion unquestioned. Meanwhile, Washington sources said the extensive FBI report, just being completed, would depict Oswald as a lone and unaided assassin.

On December 8, the Hearst-owned *New York Journal-American* ran a misleading article by reporter Guy Richards, who was close to FBI assistant director John Malone. False or inaccurate information regarding Oswald's associates included:

> [V.T.] Lee [Fair Play for Cuba Committee] was the friend and advisor who guided Oswald on many moves down South.... Lee's name and the extent of his role as a mentor for Oswald have been kept secret by the FBI and Dallas authorities...

> [V.T.] Lee ... from the militant pro-Castro PL faction of the Communist party.... The FBI is maintaining enormous interest in the elusive violently pro-Castro Mr. Lee Oswald's friend and sponsor...[1]

Since Oswald had met regularly with FBI agent Hosty in Dallas, FBI agents Quigley and de Brueys in New Orleans, and had worked with "retired" FBI man Guy Banister in New Orleans, how could these assertions crop up? This appears to be another "phase one" story to justify the "phase two" – Oswald the lone nut, version.

Earlier, in 1963 Guy Richards used his FBI connections and arranged a meeting with John Malone and reporter Michael Eddowes to be briefed for a story on JFK's affair with London call girl, Mariella Novotny. This story, which referred to "one of the biggest names in American politics," appeared just after Kennedy's peace speech at American University, and caused Robert Kennedy to threaten the *New York Journal-American* with an anti-trust suit if it did not drop the matter.[2]

Philadelphia Inquirer reporter Joseph Goulden, 12/8/63, revealed in his story that Oswald had at one time been contacted by the FBI to become an informant. Goulden said he obtained this from a law enforcement officer in Dallas whom he declined to identify. Goulden was an old friend of Lonnie Hudkins, who would soon develop the story of FBI connections to Oswald.

On December 9, 1963, J. Edgar Hoover gave President Johnson a confidential 5-volume summary of the FBI report which concluded that Oswald was a lone assassin, that Jack Ruby acted alone, and that there was no conspiracy. FBI Assistant Director Cartha "Deke" DeLoach leaked the report to the *Washington Star* and the *Chicago Tribune*. The wire services then picked up the story from the *Star*. Earl Warren confided to Senator Russell, "I tell you frankly; I just don't find anything in the [FBI Summary] report that had not been leaked to the press." *Wall Street Journal* editor, Vermont Royster, absolved the nation of guilt by emphasizing negligence as the cause in his editorial (12/9/63). Any public indictment of American society or the people of Dallas were described as vicious. The word negligence was used seven times: "... some of this negligence could be laid to all of us ... But this is something different than indictment ... the tragic acts of madmen [should not] cast a shadow on the whole of America."

A December 11, 1963 teletype from the FBI office in New York to J. Edgar Hoover indicated that NBC had given the FBI assurances that it would "televise only those items which are in consonance with the bureau report [on the assassination]." This eight-page message details the nature of NBC's research. "NBC has movie film taken at some one hundred and fifty feet showing a Dallas Police Department officer rushing into the Book Depository building while most of the police and Secret Service were rushing up an incline towards the railroad trestle in front of the motorcade."

Hoover also released information to "very friendly" journalists such as Jeremiah O'Leary, and others, such as Drew Pearson. Pearson had worked closely with CIA-directed Radio Free Europe which led to the North American Newspaper Alliance (NANA) in the 1950s, and work as a contact agent for the CIA in the 1960s. The *Dallas Morning News* (12/13) was unconvinced. Without naming witness James Tague, they asked "Did a bullet from Lee Harvey Oswald's rifle clip the curb on Main Street near the triple underpass?"

U.S. News & World Report, (12/16/63), firmly backed the FBI Report. "Facts of the shooting appear to be established beyond doubt. The facts of the assassination of President Kennedy uncovered by the Federal Bureau of Investigation have led officials to these firm conclusions:

1. "President Kennedy was murdered by one man—Lee Harvey Oswald.

2. "Oswald had no accomplices, at any stage. He alone planned the crime and fired the fatal shots from a sixth floor window of the Texas School Book Depository building in Dallas.

3. "Jack Ruby, who killed Oswald, also acted alone. There was no conspiring to silence Oswald, no connection of any kind between Oswald and Ruby.

4. "No plot, by groups in the U.S. or abroad, underlay the murders of the President and his assassin. It was an American tragedy from beginning to end – the acts of two unstable individuals out of 190 million Americans.

"These are the bedrock facts about the Kennedy assassination and its aftermath that the FBI, after the most exhaustive investigation of its type in history, feels it has nailed down beyond doubt." The story proceeded to psychologize about Oswald's motive, and then defended the weary and often overworked Secret Service. *Newsweek*, 12/16/63, ran a headline to its article, "Portrait of a Psychopath" about Oswald.

The *St. Louis Post-Dispatch*, 12/18/63, revealed that [the Secret Service] obtained a reversal of their original view that the bullet in the neck entered from the front. The investigators did so by showing the surgeons a document described as an autopsy report from the U.S. Naval Hospital in Bethesda.

We now know that Secret Service agents Elmer Moore and Roger Warren pressured Dr. Malcolm Perry for hours the evening of the assassination to stop describing Kennedy's throat wound as one of entrance. Moore told grad student James Gochenaur in 1970 that he "leaned on Dr. Perry."[3] Former Chief Operating Room nurse at Parkland Hospital, Audrey Bell, told ARRB member Doug Horne that "Dr. Perry was in a state of torment on November 23, 1963, after being pressured all night long to change his mind."

In December 1963, FBI agents attempted to dissuade *Saga*, a men's magazine, from printing a critique of FBI security measures related to the assassination authored by ex-FBI agent William Turner. After quitting the FBI, Turner had blown the whistle on FBI practices – thus spurring the FBI to closely track his actions. Turner's revelation was that the Dallas FBI was not only meeting with Oswald but did not inform the Dallas Police or the Secret Service through the usual procedure of a "risk list." FOIA releases determined that FBI supervisor William Clark, who tracked Turner, had been notified from a source in the publishing industry about the upcoming *Saga* article. Attempts to thwart the critical story had started too late. Editor Al Silverman resisted the efforts of two FBI agents to withhold the piece and he boldly printed "The FBI Could Have Saved President Kennedy's Life" in March 1964. Hoover's "good friends" at the *Chicago Tribune*, Herb Lyons and Ed Sullivan, quickly denounced the article.[4]

FBI files show "corrective" interviews with the employers and backers of journalists who had touched upon Oswald's relationship with the FBI. Drew Pearson, for example, reported that the FBI had interviewed Oswald six days before the assassination, yet failed to notify the Secret Service about him. Assistant FBI Director Cartha DeLoach interviewed one of the chief stockholders of Pearson's distribution syndicate and "furnished him sufficient information to refute all of Pearson's facts," and arranged for a stockholder to report back on his corrections of Pearson.[5]

The ACLU explored the impact of the mass media on Oswald's legal rights at the end of 1963. They argued that journalists had significantly interfered with Oswald's right to a free trial, and that he was "tried and convicted many times in the newspaper, on the radio and over television."[6]

By the end of 1963 the Associated Press released their version of the assassination, *The Torch is Passed*, an undocumented account attributed to over 100 AP reporters. This brief account faithfully echoed the 5-volume FBI report. No questions were raised as to Oswald's guilt, his ties to intelligence agencies, or for that matter, his ties to anyone. The three-shot scenario was not questioned, and they failed to even account for the bullet wound in President Kennedy's neck, just as the FBI reports had done. Recall that an AP representative had seen the Zapruder film prior to Time-Life purchasing it. No questions were raised regarding the paraffin test or the reports of a German Mauser rifle found by Dallas police. No questions were raised regarding Oswald's past – he was simply viewed as "a confused Marxist." No questions were raised regarding his trip to Mexico City and his "visits" to the Cuban and Russian embassies there.

Priscilla Johnson, referred to as an "American expert on Russia," was quoted as observing that when she met Oswald in Russia, "that this boy was the stuff of which fanatics are made." The six pages overviewing Oswald's troubled childhood were intended to clarify his adult actions.

> Surely there was enough to make the pensive psychiatrist nod his
> head sagely: the boy's wandering, fatherless, friendless, childhood;

his thirsty absorption of a shattering creed which offered promise to a life that had little; the dreary reality that rusted his promise away.

An insecure, "generous," "brutal," "classy," admirer of President Kennedy killed Oswald. Unnoticed Jack Ruby, freelance avenger, walked past them (police) and down the ramp into the basement of the building."[7]

The UPI book, *Four Days*, published in conjunction with American Heritage, was notably similar to the AP book. Though more condensed, it too failed to raise any challenges to the FBI report.

> The evidence against him [Oswald] was impressive: ballistics tests proved that the rifle bearing Oswald's prints was the murder weapon; an order, in Oswald's handwriting, showed he had purchased the rifle from a mail order house; paraffin tests for gunpowder on his hands were "positive." ... The case, that Saturday, looked air-tight.

Somehow based on a New York City school psychiatrist's report "Oswald was a potentially dangerous schizophrenic." "Oswald traveled to Moscow in 1959, and tried to renounce his American citizenship. He returned to America with the help of – and a loan from – the U.S. Government in 1962, bringing a Russian wife. He preached Marxism." The UPI raised no questions on any of these seeming contradictions regarding Oswald's life – or Jack Ruby's.

Ruby was reported as a "one man vigilante," who put great emphasis on "class" and who "admired" the police. Regarding motive, UPI simply reported "his sister told reporters that his motive for killing Oswald must have been his intense admiration for Kennedy."[8] Thus the major news services seemed content to consolidate the government position on the assassination.

Generally the mass media trade publications proudly praised the American mass media coverage of the assassination. In its 1963 report the Associated Press declared that it had "thrown more resources into covering the assassination than any single news event in its history." An editorial in *Editor and Publisher* effusively proclaimed that the assassination story was "the most amazing performance by newspapers, radio and television that the world has ever witnessed." *Broadcasting* magazine similarly deemed self-congratulations to be apt regarding the coverage of the assassination.[9]

While the American press reacted with excessive caution and what appears to have been a widespread voluntary prior restraint, the leading French press was highly critical of a U.S. government cover-up. Influential conservative journalist Raymond Cartier, writing in *Paris Match*, a journal similar to *Life*, observed in December 1963:

> There exists a remarkable contrast between America and Europe in regard to the assassination of President Kennedy … Europeans are convinced the Dallas drama hides a mystery which, if uncovered, would dishonor the U.S. and shake it to its foundations.

The leading French conservative newspaper *Le Figaro* charged the U.S. investigators with "contradictions, obscurities, intentional omissions, and deliberate lies." *Le Monde* argued that the contradictions were the result of inadequate security precautions or "they considered it advisable to choose a 'suspect' in advance, who could be charged with full responsibility … while at the same time shielding the real criminal."

One month after the assassination the *Washington Post* briefly raised a red flag by running an editorial from former President Harry Truman warning a still stunned nation about CIA excesses. "[The CIA] has become an operational and at times policy-making arm of the Government.… There is something about the way the CIA has been functioning that is casting a shadow over our historic position and I feel that we need to correct it." This editorial only appeared in the morning edition and was not picked up by other media outlets. Truman's admonition along with that of conservative reporter, Arthur Krock, on the front page of the *New York Times*, back on 10/03/63, clearly called for exploring the role of the CIA in the event of a cover-up. Yet, these explicit warnings failed to motivate the media to examine CIA involvement. Truman reiterated his concerns to *Look*'s managing editor, 6/10/64.

The experiences of an early critic, former New York State Senator Mark Lane, suggest that the chilling impact of the McCarthy hearings on the news media remained a vivid memory even after a decade. Some newsmen, such as staunch anti-communist James Wechsler, editor of the then-liberal *New York Post*, had been vigorously grilled for their past associations as well as criticisms of Senator Joe McCarthy's methods. Lane, a criminal attorney, had contacts in both alternative and mainstream media, and tried to publish gratis a critical review of the public statements from Dallas D.A. Henry Wade. He first called his friend Carey McWilliams, editor of *The Nation*, but McWilliams told him "don't bring it over … I am sorry but we have decided not to touch that subject." *Look, Life, Saturday Evening Post, The New Republic, Progressive* and *Fact* also turned down Lane. Lane's friend, James Wechsler, still an editor of the *New York Post*, was unable to find anyone to publish it and turned him down as well. Lane was turned down by seventeen media outlets, and was reluctant to run it in a leftist journal whose circulation would not be as broad as necessary. The only journal which did publish the article was *The National Guardian*, an independent left publication, edited by James Aronson. *The National Guardian* sent advanced proofs to UPI, but UPI stated that, "They wouldn't touch it." Aronson called his old employer, the *New York Times*, and was told "they would not do it." The 12/19/63 issue of *The National Guardian* sold out quickly, as did the additional 50,000 reprints. A number of publications in other countries, however, printed Lane's critique, including *Paese Sera* and *Oggi* in Italy, *Liberation* in Paris, as well as newspapers in Japan and Mexico.

In an impassioned defense of Oswald's civil liberties, "Oswald Innocent? A Lawyer's Brief" Lane confronted Dallas D.A. Henry Wade's statements.[10]

> "That which intervenes between the zealous investigator and the jury is due process of law, developed at great cost in human life and liberty over the years. It is the right to have facts … cross-examination … perhaps above all the right to counsel of one's own choice, so that all the other rights may be protected…

Lane disputed 15 assertions in the FBI's "airtight case."

> 1—A number of witnesses saw Oswald at the window of the sixth floor of the Texas School Book Depository.
>
> 2—Oswald's palm print appeared on the rifle.
>
> 3—Oswald's palm print appeared on a cardboard box found at the window.
>
> 4—Paraffin tests on both hands showed that Oswald had fired a gun recently.
>
> 5—The rifle, an Italian carbine, had been purchased by Oswald, though the mail, under an assumed name.
>
> 6—Oswald had in his possession an identification card with the name Hidell.

7—Oswald was seen in the building by a police officer just after the President had been shot.

8—Oswald's wife said that his rifle was missing Friday morning.

9—Oswald had a package under his arm Friday.

10—On a bus ride from the scene, Oswald laughed loudly as he told a woman passenger that the President had been shot.

11—A taxi driver, Darryl Click, took Oswald home, where he changed his clothes.

12—Oswald shot and killed a police officer.

13—A witness saw Oswald enter the Texas Theater.

14—Oswald drew a pistol and attempted to kill the arresting officer.

15—A map was found in Oswald's possession showing the scene of the assassination and the bullet's proposed trajectory.

… Our national conscience must reject the massive media conviction of Oswald – presumed to be innocent – and begin to examine and analyze the evidence … Our national renaissance must begin with a respect for law and disdain for the hysteria that has thus far made fair consideration of this case impossible.

Lane formed the Citizens Committee of Inquiry, which interviewed witnesses. He then presented his views countering the lone nut scenario; each night, for months, at a New York theater.

The Nation presented a policy of skeptical editorial caution in its 12/28/63 issue:

The Nation, too has been curious about the obvious discrepancies, inconsistencies, gaps and unexplained aspects of the three murders [Kennedy, Tippit, and Oswald], but has resisted the temptation to enter [the process of speculation … until an 'official' version of the facts is available. The public is entitled to nothing less [than all the known facts] … For our part, we intend to make an independent assessment of whatever 'official' report is eventually released.

The New Republic, a leading alternative magazine, 12/21/63, ran a critical piece by Stoughton Lynd and Jack Mimms, "Seeds of Doubt," which raised contradictions in the FBI report as well as mass media accounts. They questioned the number and location of the shots, the weapon, the palm print on the Mannlicher-Carcano, and the Tippit murder. They reported "police officers were examining the area at the side of the street where the president was hit, and a police inspector told me they had just found another bullet in the grass." [Photographs show an FBI agent bending to pick up the bullet – which does not become part of the official record] Like Mark Lane, but more measured in tone, they examined the inconsistencies in the mass media coverage and, in particular the *New York Times*.[11]

Reporter Richard Dudman, of the *St. Louis Post-Dispatch* and *The New Republic* clarified Parkland doctor Robert McClelland's statement that the throat wound was one of entrance. Dudman noted the hole in the windshield of the presidential limousine, and that a police inspector told him of a bullet found in the grass. Dudman was critical of the lack of security on the triple overpass, noting that the Secret Service orders were to keep the overpass clear. Dudman has declined to discuss the assassination with anyone for years. Neither the mainstream media, the press services, nor the alternative press apparently pursued these leads.

On January 1, 1964, *Houston Post* reporter Lonnie Hudkins, (an alleged CIA asset), probed Oswald's ties to FBI Agent Hosty, "Oswald Rumored as Informant for U.S." Hudkins alleged sources were Assistant District Attorney Bill Alexander, who listened to the grilling of Oswald, along with Dallas Sheriff Chief of Command Division Allan Sweatt – the alleged source of Hudkins' information. Hudkins wrote that "Oswald had Hosty's home phone, office number, and car license number." He also noted that Oswald's mother had been quoted in the *Philadelphia Inquirer* as stating that a government agent had approached her son. W.R. Hobby, the Executive Vice President and the Executive Editor of the *Houston Post*, was a member of the Hobby Foundation, a CIA front. The FBI, Secret Service, and Warren Commission counsels quickly denied any connection to Oswald. Whether the CIA was scapegoating the FBI remains unclear.

Norman Podhoretz of *Commentary*, then a center-left journal, raised concerns about the processes and power of the Warren Commission as well as power and public opinion (1/64). He asked if the FBI would act as the commission's staff. Are no public hearings to be held? Will no effort be made to evaluate the job that was done by the Secret Service, the Dallas police, and the FBI itself? Is the possibility of a treasonous political conspiracy to be ruled out? He opined, "Not the least fantastic aspect of this whole fantastic nightmare is the ease with which respectable opinion in America has arrived at the conclusion that such a possibility is absurd;

in most other countries, what is regarded as absurd is the idea that the assassination could have been anything but a political murder."

The Minority of One, "the small independent monthly dedicated to the eradication of all restrictions on thought" (January 1964) boldly explored "Who Killed Whom and Why? Dark Thoughts about Dark Events." Editor M.S. Arnoni, a holocaust survivor, insightfully speculated:

> The possibility can by no means be dismissed that important men in Washington do know the identity of the conspirators, or at least some of them, and that these conspirators are so powerful that prudence dictates that they not be identified in public. ... Let us make the 'fantastic' assumption that President Lyndon Johnson and Attorney General Robert F. Kennedy know or believe that the murder was planned by a group of high ranking officers who would stop at nothing to end American – Soviet negotiations. However strong their desire to avenge John F. Kennedy, what course would be open to them? To move against such formidable conspirators might start a disastrous chain of events ... to avert such catastrophes; it might well be considered prudent to pretend utter ignorance, in the hope that the conspirators might be removed from power discreetly, at a later date, one by one.

Freelance reporter Eric Norden's critical overview coupled media coverage with careful skepticism in his article "The Death of a President." He contrasted the early reports from the *N.Y. World-Telegram & Sun* and the *N.Y. Post* that described a 7.65 German Mauser, with the later *N.Y. Post* reports of a Mannlicher-Carcano. Norden shared the sarcasm regarding the Mannlicher-Carcano from the Italian newspaper *Carrier Lombardo*, "if more than one shot was fired there must have been a second attacker," as well as the skepticism of *The Paris Jour* that a non-automatic rifle was fired.

Norden noted Oswald's marksmanship, his location directly after the shooting, the specifics of the Tippit murder, Oswald's background, his trip to Mexico, the mistakes of the Secret Service, the action of the Dallas Police, Ruby's connections, the disputed palm print on the rifle, as well as the doubts and critiques of the foreign press from France, England, Germany, Austria, Soviet Union, India and Poland."

Norden quoted Scripps-Howard columnist Richard Starnes (12/3)

> Realism instructs us to expect little from the special commission created by President Johnson to investigate the death of his pre-

decessor ... no member of the commission has any competence as an investigator, nor does any have access to a disinterested staff. The commission will be almost wholly dependent upon the facts made available to it by the Secret Service, the FBI, and the Dallas Police Department ... it is manifestly naïve to expect these cops to bear witness against themselves, or indeed, each other. With the presence on the panel of Allen Dulles, erstwhile headmaster at the CIA, will Oswald's sojourn in the Soviet Union ever be known...?

Norden warned "if the death of the President was a well-organized conspiracy to change the military and political direction of the United States, dark days are ahead of our country.... Americans can best avenge the slaying of John F. Kennedy by searching out those behind the murder ... and by making sure that the policies and vision the president's enemies sought to destroy do not go to the grave with him."[12]

In January, nationally syndicated columnist Walter Winchell attacked critic Mark Lane in his column as an "agitator." and the *National Guardian* as a "virtual propaganda arm of the Soviet Union." Ironically, Winchell had cooperated with the CIA's Operation Mockingbird, a media-CIA propaganda program.

The Nation, 1/27/64, pursued the FBI connection in an article they had previously rejected, "Oswald and the FBI" by Harold Feldman, (collaborating with Vince Salandria) and also in an editorial "The Tasks of the Warren Commission." The article raised possible connections between Oswald and the FBI and CIA, yet the accompanying editorial focused only on the FBI connections. By neglecting the CIA connections *The Nation* was more easily able to avoid explaining the appointment of former CIA Director Allen Dulles to the Warren Commission. *The Nation* declared that there was "ample assurance that the Commission will ably discharge the extraordinary responsibilities which it has assumed." *The Nation's* editors did, however, declare that "The American public was gradually coming to the conclusion that the CIA was a self-perpetuating, ever-growing, tax-eating organization of spies, schemers, and bunglers, with a few murderers thrown in."

Early use, analysis, and handling of vital video footage raised more questions about the UPI, as well as the FBI. Abraham Zapruder was not the only amateur photographer well situated to film the assassination. Orville Nix and Mary Muchmore also used 8 mm movie cameras from the opposite side of Elm Street. Nix filmed what many researchers believe to be a second gunman on the grassy knoll. He told his friends what he had seen, including his friend in the Secret Service, Forrest Sorrels.[13] The FBI then obtained the film from the developing lab, screened it, and returned it to Nix in January 1964. The film was now badly scratched, and the FBI claimed that it was of no further use to the investigation. Nix then sold the film to UPI for $5,000. Some stills from the Nix film appeared in the UPI book *Four Days*, and some of the footage was used in David Wolper's documentary movie of the same title.

Nix used one of the cheapest brands of film, and the developing lab had either underexposed it or underdeveloped it. Although much could still be seen, UPI did not attempt to enlarge and analyze the film until private researchers Jones Harris and Bernie Hoffman began investigating in early 1965 along with UPI news film editor Maurice Schonfeld.[14] A more thorough analysis revealed a moving shadow on the grassy knoll while the presidential limousine was in front of it.

Based on a letter from the CIA-funded Cuban Student Directorate, (DRE), 1/29/64, AP, UPI, and the *Miami News* publicized Jack Ruby's visits to Cuba. This, belatedly, again pointed the finger at Cuba. Perhaps this was coordinated with a story 1/30/64, in the *Memphis Press-Scimitar*. "Oswald was paid Gunner for Castro." The source John Martino, (Bayo-Pawley raid) claimed that the assassination was prompted by Kennedy's plan "to get rid of Castro." Martino described portions of the top secret interagency invasion plans for Cuba, which slowed after the assassination. Before his death in 1975 he confessed to *Miami Newsday* reporter John Cummins, that he had disseminated false stories implicating Oswald in the assassination.[15]

On February 21, 1964, *Life* printed on its front page the now infamous photo of Oswald holding a rifle and two radical newspapers. The caption proclaimed Oswald's guilt. "Lee Oswald and the weapons he used to kill President Kennedy and Officer Tippit." While this picture helped convict Oswald in the minds of the American public, its origins remain unclear. *Life* neglected to mention that this photograph was not listed on the report of the Dallas police which itemized all of Oswald's possessions, or that when Oswald was shown the picture by the Dallas police, he repeatedly claimed that it was a forgery. The chin in the *Life* picture is square, whereas Oswald's chin was somewhat pointed. Oswald's assertion finds support in a number of other quarters. For example, FBI agent Lynn Shaneyfelt, a photography expert, was unable to state whether the rifle in the photo was the alleged murder weapon. The body and head shadows in the photo do not point in the same direction, which led many forensic photographic experts in the U.S., England and Canada to conclude that the picture was a forgery. Superintendent Malcolm Thompson of England, head of Police Forensic Science Laboratory Identification Bureau of Scotland Yard declared that the photos were fakes.

The Warren Commission later asserted that the FBI could duplicate the shadows in the picture, yet the FBI picture has the head blacked out.[16] Two years later, in 1966, the *London Times* conducted an inquiry into the shadow disparity and concluded that the pictures were fakes. Years later, the BBC shared that assessment with the House Select Committee on Assassinations.

In addition to internal inconsistencies with *Life's* Oswald picture, there were conspicuous differences amongst the prints of the picture that appeared in various publications. The *New York Times* published an AP version of the picture with no telescopic sight on the rifle. *Life* ran a picture with a prominent telegraphic sight. *Newsweek* published a picture which differed from the ones shown in *Life* and the *New York Times*, as well as one from the *Detroit Free Press* – from which *Newsweek* had obtained it.[17] Mark Lane called this to the attention of the Warren Commission, which submitted the charge to the FBI photographic expert, who confirmed that this was so.

The Warren Commission then wrote the *New York Times, Newsweek* and *Life* to clarify the various aspects of retouching.[18] The *Times* was unable to trace the origins of the picture and was unable to state what changes had been made before they got the photo. The Warren Commission concluded that the picture had been altered by the various publications *Life, Newsweek* and the *New York Times.* Those publications then notified the Commission that they had retouched this picture. In doing so, they admitted that they had altered details of the configuration of the rifle.[19]

Dorothy Kilgallen, a nationally syndicated reporter, gossip columnist and popular TV personality, emerged as the preeminent mainstream investigative reporter covering the assassination by continually raising questions in the *New York Journal-American* about the FBI and Jack Ruby.

> One of the best-kept secrets of the Jack Ruby trial is the extent to which the Federal Government is cooperating with the defense... An arrangement that was made last month between the defense counsel and the FBI has a fascinating "Kicker." It provides Ruby's side with reams of helpful information that they would never have

been able to get without the G-Men – on the condition that they do not ask for anything at all about Ruby's alleged victim, Lee Harvey Oswald. ... At many trials, the defense or the state takes pains to introduce evidence tending to show the state of mind of the victim prior to the crime. This is not merely permissible under the law, it is frequently vital to the truth. ... Why not in Oswald's case? Why is Oswald being kept in the shadows, as dim a figure as they can make of him, while the defense tries to rescue his alleged killer with the help of information from the FBI? Who is Oswald anyway?[20]

Kilgallen also reported that Dallas police patrolman Weitzman and another policeman found "a 7.65 Mauser" on the sixth floor of the TSBD, not a Mannlicher-Carcano. Kilgallen was the only reporter to interview Jack Ruby beyond the earshot of Dallas Police. She persuaded defense counsel Joe Tonahill to arrange for a small office behind the judge's bench to enable a private short interview. Although the rest of the media protested, this episode was not printed until after Kilgallen's death, when Penn Jones, Jr. noted it in his tiny newspaper, the *Midlothian Mirror*. By 2/24/64 Kilgallen posited:

> Among those who know the seamier side of Dallas show business the betting is 10 to 1 that District Attorney Hank Wade will produce witnesses who will testify that Jack Ruby and Lee Harvey Oswald were acquainted. Ruby had said repeatedly that he didn't know the alleged assassin of President Kennedy-but then Ruby's plea is temporary insanity and there are a great many things he doesn't remember, and isn't about to.

> The point to be remembered in this historic case is that the whole truth has never been told. Neither the state of Texas nor the defense put all of its evidence before the jury. Perhaps it was not necessary, but it would have been desirable from the viewpoint of the American people.[21]

The *Northern Virginia Sun*, 2/28/64, ran a remarkable revelation – "Oswald had meetings with the CIA representative in the U.S. in Moscow." How their reporters Robert Allen and Paul Scott got the State Department Cable #234 11/2/59 remains unclear. This story, like most from small newspapers, never moved from the margins to larger outlets.

Meanwhile at a broadcast media conference sponsored by the Radio-Television News Directors Association and Time-Life Broadcast, the Zapruder film was shown to 235 news directors, cameramen, writers, and editors from 35 states and Canada. According to a brief, cryptic article in the trade journal *Variety*, on 3/4/64, the conference focused on news film standards. When news directors from three Dallas TV stations were asked if they would have aired the film if they had had access to it at the time, all said that they would, with certain audience pre-warning. When asked if they would have pooled it, all three decisively rejected the idea. Conference notes could clarify broadcast media perspectives regarding the subsequent minimal coverage regarding the Zapruder film and its implications. It remains perplexing to reconcile support for airing the Z-film with the lack of coverage regarding the footage and its implications.

In March 1964, *Commentary* ran a rambling yet revealing report by Leo Sauvage, "The Oswald Affair." As the New York correspondent for *Le Figaro*, Paris' leading morning newspaper, he asserted that Oswald was innocent, regardless of the "press and media conviction" in both Dallas and Washington. Sauvage questioned Oswald's location at the time of the shots; the quality of the Mannlicher-Carcano, the lack of fingerprints on the alleged rifle; the time necessary to fire the shots, Oswald's marksmanship, the number of bullets found, whether Oswald's rife was ordered fully equipped as Captain Fritz stated; who killed Officer Tippit, the changing story of Oswald's map, the location of the wounds to the president, how many shots were fired and Dallas D.A. Wade's contradictory statements. He posited, "Is the possibility of political conspiracy to be ruled out? Not the least fanatic aspect of this whole fantastic nightmare is the ease with which respectable opinion in America has arrived at the conclusion that such a possibility is absurd; in most other countries, what is regarded as absurd is the idea that the assassination could have been anything but a political murder." Raymond Cartier observed in *Paris-Match* that "Europeans are convinced the Dallas drama hides a mystery, which if uncovered, would dishonor the United States and shake it to its foundation."

Robert Kennedy, weary with depression, was surreptitiously exploring the assassination with his closest aides, while publicly backing the Warren Commission and the FBI investigation. The Attorney General was surrounded by political enemies and knew he would need the power of the White House to unearth what he knew was a conspiracy to assassinate his beloved brother. "If the American public knew the truth about Dallas, there would be blood in the streets," he told a family friend. He figured that factions of the CIA-backed anti-Castro Cubans, which he was supposed to oversee, were involved. The day of the assassination RFK called Harry Ruiz-Williams, his closest contact in the Cuban-exile community and said, "One of your guys did it."[22] According to JFK's trusted friend, anti-Castro Cuban exile Angelo Murgado, when Oswald's suspicious activities in New Orleans in August 1963 were reported to Bobby, he told them it was OK to ignore Oswald, since he seemed to be under the direction of the FBI.

Blacklisted American journalist Thomas Buchanan, writing for the French weekly *L'Express*, asserted that a right-wing faction including LBJ and Texas "oil interests," assassinated President Kennedy. He charged that Oswald was a low-level CIA agent who knew Ruby, and the motive was to disrupt momentum for détente. This series caught the eye of JFK's best friend in the media, Ben Bradlee, who urged Bobby to meet with Buchanan. Bobby instead directed him to Ted, who connected him with Nicholas Katzenbach, the trusted Assistant Attorney General. Katzenbach fobbed him off to a commission staffer who buried Buchanan's research in the massive file.[23]

Freelance journalist, Joachim Joesten, like other early critical authors, was forced to get his book *Oswald: Assassin or Fall Guy?* published outside of the country. Joesten viewed Oswald as connected to the CIA and FBI, Texas oilmen, and the Dallas Police Department, and believed that two shooters were involved. The Warren Commission requested his manuscript, but since it was at the publisher, Joesten granted a four-hour interview with an "embassy man" at the American Consulate in Hamburg.

By early 1964, a few American periodicals criticized the press for failing to protect Oswald's rights. Most notable were: *Editor and Publisher* in "Accused or Assassin," *Saturday Review* in "When the Press Shapes the News"; *Columbia Journalism Review* in "Judgment by Television," and *Current* with a section entitled "Trial by Mass Media." These articles prompted an industry-wide review of journalistic practices at an October 1964 forum where notions of journalistic self-restraint prevailed.[24]

The intrepid and ingenious Dorothy Kilgallen convinced Ruby's lawyer, Melvin Belli, to grant her access to Ruby. Whatever Kilgallen learned from Ruby was never released – but she realized that Ruby wanted to tell his story and did not agree with the insanity" defense.

Just as the Warren Commission started its field investigation, the AP benefited from early "leaks." The *L.A. Times*, 3/25/64, ran an AP story "Man Tells of Seeing Killer Fire at Kennedy," just seven days into the field investigation. The story quoted active Warren Commission member Allen Dulles about the person who claimed to have seen the shot fired, "Is one case enough to identify the person [firing]." They used portions of

H.L. Brennan's testimony, which supported a lone shooter, but Brennan's subsequent contradictions were somehow omitted. "I saw him. The gun was sticking out the window. I saw him fire a second time."

The *New York Times* 3/30/64 carried an AP story reporting that the Warren Commission had "found no evidence that the crime was anything but the irrational act of an individual, according to knowledgeable sources." This leaked "Report" occurred only twelve days after the field investigation had begun.[25]

Meanwhile, a few media outlets and organizations briefly explored early media efforts. *Reader's Digest*, whose president Eugene Lyons had worked with the CIA's Radio Free Europe during the Cold War, trumpeted the broadcasting efforts to report on the assassination in their April 1964 issue. They proclaimed them, "an unprecedented achievement of voice and video.... Forgetting costs and rivalries, the broadcasters cooperated to keep the world completely and continuously informed." An ebullient FCC Chairman E. William Henry avowed: "In meeting this tremendous challenge the broadcasting industry earned the heartfelt gratitude of people everywhere for the manner in which it fulfilled its vital public trust. In the hour of tragedy, broadcasting achieved greatness."[26]

The American Society of Newspaper Editors, however, belatedly critiqued journalistic practices at their April 1964 meeting. Some members argued that the reporting was "sloppy," "bad," "sensational" and "a planned distortion of facts."[27] *The Saturday Review*, 1/64, foreshadowed concerns regarding the role of reporters, which were later noted in the Warren Report. Herbert Brucker, the chair of the American Society of Newspaper Editors admitted in "When the Press Shapes the News" that "pressure from the press ... had set the stage for [Oswald's killing, with] little doubt that television and the press must bear a share of the blame." He saw Oswald's murder as "related to police capitulation in the glare of the publicity... to suit the convenience of the news media ... [The problem grew] principally out of something new in journalism ... the intrusion of the reporter himself in the news."[28]

The *U.S. News & World Report*, 4/6/64, also briefly discussed, "Did Press Pressure Kill Oswald" in a commentary by Larry Grove of the *Dallas Morning News*. Dallas was already being reported as a right-wing, mean-spirited city, so a lack of media access to Oswald could aggravate that impression. The Dallas police, and in particular Chief Curry and Captain Will Fritz were portrayed as competent and accommodating. Reporter Hugh Aynesworth (an FBI asset) observed, "There is no doubt in my mind that a larger number of newsmen working the story hindered police." There were instances of radio newsmen barging into offices, grabbing police telephones and relating their stories ... Jim Ewell of the *Dallas Morning News* was "certain that the insistence of the press, notably television, people forced the police department to call moves it would not normally have made." Ewell suggested that the Dallas Police needed a liaison man "to brief the reporters and prevent them from running all over the place."

Kilgallen's column 4/14/64 probed "Why Did Oswald Risk All By Shooting Cop?"

> A mysterious and significant aspect of the events following the assassination of President Kennedy in Dallas has never been explored publicly, although it must have occurred to crack reporters covering the case as well as authorities ... why did Lee Harvey Oswald, presumably fleeing from the police after the assassination approach Patrolman Tippitt's car – in broad daylight with witnesses standing by – and shoot the policeman three times, although he did not say a word to Oswald.... A whodunit fan would infer that the policeman knew something about Oswald that was so dangerous that [he] had to be silenced at any cost...

To further solidify support from an already compliant mass media, Commission Chairman Earl Warren made a surprising suggestion during an executive session on 4/30/64, that the Commission involve the heads of the Associated Press and United Press International in the investigation.

A May 1964 letter from then Assistant Managing Editor of the *New York Times*, Clifton Daniel, to J. Lee Rankin, Chief Counsel to the Warren Commission, concerning the Warren Commission Report is revealing of Cold War mass media-government cooperation: "It happens to be our interest, as well as the interest of the Commission and the country, to obtain as wide a distribution as we can."[29] Subsequent cooperation will be evident, as we shall later explore.

L'Express French weekly ran more pieces by American journalist Thomas Buchanan arguing that President Kennedy was killed by a rightwing plot. Meanwhile, *Washington Post* columnist Chalmers Roberts reminded his readers that Buchanan had been fired in 1948 as a *Washington Star* reporter, after confessing a brief membership in the Communist Party. "On the face of it, it is absurd to call Buchanan, an admitted former

Communist now living in Paris, a rival to the group of seven distinguished Americans headed by the Chief Justice of the United States... [He has] sown vast quantities of seeds of doubt about assassination..."[30]

Sometimes photographic evidence cannot be easily interpreted. James Altgens, an Associated Press photographer, snapped a picture of the presidential limousine from about thirty feet away, just as he heard a shot. Oswald, or someone closely resembling Oswald, Billy Lovelady, was in the background, standing on the steps of the Book Depository Building. The *San Francisco Chronicle* (12/3/63) published the photograph together with one of Oswald taken after the arrest and asked if Oswald was the man in the doorway of the Book Depository. This lead did not resonate with the AP nor much of the media.

By May 24, 1964, the *New York Herald Tribune* followed the lead and asked why Altgens "was never questioned by the FBI or the Warren Commission." The next day a columnist for the *Chicago American* posed the same question. When the *Herald Tribune* requested a photograph of Lovelady, the FBI falsely told them that it had turned over to the Warren Commission everything it had on the assassination and that it could not furnish a picture of Lovelady at this time.

The *San Francisco Chronicle* asked the Associated Press for a picture of Lovelady, but the AP was unable to comply. None existed or none could be taken. Private photographer Bill Beckman attempted to take Lovelady's picture – but he was taken into custody, questioned by the Dallas police, and advised to leave Dallas, according to the *Herald Tribune*. The Commission identified the man in the photograph as Billy Lovelady.

That day the American newspaper of record, the *New York Times*, however, was taking another approach. Clifton Daniel of the *NYT* wrote Warren Commission Chief Counsel Lee Rankin expressing gratitude to Chief Justice Earl Warren for facilitating the *New York Times* publication of the Warren Report. A vigorous evaluation of the Commission's findings would have jeopardized this unique relationship between the *Times* and the Warren Commission.

Fully four months before the Warren Report was officially released, the *New York Times* on 6/1/64 ran a supportive preview on the front page. Its author, Anthony Lewis, years later lamented his article "Panel to Reject Theories of Plot in Kennedy's Death." "Maybe with all that has happened, Vietnam and Watergate, today's reporters would have come to it with some resistance. There was at the time a predisposition for the society as a whole to believe."[31]

The *Dallas Times Herald* ran a story by Jim Lehrer, on 6/6/64, clarifying the evidence about motorcade witness James Tague, without naming him. Tague, who preferred anonymity, recounted his experience of being wounded by a shot in Dealey Plaza with the sheriffs and police. "The FBI talked to me for about fifteen minutes and seemed mainly concerned about whether I knew Jack Ruby." What made him finally decide to talk about it again was the revelation that the Warren Commission had come around to the belief that only two of the three bullets actually hit President Kennedy and Governor Connally.[32]

The determined critic Mark Lane was able to reach the public through lectures as well as some radio talk shows, but television proved resistant. Some radio shows pursued the case, including Barry Gray, Murray Burnett, and *The Randy Show* (WOR) in New York, as well as Jerry Williams in Chicago. WOR, however, subsequently banned Lane for life. *The David Susskind Show* on WPIX-TV initially showed interest, and then concluded that there were too many "political shows that week." ABC-TV was starting an evening entertainment and interview program with Les Crane, who wanted to host a discussion of the assassination with Lane and Ruby lawyer Melvin Belli. Crane and his producer supported the concept but the ABC brass vetoed Lane's appearance. Crane's producer incredibly stated, "They say you have the facts and the affidavits and that would just confuse the audience." So, the first network broadcast presenting both sides actually pitted Ruby's lawyer Melvin Belli against Oswald's mother.[33]

Time, 6/12/64, confronted the growing chorus of conspiracy rumors in Europe and to a lesser extent at home, with an article "J.F.K.: The Murder and the Myths," which castigated "rightists" as well as "leftists." Thomas Buchanan, who wrote the first book critical of the official findings, was again delegitimized because he had allegedly been "fired by the *Washington Star* in 1948 after he admitted membership in the Communist party."

The New Republic responded critically to previews of the Warren Report in a piece by Murray Kempton, 6/14/64, "Oswald – May We Have Some Facts Please?" Since the Chief Counsel Lee Rankin told Kempton that the Commission still had a long list of unheard witnesses, as well as 12,000 pages of testimony to examine – the "vulgar and aggressive" dismissal of critics [by a spokesman for the commission] "…is the voice of a court which has not yet finished hearing the case." The pattern has been to say "what the evidence shows without ever showing the evidence." Kempton declared that the Warren Commission was "primarily – to reassure and unite America and to reassure and quiet down Europe ... salesmanship is a prime function of the patriot."

Years later, former ABC news president Reuven Frank wryly noted: "News is information that somebody, somewhere, wants to suppress ... everything else is just advertising." Recall that members of NBC News who covered the events in Dallas told former CBS producer Peter Noyes they were "convinced their superiors wanted certain evidence suppressed at the request of someone in Washington D.C." One former member of an NBC camera team, Gene Barnes, who had been in Dallas, told Noyes that "An FBI agent said that I should never discuss what we discovered [about the assassination] for the good of the country." Noyes speculated that Barnes' testimony in Volume XXIV of the Warren Report regarding Oswald's reported attempt to purchase a car on 11/9/63 at the Downtown Lincoln-Mercury in Dallas – may constitute the "discovery." The Warren Commission neglected to print that the NBC newsman had learned that Oswald, or a look-alike, test-drove the car over the motorcade route of 11/22/63. Subsequently, the auto salesman and his associates were unclear as to whether the man identifying himself as "Lee Oswald" was in fact Lee Harvey Oswald.[34]

Dorothy Kilgallen returned to reporting the assassination after a five-month break. During this time Ruby attempted suicide in jail and Chief Justice Warren, Gerald Ford and Warren Commission staffers spent a number of hours with him on June 7th. Ruby pleaded to be relocated since he feared for his life and feared revealing what he knew. His requests were denied. Kilgallen somehow obtained a verbatim copy of that testimony but the *New York Journal-American* refused to publish it until Kilgallen took full responsibility for the document. She did, and all 50,000 words of it ran under her byline in mid-August in New York, Albany, Boston, Baltimore, San Antonio, Seattle, Los Angeles and San Francisco. Her commentary observed that Ruby, the self-proclaimed lover of Kennedy "did not bother to watch the Presidential motorcade." She openly pondered why the Chief Justice refused to allow Ruby to testify in Washington. "Thousands of New Yorkers were shocked at the hopelessly inept questioning of Ruby by Chief Justice Warren, by Warren's almost deliberate failure to follow up the leads Ruby was feeding him."[35]

The *New York Times*, which had earlier printed leaked portions of the Warren Report, was rewarded with access to the entire report for publication. Kilgallen's leaks, which explored contradictions in the FBI report as well as unexplored leads, led to an FBI investigation of her. According to

Kilgallen's FBI dossier, which contained notations from J. Edgar Hoover, two FBI agents attempted to induce Kilgallen to reveal her source. She refused.

Undaunted, Kilgallen then exposed a secret document from the Dallas police in her column, 8/23/64. It was a private log, revealing that Chief Curry, who traveled in the presidential motorcade, initially ordered an officer to "the triple overpass towards which the presidential car was moving at about 8 miles an hour when the fatal shots were fired." Curry's comments for television, though, attributed gunfire to someone in the TSBD.

Kilgallen befriended Mark Lane, and soon he too was giving her leads. Lane was also researching areas for presentation to the Warren Commission, particularly the alleged meeting in Ruby's Club eight days before the assassination, which included Ruby, Officer J.D. Tippit and Kennedy critic Bernard Weissman. Kilgallen re-examined the Ruby testimony and noted that Chief Justice Warren had included "a rich oil man" in this group. By September 3rd, in a front-page article in *The Journal American*, Kilgallen revealed that the mention of the "rich oil man" by Chief Justice Warren would indicate that the commission was informed of the meeting by a source other than Mr. Lane, and that this second source provided the name of a fourth party – the oil man.[36]

Three weeks later, before the Warren Report was released, Kilgallen revealed two witnesses to the Tippit shooting who had kept quiet out of fear.

> **Mark Lane:** Did FBI agents tell you it was best not to discuss the case?
>
> **Mrs. Markham:** Yes.
>
> **Mark Lane:** They did? And did the Secret Service tell you it's best not to discuss this case?
>
> **Mrs. Markham:** Yes sir.

Mrs. Acquila Clemons, another witness to the shooting of Officer Tippit, stated that she saw two men running from the scene; neither of them fitted Oswald's description.

> **AC:** I'm not supposed to be talking with anybody; I might get killed on the way to work.
>
> **Q:** Is that what the policeman said?

AC: Yes. See they'll kill people that know something about that.

Q: Who?

AC: There might be a whole lot of Oswald's and things. You know, you don't know who to talk to, you just don't know.

Kilgallen also reported that patrolman Seymour Weitzman and another Dallas policeman had initially found "a 7.65 Mauser equipped with a 4/18 scope, a thick black sling on it," and they said so under oath.[37]

Life July 10, 1964 somehow obtained and printed Oswald's "Historic Diary" of his experiences in the Soviet Union. The subtitle reiterates *Life's* assertions prior to the release of the Warren Report, "Here published in full for the first time as he wrote and spelled it, is the assassin's diary inside Russia." The article, without by-line, never questioned the authenticity of the diary. Nonetheless, an unidentified prescient "expert who was unaware of whom the author was" divined that it showed "intelligence and cunning… [That] he can exert power over others, even annihilate them." The final picture in the story, "Wife and Child," has a caption, which again underscored the drumbeat of *Life's* assassination conclusions. [Marina Oswald was] "En route to the U.S. 18 months before her husband assassinated President Kennedy…"

This story could have been part of the old FBI leak system. As journalist and author Fred Cook insightfully wrote:

> Day after day we were treated to stories that contained only a smidgeon of new information in their leads-stories that went on to point out that the FBI report, whose details nobody was permitted to know, concluded definitely that Oswald was the killer; that he acted alone; that there was no conspiracy. By the time the public is permitted to get a peep at the FBI details that justify this conclusion, the conclusion will have been so drummed into us, so thoroughly accepted that it will take a bold man indeed … who questioned the details.[38]

Joachim Jostens' book, *Oswald: Assassin or Fall Guy*, was essentially ignored by the media but was caustically reviewed by Hugh Aynesworth in the August edition of *Editor and Publisher*. "Joesten, an ex-German who became a U.S. citizen in 1948 … states that Oswald was an agent of both the FBI and the CIA…. It's the same old tripe with some new flavoring." Aynesworth claimed that "Lane is the troublemaker who spent two days in Dallas in January on his investigation and now pretends to be an expert on all aspects of the tragedy." The next month in the alternative journal *New Times* Victor Perlo praised the book as well as the courage and skill of publisher-editor Carl Manzani.

Mark Lane's nightly lectures "Who Killed Kennedy" at the Jan Hus Theater on the upper east side of New York finally got coverage in the *New York World-Telegram*, "Oswald is Innocent Nightly on 74th St." They asserted. "A dragon-slayer in horn-rimmed glasses ... Lane is pulverizing the arguments of the Dallas police, the Federal Bureau of Investigation, the Secret Service and the Warren Commission.... It doesn't matter to Lane that they can supply evidence that Oswald was the killer. They have their truth and he has his."

Philosopher Bertrand Russell penned a prophetic op-ed. "16 Questions on the Assassination" in *The Minority of One*, 9/6/64. The muckraking tones and awkward timing, printed two weeks before the release of the Warren Report, perplexed even some progressives. Nonetheless, Russell developed the investigation and clarified the context of media confusion and collaboration.

> Blatant fabrications have received very widespread coverage by the mass media, but denials of the same lies have gone unpunished. Photographs, evidence and affidavits have been doctored out of recognition.... Meanwhile, the F.B.I., the police and Secret Service have tried to silence key witnesses or instruct them what evidence to give.... Why were all of the members of the Warren Commission closely connected to the U.S. government?... If the government is so certain of its case, why has it conducted all of its inquires in the strictest secrecy? Why did the Warren Commission not establish a panel to deal with the question of who killed President Kennedy?... Why has the F.B.I. refused to publish [the Dealey Plaza photos which] could be the most reliable evidence in the whole case?... How is it that millions of people have been misled by complete forgeries in the press?... Why was the result of the paraffin test altered before being announced by the authorities?... We view the problem with the utmost seriousness. U.S. Embassies have long ago reported to Washington worldwide disbelief in the official charges against Oswald, but this has scarcely been reflected by the American press. No U.S. television program or mass circulation newspaper has challenged the permanent basis of the allegations.... It is a task which is left to the American people.[39]

Imagine the impact of a coup d'état in America at the height of the Cold War? What a global challenge for capitalism and democracy in the battle for the hearts and minds. Millions would wonder if socialism deserved a second serious look.

Considerable portions of the press had now seen the Zapruder film and had read critiques of the previews of the Warren Report. Confidence in the Warren Commission, along with perceptions of patriotism, profound caution in contradicting the government on national security matters, especially since no national leader openly opposed the Commission, all contributed to self-censorship of the mainstream media. Selected Commission "leaks," a historical choreography of Oswald, and government non-cooperation regarding contradictory evidence on a complex case, contributed to promoting the Commission's findings at the height of the Cold War. Dorothy Kilgallen's columns courageously countered their pressures. Yet in a far more trusting nation than today, concerned with nuclear war, civil rights, and elections, most of the mass media reverentially waited for the Warren Commission findings.

The irony of Allen Dulles, the former Director of Central Intelligence (DCI) fired by President Kennedy, now informally leading the inquiry into the assassination went unmentioned in the mainstream media. Just a handful of investigative reporters succeeded in getting their assassination stories printed; so these scattered reports failed to resonate widely. Meanwhile, Time-Life, UPI, AP, the TV networks, The *L.A. Times* and the *New York Times* actively promoted the subsequent Warren Commission conclusion of Oswald as a "lone nut." Just five years earlier, Edward R. Murrow admonished the Radio-Television News Directors Association in 1958.

> ...For surely we shall pay for using this most powerful instrument of communication to insulate the citizenry from hard and demanding realities which must be faced if we are to survive.
>
> I am frightened by the imbalance, the constant striving to reach the largest possible audience for everything; by the absence of a sustained study of the state of the nation ... television in the main is used to distract, delude, amuse and insulate us...

The alternative press remained marginalized. While *The New Republic* and *The Minority of One, Commentary, New Times* and *The New Leader*, ran documented critiques of the FBI Report and the Warren Commission processes, *The Nation* cautiously ran one critical piece and then waited for the official conclusions. Our democracy was on trial. How did the Warren Commission confront the crisis?

5

THE WARREN COMMISSION – THE NOBLE LIE

I've got to appoint a Commission and issue an Executive Order tonight on investigation of the assassination of the President because this is getting pretty serious and our folks are worried about it … it has some foreign complications … CIA and other things…
> – President Johnson to Congressman Charles Halleck

The Warren Commission will stand as a Gibraltar of factual literature for years to come.
> – Congressman Gerald Ford, 1964.

There is always a tendency in government to confuse secrecy with security.
> – Robert Kennedy

Doubts are crueler than the worst of truths.
> – Moliere

Former President Truman admonished, "Political truth can be the biggest damnedest lie ever, but if motivated toward a pragmatic political goal … and stated with total belief and fervor, it becomes true." But what if the political truth provides only temporary protection and produces a legacy of lost legitimacy? This brief overview of the Warren Commission can refresh recollections.

President Johnson was confronted with allaying the fears of Americans, avoiding competing investigations in Congress and Texas, finessing the emerging connections between the alleged assassin and the Soviet Union, Cuba and the U.S. intelligence agencies, and slowing possible public sentiment for military retaliation. This political maneuvering needed to be accomplished before the next national election. One week after the assassination Johnson signed Executive Order 11130 establishing the Warren Commission. Johnson chose mainly Southern conservatives and trusted establishment figures, most with extensive experience with the intelligence community. They included Congressman Hale Boggs of Louisiana, Senator John Sherman Cooper of Kentucky, Congressman Gerald Ford of Michigan, according to *Newsweek*, "the CIA's best friend in Congress," Senator Richard Russell of Georgia, darling of the conservatives, the senior Senator responsible for oversight of the CIA and chairman of the Senate Armed Services Committee, John McCloy, former World Bank president, preeminent Rockefeller attorney and foreign policy advisor to many presidents, Allen Dulles, former corporate attorney and past chair of the Council on Foreign Relations, Director of the CIA from 1953-1961, and the first head of the CIA ever fired by a president, and Chief Justice Earl Warren, darling of the liberals, who very reluctantly joined only after Johnson convinced him that it was a matter of grave national security. Ford handled all matters dealing with the FBI and Dulles handled all matters dealing with the CIA.[1] Dulles was the only member without a day job, and along with John McCloy they became the most active members of the Warren Commissioners.

None of these men were strong supporters of President Kennedy, and none of them had experience as criminal investigators or as criminal jurists. The FBI had already framed the context for the case and they were running the fieldwork for a commission which acted more like a board of directors. President Johnson had assured Senator Russell that the investigation would "not take much time." Commissioner attendance at meetings was erratic; one member attended five meetings, another only sixteen. All seven commissioners never actually sat together for one full commission hearing. The majority of members missed most of the 51 hearings of testimony the Commission held. More than 80 percent of the listed Warren Commission witnesses never even saw a Warren Commissioner; instead staff members questioned witnesses. Essential leads and evidence were repeatedly not probed. The majority of the Commission did not look at the autopsy pictures or the autopsy x-rays. They never questioned President Johnson, who was technically a prime suspect. Army intelligence files were not subpoenaed by the Warren Commission and were supposedly routinely destroyed in 1973.

Initially the Commission thought that they would simply review the FBI Report. At first there was no method for even examining witnesses, and Senator Russell and Justice Warren did not even want to call witnesses. Dulles already sought to frame the investigation by distributing copies of *The Assassins* by Robert Donovan to members of the Warren Commission and it lawyers. Donovan argued that the seven previous assassination attempts on American presidents came from the actions of lone nuts. Since the Lincoln assassination was seen as dominated by the spirit of Booth, Donovan and Dulles somehow maintained that it was not a conspiracy. None of the members wanted or expected a lengthy investigation, until the Warren Commission meeting, 12/16/63, when they started to discuss the FBI Report.

> **Boggs**: There's nothing in there about Governor Connally.
>
> **Cooper**: And whether they found bullets in him.
>
> **Warren**: It's totally inconclusive.
>
> **McCloy**: This leaves me confused.
>
> **Boggs**: Reading this report leaves a million questions.

On New Year's Day 1964 the *Houston Post* ran a story by reporter Alonzo Hudkins, "Oswald Rumored as Informant for U.S." Two weeks earlier Hudkins told Secret Service agent Lane Bertram that the Chief of the Dallas Sheriffs Criminal Division, Allan Sweatt had information that Oswald was an FBI informant.[2]

The rumor of Oswald's ties to the FBI was brought to the Commission by Wagoner Carr, the Attorney General of Texas, and Henry Wade, the D.A. of Dallas. The stunned Commission met in Emergency Session, 1/22/64, amid a fear of Hoover, and that the Warren Commission would be seen as an investigation of Hoover.

> **Chief Counsel J. Lee Rankin**: if that was true the people would think there was a conspiracy and nothing the Commission did could dissipate it.
>
> **Boggs**: The implications of this are fantastic; I don't think this should be taken down.
>
> **Dulles**: Yes. I think the records should be destroyed.
>
> **Warren**: Except, we said that we would keep a record of the meetings.

After Wade and Carr met with Rankin and Warren, key challenges confronted the commissioners at that session.

> **Dulles**: Establishing the facts would be virtually impossible. The FBI, like the CIA, would commit perjury rather than admit that they employed Oswald.

Boggs: The man who recruited him would know wouldn't he?

Dulles: Yes, but he wouldn't tell.

Warren: He wouldn't tell if under oath?

Dulles: He ought not tell it under oath.

Warren Commission Chief Counsel Lee Rankin never placed Hudkins, Sweatt, or the Dallas Assistant D.A., Will Alexander under oath to have his staff or the Commission question them.[3]

The remarkable choice of Dulles as a member of the Warren Commission seems no accident, considering the connections of intelligence agencies to the assassination, Kennedy's threatening new directions for the CIA, as well as Kennedy's firing of Dulles after the Bay of Pigs. Other people who were fired from the CIA after the Bay of Pigs, were Deputy Director General Charles Cabell, whose brother was the Mayor of Dallas in 1963, and the Director of Planning Richard Bissel, who was in charge of "Executive Action," an assassination squad.

Former President Ford is recognized as the FBI's man on the Warren Commission, as confirmed by a memo from Cartha DeLoach, a close aide to Hoover.

> I had a long talk this morning (12/12/63) with Congressman Jerry Ford.... He asked that I come up and see him.... Ford indicated he would keep me thoroughly advised as to the activities of the Commission. He stated this would have to be on a confidential basis; however, he thought it should be done. He also asked if he could call me from time to time and straighten out questions in his mind concerning our investigation. I told him by all means he should do this. He reiterated that our relationship would, of course, remain confidential.[4]

It was Richard Nixon who recommended Ford as a member of the Warren Commission to President Johnson. Ford became the Commission's most industrious member, hearing seventy out of ninety-four witnesses who actually met with commissioners.[5]

The FBI had a number of motives for complicity in the cover-up. FBI meetings with Oswald and Ruby would have made the FBI appear to be a co-conspirator. Hoover's animosity for the Kennedys has been well substantiated, as well as his close cooperation with his long-time friend and neighbor Lyndon Johnson. His carefully nurtured reputation and the reputation of the FBI were at risk. Hoover's virulent anti-communist policies led him to fear Kennedy's new directions in foreign policy.

Hoover, who referred to himself as "Seat of Government," refused to cooperate fully with the crackdown on organized crime under the Kennedys, because he had long maintained that organized crime did not exist. Yet Hoover spent some of his vacations at the Del Mar racetrack and the Del Charro motel, known hangouts for powerful mafia leaders, which were owned by Texas oilmen Sid Richardson and Clint Murchison, close friends of Hoover and LBJ. Hoover was a heavy racetrack gambler at a time when racetrack gambling was controlled by organized crime. Allegedly organized crime would give him racing tips. Further, Hoover's very close and possibly romantic relationship with his longtime assistant, Clyde Tolson was well known by Mafia leaders; thus, Hoover was possibly vulnerable to blackmail.[6]

At 69, Hoover was nearing the mandatory retirement age of 70; and if Kennedy was to be re-elected in 1964, which seemed likely, then Hoover could be forced into retirement. According to former Attorney General Ramsey Clark, who served in the Justice Department under both Kennedy and Johnson, "it was pretty clear that Kennedy would not have extended Hoover." This change was problematic since Hoover had a file full of evidence confirming JFK's extramarital affairs. Retirement would not be a concern, however, under his close friend Lyndon Johnson.

The relationship between the Warren Commission and the FBI is revealing. Earl Warren originally wanted his old friend, Warren Olney III, to be the Chief Counsel of the committee. Olney had served as head of the FBI Criminal Division from 1953 to 1957, then as assistant U. S. Attorney General. In that capacity he was asked by the CIA to hold back on prosecuting a New York company that was a CIA front that had been caught smuggling arms into pre-revolutionary Cuba. Olney refused the request and pursued the charges. However, the experienced and independent Olney, an outspoken critic of Director Hoover and knowledgeable about the internal workings of the Bureau, was rejected after Hoover and Dulles, Ford, McCloy and Boggs voiced fierce opposition to his appointment.

Warren Commissioner John J. McCloy had ties to intelligence agencies as well, and his strong support for the single bullet theory and the Report's conclusions may not be coincidental. According to Harvard historian Alan Brinkley, "McCloy has been actively involved in more areas of national policy, in more critical decisions, than perhaps any political figure of his generation." He has advised nine presidents and has been referred to by numerous authors as "the chairman of the American establishment."[7] His varied assignments have included: War Department Liaison to the Joint Chiefs of Staff, where among other decisions he decided not to bomb the Nazi concentration camps; ignored FBI investigators and pushed for Japanese Internment, World Bank president in 1948; American High Commissioner to Germany from 1949-1952, where he commuted most of the sentences handed down at Nuremberg to Nazi war criminals; as well as a participant in the major foreign and military planning commissions, NSC-68 (1950) and the Gaither Report (1957), both of which promoted increased military spending which was justified as containment militarism and military Keynesianism.

In 1952 McCloy left Germany to become President of Chase Manhattan Bank, and served on the board of directors of a number of blue-chip corporations and as legal counsel to the Seven Sisters of American Oil. By 1953 McCloy worked closely with Eisenhower on foreign policy and intelligence matters. He worked on a number of projects with his fellow Warren Commissioner Allen Dulles and with C. D. Jackson, the new chief of the Psychological Strategy Board and later the editor of *Life* Magazine

On the first day of the investigation, McCloy was concerned that the Warren Report "lay the dust" expeditiously. He used his considerable skills in negotiation to mediate compromises regarding the single bullet theory, the possibility of a conspiracy, and the method of reviewing the autopsy. After the Warren Commission finished its work, McCloy proclaimed, "I have never seen a case that was more completely proven."

When Russell, Boggs and Cooper had "strong doubts" regarding the single bullet theory, and Russell threatened to not sign a report advocating it, McCloy prevailed with compromise language. He claimed that there was, "very persuasive evidence from the experts to indicate that the same bullet which pierced the President's throat also caused Connally's wounds." The Warren Commission staff stated that there was "no conspiracy," and Ford noted that "they found no evidence of a conspiracy." McCloy's language prevailed in the Final Report: "Because of the difficulty of proving a negative to a certainty the possibility of others being involved with either Oswald or Ruby cannot be rejected categorically, but if there is any such evidence it has been beyond the reach of all investigative agencies and resources of the U.S. and has not come to the attention of the Commission."[8]

McCloy agreed with Warren regarding the potentially morbid nature of the autopsy photos, and proposed that they not become part of the record provided "at least one Commissioner, accompanied by a doctor, is allowed to inspect this critical evidence." By 1967 McCloy regretfully observed on *Face the Nation* that, "there was one thing I would do over again. I would insist on those photographs and x-rays having been produced before us." However, he still argued that the best evidence on the autopsy came from the sworn testimony of the Navy and Army doctors who conducted it.[9]

After his work with the Warren Commission, McCloy became Chairman of the Council on Foreign Relations. His close friends ranged from the Rockefeller family to Texas oilman Clint Murchison, to CIA and media elites.[10] Less than two years after the assassination McCloy joined with David Rockefeller, Eugene Block of the World Bank, and former Treasury Secretary C. Douglas Dillon to form the Committee for an Effective and Durable Peace in Asia – a group which advocated widening the war in Vietnam.[11]

The powerful Senator Richard Russell of Georgia was Lyndon Johnson's close friend and mentor, and as Chairman of the Senate Armed Services Committee he oversaw the CIA. He resisted serving on the Warren Commission but LBJ pressured him, and actually announced Russell's appointment to the media, before Russell agreed to serve.

Hoover immediately took over the investigation without jurisdiction. FBI agents questioned Oswald less than two hours after the assassination. About one hundred and fifty agents were ordered to question witnesses and develop reports. An early lead pointing to the National States Rights Party was met with "Not necessary to cover as the true suspect located" – before the Dallas authorities charged Oswald with shooting the President.

By about 10 PM Friday night FBI agents had located the place where Oswald allegedly bought the Mannlicher-Carcano rifle, Klein's Sporting Goods in Chicago. When the Secret Service arrived the next day for questioning they found Klein's senior vice president, William Waldman, had been pressured by the FBI to "not discuss this with anyone."[12] Recall that the FBI was to become the sole investigative organization for the Warren Commission.

Basic evidence at the scene of the assassination was improperly investigated, covered up or ignored by factions of the Dallas police force, the FBI, the Secret Service, and the Warren Commission. Even the standard forensic paraffin test showed that Oswald did not fire a rifle that day. This was noted in the unindexed Warren Commission Hearings and Evidence in volume 22, which was released ten months after the assassination. Suspiciously, Oswald's fingerprints were not found on the Mannlicher-Carcano rifle he was alleged to have used until three days later, after Oswald was shot. Years later it was determined that FBI agents had visited Oswald's body at the morgue, with the alleged rifle to fingerprint him.[13]

The contradictory evidence regarding the murder weapon has remained unresolved through the years. According to Dallas Police Officer Seymour Weitzman and Dallas Homicide Chief Will Fritz, the rifle reportedly found initially on the sixth floor of the Texas School Book Depository was a 7.65 Mauser, a highly accurate German-made weapon. Deputy Sheriff Roger Craig also searched the Depository and he later recalled seeing the word "Mauser" inscribed on the gun. Deputy Sheriff Eugene Boone executed an affidavit in which he described the rifle as a Mauser. As late as November 23rd, Dallas D. A. Henry Wade told the media that the weapon found was a Mauser. In another affidavit, Weitzman noted that the Mauser had a 4/18 telescopic sight – this, too, was different from the scope on the Mannlicher-Carcano. Although Weitzman clearly described the weapon; the Warren Report stated Weitzman had "little more than a glance at the rifle."[14]

No marksman from the FBI or military was able to duplicate Oswald's alleged proficiency to either the Warren Commission or the HSCA. Other evidence surrounding the rifle was also either inconsistent or suppressed.[15] The Mannlicher-Carcano was known to be an inaccurate rifle, so unreliable on repeat shots that it was nicknamed "the humane weapon" during WWII. The cheap scope was off-center, and Oswald was not a good marksman. Sergeant Nelson Delgado, Oswald's Marine sergeant during training, confirmed Oswald's mediocre marksmanship. In an interview with attorney Mark Lane for Emile de Antonio's film *Rush to Judgment*, Delgado stated that the FBI pressured him to stay quiet about Oswald's mediocre marksmanship. The Mannlicher-Carcano required 2.3 seconds to shoot and reload, but that did not take into account that the President was in a moving vehicle and about 88 yards away. FBI agent Robert Frazier testified to the Warren Commission that approximately one second more per shot would be needed under those conditions.[16] For the Warren Commission and the HSCA, this mail-order $12.88 Mannlicher-Carcano rifle was the major link between Oswald and the assassination. The order for Alex Hidell did not have Oswald's signature.

A widespread pattern of cover-up occurred regarding significant evidence, which was given to the FBI and deliberately not pursued after the assassination. Years later, the HSCA concluded that "The FBI gradually exhausted its resources in confirming the case against Oswald as the lone assassin," a case that FBI Director Hoover seemed determined to make, within hours of the assassination. Recall that by November 25th the FBI agreed with Acting Attorney General Nicolas Katzenbach that "the public must be convinced that Oswald was the assassin and that he did not have confederates…"

On November 25th reports from U.S. Ambassador to Mexico, Thomas Mann, and CIA Station Chief, "Win" Scott, claimed that Kennedy could have been the victim of a communist plot. They thought that somehow Oswald had been paid by Cubans with possible KGB complicity. Hoover sent FBI agent Lawrence Keenan to meet with Mann and Scott to share the "facts" of the case – the lone nut case.

An hour prior to the assassination, Julia Ann Mercer was driving past the grassy knoll on Elm Street, where she saw a man with a rifle case dismount a pickup and climb up the knoll. The day after the assassination she reported this to both the FBI and the Dallas Sheriff's office; however, she was never questioned by the Warren Commission staff.[17] When Mercer saw Ruby kill Oswald on TV, she positively identified him as the driver of the pickup truck and notified the local Bureau official. The FBI altered her statement. In 1978 Garrison sent the Julia Ann Mercer statements to the HSCA, but never received a reply. The HSCA reported that the alleged statements made by Julia Ann Mercer had been sent, but the report noted, "they had been unable to locate her."

The FBI did not check out the most essential leads given them by the Dallas deputy sheriffs. The well-respected Dallas Deputy Sheriff Roger Craig reported to the FBI that he had seen a Nash Rambler station wagon carrying four men, including one who resembled Oswald, leave from in front of the Depository directly after the assassination. The FBI denied ever hearing this.[18]

Some of the witnesses to the assassination, contrary to the Warren Commission's conclusions, said that they not only heard shots from the grassy knoll but that they saw smoke as well. At least fifty-one witnesses stated or testified that some of the shots came from the grassy knoll, which would be consistent with the reaction of Kennedy's head slamming backward from the fatal shot as seen in the amateur video taken by Abraham Zapruder.

The transcript from the Dallas Police Department dictabelt recording seconds after the assassination indicates that Police Chief Curry and Sheriff Bill Decker were convinced shots came from the knoll. Sheriff Decker: "Have my office move all available men out of my office into the railroad yard area to try and determine what happened there and hold everything secure until Homicide and other investigators get there." Many of the people who were in Dealey Plaza testified that all of the shots didn't sound the same, meaning that they came from different directions or from different rifles, or most likely both.[19]

The responses of the Secret Service before and after the assassination were further complicated by allegations of what occurred in and around Dealey Plaza. After shots were fired, a Dallas traffic officer, Joe M. Smith, rushed from the intersection of Elm and Houston Streets to the area behind the knoll. He pulled a gun on a man who was there, who then showed him a Secret Service I.D. card. However, according to the Warren Commission, all of the Secret Service agents assigned to the motorcade had gone along with the motorcade to the hospital.[20]

When Dallas police Sergeant Harkness first arrived at the rear of the Book Depository, even before the search of the railroad yards, some of the men in the yards identified themselves to Harkness as Secret Service agents. A Dallas schoolteacher named Jean Hill had a similar experience. She witnessed a man running from the scene and chased him into the parking lot behind the fence on the knoll; he halted and identified himself as Secret Service. Despite these indications that some men falsely represented themselves as Secret Service agents, and that the Secret Service claimed that it had no agents in Dealy Plaza, the Warren Commission (and later the House Select Committee on Assassinations) dropped the matter.[21] Jean Hill has resolutely maintained that the Dallas police threatened her on 11/22/63 to stay quiet about what she had seen and heard.

During most of the hours between his arrest and being charged with the murder, local, state and federal officials questioned Oswald. Astonishingly, the Dallas police initially claimed that no records were kept of this interrogation, yet it is known that Oswald repeatedly denied his guilt.[22] (Captain Fritz's notes were found years later.)

Warren Commission testimony twice referred to three transients taken off of the trains in an area not far from the grassy knoll immediately after the assassination. Warren Commission counsel Joseph Ball and later David Belin both avoided further questions in this area. Neither the Dallas Sheriff's office nor the Dallas Police Department had any record of their arrest or questioning, yet they were booked and pictures of them being escorted by the Dallas police somehow surfaced after the Warren Commission Report was published.[23]

Many other pertinent witnesses were never asked by any investigative agency to tell what they knew. These included among others:

James Chaney, the motorcycle policeman closest to Kennedy during the assassination, who told newsmen he saw the President "struck in the face" by the fatal shot. Bill and Gayle Newman, two of the bystanders closest to Kennedy at the time of the fatal head shot, who have consistently said that shots came from directly behind them on the grassy knoll; Charles Brehm, a former Army Ranger combat vet, and one of the closest bystanders to Kennedy when he was shot; J.C. Price, who had a clear view on top of the Terminal Annex building, witnessed the entire assassination, and then told of seeing a man with a rifle running behind the wooden fence on top of the grassy knoll; James Simmons, a Union Railroad employee who supported Sam Holland in his contention that shots came from behind the picket fence on the grassy knoll; Alonzo Hudkins, the Houston newspaper reporter who stated that Dallas officials told him that Oswald was an informant for the FBI; witnesses to the Tippit shooting Acquilla Clemons and Mr. and Mrs. Frank Wright; Admiral George Burkley, Kennedy's personal physician who rode in the motorcade, was with Kennedy at Parkland Hospital, rode with Air Force One on the trip back to Washington, was present at the Bethesda autopsy, and received all of the official medical evidence, much of which is now in controversy; James Sibert and Francis O'Neill, two FBI agents who attended Kennedy's autopsy and whose report contradicts some of the official conclusions; Mary Woodward, Maggie Brown, Aurilea Lorenzo and Ann Donaldson, who all worked for the *Dallas Morning News* and who reported "a horrible ear shattering noise coming from behind us and a little to the right." This statement was in the newspaper on November 23rd, but none of these statements were mentioned or questioned by the Warren Commission; Tom G. Tilson Jr., an off-duty Dallas policeman, who saw from his car "a guy coming from the railroad tracks" after the assassination. "He came down the grassy slope on the west side of the triple underpass, on the Elm Street side. He had a car parked there, a black car. And he threw something in the back seat.... hurriedly got in the car and took off." Tilson followed the car, got the license plate number and telephoned the police homicide bureau, but they never contacted him – neither did the Warren Commission.

The FBI pressured, threatened and cajoled witnesses, physicians at Parkland Hospital and even presidential aides. Former House Speaker Tip O'Neil stated in 1992 that former Kennedy aides Kenny O'Donnell and Dave Powers told him that the FBI persuaded them not to testify that they thought shots came from the grassy knoll. They were told that there was an echo, that they were mistaken, and that the family wanted to get this behind us. So both men changed their testimony to match the FBI version.

Secret Service Agent Paul Landis, who rode in the car behind President Kennedy, said that "the shot came from in front ... and I looked along the right hand side of the road." The Warren Commission did not call Landis to testify. A. C. Millican, who stood in front on the colonnade in Dealey Plaza, said "I heard two more shots come from the arcade between the bookstore and the underpass and then three more shots came from the same direction only farther back. Then everyone started running up the hill." Millican was also not called to testify before the Warren Commission.[24]

Richard Randolph Carr had watched the motorcade from the Dallas County Government Center. During the assassination he observed a heavyset man wearing a tan sport jacket and glasses on the sixth floor of the TSBD. After the shooting stopped he saw two men from the vicinity of the TSBD jump into a Rambler wagon and drive north on Houston Street. He was never called to testify.

Senator Ralph Yarborough, who rode beside Lyndon Johnson in the motorcade, smelled gunpowder as they passed the grassy knoll.

Mary Muchmore was an amateur photographer who was shooting video close to the motorcade in Dealey Plaza. Although she sold her film to UPI for $1000.00, the FBI and the Warren Commission did not interview her as a witness.

Wilma Bond, also an amateur photographer who was photographing the presidential motorcade, was interviewed by the FBI; however, although FBI agents looked over her slides, no copies were made and she is not mentioned anywhere in the Warren Report.

Sam Kinney – Secret Serviceman in the motorcade who saw blood and brain matter on the windshield of the following motorcycle and who claimed he found the back part of the president's head, was never interviewed as a witness.

Some witnesses who were questioned by the Commission, either at the hearings or by deposition, have stated to researchers that their testimony was altered. Butch Burroughs, Jean Hill, Phil Willis, Orville Nix, James Tague, and others have stated that their oral testimony was not accurately reflected in the Warren Commission Report.[25]

The experience of Texas Senator Yarborough revealed the manner in which the Commission allowed key witnesses to be treated. Yarborough recalled:

After I wrote them, you see, a couple of fellows came to see me. They walked in like they were a couple of deputy sheriffs and I was a bank robber.... As a senator I felt insulted. They went off and wrote up something and brought it back for me to sign. But I refused. I threw it into the drawer and let it stay there for weeks. And they had on there the last sentence, which said, "This is all I know about the assassination." They wanted me to sign this thing, then say this is all I know. Of course, I would have never signed it. Finally after some weeks, they began to bug me. "You're holding this up, you're holding this up" they said, demanding that I sign the report. So I typed one up myself and put basically what I told you about the cars all stopped. I put in there, "I don't want to hurt anyone's feelings, but for the protection of future presidents, they should be trained to take off when a shot is fired." I sent that over. That's dated July 10, 1964.... When the volumes were finally printed and came out, I was surprised at how many people down at the White House didn't file their affidavits until after mine, waiting to see what I was going to say before they filed theirs. I began to lose confidence then in their investigation and that's further eroded with time.[26]

An internal FBI memo 11/23/63 noted that Agent-in-Charge J. Gordon Shanklin of the FBI's Dallas field office: "Stated he did not believe that the (Zapruder) film would be of any evidentiary value; however, he had to take a look at the film to determine this factor." Later in the memo the FBI assumed that it had sole possession of the original and that "... later a determination would be made as to whether the film would be given back to Zapruder or not." This was speculation, since Abraham Zapruder had already sold it to Time-Life for $150,000.[27]

Another amateur photographer caught critical footage of the assassination, Charles L. Bronson, a metallurgist from Dallas. Located on Houston Street, Bronson's photographs were "crisp and clear" (*Dallas Morning News*) and showed Kennedy as he was hit in the head. "The slides were clear enough to show that seconds before the assassination no one was at the sixth floor window of the TSBD. Dozens of witnesses could have been located and questioned. Dallas FBI agents Melton Newson and Emory Horton claimed that the films were not "sufficiently clear" and did not forward them to FBI Washington headquarters.[28] The pictures were unknown to the Warren Commission. Citizen researchers Harold Weisberg and Jim Lesar unearthed the pictures in 1978 using the Freedom of Information Act. Actually 21 law enforcement officers said and testified that a shot came from the grassy knoll area, although the Warren Commission found "no evidence" of a shot from the front.

Secret Serviceman Paul Landis, riding the right rear running board of the third car of the presidential motorcade, as well as Forrest Sorrels riding on the lead car of the motorcade, both stated that shots came from the right front.

> **Dallas Police Chief Jesse Curry** riding in the lead car told the Warren Commission "I said over the radio, "Get someone up in the railroad yard and check."[29]

> **Deputy Sheriff Eugene Boone** ran toward the knoll and the railroad yard as soon as he heard the shots.[30]

> **Roger Craig, Deputy Sheriff**, ran to "the terrace on Elm St" and then to the railroad yards.[31]

> **Dallas Police officers Harold Elkins, "Lummie" Lewis, A.D. McCurley, Luke Mooney, and W.W. Mabra** all ran to search the grassy knoll and the freight yard.[32]

> **Deputy Sheriff J.L. Oxford** ran toward the triple underpass.[33]

> **Dallas policeman L.C. Smith** climbed the fence behind the grassy knoll and searched the parking lot.[34]

> **Deputy I.C. Todd** ran to the railroad tracks as did Ralph Walters and radio officer Jack Watson.[35]

> **Dallas policeman Harry Weatherford** ran "toward the railroad yards where the sound seemed to come from." [36]

> **Deputy Sheriff Walthers** riding behind the presidential limousine ran across Deale Plaza to the "concrete structure on the knoll"[37] His second choice for gunfire was the TSBD. [38]

> **Dallas motorcycle policeman Clyde Haywood** ran to the knoll. [39]

> **Dallas policeman Joe M. Smith** "ran to an area immediately behind the concrete structure" [40]

> **Dallas policeman "Edgar L. Smith** thought the shot came from the concrete structure on the grassy knoll. [41]

> Ear witness testimony is not disposition, yet 21 cops join 30 citizens in placing a shooter on the grassy knoll.

The Commission argued that all of the shooting took place in approximately six seconds. The alleged murder weapon was an old Mannlicher-Carcano bolt-action rifle, which could be loaded and fired once in 2.3 seconds. The 6th floor of the Texas School Board Depository presents a difficult angle of engagement, partly obscured by a live oak tree. The first shot, normally the most accurate, supposedly missed. No government "reenactment" could duplicate the shooting scenario. The Zapruder film shows a timing gap of 1.6 seconds between the second and third shots. The Warren Commission acknowledged that. "The rifle couldn't be perfectly 'sighted in' in order to raise the scope without installing two metal shims, (small metal plates) which were not present when the rifle arrived for testing, and were never found."[42] Supposedly of the three bullets fired, one shot hit the curb, one shot hit the president's head, and the other bullet supposedly damaged the president's neck, Connally's ribs, wrist and leg. Incredibly, after breaking both the wrist and rib bones, the bullet produced by the Commission (CE 399) supposedly emerged from Connally's leg appearing as though it had hit nothing, showing no traces of blood or tissue.

In addition to obvious leads not followed, standard procedures inexplicably broken, basic information withheld, and many agencies confirming these irregularities, the Warren Commission broke the laws of physics as well. The whole notion of a single bullet passing through Kennedy, shattering Governor Connally's fifth rib, and emerging in "pristine form" is "semantical sophistry and intellectual gymnastics" according to Dr. Cyril Wecht, former President of the Academy of Forensic Sciences. Wecht has pointed to the condition of Mannlicher-Carcano ammunition after test firing into a goat carcass that sustained a broken rib. All of the bullets tested at the Army Ballistics Arsenal were visibly more damaged than the bullet alleged to have gone through seven layers of skin, numerous layers of tissue and then shattered multiple bones in Connally.[43]

The author of the "single-bullet theory" was Arlen Specter, formerly a special agent of the Office of Special Investigations for the Air Force, and later a U.S. Senator from Pennsylvania. If the bullet fragments in Governor Connally's wrist and leg are added to the weight of the so-called "magic bullet," the total weight is more than one bullet. Yet one bullet had to account for all of the body wounds to Kennedy and Connally.

The Chairman of the U.S. Army's Wound Ballistics Board, Dr. Joseph Dolci, stated that the Warren Commission case for this bullet was forensically not possible. Pictures of the test bullets do not appear in the twenty-six volumes of hearings and exhibits. [44] The Warren Commission never explored the possibility that some of the bullets could have been hollow-nosed ammunition, so-called exploding ammunition.

Connally has testified repeatedly that he was hit by a separate shot. Even the FBI and the Secret Service argue in their reports that Kennedy and Connally were hit by separate bullets. Nellie Connally notes that her husband "reared up like a wounded animal" before she heard the shot which hit him, hardly the "delayed reaction" argued by Arlen Specter in the Warren Report. According to the Warren Commission, Connally held his Stetson hat 1.6 seconds after his wrist was shattered. Almost every critical account has pointed this out; however, the necessity of another shot has somehow eluded both the Warren Commission and the HSCA. This point is crucial, since more than one bullet would indicate there was more than one assassin. Amazingly, the alleged bullet was not even found on Connally's stretcher. William Alexander, Dallas County Assistant D. A. in 1963, observed, "The Magic Bullet is like the Immaculate Conception. You either accept it or you don't." Earl Warren listened to Specter explain the trajectory of Oswald's bullet, and walked away without say a word.[45]

FBI photo analysts concluded that the first shot came before Zapruder frame 170, since the view from the TSBD was blocked by a live oak tree. CIA photo analysts at the National Photographic Intelligence Center (NPIC) agreed; nonetheless, The Warren Commission rejected these findings.

Further, none of the autopsy doctors at Bethesda Naval Hospital thought that the President and Connally were struck by the same bullet, until they later changed their stories.

The Warren Commission did not acknowledge running neutron activation analysis tests. In 1973 a declassified memo to the Commission from J. Edgar Hoover, 7/8/64, stated that NAA tests had been run and admits that they prevented "positively determining" which bullet the fragment came from.

Dallas Police Chief Jesse Curry admitted to reporters: "We don't have proof that Oswald fired the shots." Citizen Critic Sylvia Meagher observed: "No link between the clip and Oswald has been established—by purchase, possession, fingerprints or other methods."[46]

Oswald had only four cartridges for the purported assassination rifle and FBI investigations never established a source for this limited supply of ammunition. While the Warren Commission argued that this ammunition was readily available and of high quality, the reverse was true. One unpublished memorandum was seen by researchers regarding the manufacturer, Western Cartridge, of the 6.5 caliber Mannlicher-Carcano ammunition for the Marine Corps in 1954. This ammunition does not fit and cannot be fired in any Marine Corps weapons. Was the contract for ammunition placed by the CIA for Western Cartridge under a Marine Corps cover for concealment purposes?"[47] Years later the HSCA allowed two documents pertaining to the Western Cartridge Company to be locked away in the National Archives for fifty years. And why would an assassin leave three cartridges, in plain view at the scene of the crime? The cartridge case evidence was never analyzed. One of the cartridges, CE 543, contained a dent so deep it could not house a bullet. The bolt of the Mannlicher-Carcano rifle had not marked two of the cartridges, which means they had not been ejected from the rifle. CE 543 had markings on its base from the firing pin strikes that could only be present if the cartridge had been empty, according to FBI tests.[48]

Oswald told Dallas police that he was eating lunch on the first floor of the Texas School Book Depository at the time of the assassination. Carolyn Arnold, secretary to the vice-president of the TSBD, saw Oswald in the lunchroom on the second floor at 12:15. Oswald had no way of knowing if the motorcade was late, and if he had planned an assassination, he would have been getting into position to fire. The Warren Commission and the HSCA, however, concluded that Oswald stayed on the sixth floor. In the TSBD second floor lunch room Dallas policeman, Marion Baker, encountered Oswald less than 90 seconds after the final shot was fired. It is hardly conceivable that after shooting a President an assassin could hide the rifle, rearrange the boxes in the window, run down five flights of stairs, and be standing calmly drinking a soda when a policeman rushed into the lunch room. When independent researchers, in excellent physical condition, attempted to duplicate this sequence of actions, it took them close to four minutes.

Less than 45 minutes after the assassination Dallas police officer J.D. Tippit was shot to death in the Oak Cliff area, several miles from Dealey Plaza. Tippit was hit four times. Officer Gerald Hill, who had custody of the .38 revolver supposedly found on Oswald at the time of the arrest, testified to the Warren Commission that he discovered six live rounds in the chamber and two empty cartridges at the murder scene – revolvers, however, do not discharge shells after firing. According to the police radio report, the shells found at the scene were from an automatic pistol and could not have been fired from Oswald's .38 revolver.

The FBI Crime Lab (BuLab) claimed that the cartridge cases at the scene of the Tippit shooting matched Oswald's revolver. Warren Commission attorney Melvin Eisenberg knew that BuLab had examined only one of the four bullets recovered from Tippit's body and that the bullet was so damaged that it could not be matched to Oswald's revolver. The FBI did not even ask for Tippit's autopsy report for three months after Dr. Rose released it to the Secret Service on 12/10/63. The FBI blamed the Dallas police – yet only after Eisenberg's request 3/64 for the BuLab report did three bullets mysteriously turn up in Dallas Police Captain Will Fritz's file. After testing the three bullets BuLab noted that, "no conclusion could be reached as to whether or not they were fired by Oswald's revolver. BuLab's examination of the four empty .38 hulls from the crime scene determined, "the firing pin would not strike one or more of the cartridges with sufficient force to fire them." (Gerald McKnight. *Breach of Faith*. (p.116-122).

Almost every eyewitness to the shots originally stated that the man who fired the weapon did not look like Oswald; however, they changed their testimonies to the Warren Commission, stating that the killer did look like Oswald. One eyewitness to the Tippit killing who saw two men was Acquilla Clemons. She described the man who shot Tippit as heavyset, with short hair. She never changed her story, even after men came to her house and warned her, "She'd better keep her mouth shut if she didn't want to get hurt." Ms. Clemons was never called to testify before the Warren Commission.[49]

The actions of the Secret Service, a branch of the Treasury Department, before, during, and after the assassination suggest complicity as well as an early pattern of suppression of evidence. Contrary to its own manuals on "protection," the Secret Service had (1) not provided the President with a protective bubble for the limousine; (2) had not bracketed the Presidential limousine with motorcycle cops at each fender; (3) had not secured the roofs and windows of the parade route; (4) had deleted the Dallas police squad car; (5) had declined to augment their forces either with military personnel or the Dallas sheriffs; (6) planned an unnecessary 120 degree turn; and (7) The Presidential limousine almost halted during the shooting. Although on 11/21/63 Dallas Sheriff Bill Decker had been told to use his men to augment security, the order was reversed the next day by a call from Washington. Researcher Vincent Palamara argues that ASAIC Floyd Boring, who was responsible for the trip, probably gave those unusual orders. Many agents, contrary to Secret Service regulations, were drinking heavily until 4:00 AM on 11/21/63 at Pat Kirkwood's club, with girls from Jack Ruby's club. The Secret Service were not even positioned on the ground in Dealey Plaza, yet somehow two imposters convincingly identified themselves as Secret Service agents to three Dallas policemen, and others, after the assassination.[50] Advance Agent David Grant appears to have been critical in the decision to place the press car to the rear of the motorcade procession, instead of its usual position in front of the presidential limousine.[51]

The role of the Secret Service in the investigation is also troubling, and under-researched. About an hour and a half after the assassination Secret Service agents pressured Dr. Earl Rose, the Dallas County Medical Examiner, and Judge Theron Ward to release the corpse for transit to the U.S. Naval Hospital in Bethesda, Maryland. Dr. Rose argued that under Texas law the body of the murder victim could not be removed until an autopsy had been performed. The Secret Service agents then forced the judge and doctor against the wall at gunpoint and forcibly took Kennedy's body from Dallas to Bethesda. Then, on orders from Lyndon Johnson, the Secret Service flew the Presidential limousine to Washington, D.C., allowed the FBI to assist in inspecting it, before it was scrubbed, washing away important traces of blood, bones and bullets. Deputy Secret Service Chief Paul Paterni, a member of the OSS during WWII and a former partner of CIA Counter Intelligence chief James Angleton, would provide the only significant hands-on input from the Chief's office on the day of the assassination. Paterni and Boring were involved with the limousine inspection at the White House garage, and vehicle damage was "noted" before the FBI got their hands on the limousine.[52] This destruction of evidence has yet to be accounted for.

When the Warren Commission investigated Lee Oswald's office in Guy Banister's New Orleans operation, they claimed to have found nothing remotely suspicious.[53] Guy Banister, a past supervisor of the FBI office in Chicago, who supposedly ran a private detective agency in New Orleans in 1962-3, had CIA and Mafia operatives working out of his office at 544 Camp Street (the same location as 531 Lafayette Street, Banister's address of record). Oswald also worked out of Banister's office, and he handed out "Fair Play for Cuba Committee" leaflets with the address 544 Camp Street. Yet the Secret Service synopsis to the Warren Commission stated, "Extensive investigation conducted thus far has failed to establish that the 'Fair Play for Cuba Committee' had offices at 544 Camp Street. It has likewise been impossible to find anyone who recalls ever seeing Lee Harvey Oswald at this address."[53]

The front entrance of the Secret Service's office was located about 50 feet from 544 Camp Street. As former FBI man Bill Turner discovered for Jim Garrison, after walking those 50 feet, if the Secret Service agents had gone up the stairs, they would have found themselves on the landing outside the door of Guy Banister's office with Banister's name printed on the door. If they had obtained a search warrant, they would have found a stack of leftover "Fair Play for Cuba Committee" leaflets in the office.[54]

The investigations of the Secret Service actions in Dallas were uneven. The Assistant Special Agent in charge of White House Detail, Floyd Boring was in charge of planning the Dallas trip. However, neither the Warren Commission nor the HSCA ever questioned him. Advance agent David Grant, who was involved in the aforementioned changes on November 18, 1963, was not questioned either. In Dallas, SAC Winston Lawson, formerly of the Army Counter Intelligence Corps, took the lead in changing the motorcade route, and limiting the number of Dallas police and motor-cycle escorts to protect the president.

A number of agencies have seemingly tampered with evidence. The most dramatic of which is that Kennedy's brain was "missing" from the National Archives in 1965.[55] Also missing are supplemental photographs taken of the interior of the President's chest. The CIA had destroyed its alleged tape recordings of Oswald supposedly recorded at the Cuban and Russian embassies in Mexico City in 1963.[56] Witness Beverly Oliver claimed to have filmed the assassination and her movie camera was immediately taken by the FBI; it was never returned. The FBI also supposedly destroyed the transcripts of tape recordings and was never able to produce any pictures of Oswald at Cuban and Russian Embassies in Mexico City.[57] In 1976, the National Archives disclosed that two letters written to Warren Commission General Counsel Rankin were missing from the National Archives collection: a "Letter of David Belin to J. Lee Rankin (chief counsel of the Warren Commission) on the interrogation of Oswald by the Dallas Police Dept," and a "Memorandum of Griffin to Rankin in August 1964" dealing with a number of inquiries to be made of various agencies, including unidentified prints found on the book cartons in the Texas School Book Depository.

The official copy of the Dallas police dictabelt of the police radio transmissions made during the assassination, and the shots recorded on it, is missing from the National Archives. Also two sets of reports dealing with "operational security involving the transfer of Lee Harvey Oswald" were found to be missing in 1976.

The FBI explanations about Jack Ruby provide useful insights into the investigation. The FBI could find "no significant links between Ruby and organized crime" for the Warren Commission, even though Ruby's entire adult life had been linked to organized crime. A few weeks prior to the assassination, Ruby made three calls to organized crime figures and their representatives.[58] One call was to Jimmy Hoffa's personal strong-arm man, "Barney Baker," one was to a Hoffa lieutenant, Dusty Miller, and one was to Nofio Pecora, a lieutenant of New Orleans mafiosi Carlos Marcello.

Further, Ruby had a special relationship with the Dallas office of the FBI, and in 1959 he met with agent Charles Flynn nine times. At that time he also purchased a microphone-equipped wristwatch, a bugged tie clip and other intelligence paraphernalia.[59] The FBI claimed that no useful information was ever obtained. Ruby repeatedly requested transfer to a safer prison, yet this was denied. When Chief Justice Earl Warren interviewed Ruby he inexplicably told him, "If you don't think it's wise to talk, that's ok."

The Warren Commission conceded that Ruby was "familiar if not friendly" with gangsters but found no "grounds for believing that Ruby's killing of Oswald was part of a conspiracy." Burt Griffin, the Commission's expert on Ruby, questioned aspects of this finding. "I think that we should have considerably more information about Ruby's visit to Cuba before we arrive at such a conclusion." (August 1964 memorandum)

Ruby's connections with organized crime were not difficult to ascertain and would have widened the investigation. By 1963, the Justice Department under Bobby Kennedy was effectively prosecuting the Mafia and had increased the Organized Crime section of the Justice Department by about 400%. Investigations of Mafia figures to be targeted for prosecution increased from 40 to 2,300. After the assassination of President Kennedy, the number of convictions dropped by 83%.[60]

Years later, the House Select Committee on Assassinations was able to tie Mafia kingpins Carlos Marcello and Santos Trafficante to Oswald and Ruby. Oswald had been connected in Louisiana with David Ferrie, who had worked as a pilot for Marcello (a New Orleans Mafioso who was deported by Attorney General Robert Kennedy in 1962) and anti-Castro Cubans. Oswald's uncle was a runner for Marcello. Further, four dancers at Ruby's club stated that they saw Oswald and Ruby together two weeks prior to the assassination. Ruby had been a runner for Al Capone in Chicago, had co-operated and worked with the Mafia in developing his strip joints in Dallas, and seemed to have visited Santos Trafficante in the Cuban prison Triscomia. Four witnesses claimed to have seen Ruby in Dealey Plaza during the time of the assassination: Julia Ann Mercer, Jean Hill, off-duty policeman Thomas Tilson, Jr., and TV cameraman Malcolm Couch. Tilson and Couch never were called to testify by the Warren Commission. In attempting to convince Jean Hill that she was mistaken, FBI Agent J. Gordon Shanklin told her that Jack Ruby had an unimpeachable witness who could place him in the *Dallas Morning News* at the time of the assassination.

Ruby was seen in the Dallas Parkland Hospital while Kennedy's body was there. According to Ruby's friend, journalist Seth Kantor, Ruby spoke with him for about 30 seconds. The Warren Commission accepted Ruby's denial about being in the hospital rather than Kantor's testimony.

Dallas police Chief Jesse Curry chose the basement route for Oswald's transfer to the Dallas County jail despite Ruby's phone calls to Officer Billy Grammer warning of a plot to kill Oswald in the basement. The officer in charge of basement security was Lt. George Butler, an old friend of Ruby and a member of the KKK, who moonlighted as a security guard for oil man H.L.

Hunt. Moments before the shooting, Ruby hid himself in the garage behind his old friend, Detective William Harrison, as well as a bevy of reporters.[61]

There was an inadequate investigation of the evidence of assassination plots prior to the assassination, interviews with Parkland Hospital employees, as well as distribution of evidence, which suggests another case of FBI and Secret Service suppression.

In Miami, on November 9, 1963, a right-wing extremist named Joseph Milteer informed a Willie Somerset, a police informant that an assassination of JFK was "in the works." Milteer stated that Kennedy would be killed "from an office building with a high power rifle.... (Then) they will pick up somebody...within hours afterward ... just to throw the public off." He continued, "It's in the works.... There ain't no countdown to it.... We just got to be sitting to go." Tapes of Milteer's comments were turned over by the Miami Police to the Secret Service. After some inquiries the case was quickly closed. The information apparently was not relayed to the Secret Service agents in charge of the President's Dallas trip.

The day of the assassination Milteer phoned his "friend" Somerset to say that Kennedy was expected in Dallas that day and would probably never again visit Miami. After the assassination Milteer boasted that the plot he had described had succeeded. Five days later the FBI asked Milteer about these statements. He denied making any threats. As the Warren Commission was winding down, the FBI passed along its documents on Milteer. The matter is ignored in the Warren Report and the twenty-six volumes of published evidence.

Another instance where vital information was suppressed prior to the assassination and from the Warren Commission comes from former FBI employee William S. Walter, who received warning of a possible presidential assassination attempt over the FBI Teletype in the New Orleans office on November 17, 1963. He called five agents who handled investigatory units. In 1976 Walter gave a recollection of the FBI telex to the Senate Intelligence Committee chaired by Richard Schweiker. After the Freedom of Information Act was passed, it was possible to get this telex:

URGENT: 1:45 AM EST 11-17-63 HLF 1 PAGE
TO: ALL SACS
FROM: DIRECTOR

THREAT TO ASSASSINATE PRESIDENT KENNEDY IN DALLAS TEXAS NOVEMBER 22 DASH TWENTY-THREE 1963.
MISC INFORMATION CONCERNING. INFORMATION HAS

BEEN RECEIVED BY THE BUREAU (SIC) BUREAU HAS DE-
TERMINED THAT A MILITARY REVOLUTIONARY GROUP
MAY ATTEMPT TO ASSASSINATE PRESIDENT KENNEDY
ON HIS PROPOSED TRIP TO DALLAS, TEXAS NOVEM-
BER 22-23 1963. ALL RECEIVING OFFICES SHOULD IMME-
DIATELY CONTACT ALL CIS, PCIS LOGICAL RACE AND
HATE GROUP INFORMANTS AND DETERMINE IF ANY
BASIS FOR THREAT. BUREAU SHOULD BE KEPT ADVISED
OF ALL DEVELOPMENT BY TELETYPE. OTHER OFFICES
HAVE BEEN ADVISED. END AND ACK PLS.

Shortly after Kennedy was shot, Walter asserts that he checked the file again to see if the warning was still there, but it had been removed. Months earlier, President Kennedy's motorcade was cancelled in Chicago due to murder threats that the Secret Service were aware of. Former Chicago Secret Service agent Abraham Bolden has confirmed that "there were to be no written reports, and information was to be given to [Chicago Secret Service Chief Maurice Martineau] by him orally. After the assassination the Chicago Secret Service Chief showed them a memo from Washington "that the Secret Service was to discuss no aspect of the assassination and investigation with anyone from any other federal agency now or any time in the future." Bolden disregarded these orders and went to Washington to talk with Warren Commission staffers about the Secret Service laxity and the assassination attempts in Chicago and Tampa. He was arrested the next day based on "information" from two mafia criminals that Bolden had previously put in jail.

Remarkably, Secret Service and FBI interviews with more than 30 employees at Parkland hospital were not included in the Hearings and Exhibits.[62]

The FBI also ignored repeated warnings from exiled Cuban businessman and FBI informant Jose Aleman. Aleman spoke with Miami Mafioso Santos Trafficante in September 1962 when Trafficante stated: "Kennedy's not going to make it to the election. He is going to be hit." Aleman told investigators that he was "given the distinct impression that Hoffa (who's Teamsters Union was a major source of Mafia loans) was principally involved in the elimination of Kennedy." Aleman told the FBI "something was going to happen.... I was telling them to be careful." Aleman was noticeably fearful in testifying before the HSCA in 1978, as noted by Chairman Louis Stokes. Jose Aleman died in 1983, broke and crazy. He did live in fear for his life.[63]

Soon after Oswald was arrested in a movie theater, Dallas police found a Selective Service card in his possession, which identified him as Alek James Hidell. By 3:15 PM November 22, Colonel Robert E. Jones of the

112th Military Intelligence Group contacted the FBI in both San Antonio and Dallas and stated that the Hidell/Oswald file was available to investigators. The FBI never picked up this file and the Warren Commission never questioned Colonel Jones. Although the Warren Commission specifically asked to see any military files on Oswald, the files were withheld from the Commission. Later, the Army claimed that the file was "destroyed routinely" in 1973, in accordance with normal file management procedures, as are thousands of intelligence files annually.

The inconsistencies between the reports regarding Kennedy's wounds at Parkland Hospital in Dallas and at Bethesda Naval Hospital are infamous. The six doctors at Parkland Hospital in Dallas observed Kennedy's head wound to be about 35 square centimeters with the massive exit wound on the rear of the head. They established that a small wound of 3-5 mm, which would indicate an entrance wound, existed in the throat area. Also, a wound six inches down from the right shoulder, 5 3/4-6 inches down from the collar of his shirt, at the third thoracic vertebra, was confirmed on the death certificate by Dr. Burkley, the President's doctor. Kennedy's body was wrapped in sheets and placed in an expensive bronze ceremonial casket.

Two hours later, the report of the military-controlled autopsy at Bethesda differed markedly from that of the doctors at Parkland on both the location and size of all of these wounds. Kennedy's body somehow arrived in a slate gray body bag in a plain gray shipping casket. The head wound expanded to 130 square centimeters, with the location four inches higher and on the right side of the head. The throat wound had somehow become a three-inch gash. This confused the doctors at Parkland. Logically, if an assassin had fired from the sixth floor, a bullet couldn't penetrate nearly six inches below the shoulder, as the death certificate, the autopsy chart, and Kennedy's clothing indicate, and then emerge from the front of the neck. Thus, after the Warren Commission needed "evidence" to be consistent with the lone assassin theory, the back wound was relocated to the base of the neck in the final autopsy report.

Parkland surgeon Charles Crenshaw, who attempted to revive Kennedy, revealed in his book *JFK: Conspiracy of Silence* that "I have wanted to shout to the world that the wounds to Kennedy's head and throat were caused by bullets that struck him from the front, not the back." Crenshaw noted that he was given an edict of secrecy by Dr. Charles Baxter; the director of the emergency room at Parkland, and he feared for his job if he spoke out. Dr. McClelland stated to the Warren Commission "I was in such a position that I could clearly examine the head wound. I noted that the right posterior portion of the skull had been blasted."[64]

The descriptions of the wound in the lower back of the president written in the report by FBI agents Sibert and O'Neill 11/26/63, and the FBI summary and Supplemental Reports 12/9/63 and 1/13/64, are not mentioned in the Warren Report, nor the Hearings and Exhibits. The report of a low back wound should match with the President's shirt and coat as well as the autopsy diagram – but would not be consistent with a shot from the 6th floor of the TSBD, with a downward trajectory, exiting the neck.

The autopsy pictures were not shown to the Commission. They were viewed by Chief Justice Warren, and supposedly on grounds of sensitivity, the Commission elected to have an artist draw autopsy pictures. Harold "Skip" Rydberg, the artist, and junior counsels Specter and Belin were angry that they were not allowed to view the autopsy pictures.

Dulles, Ford and McCloy were the most active members of the Warren Commission, and they were the most effective in avoiding an examination of the intelligence agencies. Oswald was portrayed to the Commission as a Marxist, an organizer for the Fair Play for Cuba Committee, and a defector to the Soviet Union who was preparing to defect again to Cuba. On the first day of hearings Dulles promoted copies of a book *The Assassins* that portrayed all major American political assassinations as the work of crazed lone gunmen. The FBI knew that the CIA pictures of "Oswald" entering the Russian and Cuban Embassies in Mexico City in 1963 were clearly not pictures of Oswald. Evidence seemingly had been manipulated to make it appear that Cuba and or Russia were directing Oswald, evidence the Warren Commission chose to ignore.

An internal Warren Commission memo by staff lawyer Melvin Eisenberg, dated 2/17/64, regarding the goal of the Commission is revealing:

> The President stated that rumors of the most exaggerated kind were circulating in this country and overseas. Some rumors went as far as attributing the assassination to a faction within the government wishing the Presidency assumed by Johnson. Others if not quenched, could conceivably lead the country to a world war, which would cost forty million lives. No one could refuse to do something, which might prevent such a possibility. The President convinced him (Warren) that this was an occasion on which the actual conditions had to override general principles.

Members and staff of the Warren Commission saw the Zapruder film; however, they failed to mention the backward motion of the president's head. Although still frames of the Zapruder film were published in the

Warren Commission volumes, the two frames following the headshot were printed in reverse order. J. Edgar Hoover later explained that this was an FBI printing error.

Johnson and some of his advisors thought that public knowledge of the apparent Cuban and Russian involvement in the assassination could have prompted a mass response for revenge – which could have led to a world war. So, a patriotic motive was given to the Warren Commissioners to pacify the public and classify the documents. When alleged "pictures" of Oswald entering the Cuban and Russian Embassies in 1963 were sent by the CIA to the HSCA, the pictures were of a balding man about fifty pounds heavier than Oswald. CIA document 657-831 indicates that Allen Dulles privately coached CIA officers on how best to discuss whether Oswald was an agent.

By January 1964 Chief Counsel Rankin had learned from Dallas D.A. Henry Wade that Wade was aware of an allegation that Oswald was a CIA informant with the number 110669. Rankin and Warren never made the Warren Commissioners aware of this number.[65]

According to respected researcher Dr. Gerald McKnight the FBI and CIA quickly ended an investigation of Oswald's pro-Castro activities after September 1963:

> The day following the assassination Hoover canceled orders to Contact the FBI's Cuban sources ... he excluded all of the Bureau's Cuban experts and supervisors from the investigation abandoning any Cuban angle.... Hoover turned the investigation over to the Bureau's Soviet experts. Senior CIA officers, in concert with the FBI, maneuvered to keep the public in the dark about any possible connection between the agency and Oswald's movements in Mexico City or his tagged pro-Castro activities in New Orleans. In late December Deputy Director of Plans Richard Helms removed John Whitten from the CIA's investigation and replaced him with James Angleton, the Chief of the agency's counter intelligence staff. According to Whitten, Angleton had "direct ties' with Hoover.[66]

Proof of Oswald's purported weeklong visit to Mexico was still nonexistent as late as September 1964. Marina Oswald maintained that the trip never occurred and FBI searches had revealed no evidence of it. Marina had been cloistered in a motel room for months after the assassination for extensive questioning. Suddenly, days before the Warren Commission's Final Report, "evidence" was found in the presence of "reporter" Priscilla Johnson, a witting asset of the CIA. Marina somehow supposedly found ticket stubs for a trip to Mexico City tucked in a Spanish language television schedule.

Senator Russell was unconvinced. Why would Oswald bring back a Spanish language television guide if he spoke almost no Spanish? Why would Marina bring it to the motel room? Why were previous FBI searches unable to uncover this? Nevertheless other Commissioners prevailed regarding the reliability of this evidence.[67]

Critics later asked: (1) why was Priscilla Johnson not a suspect? And (2) why was Priscilla Johnson allowed to visit with Marina Oswald when her relatives and other reporters could not get approval from the CIA and FBI?

Priscilla Johnson "had also met Lee Oswald in Moscow in 1959." In an almost obliterated CIA document, #646-277, the reason Johnson's name appeared in Oswald's personal notebook was stated. Priscilla Johnson "has apparently been employed on a part-time basis within the U.S. Embassy during two periods of residence in Russia." A "part-time basis" is often a euphemism used by the CIA in referring to its contract agents. CIA asset Richard Snyder could have used the U.S. Embassy in Moscow as a cover and sent cables to the State Department and CIA that Johnson supplied for him.

Priscilla Johnson later wrote a book, *Marina and Lee*, yet according to Marina, much of it was false. In 1967, Priscilla Johnson was assigned by the CIA to be the household companion of Alliluyeva Stalin (Stalin's daughter) who had recently defected. Some of these files remain heavily redacted.

The Warren Commission assumed that Soviet journalists who interviewed Oswald in Russia were KGB agents but they never explored whether the U.S. journalists who interviewed him had U.S. intelligence connections.

The Warren Commissioners did not agree among themselves on the final conclusions, and some members openly criticized the process and conclusions years later. Senators Russell and Cooper along with Congressman Boggs disagreed with the single bullet theory, and wrote a formal dissent. Somehow this dissent was lost from the record.[68] Boggs had been the most vocal critic of the Warren Commissioners and stated that he had strong doubts about the "magic bullet." Boggs had been the recipient of damaging material on the lives of critics of the Warren Commission and the FBI investigation of the President's death, which led him to attack the FBI. Years later, Boggs declared "Hoover lied his eyes out to the Commission on Oswald, on Ruby, and their friends ... you name it." He also accused them of "Gestapo tactics." Boggs, who would have soon become Speaker of the House and a powerful ally in reopening the investigation, disappeared without a trace on a military junket flight in Alaska on October 16, 1972.

The Warren Commission staffers did not have access to the deliberations of the executive sessions. And while the Commission lacked the authority to classify documents, it classified the transcripts of its proceedings "Secret" or "Top Secret." In 1965 President Johnson signed an executive order which provided that all of the Warren Commission's materials would be kept in the National Archives, but which also permitted the various government agencies, such as the CIA and FBI, to require continual classification of the documents until the year 2039. So only a fraction of the CIA records found their way to the Commission in the first place. By 1977, Oswald's CIA 201 files alone contained 1,194 documents, but until 12,300 pages were released in 1993 only 66 were made public in their entirety.

Commission General Counsel of J. Lee Rankin noted in executive session:

> Part of our difficulty ... is that [the FBI officials] have no problem, they have decided that it is Oswald who committed the assassination, they have decided that no one else was involved ... (WC Executive Session 1/27/64) in 1978 former Warren Commission assistant counsel Burt Griffin told HSCA that – 'I felt betrayed, if feel like the CIA lied to us. (BBC Special on the Kennedy Assassination: "What Do We Know Now that We Didn't Know Then").

Thus the Warren Commission ratified a "Noble Lie," preferring official dignity and perceived national security, over truth. The Warren Report was more improvised public relations than a real investigation. After the Warren Report was released, FBI Director J. Edgar Hoover asked for all derogatory material on Warren Commission members and staff contained in FBI files.[69]

Chief Justice Earl Warren was asked by a reporter 2/4/64 whether testimony taken by the Commission would be made public; He responded: "Yes, there will come a time. But it might not be in your lifetime... there may be some things that involve security. This would be preserved but not made public."[70] This statement was seen by some of Warren's friends as a blunder which damaged the commission's reputation. Katherine Graham wrote Warren, "It seems to me that you are courting an undesirable and unnecessary impression by publicly discussing the investigation, however guardedly, while it is in progress."[71] Warren agreed, and lamented that "We desired no publicity whatsoever, but for a time, the pressure was almost hysterical." Junior counsel Arlen Specter was convinced that Chief Justice Warren determined early on that Oswald acted alone. Warren's attitude was "let's get this goddamn thing over with … in a hurry." [72] The Warren Report was not consistent with the 26 volumes of Hearings and Exhibits, but the biases, gaps and contradictions would only be painstakingly revealed over time.

The final Warren Report issued in September 1964 focused on biographical information of the alleged assailant, Lee Harvey Oswald. Only about 11% of the report addressed the alleged facts of the case. More time was spent on the Secret Service than on the Kennedy autopsy.[73]

Years later, the Senate Special Committee on Government Operations in 1975-6, determined that the FBI and CIA kept evidence of whole areas of overwhelming importance from the Commissioners.

Some of these major areas include:

> CIA attempts to kill Castro.
>
> CIA realization of Castro's knowledge of the plots.
>
> FBI failure to investigate the Cuban exile plots in New Orleans and their possible connections to Oswald.
>
> CIA cover-up of Oswald's alleged trip to Mexico City.
>
> Hoover's almost immediate release of a report incriminating Oswald.
>
> Hoover's leaks of the FBI investigation to the press that were meant to shut off the possibility of an independent inquiry.

The upcoming media coverage of the Warren Report can be glimpsed when CBS taped Mark Lane's critical lecture just prior to the release of the Report. A CBS representative called Lane to say that the lecture had been edited to "about the finest nine minutes of television viewing that I have ever seen…. It will be shown tomorrow evening, or the next evening." It was never shown.[74] The Warren Report coverage revived Mark Twain's notion that "A lie can get halfway around the world before the truth can even gets its boots on."

6

WARREN REPORT COVERAGE: MAINSTREAM SPIN VS. JOURNALISM

The liberty of the press is indeed essential to the nature of a free state, but this consists in laying no previous restraint on publications.
                                        –William Blackstone, English Jurist

If thou art privy to thy country's fate, which, happily, foreknowing, may avoid, O speak.
                                        – Shakespeare, *Hamlet*

All the news that is fit to print.
                                        – *New York Times*

What we don't say is often more important than what we do say.
                                        – Edward R. Murrow, CBS Reporter,
                                        CBS Vice-President, Director of USIA

The release of the Warren Report on September 25, 1964 preceded the release of the 26 volumes of Hearings and Evidence upon which it was based. That didn't seem to matter as the mass media greeted the report with staunch support, while the alternative media coverage varied widely – from support to caution to dissent. All of the major networks devoted special programs which faithfully backed the Report. CIA assets strengthened the Cold War mass media-government cooperation during this crisis, while trusted establishment sources avoided and denigrated critics as well as contradictions in the evidence.

The Warren Report reached an American public where 70% still had confidence in government. Years later, former PBS anchor Robert Mac-Neil observed that "the report fell on receptive ears and fitted a psychological and emotional matrix of a nation disposed to blame a deranged gunman rather than the wholesome society from which he came." (John Barbour *The Garrison Tapes*).

Immediately after its release, foreign political and media leaders were sent copies of the Warren Report to counter "the strong belief in many countries" that a "political plot" occurred, according to CIA Propaganda Notes Series A – Bulletin 9/22/64.

> The long awaited Warren Commission Report, on its exhaustive investigation ... will probably be released over the weekend. The Department of State is air pouching copies of the report to ports for selective presentation to "editors," jurists, government officials, and opinion leaders... the unwarranted interpretation that Ruby's murder of Oswald was committed to prevent Oswald from revealing the purported conspiracy adds to the belief. Communist regimes have used both murders to denigrate American society and the release of the Report will undoubtedly be used as a new peg for the same purpose.... Covert assets should explain the tragedy wherever it is genuinely misunderstood and counter all efforts to misconstrue it intentionally.... Communists and other extremists always attempt to prove a political conspiracy behind violence. In countries accustomed to assassination by political conspiracy, American dedication to institutions of law and government with stable administration procedures can be described; and American Presidents can be shown to have been victims (with the exception of Lincoln) of single, fanatical individuals. Three commercial editions will be published as soon as possible after the formal release. _____ has ordered 150 _____ publications but will evaluate the introductions of all three and inform operating Divisions of any drawbacks. Divisions should make bulk purchases for field use through regular channels.[1]

The *New York Times* passionately supported the Warren Report with a special news supplement, opinion pieces, and by publishing a paperback version of the Report with Bantam Books. The *New York Times* lead story by Anthony Lewis of September 27, 1964 declared: "The Warren Commission analyzed every issue in exhaustive, almost archeological detail..." An editorial proclaimed "The facts, exhaustively gathered, independently checked and cogently set forth, destroy the basis for conspiracy theories that have grown weed-like in this country and abroad." C.L. Sulzberger wrote, "It was essential in these restless days to remove unfounded suspicions that could excite latent jingo spirit. And it is necessary to reassure our allies that ours is a stable reliable democracy." Reporter Arthur Krock, an old friend of JFK, declared the Warren Report as the "definitive history of the tragedy." Harrison Salisbury declared in the *New York Times* paperback edition of the Warren Report, "the evidence of Oswald's single handed guilt is overwhelming."

The lead editorial from the *Washington Post* was stridently supportive.

> The Warren Report has given the American people, and the world, a report, which deserves acceptance as the whole truth and nothing but the truth about the assassination of President Kennedy.... No doubt rumor and speculation will continue to be disseminated among the gullible, the perversely romantic and the morbid as they have circulated for years concerning other presidential assassinations... It is impossible for rational men to believe that this commission could have been either corrupted or deceived into error...

The *Washington Post* of 9/28/64 devoted seven pages reprinting portions of the Warren Report, along with numerous euphoric stories. One story was titled, "A masterpiece of its kind, if not elegant literature." One article, drawn from dispatches, briefly noted disapproval of the report, but none of the critical arguments were discussed.

On September 27, 1964, the very day the Warren Report was released, CBS broadcast a two-hour Warren Report "illustration," reverentially backing it. Actually the piece was ready by July, the expected release date, but the Warren Commission lawyers needed more time. Years later, CBS Executive Producer Les Midgely attempted to clarify:

> The 1964 effort was not an investigation of the circumstances of the assassination itself but solely an illustration, translated into a television broadcast of the Report. The findings were not questioned; they were illustrated.[2]

In early September 1964, Mark Lane and filmmaker Emile de Antonio, a Harvard classmate of JFK, viewed CBS outtakes in the CBS film library for five hours, focusing on interviews related to the assassination. When a witness said something which contradicted the Warren Report the interview was snipped away and turned into an outtake. Lane stated, "If a witness said, for example, that he heard the shots and at the time believed that they had come from the knoll, the interview might be halted and begun again. What was said in the interim is as puzzling as the Warren Commissions 'off the record' discussions." The CBS program, as with the Summary of the Warren Report, proclaimed, "there is no hint" of differences of opinion.[3]

Lane and de Antonio immediately signed a "blue sheet contract," essentially an official offer to buy the outtakes. According to Lane, the next morning de Antonio called the CBS library to arrange for another appointment to view footage and was told "CBS would not sell any of the footage to us; in fact, CBS was soon to destroy the film." The librarian added, "we could, of course, view no more film ... and that its decision was final and there was no appeal to it."[4]

George Orwell surmised in *1984* that:

> The process has to be conscious, or it would not be carried out with sufficient precision, but it also has to be unconscious or it would bring with it the feeling of falsity and hence of guilt.... To tell deliberate lies while genuinely believing in them, to forget any fact that became inconvenient, and then, when it becomes necessary again, to draw it back from oblivion for just as long as it is needed, to deny the existence of objective reality and all the while to take account of the reality which one denies – all this is indispensably necessary."[5]

The procedures used by CBS challenged the canons of journalism, censorship, and private property. How was CBS linked to the Warren Commission? Why did they proceed from a script? Why did they selectively edit to support the Warren Commission? When does the public have a right to know about critical historical moments?

The following day, 9/29/64, the *Washington Post's* venerated columnist Walter Lippmann pronounced that:

> The report deals with all points factually and authoritatively.... We may be confident that historians will find nothing to make them question the perfect good faith of the record, which the seven commissioners have compiled ...

The Warren Report ironically criticized the Dallas police, the bar, and the media for the confusion during Oswald's time in jail, and recommended the development of ethical standards on collecting and presenting information to the public. *Washington Post* managing editor Al Friendly glowingly supported early press coverage.

> This quick intelligence in spite of imperfection kept the whole nation on an even keel, sufficiently satisfied the public curiosity to

prevent hysteria and panic and was detailed enough to prevent rumor and suspicion that might have otherwise directed popular vengeance against innocent individuals or groups.

The *Wall Street Journal*, 9/28/64, succinctly agreed with the Warren Report that "Kennedy's Killer was Beyond Doubt, Lee Harvey Oswald." A lengthier piece by Jonathan Spivak recounted the findings of the Warren Report, and raised no concerns.

The *Atlanta Constitution*, 9/28/64, carried four *New York Times* reports and three AP reports, and all but one gave unqualified support to the Warren Report. One short report quoted American communists as well as Bertrand Russell as viewing the report as incredible; however, no facts or arguments were mentioned. A front-page piece by AP reporter Hugh Mulligan ran under the headline, "Report is Rebuff to Witch-Hunters."

The *L.A. Times*, 9/28/64, forcefully backed the findings in the Warren Report with a large headline "No Conspiracy in Kennedy Slaying," and a number of writers summarized its findings. The headlines for Robert Donovan's articles read "Oswald Acted Alone in Kennedy Assassination" and "Full Account of Tragedy a Masterpiece – Report Carries Stamp of Honesty and Authenticity." The lengthy summary was printed in full with an AP byline. Vincent Burke's piece, "Assassination Termed Act of Man 'Alienated' from Real World" underscored the lone-nut thesis.

Remarkably, *Life* (10/2/64) chose to have Commissioner Gerald Ford review his own work. Perhaps as noteworthy, *Life* printed three different versions of this issue in the same day. At first a still frame from the Zapruder film, depicting Kennedy's rearward motion at the moment of the head shot, was replaced with an earlier frame that gave no indication of the direction in which his head moved. The caption stated, "The assassin's shot struck the right rear portion of the President's skull, causing a massive wound and snapping his head to one side." The accompanying photo (frame 323) showed the president slumped back against the seat, and leaning to the left, an instant after the fatal shot. The photo gave the impression that shots came from the front or the right. The second version of this issue replaced frame 323 with frame 313, the graphic picture of the president's head exploding. The caption, though, remained the same. Then, a third version was developed, the resetting plates broken again at considerable expense, to create a new caption, which fit the Warren Commission findings. "The direction from which the shots came was established by this picture taken at the instant the bullet struck the rear of the President's head, passing through, caused the front part of his skull to explode forward."

These changes were inexplicable according to *Life* editor Ed Kearns in a talk with citizen researcher Vincent Salandria:

> I am at a loss to explain the discrepancies between the three versions of *Life*, which you cite. I've heard of breaking a (printing) plate to correct an error. I've never heard of doing it twice for a single issue, much less a single story. Nobody here seems to remember who worked on the early Kennedy story...[6]

The Warren Commission Report never addressed the backward motion of the president's head. This omission was facilitated by the reversal of the two frames following the explosive frame 313 in the Warren Commission's published volumes, which confused this issue by making it appear as if the head jerked forward. J. Edgar Hoover later claimed that the switch was a "printing error."

U.S. News & World Report, 10/5/64, devoted twelve pages to summarize and quote the Warren Report. Its reverence rested upon: "A White House Commission which collected every fact, followed every clue, and studied every rumor."

Newsweek, 10/5/64, devoted 24 pages of homage to the Warren Report. "The report was calm, measured, and overwhelming – in the weight of its evidence against Oswald, in the glint of fresh and authentic detail, and the sheer scope, intensity and thoroughness of the investigation ..." The Warren Report psychologizing of Oswald began in the second paragraph. Oswald supposedly had a "deep rooted resentment to all authority" and "a hostility toward every society in which he lived" and was dogged by "isolation frustration and failure and an urge to find a place in history."

Newsweek contended that Oswald's connections were interviewed, and both Cuba and the Soviet Union cooperated with the investigation – the information they furnished was independently checked on the spot by agents of the CIA. *Newsweek's* national affairs editor, John Iselin sent Dulles a note thanking him for his judicious findings and that the magazines coverage of the report "was made easier through your kindness in giving us some idea of what to be on the watch for."[6a]

Time's ten-page overview also extolled the thoroughness of the Warren Commission and posed no questions or concerns.

The Nation, 11/2/64, clarified their early concerns and then strongly backed the Warren Report as well. At the time the Warren Commission was appointed, the respected liberal journal took the position that "it would stoutly resist the temptation to enter the ranks of the rapidly expanding army of amateur 'private eyes' and miscellaneous freelance James Bonds, who were even then busy as beavers mass producing conspiracies among unnamed 'oil millionaires' and offering each day a new theory of President Kennedy's assassination."

In their feature article, Stanford Law Professor Herbert Packwood, passionately praised the Warren Report as having,

> Admirably fulfilled its central objective ... that is adequate to satisfy all reasonable doubts about the immediate essential facts.... If there are minor flaws ... they are thrown into shadow by the conscientious and at times brilliant job that the commission has done.... Only those who for whatever reasons of personal or political myopia cannot bring themselves to face reality will continue to think that the tragedy was proximately the work of more than one man...

Packwood regretted the committee leaks, the lack of simultaneous distribution of the Hearings and Exhibits, the "mischievous" Mark Lane, the gingerly treatment of Messrs. Curry and Wade, Oswald's lack of counsel, and a perceived discouragement of dissenting opinions by Earl Warren. While noting that we have not seen the end of this affair, Packwood condescendingly concluded,

> What the Warren Commission has done is to refute or render irrelevant the speculation of those who, out of whatever aberrant needs, still refuse to believe that Oswald, Ruby, and the Dallas authorities were what they appear to be and not something sinister.

Independent leftist journalist I.F. Stone also strongly backed the Warren Commission for its "first class job," and condemned the critics in *I.F. Stone's Weekly* (10/5/64). His story, "The Left and the Warren Commission" disparaged the "slanderous" style of some of the dissenters and admonished the need to [not] write and speak in just that hysterical and defamatory way from which the Left has suffered in the last quarter century. He claimed that journalists Joesten, Marzani and Buchanan had published "rubbish."

Isador Feinstein Stone had previously been the Washington editor for *The Nation*, and then worked for mainstream liberal dailies, *P.M.*, the *New York Star* and the *New York Daily Compass* before launching his weekly one-man operation in 1953. (The circulation eventually reached 70,000.) His ringing praise for the Warren Report stunned many of his followers. It ran contrary to his usual working methods, as well as his perspective that "all governments lie." When critic Raymond Marcus called Stone three years later to clarify his position Stone bellowed, "I don't care about that asshole case!" (Marcus, Ray unpublished manuscript)

After the Warren Report was officially released, Kilgallen critiqued FBI and Dallas Police procedures and conclusions in her syndicated column.

> I would be inclined to believe that the Federal Bureau of Investigation might have been more profitably employed in probing the facts of the case, rather than how I got them – which does seem a waste of time to me. At any rate, the whole thing smells a bit fishy. It's a mite simple that a chap kills the President of the United States, escapes from that bother, kills a policeman, eventually is apprehended in a movie theater under circumstances that defy every law of police procedure, and subsequently is murdered under extraordinary circumstances.[7]

The New Republic, 10/10/64, piece by Murray Kempton, "Warren Report Case for the Prosecution," viewed a report "which drastically narrowed the area of doubt," yet needed less psychologizing along with a commitment to the adversarial process. He questioned: Oswald's marksmanship as "implausible but not impossible"; Howard Brennan's inconsistency as a witness – positively identifying Oswald fully four weeks after the assassination; Brennan's supposed statement to the Dallas Police, the source of the police alarm describing Oswald at 12:45. Kempton then assessed police-media relations:

> The reporters should not have baited Lee Oswald; but much more fundamental the police should not have brought him out to be baited. Reporters go so far as society will let them; it was the duty of the cops to throw the reporters out. And the Commission has to be harsher on private citizens that were doing their job than on policemen who refused to do theirs.... For two days Chief Curry had been blatting to the papers any piece of evidence useful to his image. After Oswald was murdered, J. Edgar Hoover called Cur-

ry and told him to shut up. Thereafter the chief stopped talking to reporters. On Sunday night District Attorney Henry Wade came to Curry, said the world was full of rumors that Oswald died an innocent victim and he proposed to go before the press and set the record straight ... Curry, with the wrath of Hoover still hot upon him, refused to give Wade any of the police case. Wade went doggedly ahead from what he remembered ... and appeared on television to reassure the police that Oswald was guilty beyond any possible debate. "Unfortunately," the Commission says, "he lacked a thorough grasp of the evidence and made a number of errors ... [which provided much of the basis for myths and rumors ..."

The *New Leader* 10/12/64 revealed inconsistencies and omissions in the Warren Report's investigation of the Tippit shooting. "The Other Witnesses" by George and Patricia Nash explored three witnesses they had found whose descriptions of the murder differed markedly from the Warren Report. Frank Wright stated that he witnessed the shooting about half a block from his apartment and his wife called for an ambulance. Wright seemed certain that a man of medium build with a long coat was close to Tippit and then ran to his grey car after Tippit fell. He was not interviewed by the Dallas police nor the Warren Commission. Another witness, Acguilla Clemons, saw two men around Tippit's squad car but her statement was not officially taken supposedly because of health reasons. These witnesses significantly disagreed with witness Helen Markham on how soon the ambulance arrived and undermine her credibility.

The *New York Times* remained effusive when the 26 volumes of exhibits and testimony were released on November 24th. Their instant analysis of the more than 10 million words evoked this commentary 11/25/64: "(it) brings to a close its inquiry, at once monumental and meticulous."

The 26 volumes, however, did not match the 888-page Warren Report. Evidence was edited which could have indicated a shot from the front, as well as the connections between Oswald and Ruby, which suggested conspiracy. Apparently that was not "all the news that is fit to print."

Reader's Digest, with psychological warfare expert Eugene Lyons (Radio Free Europe) as a senior editor, ran a story in September of 1964 supportive of the Warren Commission. Although they did not write on the Warren Report, in the November 1964 issue they ran a story from former Vice-President Richard Nixon. "Cuba, Castro and John F. Kennedy: Reflections on U.S. Foreign Policy" viewed Oswald as "demented ... and driven ... by Communism in particular ... Castro was the indirect cause of the tragic snuffing out of John F. Kennedy's life…" Nixon proclaimed that, "The last four years have seen the greatest series of foreign policy failures in any comparable period in our history."

"The Doubts Remain" by Mark Lane in the *National Guardian*, 10/3/64, attacked the Warren Commission procedures and partiality. "All seven members were associated with the government." Further, Oswald's family could not choose a counselor to defend his interests.

The Legal Intelligencer, a law journal from Philadelphia, ran the riveting dissent of Vincent Salandria 11/2/64, "The Warren Report – Analysis of Shots, Trajectories and Wounds: A Lawyer's Dissenting View." Salandria cited the auditory, visual and olfactory stimuli indicating a shot from the front which was ignored, as well as the trajectory of the shot which hit James Tague not emanating from the TSBD. The Warren Report disregarded testimony of Secret Service Agent Glen Bennett, stationed to the right rear of the President's follow-up car. Although the Report gave "substantial weight" to Bennett's other observation – that the first shot missed. "Connally's body did not react immediately after the President's body reacted. Therefore, the same bullet that hit the President did not hit him. The Commission would have us believe that Governor Connally was wrong, his wife was wrong, the FBI's initial findings were wrong, the Zapruder film was wrong, and that there is no law of physics called action and reaction. Governor Connally was not hit by the first bullet to hit President Kennedy."

Salandria noted inconsistencies in the description of the President's back wound, the trajectory of a sixth-floor shot, and the wounds in Connally. He concluded there was more than one gunman.

In November, a team of NBC newsmen came to Dallas and contacted Jim Kerr of the *Dallas Times Herald*. Kerr contacted Dallas Deputy Sheriff Roger Craig, a witness to events in Dealey Plaza after the assassination, to set up an interview. NBC had been calling Craig since October but Craig was reluctant to talk – fearful of the reaction of his boss, Sheriff Bill Decker. The powerful chief, who ran his office like a Field Marshal, ordered Craig to "Tell them you didn't see or hear anything." After that, Decker assigned officers to spy on Craig. Craig followed orders, but a few years later he talked with journalist Penn Jones and worked for Jim Garrison.[8]

In December 1964 the *New York Times* and Bantam Books issued *The Witnesses*, which claimed to be "the highlights of the Hearings before the Warren Commission… selected and edited by the *New York Times*." All testimony which contradicted the conclusions of the Warren Commission was eliminated. Excerpts from Abraham Zapruder's testimony do not include his statements where he considered it likely that some of the shots came from behind him on the grassy knoll. Numerous other witnesses, who reported that at least some of the shots were fired from in front, also had their testimony omitted. Excerpts from the testimony of Naval Commander J.J. Humes omitted his acknowledged burning of the first draft of the autopsy report. Excerpts from the testimony of Major Eugene D. Anderson and Sergeant James A. Zahn (who served with Lee Harvey Oswald in the Marines) suggest that the shots were not difficult and that Oswald had the capability to have fired them. However, the statement that Nelson Delgado, Oswald's Marine Sergeant, gave to the FBI that Oswald was a poor rifleman was omitted from the Warren Report.[9]

Deleted from the testimony of Secret Service agents William Greer, Clint Hill and Roy Kellerman were statements which placed the wound in the back of the president approximately six inches below the shoulder, a description at significant variance with the official autopsy report. *The Witnesses* also excluded testimony from witness Arnold Rowland in which he told the Warren Commission that he had actually seen two men on the sixth floor of the TSBD at the time of the assassination, but that the FBI told him to "forget it," and in which he stated his conviction that the shots had been fired from the railroad yards in front of the President.

The Witnesses also omitted the testimony of: James Tague, Billy Lovelady, Roy Truly, Lee Bowers, James Underwood, Frank Reilly, S. M. Holland, special assistant to the President David Powers and others who reported seeing some shots fired from the front, as well as Jean Hill who reported seeing a man fleeing the grassy knoll area after the shooting, Wilma Tice and reporter Seth Kantor, and many others.

By the end of the first week Bantam had printed over one million copies of the book. Ironically, the *Times* would later imply that the critics of the report were guilty of exploitation because of the "minor if lucrative industry" that arose from challenges to the official version of the assassination. So *The Witnesses,* compiled by America's "newspaper of record," manufactured consent for the Warren Commission. At about this time the Associated Press published their own strongly pro-Warren Report book, *The Torch is Passed.*

A year after the assassination, the AP ran two articles by Sid Moody, one of the major authors of the book. These pieces were as strongly pro-Warren Report as the book. The lone faint note of dissent was from Oswald's mother who called him a "patsy." Abraham Zapruder was interviewed for the first time but was not asked about the direction of the shots. Ruth Paine was portrayed as a warm person, "troubled" by her closeness to the Oswalds, who wondered what "demons" drove Oswald, and "laughs" at rumors of a plot. Jack Ruby was portrayed as a strange, suicidal, patriotic loner who talked more with (Dallas D.A.) Henry Wade, than to his own lawyer. Governor Connally's feelings were probed, but not his beliefs regarding the sequence and number of shots.

In his other story "Dallas' Everyday Places ... JFK's There in Death," Moody described Oswald's flophouse; Marina Oswald's new home; Ruth Paine's feelings, patriotism and cooperation with law enforcement; and Pat Kirkwood's joint – where the Secret Service "had stopped" before the assassination. These backgrounders offered vivid impressions, but avoided any investigation.[10]

December 4, 1964, Mark Lane debated Warren Commission attorney Joseph Ball, A.L. Wirin, a civil liberties attorney and Herman Selvin, president of the L.A. County Bar. Lane carried the day, and the "debate" was aired on KPFK, a Pacifica radio station.

Liberation, 1/65, a new left magazine published by Dave Dellinger and A.J. Muste, ran Vincent Salandria's expanded critique "A Philadelphia Lawyer Analyzes the Shots, Trajectories and Wounds." Salandria cited Dr. Charles R. Baxter's testimony to the Warren Report that the President's neck wound would be unusual and unlikely for a point of exit for a high velocity missile. Dr. Ronald Jones (at Parkland Hospital) also saw the neck wound as one of entry. Warren Commission counsel Arlen Specter had asked Jones if this neck wound could be an exit wound from a low-velocity rifle (like the Mannlicher-Carcano) and Jones agreed. This though did not fit with the other high velocity wounds to the President and Connally.

Salandria examined the testimony of Special Agent Roy Kellerman, who was at the autopsy in Bethesda, to clarify the finding of Col. P. Finck "...we were standing right alongside of him, he is probing inside the shoulder with his instrument and I said, 'Colonel where did it [the bullet] go.' He said, There are no lanes for an outlet of this entry in this man's shoulder."[11] Such a finding would make the back wound a separate hit.

Salandria contrasted the Warren Commission Exhibits 385 and 386, which showed an entrance wound in the back of the President's neck, slightly higher than the supposed exit wound from his throat, with the autopsy reports and evidence. According to the testimony of FBI agent

Robert A. Frazier, the holes in the President's coat and jacket were 5⅜"
and 5¾" below the collar, Commander Humes attempted to reconcile
these evidentiary differences by suggesting that the President was waving
which "would further accentuate the elevation of the coat and the shirt."
However, Exhibit 396 shows President Kennedy gesturing to the crowd
waving no higher than his forehead. Dr. Humes conceded that the drawings were not "absolutely true to scale." Salandria noted that "no criminal court in the land would have admitted those drawings as evidence
without having first required the production of autopsy x-rays with the
colored and the black and white pictures of the body."

Humes stated to Specter that "the availability of the x-rays would not
assist the Commission." Salandria then noted that Humes "destroyed certain preliminary draft notes relating to the Naval Medical School Autopsy
Report."[12]

Salandria outlined the criticisms to the single-bullet theory by quoting
Connally's testimony, his wife's, noting the lack of any eyewitness testimony, the Zapruder film, and the ballistics evidence of Dr. Robert Shaw
(Connally's doctor) that more than 3 grains of metal were in the Governor's body – more than were lost from CE 399.

He noted witnesses stating they thought the head shot to the President
came from the front – a right temporal wound, including Dr. McClelland
at Parkland Hospital and Father Oscar Huber, Secret Service Agents and
Dr. Marion Jenkins. Numerous witnesses at Parkland Hospital testified to
seeing not a small entry wound in the back of the head but rather a gaping
wound – contrary to the reports from the Bethesda doctors.

Life's relationship with the CIA seemingly led them to run a cover picture of a North Vietnamese stamp that showed the Vietnamese shooting
down American planes (2/26/65). These gruesome stamps showed that
the Vietnamese were glorifying the killing of Americans. We later learned
that the North Vietnamese had no such stamps – they were actually CIA
forgeries.

The Atlantic Monthly, March 1965, ran a hyperbolic defense of the
Warren Report in Lord Patrick Devlin's "Death of a President: The Established Facts." Previously a Justice to the British High Court, Devlin
concluded that the Warren Report painstakingly proved the case against
Oswald; however, the actions of the Dallas authorities created suspicions.
"Everything big and little that was said and done in this great tragedy is
here set down." Devlin's discussion of witness Howard Brennan glossed
over the inconsistencies in his testimony and an inattention to what was

printed in the Warren Report. This abuse of his discretion led to a derisive challenge to critics, "if they can suggest one [theory] that is even faintly credible, they will deserve more public attention then they are likely to get by making charges of suppression that are more than faintly ridiculous."

The March 1965 issue of *Esquire* saw things differently in Dwight Mc-Donald's review of the "Report of the Presidents Commission Investigating the Assassination of John F. Kennedy." McDonald viewed the Report as an imaginary American "anti-Iliad," rather than a murder investigation. *Esquire's* bold journalism also piqued the interest of New Orleans Judge Jim Garrison.

The Minority of One ran "Fifty-One Witnesses" by Harold Feldman, 3/65, exploring the witnesses who stated shots from the grassy knoll. They also ran a letter to the editor, "Oswald Censored" where Lillian Castelano noted that the CBS 1964 program on the Warren Report omitted Oswald's remark "I'm a patsy."

Journalist Fred Cook composed a short piece raising contradictions in the Warren Report version of the firing sequence and submitted it to Carey McWilliams, the editor of *The Nation*. After three weeks McWilliams rejected the article, although he could not find flaws in Cook's reasoning. Cook surmised that McWilliams and others were concerned that, "if the assassination proved to be the work of a conspiracy, it might start another irresponsible witch-hunt comparable to that of the McCarthy era."

Cook then tried to get other magazines to publish his piece but *True*, *Playboy* and *Ramparts* all rejected it – without objecting to anything in the piece. Finally, after delaying for more than a year, *The Nation* published it, in June of 1966, though they printed a rebuttal soon afterwards.[13]

While most of the mass media was suppressing assassination news for the sake of national security, President Johnson and the Defense Department were creating inflammatory fake news. Johnson's apparent news management was demonstrated with the Tonkin Gulf crisis. Professor Jerel Rosati noted:

> Government officials charge that American destroyers sustained two unprovoked attacks by North Vietnamese warships in international waters. This led to the passage of the Tonkin Gulf resolution, which supported any presidential action taken in Vietnam and helped legitimize the subsequent American support of the war. In fact, accounts now reveal that one of the two North Vietnamese attacks on American destroyers probably never took place and that American ships were providing intelligence support for

South Vietnamese covert military attacks of North Vietnam. Furthermore, the congressional resolution was actually prepared by the Johnson administration before both the Tonkin Gulf crisis and the 1964 election. This suggests that President Johnson and his administration were able to use the Tonkin Gulf crisis to manipulate the media and maximize domestic political support in order to "get tough" and exercise greater force in Vietnam. In other words because of the secrecy and covert nature of the operation, because of administration lies, both the Congress and the public were seriously misled.[14]

In contrast, in June 1965 Kilgallen tried to present her findings on the ABC show *Nightlife*, a talk show that competed with Johnny Carson. While in the dressing room ABC producer Nick Vanoff approached her and prohibited her from discussing the "too controversial" subject, the source of Vanoff's concern was never clear.

Penn Jones, a former army officer, and reporter, editor and owner of the tiny *Midlothian Mirror*, courageously wrote 6/3/65, of the untimely and strange deaths of witnesses in the assassination case.

In mid-June Kilgallen was booked to appear on ABC's *Nightlife*, expecting to talk about the Kennedy assassination. Yet minutes before she was on air, a producer warned her not to discuss the Kennedy assassination because it was "too controversial."

Early critic Harold Weisberg self-published *Whitewash*, August 1965, after a series of rejections from publishers. None of the rejections "contained any adverse editorial comments." Further "seven literary agents … found themselves too busy to do justice to the book once they learned of the subject matter." One agent noted, "No American publisher will now touch this subject."[15]

In August of 1965, *Life* reiterated its position on Oswald's guilt in Keith Wheeler's piece "Cursed Gun: The Track of C2766," which traced the history of the Mannlicher-Carcano as well as the handgun reported to have been Oswald's. Considerable attention was given to the history of the rifle, yet the lack of powder burns on Oswald's cheeks based on a negative paraffin test was unmentioned. Although Dallas police initially reported the rifle found on the sixth floor to be a German Mauser 7.65, a .30-30, a high powered army or Japanese rifle of .25 calibers, an Argentine made Mauser or a British .305, the early confusion was not noted. The initial lack of fingerprints on the rifle didn't seem noteworthy to Wheeler either. The Mannlicher-Carcano had long been the butt of jokes in Italy where it was called "that cursed gun" and "the humane weapon." Wheeler however, declared that a man of "impeccable credentials ... Robert Frazier, an FBI firearms specialist who test fired the gun, has testified. It is a very accurate weapon."

Dorothy Kilgallen's last published piece on the assassination ran in her column of September 3, 1965:

> Those close to the scene realize that if the widow of Lee Harvey Oswald ... ever got out the "whole story" of her life with President Kennedy's alleged assassin, it would split open the front pages of newspapers all over the world. Even if Marina explained why her late husband looked so different in an official police photo and the widely printed full-length picture feature on the cover of *Life* magazine, it would have caused a sensation. This story isn't going to die as long as there's a real reporter alive – and there are a lot of them.

On September 9th Jack Ruby granted an interview to KTVT Fort Worth, which was taped in the Dallas County Courthouse.

> The only thing I can say is – everything pertaining to what's happened has never come to the surface. The world will never know the true facts of what occurred – my motive, in other words. I am the only person in the background to know the truth pertaining to everything related to my circumstances.

Ruby was then asked if he thought that the truth would ever come out.

> No. Because unfortunately these people have so much to gain and such an ulterior motive to put me in the position I'm in, will never let the true facts come above board to the world.
> "Are these people in high places Jack?"
> "Yes."
> One of the reporters then asked Ruby "Jack, you said that the people will probably never get the truth – Why's that Jack?"
> At that point either Ruby was silent or the tape in the National Archives was cut.[16]

In early November 1965, Dorothy Kilgallen had confided to friends that she would "blow the lid" off of the Kennedy case. These friends included her old friend and lover Johnnie Ray, Bob Bach, associate producer of *What's My Line*, her makeup man Carmen Gebbia, her hairdresser

Marc Sinclair, her lawyer Mort Barber, as well as Mark Lane.[17] By then her phone was tapped and she was calling other critics from phone booths. She was the last journalist to interview Jack Ruby, and apparently was intending to print it in her forthcoming book, *Murder One*. But before she published her story she died, victim of what police said was a drug overdose, yet no quantities were given in the autopsy report. No notes relating to her chapter on Jack Ruby were ever found.[18]

The junior NYC medical examiner, Dr. James Luke, officially estimated that she overdosed on barbiturates and alcohol "circumstances undetermined," between 2:00 and 4:00 AM, November 8th, just 3-5 hours after appearing on the popular television show *What's My Line?* After the show she had cocktails with friends and mentioned that she had "shocking" information and was excited about her upcoming book. In a 1978 interview Dr. Luke noted that Kilgallen probably did not commit suicide: "the pills were not what we might expect to find in cases that are suicide." Curiously, Kilgallen was found to have 50 cubic centimeters of "pink fluid" in her stomach, which was sent to toxicology for analysis. If the analysis was done it was never made available to Dr. Luke. The Director of Toxicology at the New York City Medical Examiner's Office, (Dr. Charles Umberger), believed that Kilgallen had been murdered, according to his top assistant, chemist John Broich. Broich agreed and recounted that in 1968 Dr. Umberger advised that he should "keep it under your hat."

The City of New York was not yet regularly using tests that could determine which drug or drugs from three fast-acting barbiturates had been involved in the death. Umberger, using more sophisticated tests, found that secobarbital, (seconal) amobarbital, (tuinal) and pentobarbital (trademark Nembutal), were particularly dangerous in the right amount and in combination. Nembutal is now a controlled substance sometimes used in executions. The chemist who ran the tests for the Department of Toxicology, which were to be given to the Department of Pathology, determined that quinine, which might have covered the bitterness of the secreted barbiturates, was found in "brain, bile and liver." The quinine somehow was not reported to the Department of Pathology. Further, Kilgallen was found lying on a bed which her friends and family said that she never used, somehow sitting in an upright position. Years later Dr. Broich revealed that it was "not unusual for the medical examiners to screw up a case, there weren't too many people working there who could get a job anywhere else."[19]

Mark Lane contacted Dorothy Kilgallen's husband, Richard Kollmer, about a month after her death and asked to see her notes on the assassination. Kollmer declared, "I'm going to destroy all that. It's done enough damage already." Kilgallen's assassination notes were never found.

Kilgallen was not the first reporter researching Jack Ruby to die under suspicious circumstances. Bill Hunter, a reporter for the *Long Beach Press-Telegram* and Jim Koethe a respected reporter for the *Dallas Times Herald* had visited Ruby's apartment on the evening after Oswald's murder. Before the police had an opportunity to search the premises, they met with Ruby's roommate George Senator, Ruby's attorney Tom Howard, and attorney Jim Martin. Hunter was killed when a detective's gun discharged, ostensibly by accident, in the hands of a policeman "playing a game of quick draw" at the Long Beach police station in April of 1964. Jim Koethe, who was writing a book on the assassination, was mysteriously found dead in his apartment five months later. His neck had been broken as he emerged from a shower. None of his writings or notes was found. No investigation of the murder was ever conducted.[20]

The universally strong support among the major mass media for the Warren Report strengthened the early "lone nut" consensus. The often-derisive characterizations of those who questioned the Report, along with the deaths of Hunter, Koethe and Kilgallen, sent a chilling message to independent voices in the mainstream and alternative media. The sole mainstream media sources to challenge the "Noble Lie" were *Esquire* and the *New York Journal-American*.

Close Kennedy aide Fred Dutton recounted reasons for supporting the Warren Report, although many elites saw it as a PR job. Author David Talbot observed:

> … If one wanted to remain a member in good standing in Washington political and social circles, it was wise not to say something intemperate about the assassination. This expedient position was couched as doing what was right for the country, and helping it get along with business… while the country's ruling caste – from President Johnson on down--muttered among themselves about a conspiracy, these same leaders worked strenuously – with the media's collaboration – to calm the public's fears.[21]

Ironically, in 1965 Congress funded a quarterly magazine called *Censorship*, as part of the cultural Cold War, which investigated limitations on free expression around the world. Although most of the articles concerned communist and authoritarian regimes, they also included thought control and press taboos in Japan, Western Europe and the U.S., written by presumably unwitting assets in academe. The editor, Meir Mindlin, admitted years later that he should have guessed that *Censorship* was a CIA front.

Deceptive efforts to support the Warren Report by CBS, the *New York Times* and *Life,* the Associated Press and UPI, proved central to the circling of the wagons. These mainstream sources acted solidly supportive of the Warren Report, even two months before the 26 volumes of Hearings and Evidence were released. Cold War media-elite-government cooperation, along with fears of a nuclear war, and the fear of appearing like a banana republic, galvanized the faithful support. Author Gay Talese viewed the relationship between the *New York Times* and the highest levels of the U.S. government as "a hard alliance," which in any large showdown would "undoubtedly close ranks and stand together." Cold war cooperation at the *Washington Post* centered on the Graham family, and the death of Phil left his wife, the inexperienced and cautious Katherine, at the helm. Since no major American political leader challenged the Report, it made it easier for the media to avoid confronting the confusing contradictions.

The Minority of One steadily unraveled contradictions in the official story with monthly reporting which included the investigations of Penn Jones, Sylvia Meagher, Eric Norden, Cedric Belfrige, Mark Lane, Harold Feldman, and Vincent Salandria. Soon they would print articles by Martin Seboty, Jim Garrison and Conner Cruise O'Brien among others.

For the second anniversary of the assassination *The New Leader* ran Leo Sauvage's critique of the Warren Commission that "we prefer not to be confronted once again by the ugly details of that day." Letters to the editor supportive of Sauvage's article regularly found their way into print.

Meanwhile, *Ramparts* equivocated on a commitment to work to "reopen the warren Commission" by electing not to publish a piece by Fred Cook.

November 25, 1965 Penn Jones warned in the *Midlothian Mirror*:

> I have a concern for the strange things happening in America in recent months … Miss Dorothy Kilgallen joins the growing list of persons who have died after a private interview with one of the two members of the Jack Ruby-George Senator Team. We have printed the strange deaths of Bill Hunter and Jim Koethe after they had a private interview with George Senator and Ruby's attorney Tom Howard. Hunter and Koethe were murdered. Lawyer Tom Howard died under strange circumstances. Now Miss Kilgallen dies under clouded circumstances. During the Ruby trial in Dallas, Judge Joe B. Brown granted Miss Kilgallen a privilege given no other news-

man. She had thirty minutes alone with Jack Ruby. Even the guards were outside the door. Miss Kilgallen told some of what went on in the interview in her columns. But was someone afraid of the interview in her columns? But was someone afraid that she knew more? What is happening in our land...? How many murders of persons connected in some way with the assassination principal can go unnoticed by our people?

The responses of the alternative media were mixed. *I.F. Stone's Weekly* strongly supported the official findings. *The Nation* essentially supported the conclusions of the Warren Report while raising some concerns. *Ramparts,* a new left-liberal monthly remained cautiously quiet. *The Legal Intelligencer* and some alternative media outlets, *A Minority of One,* the *New Republic, The New Leader, Liberation, National Guardian, Saga,* and the *Village Voice,* along with the *Midlothian Mirror* were critical but faint voices. Independent investigators increasingly posed contradictions and omissions in the Warren Report and prodded media coverage.

In Europe the press was much more skeptical of the official findings, and the assassination was widely controversial. A critical book, *Who Killed Kennedy?* by American expatriate Thomas Buchanan, was already a best seller, and critical books by Leo Sauvage and Joachim Joesten were available. The *Sunday Times* of London ran a piece by the respected British historian Hugh Trevor-Roper, accusing the Warren Commission of setting up a smokescreen which failed to ask basic questions.

7

Citizens Prod the Press

*Liberty cannot be preserved without a general knowledge of the people,
who have a right and desire to know… they have a right, an indisput-
able, unalienable divine right to the most envied and dreaded kind of
knowledge, I mean the character and content of their rulers."*

– John Adams

*While the people retain their virtue and vigilance, no administration,
by any extreme wickedness or folly, can seriously injure government in
the space of four years.*

– Abraham Lincoln

A nation of sheep will beget a government of wolves.

– Edward R Murrow

Citizen researchers persevered, sacrificing time not normally available to most media outlets, pouring over the 26 volumes of hearings and evidence. Early books and articles critical of the Warren
Report, particularly *Rush to Judgment* by Mark Lane, and a front page piece
in the *Washington Post*, prompted responses from the mainstream and alternative media, as well as from the FBI and CIA. Steadily the marginalized citizen critics, like a modern Committee of Correspondence, contributed to
moving many reluctant mainstream media sources to call for a reinvestigation. The first actual meeting of the critics of the Warren Report, "Warrenol-
ogists" as Sylvia Meagher called them, was October 3, 1965, at Meagher's
apartment in New York. The group included Maggie Field, Leo Sauvage,
Sylvia Meagher, Isabel Davis, Edward Epstein, Joe Lobenthal, and Tom
Stamm, Vince Salandria and his wife and Bill Crehan. The group wondered
how Epstein had gained access to many Commission attorneys and Warren
Commission members. The meeting proved useful but contentious, so letters and phone calls continued to connect the critics.

The Minority of One published March 1966, "The Impossible Tasks of
One Assassination Bullet," based on an article that Vincent Salandria had

read in draft form at the meeting at researcher Sylvia Meagher's home. A companion piece, "A Separate Connally Shot" by Salandria, explored the FBI Report (exhibit 23).[1]

Immediately after President Kennedy and Governor Connally were admitted to Parkland Memorial Hospital, a bullet was found on one of the stretchers. Medical examination of the President's body revealed that one of the bullets had entered just below his shoulder to the right of the spinal column at an angle of 45 to 60 degrees downward, that there was no point of exit, and that the bullet was not in the body. An examination of this bullet by the FBI Laboratory determined that it had been fired from the rifle owned by Oswald.

The Warren Report criticisms resurfaced nationally when on May 29, 1966, the *Washington Post* ran an eight-column banner headline on the front page, "An Inquest: Skeptical Postscript to Warren Group's Report on Assassination." Lengthy discussions of Harold Weisberg's book *Whitewash* and Edward Epstein's *Inquest* warned that these authors raised "grave doubts about the Commission's work." Epstein noted the inconsistent documentary and evidentiary placement regarding the back wound, as well as the bureaucratic time pressures that handicapped the Commission. He argued that the Warren Commission was more interested in dispelling rumors that in exposing the truth.[2]

Epstein examined discrepancies regarding the location of the President's back wound by noting that the holes in the President's shirt and jacket matched the FBI reports from Sibert and O'Neill, as well as the testimony of three Secret Service agents, by placing the location in the back below the shoulder. The official autopsy report, though, located the wound much higher, at the base of the neck.

Weisberg analyzed: Oswald's marksmanship; Oswald's location at the time of the assassination; the single bullet theory; witnesses around the grassy knoll; the head snap (Zapruder film); the shooting of Officer Tippit, and the throat wound. When the *New York Times* reviewed these books (6/5/66) they buried their story on page 42, and focused solely on a defense of the single-bullet theory.

Later that month, Mark Lane's book *Rush to Judgment* made the bestseller list. The *Times* of London and the *London Observer* also called for a new investigation. Investigative reporter Fred Cook tried to get his critique of the Warren Commission published by *Ramparts* but after first agreeing, they refused. Then *The Nation*, after deliberating more than a year, ran Cook's critique in a two-part series on 6/13/66 and 6/20/66.

He observed that, "not a single eyewitness to the Commission heard or saw the action in a way that the commission decided it had happened. All, without exception, were convinced that the President and Governor Connally were felled by separate, wounding shots." These probing pieces, based largely on contradictions in the Warren Report, were atypically prefaced by an editors' statement which reiterated "…we never doubted the good faith of the Commission or the good faith or high quality of its staff. But the facts disclosed by the transcript, as they relate to points which trouble Mr. Cook, are not conclusive, and from them reasonable men may reach different or, as in this case, variant conclusions." Less than two weeks after *Rush to Judgment* was published, the CIA circulated a detailed memorandum critiquing the book. This memorandum was followed by another memo, which raised objections to Lane's research regarding Oswald's trip to Mexico as well as the intelligence links to Oswald and Ruby.[3]

Fred Graham, a close social friend of Assistant Attorney General Nicholas Katzenbach, reviewed *Whitewash* and *Inquest* in the July 3rd *New York Times Book Review*. The first half of the review largely defended the methods used by the Warren Commission. Graham called Weisberg a "painstaking investigator," but asserted, "It is difficult to believe that any institution could be that inept, careless, wrong or venal as he implies. Rather, the reader is impressed with the elusiveness of the truth…"[4]

Graham saw *Inquest* as "superficial," since Epstein spent only two days in the National Archives. While he admitted that the single-bullet theory was "porous," he somehow declared that no other explanation made sense. Conveniently he concluded that "a major scholarly study is not feasible now because the crucial papers in the archives … have not been declassified."

Citizen researchers, led by Jim Lesar, Bud Fensterwald and Harold Weisberg, joined with a range of political activists, a handful of newspaper editors, and Congressman John Moss, to push for the Freedom of Information Act. Bill Moyers, then in the LBJ inner circle, recalls that Johnson "hated the thought of journalists rummaging in government closets … only some last minute calls from some newspaper editors overcame the president's reluctance." He signed "the f_ _ _ ing thing" as he called it, on July 4, 1966, and then went out to claim credit for it."[5]

Newsweek saw *Inquest* as "serious and scholarly." *The New Republic* asserted that Weisberg and Epstein have independently "ransacked the twenty-six volumes of testimony and exhibits and the FBI reports on which the Warren Report is based." *The New Leader* and the *Minority of One* echoed that sentiment.[6]

Talk radio stations at times provided an outlet for critics of the Warren Report. A notable exchange regarding the role of the FBI occurred on a radio program in July of 1966 between reporter Fred Cook and Warren Commission Counsel Burt Griffin. Griffin was asked if he thought that Oswald had been connected with the FBI and he responded by saying that no one was ever going to know. Cook prodded Griffin on this point and Griffin observed, "I am just stating a fact of life ... if anyone from an important federal agency was involved, the record would have been so thoroughly covered up that no one would ever find out." After the program Griffin told Cook, "I admire what you are trying to do, but I have to tell you that you're not going to get anywhere."[7]

The Nation then ran an article defending the Warren Report conclusions written by Jacob Cohen, "The Vital Documents," on 7/11/66. Cohen contended that Cook, Salandria and Epstein had accused the autopsy doctors of deliberately falsifying their report or that the autopsy report reproduced by the Warren Report was a forgery. However, Cook's articles clearly do not state that. Cohen called for a release of the autopsy x-rays and photos, while staunchly defending the Warren Report's conclusions. Cook demanded that *The Nation* editor Carey McWilliams give him an unedited response or he would no longer write for the magazine – which was granted. Cook then dismantled Cohen's arguments. Months later, after debating researcher Vincent Salandria, Cohen did not deny that he was working with the CIA.[8]

Ray Marcus tried unsuccessfully to get Dell and Pocket Books to print *The Bastard Bullet* (CE 399). *The Minority of One* offered to publish it if he could cut it by half but Marcus thought those cuts to be too deep. Undaunted, he explored ballistics tests, interviewed coroners about the likelihood of a bullet falling from a wound, and interviewed Darrell Tomlinson, the hospital engineer credited with finding the bullet on a stretcher other than Connally's stretcher. Tomlinson "told Marcus that the FBI telephoned him about one o'clock in the morning and told him to keep his mouth shut."[9]

Dr. Cyril Wecht, the young director of the Institute of Forensic Sciences at Duquesne University School of Law, condemned the medical aspects of the Warren Report at a meeting of the American Academy of Forensic Sciences. "By standards found in most competent medical legal investigative facilities the autopsy report would not be deemed to be a complete one." Reporter Gaeton Fonzi, after collaborating with Vincent Salandria, interviewed Warren Commission attorney Arlen Specter for the *Greater Philadelphia Magazine* August 1966; Specter argued that Oswald had an easy shot, that it is not possible to tell when Kennedy was first hit, that Kennedy waving to the crowd accounts for the location of the location of the holes in his jacket, and that the Warren Commission did not view the x-rays due to considerations of taste and respect for the dead president...

The article stated:

> It is difficult to believe that the Warren Commission Report is the truth. Arlen Specter knows it.
>
> It is difficult to believe that all the shots which caused the President's and Governor Connally's wounds were fired from the sixth floor of the Texas School Book Depository. Arlen specter knows it.
>
> It is difficult to believe that "the same bullet which pierced the President's throat also caused Governor Connally's wounds." Arlen Specter knows it.

CBS radio Mike Wallace, at-large correspondent George Herman interviewed Harold Weisberg 7/24/66. Weisberg argued that the Warren Commission "set out to prove Oswald guilty.... It did it by selecting what evidence it wanted to use, by ignoring the evidence it didn't want to use, by not looking for what it did not want to find, and above all, as with any such inquiry, you have the built in weakness of no representation of the other side.... The only man who saw Oswald go into the building stoutly maintained that Oswald carried nothing.... There is only one explicit conclusion in Whitewash ... the job hasn't been, and must be done – and entirely in public."

A *London Observer* review of Epstein's book, reprinted by the *San Francisco Chronicle*, 8/13/66, wryly noted, "How long the dead president's political heir can manage to retain a non-committal attitude is perhaps the most intriguing question in American politics today."

Kennedy aide Richard Goodwin stirred Washington with his strongly supportive review of *Inquest* in the *Washington Post*, 7/24/66. He called for an independent panel to review the Warren Report, and if necessary, a new investigation. The *New York Times* noted that this was "the first member of the president's inner circle to suggest publicly that an official re-examination be made..."

Sylvia Meagher's painstaking work to create the only index of the 26 volumes of Warren Commission hearings and evidence broadened her reputation, even prior to the publication of her book *Accessories After the*

Fact. She was asked to consult for a piece in *Esquire,* to write assassination book reviews for studies on the left, CBS requested her advice, and the *London Times* asked for a copy of her Subject Index.[10]

Strong support for the Warren Report from the *New York Times* continued when Fred Graham reviewed Mark Lane's *Rush to Judgment* and Leo Sauvage's *The Oswald Affair* for the *New York Times Book Review* 8/28/66. He ignored the forensic evidence in both books and concentrated upon their reliance on eyewitness testimony. Graham argued that the main source of the Warren Commission's dilemma was that it had to issue a report before the 1964 election. The broad proof against Oswald and the lack of evidence pointing to any other possible assassin gave the Warren Commission no choice "but to smooth over the inconsistencies to the extent possible and brand Oswald the lone assassin." He avowed, "It is clear that any jury, faced with the material before the Warren Commission and in these books, would easily convict Oswald of murder."

A Harris Poll released in September 1966 showed that less than one third of the American public believed that the Warren Commission had told the whole story. So despite the extensive governmental and mass media efforts to support the official story, already a clear majority of the public felt that major questions remained unanswered.

Amid the growing controversy, the *New York Times Magazine* ran an astonishing story 9/11/66, "No Conspiracy, But – Two Assassins, Perhaps?" by Henry Farlie. He acknowledged that the Warren Commission "did a hurried and slovenly job." Then he creatively claimed that there could be more than one assassin but "it still does not justify making the long leap to a conspiracy theory of the assassination … none of this is to deny that there may have been two or more people involved in the assassination... it is possible to regard such people as fanatics or nuts and nothing more." It was a coincidence theory. Farlie fearfully opined, "To set up another independent body with no promise that it will succeed, would be to agitate public doubt without being certain that it could in the end settle it. Popular fear and hysteria are dangerous weird to excite…"

Meanwhile, the UPI handling of the Nix film taken from Dealey Plaza during the assassination took more perplexing twists. Maurice Schonfeld, the managing editor of the UPI news film service, after working with the film for two years, stated that he saw enough shadows on the grassy knoll to be fearful for his own life. Yet when UPI reporter Jack Fox reported on it, he asserted that there might have been a gunman on the knoll – although it could be "a brown cow grazing."[11]

UPI was unwilling to pay for additional research, stating that it would be costly and there would be no financial return, since "UPI does not sell exclusive stories and it is impossible to assign a dollar value to a wire service scoop." Schonfeld then approached *Life* and spoke with assistant editor Dick Billings. Billings was purportedly unable to interest his superiors at *Life* who "felt they had already given sufficient space to the Kennedy assassination."

Schonfeld then offered the film to *Newsweek* photo editor Tim Orr, who said that he didn't know what to make of the pictures. Orr made it clear that as a UPI client he was entitled to the pictures as a matter of routine. Schonfeld left and curiously "locked the film in a vault to avoid trouble." As the value of the film steadily grew, CBS came over to view it; however, they too supposedly "did not know how to handle the story." According to Schonfeld "nobody wanted to assume the cost of further investigation." So despite widespread public doubts about the Warren Report, this lead languished.[12]

Comedian Mort Sahl invited Mark Lane on his shows 9/4/66 and 10/9/66, in part because critic Ray Marcus had shared his research with Sahl. Lane stated that two-thirds of the Dealey Plaza witnesses reported hearing shots from the grassy knoll. He shared taped clips of witnesses from his upcoming documentary *Rush to Judgment* – the first time most Americans had seen testimony contradicting the Warren Report. Sahl quipped, "It isn't fun to awaken America now. It is like walking into a party – everyone's been drunk for 175 years, and you're getting the tax for the liquor.... But we gotta keep this thing going ... America is at stake."

Finally, by the end of September 1966, the *New York Times* raised concerns regarding the Warren Report. Tom Wicker questioned the Warren Commission procedures, objectivity and diligence. "The damaging fear has been planted, here as well as abroad, that the commission ... was more concerned to quiet fears of conspiracy and treachery than it was to establish the unvarnished truth, and thus made the facts fit a convenient thesis." Wicker endorsed the call for a Congressional review.

Penn Jones's impact increased with his self-published book *Forgive My Grief* – it led to an interview on *CBS Evening News* 10/29/66. He declared, "I would rather be the sorriest bootlegger in Midlothian than be in the shoes of Earl Warren in the eyes of history. If this is the democracy that we claim it is, then he flunked his final when his country needed him most."

The *Washington Star* ran a range of views, while denigrating the critics. On 10/5/66, reporter Richard Wilson called for a "supplementary report" to examine the x-rays and autopsy pictures ostensibly because "conspiracy theory critics" have played on the "natural gullibility of the American public." A month later, reporter Jeremiah O'Leary reviewed Leo Savage's *The Oswald Affair* and dismissed all critiques of the Warren Report as "dreamed theories." Recall that O'Leary was a "very friendly source" for the FBI and the CIA.

Allen Dulles responded to the rising tide of dissent by pressuring his "old and close friend" David Lawrence, the owner of the *U.S. News & World Report*.[13] The 10/10/66 issue of *USNWR* created a faithful defense, "Truth about Kennedy Assassination: Questions Raised and Answered." Based on "exhaustive research;" all questions regarding evidence as well as the credibility of the Warren Commission were seen as resolved:

> Officials familiar with the inner workings of the Warren Commission say that all of these points are covered in the official report.... The answers, they say, are in the Commission documents, for anyone who wants to look them up.

The controversy regarding the discrepancy between the FBI Report and the Autopsy Report was "resolved" by merely noting that the FBI did not receive the report until December 23, two weeks after it issued its report. The x-rays and autopsy photographs were quickly taken by Attorney General Robert Kennedy, and then released to the National Archives. Under a "deed of gift," they remained under lock and key. Warren Commission counsel Arlen Specter, who headed this phase of the investigation, said, "The Commission decided that it would not press for the photographs, as a matter of deference to the memory of the late President, because the Commission concluded that the photographs and x-rays were not indispensable."

USNWR conducted a ten-page interview with Warren Commission Counsel Arlen Specter, "Overwhelming Evidence Oswald was Assassin." Specter somehow determined, "There has not been a scintilla of new evidence," "we did a responsible and thorough job," and "that reopening the investigation would not disclose any additional evidence based on all that is known at the present time."

By November 1966, the work of citizen researchers Shirley Martin, Harold Weisberg, Mark Lane, Vincent Salandria, Penn Jones, Sylvia Meagher, Leo Sauvage, Penn Jones, Mary Ferrell, Ray Marcus, Maggie Field, Lillian Castelano, Jim Lesar, Bill Turner, Jerry Policoff, Josiah Thompson, and Bud Fensterwald, along with dozens of others, had significantly contributed to calls for a new investigation from a range of mass media outlets: the *Boston Globe*, the *Boston Herald*, the *Louisville Courier-Journal*, the *Louisville Times*, the *Cleveland Press, Washington Post*, the *Denver Post*, the *Montgomery* (Alabama) *Advertiser, The Progressive, Esquire, Ramparts, Commentary, The National Review, Perspectives, Chicago American* and even *Life*. In France *Paris-Match* declared, "No legal expert today would dare to affirm that Oswald would be judged guilty by a court." The *London Times* and *L'Obsservatore*, the Vatican newspaper, also called for a reopening of the case. *Time*, though, steadfastly maintained that "there seems little valid excuse" for a new probe.

On the third anniversary of the assassination the *Washington Post* ran an AP story, which reviewed dissent by John Connally regarding the shots and bullets. "There is absolute knowledge ... that one bullet caused the President's first wound and that an entirely separate shot struck me. It is a certainty." It noted Senator Russell's objections to the single-bullet theory, Oswald's past regarding Russia and Cuba, as well as witness S.M. Holland's eyewitness statements regarding shots coming from the grassy knoll. The Associated Press, however, did not call for a new investigation. Notably, none of the contradictions and uncertainties in the case, even those mentioned in AP stories, were printed in the redistribution of the AP book *The Torch is Passed* in 1967.

The afternoon *Merv Griffin Show* invited Penn Jones on 11/14/66, and Mark Lane 11/23/66. Lane sparred with pundit David Susskind who accused him of "alarming the American public" – Lane retorted that "the American should be alarmed, and that evidence, not faith in distinguished Americans, was needed."

The November 25, 1966, issue of *Life* reassessed the assassination in a series of articles entitled "A Matter of Doubt," which narrowly focused on the single-bullet theory. The composition of the research team raised questions about the seriousness of the investigation. Hugh Aynesworth, an FBI informant and a CIA applicant, teamed with Dick Billings, the *Life* editor who worked with the CIA on the failed 1963 Bayo-Pawley mission, *Life* stringer David Chandler, a major opponent of Jim Garrison's investigation, and Holland McCombs, a close friend of Clay Shaw.[14]

Aynesworth's unpublished report to *Newsweek*, 2/22/67, reveals that he as well as *Life* were on to some of the same leads as New Orleans District Attorney Jim Garrison. Billings made at least two trips to New Orleans to confer with Chandler, some Cubans, and in particular, David Ferrie, the pilot and right-wing mercenary who worked with Oswald and New Orleans businessman Clay Shaw and had FBI, CIA, and mafia connections.

Life did not mention the widening critique of the roles of the FBI, CIA, the Secret Service, or the new witnesses who had been interviewed by Mark Lane. Lane's book was derided as "a grab-bag of virtually all of the conceivable theories that offer an alternative to the Commission. The book is wildly speculative ... peripheral and indiscriminate." Although *Life* called for a new investigation, it printed only 31 frames of the Zapruder film in the story, and again did not print any frames of President Kennedy being hit in the head. By 1965 the Zapruder film was available in the National Archives but the mass media never seemed to mention this to the public. Author Josiah Thompson asserted that the *Life* article was originally more extensive, but 17 editors significantly limited it. Thompson attributed organizational caution as blunting the probe. Nonetheless, *Life* shed further doubt on the "single-bullet theory," and opined that "a new investigative body should be set up, perhaps at the initiative of Congress." But *Life* published no other story from this team of reporters.

Life's business partner *Time*, however, editorialized against the "phantasmagoria" of Warren Commission critics and argued: "...there seems little valid excuse for so dramatic a development as another full scale inquiry." When asked about the opposing editorial positions, Hedley Donovan, editor-in-chief of both magazines arrived at consistent positions on major issues, "and I am sure in due course we will on this one." *Life* reporter Richard Billings stated that a superior told him "it is not *Life's* function to investigate the Kennedy assassination." Billings investigation was ended.

Hugh Aynesworth informed the FBI of a research strategy he was using in connection with the *Life* story, 12/13/66. He passed along information on a Dealey Plaza witness, George Davis, who had not been interviewed, and who thought that the smoke, which came from a point on the overpass, probably came from the motorcycle of Dallas Police Officer Harkness. Aynesworth also mentioned that he had information on critic Mark Lane's sex life.[15]

Harrison Salisbury, an editor at the *New York Times*, reversed his early support for the Warren Report in his article in *The Progressive*, a small alternative monthly. His readings of *Rush to Judgment* and *Inquest* convinced him that major questions remained unresolved. Salisbury now supported Congressman Theodore Kupperman's resolution for a congressional review.

Within this changing political climate, the *New York Times* seemingly started an investigation of its own in November 1966, under the direction of Harrison Salisbury. This investigation, however, was somehow derailed almost as quickly as it began. It was "temporarily suspended" in December and was never completed. Salisbury received permission to visit Hanoi in December. Another member of that research team, Martin Waldron, noted that he and others came up with "a lot of unanswered questions that the *Times* didn't bother to pursue ... I'd be on a good lead and then somebody would send me off to California on another story or something. We never really detached anyone for this. We weren't really serious."[16]

Gene Roberts, *New York Times'* Atlanta bureau chief and a member of their investigation team, told researcher Jerry Policoff:

> There was no real connection between Salisbury going to Hanoi and the decision not to publish, or to continue the inquiry ... the basic conclusion was that we couldn't find that there was supporting evidence to the contentions of the critics ... we found no evidence that the Warren Report was not right.... We are not in the business of printing opinion... [17]

As Salisbury told it to researcher Bernard Fensterwald "there wasn't even an overt decision to drop it. He just had other things to do." Reluctantly the *New York Times* editorial, 11/22/66, observed, "Further dignified silence, or merely more denials by the commission or its staff, is no longer enough."

Amid a political milieu of distrust regarding the Warren Report in Europe and at home, the revered columnist Walter Lippmann cautiously advocated a new investigation, which would circumvent the Constitution. Though "a certain amount of reasonable doubt exists" that it might be desirable to "open the case unofficially." He suggested "a reputable agency, politically and financially independent" which could "examine new interpretations of the old evidence and any new evidence that might be brought forward in the future."

Newsweek, 11/7/66, remained stoutly resistant to covering the new contradictions raised by citizen researchers. They were mocked as "a cult ... a subculture of assassination buffs who obsessively probe the massive record.... And they have created a growing market: a recent Louis Harris poll showed that three-fifths of the American public doubts the assassination was the work of one man, nearly double the level of two years ago."

The rapidly growing alternative monthly magazine, *Ramparts*, in a much delayed assassination issue, explored the untimely deaths of numerous witnesses to the assassinations of President Kennedy and officer Tippit. "In the Shadow of Dallas" by (Ret.) Brig. General Penn Jones prophetically predicted "that more killings are to be necessary to keep this crime quiet." *Ramparts* started five years earlier as a critical quarterly with a highbrow Catholic identity, and was transformed under the leadership of muckraker Warren Hinkle. By its peak a few years later, circulation would rise to 250,000, and it would soon be confronted by American intelligence agencies.

Time, 11/11/66, quickly responded by attempting to rebut some of the issues raised by Penn Jones and *Ramparts*. Jones was labeled a "mythmaker," "engaged in a macabre and mischievous exercise." *Time* neglected to respond to a number of areas: Tom Howard (Ruby's lawyer); incessant police harassment of Mrs. Earlene Roberts, Oswald's rooming house manager; witness Julia Ann Mercer; Carroll Jarnagin, witness to Ruby-Oswald meeting; policeman Harry Olsen, the death of Hank Killen, a friend of Ruby and roommate of Oswald's at the time of the assassination, whose throat was slit; Warren Reynolds, witness to the Tippit shooting, who "would hesitate to identify Oswald as the individual," was shot in the head two days after talking to the FBI while he was closing up his car lot – nothing was stolen; Lee Bowers, the witness who had a good view from a 14-foot train tower directly behind the grassy knoll, somehow veered off the road though traveling at a slow speed, 8/9/66, and hit a bridge abutment. No skid marks were found. A doctor riding in the ambulance stated that Bowers was "in a different state of shock than an accident victim experiences. I can't explain it. I've never seen anything like it." There was no autopsy.

The *Washington Star* summed up the national sentiment in their third year anniversary article headlined, "Assassination Controversy at New High." They led with the calls from Sen. Russell Long and former Kennedy advisor Arthur Schlesinger to start a new investigation.

They expanded Governor Connally's statement that he was not hit by the bullet that struck the president, as well as Senator Russell's objections to the Warren Commission.

Newsweek, 12/5/66, dismissed the *Life* questions regarding the single bullet theory as "a good deal of fuss." They creatively claimed that, "As the pictures (of the Zapruder film) suggest ... Connally was hit earlier than he thought" – thus he was hit by the same bullet that wounded the president. They questioned the location of Connally's wrist when it was hit, but made no call for a new investigation to resolve the differences.

Newsweek then argued that the notes on the autopsy drawing clarified the discrepancy regarding the location of Kennedy's back wound. They failed to mention that the bullet hole in President Kennedy's coat and shirt, as well as the signed death certificate, all indicate a wound 5 3/4" below the neck, which does not match the autopsy drawing. They deferred to J. Edgar Hoover who proclaimed that there is "not one shred of evidence" of a conspiracy, before he admitted that there were "no final certainties."

U.S. News & World Report, 12/5/66, conceded some limited contention on specifics of the Warren Report, while strongly reinforcing its conclusions. They noted Governor John Connally's "disagreement with the Commission on one point – its conclusion that he was hit by a bullet that had passed through the President's body," while declaring that "a new investigation would be neither warranted, justified, nor desirable." They called critics of the Commission "journalistic scavengers."

Nonetheless, the rising chorus of calls for reinvestigation led to a Justice Department review by the autopsy team of photos and X-rays in late 1966, although no significant new evidence was released.

Esquire, December 1966, printed one of the most insightful pieces during that era, written by citizen-researcher Sylvia Meagher. She examined the contradictions and gaps regarding Oswald's arrest and interrogation, the autopsy, the stretcher bullet, and culpable law enforcement procedures. She also explored the allegation that Oswald fired at the home of outspoken right-wing General Edwin Walker. Meagher then proposed fourteen new evidentiary tests for the case, and then developed these proposals in her book *Accessories After the Fact*, which was published in 1967.

Esquire also printed Edward Epstein's article, "Who's Afraid of the Warren Report – A Primer of Assassination Theories" which prompted UPI to further analyze the Nix film. UPI managing editor Schonfeld chose to try a firm "which (he) had never heard of, Itek." Schonfeld regretted that he did not know that former OSS and CIA officer Frank Lindsey, and a close collaborator with Allen Dulles and Frank Wisner in the 1940s and 1950s, headed Itek. Nor did he know that Time Inc. owned 5% of Itek stock, or that 60% of Itek's business came from the government, mostly for intelligence purposes. Nor did he realize then his contact man at Itek, Howard Sprague, was a former CIA employee. Perhaps it is not a coincidence that Itek found nothing significant on the film, and *Time* and UPI and many newspapers reported it as such in May of 1967.[18]

Schonfeld later wrote,

> I gave up. Enough was enough. But I love to tell the story on myself, and maybe all of us, of how, in the end, the only people I could get to investigate a picture that might involve the CIA were people who worked for the CIA.

Schonfeld later wrote that an RCA public relations executive suggested that devices that RCA had developed for the government could scan the Nix film. "The executive attempted to get RCA clearance, but RCA found the project too controversial."[19]

Penn Jones, of the *Midlothian Mirror*, published *Forgive my Grief*, which developed his analysis of disappearing witnesses in the case. "Kilgallen said that she was going to New Orleans and break the case wide open, also strangely Miss Kilgallen's close friend Mr. Earl Smith died two days after Miss Kilgallen. Mr. Smith's autopsy read that the cause of death was unknown."

The CIA responded to the widening disbelief with a memo "Countering Criticism of the Warren Report" On 1/4/67 they distributed the memo to their media assets at the *New York Times*, CBS, NBC, ABC, *Washington Post* etc., suggesting arguments to discredit Warren Report critics. "Conspiracy theorists have frequently thrown suspicion on our organization, for example, by falsely alleging that Lee Harvey Oswald worked for us…. This affects … the whole reputation of the American government…. Note that Robert Kennedy, attorney general at the time … would be the last man to overlook or conceal any conspiracy."

Robert Kennedy, though, repeatedly told his friends and aides that he needed the power of the presidency to realistically re-investigate the assassination. One of his friends, CBS News producer Don Hewitt, worked up the courage to ask him "the million dollar question … Bobby, do you really believe Lee Harvey Oswald, all by himself killed your brother? Hewitt noted "he dismissed the question with almost studied indifference…. What difference does it make? It won't bring him back." Hewitt was deeply suspicious of RFK's response as well as of the Warren Report.[20]

Public and media pressure to pursue a comprehensive investigation pushed the CIA to delegitimize new critical books. This CIA memo, 1/4/67, alleged that many of the critics were anti-American, far left, or Communist sympathizers, some of whom were in search of financial reward, some in love with their theories, and some "raise as many questions as possible while not bothering to work out the consequences." This document along with two others was released through the Freedom of Information Act (FOIA) in 1976.

"CIA Document ll:
Background Survey of Books Concerning
The Assassination of President Kennedy
Dated 4 Jan 67

1. (Except where otherwise indicated, the factual data given in paragraphs 1-9 is unclassified.) Some of the authors of recent books on the assassination of President Kennedy (e.g., Joachim Joesten, *Oswald: Assassin or Fall Guy*; Mark Lane, *Rush to Judgment* [sic]; Leo Sauvage, *The Oswald Affair: An Examination of the Contradictions and Omissions of the Warren Report*) had publicly asserted that a conspiracy existed before the Warren Commission finished its investigation. Not surprisingly, they immediately bestirred themselves to show that they were right and that the Commission was wrong. Thanks to the mountain of material published by the Commission, some of it conflicting or misleading when read out of context, they have had little difficulty in uncovering items to substantiate their own theories. They have also in some cases obtained new and divergent testimony from witnesses. And they have usually failed to discuss the refutations of their early claims in the Commission's Report, Appendix xii ("Speculations and Rumors"). This Appendix is still a good place to look for material countering the theorists.

2. Some writers appear to have been predisposed to criticism by anti-American, far left, or Communist sympathies. The British "Who Killed Kennedy Committee" includes some of the most persistent and vocal English critics of the United States, e.g.' Michael Foot, Kingsley Martin, Kenneth Tynan, and Bertrand Russell. Joachim Joesten has been publicly revealed as a onetime member of the German Communist Party (KPD); a Gestapo document of 8 November 1937 among the German Foreign Ministry files microfilmed in England and Now returned to West German custody shows that his party book was numbered 532315 and dated 12 May 1932. (The originals of these files are now available at the West German Foreign Ministry in Bonn; the copy in the U.S. National Archives may be found under the reference T-120, Serial 4918, frames E256482-4. The British Public Records Office should also have a copy.) Joesten's American publisher, Carl Marzani, was once sentenced to jail by a federal jury for concealing

his Communist Party (CPUSA) membership in order to hold a government job. Available information indicates that Mark Lane was elected Vice Chairman of the New York Council to Abolish the House Un-American Activities Committee on 28 May 1963, he also attended the 8th Congress of the International Association of Democratic Lawyers (an international Communist front organization, in Budapest from 31 March to 5 April 1964, where he expounded his (pre-Report) views on the Kennedy assassination. In his acknowledgements in his book, Lane expresses special thanks to Ralph Schoenman of London "who participated in and supported the work"; Schoenman is of course the expatriate American who has been influencing the aged Bertrand Russell in recent years. (See also paragraph 10 below on Communist efforts to replay speculation on the assassination.)

3. A factor has been the financial reward obtainable for sensational books. Mark Lane's *Rush to Judgment*, published on 13 publishers had printed 140,000 copies by that date, in anticipation of sales to come. The 1 January 1967 *New York Times Book Review* reported that book as at the top of the General category of the best seller list, having been in top position for seven weeks and on the list for 17 weeks. Lane has reportedly appeared on about 175 television and radio programs, and has also given numerous public lectures, all of which serves for advertisement. He has also put together a TV film, and is peddling it to European telecasters; the BBC has purchased rights for a record $45,000. While neither Abraham Zapruder nor William Manchester should be classed with the critics of the Commission we are discussing here, sums paid for the Zapruder film of the assassination ($25,000) and for magazine rights to Manchester's *Death of a President* ($665,000) indicate the money available for material related to the assassination. Some newspapermen (e.g. Sylvan Fox, *The Unanswered Questions about President Kennedy's Assassination*; Leo Sauvage, *The Oswald Affair*) have published accounts cashing in on their journalistic expertise.

4. Aside from political and financial motives, some people have apparently published accounts simply because they were burning to give the world their theory, e.g., Harold Weisberg, in his *Whitewash*; Penn Jones, Jr., in *Forgive My Grief*, and George C. Thomson in *The Quest for Truth*. Weisberg's book was first published privately, though it is now finally attaining the dignity of commercial publication. Jones' volume was published by the small-town Texas newspaper of which he is the editor and Thomson's booklet by his own engineering firm. The impact of these books will probably be

relatively slight, since their writers will appear to readers to be hysterical or paranoid.

5. A common technique among many of the writers is to raise as many questions as possible, while not bothering to work out all the consequences, Herbert Mitgang has written a parody of this approach (his questions actually refer to Lincoln's assassination) in "A New Inquiry is Needed," *New York Times Magazine*, 25 December 1966. Mark Lane in particular (who represents himself as Oswald's lawyer) adopts the classic defense attorney's approach of throwing in unrelated details so as to create in the jury's mind a sum of "reasonable doubt." His tendency to wander off into minor details led one observer to comment that whereas a good trial lawyer should have a sure instinct for the jugular vein; Lane's instinct was for the capillaries. His tactics and also his nerve were typified on the occasion when, after getting the Commission to pay his travel expenses back from England, he recounted to that body a sensational (and incredible) story of a Ruby plot, while refusing to name his source. Chief Justice Warren told Lane, "We have every reason to doubt the truthfulness of what you have heretofore told us" – by the standards of legal etiquette, a very stiff rebuke for an attorney.

6. It should be recognized however, that another kind of criticism has recently emerged, represented by Edward Jay Epstein's *Inquest*. Epstein adopts a scholarly tone, and to the casual reader, he presents what appears to be a more coherent, reasoned case than the writers described above. Epstein has caused people like Richard Rovere and Lord Devlin, previously backers of the Commission's report, to change their minds. The *New York Times'* daily book reviewer has said that Epstein's work is a "watershed book" which has made it respectable to doubt the Commission's finding. This respectability effect has been enhanced by *Life* magazine's 25 November issue, which contains an assertion that there is a "reasonable doubt," as well as a republication of frames from the Zapruder film (owned by *Life*), and an interview with Governor Connally, who repeats his belief that he was not struck by the same bullet that struck President Kennedy. (Connally does not, however, agree that there should be another investigation.) Epstein himself has published a new article in the December 1966 issue of *Esquire*, in which he explains away objections to his book. A copy of an early critique of Epstein's views by Fletcher Knebel, published in *Look*, 12 July 1966, and an unclassified, unofficial analysis (by "Spectator") are attached to this dispatch, dealing with specific questions raised by Epstein's.

7. Here it should be pointed out that Epstein's competence in research has been greatly exaggerated. Some illustrations are given in the Fletcher Knebel article. As a further specimen, Epstein's book refers (pp., 93-5) to a cropped-down picture of a heavy-set man taken in Mexico City, saying that the Central Intelligence Agency gave it to the Federal Bureau of Investigation on 18 November 1963, and that the Bureau in turn forwarded it to its Dallas office. Actually, affidavits 1 the published Warren material (vol, XI, pp. 468-70) show that CIA turned the picture over to the FBI on 22 November, the fact is that the FBI flew the photo directly from Mexico City to Dallas immediately after Oswald's arrest, before Oswald's picture had been published, on the chance it might be Oswald. The reason the photo was cropped was that the background revealed the place where it was taken.) Another example where Epstein reports (p. 41) that a Secret Service interview report was even withheld from the National Archives, this is untrue; an Archives staff member told one of our officers that Epstein came there and asked for the memorandum. He was told that it was there, but was classified. Indeed, the Archives then notified the Secret Service that there had been a request for the document, and the Secret Service declassified it. But by that time, Epstein (whose preface gives the impression of prolonged archival research) had chosen to finish his searches in the Archives, which had only lasted two days, and had left town. Yet Epstein charges that the Commission was over-hasty in its work.

8. Aside from such failures in research, Epstein and other intellectual critics show symptoms of some of the love of theorizing and lack of common sense and experience displayed by Richard H. Popkin, the author of *The Second Oswald*. Because Oswald was reported to have been seen in different places at the same time, a phenomenon not surprising in a sensational case where thousands of real or alleged witnesses were interviewed, Popkin, a professor of philosophy, theorizes that there actually were two Oswald's. At this point, theorizing becomes sort of logico-mathematical game; an exercise in permutations and combinations; as Commission attorney Arlen Specter remarked; "Why not make it three Oswald's? Why stop at two? "Nevertheless, aside from his book, Popkin has been able to publish a summary of his views in the *New York Review of Books*, and there has been replay in the French *Nouvel Observateur*, in Moscow's *New Times*, and in Baku's *Vyshka*. Poplin makes a sensational accusation indirectly, saying the "Western European critics" see Kennedy's assassination as part of a subtle conspiracy attributable to "perhaps even (in rumors I have heard) Kennedy's

successor." One Barbara Garson has made the same point in another way by her parody of; Shakespeare's *Macbeth* entitled *MacBird!*, with what is obviously President Johnson (Mac Bird) in the role of Macbeth. Miss Garson makes no effort to prove her point; she merely insinuates it. Probable the indirect form of accusation is due to fear of a libel suit.

9. Other books are yet to appear. William Manchester's not-yet-published. *The Death of a President* is at this writing being purged of material personally objectionable to Mrs. Kennedy. There are hopeful signs: Jacob Cohen is writing a book which will appear in 1967 under the title *Honest Verdict*, defending Wesley J. Libeler, is also reportedly writing a book, setting forth both sides. But further criticism will no doubt appear; as the *Washington Post* has pointed out editorially, the recent death of Jack Ruby will probably lead to speculation that he was "silenced" by a conspiracy.

10. The likelihood of further criticism is enhanced by the circumstance that Communist propagandists seem recently to have stepped up their own campaign to discredit the Warren Commission. As already noted, Moscow's *New Times* reprinted parts of an article by Richard Popkin (21 and 28 September 1966 issues), and it also gave the Swiss edition of Joesten's latest work an extended, laudatory review in its number for 26 October. (In view of this publicity and the Communist background of Joesten and his American publisher, together with Joesten's insistence on pinning the blame on such favorite communist targets as H.L. Hunt, the FBI and CIA, there seems reasons to suspect that Joesten's book and it exploitation are part of a planned Soviet propaganda operation.) Tass, reporting on 5 November on the deposit of autopsy photographs in the National Archives, said that the refusal to give wide public access to them, the disappearance of a number of documents, and the mysterious death of more than 10 people, all make many Americans believe Kennedy was killed as the result of a conspiracy. The radio transmitters of Prague and Warsaw used the anniversary of the assassination to attack the Warren report. The Bulgarian press conducted a campaign on the subject in the second half of October; a Greek Communist newspaper, *Avgi*, placed the blame on CIA on 20 November. Significantly, the start of this stepped-up campaign coincided with a Soviet demand that the U.S. Embassies in Moscow stop distributing the Russian-language edition of the Warren report. *Newsweek* commented (12 September) that the Soviets apparently "did not want mere facts to get in their way."

The first week in January of 1967 *The Saturday Evening Post* ran a pro-Warren Report story by Richard Whalen, a reporter friendly to the FBI. An FBI memorandum from W.C. Sullivan (head of FBI Domestic Intelligence Division) to Cartha DeLoach recommended FBI cooperation:

> In providing facts for Mr. Whalen to use in an article to appear in *The Saturday Evening Post* in the near future, aimed at silencing critics of the Warren Commission Report.... Whalen states that this [cooperation] is absolutely necessary since he believed he and the Bureau shared a rising apprehension at the new-won respectability and acceptance of the various conspiracy mongers. [21]

At the outset of the piece Whalen declared, "Had he (Oswald) been prosecuted for murdering an ordinary citizen the evidence arrayed against him would almost certainly have brought a verdict of guilty." After summarizing the major critics, Whalen claimed, "The critics raise a great many trivial questions and some troublesome ones, particularly regarding the Kennedy head snaps, the Tague hit and the possibility of misinterpreted photographic evidence. However, they are almost barren of plausible answers when asked what they think happened in Dealey Plaza." He printed Commander J. Thornton Boswell's autopsy room chart, in which a bullet hole is shown about six inches down from the president's neck. Yet the discrepancy from this and the neck wound noted in the Warren Report was attributed merely to Boswell's carelessness. "Recently he [Boswell] said if he had known his sketch would be made public, he would have been more careful." Whalen neglected to mention existing contradictory evidence of the signed death certificate, and the location of the holes in the president's shirt and coat which indicate a wound about six inches down from the base of the neck – all of which were consistent with Boswell's chart.

Whalen conceded, "there is still room for some doubt about the essential findings." He questioned Oswald's marksmanship, CE 399 (the bullet which supposedly went through Kennedy and Connally), the lack of autopsy pictures and X-rays, which were not examined by the Warren Commission and the inconsistencies regarding the wound in the president's back.

He claimed that "the critics who allege a cover-up of the 'true facts' by the Warren Commission can as easily argue their case on the basis of the appearance of concealment as they can on the grounds of actual conspiracy." He concluded that the "evidence against Oswald remains as 'hard' as it was when Ruby's bullet killed him." Nonetheless, he advocated a pursuit of the "soft" evidence by a Congressional Committee or a "citizen's panel with unlimited access to the records."

The *Philadelphia Inquirer* reporter Joe McGinnis, 1/6/67, interviewed Vincent Salandria for "The Fine Edge of Believability." Salandria over-viewed the critical perspective and then speculated on who was responsible. He noted the condition of CE 399, the Zapruder film showing the president pushed backward and to the left, that there were "at least three or four assassins ... and Oswald was not one of them. He was standing on the front steps of the Depository when the shooting took place. The CIA set him up to be a patsy." Salandria viewed the CIA and the military leaders as fearful that Kennedy would end the Cold War, and that they would lose their power. Johnson would not make those changes and John-son would go along with the assassination "They will get Bobby killed. ... They'll turn us into a closed totalitarian society." McGinnis thought that Salandria had been working too hard, and that "the sad part was that Vin-cent Salandria really believed in everything he said."

The *New Republic* 1/7/67 joined the critics calling for a government re-view of the Warren Report. Yale Law Professor Alexander Bickel counseled caution and comprehensiveness in "Re-examining the Warren Report":

> It is important that legitimate questions are asked that are answer-able but are unanswered in the report, then even for those who may find the answers implicit, or who reach them for themselves by an imaginative leap or by an act of faith, a fresh investigation is not merely desirable; it is as imperative as the first one was.
>
> The next task of a new commission would be.... To exclude the possibility of a second assassin. The Warren Commission never really tested theories of how the assassination might have been ac-complished other than its own hypothesis concerning the timing of the shots, and the initial wounding of both President Kennedy and Connally with a single bullet. [22]

He questioned the Tippit murder, autopsy photos, and X-rays, the ac-tions of the Dallas police and the location of the wounds in the President. The new commission, Bickel admonished, should consist of federal and state judges with subpoena power and resources.

Ramparts, January 1967, weighed in with a detailed critique of the Warren Report, "The Case for Three Assassins" by citizen investigators David S. Lifton and David Welsh. They explored contradictions in the *New York Times* coverage as well as the major conclusions of the Report primarily through testimony from the 26 volumes of Hearings and Ex-hibits in the Warren Report itself. The areas included: 1) How Could the President Have Been Shot in the Front from the Back; 2) The Park-land Doctor's Testimony; 3) The 64 Witnesses Indicating Firing from the Grassy Knoll area – Witnesses from the Overpass, Standing on the Knoll, Standing in Dealey Plaza; In or Immediately Outside the De-pository; Members of the Dallas County Sheriff's Department, Secret Service Agents, Dallas Police Officers, Witnesses in the Motorcade as well as Other Witnesses.[23]

Because the un-indexed 26 volumes of Hearings and Exhibits were written in legal language, it presented researchers and reporters with lay-ers of fog amid the mountains of evidence. Citizen researchers, often net-works of correspondence, penetrated some of the fog, and clarified por-tions of the case.

BBC seemed more open to debate the assassination controversy than the American networks but this proved illusory. On January 29, 1967, BBC ran a five-hour program starting with the premiere airing of the doc-umentary *Rush to Judgment* by Emile de Antonio and Mark Lane. This was to be followed by a discussion including three supporters of the War-ren Report, Professor Bickel, Warren Commission counsel Arlen Specter, who had not debated Lane in the U.S.; and Britain's Lord Devlin, con-fronting Mark Lane. They were to dress in black robes and were to act as judges, while journalist Kenneth Harris was to moderate. Lane argued for a more balanced discussion but to no avail.

An inaccurate model of Dealey Plaza bolstered their defense of the Warren Commission. Major areas of the investigation had been rehearsed without Lane's knowledge. Harris once even apologized off camera to Specter for asking a question regarding the location of shots, which they had not rehearsed. Twice Lane's efforts to contend with Warren Com-mission counsels David Belin and Specter were cut off by the modera-tor. Lane then shifted to commenting on the single-bullet theory when Specter walked over to Harris and loudly declared, on camera, that Lane should not be allowed to trifle with his theory. Harris yielded again. The program curiously closed with Lord Devlin's sophistry: "we let President Kennedy's soul rest in peace, and if there were another assassin, no one had proved he was a subversive, and if he wasn't subversive what differ-ence did it make?"[24]

In the spirit of Mark Twain some of the citizenry passionately plodded on to protect democracy.

My loyalty was loyalty to one's country, not to its institutions or its officeholders. The country is the real thing, the eternal thing ... to be loyal to; institutions are extraneous, mere clothing, and clothing can wear out, become ragged ... cease to protect the body from winter disease and death. To be loyal to rags, to shout for rags, to worship rags to die for rags – that are loyalty of unreason ... it belongs to monarch; let monarchy keep it ... I was from Connecticut, whose constitution declares, "that all power is inherent in the people.... The citizen who thinks he sees that the commonwealth political clothes are worn out and yet held his peace and does not agitate for a new suit; is disloyal; he is a traitor. That he may be the only one who thinks he sees this decay, does not excuse him; it's his duty to agitate anyway. [25]

The virtue and vigilance of citizen investigators revealed major contradictions in the Warren Report and catalyzed coverage by elements of the alternative and mass media. While the alternative press was slowly growing in strength, limited resources and modest circulations constrained their impact. *The Nation* ran articles critiquing as well as supporting the Warren Report. *The New Republic* was somewhat more critical and called for a new investigation. *The Minority of One* and the *Midlothian Mirror* steadfastly continued their critiques. *Ramparts* regularly ran critical reporting, and rapidly increased their circulation. The CIA responded with dirty tricks to hurt their circulation and financing. A few elements of the mass media periodically probed the case, notably some radio stations along with the *Washington Post* and *Esquire*, while most of the mainstream media, including the television networks and news services, skepticly reviewed the contributions of the citizen-critics. Nonetheless, in spite of the propaganda of the CIA and FBI, by early 1967, many in the mainstream media called for some form of reopening the case.

During a Cold War period of urban riots and a floundering and increasingly unpopular war in Vietnam, government-corporate-media elites probably viewed a limited reinvestigation as a tactic to strengthen systemic legitimacy. But the possibility of an independent, aggressive, maverick, district attorney revealing the seamy sides of American power generated a widespread establishment backlash. By early 1967, when New Orleans D.A. Jim Garrison's investigation began, the mass media rushed to cover it. The *Washington Post*, 3/1/67, ran a political cartoon of Garrison as a strip-tease artist covering himself with fans labeled "D.A. Publicity Stunts," which foreshadowed the daunting challenge. The CIA and FBI efforts to mislead the public would unleash a stunning new phase of psychological warfare.

8

THE GARRISON INVESTIGATION: CONFRONTING PSYCHOLOGICAL WARFARE

> *Those who expect to reap the blessings of freedom must, like men, undergo the fatigue of supporting it.*
> – Tom Paine, 1777

> *You know that the first amendment is only an amendment...one journalist is worth twenty agents.*
> – Ray Cline, CIA Officer

> *Secrecy and a free democratic government don't mix.*
> – Harry Truman

The bold and flamboyant New Orleans District Attorney Jim Garrison unraveled many aspects of the assassination, although his unorthodox style contributed to a problematic relationship with most of the media. He challenged the government and the media were challenged to revisit our national nightmare at a time when the Vietnam War protests were expanding and race riots had scarred several cities. Federal non-cooperation with the Garrison's investigation was bolstered by a wide gamut of tactics including: FBI wiretapping and infiltrating Garrison's investigation; mass media covers for spying, FBI and CIA-linked reporters weakening Garrison's credibility, biased network specials on NBC and CBS; slanted wire service reporting and book publications; and even a biased interview on a famous evening TV talk show. Detailed CIA memos, designed to counter Warren Commission critics, clouded key issues. The closer Garrison got to the truth, the more vicious the psychological war became.

In this David vs. Goliath drama Garrison was passionately dedicated, insightful and witty but also, at times self-righteous and sarcastic. In a critical, convoluted case, with controversy at every turn, misperceptions of style and substance, as well as misstatements, provided fodder for those committed to the Warren Report. Media attacks put Garrison on the defensive on complex issues, not amenable to sound bites. Unaccustomed to the media glare, Garrison needed a P.R. team as well as a few dozen more investigators. He also needed cooperation from the CIA, FBI, Secret Service, IRS and the DOD – but this was not the time for governmental atonement.

In November 1966, Garrison mentioned his assassination conspiracy case with reporter David Chandler. Chandler told Richard Billings of *Life* (and "Operation Tilt") who met with Garrison in January of 1967. According to Garrison, Billings said that the top management at *Life* thought that he was "moving in the right direction" and he offered to work closely with Garrison. Billings also suggested that "the magazine would be able to provide … technical assistance, and … a mutual exchange of information."[1] This seems to have been merely a ruse. On January 23rd, 1967 the *New Orleans States-Item* ran a brief report by Jack Dempsey stating, "At least five persons have been questioned by the District Attorney's office in connection with another investigation into events linked to the Kennedy assassination." Garrison was furious and threatened to take Dempsey before the grand jury to determine his sources. Dempsey was replaced, and the story was given to Rosemary James.[2]

Garrison's investigation quietly made considerable progress through early 1967, but on February 17, a *New Orleans States-Item* story by Rosemary James decried the expenses for a probe of an assassination plot as scandalous. This unexpected early attention hampered the investigation and enabled disinformation and biased coverage to significantly delegitimize the case. Hundreds of reporters then stormed into New Orleans to focus on this shoestring investigation. Less than a week later two key suspects in the case died mysterious deaths. David Ferrie supposedly committed suicide and Eladio Del Valle was shot at point-blank range.

Just two weeks earlier Garrison had interviewed Carlos Bringuier, an active anti-communist and CIA contact, who had interacted with Oswald. Bringuier was also a member of both INCA, (Information Council of the Americas) an elite right-wing New Orleans organization, and DRE, the CIA-backed Cuban Student Directorate. After that interview, Bringuier immediately requested an interview with Hunter Leake of the New Orleans CIA office. In a CIA memo from the Chief of the New Orleans office Lloyd Ray to the Director of the Domestic Contact Service, Ray noted his belief that the Garrison investigation was credible.

The suspicious suicide of key witness David Ferrie, who had ties to Oswald and Clay Shaw as well as the CIA, FBI and Mafia, forced Garrison to move quickly or lose other witnesses. The next day, 3/3/67, Garrison arrested socialite, international businessman, and CIA asset Clay Shaw, who had been seen with Oswald in both New Orleans and Clinton, Louisiana. Neil Strawser of CBS News asked newly confirmed Attorney General Ramsey Clark if he had information about Shaw. Clark stated that Shaw "was involved in an FBI investigation – in the New Orleans area in November-December 1963. Shaw was checked out and found clear." His comments were carried in all the major newspapers. The *New York Times* 3/3/67, added that "a Justice Department official said tonight that his agency was convinced that Mr. Bertrand (an alias used for social occasions) and Mr. Shaw were the same man, and that this was the basis for Mr. Clark's assertions." Cryptically they noted, "Mr. Clark's statement however caused a certain amount of bewilderment in some quarters." The determination that Clay Bertrand was Clay Shaw inadvertently strengthened Garrison's case; however, three months later the Justice Department issued a statement that the FBI did not investigate Clay Shaw, and that Clark's 3/2/67 statement was in error.[3] The *New York Times* printed no reason for the reversal.

An FBI memo 3/2/67 from Cartha DeLoach to Clyde Tolson indicates Clark's original statement was accurate.

> The A.G. asked whether the FBI knew anything about Shaw. I told him Shaw's name had come up in our investigation in December 1963 as a result of several parties furnishing information.

Revealingly, J. Edgar Hoover had noted on that memo, "I hope A.G. is not going to peddle this information we send him."

The FBI seemingly utilized some of its reporter/assets to gather information for Clay Shaw as well as for spin control during this period. Lawrence Schiller, Jack Ruby's former "business agent," authored a vicious, pro-Warren Commission book. Widely syndicated columnist Jack Anderson, reporters Hugh Aynesworth and Charles Roberts from *Newsweek*, James Phelan from the *Saturday Evening Post*, and UPI reporter Merriman Smith all worked with the FBI. Some reporters, such as Hugh Aynesworth, also appear to have cooperated with the CIA.

In March 1967, Jack Anderson ran two pieces in his "Washington Merry-Go-Round" column, asserting Castro's role in the assassination

(3/3/67 and 3/7/67). Anderson mentioned a "political H-bomb- an unconfirmed report that Senator Robert Kennedy may have approved an assassination plot which then backfired against his brother."

Anderson then briefed the FBI about his lengthy interview with Jim Garrison.[4] The unsuspecting Garrison invited Anderson into his home for a six-hour interview. According to the FBI report, Anderson told the Bureau that Garrison was a convincing talker who had considerable facts at his disposal that the CIA had coordinated the assassination of JFK. In public news reports, however, Anderson argued that President Kennedy was assassinated by elements of the Mafia working with the CIA as the Castro assassination plots "backfired." Years later Anderson claimed that Castro retaliated against Kennedy.

The popular Mormon muckraker aggressively pursued leads and had boldly reported his findings. His sources in the mafia confirmed stories of Nixon's ties to West Coast mobster Mickey Cohen, among others. Widely viewed as Nixon's nemesis, and the source of straight-forward reporting and colorful commentary, this style was often viewed with disdain by the mainstream media. He utilized a remarkable range of contacts without remaining loyal to them. Later in his career, when he was more popular and more accepted by the mainstream media, he exposed major scandals with the CIA, State and Defense Departments and the Nixon White House.

Anderson's major source on the assassination was Mafia lieutenant Johnny Roselli, who had been involved with the CIA-Mafia plots against Castro. Roselli, however, had just been convicted of fraud, and was facing deportation. According to former FBI man William Turner, the story originated from Robert Maheu, a CIA-Mafia intermediary, who gave it to Edward P. Morgan, a former FBI man and well-known lawyer, who passed it on to Anderson.[5]

Perhaps I. Irving Davidson, the powerful lobbyist who had been his office mate and at times his benefactor from 1954-1964, also influenced Anderson. Davidson had a wide range of contacts including Carlos Marcello, J. Edgar Hoover, Teamster Union boss Jimmy Hoffa, the CIA, the Somozas, and the Murchisons of Dallas.[6] Also, Anderson's longtime mentor and senior partner in journalism, Drew Pearson, was a CIA asset. (Commission Document 990).

Author Jim DiEugenio has revealed some of reporter Hugh Aynesworth's intelligence ties as well as his cooperation with the Shaw defense team. One month before the assassination, CIA agent J. Walton Moore, who had been meeting with Oswald's friend George de Mohrenschildt, was also meeting with Aynesworth about traveling to Cuba (Moore, Walton, Ford, *Ford Report* 9/28/62). In Aynesworth's reports to *Newsweek*, 2/24/67, he described David Ferrie's ordination into the Old Catholic Church of North America. He noted parenthetically, "We're trying to protect our own in this group and would appreciate your not using the church's name." This suggests that Aynesworth knew that the CIA was using this strange religious sect as a front organization.

In another report, 3/3/67, Aynesworth wrote that the CIA attempted to get Nazi intelligence officer turned CIA mercenary Otto Skorzeny in on a Castro kidnapping plot in 1963. Since this was not even revealed in the 1967 Inspector General Report on CIA plots to kill Castro, it indicates Aynesworth's connections. Aynesworth later cooperated with Clay Shaw's defense team and a number of his investigative interviews were given to Shaw's lead attorney Ed Wegmann.

The positive public response to new critical books, as well as the Garrison investigation, prompted the CIA to generate a wider range of defensive strategies. A CIA memo distributed to CIA media assets at the *New York Times*, CBS, NBC, ABC, and elsewhere (4/1/67) focused on "Countering Criticism of the Warren Report."

> Document 1:
> Chiefs, Certain Stations and Bases
> Document Number 1035-950
> For FOIA Review on Sept 1975
> Countering Criticism of the Warren Report
> Dated 4/1/67
> PSYCH
>
> 1. Our Concern. From the day of President Kennedy's assassination on, there has been speculation about the responsibility for his murder. Although this was stemmed for a time by the Warren Commission report (which appeared at the end of September 1964), various writers have now had time to scan the Commission's published report and documents for new pretexts for questioning, and there has been a new wave of books and articles criticizing the Commission's findings. In most cases the critics have speculated as to the existence of some kind of conspiracy, and often they have implied that the Commission itself was involved. Presumably as a result of the increasing challenge to the Warren Commission's Report, a public opinion poll recently indicated that 46% of the American public did not think that Oswald acted alone, while more than half of those polled thought that the Commission had left some ques-

tions unresolved. Doubtless polls abroad would show similar or possibly more adverse results.

2. The trend of opinion is a matter of concern to the U.S. government, including our organization. The members of the Warren Commission were naturally chosen for their integrity, experience, and prominence. They represented both major parties, and they and their staff were deliberately drawn from all sections of the country. Just because of the standing of the Commissioners, efforts to impugn their rectitude and wisdom tend to cast doubt on the whole leadership of American society. Moreover, there seems to be an increasing tendency to hint that President Johnson himself, as the one person who might be said to have benefited, was in some way responsible for the assassination. Innuendo of such seriousness affects not only the individual concerned, but also the whole reputation of the American government. Our organization itself is directly involved: among the other facts, we contributed information to the investigation. Conspiracy theories have frequently thrown suspicion on our organization, for example by falsely alleging that Lee Harvey Oswald works for us. The aim of this dispatch is to provide material for countering and discrediting the claims of the conspiracy theorists, so as to inhibit the circulation of such claims in other countries. Background information is supplied in a classified section and in a number of unclassified attachments.

3. Action. We do not recommend that discussion of the assassination question be initiated where it is not already taking place. Where discussion is active, however, addresses are requested.

a. To discuss the publicity problem with liaison and friendly elite contacts (especially politicians and editors), pointing out that the Warren Commission made as thorough an investigation as humanly possible, that the charges of the critics are without serious foundation, and that further speculative discussion only plays into the hands of the opposition. Point out also that parts of the conspiracy talk appear to be deliberately generated by Communist propagandists. Urge them to use their influence to discourage unfounded and irresponsible speculation.

b. To employ propaganda assets to answer and refute the attacks of the critics,. Book reviews and feature articles are particularly appropriate for this purpose. The unclassified attachments to the guidance should provide useful background material for passage to assets. Our play should point out, as applicable, that the critics are (i) wedded to theories adopted before the evidence was in, (ii) politically interested, (iii) financially interested, (iv) hasty and inaccurate in their research, or (v) infatuated with their own theories. In the course of discussions of the whole phenomenon of criticism, a useful strategy may be to single out Epstein's theory for attack, using the attached Fletcher Knebel article and *Spectator* piece for background. (Although Mark Lane's book is much less convincing than Epstein's and comes off badly where contested by knowledgeable critics, it is also much more difficult to answer as a whole, as one becomes lost in a morass of unrelated details.)

4. In private or media discussion not directed at any particular writer, or in attacking publications which may be yet forthcoming, the following arguments should be useful:

a. no significant new evidence has emerged which the Commission did not consider, the assassination is sometimes compared (e.g. by Joachim Joesten and Bertrand Russell) with the Dreyfus case; however, unlike that case, the attacks on the Warren Commission have produced no new evidence, no new culprits have been convincingly identified , and there is no agreement among the critics. (A better parallel, though an imperfect one, might be with the Reichstag fire of 1933, which some competent historians (Fritz Tobias, A.J. P. Taylor, D. C. Watt) now believe was set by Nazis or Communists; the Nazis tried to pin the blame on the Communists, but the latter have been much more successful in convincing the world that the Nazis were to blame.)

b. Critics usually overvalue particular items and ignore others. They tend to place more emphasis on the recollections of individual eyewitnesses (which are less reliable and more divergent – and hence offer more hand-holds for criticism) and less on ballistic, autopsy, and photographic evidence. A close examination of the commission's records will usually show that the conflicting eyewitness accounts are quoted out of context, or were discarded by the Commission for good and sufficient reason.

c. Conspiracy on the large scale often suggested would be impossible to conceal in the United States, esp., since informants could expect to receive large royalties, etc. note that Robert Kennedy, Attorney General at the time and John F. Kennedy's brother, would be the last man to overlook or conceal any conspiracy. And as one reviewer pointed out, Congressman Gerald R. Ford would hardly have held his tongue for the sake of the Democratic administration, and Senator Russell would have had every political interest in exposing any misdeeds on the Part of chief Justice Warren. A conspirator moreover would hardly choose a location for a shooting where so much depended on conditions beyond his control: the route, the speed of the cars, the moving target, and the risk that the assassin would be discovered. A group of wealthy conspirators could have arranged much more secure conditions.

d. Critics have often been enticed by a form of intellectual pride: they light on some theory and fall in love with it; they also scoff at the Commission because it did not always answer every question with a flat decision one way or the other, actually, safeguard against over commitment to anyone's theory, or against the illicit transformation of probabilities into certainties.

e. Oswald would not have been any sensible person's choice for a co-conspirator. He was a "loner," mixed-up of questionable reliability and an unknown quantity to any professional intelligence service.

f. As to charges that the Commission's report was a rush job, it emerged three months after the deadline originally set. But to the degree that Commission tried to speed up it's reporting, this was largely due to the pressure of irresponsible speculation already appearing, in some cases coming from the same critics who, refusing to admit their errors, are not putting out new criticisms.

g. Such vague accusations as that "more than ten people have died mysteriously" can always be explained in some more natural way: e. g., the individuals concerned have for the most part died of natural causes; the Commission staff questioned 418 witnesses (the FBI interviewed far more people, conducting 25,000 interviews and re-interviews), and in such a large group, a certain number of deaths are to be expected. (When Penn Jones, one of the originators of the "ten mysterious deaths" line, appeared on television, it emerged that two of the deaths on his list were from heart attacks, one from cancer, one was from a head-on collision on a bridge, and one occurred when a driver drifted into a bridge abutment.)

5. Where possible, counter speculation by encouraging reference to the Commission's Report itself, Open-minded foreign readers should still be impressed by the care, thoroughness, objectivity and speed with which the Commission worked. Reviewers of other books might be encouraged to add to their account the idea that, checking back with the Report itself, they found it far superior to the work of its critics.

[At the bottom of the first page of this document are the words:] **DESTROY WHEN NO LONGER NEEDED** (Lane 114-118)

More than a year before the Shaw trial began, *The Saturday Evening Post, Newsweek, Time,* the *New York Times* and NBC had already characterized Garrison as irresponsible and power hungry.

The Saturday Evening Post, then owned by Curtis Publishing, whose president, Martin Ackerman, was also a friend of CIA operative Robert Maheu, printed a highly misleading story on April 6, 1967, entitled "Rush to Judgment in New Orleans." The reporter, James Phelan, an FBI contract agent, claimed that after ten hours of talking with Garrison he felt the case was "wildly speculative." "Boiled down... [It was] the result of a homosexual conspiracy masterminded by David Ferrie." Phelan made no mention of Garrison's evidence raising questions about the FBI, CIA, or the Secret Service. Phelan also omitted Perry Russo's confirmation that he had told Garrison's office that he had identified Shaw as Bertrand. When questioned by Mark Lane about this omission Phelan complained that he was facing a tight deadline.[7] Since the piece appeared almost two years before the trial date, Mark Lane noted that Phelan and *The Saturday Evening Post* had rushed to judgment, to delegitimize Garrison and his case.

Some of "reporter" Phelan's activities on this case raise significant concerns. Phelan, like his boss Ackerman, was friends with Robert Maheu, Howard Hughes's contact man with the CIA and the Mafia. Surreptitiously he visited witness Perry Russo four times to entice him to change his testimony and wreck Garrison's case. Phelan was later accompanied and aided by ex-FBI and NSA asset, and RFK confidant, Walter Sheridan in these attempts to bribe Russo in order to discredit Garrison.[8]

During the trial Phelan rented a house and would invite reporters over every evening to serve refreshments and give his views. On the day that Garrison showed the Zapruder film, journalists were shocked. That evening Phelan expounded on the "jet effect" theory to counter the strong impression of the fatal head shot coming from the front. Garrison's staff then made several bootleg copies of the Zapruder film and distributed them to assassination researchers.

By 4/21/67 the CIA seemingly generated another line of attack to rebut Mark Lane's book *Rush to Judgment.* Edward Epstein, author of *Inquest,* claimed that "Lane is guilty of the same fault he charges the Warren Commission – a rush to judgment."

The intelligence community's connections with *The Saturday Evening Post* were utilized in a story 5/20/67, "I'm Glad the CIA is Immoral" by Tom Braden, formerly head of the CIA's International Organizations Division. Years later Braden revealed his role in Operation Mockingbird. (The CIA's media operation)

"If the director of the CIA wanted to extend a present ... he could hand it to him and never have to account to anybody ... there was simply no limit to the money it could spend and no limit to the people it could hire and no limit to the activities it could decide were necessary to conduct the secret war.... Journalists were a target, labor unions a particular target – that was one of the activities in which the communists spent the most money"[9] (Granada Television, *World in Action* 1975).

Another response to the critics of the Warren Report came from nationally acclaimed Merriman Smith, the UPI White House reporter. Smith coarsely proclaimed in a *Dallas Times Herald* editorial on 4/27/67 that decent folks should tell [The Warren Report critics] "to shut the hell up." Quite a statement from a reporter who won a Pulitzer Prize for his reporting on the assassination. Back in November 1966, Smith imaginatively wrote:

> The car in which I rode was not far from the presidential vehicle and in clear view of it. We were coming out of an underpass when the first shot was fired. The sound for a split second resembled a big firecracker. As we cleared the underpass, then came the second and third shots. The shots were fired smoothly and evenly. There was not the slightest doubt on the front seat of our car that the shots came from a rifle to the rear.

There is only one underpass in Dealey Plaza and the Presidential limousine was proceeding toward it. When the President was about 350 feet from the underpass the first shot was fired, and about 260 feet from it when the last shot was fired. Smith clearly was not where he claimed to be when the shots were fired. (Perhaps he deserved a Pulitzer Prize for fiction.) We now know that Smith was an FBI informant, according to documents released in 1995.

Reporter Hugh Aynesworth not only had FBI and CIA connections, he also served as an informant for President Johnson. In a Western Union memorandum dated 5/13/67, he forwarded a rough draft of his *Newsweek* story of 5/15/67 to President Johnson's Press Secretary George Christian, in order to make "a complete report of my knowledge available to the FBI, as I have done in the past."[10] He indicated in his memorandum that the wire services would carry this story, which they did. Whether the wire services knew of Aynesworth's connections remains unclear. Aynesworth piled on unproven allegations in a vicious smear.

Jim Garrison is right. There has been a conspiracy in New Orleans – but it is a plot of Garrison's own making. It is a scheme to concoct a fantastic "solution" to the death of John F. Kennedy, and to make it stick; in this cause, the district attorney and his staff have been indirect parties to the death of one man and have humiliated, harassed, and financially gutted several others.... I have evidence that one of the strapping D.A.'s investigators offered an unwilling "witness" $3,000 and a job with an airline – if he only would fill in the facts of an alleged meeting to plot the death of the President...

When the New Orleans Police Department and the Deputy Superintendent of Police conducted an internal investigation of the Beauboef bribery matter (Al Beauboef was Dave Ferrie's friend) they completely exonerated New Orleans Assistant D.A.'s Lynn Loisel and Lou Ivon of any wrongdoing. Beauboef then retracted his charges of bribery in a sworn statement. Although this material was released on June 12, 1967, Aynesworth never included this in his subsequent reporting. He then implied incompetence or foul play by asserting that key witness Perry Russo had been hypnotized just "hours before he testified" at the preliminary hearing. Aynesworth neglected to mention that Russo had been hypnotized 50 hours prior to the hearing, in a controlled setting, with both Dr. Esmond Fatter, a court accredited expert on hypnotism and Dr. Nicholas Chetta, a coroner of Orleans parish, present. Aynesworth nonetheless derisively declared: "The real question in New Orleans is no longer whether Garrison has solved the assassination. The question is how long the people of the city and the nation's press will allow this travesty of justice to continue."

Aynesworth's suspicious involvement in the assassination coverage from the outset warrants review. Immediately after the assassination Aynesworth, who was friendly with the Dallas police, somehow incredibly "felt a story breaking near the TSBD building when all of the other newsman had followed the dying President to Parkland Hospital." Remarkably, he then got a ride in a police car not only to the Tippit slaying, but then directly to the Texas Theater. Aynesworth was also somehow the recipient of Oswald's alleged diary, and it was published under his byline. One of his newspaper friends, Holmes Alexander, wrote in 1964 that Aynesworth was putting pressure on both the Warren Commission and the FBI to portray Oswald as a crazy leftist assassin.[11]

Perhaps it was no coincidence that Aynesworth's colleague at *Newsweek*, White House correspondent Charles Roberts, wrote a book *The Truth*

About the Assassination, which coincidentally followed the CIA memo "Countering the Criticism of the Warren Report," almost point for point. Roberts took the statements of witness S.M. Holland out of context. He criticized Mark Lane's arguments regarding the location of the shots and claimed that "the Commission found witnesses who were near the Book Depository who thought the shots came from the building."[12] The Warren Report noted, however, that "When the shots were fired, many people near the Depository believed that the shots came from the railroad bridge over the triple underpass or from the area to the west of the Depository."[13]

He distorted the testimony of witness Julia Mercer who claimed to have seen someone with what appeared to be a "so-called gun case" "near" the scene of the murder. He viewed this as "insignificant" since "60-odd" similar statements were made to the Warren Commission. Actually 30 statements were made, and Mercer's testimony places a gunman precisely at the scene of the murder, not "near" it.[14]

Roberts claimed that Lane was a scavenger out for profits not truth – paralleling points 3, 4 and 5 of the CIA memo, "Countering the Critics."

> Are they bona fide scholars, as the reviewers took them to be, or are they "journalist scavengers" as Connally has suggested ... unlike Emile Zola and Lincoln Stephens, who rocked the nation by naming the guilty, the Warren Report critics never tell us who's in charge of the scheme that has victimized us all. Nor are they able to define its purposes, although they offer half a dozen conflicting theories ... clearly the pattern of the Warren Commission critics is: If the experts agree with you, use them. If they don't ignore them.[15]

In an anonymous *New York Times* review, 5/21/67, Roberts' book was roundly praised.

> By selecting the incredible and contradictory, scavengers like Mark Lane sowed confusion. In the case of the Warren Commission and the book business, you get a fabulously successful spin-off called the assassination industry, whose products would never stand the scrutiny of Consumers Union. Consumers buy it as they buy most trash: the packaging promises satisfaction but the innards are mostly distortions, unsupported theories, and gaping omissions. By writing an honest guide for the perplexed, Roberts performs a public service.

CIA "Propaganda Notes" not only praised Roberts' book, they obtained a supply of them for distribution. CIA "Propaganda Notes –

Background Materials," 5/15/67 admonishes that Robert's book "Gives convincing answers to the major criticism of the report…" (Document #1081-963) Point four of 5/15/67 "Propaganda Notes, Series B: Background Materials" reads:

> 1.- Deleted - have obtained a supply of copies of Robert's book and can provide these and reproductions of the Goodhart article. We also have reproductions of *Newsweek*'s exposé of Garrison. Furthermore, a limited number of copies of the Warren Commission Report are available if needed. (CIA document 180-10098-10194)

ABC decided to explore Garrison's investigation on its "Issues and Answers" (5/28/67) show hosted by Bob Clark. The questioning was tough but Garrison was allowed to develop his case and clarify a number of forensic issues.

> I think that the Warren Report in many respects unfortunately is in the position of Humpty Dumpty…. the conclusion is totally indefensible … a study of the Zapruder film, which was never studied by the Warren Commission before it reached that conclusion, shows that his head went to the back, to the back and rear as if he were hit with a baseball bat … this is one of many areas which would have come to light had there been an adversary proceeding.

NBC and CBS would not be so straightforward.

By May of 1967 the *New Orleans States-Item* ran a series of articles by Hoke May and Ross Yockey that treated the Garrison case seriously and revealed some of the CIA connections around Gordon Novel and his lawyers. Ross Yockey's piece 7/1/67 was titled "CIA Hiding 51 Documents Vital to Probe – D.A. Aide." Reactions were rapid. CIA General Counsel Lawrence Houston had his assistant, John Greaney meet with local CIA officer Lloyd Ray in New Orleans to discuss the Garrison investigation. This memo remains partly redacted. Then, Bill Gurvich, a short-term volunteer with unknown CIA connections, who had left the DA's office, met with the hierarchy at the *States-Item*. Quickly and inexplicably, Yockey and May were pulled from the Garrison case. Gurvich later admitted to stealing the DA's master file and contacting Walter Sheridan, who coordinated and produced the NBC "White Paper" on Jim Garrison.[16]

Walter Sheridan, a former member of the DOJ "Get Hoffa" team, and a former chief of Counterintelligence at the NSA, also provided information to the former DOJ head of Criminal Division, then a CIA attorney. Attorney Herbert Miller stayed in touch with CIA Associate General Counsel Richard Lansdale regarding Garrison's case, and in particular Al Beauboef. Beauboef refused to cooperate with Garrison after his trip to Washington. A CIA memo 5/11/67 reveals that Sheridan wanted to meet with the CIA "under any terms we propose."[17]

In another effort to blunt the momentum of Jim Garrison, NBC crafted a program to discredit him. The Counterintelligence Chief of the CIA, James Angleton, issued a memorandum for the Deputy Director of Plans, 5/12/67:

> Richard Lansdale, Associate General Counsel, has advised us that NBC plans to do a derogatory television special on Garrison and his probe of the Kennedy assassination; that NBC regards Garrison as a menace to the country and means to destroy him. The program is to be presented within the next few weeks. Mr. Lansdale learned this information from Mr. Walter Sheridan.

A memo released three decades later by the Assassination Records and Review Board (ARRB) states:

> A local FBI agent reported that Richard Townley, [of NBC affiliate] WDSU-TV, New Orleans, remarked to a special agent of the New Orleans office last evening that he received instructions from NBC, New York, to prepare a one hour television special on Jim Garrison with the instruction "shoot him down."

NBC led its "White Paper," entitled "The Case of Jim Garrison," 6/19/67, with interviews of three people, unknown to Garrison personally, who accused him of pressuring witnesses and bribery. None of these "witnesses" ever repeated their charges under oath, and all later pleaded the Fifth Amendment before the Orleans Parish Grand Jury.

Next, attorney Dean Andrews claimed that Clay Shaw had not called him the day after the assassination. Following the NBC show Andrews was indicted and found guilty by the Orleans Parish Grand Jury for committing perjury when he testified that Clay Shaw was not the "Clay Bertrand" who called him to be Oswald's lawyer.

On the program, businessman Fred Leemans asserted that Garrison and reporters offered him money if he could remember that Clay Shaw also used the name Bertrand and frequented his New Orleans Turkish bath with a young man named "Lee." After the NBC special Leemans admitted in a sworn statement that he had received threatening phone calls "relating to the information that he had given Garrison." Leemans was told to contact Irvin Dymond, one of Shaw's attorneys, and was offered an attorney and bond in the event he was charged with giving false testimony to the D.A.'s office. NBC included a jailhouse interview, wherein Miguel Torres claimed that Garrison had offered him his freedom, $75 worth of heroin and a vacation in Florida in exchange for his incriminating testimony. Another convict, John "The Baptist" Cancler, who Garrison had recently prosecuted for burglary, claimed that Garrison had promised him freedom if he would break into Clay Shaw's home and plant incriminating evidence. After the NBC special, Garrison called Torres and Cancler to repeat their stories to a Grand Jury. Both pleaded the Fifth Amendment and were convicted for contempt.

The NBC-TV program also claimed that lie detector tests cast doubts on the testimony of prospective witnesses Vernon Bundy and Perry Russo. Recall that a three-judge panel in New Orleans had already decided on the basis of their testimony to try Shaw.

The day after the "White Paper," the *New York Times*, to their credit, reported, 6/20/67, about a press conference in Garrison's office, where Perry Russo charged that Walter Sheridan and other NBC-TV employees sought his help to wreck the investigation. Russo also declared that Richard Townley of WDSU-TV and James Phelan (*The Saturday Evening Post*) spoke to him on behalf of NBC-TV. Russo said that the NBC-TV team used threats and promises of a job in California to persuade him to appear on the program. Russo's charges have been confirmed, because Jim Garrison had secretly wired Russo to record the meeting.[18]

According to two sources, Sheridan was the NSA liaison to a CIA cover organization named International Investigation Incorporated. NBC also hired CIA operative Gordon Novel, the man who wiretapped Garrison's office, as a consultant for the show.[19] Sheridan put Novel on a $500 a day retainer, then urged him to skip town to avoid being indicted, and paid him an additional $750 while he was in Columbus, Ohio.[20]

Newsweek, nonetheless, reported that the program was a "tough ... hard-nosed analysis" (7/3/67). The *L.A. Times* condemned Jim Garrison's "fantastic allegations and weird evidence" and supported Walter Sheridan's "White Paper." Later that year though, the FCC, in an unprecedented decision based on the "Fairness Doctrine," provided Garrison one-half-hour to respond to the hour long White Paper.[21] Garrison calmly observed,

> The people of their country don't have to be protected from the truth. The country was not built on the idea that a handful of nobles, whether located in our federal agencies in Washington D.C., or in the news agencies in New York, should decide what was good for the people to know and what they should not know ... I would rather put my confidence in the common sense of the people of this country.

Garrison's brief overview on NBC was clear and compelling, but the better advertised and more reported "White Paper" had recast the public perception of Garrison, from a crusader to merely a character. Garrison also moved to arrest Sheridan for bribing witnesses, although the charges were later dropped. Author David Talbot argues that RFK stepped in to assist his old ally Sheridan.

Back then NBC was owned by RCA, whose Pentagon contracts had increased more than $1 billion from 1960 to 1967. Questions linger regarding the role played by NBC's chairman, retired General David Sarnoff, and CEO Robert Sarnoff, both noted cold warriors, in the coverage of Garrison's investigation. General Sarnoff was the former president and a permanent director of the Armed Forces Communications and Electronics Association (AFCEA), a network of the American electronics industry and the military establishment. In an address at an annual AFCEA banquet, 5/26/65, Sarnoff connected:

> The working alliance of industrial and military leadership represented in this organization... It took nearly two centuries and several prolonged conflicts to teach us that the absence of this vital alliance in times of peace could be costly in time of war ... AFCEA has fashioned a community of interest as closely interwoven that whatever affects the progress of one partner is reflected in the progress of the other.[22]

RCA's technology soon became a major part of the core of the NSA.[23]

These NBC connections cast new light on the reporting of Oswald's activities in the summer of 1963 by NBC New Orleans affiliate WDSU-TV, owned by Edith and Edgar Stern, who were close friends with Clay Shaw. Strangely, WDSU-TV filmed Oswald outside the New Orleans Municipal Court after receiving a $10 fine for a fracas with CIA operative Carlos Bringuier, while distributing "pro-Castro" leaflets in front of the Trade Mart. These actions hardly constitute news in a big city; they do, however, appear to be pre-planned elements of a "lone communist nut" scenario.[24] After this incident, Oswald was invited to "debate" CIA operatives Carlos Bringuier and Ed Butler on WDSU radio, which had the effect of publicly identifying Oswald as a Marxist Soviet defector. Later, as the Garrison case unfolded, another WDSU-TV reporter, Ed Planer, offered to share information he had on the Garrison investigation with the FBI.

The context for these connections is revealing. The Sterns, heirs to the Sears Roebuck fortune, were active members of INCA, the Information Council of the Americas. The Stern's son, Philip, worked for the CIA as "liaison clearance" with the Deputy Asst. Secretary Of State for Public Affairs. Dr. Alton Ochsner, (a cleared source for the CIA since 1955) and Edwin S. Butler who founded INCA in 1961, attempted to protect the interests of the New Orleans economic elite and stimulate anti-communism. Standard Oil, the Reily Foundation, Hibernia Bank, and Mississippi Shipping Company funded it, along with the International Trade Mart, whose managing director was Clay Shaw. Butler openly bragged about his relationship with CIA Deputy Director Charles Cabell, who was fired by President Kennedy. Ochsner was a member of the exclusive Boston Club and had been a guest at the elite Bohemian Grove in California. His friends included Samuel Zemurry of United Fruit, Turner Catledge, managing editor of the *New York Times*, Clay Shaw, Edgar Stern owner of WDSU radio and many of the New Orleans elite.[25]

By early 1967, three members of INCA helped form a group called "Truth or Consequences," which raised funds for Jim Garrison's investigation. Willard Robertson and Cecil Shilstone were also founding members of INCA, and attorney Eberhard Duetch was a director for INCA who had been Garrison's former law partner. Critics have long contended that Truth or Consequences was well situated for surveillance of Garrison's investigation.

In May, stories from UPI, *Life* and *Time* reported Itek's findings that the Nix film proved nothing. What appeared to be a man on the knoll "must be taken for a shadow."[26] Recall that former CIA officer Frank Lindsey headed Itek.

Some of the best reporting during this period appeared in Fred Powledge's 6/17/67 piece in *The New Republic*. He outlined Oswald's links to an anticommunist group, the fictional New Orleans chapter of the Fair Play for Cuba Committee. He then explored Garrison's research regarding 19 witnesses who had originally testified before the Warren Commission that they had heard shooting coming from the grassy knoll.

Powledge examined some of the links between Gordon Novel and Clay Shaw to the CIA, as well as the possibility of a CIA and media cover-up. He determined that Garrison had uncovered the connection of witness Gordon Novel to the CIA, which led to the *New Orleans States-Item* headline "NOVEL CIA AGENT, ATTORNEY ADMITS" on May 23, 1967. The *New York Times* also printed the acknowledgement by Novel's lawyer that he had been a CIA agent, but buried their brief story on page 44.[27] Even the Associated Press noted "When Novel first fled from New Orleans, he headed straight for McLean, Virginia, which is the Central Intelligence Agency suburb, this is not surprising, because Gordon Novel was a CIA employee in the 1960s."

Years later, Victor Marchetti, a former high-ranking CIA officer, revealed a glimpse of CIA concern for Garrison in an article in *True* magazine in April of 1975:

> I used to attend, among other things, the Director's morning meeting. This was Richard Helms at the time and he held a meeting every morning at 9, which was attended by 12 or 14 of his leading Deputies plus 3 or 4 staffers ... I used to take minutes of this meeting.... But during the Clay Shaw trial I remember the Director on several occasions asking questions like, you know, "Are we giving them all the help they need?" I didn't know who they or them were. I knew they didn't like Garrison.... They would talk in half sentences like "is everything going all right down there ... yeah ... but talk with me about it after the meeting" or "we'll pick this up later in my office" ... I began to ask around ... I was told "Shaw, a long time ago, had been a contact of the Agency ... He was in the export-import business ... he knew people coming and going from certain areas – the Domestic Contact Service ... and he's been cut off a long time ago" ... "well of course the Agency doesn't want this to come out now because Garrison will distort it, the public would misconstrue it."

Bill Small, then head of CBS Washington Bureau and reporter Dan Schorr proposed a program to review the new critical books about the assassination. How CBS management mangled their proposal is revealing. This proposal, promoted by CBS Senior VP Gordon Manning, was rejected by Richard Salant, president of the CBS News Division. By November 1966 Manning, along with Executive Producer Leslie Midgely, then proposed a 3-hour even-handed debate of the Warren Report. The final hour would consist of deliberations by a panel of law school deans. Salant's revised this proposal and advocated putting the Warren Report on trial. When this was presented to the president of CBS Broadcast Group, John Schneider he told Salant to bring it to CBS News Executive Committee (CNEC).

Former CBS attorney Roger Feinman revealed the editorial power of the little known CNEC in rapidly transforming the series. Weekly meetings of the CNEC, which determined CBS News policies and operations, consisted of William Paley, Frank Stanton, (LBJ's friend and business partner) Richard Salant, Sig Mickelson, and John Schneider. Richard Salant, Frank Stanton's protégé, started to get second thoughts and then sent Gordon Manning and Leslie Midgely to California to meet with two prominent lawyers to dissuade them. They were Edwin Hudelson, board member of RAND Corporation and a Harvard law school classmate of Frank Stanton (also a State Department of Intelligence attorney) and Bayless Manning, Stanford Law School Dean, and a Chair on the Board at RAND with Stanton. Both feared national security risks and strongly advised that CBS should let the JFK assassination rest. Gordon Manning then changed his proposal to "A Defense of the Warren Report," while Midgely continued to lobby for at least some pertinent inquiry. Midgely suggested running experiments more scientific than the FBI, as well as holding a mock trial. Salant responded with an anonymous attack crafted by Warren Commissioner John McCloy.

The CNEC, through Salant, then invited Warren Commissioner John J. McCloy to be kept posted on the series through his daughter, CBS producer Ellen McCloy, and her Executive producer Les Midgely.

The *Boston Herald-Traveler* television editor, Eleanor Roberts, revealed 4/19/67, some of the CBS infighting on the series. "A most unusual television experiment is taking place at CBS News – the preparation of a documentary on another look at the Warren Commission Report – which may never be telecast." The series could be tabled unless CBS could find new information to counter the Commission's critics. After reading the article, critic Ray Marcus called CBS reporter Bob Richter to opt out of the project. Richter retorted, "If those of you who have important information don't cooperate with us you're just guaranteeing that the other side wins."

Marcus met several times with Richter, and at one point they took the Mary Moorman photo #5, enlarged, (taken at the time of the assassination looking at the grassy knoll) to CBS program producer Leslie Midgely. Midgely thought he saw someone in the photo – then clammed up.[28]

Five days prior to this program airing, author Richard E. Sprague met with reporters Bob Richter and Dan Rather and both agreed that the conclusions stating conspiracy had to be made stronger. Last minute changes, which gutted this critique, caused an outraged producer Bob Richter to resign. Sprague's correspondence with Walter Cronkite showed that script changes came from Midgely and reporter Robert Lister.[29] Richter told author Bill Turner that the series started out objective, but somewhere along the line the whole tone was changed so as to completely reinforce the Warren Report. The change came, Richter observed, after a phone call from Washington to CBS President Frank Stanton. The caller was a top government official, possibly Stanton's old friend and business partner Lyndon Johnson.

In June of 1967, CBS broadcast their highly touted four-hour program which strongly supported the Warren Commission's findings. The *New York Times* billed it as "very well the most valuable four hours you ever spent with television." CBS President Richard Salant asserted in a press release that the program was a work of "genius." The Special Reports unit, which had developed the two-hour "illustration" of the Warren Report for CBS in 1964, did the reporting. Upper-level management at CBS, Richard Salant President of CBS News, and Gordon Manning, Vice President of News, were "unusually concerned and involved," according to Executive Producer Les Midgely. Salant claimed, "that it would not be a documentary marshaling of facts." He said long before the work was done that CBS News would reach and state its own conclusions – "no matter what they might be."

Actually, according to an FBI memo, CBS cooperated with the FBI, the CIA and former Warren Commissioners. FBI memo 1/27/67, #62-109090, Urgent, to Director:

> (Deleted two lines) advised me confidentially that the Columbia Broadcasting Company was planning a five-hour documentary on the assassination. He stated the primary purpose of this was to take the books, which are critical of the Warren Report, particularly *Rush to Judgment* by Mark Lane and tear the same apart. He indicated this documentary was certainly not going to be critical of the FBI and in fact would support the Warren Report. He stated he understood that Columbia officials in New York had been in touch with John J. McCloy, Allen Dulles and J. Lee Rankin. He was of the opinion that they were certainly cooperating, or were going to cooperate in this production. (Deleted word) requested that this

information be kept confidential, and he said he would furnish me more details at a later date. Bureau will be kept advised of any further development.

One CBS reporter on the documentaries, Eddie Barker, had previously worked on the first two pro-Warren Commission CBS documentaries. He was by then the news director of KRLD in Dallas and also an FBI informant.

In the program CBS alluded to Oswald's marksmanship. A fellow serviceman noted "he was not a genuine marksman." CBS could have also interviewed Oswald's Sergeant, Nelson Delgado, as had filmmaker Emile de Antonio, since Delgado had already stated that he was threatened by the FBI to remain silent about Oswald's poor marksmanship. This line of inquiry then shifted to whether the rifle could be shot quickly enough.

CBS attempted to replicate the alleged marksmanship of Oswald using 11 marksmen. Out of 37 attempts to fire three shots, seventeen of those attempts were not counted "because of trouble with the rifle," yet CBS did not state what the trouble was. In the 20 attempts [remaining] where time could be recorded, the average was 5.6 seconds. CBS divulged only four of the twenty attempts – one had three hits in 5.2 seconds; one had 2 of 3 hits in slightly less than 5 seconds; one had one hit in 4.1 seconds and one had one hit in 5.4 seconds. Walter Cronkite, the respected CBS anchorman, often referred to as an American television father figure, creatively claimed that:

> It seems reasonable to say that an expert could fire that rifle in five seconds.... It seems reasonable to say that Oswald, under normal circumstances, would take longer [than experts]. But these were not normal circumstances. Oswald was shooting at a President. So the answer is: probably fast enough.

Dan Rather chose to reject previous FBI test firings as well as the results of the marksmen hired by CBS and deduced that it was, "A much easier shot than even it looks in our pictures."[30] In a documentary 26 years later CBS finally revealed that only four of the eleven marksmen managed two hits out of three.

Notably the discussion of the single bullet theory neglected to mention the Army ballistics test, which determined that a bullet hitting dense objects would be deformed. Also unmentioned was the critical fact that more grains of a bullet were found in Governor Connally's body than

were lost from the magic bullet. According to CBS attorney Roger Fein-
man, the questions to be asked of former Warren Commission counsel
Arlen Spector were provided in advance, sidestepping CBS's own book of
Standards and Procedures.

Warren Commissioner John McCloy was questioned by CBS, but
not regarding the evidence raised by critics like Lane, Epstein, or Weisberg. Jim Garrison's criticisms were shown for only about thirty seconds.
McCloy confirmed his continued support for the findings of the Warren
Commission. Internal memos indicate that John McCloy's daughter Ellen had indeed kept her dad posted regarding the script.

> One comment that Dad made after reading the "rough script" Mr.
> Salant wanted me to pass along to you. It concerned a sentence that
> appears on the top of page 5C … Dad said: 1) he has no recollec-
> tion of President (LBJ) asking or urging the members of the War-
> ren Commission to "act with speed." 2) The phrase "in less than a
> year" again implies that the Commission might have acted in haste.
> Dad suggests that you say 8 ½ months." Ellen, (to Les Midgely the
> producer of the series). [31]

The transfer of this internal memo to John McCloy again ignored the
CBS book of Standards and Procedures. Midgely later sent a letter to John
McCloy thanking him for his "extremely kind and generous comments."

In the first of the four one-hour programs, CBS attempted to examine
whether Oswald owned a rifle. The controversial picture of Oswald holding the alleged murder weapon was analyzed by, according to Cronkite,
"a professional photographer and photo analyst," yet remarkably the "independent study" was made by FBI informant Lawrence Schiller, the
alleged former business agent for Jack Ruby. Although the FBI and the
London Times (1966) had failed to prove the authenticity of the backyard
photo of Oswald, CBS "expert" Lawrence Schiller claimed to succeed.[32]

The 1967 CBS interview with Orville Nix, who, like Zapruder, filmed
the assassination, recycled some of the procedures used in the 1964 CBS
documentary. When asked where the shots came from, Nix said, "From
over there on the grassy knoll behind the fence." This was then disregarded and Nix was again asked the same question, to which he gave the same
response – this sequence was repeated six or seven additional times. Then
a producer asked him where the Warren Commission said the shots came
from? Nix answered, "From the Texas School Book Depository." Only
Nix's last response was used. CBS producer Bernard Birnbaum, who

worked on the documentary, denied the exchange. He asserted, "We never tried to put words in anyone's mouth."[33]

According to Nix's granddaughter Gayle Jackson, her grandfather told CBS that there were four shots fired; however, CBS ran Nix saying, "bang, bang, bang" suggesting only three shots were fired. After the CBS interview the normally gentle Nix became furious. He was hitting the steering wheel on the ride back home saying "Why are they trying to make me feel like I am insane?" Jackson recalls. A year later when Jim Garrison called for Nix to testify, he refused. Jackson thought he feared for his life.[34]

Regarding the question "Was Oswald's rifle fired from the building?" CBS appeared to gloss over the equivocating responses from a key witness, Dallas Deputy Sheriff Seymour Weitzman, who had managed a sporting goods store and was known as an expert with rifles. Weitzman originally stated to the Dallas police that he found a German Mauser 7.65 in the TSBD. Curiously, he changed his story when questioned by the Warren Commission. Weitzman repeated to CBS essentially what he told the Warren Commission: "that he had seen the weapon at a glance ... it's a German Mauser, that it's an Italian type gun and that it looked like a Mauser, which I said it was mistaken, and it was proven that my statement was a mistake..." Rather reported, "So Mr. Weitzman now seems sure that the rifle was indeed Oswald's Mannlicher-Carcano."[35]

CBS was given a blow-up of a snapshot taken by Mary Moorman who was facing the grassy knoll when the shots were fired. Researcher Raymond Marcus gave the picture to producer Robert Richter who said he strongly believed that he discerned a man. Executive producer Les Midgely, who had the final say, disagreed, and viewers only briefly saw the picture with a denigrating description, "If there are men up there, they definitely can't be seen with the naked eye." Marcus asked a dozen experts, some from MIT and UCLA, to examine the blow-up without mentioning its connection to the assassination and 10 of them concluded that at least "probably" they saw a man in the photograph.[36]

In a creative attempt to scientifically bolster the findings of the Warren Report, CBS included a "jiggle analysis" of the Zapruder film. Dr. Luis Alvarez, a physicist at UC Berkeley, noted that Abraham Zapruder would not be able to hold his camera steady when he heard the shots fired, thus significant blurring would occur after each shot was fired. Although blurring could occur due to panning errors as Zapruder turned his camera, if only three blurs existed it would constitute important evidence that three shots were fired.

The fatal headshot occurred at frame 313 and frames 318-322 are unquestionably blurred. CBS claimed to have found blurring at 186 and at 222, and concluded that only three shots were fired. CBS neglected to reveal that Dr. Alvarez thought that the blurred frames occurred at frame 177 and again at frame 216.

Another problem with the CBS and Alvarez analysis was that the first and second shot were placed too closely together. The Warren Commission found that an expert marksman using the Mannlicher-Carcano could not fire two shots in less than 2.3 seconds.[37] This translates to about 43 frames of film, since Zapruder's camera ran at 18.3 frames per second. In the CBS study the first two shots differ by 36 frames (less than 2 seconds) and in Dr. Alvarez's study they differ by 39 frames (2.1 seconds). Actually, if either CBS News or Dr. Alvarez were correct, either would have inadvertently proved that Oswald ... was not the lone assassin.

CBS photo-analyst Charles Wyckoff noted 4 jiggles in the film but determined that one of them was caused by a car backfire. Since the Zapruder film is 8mm and silent, the determination of a car backfire was quite intuitive.

CBS used a military doctor and former Warren Commission consultant to test whether a bullet could penetrate both Kennedy and Connally. In all four tests the bullet failed to penetrate the equivalent of Connally's thigh, nonetheless the doctor concluded it would have taken very little more velocity to cause a similar wound. CBS did not announce the distance from which the test bullets were fired and neglected to duplicate the strange path of the "magic bullet."

To clarify the location of the President's back wound CBS chose Commander Humes, the pathologist who had directed the autopsy and had subsequently burned his preliminary draft of the autopsy. Humes confirmed that one wound was in the back of the neck; disregarding the reports of four Secret Service agents, two FBI agents, the signed death certificate, the autopsy description sheet, and the President's shirt and jacket, which all pointed to a hole 5 ½ inches below the collar, in the back.

As noted author Jim DiEugenio revealed in his article in Kennedys and King, 10/16/10 regarding CBS coverage:

> In their research for the series, CBS had discovered a document that the Warren Commission did not have. The afternoon of the assassination, Perry had given a press conference along with Dr. Kemp Clark. Although it was filmed, when the Commission asked

for a copy or a transcript, the Secret Service said they could not locate either. (Doug Horne, *Inside the ARRB*, vol. 2, p. 647) This was a lie. The Secret Service did have such a transcript. It was delivered to them on November 23, 1963. The ARRB found the time-stamped envelope. But Feinman discovered that CBS had found a copy of this transcript years before, White House correspondent Robert Pierpont found a transcript through the White House press office. One reason it was hard to find was that it should not have been at the White House; it should have been at the Kennedy Library. But as Roger Feinman found out, it had been relabeled. It was not a Kennedy administration press conference anymore; but the first press conference of the Johnson administration. So it ended up at the Johnson Library.

None of this was revealed on the program by either Cronkite or Rather. And neither the tape nor transcript was presented during the series. In fact, Cronkite did his best to camouflage what Perry said during this November 22nd press conference, specifically about the anterior neck wound. Perry clearly said that it had the appearance to him of being an entrance wound, and he said this three times. Cronkite tried to characterize the conference as Perry being ushered out to the press and badgered. Not true, since the press conference was about two hours after Perry had done a tracheotomy over the front neck wound. The performance of that incision had given Perry the closest and most deliberate look at that wound. Perry therefore had the time to recover from the pressure of the operation. And there was no badgering of Perry. News men were simply asking Perry and Clark questions about the wounds they saw. Perry had the opportunity to answer the questions on his own terms. Again, CBS seemed intent on concealing evidence of a second assassin. For Oswald could not have fired at Kennedy from the front.

Walter Cronkite, who reportedly read the script given to him, disregarded the limited number of eyewitnesses in Dealey Plaza who were interviewed by CBS invoking "an old axiom among lawyers that nothing carries more weight with a jury, or is less reliable, than eyewitness testimony." The preponderance of witnesses running up the grassy knoll was not mentioned.

Dr. Alvarez, who declared that the backward motion of the President's head was due to the "spalling" [shattering] effect, refuted the possibility of frontal shots. Cronkite hedged, "That is one explanation from a physicist as to how a head could move backwards after being struck from behind."

One of the autopsy doctors James Humes endorsed the Rydberg drawings of the wounds. This is remarkable because Rydberg never had access to photos, x-rays or official measurements. Further those drawings do not correspond to existing pictures, measurements or the Zapruder film.

When critic William Turner was interviewed he asserted, "That the massive head shot … came from a quartering angle on the grassy knoll." Turner also rebutted one of Cronkite's earlier statements regarding a lack of cartridge shells, because "with a revolver or pistol the shells do not eject…. Number two they can slip the gun under their coat." Cronkite determined "that it was difficult to take such versions seriously…"

Regarding Jack Ruby's motive, Cronkite stated, "…maintaining to the last that he was no conspirator, that he killed Oswald out of anger and a desire to shield Jacqueline Kennedy from the ordeal of a trial …" Three months earlier *Newsweek* reported that Ruby's new lawyer, Joe Tonahill, said that Ruby wrote him a note stating, "Tom Howard (Ruby's first lawyer) told me to say that I shot Oswald so that Caroline and Mrs. Kennedy wouldn't have to come to Dallas to testify." Cronkite nevertheless posited, "the Oswald murder still appears to have been not a conspiracy but an impulse – meaningless violence born of meaningless violence."

CBS commentator Eric Sevareid caustically closed the series by denigrating critics of the Warren Report. Those who do not accept Oswald's lone guilt were compared with "people who think Adolph Hitler is alive, people who think the so-called Elders of Zion are engaged in a Jewish plot to control the world…. It would be utterly impossible in the American arena of a fierce and free press and politics to conceal a conspiracy among so many individuals who live in the public eye." He proclaimed that the notion that the Commission members "knowingly suppressed or distorted decisive evidence … is idiotic." Dan Rather's summation perplexed many viewers.

> I'm content with the basic findings of the Warren Commission, that the evidence is overwhelming that Oswald fired at the President, and that Oswald probably killed President Kennedy alone. I am not content with the findings on Oswald's possible connections with government agencies, particularly with the CIA. I'm not totally convinced at some earlier time, unconnected with the assassination, Oswald may have had more connections than we've been told about, or that have been shown. I'm not totally convinced about the single-bullet theory. But I don't think it's absolutely necessary to the final conclusions of the Warren Report.

How were past CIA connections not relevant? How was the single bullet theory not necessary? Cronkite intoned in the last hour of the series that CBS had found:

> There has been a loss of morale, and a loss of confidence among the American people toward their government and the men who serve it. And that is perhaps more wounding then the assassination itself.... The damage that Lee Harvey Oswald did to the United States of America, the country he first denounced, and then appeared to embrace, did not end when the shots were fired from the Texas School Book Depository. The most grievous wounds persist and there is little reason to believe that they will soon be healed.

Remarkably, just a day after the series, a CBS press release ran a headline "[CBS] Says Question of Oswald Connection to CIA, FBI Not Frivolous." Recall the statements in the series by Rather and Cronkite noting, "the Commission's handling of that question is scarcely justifiable ... there remain disturbing indications {of} some kind of link between Oswald and various intelligence agencies of the United States." So how could CBS claim in their series that Oswald had "denounced" his country, "was the sole assassin" and now concede that he may have been working for the government intelligence agencies?

Viewers did not even see a critic until the end of the third night of the series. A thirty minute taped interview of critics Mark Lane and William Turner was somehow sliced to one-minute segments. Garrison's lengthy interview was also cut to about 30 seconds. Garrison later cracked to Turner that "This gave me just enough time to be a discordant bleep in the network's massive four hour tribute to the Warren Commission." Similarly, the interview with noted forensic pathologist and critic Dr. Cyril Wecht was edited so that the aired excerpt contained only Wecht's concession that it was possible that the backward motion of Kennedy's head could have been the result of a neuro-muscular reaction.

TV Guide, 6/24/67, then owned by *Philadelphia Inquirer* publisher Walter Annenberg, gushed that the program "ranks as a major journalistic achievement.... It was a masterful compilation of facts, interviews, experiments and opinions – a job of journalism that will be difficult to surpass." Coincidentally, Walter Annenberg's father Moe had been heavily involved with organized crime, and John Roselli was Moe's primary business representative in Los Angeles in 1929. A facet of Moe Annenberg's rise involved hiring "gangs of sluggers and ex-boxers" to defend the Hearst newspaper empire in its circulation wars. Ex-boxer Jack Ruby worked for Moe Annenberg and his successor in this capacity in the 1930s.[38]

An Associated Press story, 6/26/67, backed the CBS series, asserting in "CBS Supports Findings of Warren Commission":

> 1) That a Mannlicher-Carcano can be fired at least as accurately and rapidly – and probably more – as the Commission believed;
>
> 2) That the first shot was fired from the TSBD building sooner than the Warren Commission said;
>
> 3) That the amateur film taken by Abraham Zapruder was quite possibly running slower than the Commission thought;
>
> 4) That the shot that Governor John Connally heard missed its mark.

No other criticisms of the CBS special or the Warren Commission were mentioned.

While the CBS series was on, Garrison aide William Gurvich resigned from the New Orleans D.A. office and blasted Garrison's investigation. Jack Nelson of the *L.A. Times* covered the murky charges and counter-charges for three days. Comments from Gurvich (who was influenced by former NSA agent Walter Sheridan) and Clay Shaw were far more prominent than statements from Garrison. The *L.A. Times* story by Jack Nelson, 6/28/67, "Shaw Hopeful 4-Month 'Nightmare' is ending" discussed Shaw's feelings, rather than Garrison's case. This perspective was probably influenced by former FBI agent Aaron Kohn working with Nelson as well as *L.A. Times* reporter Jerry Cohen working with FBI asset Lawrence Schiller. *Times* chief editor Ed Guthman spoke with Garrison, and publicly decided that Garrison did not have a case. Yet Guthman had told Wesley Liebeler (Warren Commission counsel) that Garrison had shown two months before that Clay Shaw was actually Clay Bertrand – a central contention of the Garrison case. The *L.A. Times* omitted this contention from their coverage, yet proclaimed in an anti-Garrison editorial, 7/14/67, that "Whatever the outcome, the press will not be muzzled in its search for the truth in New Orleans"[39]

The New Republic 7/15/67 gave the CBS series a mixed review. Alexander Bickel opined:

> The first hour was a brilliant achievement, which demonstrated what an incomplete job the Warren Commission had done, and how much new light a second, more effective official inquiry could

shed. After that, the more accustomed TV atmosphere closed in again, and things got evasive and fatuous. The first program showed convincingly, taking full advantage of the visual medium that three shots had been fired, and that Oswald's rifle could have fired all three from the Texas School Book Depository.

Bickel argued that the CBS tests were more "complex and realistic" than any done by the FBI. He accepted CBS's jiggle analysis of the Zapruder film but was unconvinced with the CBS case for the single-bullet theory. He credited CBS for its retesting of the bullet but noted that the test "disproved" the conclusion and that the CBS expert Dr. W. F. Enos had stated "it's highly improbable." Bickel observed that Cronkite's conclusion on behalf of CBS evaded the fact that there were more fragments left in Governor Connally than the bullet accepted by the Commission was likely to have lost.

Bickel blasted Garrison, "who cuts a preposterous figure," while approving of the statements by Eric Sevareid and John McCloy. He closed by castigating historian Henry Steele Commager for declaring he saw "no value, really, in another investigation," since anyone who disbelieved the first investigation would disbelieve "a second, third and fourth." This review generated a brief exchange between CBS and *The New Republic* a month later. CBS Special Reporter Walter Lister responded to Bickel and focused on "one major error of fact and … specious arguments against the single bullet theory." Lister in some way declared that the autopsy pathologists were mistaken in describing that more particles were embedded in Connally's wrist than were lost from [CE 399] the single bullet.

> Three particles were removed; the largest weighed half a grain. The other two and those left in his wrist was far tinier. There was also a tiny particle in his thigh. The total weight of these particles could easily be less than two grains. There were two or three grains missing from the bullet so this did not disprove the single bullet theory, nor prove it.

Lister asserted that the ballistics tests conducted by Dr. Alfred Oliver, Chief of Wound Ballistics at the Army's Edgewood Arsenal, show that one bullet could have caused all of the wounds. Lister's third point clarified that pathologist Dr. Cyril Wecht made the statement that the single bullet theory was "highly improbable." Bickel's brief reply conceded that the single-bullet theory was possible. Bickel noted that he had never argued that the throat wound was one of entrance and that he had never challenged the physical findings of the autopsy report. Bickel's lone rejoinder was that Dr. Humes, the autopsy surgeon, and Dr. Finck, who assisted in the autopsy, both said that CE 399, the stretcher bullet, could not have caused all of Connally's wounds.

A few days later the *L.A. Times* ran a useful report of the CBS special but buried it on page 17 of part four, 6/30/67. Hal Humphrey's article noted that only one major criticism was made of the Warren Report – that the CIA and FBI were allowed to investigate themselves on matters involving those organizations. "Otherwise the CBS inquiry tended to turn its back on all of the chief critics of the Warren Report.... An overall evaluation ... seems to indicate that it was done primarily to allay fears and doubts of much of the public, not just on the matter of the Kennedy assassination but on the subject of trusting our government per se..."

Newsweek declared, 7/3/67, that the "CBS documentary thoroughly probed into aspects of the assassination which, if examined more closely by the Warren Commission might have dispelled at least some of the doubt that Oswald was the lone assassin....The network argues that the failure of some persons to accept the bulk of the Commissions' voluminous report is due simply to irrationality." Those believing in conspiracy were referred to as "cultists."

During this period, unidentified phone callers attempted to manipulate reporters. Reporter Jack Payton of the *St. Petersburg Times* observed,

> ...Somebody put together a carefully orchestrated campaign to discredit him (Garrison) right from the beginning.... Reporters, myself included, started getting strange telephone calls from people who wouldn't identify themselves.... You would try to check these things out and always end up getting nowhere. Even so, some of it would show up in the media, attributed to unnamed sources. One I remember in particular was a noted pederast ... others suggested marital infidelities, financial improprieties, or ties to the local mafia clan.[40]

By mid-1967 the Associated Press re-released *The Torch is Passed*, yet remarkably they just reprinted their 1963 version unchanged. No new questions were even raised. Simon and Schuster, the new publisher, ironically reprinted the acknowledgment which claimed: "...While a nation could be halted, dazed and inert with grief and horror – the newsman could not. The story required the best from the Associated Press writers

..." The writers for this eloquent tale were Saul Pett, Sid Moody, Hugh Mulligan, and Tom Henshaw. The member organizations of AP include: the *Dallas Morning News*, the *Dallas Times Herald*, CBS, NBC, ABC, the *Washington Post*, the *Washington Star*, and the *New York Daily News*. In an unprecedented action AP then published a three-part report, completely supporting the Warren Commission Report. Nine full pages of this AP editorial, which posed as news, was run in hundreds of newspapers across the country, usually without opposition commentary.[41]

The *New York Post* hammered away at Garrison's investigation with Clayton Fritchey's screed, "Can Garrison Be Stopped?"

"Garrison has concocted so many different plots ... American criminal justice is full of cases where prosecutors have abused their office with impunity, but records show few parallels for ruthlessness with which Garrison has apparently violated the rights and liberties of various individuals in building up his Kennedy assassination extravaganza.... If Garrison gets away with this, no critic of his investigation will be safe from prosecution on one charge or another." Garrison responded to Fritchey with a letter but received no response.

Life ran a lengthy two-part piece on "The Mob," written by Sandy Smith and assisted by David Chandler, Dick Billings and Robert Blakey that implicated Jim Garrison (9/1/67 and 9/8/67). Robert Kennedy's extensive organized crime prosecutions were omitted, as well as the rapid drop off in mob prosecutions under Lyndon Johnson. The only official *Life* deemed worthy of examining was Jim Garrison. According to *Life* reporter and chief researcher for the article, Richard Billings, "The Director (FBI) likes to do things for Sandy [Smith]."[42] Assisting Billings was *Life* stringer David Chandler, a close friend of Clay Shaw. Just month's earlier Chandler had written that Garrison was "an incorruptible crusader for justice" in the November 1966 issue of New Orleans. Chandler, coincidentally, moved into the New Orleans apartment of Ruth Kloepfer, a Quaker, who after being contacted by Ruth Paine, visited Marina a number of times. Billings and Chandler wrote,

> The well-known New Orleans District Attorney was the guest of Marcello mobster Mario Marino at a Las Vegas hotel. Garrison denies knowledge of Marino's connection with Marcello ... Garrison knows Marcello's bookmaking brother Sammy – but denies knowing he is a bookie. Three times since 1963 Sammy has paid Garrison's hotel bill.... On his last visit in March the tab was signed by Marino himself. Garrison was also rated a $5000 credit. Garrison con-

tends that he didn't gamble and that Marino gave him the credit so he could cash checks.... He is unable, he told Life, "to see anything wrong with a prosecutor freeloading at a mob-controlled casino... "

The wide-ranging critiques of Garrison's investigation seemed to have peaked by late summer of 1967, but his credibility already had been significantly tarnished. Garrison's impatience and inexperience with the mass media hurt his credibility as well. He was an uneven public speaker, sometimes ponderous and unfocused. His case could not be recapped in sound bytes.

Reporter and former FBI agent William Turner recounted that once, after working all night, Garrison was confronted by a group of aggressive reporters pushing to be updated on his progress. "When are the arrests going to be made?" Garrison reiterated past statements by noting, "Of course there will be arrests." A reporter then asked, "You mean you've solved the case?" Garrison retorted, "Of course. We solved it weeks ago in its essentials." The New Orleans newspaper ran the caption, "Case Solved Says Garrison," and the wire services ran this story. Although Garrison knew far more than he could prove, his sobering speculation along with fragmentary evidence contributed to the confusion.

In another instance Garrison poetically avowed to reporters that, "The key to the whole case is through the looking-glass. Black is white, white is black. I don't want to be cryptic, but that's the way it is." Some media outlets claimed that the case was like Alice in Wonderland, missing the metaphoric description of an intelligence operation.[43]

Reporter Peter Noyes found Garrison's lack of clarity a source of frustration. His statements regarding the complicity of mobster Eugene Hale Brading plotting with Shaw, Ferrie and Oswald seemed vague. The indictment claimed that a meeting among these four suspects occurred in New Orleans sometime in the middle of September 1963. Noyes thought the witnesses should know the exact date of the conspiracy. Developing the Brading connection was rendered impossible since California Governor Ronald Reagan refused to extradite him to stand trial.

Look's editor-in-chief, William Attwood, formerly the secret liaison to Cuba under JFK, met with Garrison and was impressed with the case. Attwood urged Bobby Kennedy to so something and mentioned that Look was going to report on the investigation. Soon thereafter, Attwood suffered a heart attack, and when he returned to work three months later, Look had decided that it had other priorities.

CIA defensive strategies were revised in a late September 1967 memo, which outlined two main courses of action. First get sympathetic members of Congress, and/or the Executive branch to attack Garrison and support the Warren Report. The second strategy was to use the media, both at home and abroad, to smear the DA.

To prepare for the trial of Clay Shaw the CIA memo stated, "it would be prudent to have carefully selected channels of communication lined up in advance." It suggests that CIA Director Richard Helms should "assure that the newspaper outlets receive a coherent picture of Garrison's 'facts' and 'motives.'" The memo also suggests using the United States Information Agency (USIA) for foreign media and urges Helms to ensure their cooperation through Secretary of State Dean Rusk. A week later, Donovan Pratt (of CIA Director of Counterintelligence James Angleton's staff) was suggesting specific "story lines" for press contacts to use.[44]

Garrison found the mass media reporting of his statements to be often inept and biased. Years later he lamented that his public statements got twisted so often that he stopped speaking to the press. This self-censorship contributed to even less accurate and less favorable coverage. A Harris poll showed a marked decline in confidence that Garrison would "shed light on the JFK death" – from 45% in March 1967 to 32% in September 1967.

Bill Turner's piece in *Ramparts* (9/67), "The Press verses Garrison," critiqued the CBS and NBC specials as "designed to revitalize the sagging public confidence in the Warren Report. Turner lamented that the half hour interviews with Mark Lane and himself were both cut to one minute segments.... Meanwhile, a string of handpicked witnesses and "experts" were heard from." He recounted Garrison's top volunteer, William Gurvich, defecting to speak with Walter Sheridan, as well as the NBC threats to Garrison witness Perry Russo.

Garrison's most compelling public statement appeared in the October 1967 *Playboy*. Although limited in his pre-trial comments by Judge Haggarty, Garrison explored Oswald's ties with CIA agents, the CIA manipulation of the Warren Commission, and the CIA threat to democracy. The CIA memorandum 10/3/67 regarding this article remains partly redacted. He colorfully declared:

> In over five years of office, I have never had a single case reversed
> because of improper methods, a record I'll match with any D.A.
> in the country. I only wish the press would allow our case to stand

or fall on its merits in court. It appears that certain elements of the mass media have an active interest in preventing this case from ever coming to trial at all and find it necessary to employ against me every smear device in the book. To read the press accounts my investigation, my "circus," I should say, I'm a cross between Al Capone and Attila the Hun, ruthlessly hounding innocent men, trampling their legal rights, bribing and threatening witnesses and in general violating every canon of legal ethics. My God, anybody who employs the kind of methods that elements of the media attribute to me should not only not be a district attorney, he should be disbarred. This case has taught me the power of the mythmakers.

Playboy confronted Garrison about allegations on NBC's special "The J.F.K Conspiracy: The Case of Jim Garrison." NBC reporter Frank McGee claimed that NBC investigators had discovered that two key witnesses against Clay Shaw, Perry Russo and Vernon Bundy, both failed polygraph tests prior to their testimony to the grand jury. Garrison defiantly challenged NBC:

> NBC's allegations in this area are about as credible as its other charges. The men who administered both polygraph tests flatly deny that Russo and Bundy failed the test.... I want to make a proposition to the president of NBC: If this charge is true, then I will resign as district attorney of New Orleans. If it's untrue, then the president of NBC should resign. Just in case he thinks I'm kidding, I'm ready to meet with him at any time to select a mutually acceptable committee to determine once and for all the truth and falsehood of this charge.

Garrison probed some of the procedures of the Dallas police:

> At 12:45 p.m. on November 22nd, the Dallas police had broadcast a wanted bulletin for Oswald, over a half hour before Tippit was shot and at a time when there was absolutely no evidence linking Oswald to the assassination. The Dallas police have never been able to explain who transmitted this wanted notice or on what evidence it was based; and the Warren Commission brushed aside the whole matter as unimportant...
>
> As I said earlier, the evidence we've uncovered leads us to suspect that two men, neither of whom was Oswald, were the real murderers of Tippit.... The critics of the Warren Report have pointed out that a number of witnesses could not identify Oswald

as the slayer, that several said the murderer was short and squat, Oswald was thin and medium height, another said that two men were involved. [Beyond the time factor.] The clincher ... is that four cartridges were found at the scene of the slaying. Now, revolvers do not eject cartridges, so when someone is shot, you don't find gratuitous cartridges strewn over the sidewalk, unless the murderer deliberately takes the trouble to eject them. We suspect that cartridges had been previously obtained from Oswald's .38 revolver and left at the murder site by the real killers as part of the setup to incriminate Oswald. However, somebody slipped up there. Of the four cartridges found at the scene, two were Winchesters and two were Remington's, but of the four bullets found in Officer Tippit's body, three were Winchesters and one was a Remington!

Jack Ruby died of cancer a few weeks after his conviction for murder had been overruled in appeals court and he was ordered to stand trial outside of Dallas, thus allowing him to speak freely if he so desired.

What worries me deeply, and I have seen it exemplified in this case, is that we in America are in great danger of slowly evolving into a proto-fascist state.... Its origins can be traced in the tremendous war machine we've built since 1945, the military industrial complex that Eisenhower vainly warned us about ... In a very real and terrifying sense, our Government is the CIA and the Pentagon, with Congress reduced to a debating society. Of course, you can't spot this trend of fascism by casually looking around ... the clever manipulation of the mass media is creating a concentration camp of the mind that promises to be far more effective in keeping the populace in line.... The test is what happens to the individual who dissents?

A number of the men who killed the President were former employees of the CIA involved in its anti-Castro underground activities in and around New Orleans. The CIA knows their identity. So do I...

We must assume that the plotters were acting on their own rather than on CIA orders when they killed the President. As far as we have been able to determine, they were not in the pay of the CIA at the time of the Kennedy assassination.

The CIA could not face up to the American people and admit that its former employees had conspired to assassinate the president, so from the moment Kennedy's heart stopped beating the agency attempted to sweep the whole conspiracy under the rug ... it has become an accessory after the fact in the assassination.

The *New York Times* 9/11/67, review of the *Playboy* interview, not its usual grist for the mill, merely noted that Garrison expanded on earlier charges that CIA ex-aides were involved in the assassination. "Garrison rose to at least 7 the number of men he says took direct part in the killing of President Kennedy.... Garrison says the plotters were disturbed by Kennedy's peace overtures to Cuba."

Garrison's efforts generated a response from the Justice Dept. U.S. Attorney General Ramsey Clark said (10/13/67) "he might have to prosecute Garrison" for accusing him of ruining prominent businessman Clay Shaw.

In November Jim Garrison spoke to the L.A Press Club, though only The *L.A. Free Press* (The Freep), an independent weekly, printed much of his scathing statement. (11/17/67) He declared a "Fascist cover-up" was continued by constant government lies, destruction of evidence and "blowing up the case." Garrison challenged the "apathetic" American press to ask as many questions of the government as they had asked about him. Revealing their ties to Dallas officer Joe Cody, Garrison developed the links between Ruby, Oswald, and the Dallas Police. He clarified Oswald's Armed Forces Russian Test, P.R.T. 21, indicating military training. He closed by pleading to the press "If you ever wished for an opportunity to do something for your profession and do something for your country, then you have such an opportunity ... if you can only get interested ... Your country needs you now, as it never has before." Few media outlets rose to the challenge.

The *L.A. Free Press* 11/24/67 also published Raymond Marcus's work on the Mary Moorman photo of the grassy knoll at the time of the fatal assassination shot. Marcus noted that the Warren Commission neither interviewed Moorman nor presented her photo as evidence. He showed blowups of the picture to professional photographers, and asked if they saw the outline of a man holding a rifle. Many did.

By early December 1967 *The Saturday Evening Post* shifted its stand on the assassination in its review of *Six Seconds in Dallas*, written by philosophy professor Josiah Thompson. Its editorial called for a new investigation stating it had now been "demonstrated fairly conclusively that the Warren Commission was wrong."

A brief book review in *The New Republic*, "Return to Dallas" by Alexander Bickel, 12/23/67, surmised the social costs of continued national denial, "it would be a devastating commentary on the American spirit if we were all content to let the matter rest ... the Warren Commission ... failed to satisfactorily establish the central facts about the awful event."

Bickel found *Accessories After the Fact* by Sylvia Meagher to be "indiscriminate and unfocused" though he had praised her "welcome" index, published in 1966. Josiah Thompson's *Six Seconds in Dallas* was viewed as "pretentious" but useful in carefully exploring the possibility of a frontal shot by analyzing the Zapruder film. Bickel concluded that testimonial evidence had gone stale but "physical evidence is as good as ever" and this could be "fruitfully reinvestigated even now.... The attempt should, however, be made by another official body, for the Warren Commission did not try hard enough." *Life* magazine then exercised its proprietary rights to own American history. *Life* sued its former reporter Josiah Thompson, his publisher Random House, and Bernard Geis Associates, to stop the distribution and sale of his book. *Life* alleged that its copyright of pictures from the Zapruder film had been violated, and that the film had been "stolen" by Thompson at the instigation of Bernard Geis. The court determined that *Life* could not claim financial damage since Thompson offered all of the profits to *Life*. So *Six Seconds in Dallas* was published without the photographic evidence, using instead charcoal drawings of the different frames of the Zapruder film, thus giving America its first view of this compelling evidence.

Soon thereafter *Life* scuttled their investigation of the assassination that they had assigned to editor Richard Billings. Notably, Billings worked with Holland McCombs, formerly of the Office of Naval Intelligence, and a friend of Clay Shaw. Photo researcher Richard Sprague, who was working with Billings, asserted that the *Life* team was ordered to stop all work on the story. "All of the research files, including the Zapruder film and slides, and thousands of film frames and photographs, were locked up tight." Billings resigned claiming that he was outraged.[45]

Two Dallas newspapers may have suppressed potentially significant photo and video evidence. Researcher Richard Sprague asserts that the *Dallas Morning News* in late 1967 locked up a picture taken by its photographer Jack Beers which showed cartons on the sixth floor "snipers nest" before the Dallas police moved them, and that the *Dallas Times Herald* pictures taken by their photographer Bob Jackson of the TSBD 6th floor at the time of the assassination, which could have indicated no one in the "snipers nest," were locked in DTH files in 1968.[46]

At a press conference in December 1967 Jim Garrison revealed that the FBI had prior knowledge of the assassination attempt. Former FBI security clerk William Walter said that he received a TWX (now Telex) message November 17th, which was directed to all southern regional offices of the FBI regarding the attempt to assassinate President Kennedy. Another TWX came in a few hours later, countermanding the first one. After the assassination, agents "were ordered to resolve the conflicts with the new reports and to destroy old ones."

The FBI stonewalled the press on this matter. Perhaps not coincidentally, three days later *Chicago Tribune* reporter Russell Freiburg questioned Garrison's mental capacity. Freiburg was somehow given Garrison's leaked Army 201 file, which he misreported. When confronted by ex-FBI agent William Turner as to J. Edgar Hoover being the source of the 201 file, Freiburg did not categorically deny it.

Coverage of the Garrison investigation in *The New Republic* abruptly changed from support in June 1967 to a vicious condemnation in March 1969. Possibly the 1968 appointment of former high ranking CIA agent Robert Myers to the position of publisher explains this reversal. Myers' career took him from army intelligence to 12 years with the CIA, where for a while he was an aide to William Colby, who later directed the CIA.

Their March 1969 editorial condemned Garrison as "paranoid," and "potentially the most dangerous demagogue since Huey Long." While conceding that Garrison made some points, *The New Republic* claimed that they were not new, and did not develop them.

During the Shaw trial "reporters" James Phelan and Hugh Aynesworth abandoned all guise of being journalists. Phelan appeared as a witness for the defense. Aynesworth helped Shaw's attorneys by sandbagging the prosecution, obtaining its witness list, and then running background checks to provide information for the defense.[47]

Drew Pearson, an eminent syndicated columnist who had worked with Jack Anderson, took some of his leads to Chief Justice Earl Warren in 1967. According to revelations from the 1976 Schweiker-Hart Report (Senate Intelligence Subcommittee), Drew Pearson conferred with the Chief Justice about the Roselli-Maheu story regarding CIA-Mafia efforts to assassinate Castro. The Secret Service was then alerted, as was the FBI, although neither agency followed the new leads. Pearson's actions can perhaps be clarified by reviewing Commission Document 990, which had been suppressed for twelve years. Previously, Pearson had worked with the CIA as a reporter to "interview" Khrushchev regarding his response to President Kennedy's assassination.[48]

By late 1967, Senator Robert Kennedy was quietly inquiring about Garrison's investigation. In November of 1967 Mark Lane asserted on the *John Hightower Show*, WFAN-TV, Washington, and later in the *New*

York Free Press, that "over a period of several weeks, two different emissaries had arrived in New Orleans.... Each had sought out Jim Garrison.... Each stated that he was carrying a message from Robert Kennedy.... Each was known by Garrison to be associated with Kennedy.... Each said that Robert Kennedy did not believe the conclusion of the Warren Commission and agreed with Garrison that a conspiracy had taken the life of his brother." According to comedian Mort Sahl, who was actively researching and publicly speaking about the case, the message from Bobby Kennedy was "I must wait until I reach the White House ... [to] get the guys who killed Jack." Garrison's response was that RFK's only chance was to speak out about the conspiracy, which could delay his enemies from attacking him. RFK's circle disagreed. Also, conceivably Garrison could uncover and reveal RFK's role with the CIA's violent anti-Castro Cubans, and even of RFK's knowledge of Oswald. This could prove devastating politically and personally. This might also explain RFK's apparent silence to the "reporting" of his old friend Robert Sheridan.

The day after Christmas 1967, Garrison and Turner appeared at a press conference in the Monteleone Hotel to announce a forthcoming article for *Ramparts*. Turner returned to his room after the press conference to get some documents but the door had been jammed shut, someone had pushed a chair under the inside doorknob. Through a crack in the door Turner could see a man in a business suit climbing out onto the fire escape. He told chief D.A. investigator Lou Ivon, "We must be getting close ... someone out there wants very badly to know what we know."

Pacifica Radio, 12/29/67, ran an hour-long interview with Josiah Thompson, soon after his book *Six Seconds in Dallas* had been published. Thompson carefully analyzed trajectories, wounds, ballistics to present a compelling case for conspiracy and cover-up. Further, he declared that the assassination was in fact a coup d'état, but that "evidence did not yet support this."[49]

In January 1968 *Ramparts* ran an extensive expose by William Turner, "The Garrison Commission on the Assassination of President Kennedy," which expanded Garrison's *Playboy* interview. Again the alternative media significantly deepened the inquiry, and this piece foreshadowed portions of the movie *JFK*. Garrison was finally humanized as insightfully pragmatic, patriotic, and professional. Progress on reporting the case included: Guy Banister's links to the CIA, Clay Shaw and the ONI (Office of Naval Intelligence) and CIA; Gordon Novel's activities for the CIA; clarification regarding Oswald's statements during a New Orleans radio interview 8/21/63; Oswald's interest in Soviet military deployment as well as "microdots" and spy cameras; connections between Oswald and Clay Shaw; inconsistencies regarding the bullets in the Tippit killing; Rose Cheramie's statements warning of a pending assassination of President Kennedy; Ruby's links to certain Dallas policemen including Dallas Police Department's Joe Cody, who escorted Oswald; the two honks in the Dallas Police Department headquarters prior to Ruby shooting Oswald; as well as Jules Kimble's statement connecting Ruby to the right-wing Minutemen.

By January 1968 it appears that archival files denied to researcher Harold Weisberg were eagerly released to Fred Graham of the *New York Times*. Graham's piece in the *Times* 1/6/68 incorrectly placed responsibility for the suppression of the photographic evidence of the autopsy on the Kennedy clan. In 1972 Graham told Weisberg that the Assistant Archivist Dr. James Rhoads had begged him to request that material through the F.O.I.A.[50]

NBC invited Jim Garrison to appear on *The Tonight Show Starring Johnny Carson* on 1/31/68, based on an overwhelming audience reaction to a Mort Sahl suggestion on one of his previous shows. Bobby Kennedy tried to get Carson to withdraw the invitation. "CNN political reporter Jeff Greenfield, who was a young aide at the time, remembers walking into his Senate office and overhearing Bobby Kennedy on the phone. He was telling Carson that Garrison was full of crap.... Don't believe him, if I thought there was anything to this, I would have done something.[51]

The afternoon of his appearance though, NBC attorneys questioned Garrison for several hours in Carson's offices. On stage Garrison saw that Carson had cards which recorded his answers with responses inserted, hardly an open discussion. During the show, when Garrison tried to show a picture of the three "tramps" being marched off by Dallas police immediately following the assassination, Carson lunged to pull down Garrison's arm. After disagreeing about whether the pictures would show up on television, Carson again yanked down Garrison's arm. At this point, the director of the show turned off the cameras. Carson had inadvertently meandered into the ongoing NBC fight with Garrison.[52]

The *L.A. Free Press*, 2/9/68, presented the interview in its entirety. Garrison summed up the heated and bitter exchange by declaring, "I'm trying to tell the people of America that the honor of the country is at stake. And if we don't do something about this fraud, we will not survive."

Garrison also faced the loss of a considerable number of his case files. William Wood, a Garrison investigator, admitted that he had worked with the OSS. He worked previously as a journalist for various newspapers, and in 1967 applied to work for the CIA. According to CIA records he was turned down and soon thereafter worked for Garrison. When the staff became suspicious of Wood toting an oversized briefcase, Garrison asked to meet Wood at Garrison's home. Wood never showed up. Garrison then visited Wood's rented apartment and found out from his landlady that he had never stayed at the apartment.[53]

Playboy February 1968 ran strongly supportive reviews of Sylvia Meagher's book *Accessories After The Fact* and Josiah Thompson's *Six Seconds in Dallas. Playboy* saw Meagher's book as "the best of the crop of books and the most chilling in its implications." Both books clarified "the failure of the Warren Commission to investigate, evaluate – or even acknowledge – the huge body of evidence in its possession indicating the possible presence of more than one gunman … [and] lend weight to widening appeals by Congressmen and the press for an independent new investigation."

Fred Graham's *New York Times Book Review*, 2/28/68, of *Six Seconds in Dallas* and *Accessories After the Fact* found it "astonishing" that there was such disbelief "in a document that has the endorsement of some of the highest officials in government." Graham avowed that "despite the fact that embarrassing gaffes by the Commission and inconsistencies in the evidence have been pointed out, none of the critics have been able to suggest any other explanation which fits the facts better than the Warren Commission's."

Capital City broadcasting, owners of several radio stations, in 1968 had a producer Erik Lindquist, who wanted to do a series of programs on the assassination of President Kennedy. However, after several months of work the project was canceled, presumably by upper level management.

Another New Orleans reporter, Sam DePino of WVUE-TV, fed information to both the FBI and CIA on the Garrison probe. The CIA's Lloyd Ray noted in a memo that DePino was offering information to the CIA. Ray then discussed DePino with the FBI, who confirmed that DePino had talked to the FBI on many occasions, and was considered "an eager beaver."

After the assassination of Martin Luther King, reporter William Turner wrote in *Ramparts* about parallels with the JFK assassination. Rifles conveniently left at the crime scene were easily traceable to men with aliases. Immediately police radio reports emanated from unknown sources, they described Oswald, and in the MLK assassination a white Mustang getaway car in what is now known to be a non-existent "police chase." Purported maps surfaced in Oswald's possessions with circled points on the parade routes and one was found in "Galt's" (James Earl Ray's alias) car. The FBI also determined that since August 1967 (Ray) had spent about $10,000, although no source of income was known. Turner admonished that, "Congress has shown little inclination to take on such a controversial and politically loaded task, and the citizen's committee might serve as an interim force until public opinion compels Congress to act."

The Saturday Evening Post, 4/6/68, in "Secret Evidence on the Kennedy Assassination" by David Wise, defended the Warren Commission, findings, while blaming the suppression of evidence on Earl Warren. Oswald was portrayed as possibly a KGB operative who might have revealed radar information leading to the first Soviet shoot-down of Gary Powers U-2 spy plane; this incident led to the canceling of the U.S.-Soviet Summit. Powers claimed in his book *Operation Over-flight* that Oswald's information allowed the Soviets to down the U-2.

The National Archives somehow estimated that 25,000 pages of Warren Commission files remained classified, and a sampling of the Chief Archivists estimated that "very little would be closed by 1975." According to author and researcher Harold Weisberg, Assistant National Archivist James Rhoads declassified benign intelligence documents exclusively to Wise.

Wise reviewed the declassified transcripts of 11 commission meetings and highlighted: The timing of an interview with Jackie Kennedy; whether the FBI report could be turned over to the CIA; avoiding a subpoena from Ruby's lawyers; the agreed upon suppression of the autopsy photos from the public record, although Chief Counsel Rankin and Warren could view them. Wise noted that CD 931, Helms' memo to Hoover on "Lee Harvey Oswald's access to classified information about the U-2," remains classified.

The memos regarding Oswald in Mexico City remained classified. Chief of Archives, Dr. Robert Bahmer, asserted that nothing in the sealed files "from what I know of the records," would contradict the Warren Report's conclusions. Wise admonished that as long as 20% of the Commission's files remain locked in the Archives, doubts will continue to multiply. The vagueness of classification standards was not questioned. Attorney General Nicholas Katzenbach was viewed as proactive, submitting guidelines for declassification on 1/28/65. The Warren files were to remain closed: when existing law required it; when national security is involved; when disclosure might "be a source of embarrassment to innocent persons."

The CIA was aggressive in distributing anti-Garrison articles. *The New Yorker* magazine, 7/13/68, ran a fiercely anti-Garrison tract by Ed Epstein. Epstein had worked closely with CIA counterintelligence Chief James Angleton for *Inquest*, his book on the Warren Commission. A subsequent CIA memo to Chiefs of Staff worldwide cautioned against attacking Garrison personally but provided them with Epstein's article to "use the article to brief interested contacts."[54]

Garrison had doubted Epstein's credibility but accommodated him for the article. Epstein spent two days in New Orleans but only three hours at Garrison's office. According to former FBI man Bill Turner, Garrison was heartbroken when the piece was printed. Turner responded in *Ramparts*, 9/7/68, where he quoted author Richard Popkin's reactions to Epstein's tract:

> I found it a queer mix of facts, rumors, and very dubious information from people hostile to Garrison. Epstein has compressed all of this to make it look like everything's on the same level. I think it will take a lot of work to disentangle what he's saying…

Turner learned that Clay Shaw's attorneys later entered Epstein's piece as evidence. Epstein was also in regular contact with the lawyers for Shaw, Gordon Novel and Jack Ruby.

Nationally, the violence at the Democratic Convention in Chicago by the police and the National Guard, which targeted photographers, journalists and cameramen, served to deepen both government and media caution.

Toward the end of 1968 Garrison tried to legally secure the release of the photos and x-rays. The Justice Dept. under Attorney General Ramsey Clark tried to block this action by releasing a report by a panel of forensic pathologists who had examined the photos and x-rays a year earlier – confirming the medical findings of the Warren Commission. Fred Graham's supportive coverage of the Panel Report for the *New York Times* ran on page 1, 1/17/69. But the Panel Report raised new and troubling questions. The Clark Panel Report differed from the original autopsy report and the Warren Commission testimony regarding the autopsy surgeons – and the fatal head wound had mysteriously moved up about four inches. Researcher Sylvia Meagher brought this to Graham's attention, but no follow-up story was written.[55]

The *New York Times* coverage of the Shaw trial (2/25/69), as with most of the mass media, buried the lead. Colonel Pierre Finck, an Army pathologist, who assisted with the autopsy of President Kennedy, testified that he had been ordered by one of the generals or admirals at the autopsy to not dissect the President's neck. This appeared on page 18, six paragraphs into the piece, which was headlined "Kennedy Autopsy Doctor Tells Shaw Jury Shots Came from Rear.'" Dr. Finck testified that he was told that the President's family wanted no examination of the neck organs. Finck also testified that the autopsy would not meet the standards of the American Board of Pathologists, since it omitted a study of a number of the President's organs.

The two most reliable mainstream sources for covering the Clay Shaw case were the *New Orleans Times-Picayune* and the *New Orleans States-Item*. Off the record, the reporters at both newspapers supported Garrison's investigation, as seen in *Plot or Politics* by two reporters, Rosemary James and Jack Wardlaw. The average New Orleans citizen was aware of far more than the rest of the country. They had heard of: the justice department delays; CIA payments to Shaw's lawyers; the FBI search for Shaw under his alias Clay Bertrand even before Dean Andrews mentioned it; that twelve people saw Shaw, Ferrie, and Oswald together on many occasions; and Colonel Pierre Finck's testimony that during the autopsy he was ordered by an unidentified general not to probe the president's neck wound. It was only after the final verdict that the papers savagely attacked Garrison in their editorial pages.

The mass media reaction to Garrison's prosecution of Clay Shaw was generally to overlook the many pearls amid the slime. The *New York Times* accused Garrison of the "prosecution of an innocent man" and called the case "one of the most disgraceful chapters in the history of American jurisprudence" (3/2/69). Reporter Sydney Zion claimed that Garrison "restored the credibility of the Warren Report." The *New Orleans States-Item*, 3/1/69, demanded that Garrison resign; "...[He was] a man without principle who would pervert the legal process to his own ends."

Look published a piece by Warren Rogers, "The Persecution of Clay Shaw," which attacked Garrison for his venality and mafia connections. Years later the public would find out from FBI Counterintelligence Chief William Sullivan's book that Rogers routinely cooperated with the FBI.

Newsweek, 3/10/69, relegated the case to two derisive sentences in "TRIALS: FACT AND OPINION":

Acquitted: By a jury in New Orleans, exactly two years to the day after his arrest on charges of conspiracy to murder John F. Kennedy, retired Louisiana businessman Clay Shaw, 55.

Convicted: In a case that collapsed at every seam, District Attorney, Jim Garrison, 47, of incompetence and irresponsibility as a public official.

The cumulative impact on Garrison's case of federal non-cooperation, FBI spying, files mysteriously disappearing, the loss of key witnesses, FBI and CIA media manipulation and significant aid to the defense team, all tarnished Garrison's image and gutted the case. The leads and implications were startling, but by the time the case got to trial the evidence was fragmentary. The courageous gamble by the out-manned D.A. unearthed vital aspects of the assassination, however, the rapid acquittal of Shaw provided the basis for a mass media response that Garrison lacked a case, and that the Warren Report may have been right. Some reporters and editors knew that promising leads were generated but the political turmoil of the Vietnam War, race relations and cultural change competed for coverage. Citizen researchers emerged divided, with their reputations and momentum diminished. The investigation languished in the media for two more years before even the alternative press would clarify the new information and outline a critical case.

In the spring of 1969 some journalists finally critiqued Jim Phelan and Hugh Aynesworth for their roles as participants and biased observers. Roger Williams from *Time* and Michael Parks from the *Baltimore Sun* wrote in the *Columbia Journalism Review*:

Jim Phelan and Hugh Aynesworth, both fiercely anti-Garrison, became in effect special advisors to the defense. They consulted frequently with Shaw's attorneys, passing along tips.... The two of them, says chief defense attorney F. Irvin Dymond, were "extremely valuable" to the defense case ... Aynesworth could have chosen between his twin functions of reporter and participant ... *Newsweek's* editors should have made the choice for him, to protect their own interests and the interests of the readers.

What *Newsweek* editors knew of Aynesworth's intelligence connections remains unclear.

The next *New York Times* story, 4/20/69, bolstering the Warren Report, was a bitter attack from Edward Epstein, "The Final Chapter in the

Assassination Controversy." He impugned the motives and integrity of the critics, asserting that many of them had been "demonologists" with "books as well as conspiracies to advertise." He neglected, however, to mention his own past reliance on CIA Counterintelligence Chief James Angleton.

Epstein discussed the single-bullet theory by citing a 1967 CBS inquiry, which had theorized that three jiggles in Zapruder's files represented reactions by Zapruder to the sound of shots, thus allowing the determination of the timing of the shots. CBS had speculated that the first shot had been fired earlier than the Commission had reasoned likely – at the point where the presidential limousine would have been briefly visible (1/10 second) from the sixth-floor window through the foliage of a large oak tree. "In other words, the President and Governor could have been hit by separate bullets by a single assassin. The CBS analysis which persuasively argues that this was the case renders the single-bullet theory irrelevant." CBS however, ignored the fact that there were several jiggles in the Zapruder film and five not three, in the frame sequence in question. *Life* magazine, which owned the original Zapruder film, rejected the "jiggle theory," attributing all but the most pronounced jiggle that coincided with the headshot, to imperfections in the camera mechanism. Moreover, CBS did not allege an earlier hit, but an earlier miss. Epstein misrepresented its conclusions. CBS had recognized that an earlier hit meant a steeper trajectory which precluded the throat wound being one of exit and which again implied a fraudulent autopsy report. Epstein dismissed the head movement on the Zapruder film by citing a Justice Department Report in which a panel of forensic pathologists who had studied the sequestered autopsy photos and X-rays had supported the Warren Report. The Clark Panel Report (so-called, after Attorney General Ramsey Clark) however, revealed glaring differences between its findings and the original autopsy such that serious doubts had been raised as to whether the Panel had seen the "genuine" material.

When critical authors Sylvia Meagher and Harold Weisberg proposed responses in letter or article form, The *New York Times* rejected them. Ostensibly due to space limitations, they ran only the response from Josiah Thompson.[56]

Ironically, in September 1969 it was former President Johnson who nearly revealed a useful perspective about the case. In an interview for CBS-TV Johnson remarked, "I don't think that they [the Warren Commission], or me, or anyone else is absolutely sure of everything that might have motivated Oswald or others that could have been involved. But he was quite a mysterious fellow, and he did have connections which bore examination." Although this seems a modest understatement, Johnson felt he had said too much, and he asked CBS to withhold this section of the interview on the grounds of "national security." Although the CBS news department wanted to run this story, the CBS management obliged, and suppressed those statements until 1975.[57]

Remarkably, in 1969 Nicholas Johnson, a member of the Federal Communication Commission, bluntly declared that: "The networks in particular … are probably now beyond the check of any institution in our society. The President, the Congress of the United States, the FCC, the foundations, and universities are reluctant even to get involved. I think that they may now be so powerful that they're beyond the check of anyone."[58]

By 1969 America was convulsed and bitterly divided over the Vietnam War. Chaotic race relations, as well as the cynicism surrounding the assassinations of Martin Luther King and Robert Kennedy, amplified anti-government sentiment. The tumultuous times strengthened an already strong rationale for national security for the FBI and CIA to influence the press to dampen the public dissent. Those in power could easily imagine how strongly the country might have reacted to a fair reporting of Garrison's investigation and its implications.

In January 1970 Senator Richard Russell granted an interview to Cox Television to discuss the Warren Report. Russell declared that he "never believed that Lee Harvey Oswald assassinated President Kennedy without at least some encouragement from others … that's what a majority of the committee wanted to find. I think someone else worked with him…"

The *New York Times* book reviews by John Leonard, 12/1/70, on books critical of the Warren Report illustrate their continuing policy. Between the early and late editions the title of the review changed from "Who Killed John F. Kennedy?" to "The Shaw-Garrison Affair." A paragraph headed "Mysteries Persist" was cut, along with the last 30 lines of the review, which were critical of the Warren Report. This portion includes:

> Frankly I prefer to believe that the Warren Commission did a poor job, rather than a dishonest one. I like to think that Mr. Garrison invents monsters to explain incompetence. But until somebody explains why two autopsies came to different conclusions about the President's wounds, why the limousine was washed out and rebuilt without investigation, why certain witnesses near the "grassy

knoll" were never asked to testify by the Warren Commission, why we were all so eager to buy Oswald's brilliant marksmanship in split seconds, why no one inquired into Jack Ruby's relations with a staggering variety of strange people, why a "loner" like Oswald always had friends and could always get a passport - who can blame the Garrison guerrillas for fantasizing?

Something stinks about the whole affair, *A Heritage of Stone* rehashes the smelliness; the recipe as unappetizing as our doubts about the official version of what happened. Would then – Attorney General Robert Kennedy have endured his brother's murder in silence? Was John Kennedy quite so liberated from the cold war clichés as Mr. Garrison maintains? But the stench is there and it clings to each of us. Why were Kennedy's neck organs not examined at Bethesda for evidence of a fatal shot? Why was his body whisked away to Washington before the legally required Texas inquest?

Apparently the *New York Times* did not deem this as "all the news that's fit to print." John Leonard was told that a "night editor" felt it [the review] was overly editorial. Leonard was upset and attempted to determine the source of the editing – yet he was never able to find out. Leonard remarked once to researcher Jerry Policoff in his new position as a book reviewer for the *Sunday Times* that new books on the JFK assassination were already pre-assigned to others, sometimes to David Belin, Warren Commission counsel, or to Priscilla Johnson McMillan.

In January of 1971, popular maverick columnist Jack Anderson revised his earlier reporting regarding his Cuban retaliation theory for the assassination. He clarified the CIA-Mafia assassination plots against Castro, which ostensively prompted the highly risky Cuban response. (1/17 and 1/18) Anderson's February column about Roselli, from confidential FBI files, identified him as "a top mafia figure" who "handled undercover assignments for the CIA." Roselli's lawyers were now "trying to get clemency for their client." Anderson also mentioned ex-CIA officer William Harvey and CIA contract agent Robert Maheu, the liaison on the CIA-mafia plots of 1960 (plots involving Nixon but not Kennedy). This column "caused a flurry of investigative memos inside the Nixon White House including a warning from one of the White House dirty tricks operatives, Jack Caulfield, that Maheu's covert activities ... with CIA ... might well shake loose Republican skeletons from the closet" (P.D. Scott *The Assassinations*, p. 375). According to journalist Anthony Summers, Attorney General John Mitchell arranged a deal with Maheu that if he stayed quiet on "the entire Castro story," he would not have to testify before a grand jury on a Las Vegas gambling prosecution. [59]

Senate Watergate Committee staffers later concluded that White House concern about Anderson's story "could have been a possible motivation for the Watergate break-in to the office of the DNC"[60]

Anderson then got targeted by Nixon's Plumbers Unit, "supposedly to plug leaks." G. Gordon Liddy and E. Howard Hunt later confessed during the Watergate hearings that they met with a CIA operative in 1972 to consider poisoning, drugging or killing Anderson.[61]

Meanwhile, CBS boldly reported on Pentagon public relations in their documentary "The Selling of the Pentagon." (2/23/71). The Congressional reaction deepened mass media caution on national security issues. Following its airing, a Special Investigations Subcommittee of the House of Representatives Interstate and Foreign Commerce Committee announced that they would investigate CBS News and the documentary. The committee feared the growing power of the press and subpoenaed the outtakes of the documentary to determine bias. CBS President Frank Stanton refused, calling this an "assault by Congress on the independence of editorial judgment." The FCC backed CBS. The Committee then pushed for a Congressional vote on contempt of Congress. Although Congress voted that CBS was not in contempt, a chilling message was sent.

After an extended media silence on the JFK assassination, Fred Cook in "The Irregulars Take the Field" reassessed the status of assassination investigations in *The Nation*, 7/19/71. Cook broke new ground on the cases of both President Kennedy and Martin Luther King, Jr., and summarized Congressional caution and citizen activism.

He praised the efforts of Bud Fensterwald, researcher and former Senate Administrative Aide, who revealed senatorial constraints.

> I tried to interest some of these men in the Senate, many of them good friends of mine, in doing something about the Warren Report. I got no response at all, largely, I think, for two reasons: the great regard a lot of these men had for Chief Justice Earl Warren, and the fact that other distinguished members of Congress, like Senator Richard Russell of Georgia, had their reputations on the line – and so nobody wanted to mess with the case.
>
> I talked to Senator Long about it. I'm sure that he, like many of the others, didn't believe the Warren Report, but he didn't think anything could be done about it and he thought that politically it

was suicidal. He was sympathetic to what I was trying to do, but that was it.

Cook clarified the material from the former Miami Chief of Police, Walter Headley, Jr., regarding the tape-recorded assassination threat from Minuteman Joseph Milteer, which was not included in the Warren Report. He summarized the key points from Dallas Police Chief Jesse Curry's book *JFK Assassination File*:

> 1. A paraffin test taken of the right side of Oswald's face did not reveal any nitrates from having fired a rifle ...
>
> 2. Howard Brennan, the Warren Commissions star witness gave testimony to FBI agents, which apparently changed from month to month.
>
> 3. Eyewitnesses who reported seeing Dallas police interview two men on the 6th floor of the depository, turned over to the FBI and No statement about the second man or mention of an accomplice was in the FBI report.
>
> 4. We don't have any proof that Oswald fired the rifle. No one has been able to positively put him in that building with a gun in his hand.

Cook then reviewed the discrepancies between the Secret Service rulebook and Secret Service practices in Dallas, as well as the book by JFK advanceman Jerry Bruno which clarified the Secret Service approval of the Trade Mart site for Kennedy's speech – bringing the president through Dealey Plaza.

In August 1971 the small but influential weekly, the *Texas Observer,* printed a lively exchange between Sylvia Meagher (*Accessories After the Fact*) and David Belin, a junior counsel for the Warren Commission. The exchange focused on the statements of an Oswald co-worker named Charles Givens. Meagher pointed out that Givens had repeatedly told authorities that he had last seen Oswald on the first floor of the Depository reading a paper, rather than on the sixth floor at 11:45 a.m. as he told Belin. Meagher noted an FBI document quoting Lt. Jack Revill of the Dallas Police Department to the effect that Givens would "probably change his testimony for money." Belin ignored this contention and attacked "assassination sensationalists" in general.

Meagher sent a copy of the exchange to Harrison Salisbury, then the editor of the *New York Times* op-ed page. Salisbury chose, however, to print a condensed version of only Belin's *Texas Observer* piece for their story on the eighth anniversary of the assassination. Belin concluded by proclaiming that "...the Warren Commission Report will stand the test of history for one simple reason: The ultimate truth beyond a reasonable doubt is that Lee Harvey Oswald killed both President Kennedy and Officer Tippit..." Meagher's repeated efforts to respond were rejected.

Ironically, the *New York Times* was then boldly defending freedom of the press in the Pentagon Papers case. When the FBI stopped the *New York Times* from printing the Pentagon Papers, the *Washington Post* took over, then the *Boston Globe*. The courageous Dan Ellsberg and Tony Russo distributed the RAND study widely, and 17 newspapers ultimately confronted the government and printed portions of the leaked national security documents. Exposing the history of U.S. involvement in Vietnam during a deeply divisive, failed policy was worthy of a major legal battle, but exposing the assassination of President Kennedy questioned the political legitimacy of government as well as the mass media.

Leslie Gelb, who produced and revealed the report, commented, "most of the elected and appointed leaders in the national security establishment felt they had the right – and beyond that the obligation – to manipulate American public opinion in the national interest as they defined it. Supreme Court Justice Hugo Black asserted in his concurring opinion on the Pentagon Papers case that,

> In the First Amendment the Founding Fathers gave the free press the protection it must have to fulfill its essential role in our democracy. The press was to serve the governed, not the governors. The government's power to censor the press was abolished so that the press would remain forever free to censure the government. The press was protected so that is could bare the secrets of government and informs the people.[45] Only a free and unrestrained press can effectively expose deception in government. And paramount among the responsibilities of a free press is the duty to prevent any part of the Government from deceiving the people.

The *L.A. Free Press* (5/7/71) bluntly declared that Dealey Plaza was an assault on civilian control. "When an assassination has been supported by elements of the federal government an independent investigation is as welcome as a snake dropped inside one's shirt.... Every possible government agency will be used in the counter attack against the menace presented by an outside agency."

Daniel Ellsberg and Anthony J. Russo, the DOD and RAND researchers who leaked the Pentagon Papers to the media, triggered the "Plumbers" unit from the White House to break into Ellsberg's psychiatrist's
office, with help from the CIA's Office of Security. Further, Ellsberg was
friendly with Frances FitzGerald, the author of *Fire in the Lake*, a critical
history of Vietnam, and the daughter of the late Desmond FitzGerald, a
former deputy director of the CIA. Desmond FitzGerald had coordinated
the anti-Castro plots in 1963, as well as directing his special affairs staff to
follow Lee Harvey Oswald.[62]

The allegation that the Kennedy family had suppressed autopsy photos
resurfaced in Fred Graham's front page exclusive, in the *New York Times*,
1/9/72. According to Harold Weisberg, Fred Graham said that Assistant
National Archivist Rhoads had told him that a urologist and right-wing
fanatic Dr. John Lattimer, J.Edgar Hoover's doctor, had been allowed to
view the autopsy photos. Lattimer's perspective is seen in *World Medical
News*, 3/13/70, where he declared "Oswald showed what the educated,
modern-day, traitorous guerrilla can do among his own people…" This
story reads:

> The family of President Kennedy … previously allowed only rep-
> resentatives of the government to inspect pictures and x-rays of the
> assassinated leader's body…. Lattimer … said that they "eliminate
> any doubt completely about the validity of the Warren Commis-
> sion's conclusion the Lee Harvey Oswald fired all the shots that
> struck the president…. The 65 x-rays, color transparencies and
> black and white negatives taken in the autopsy have been the fo-
> cus of controversy because the Kennedy family previously guard-
> ed them so closely that they were not allowed to be seen even by
> members and staff officials of the Warren Commission…

The renowned pathologist Cyril Wecht was next granted access to the
Kennedy family materials, and again Graham had an exclusive story arranged by Rhoads, which ran in the *New York Times*, 8/22/72.

> The preserved brain of President Kennedy, plus microscopic slides
> of tissues removed from his bullet wounds, have been withheld,
> apparently by the Kennedy family from the assassination evidence
> in the National Archives … [Dr. Wecht] asserted that questions
> about President Kennedy's wounds would remain unanswered so
> long as these objects were not available for examination. Interviews
> with Government officials and President Kennedy's personal sec-

retary, Evelyn Lincoln, disclosed that the slides and probably the brain, which was removed from the body in the autopsy in 1963 and was placed in container of formalin, were delivered in a locked chest to a representative of Senator Robert F. Kennedy in 1965. When the autopsy materials were placed in the National Archives in 1966 by Burke Marshall, a representative of the Kennedy family, the brain and possibly some of the other items were not included.

Actually, this transfer was from one government safe to another. It was from the Secret Service to the Kennedy library. The library was run by Rhoads, not by Robert Kennedy – and the transfer took place in the National Archives.[63]

Washington Post reporter Carl Bernstein observed that in 1972 when he started covering Watergate there were about 2,000 reporters in Washington, yet only 6 were assigned to cover Watergate full time. And even the *Post* chose not to explore CIA complicity to any extent, even though all of the Plumbers had CIA connections.

Through 1972 and 1973 the presidential election, the Vietnam War and the Watergate scandal commanded the attention of the nation and the media. In the July 1973 *Atlantic* LBJ revealed more about the JFK assassination. He declared, "I never believed Oswald acted alone, although I can accept that he pulled the trigger.... We have been running a damned Murder Inc. in the Caribbean."

A little-noticed article in the November 1973 edition of *Esquire* regarding *Life* publisher C. D. Jackson was revealing. Richard Stolley, the editorial director of all Time, Inc. magazines and the purchaser of the Zapruder film, claimed that "...Jackson was so upset by the head wound sequence that he proposed the company obtain all rights to the film and withhold it from the public viewing at least until emotions had calmed..." So even a decade after the assassination, the frames of the Zapruder film had not yet been printed in sequence.

Meanwhile, a film exploring the assassination of President Kennedy, *Executive Action*, opened amid controversy. Several television stations refused to show trailers for the film, and very few movie theaters showed it. Critics Mark Lane and Donald Freed wrote the story along with consultants Penn Jones and David Lifton. The screenplay was written by Dalton Trumbo. It was told in a semi-documentary style, through the perspective of the conspirators, by focusing on a Texas oil baron and a former CIA black ops specialist. The movie was pulled from theaters before Christmas that year.

The gamut of psychological warfare coupled with federal non-cooperation, bugging and stealing files, along with the murder of key witnesses, had effectively decimated Garrison's investigation. Like Hemingway's great fish in the *Old Man and the Sea*, not much was left after the fight. Elements of the mass media shielded FBI spying, and gave assistance to Clay Shaw's attorneys. FBI and CIA mass media assets diminished Garrison's legitimacy. CIA memos to selected media assets influenced their critiques. Government biases from both AP and UPI impacted mass media coverage. Negative network specials at NBC and CBS, spun in part by CIA, NSA and FBI assets, reached wide audiences. The investigation of CBS by the Congressional Special Investigative Subcommittee of the Interstate and Foreign Commerce Committee deepened media caution on national security. Supreme Court Justice Louis Brandeis wrote in the landmark case *Olmstead vs. U.S.* (1928) that "our government is the potent omnipresent teacher. For good or ill, it teaches the whole people by its example. Crime is contagious. If the government becomes a lawbreaker, it breeds contempt for the law … it invites anarchy…"

The Roman historian Tacitus warned that, "Crime once exposed has no refuge but audacity." George Orwell observed that "political language … is designed to make lies sound truthful and murder respectable, and to give the appearance of solidity to the wind."[64]

Garrison, the critics and the alternative media had unearthed considerable new evidence and leads but fell short of critical mass. The trial muddied the waters for mainstream journalists on the case for a few years, although a number of new critical books on the assassination found publishers. Meanwhile, other issues dominated the national attention. For a couple of years only *Ramparts*, *The Nation* and *The Realist*, along with Mae Brussell's radio show *World Watchers International* (out of Oklahoma) continued to regularly critique the Warren Report. Due to the divisive and unending Vietnam War and Watergate, the institutions of national security become more accessible to Congressional and mass media review, but that access, as well as media assertiveness, was short-lived. Nevertheless, most media historians view this period as a golden age of journalism, one less compromised by the corporate pressures for profits than in the upcoming consolidation of media ownership.

9

Post-Watergate: Media Retreat and Congressional Investigations

Great is truth, but still greater from a practical point of view is silence about truth.

– Aldous Huxley

Freedom of the press is perhaps the freedom that has suffered the most from the gradual degradation of the idea of liberty.

– Albert Camus

A state is bound to be more dangerous if it is not governed openly by the people, but secretly by political forces that are not known or widely understood.

– Andrei Sakharov

The assassinations in the 1960s, the Vietnam War, urban riots and the Watergate scandal severely diminished trust in government as well as official history. After Watergate, the mass media appeared to have finally ascended to the role envisioned by our Founding Fathers. In late 1973 *New York Times* columnist Tom Wicker observed, "In the last few news conferences, for the first time in my experience, the press has suddenly become what it has touted itself to be all these years--an adversary."

This new role surfaced in Seymour Hersh's extensive series on CIA abuses of power, which the *New York Times* ran from late December 1973 through February of 1974. While these CIA stories reverberated, elite elements of society, including much of the mass media, thought Hersh had gone too far. Senator J. William Fulbright, a staunch critic of the Vietnam War, declared in the *Columbia Journalism Review* that the "inquisition psychology" of journalists should end, and that "voluntary restraint" was needed to reaffirm the "social contract."[1] William Greider, a progressive editor with the *Washington Post*, wrote "There is a story wish all over town, a palpable feeling that it would be nice if somehow this genie could be put back in the bottle. It is a nostalgic longing for the easy consensual atmosphere which once existed among contending elements in Washington." Ben Bradlee, after retiring from editing the *Washington Post* observed, "I think the press was appalled at what had happened as a result of Nixon, it was not clear that the press wanted that power. Many editors cautioned, 'Let's watch out for the reporters who try to act like Woodward and Bernstein.'"[2] This short-lived adversarial phase impacted the mass media coverage of the assassination of President Kennedy – but it faded almost as fast as it came.

The death of the feared J. Edgar Hoover coupled with the excesses of the FBI and CIA during Watergate opened some political space for the mainstream media to explore FBI connections to the assassination, as well as call for a new investigation. The Senate Intelligence Committee tasked a subcommittee to review the Warren Commission findings, which opened new leads, bolstering calls for a new investigation, as well as for the Senate Intelligence Committee (the so-called Church Committee) to investigate the CIA.

Mainstream media coverage of the assassination cautiously widened in many outlets and chipped away at the flaws in the Warren Report. Meanwhile, the alternative media, led sometimes by tabloids or adult magazines, pushed further and theorized more. A complicated case became more problematic, murky and ominous.

Relentless and better organized citizen critics, along with some elements of the media, revealed important lines of inquiry. The confluence of these forces pushed the House of Representatives to reinvestigate the assassinations of President Kennedy and Martin Luther King in the House Select Committee on Assassinations.

The National Tattler, a tabloid, devoted most of their November 1973 issue to assassination coverage. The lead article by James Kerr, also a staff writer for WBAP-TV Dallas-Fort Worth included witness Howard Brennan's changed stories, James Tague's wound; Dallas policeman Roger Craig's account of Oswald running from the TSBD to a honking station wagon; Eugene Brading's arrest, Mafia-oil links and listed more witnesses saying shots came from the grassy knoll. They lamented, "if only the Warren Commission could have acted like the Watergate investigation."

In late November of 1973, Dave Belin, former assistant Counsel to the Warren Commission, debuted his book *November 22, 1963: You Are the*

Jury, defending the Warren Commission findings. Harrison Salisbury, the *New York Times* editor who encouraged Belin to write the book, wrote a laudatory introduction. The book was glowingly reviewed for the *New York Times Book Review*, 11/15/73 by, of all people, George and Priscilla Johnson-McMillan. Four days later, witting CIA asset Priscilla McMillan creatively psychologized in the *New York Times* that the reason people cling to conspiracy theories is that Oswald had committed symbolic patricide. She asserted that since we all subconsciously want to kill our fathers we believe in conspiracy "as a defense, a screen, a barrier, against having to hold those feelings in ourselves."[3]

Ramparts bluntly bolstered the critics, "It is clear that a reopening of the assassination investigation is in order."[4] The secret release of the Zapruder film from Time-Life Inc., which was optically enhanced by Robert Groden (both enlarged and slowed down), and shown to public gatherings and selected members of Congress, accelerated calls to reopen the case.

Unexpectedly, one of the most useful of the assassination overviews came from the tabloid *National Examiner* 4/1/74, "Exposed conspiracy to destroy America's leaders." They quoted Dr. Cyril Wecht, Mark Lane, journalist Fred Cook and Harrison Salisbury (*NYT*) on the JFK assassination.

"Tattler Source in JFK Probe Found Shot to Death under Mysterious Circumstances" headlined *The National Tattler*. "A private detective who worked closely with *Tattler* on the continuing investigation of John Kennedy's assassination has been shot.... Joe Cooper was shot in the face while lying in bed at his Baton Rouge apartment in the early hours of 10/16 ... Cooper a WWll hero and ex-cop ... had devoted ten years to the case.... Cooper argued that naval intelligence was involved.... Cooper led *Tattler* to two pilots who claimed that they were offered $25,000 to fly two passengers from Dallas to Latin America after Kennedy was shot. One was Billy Kemp, a WWII fighter pilot and the other feared to go on the record. Cooper's wife and his attorney do not think suicide was the case."[5]

The *Washington Star-News*, 1/13/75, ran an AP piece noting that Rep. Hale Boggs' son said that his father gave him FBI files compiled on Warren Commission critics to discredit them. The files were of political and sexual backgrounds on seven critics, though Boggs declined to identify all seven.

The *New York Times* reached out to Warren Commission lawyer David Slawson regarding an FBI memo three years before the assassination that an "imposter might be using Oswald's birth certificate." Slawson then attacked the CIA, on the record in the *Times*, for not sharing more documents with the Warren Commission. A few days later Slawson got a strange and threatening call from James Angleton, former CIA Counter-intelligence Chief, stating that the CIA needed Slawson's continuing help as a "partner … we hope that you will remain a friend."[6]

Finally, on March 6, 1975, an optically enhanced version of the Zapruder film was shown on the ABC-TV show *Goodnight America* hosted by Geraldo Rivera. Robert Groden, activist Dick Gregory and Rivera successfully lobbied for the Zapruder film to be aired on ABC. Rivera threatened, "It was one of those things where I said (to ABC), 'It gets on or I walk." ABC relented, but only after Rivera signed a waiver accepting sole financial responsibility if *Time* or the Zapruder family sued.[7] Rivera thought that Time-Life did not sue because they "were blown away by the [positive] reaction to the program."

A *New York Review* article, 4/3/75, explored the CIA pictures purported to be of Oswald during his visit to Mexico City in October 1963. In "The CIA and the Man Who Was Not Oswald," researchers Bernard Fensterwald and George O'Toole examined the stated FBI and CIA positions regarding the pictures of Oswald outside of the Cuban Embassy in Mexico City, which clearly were not pictures of Oswald. They revealed Warren Commission dialogue regarding the difficulty of clarifying records on intelligence assets, the "terribly bad character of some agents," and the need to become less dependent on the FBI for the investigation.[8] Fensterwald and O'Toole proposed a Congressional investigation, and then issued a clarion call for the press to cover the case.

Without pressure from the press, government officials generally do little. Recall that, Attorney General Richard Kleindienst had promised that the Justice Department would attack the Watergate scandal with the most extensive, thorough and complete investigation since the assassination of President Kennedy. The Justice Department, ironically, prosecuted no further than Gordon Liddy. Some elements of the press didn't accept the official truth as the whole truth. The *Washington Post* pursued the story and subsequently so did the rest of the national press, until reluctantly, Congress acted.

The *Washington Post's* executive director Ben Bradlee explained why he never assigned an investigative team to the JFK assassination:

> Ron Kessler did a recent story knocking down the second gun theory in the Robert Kennedy assassination and nuts from both coasts

were all over me. Letters, telegrams, phone calls, personal visits, I've been up to my ass in lunatics.... Back in 1965 Russ Wiggins, the man I replaced here at the *Washington Post* told me there would never be an end to this story [the JFK assassination]. He said unless you can find someone who wants to devote his life to it, forget it.[9]

On April 24, 1975, CBS finally aired their 1969 interview with Lyndon Johnson regarding the Warren Commission. Johnson did not rule out foreign involvement. "I don't believe that the Warren Commission, or I, or anyone else is absolutely sure of everything that might have motivated Oswald or others that could have been involved."

Developing leads remained problematic, as seen by the reaction of how CIA Director Richard Helms exited the Rockefeller Commission hearings on CIA attempts to assassinate foreign leaders. Schorr had broadcast some stories about CIA-mafia assassination conspiracies and sought comment from Helms outside of the hearing room (4/28/75). The generally reserved Helms screamed, "You son-of-a-bitch! You killer! You cocksucker! Killer Schorr-that's what they ought to call you."[10]

Despite LBJ's statement, as well as the range and clarity of the critics, the *L.A. Times* still staunchly supported the Warren Commission. "Kennedy Conspiracy Discounted" by W. David Slawson and Richard Mosk, 5/11/75, psychologized that, "The conspiracy theory persists partly because some persons find it difficult to believe that such a momentous act could be done so capriciously, and by such an insignificant, hapless man ..." "The evidence 'supporting Oswald's guilt is overwhelming'. Thus a reopening of the inquiry would not serve any useful purpose."

Some mainstream sources adopted a different perspective, particularly regarding the FBI after the death of J. Edgar Hoover. In late spring of 1975 the *Dallas Times Herald* received information concerning an alleged visit to the Dallas FBI office by Lee Harvey Oswald, about ten days prior to the assassination. The FBI had covered up this incident. Apparently Oswald had left an envelope containing a note after asking for an FBI agent by name, and that after Oswald was murdered, the letter had been destroyed. Publisher Tom Johnson decided to delay publication until he had checked the story with FBI director Clarence Kelly. The day after the meeting, 7/8, the Attorney General was advised, "the Bureau failed to develop any information indicating Oswald had ever visited an FBI office in Dallas or that he had left a note." Senator Richard Schweiker (R-Pa) Chair of the Intelligence Committee, however, had subsequent interviews with

FBI personnel, who confirmed: 1) Oswald visited the Dallas FBI office; 2) Oswald asked to see FBI Agent James Hosty; 3) a note was left for Hosty; and 4) the note was destroyed after the assassination. The Schweiker Report determined that the FBI internal investigation was unable to establish either whether the note was threatening in nature or who directed the note to be destroyed.

In the wake of Watergate the *U.S. News & World Report*, 6/2/75, asserted the need to reopen an investigation of the assassination by exploring the newly uncovered evidence raised by Senator Schweiker. "The increased cynicism of Watergate, the Vietnam War and the revelations about CIA operations has made both officials and the American public more inclined to accept a conspiracy as possible." The report concluded by noting that many Americans will now be "watching what the Senate does with his [Schweiker's] idea."[11]

The National Tattler turned to Earl Golz (*Dallas Morning News*) to explore the role of the mafia in the JFK assassination 6/8/75.

Eugene Brading (aka Jim Braden), arrested minutes after the assassination in the Dal-Tax building, was tied to mafia and oil interests. Jack Ruby's ties to Dallas mafia boss Joe Civello were indicated by one of Ruby's piano players. Golz also mentioned the Phil Willis' picture of a man who looks just like Ruby in front of the TSBD after the assassination. Golz argued "The Warren Commission had enough evidence to make a strong case for a mafia assassination of President John F Kennedy."

Another tabloid, *National Star*, pushed to revive the investigation with an article "10 Questions to still be answered on the JFK assassination." 6/21/75. Warren Commission lawyer, now Judge Burt Griffin stated, "I don't think that the Dallas Police or the FBI told us the entire truth." Congressman Stewart McKinney (R-Conn) declared, "There are just too many questions in the minds of too many people." According to a Gallop Poll 78% of the American people no longer believed in the Warren Commission.

At the end of June 1975, the *CBS Evening News* ran a short piece by Daniel Schorr about the relationship between the CIA and Oswald. An unidentified ex-CIA agent asserted that he saw an interview report from a re-defector from the Soviet Union. This re-defector was identified as a former Marine, and he was returning to the U.S. with his family. The contents of the memo dealt mainly with intelligence at the Minsk radio plant.

Schorr: that was very similar to the story of Lee Harvey Oswald.

Ex-agent: yes, the similarities were very striking...

Schorr: CBS News has waited a week for the CIA to check on this report of a possible Oswald contact. The agency now says it did interview a redefector in 1962, a case very similar to Oswald, but an ex-Navy man, not an ex-Marine, who worked in a plant in another Soviet City, not Minsk. The Navy says it found no record of such a man ...

In "The Media and the Murder of John Kennedy," *New Times,* (8/8/75), ran researcher Jerry Policoff's critique and prescient admonition.

The Kennedy assassination cover-up has survived so long only because the press, confronted with the choice of believing what it was told or examining the facts independently chose the former. Unless and until the press repudiates that choice, it is unlikely that we shall ever know the truth.

The *Dallas Times Herald,* 8/31/75, broke the story of Oswald's note to Hosty on the uncorroborated testimony of a receptionist at the FBI who somehow read a "partly visible" note, in an unsealed envelope that Oswald wrote. She claimed that Oswald had written "I will blow up the FBI and the Dallas Police Department if you don't stop bothering my wife." Other headlines and articles in the September *Dallas Times Herald* also characterized Oswald's nature as violent – "FBI destroyed the threat note from Oswald" and "Note from Oswald threatened to bomb FBI." The purported reasons for destroying evidence, which would have bolstered the lone nut thesis, went unexplained.

The *New York Times,* for a change, took the lead and briefly probed the role at the Dallas FBI. It was easier to investigate the FBI after Hoover's death than to probe the CIA's role during Congressional hearings. Just two days later, they noted that FBI agent Hosty's immediate superior, Gordon Shanklin, asked Dallas Police Chief Jessie Curry not to disclose Hosty's previous dealings with Oswald. Chief Curry agreed to "sit on" the information, and only disclosed Shanklin's request after the *New York Times* broke the story. By September 17, 1975, the *New York Times* cited an unnamed source who asserted that the decision to destroy the note came from FBI Director Hoover. The same week, also citing unnamed sources, *Time* named John Mohr, former FBI administrative chief, and his aides as responsible.

Mike Wallace at *60 Minutes* gently probed the role of the Secret Service in an interview with agent Clint Hill. Hill had been a friend of the

Kennedy family and he broke down in tears recounting his feelings and actions in Dealey Plaza. Convulsing with emotion, Hill lamented that he had not taken the fatal head shot instead of Kennedy. Ironically, Hill, riding in the follow-up car, disregarded orders and bravely raced to the presidential limousine to push Jackie Kennedy safely back in. Only years later did researcher Vince Palamara discover that the Secret Service had ordered that no agents were to ride on the running boards of the presidential limousine or at the rear of the car. Other areas of the Secret Service non-compliance with their policies and procedures or their role in the Warren Commission investigation went unexplored.

Congress finally decided to investigate the CIA, while the mass media widened its examination of the FBI. However, key elements of the mass media rejected a thorough investigation of the CIA. Initially the mass media supported the hearings, led by conservative but independent Republican Congressman Otis Pike; however, when the State Department was probed, support not only immediately vanished – Pike was quickly castigated as a "McCarthyite." Kissinger's close friend, James Reston, the well known *New York Times* columnist, phoned the chief counsel of the Pike committee and bellowed "What the hell are you guys doing down there? Are you reviving McCarthyism?" A *New York Times* editorial referred to Pike as "hip shooting toward some high noon in a federal courtroom." Another editorial 'Neo-McCarthyism?' declared that the investigation was "clearly contrary to the national interest." (10/19/75). The *L.A. Times* also invoked the image of McCarthyism; and the *Tulsa Daily World* called Pike "a small minded egotist." Even the *Washington Post* saw Pike's committee as irresponsible:

> In its zeal, the Pike committee – unlike its Senate counterpart - has brushed by the time-tested 'political' way in which responsible standing committees can and do gain access discreetly to material which would not be forthcoming in the context of a hostile political confrontation. (11/19/75).

Journalistic challenges regarding national security reporting were partly revealed by the experiences of *New York Times* reporter Nicholas Horrock. Horrock tentatively questioned the Warren Commission access to information, after communicating with the CIA, in an article "The Warren Commission Didn't Know Everything." In respectful tones he noted that the withholding of evidence by the FBI and CIA left gaps in the "encyclopedic" work of the Warren Commission. "No one is suggesting these new inquiries will change the commission's conclusion ... [but] the age of trust in government ended in the months after John Kennedy's death. That might be a good point at which to restore credibility." The omission of CIA assassination plots to the Warren Commission kept it from giving "far greater attention to the question of whether Oswald was part of the retaliation plot [from Cuba]."

Horrock accepted the FBI acknowledgment that "a letter from Oswald was delivered to the Bureau ten days before Kennedy was shot, in which he threatened to blow up the Dallas police headquarters, was withheld from the Warren Commission and then destroyed. The destruction was reportedly ordered by J. Edgar Hoover."

The CIA version of events in Mexico City remained unquestioned perhaps due to Horrock's calls to the CIA. In a CIA memo 9/19/1975 from Mitchell Rogovin, Special Counsel to the Director to CIA Director Colby stated:

> Nick Horrock called again on the Oswald theory. He said he didn't want to barter like a fish peddler and then proceeded to do just that. He said they would be willing to leave out the Mexico source if we did give them a verbatim transcript of what was said. I told him that was undoubtedly out of the question. That we might be able to characterize the type of contract that was involved.
>
> I have seen the verbatim transcript and it raises more questions than it answers.
>
> Horrock believes that these were two separate conversations and does not appear to be clear as to whether they were with the Russian or Cuban Embassy. If we go forward with a release, I would recommend that it clearly indicate that Oswald had contacted both embassies.
>
> Horrock said that two people who knew about the conversations said that the embarrassment to the CIA was that we never told the FBI of former defectors contact with one of the embassies prior to the assassination of John Kennedy. This is clearly wrong for contact with the Soviet embassy was brought to the attention of the FBI and this is clear in the proposed press release.
>
> Finally, Horrock said that he had been told that the information had only been told to Lee Rancon [sic] and he had not gone to the members of the Warren Commission. DDO's file indicates that Chief Justice Warren and members of the Commission came out to headquarters and among other things had access to the Oswald 201 file.

Apparently Horrock included the CIA's corrections and elected not to pursue any other CIA related areas.[12]

In late 1975, *The New York Times Magazine* reverted to its staunch support for the Warren Commission and assigned James Phelan to write an overview of the assassination. In "The Assassination That Will Not Die" Phelan referred to Kennedy's backward head snap as a neuromuscular reaction; he again defended the single-bullet theory, and called the early Warren Report critics a "housewives' underground."[13]

Commentary, a moderate alternative weekly, which was turning neocon, 10/75 ran a denigrating researcher piece by Dr. Jacob Cohen where he attacked researchers as "paranoid conspiracists." Cohen told Vincent Salandria that he was CIA.

The adult magazine *Gallery*, 10/75, published a solid critique of the Warren Commission, "The Guns of Dallas" by Colonel Fletcher Prouty. After Prouty's book *The Secret Team*, which pointed to a CIA-military role in the assassination, was published by Ballantine, he was still having difficulty finding publishers to print his articles. Although previously he had been published in *The Nation, The New Republic* and *Air Force Magazine*, now he was reliant on *Gallery*.

Prouty illustrated his piece with frames of the Zapruder film, as well as with pictures from AP photographer James Altgens. Perhaps his most revealing portion clarified Secret Service procedure:

> Not only did the Secret Service disregard experienced and qualified assistance from the Armed Forces, but also they did not act in accordance with their own regulation ... William McKinney, a former member of the crack 112th Military Intelligence Group at 4th Army Headquarters, Fort Sam Houston, Texas, has revealed that both Col. Maximillian Reich and his deputy Lt. Col. Joel Cabaza, protested violently when they were told to "stand down" rather than report their units for duty in augmentation of the Secret Service in Dallas. All the Secret Service had to do was nod and these units (which had been trained at the Army's top Intelligence school at Camp Holabird, Maryland) would have preformed their normal function of protection for the President in Dallas.[14]

The journalistic challenges faced by CBS reporters echo those of Nicolas Horrock, and declassified documents prove revealing regarding the *CBS Twelfth Anniversary Special*. In September of 1975 CBS-TV reporters Dan Rather and Bruce Hall explored the nature of the FBI's relationship with Oswald. A known FBI informer, Orest Pena, who had worked with FBI Agent Warren de Brueys in New Orleans, charged that he had seen Oswald and de Brueys together at a restaurant. He further claimed that de Brueys "threatened" him into giving false testimony to the Warren Commission. Allegedly de Brueys said, "If you ever talk about me I will get rid of your ass." de Brueys, however, denied all of Pena's allegations. Former FBI clerk William Walter was carefully questioned by CBS about the FBI memo to all offices giving advance warning of assassination threats.

CBS-TV pursued CIA connections to Oswald in a more collegial manner according to documents of meetings and correspondence between Dan Rather and Les Midgely and DCI William Colby. At a meeting on September 3rd Rather and Midgely covered "a variety of matters" which CBS planned to pursue in its upcoming series *The Assassins*. This meeting appears to have conformed with the CBS Procedures Handbook, which states that prior to interviews the questions cannot be divulged, however, areas of inquiry can be discussed. Colby reiterated "that the CIA had no contact with Oswald either during his Russian period or afterwards, that the CIA's only records of Oswald came from our being aware of his visits to embassies in Mexico City, which information was made available to the Warren Commission…"

Colby's memo to the CIA hierarchy continued:

> We discussed Allan Dulles' comments about whether an intelligence agent could ever be exposed, but we left on the final comment by Mr. Dulles that he believed Mr. Hoover's comments on this matter, which Mr. Rather said he probably would himself at the time. I said that this in no way indicated a desire by Mr. Dulles to conceal any CIA activity. Mr. Rather also said that Mr. Helms had become somewhat agitated over the Garrison allegations, and I said that was easily explained by Mr. Helms' concern that such false allegations be made of the CIA…
>
> With respect to Oswald's one appearance in our records, I explained that the CIA might well have shied off from any interview with him if there was an indication of prior FBI interest. As for the military, I said the Interagency Source Register did not indicate Mr. Oswald was a clandestine source and that DCS Joint Debriefing Program with the military services from 1953 on would probably have indicated any military debriefing for intelligence purposes, but none appear in our files, so I believe none had been conducted.
>
> We parted with the assurance that anything else that arose which could cast doubt on my statements would be brought to Mr.

Rather's attention. The two gentlemen expressed appreciation for our discussions.

From their attitude, I believe there is a chance that the program will indicate that there is no CIA connection with Oswald beyond that noted above. This could make a contribution to knocking down the paranoia belief to the contrary. We must, however, insure that Mr. Rather does not learn anything, which could cause the slightest doubt on the above account before he produces the programs in November. [15]

In the light of CIA documents declassified in the 1990s, Colby may have not been fully informed of agency files. Colby's cooperation with Congress, by many accounts, contributed to his replacement by President Ford with George H.W. Bush.

A note, 10/1/75, from Rather to Colby requested a response to filmed accusations of a CIA role in the assassination of Martin Luther King, Jr., while noting Colby's explicit denials of a CIA role. There was an internal CIA memo regarding the upcoming interview with Rather, which was sent from Angus Thuermer, Assistant to DCI, to Colby, 10/21/75. Thuermer, a former AP reporter, stated that his office had been called on 10/17 by CBS reporter Daniel Schorr, and that Schorr had been told by Colby that Colby "would look into the possibility of declassifying and giving to him a memo in the file that indicated back in 1962 that the CIA did not interview Lee Harvey Oswald because the FBI was handling the case. Wanted to remind Colby of this." Thuermer admonished:

> **Bill**: Neither DDO nor DCD can figure out what this means. Please be alert to the possibility that Dan Schorr and Dan Rather … are ganging up on that old Oswald story that Schorr has been chewing on for so long.

The next day Thuermer talked to CBS Producer Les Midgely about questions that would come up Friday with Rather. The CBS Ethics and Procedures book, which precludes discussion of questions in advance, was seemingly ignored.

> Rather will ask whether the CIA had any trace of the movements of [James Earl] Ray, the convicted assassin of Reverend Dr. King. Ray crossed several borders. Midgely says CBS wonders whether we don't have something on Ray for that reason…

As you mentioned to Pat Taylor, there will be Oswald questions (although Rather did not put them into his letter).

There will be questions such as:

Did you have no record on Oswald?

Did the CIA have anything to do with Oswald's training while in the Marines?

Did the CIA have knowledge of him while in Russia (he went into the Embassy; CBS thinks it unlikely we were unaware of this)?

Did we have no knowledge when he came back from Russia?

Did the CIA not debrief him when he came back from Russia? This seems almost unbelievable to CBS that we didn't. Midgely is aware that you have said we did not and believes you. He also believes that the FBI did debrief him; CBS is working on getting the agent who debriefed him on the tube. Nevertheless Rather will ask about this for the show.

Did the CIA know about Oswald when he went to Cuba?

He will also want to talk about the misidentified picture of Oswald.[16]

Were either Thuermer or Midgely directed to further clarify the questions? Did Midgely, in an effort to be cooperative, allow himself to be co-opted again? This procedure seems consistent with his efforts during the 1967 CBS documentary when Midgely communicated with Warren Commissioner John McCloy through McCloy's daughter Ellen, an assistant producer, prior to the airing in 1967.

Rather asked most of the questions that Midgely had mentioned to Thuermer, but did not probe CIA officer David Phillips' blanket denial of CIA involvement.

The November 1975 two-part CBS special "The American Assassins" hosted by Dan Rather, essentially paralleled their previous conclusions on the JFK assassination. After six months of investigation the first of the CBS Reports Inquiry presented a number of questionable specialists who consistently omitted critical information. The second program went further and touched on Oswald's intelligence ties but chose to omit any discussion of Jack Ruby, his ties to the mafia, FBI, Dallas police, Cuba and possibly Oswald. Yet the previous spring *60 Minutes* had spent two months researching a segment "The Oswald-Ruby Connection," and while it was canceled, the research was supposedly made available to the Reports Inquiry team.

Dr. James Weston, the president-elect of the American Academy of Forensic Sciences, asked by CBS to analyze Kennedy's wounds, is the only recent Academy president still satisfied with the original Warren Commission conclusions about two shots striking from the rear. Outgoing Academy president Robert Joling, as well as four other past presidents, had called for a review of all medical evidence by a new independent panel of forensic experts.

Dr. Alfred Oliver, called on by CBS to uphold the controversial belief that a single bullet could emerge unscathed after hitting both Kennedy and John Connally, was actually a veterinarian at Edgewood Arsenal. The Warren Commission, as well as the Rockefeller Commission has called his lone approving voice the gospel on CIA activities, and now CBS.

As for the critics, CBS gave them short shrift. Despite a total of six hours of interviews with photo researcher Josiah Thompson and former Academy of Forensic science president Cyril Wecht, the strongest conclusions of both men wound up on the cutting room floor.

Former CBS editor Bob Richter, who resigned from the 1967 CBS assassination special, noted that the latest CBS effort "seems a form of unusual advocacy journalism. Especially the first program … they should have said, here's the evidence and here's what the experts say – experts who disagree. A third conclusion ought to have been considered for the evidence: not proven."

Both Wecht and Thompson privately wondered if the script didn't undergo last minute editing from CBS higher-ups. After calling him twice to go over word for word what Rather would say about Wecht's statements, Wecht says CBS then "cut the heart of my presentation." Senator Russell's critiques of CBS' version of the single-bullet theory and the fatal shot were also somehow omitted.

CBS refuted the doubters on this issue by claiming it was impossible to tell precisely how Kennedy and Connally were sitting when struck. This time the network chose to use the temporary obstruction of the freeway sign in the Zapruder film to make it's point. If the men change position in that time frame, CBS said, the strange trajectory could have occurred. Had CBS consulted available films taken from other angles, it would have been obvious that neither man moved in that less-than-a-second interval to allow the otherwise impossible flight of the so-called "magic bullet."

The program's experts also maintained that a slight visible movement on Connally's part right after Kennedy was hit indicates that the same bullet is striking him. Josiah Thompson and Dr. Wecht painstakingly showed CBS how, more than a second later in the Zapruder frames, Connally clearly reacts – his right shoulder collapsing, cheeks puffing, and hair dislodged. Connally's own doctors believe that is the momentum of a bullet hitting him, while the earlier movement is a startled reaction to hearing a shot hit Kennedy. Connally agreed. In fact, he told that to CBS in an earlier interview where he also stated his feeling that all the shots did come from the rear. CBS chose to use the latter segment but eliminated Connally's remarks about different bullets.

CBS also eliminated Dr. Wecht's discussion of the implausibility of the single bullet's remarkably pristine condition, if indeed it could do what the Warren Commission claimed. Not one scientist has ever come up with a bullet in such good condition in simulated experiments with cadavers. Yet CBS took the word of veterinarian Alfred Oliver that it could happen.

CBS asserted that Itek's image enhancement technique (of the Zapruder film) claims to show a perceptible forward movement of Kennedy's head before the backward "reaction" sets in. If so, it was invisible in CBS' rendering. CBS backed this up with the hypothesis that Jacqueline Kennedy may have inadvertently pushed her husband backward. This is nonsense, since the film shows no reaction on Mrs. Kennedy's part until ten frames after the fatal shot. Recall that Itek was run by former CIA officer Franklin Lindsey, who had worked closely with Allen Dulles and Frank Wisner. Itek Corporation had helped build the CORONA spy satellite system.

For further evidence Dan Rather asserted that the greater portion of the president's brain matter flew forward, indicating once again a shot from the rear. Almost every witness in the motorcade contradicts this statement. Both policemen riding behind the limousine were splattered, one so hard he thought he'd been shot, and two skull fragments also went flying backward. Only a small amount of debris flew in front of the limousine.

Nor was there mention of new technological tools like the Psychological Stress Evaluator (PSE), which concluded from voice tapes of Oswald after the shooting that he was telling the truth about not shooting anybody in Dallas.

The second program, which dealt with Oswald's relationships, failed to discuss Jack Ruby. Why, in interviewing ex-CIA official Victor Marchetti, didn't CBS ask about the meeting he attended in 1968 with then-director Richard Helms? At the height of Jim Garrison's conspiracy investigation in New Orleans, Marchetti recalls Helms conceding that Garrison's two principle figures – accused conspirators Clay Shaw and David Ferrie – were indeed once CIA contact employees. The Garrison probe wasn't mentioned once by CBS. . . . But the one startling revelation – an interview with Robert McKeown [mafia ties and gun running] about Oswald approaching him, to buy four high-powered rifles – wasn't pursued very far. . . [17]

The Saturday Evening Post also called to reopen the investigation December 1975 in "The Question that won't go away," in part by reassessing their past coverage.

In the wake of Watergate, the *New York Times* and particularly the *Washington Post* pushed deeper than in the past on the twelfth anniversary. The Times cautiously focused on Warren Commission counsel David Belin's comments to Congress. He called for a reinvestigation primarily to "contribute toward a rebirth in confidence and trust in government." Belin believes that "the bulk of the criticism of the commission is unfounded and "many of the most extreme and vocal critics have deliberately misrepresented the overall record of evidence." Belin also blamed the CIA, FBI and Robert Kennedy for "failing to disclose to the Warren Commission evidence concerning plots to assassinate Castro."

The next day the *Washington Post* ran Robert Sam Anson's far-reaching investigation "JFK and the CIA: Dallas Revisited," a critical overview of means and motives. Anson, a political correspondent for *New Times* and a public television producer in New York, chronicled JFK's conflict with the CIA and noted that they had never been investigated regarding the assassination. CIA bitterness built over a range of issues: the Bay of Pigs fiasco; deep disagreement with the President's policies to normalize relations with Cuba combined with the "banning of atmospheric testing of nuclear weapons; accommodation with Communists in Laos; to the reevaluation of the entire American commitment in Southeast Asia. . . . A thousand advisors were to be called home by the end of the year ... a clear sign of where Kennedy was heading. . . . Kennedy was potentially [the CIA's] most dangerous adversary ... the CIA had a motive, It had the means. It had the experience. It had the disposition. The agency could have killed him, and far better than anyone else covered its crime."

Anson saw Oswald as an intelligence agent, perhaps Army Intelligence, which had three times the number of agents as the CIA. Army Intelligence "knew the arrangements of the President's trip and "the Secret Service, chronically short-handed, worked with Army Intelligence as a matter of routine."

Anson speculated that Oswald could have gone rogue, which was possible with "bright, tough, competitive guys ... trained to win." Oswald's mafia connections to Banister, Marcello, Ferrie and Shaw further created a confluence of interests. "The two most secret and powerful organizations in America working hand in glove... that [CIA/ mafia differences] had ceased to be a distinction... the key to understanding John Kennedy's murder."[18]

Perhaps Anson's piece nudged the *New York Times* toward printing Jerry Policoff's probe of the evidence in "A Critic's View of the Warren Commission Report" (12/8/75). Policoff noted that "Recent disclosures show that both the Federal Bureau of Investigation and the Central Intelligence Agency systematically withheld evidence from the commission, and declassified executive session transcripts tell of untenable circumstances under which the commission operated." Policoff cogently clarified why the former commission staffers were mistaken since the evidence available to them "weaves a fabric pointing unavoidably toward conspiracy." He recapped the missing evidence: the views of the majority of witnesses regarding the location of the shots: the backward reaction of the President's head [when he was hit]; the doctors at Parkland Hospital seeing an apparent entrance wound; Oswald's poor marksmanship; the disparity between the President's back wound and the holes in his shirt and jacket; the time necessary to fire the rifle; and the impossibility of one bullet causing seven wounds and remaining unscratched.[19]

Dick Russell responded to the CBS special in the *Village Voice* (12/8) "JFK Assassination Probe: CBS leaves a skeptic skeptical."

> Itek, a photo-analysis corporation hired to examine the frames of the original Zapruder Film, is a Rockefeller company that gets 60 percent of its contracts with the government. Mainly the military and the CIA seek Itek's knowledge about things like development of bombsights. Itek' chairman of the Board, Franklin A. Lindsey was CIA. Lindsey's assistant writes [Maurice] Schonfeld [for CJR] Howard Sprague, has also been a CIA employee. And this CBS study was Itek's third purporting to show no photographic evidence of conspiracy in the JFK assassination. The others were from UPI and *Life*.[20]

The *Village Voice* report by Dick Russell, one week later, "Senator Schweiker Reopens Assassination Probe: The Finger Points to Fidel, but should not," widened the investigation. Senator Richard Schweiker notes from his subcommittee investigation "The more witnesses, the more they raise the fact that the Warren Commission really is a house of cards....

I've learned more about the inner workings of government in the past nine months than my previous fifteen years in Congress.... A lot of stuff is not in certain files. So when Hoover says his files show only three FBI contacts with Oswald, he could be narrowly telling the truth, where in fact he is lying through his teeth.... Why did the FBI withhold for twelve years that he'd (Jack Ruby) informed for them on nine occasions?"

Russell revealed that William Attwood, America's number two man at the UN, "held a series of talks with the Cuban ambassador to the UN to discuss opening negotiations on an accommodation between Castro and the U.S. The progress was reported regularly to the White House, where McGeorge Bundy says JFK was in favor of pushing an opening with Cuba.... In November a French journalist named Jean Daniel went off to see Castro as a quasi-official spokesman for JFK" Meanwhile, according to the CIA's 1967 inspector general's report, "it is likely that at the very moment President Kennedy was shot, a CIA officer was meeting with a Cuban agent and giving him an assassination device for use against Castro."

Russell asked, "Why should U.S. intelligence, which desperately wanted Castro gone anyway, be so scrupulous about covering up Castro retaliation against Kennedy? Was Castro – or his tie with Russia – so strong that this government then feared him? Nonsense, The Castro's revenge story is too easy."

Russell also revealed the Schweiker file on J.A. Milteer of the National States Rights Party, who told a police informant in Miami, "that a plan to kill Kennedy was in the works." Two weeks prior to the assassination, the informant passed that information to the Secret Service about an assassination plan from a window with a high-powered rifle.

As Senator Schweiker deepened his inquiry of the role of U.S. intelligence agencies in investigating the assassination he wrote of his respect for citizen-researcher Sylvia Meagher. *Accessories After the Fact* was instrumental in finally causing a committee of Congress – with full subpoena power, access to classified documents, and a working knowledge of the nuances of the FBI and CIA – to take a second official look at what happened in Dallas on November 22, 1963."[21]

By late 1975 *The Saturday Evening Post* joined the call for a new investigation, and offered a reward for information leading to the conviction of the conspirators. Meanwhile, Colonel Fletcher Prouty and *Gallery* tried to deepen the discourse and Congressional investigation of the CIA with the 12/75 piece "The Fourth Force," which explored CIA-military cooperation.

The Bay of Pigs in 1961 was a large, military exercise. It involved an air force, a navy, and a sizable over-the beach force of Cuban expatriates. The insurrection against the Sukarno government in Indonesia in 1958 involved more than 42,000 rebel troops and a good sized clandestine air force, and a navy. In Tibet in 1959-60 more than 14,000 insurgent Kham tribesmen were supported by a major airlift of arms over the Himalayan Mountains. Cold War needs and perceptions forged broad CIA-military cooperation as "The Fourth Force," in Indonesia 1958, Tibet 1959 and Cuba in 1961. The military was to shield Congress from its cooperation. Prouty asserted that the Rockefeller Commission did not look into this because it had been penetrated on behalf of the CIA by David Belin, its chief counsel and former counsel of the Warren Commission.[22]

The close relationship between CBS and the CIA reemerged a few months later regarding the release of the Pike Committee Report. By a close congressional vote the House determined that the Pike investigation should not be released to the public, but a leaked copy was given to CBS reporter Daniel Schorr. CBS rejected Schorr's efforts to either report on or write about the leaked report. Soon after, CBS chairman Bill Paley met with the new CIA director George H.W. Bush.

Schorr quickly released the report to the *Village Voice* and was then castigated by the *Washington Post*, the *New York Times*, and most of the mass media. Not long afterward, Schorr was forced to resign from CBS. Mass media coverage of Schorr's efforts was muted, and a public which was emotionally weary from the Vietnam War and Watergate, had seemly shifted somewhat from valuing transparency to desiring security. A December 1975 Harris poll showed that slightly more respondents disapproved of the Congressional investigation of the CIA than approved of them. This provocative congressional probe could have impacted coverage of political assassinations if Congress had voted to declassify it, or if the mass media would have covered it like the Pentagon Papers or Watergate.

Argosy, 4/76, ran Dick Russell's interview with former mercenary and CIA contract agent Gerry Patrick Hemming, who claimed to have been repeatedly offered money to assassinate Kennedy. Hemming, a big ex-Marine and Green Beret, knew Oswald, Sturgis, Castro and Che Guevara. He fought with Castro to overthrow Batista, and then fled to the U.S. in 1960 to train embittered Cuban exiles in guerrilla warfare. He worked with the CIA, elements of the mafia, Howard Hughes, Congress and others. Hemming clarified his statement to Senate investigators about ex-CIA contract employee Loran Hall being seen in Dallas on the day of the assassination (recall that Hall was named by the Warren Commission as visiting Sylvia Odio with Oswald). Hemming then recounted a number of CIA-mafia plots to assassinate Castro, yet he felt that Castro was being set up for the blame on the assassination to justify an invasion.[23]

Russell again broke ground with his *Village Voice* piece, 4/26/76, which pointed to inconsistencies with the CIA reports on Oswald's alleged rifle, Oswald's ties to the CIA, Khrushchev's disbelief in the Warren Report, and the mysteries of Mexico City, as well as Ruby's connections. CIA memos indicate that CIA pictures of Oswald supposedly visiting the Soviet Embassy were not pictures of Oswald. The CIA admitted so while recommending that the photographs not be reproduced in the Warren Report. British journalist John Wilson revealed Ruby's visit to Mafiosi Santo Trafficante in a Cuban jail in 1959. Wilson states that while jailed in Cuba, he met Trafficante and that Trafficante had been visited by Ruby. Russell also pointed to Oswald's other associates with purported CIA ties, Arnesto Rodriguez and "Ruedolo."[24]

The muted response of the mainstream media can be partially attributed to the public relations efforts of the Association of Retired Intelligence Officers. In 1976 retired CIA propaganda expert David Phillips (AKA Maurice Bishop) organized over 600 former spies to generate "background material" to distribute to national organizations. Guidelines for public relations on speeches, op-ed pieces, etc. were crafted to promote at first the view that CIA agents were physically endangered by the Congressional investigation. The P.R. work became vital after Senator Richard Schweiker's (R-Pa.) statement on CBS's *Face the Nation* 9/27/76. "I think the [Warren] Report … has fallen like a house of cards … the fatal mistake the Warren Commission made was not to use its own investigators, but instead to rely on CIA and FBI personnel, which played directly into the hands of senior intelligence officials who directed the cover-up."[25]

In the wake of the Senate Intelligence sub-committee report in 1976, the so-called Schweiker-Hart report, the FBI released 98,000 pages of documents on President Kennedy's death. Four major new areas of the assassination were clarified:

1. An aggressive cover-up plan was directed out of the White House which secured control of the investigation and defined Oswald as the sole assassin;

2. Jack Ruby was a "political criminal informant" for the FBI and he had strong links to organized crime and the Dallas police;

3. The FBI took deliberate and secret steps to counter the Warren Commission critics; and

4. Hart thought that the FBI misled the Warren Commission.

The Castro retaliation theory would increasingly percolate into print. Those promoting this theory either neglected or were unaware of: 1) Castro's communications with Kennedy; 2) Castro's early writings declaring that the U. S. far right was responsible for the assassination; 3) the logic in creating a significant rationale for the invasion of Cuba and conceivably a world war; 4) Castro's overtures to LBJ; and 5) Castro's views of LBJ as more hawkish than JFK.

Years later, Senator Gary Hart (D-CO) told the *Huffington Post* "It's amazing to me that American journalism never followed up on that story very much (the murders of Johnny Roselli and Sam Giancana) because if you found out who killed those two guys, you might have some really interesting information on your hands." There were "all kinds of leads ... I went down to Miami when Roselli was killed and talked to this Dade County sheriff from the Miami Police Department, and they showed me pictures of him being fished out of the water in a barrel and how he had been killed – nightmarish stuff. And [Momo Salvatore] Giancana was killed in his own basement with six holes in his throat with a Chicago police car and an FBI car outside his house."

Based on CIA documents released in 2007, the CIA offered Roselli $150,000 to kill Fidel Castro. Roselli worked with Robert Maheu (former FBI agent), Sam Giancana, and Santo Trafficante.

During his Presidential run in 1988 Senator Hart called to reopen the investigation of the JFK assassination and received death threats. In 2013 Hart admitted that in revealing the assassination story, even as a journalist, "you risk your life because whoever killed these two guys is still out there."[26]

PBS's Jim Lehrer probed the role of intelligence agencies in the assassination during the *Robert McNeil Report*, June 24, 1976. The guests included David Phillips (ret. CIA office), Senator Robert Morgan (D-NC) (and member of the Senate Select Intelligence Committee) and Nicholas Horrock, *N.Y. Times* reporter. Lehrer started by clarifying the poor performance of the CIA and FBI during the Warren Commission investigation and characterized the findings of the Senate Select Intelligence as indicating that the CIA and FBI were involved in a cover-up. Senator Morgan viewed the FBI as protecting its image, while the CIA did not offer any information not asked of it. The Senate Select Committee determined that the CIA plotted to assassinate Castro, which Morgan saw as dereliction.

Lehrer asked about the FBI dereliction in handling Oswald prior to the assassination, and Morgan agreed, noting that J. Edgar Hoover directed his agents to gather derogatory material on the Warren Commission members. Nicholas Horrock noted the FBI motto "Don't embarrass the Bureau."

Lehrer noted that the FBI used the Domestic Intelligence Division but never consulted their expert on Cuba. Horrock then suggested the underlying possibility of foreign involvement so, "On the surface it appears the bureau is just trying to cover itself." Then Horrock seemed to start revealing something. "But at that time, I don't think that the Warren Commission was overly eager to discover that sort of..." Lehrer shifted to ask, "What startled you the most?" and Horrock responded with, "a fellow boards an aircraft in Mexico City and apparently sits with the pilot, doesn't go through normal customs, and ends up in Cuba nine days after the assassination." Lehrer then turned to David Phillips to discuss the Cuban Connection, and Phillips wove quite a tale.

The first one is the story about "D." The Warren Report identified him as a Latin America secret agent. He was in fact a fabricator. "I [Phillips] am convinced he was a fabricator. I interviewed him personally.... And one of the last things he said was "that wasn't really true [seeing Oswald receive $6500 in the Cuban embassy] I said this because I hoped the United States would do something about Castro. This man represented another government, and it might very well have been a covert action by that government."

Lehrer then asked about this man entering the Cuban Embassy, and Phillips claimed that it would be inappropriate to say how thorough CIA coverage was.

Senator Richard Schweiker (R-Pa.) had already shown pictures of someone who was identified as Oswald entering the Cuban Embassy- but who was about 50 pounds heavier and had a receding hairline.

Phillips then described "D" leaving from Mexico City with a nine-member crew to Cuba. Purportedly this came from a CIA Report from Washington. Phillips then denied knowledge of AMLASH, the CIA operative attempting to assassinate Castro. Senator Morgan then claimed that when the CIA met with AMLASH, 10/29/63 that the plot "had the blessings of the President and the Attorney General."

Horrock declared that he would be uncomfortable with continued investigation of the CIA, and that America had undertaken "five investigations ... and every newspaperman has taken a crack at it ... this makes people unnecessarily uncomfortable."

Lehrer reverted to a concern about the possibility of proving Castro's involvement. Senator Morgan agreed with Horrock that an investigation into the assassination could have no satisfactory conclusion. Phillips then joked about the major industry of assassination researchers.

While this segment started with public statements regarding the dereliction of the FBI and CIA, the interviews then focused on Cuba and ambivalance regarding new investigations. No mention was made of forensic evidence, or the roles of the mafia, Secret Service, the military or LBJ. Lehrer was taken by a supposed Cuban connection, and Phillips predictably enabled that line of inquiry. Horrock advocated a notion of national security which meant a self-censoring of the press and government.[27]

On August 3, 1976, a United Press dispatch stated that "Congressman Thomas Downing had distributed a 79-page packet compiled by former CIA operative Robert Morrow ... suggested right-wing Cuban exiles sought Kennedy's assassination in retaliation for his withdrawal of air support for the Bay of Pigs invasion ... this material alleged that Nixon was the action man behind the Bay of Pigs and that Nixon promised the right-wing Cuban exile leader, Mario Kohly, that he would eliminate left-wing anti-Castro exiles after the invasion."

Meanwhile, the murders of Mafiosi Sam Giancana before he was scheduled to speak to the Senate Select Committee (Church Committee or CIA oversight), and of John Roselli, after his testimony to the Senate Select Committee, fueled government investigations). The *New York Times*, 8/14/76, commented editorially on the Giancana-Roselli-Kennedy assassination connections, and for the first time called for a new Congressional probe.

In 1976, the National Archives disclosed that two of Leon Jaworski's letters to the Warren Commission were missing from the records of the Commission: a "Letter of December 18, 1963" expressing a continuous "willingness to assist in any way" and a "Letter of Leon Jaworski to J. Lee Rankin, May 8, 1964." Also found missing from the Warren Commission documents in the Archives was a "Letter of Gerald Ford, April 7, 1964, concerning expediting the FBI investigation." Coincidentally, evidence started to disappear from the National Archives.

A 8/22/76 UPI story reported, based on Roselli's unnamed lawyer, who told the FBI in 1967 that Roselli and another client were involved with "a government approved project aimed at assassinating Castro" in the early 1960s, and that Castro planned to murder President Kennedy. The next day Jack Anderson retold his twice-printed Mafia-Castro assassination story on ABC's *Good Night America*. Anderson again disregarded the Garrison material which he had given to the FBI, and repeated the conclusions of the Warren Report. The lone nut assassin, Oswald, was portrayed as "pro-Castro."

The major networks and newspapers generally reported that the newly released FBI and CIA documents contained no evidence of conspiracy, and nothing to imply that the roles of Oswald or Ruby might need to be reassessed. ABC's *Good Morning America*, however, twice granted the Assassination Information Bureau, a citizen's research group, five minutes of airtime to comment on the documents during late 1976 and early 1977. ABC was the only major media outlet to do so.

"The Trial of the CIA," by Taylor Branch, which appeared in *The New York Times Magazine* (9/12/76) was subtitled "Not all of its covert actions have succeeded," but the agency did manage to outfox Congressional investigators. While the Rockefeller Commission had neither the time nor mandate, the Senate Intelligence Committee, referred to as the Church Committee after Chairman Senator Frank Church, D-ID continued exploring CIA foreign assassinations. Branch claimed:

> Where American efforts to kill were direct and persistent – in the case of Castro – they were unsuccessful, and where foreign leaders were actually killed – Lumumba in the Congo, Trujillo in the Dominican Republic, Diem in South Vietnam, Schneider in Chile – there was no hard proof that CIA operatives actually took part in the murders.... Certainly many thousands of people have died as a result of CIA paramilitary interventions ... [Regarding Trujillo] the Committee showed how American policy turned against the Dominican strongman, how the agency provided assurances of support to those who plotted against him, how CIA officials smuggled weapons into the country and exchanged cryptic messages on the likelihood of a successful assassination, however the committee exonerated the agency of Trujillo's murder on the grounds that the weapons it smuggled in were probably not the ones used in the killing.... By the time we finished the assassination report we lost three things, the public attention, much of our own energy, will

power and our leadership.... Church wanted to wrap up investigative chores to begin his own Presidential campaign.... The committee was floundering: Rogovin [CIA Special Counsel] pressed his advantage. We agreed with the committee that they could have access to information for six case studies in covert action provided they would go public with only one of them. They swore all sorts of secrecy oaths that they would not let the names of the other countries leak.... By December 1975 the House and Senate committees were set on opposite courses. Pike wanted to impale the CIA for its abuses. Church wanted to show that a Senate committee could handle national security responsibly.... Pike developed two thematic criticisms of the CIA ... gathering intelligence against which there is no audible dissent. He attacked covert action by revealing a few more of the startling case studies. His most poignant example involved the Kurdish minority in Iraq.... The Church committee was badly divided on the issue of reform.... These recommendations amounted to a clear, though tortured endorsement of CIA's covert action program.... A combination of events enabled the CIA to prevent a debate on whether covert action – secret wars and secret alternatives to war is justified or necessary. The CIA bowled over the Pike Committee.... The agency began these searching investigations on the ropes, and clearly emerged the winner. Its powers, so unique and hidden, remain essentially unchallenged. [28]

This insightful overview foreshadowed the challenges faced by the House Select Committee on Assassinations. But it did not motivate the mainstream media to challenge the largely hidden CIA domestic operations.

A Gallup poll, September 1976, indicated that over 80% of the public believed that a conspiracy was responsible for both the assassinations of President Kennedy and Martin Luther King, Jr. This perspective is a tribute to the assassination research community, some bold witnesses, portions of the media, a few mainstream investigations and the American public. This public sentiment, along with activist assassination researchers led by Mark Lane in a post-Watergate political climate, led to the reluctant authorization of the House Select Committee on Assassinations (HSCA) in late 1976.

Professor Peter Dale Scott now viewed the mainstream media as making "a large contribution to the mounting public pressure to reopen the investigation of the Kennedy assassination.... "The only way the press will appreciate the significance of the less sensational research is through its own sustained investigation."[29]

The *Fort Worth Star-Telegram* reporter Jim Marrs framed the HSCA challenges in his lead paragraph (12/1/76). "The new House Select Committee on Assassinations may find itself faced with the distinct possibility that a coup d etat occurred in 1963 – with the complicity of U.S. Government officials"

New challenges emerged. CIA fingerprints seemed evident in the *Houston Post* piece "No cover-up and Oswald's Mexico visit," 12/2/76, by Donald Morris, who had worked with the CIA for 17 years before joining the *Post* in 1972. It appeared to have been edited by the newly formed Association of Retired Intelligence Officers. The article characterized the interest in Oswald's visit to Mexico City as "a perfect example of paranoia at work." All CIA actions and procedures were stoutly defended. No attempt was made to clarify Senator Schweiker's questions about the purported pictures of Oswald entering the Cuban and Russian embassies clearly not being pictures of Oswald. Morris even attempted to revise the record regarding these "visits" by claiming Oswald merely called the embassies. He maintained:

> On the whole, the CIA performed commendably in catching the contact, transcribing it in passing it to the FBI through its normal channels in such a short period.... Oswald was one of a great number of left wing nuts again rebuffed in one of his efforts to make himself attractive to the Soviets ... it was not sinister in 1963 ... and it isn't sinister now.[30]

By tradition, Congress does not conduct lengthy investigations, so the HSCA was hampered by significant constraints of time, money, disinformation, the intransigence of certain agencies, and mission.

Briefly, HSCA Chief Counsel Richard A. Sprague, the effective, no-nonsense, Philadelphia D.A., planned to aggressively pursue the investigation including questioning of the CIA, FBI and Military intelligence. By November 1976 he had hired a staff of 170 and he soon became a threat to many in Washington, as he aggressively sought more money, time and subpoena power. Select committees essentially have to lobby for money, and when Congressman Tom Downing (R-Va.) retired this became more problematic.

Ben Franklin of the Washington bureau of the *New York Times* filed a balanced and accurate story about the HSCA, but he was quickly reassigned. The *New York Times* then ran an attack piece by David Burnham, "Counsel in Assassination Inquiry Often Target of Criticism," smearing

Sprague's seventeen-year record in Philadelphia solely in terms of the controversies he provoked. He recycled a discredited attack printed years earlier in the *Philadelphia Inquirer* though the Inquirer was hit with a $34 million judgment for defamation of a public official in the U.S. Burnham quoted CIA asset Walter Pincus, a *Washington Post* reporter, regarding HSCA debate, "Mr. Walter Pincus calls it [HSCA] perhaps the worst example of congressional inquiry run amok." 1/2/77. (Burnham was the reporter whom anti-nuclear activist Karen Silkwood was supposed to meet the night that she was driven off the road and killed.) Nonetheless, the Burnham articles served to almost derail the HSCA. Two days later the attempt to reconstitute the committee by voice vote failed, which delayed the HSCA for weeks.

The January 6, 1977, *New York Times* piece by Burnham ran a warning from Rep. Don Edwards (D-Cal.), an ex-FBI man who chaired the House Judiciary subcommittee on Civil and Constitutional Rights. Edwards argued that the HSCA's investigative techniques were "wrong, immoral, and very likely illegal." He was referring to alleged plans to secretly tape witnesses and then do psychological stress tests.[31] George Lardner Jr. of the *Washington Post*, 2/11/77, then crafted a story strongly critical of Sprague's proposed procedures:

> Sharp objections have been raised to the Assassination Committee's proposed purchases and investigating techniques. With Downing still chairman of the committee staff recently sought to buy five suction cup devices that are used to tape-record telephone conversations. In a letter submitted under Downing's name, the committee sought authority to install transmitter cut off arrangements for listening in purposes on two of the committee's phones.... Emphasizing that he was speaking for himself, Gonzalez not only disavowed the telephone gadgetry ... but expressed distaste for some of the equipment Sprague wants to purchase, such as two mini phone recording devices.

Curiously, Lardner had interviewed David Ferrie, Garrison's key witness, for hours on the night that Ferrie allegedly committed suicide. The *L.A. Times* recycled the *Washington Post's* criticism.

> Some of the proposed investigative techniques have stirred objections. One is the use of hidden electronic transmitters to secretly record the remarks of potential witnesses; this is a thoroughly

bad proposal that if implemented would invade the constitutional rights of the subject of the inquiry. The committee also wants to buy lie detector machines and stress evaluators ... this latter smacks of mere gimmickry, unless a need for these devices is shown. [32]

Sprague refused to resign and enlisted Rep. Tip O'Neill's support in the ensuing power struggle. When the HSCA staff and the Congress backed Sprague, HSCA Chair Rep. Henry Gonzalez then took the unusual step of quitting. During the struggle Sprague was proposing a staff of 200, a yearly budget of $6.5 million and issuing subpoenas to the CIA. The CIA stipulated that HSCA staff must comply with a policy of confidentiality which precluded them telling anything to Sprague. Some other mass media outlets then attacked Sprague.

Meanwhile, the attorney for retired Vice-Admiral Burkley, President Kennedy's personal physician, contacted Sprague to grant an interview. Although Burkley was present at Parkland Hospital, and signed the death certificate of President Kennedy in Dallas, the Warren Commission had never called him as a witness. Burkley was indicating that others besides Oswald must have been involved, but Sprague never got the opportunity to pursue the interview.

Sprague, upset with the political and media attacks, which paralleled those endured by Garrison, instructed the HSCA PR man, an experienced reporter, to contact the press around the nation and clarify the nature of the inquiry. Inexplicably, not one newspaper in the country contacted Sprague to get more information.

> Practically, all the Cabinet members of President Kennedy's administration, along with Director J. Edgar Hoover of the FBI and Chief James Rowley of the Secret Service, whose duty it was to protect the life of the President, testified that to their knowledge there was no sign of any conspiracy. To say now that these people, as well as the Commission, suppressed, neglected to unearth, or overlooked evidence of a conspiracy would be an indictment of the entire government of the United States.

The sketchy Dutch journalist Willen Oltmans, who had reported on the assassination for years, told the HSCA that he was shocked when he met again with George de Mohrenschildt in Dallas, in February of 1977. Normally confident and fit, de Mohrenschildt was "nervous, trembling, and very, very scared." De Mohrenschildt confessed or dissembled, "I feel responsible for the behavior of Lee Harvey Oswald." He admitted being the liaison between H.L. Hunt (oilman), anti-Castro Cubans, and elements of the FBI and CIA.

After de Mohrenschildt begged to leave the country, Oltmans flew with him to Holland and Belgium. In less than a week the enigmatic de Mohrenschildt fled from Oltmans back to the U.S. A few weeks later he supposedly committed suicide just hours before HSCA investigator Gaeton Fonzi was to interview him.

Two days after de Mohrenschildt's death, CBS briefly covered his role along with Oltmans' testimony to the HSCA. CBS reporter, Jim McManus, reported that Oltmans spent more than two hours answering committee questions behind closed doors and repeated his claim that de Mohrenschildt, a one-time friend of Lee Harvey Oswald, was part of a conspiracy to murder President Kennedy. Oltmans claimed that "de Mohrenschildt told me in Dallas on the 23rd of February of this year that Oswald acted at his instructions and that de Mohrenschildt and Oswald discussed the Kennedy assassination from A to Z, and that he knew that Oswald was going to kill Kennedy sooner or later." Oltmans claimed, "That there were four Kennedy assassins, and he gave the committee a picture of a Cuban as possibly one of the four, but he declined to give the name publicly." Oltmans claimed in their talk last month that de Mohrenschildt also mentioned the involvement of an anti-Castro Cuban, "Loran Hall was offered in the office of Lester Logue, with five or six people present, $50,000 to take part in the assassination of President Kennedy."[33]

Subcommittee Chairman Richardson Preyer (D-NC) wanted to work with this information on a background basis. Oltmans also implicated the late Texas millionaire H.L. Hunt in his testimony.

CBS then ran a 1968 Oltmans interview with de Mohrenschildt where he denied the involvement of Texan oil money in the assassination. De Mohrenschildt also purportedly said that "Oswald was a lunatic who killed President Kennedy." Oltmans claimed that de Mohrenschildt simply changed his story. De Mohrenschildt's lawyer told CBS's Eric Enberg that he was present in Dallas when Oltmans talked with his client. Rather than examining de Mohrenschildt's fears, strange behavior, ominous possible involvement, changed statements and suicide, CBS highlighted de Mohrenschildt's statements nine years earlier. When later questioned by researcher Jerry Policoff, Oltmans threatened "You had better watch out or you will get hurt." Policoff maintains that Oltmans acted like a spook rather than a journalist.

Remarkably, de Mohrenschildt's wife, Jeanne, granted an interview to the *Fort Worth Star-Telegram* 5/11/78, and said that she did not think that her husband committed suicide. She thought Oswald was a U.S. intelligence agent, possibly CIA, and she was convinced that he did not kill President Kennedy. "They may get to me too but I'm not afraid ... it's about time that somebody looked into this thing."[34]

Bill O'Reilly, then a reporter for WFAA-TV Dallas, briefly explored the relationship of the CIA and Lee Harvey Oswald, 4/11/77, with the help of his old friend Gaeton Fonzi, now a HSCA staffer. He reported that a "recently declassified document, now in the hands of a writer, indicates that Oswald was employed by the CIA possibly in 1962, and although it may be a coincidence, Oswald's tax return was not made public." In a related matter, Mrs. Jeanne de Mohrenschildt, wife of the late George de Mohrenschildt, told O'Reilly that she and her husband were good friends with a Dallas CIA agent named J. Walton Moore, and that Moore told George de Mohrenschildt that Lee Harvey Oswald was OK to recommend for a job. When O'Reilly called Moore who had no comment, CIA headquarters told O'Reilly that they were "astonished" by Mrs. de Mohrenschildt's comments. 35 Years later, when O'Reilly got famous with FOX network, he adopted the lone nut scenario on the assassination.

By March 27th the *Baltimore Sun* editorialized about the HSCA, "Kill it."

The HSCA limped along, though on a limited time frame and budget. Sprague knew that he had lost Congressional support, and on June 20, 1977 he resigned, realizing the fate of the HSCA was in jeopardy. Years later, in an interview with Dick Russell, Sprague tried to set the record straight.

> One, as a prosecutor, I have never wiretapped and never secretly recorded any conversation with anybody. I wanted to obtain recording equipment for the purpose of our people in the field interviewing and getting permission to tape record for the purpose of accuracy. If the person said no, we would not record it. The record will show that's exactly how we used them. Three or four weeks after we made that request to congress, stories were carried in the *Los Angeles Times*, and the *Post*, and particularly by Burnham [*NYT*] that I'd bought this recording equipment to surreptitiously record what witnesses are going to say. To this day, nobody has ever in fact produced anybody who said we did that.... Crucified not for what we did, but for what a reporter says we did ... after I resigned, Burnham was taken off the whole thing [story] ... [36]

G. Robert Blakey, a law professor at Cornell University, and a specialist in organized crime who had served from 1960-1964 in the Justice Department, replaced him. At the press conference announcing his appointment Blakey declared, "The purpose of this news conference is to announce there will not be any more news conferences." He then quoted former Republican Presidential candidate Tom Dewey:

> In general, it is my belief that a talking prosecutor is not a working prosecutor.... It is my sincere hope that the work we are doing vanishes from the newspapers.[37]

Blakey then required his staff to sign agreements, subject to a $5000 penalty if they disclosed anything. He asserted that he would follow a strategy of voluntary cooperation with the CIA. Meanwhile, the CIA brought former agent George Joannides, a former Helms man, out of retirement to work as the CIA liaison to the HSCA. Blakey was unaware that Joannides ran psychological warfare operations in 1963 with anti-Castro Cubans, including the revolutionary Student Directorate (DRE), heavily funded by the CIA, which had regular contact with Oswald. HSCA Assistant Chief Counsel. Robert Tannenbaum, who quit in frustration, summarized the process.

> We were not interested in receiving documents that were redacted. We were only interested in seeing who questioned a witness, what evidence they received and what they did ... why couldn't Congress get that material from the executive branch? There is no reason for the executive branch intelligence agencies to clear members of Congress. That's preposterous...
>
> Tannenbaum observed, [The sixth floor window] is open maybe 12" and an opaque wall of maybe 4 ft. where the window starts. At best you could just see a partial of a shooter's face, if in fact someone was shooting.... How did the Dallas police, at 12:48 pm, just about 18 minutes after the assassination, get the description of someone who was in that window?

Tannenbaum saw CIA documents from Richard Helms' office confirming much of Garrison's case. "They were intimidating his witnesses." He resigned early on because the committee "was not committed to the truth."

> Those who were subpoenaed who were lying to the committee, who were in the government, and not doing the right thing, we

needed to hold them in contempt, and or charge perjury. That required a vote of the committee, a vote of the House of Representatives and a submission to the U.S. Attorney's office. They weren't prepared to do that. Because they really didn't work to find out the truth publicly.[38]

In Tannenbaum's questioning of CIA officer David Phillips, significant contradictions emerged.

"Phillips testimony was that there was no photograph of Oswald [entering the Russian Embassy in Mexico City] because the camera equipment had broken down that day and there was no audio tape of Oswald's voice because that recycled every six or seven days."

The pictures were not of Oswald, and the FBI had heard the voice on the tape, which was not the voice of Oswald – yet the HSCA did not confront Phillips with this evidence.

Face the Nation (CBS) 6/27/76, interviewed Senator Schweiker (R-Pa), who had served on the Senate Select Committee on Intelligence Subcommittee on the John Kennedy Assassination. Schweiker's memorable response to reporter George Herman's first question about the premises of the Warren Report was:

> I think that the report, to those who have studied it closely, has collapsed like a house of cards … I frankly believe that we have shown that the John F. Kennedy assassination was snuffed out before it even began, and that the fatal mistake the Warren Commission made was not to use its own investigators, but instead to rely on the CIA and FBI personnel, which played directly into the hands of senior intelligence officials who directed the cover-up.[39]

Disinformation played a role in shaping the HSCA as well as creating obstacles for its investigators. Gaeton Fonzi, formerly a reporter with the *Philadelphia Magazine* before working as a Senate and HSCA researcher, revealed the source of false leads that Senator Schweiker had asked him to pursue in 1975. That source was Clare Booth Luce, the widow of the founder of Time, Inc., who had been a member of Congress and a former CIA contract agent, and then served as a board member of the Association of Retired Intelligence Officers.

Luce told Senator Schweiker that a militant anti-Castro Cuban, whose name was "something like" Julio Fernandez, had called her years ago to say that his "Free Cuba" group in New Orleans had kept tabs on Oswald.

Julio Fernandez supposedly gave all of the information, including tape recordings, to the FBI, and he was fearful of subsequent involvement in the case.

By 1977, after checking this lead as far he could, Fonzi set up a meeting with Clare Booth Luce. She graciously recounted the story she told Senator Schweiker, and she confirmed that she had been calling CIA Director Colby to keep him posted on Schweiker's investigation. Fonzi recalls:

> According to Colby's own notes, she admitted to him that she had concocted the name of Julio Fernandez. When I asked Luce why she had done that, she simply smiled sweetly.[40]

Fonzi also had his notes for a key witness, CIA asset Antonio Veciana, stolen and leaked by someone to reporter Jack Anderson. Anderson's column in the *Washington Post* referred to "a mysterious Mr. X" but described him in such detail that Veciana's life might have been put in danger. It had a chilling effect on Veciana's testimony as well as other actual and potential witnesses. In Anderson's second column he detailed "Mr. X's" relationship with "Morris" Bishop, (instead of Maurice) the precise misspelling of Bishop's first name used in Fonzi's notes. Anderson seemingly had somehow gotten copies of those notes. Fonzi and many other HSCA investigators were convinced that Maurice Bishop was a pseudonym for David Phillips, CIA Chief of Western Hemisphere.

The *L.A. Times* 9/18/77 story "Ex-CIA official Denies Any Oswald Link to Agency" covered a spirited debate between David Phillips and Mark Lane hosted by the University of Southern California. Reporter Myrna Oliver noted Phillips claimed he "felt like an insect pierced and mounted on a pin for public display" as the latest 'spook' suspected of trying to cover-up the assassination.

Lane later asserted that he:

> Specifically doubted CIA reports that Oswald had contacted the Soviet Embassy in Mexico City, then under Phillips' CIA eye, to ask for messages. He said FBI agents who questioned Oswald after Kennedy was shot in Dallas listened to the tapes the CIA claimed proved that Oswald called the Soviets; Lane said the FBI determined the taped voice was not Oswald's.

Rolling Stone ran Carl Bernstein's stunning revelations in "The CIA and the Media" 10/20/77. Bernstein used a range of concerns and procedures with sources to explore Senator Church's Intelligence Committee hearings on the media.

Despite the evidence of widespread CIA use of journalists, the Senate Intelligence Committee and its staff decided against questioning any of the reporters, editors, publishers or board executives whose relationships with the agency are detailed in CIA files.

According to sources in the Senate and the Agency, the use of journalists was one of two areas of inquiry which the CIA went to extraordinary lengths to curtail. The other was the agency's continuing and extensive use of academics for recruitment and information gathering.

In both instances, the sources said, former directors Colby and Bush and CIA special counsel Mitchell Rogovin were able to convince key members of the committee that full inquiry or even limited public disclosure of the dimensions of the activities would do irreparable damage to the nation's intelligence gathering apparatus, as well as to the reputations of hundreds of individuals. Walter Elder, deputy to former CIA director McCone and the principal Agency liaison to the Church committee, argued that the committee lacked jurisdiction because there had been no misuse of journalists by the CIA; the relationships had been voluntary.

Some members of the Church committee feared that agency officials had gained control of the inquiry and that they were being hoodwinked ... Church and some of the other members were much more interested in making headlines than in doing serious, tough investigating...

The Senate committee's investigation in the use of journalists was supervised by William B Bader, a former CIA intelligence officer... now a high-level intelligence official at the Defense Department. Bader was assisted by David Aaron, who later served as the deputy to Zbigniew Brzezinski...

According to colleagues on the staff of the Senate inquiry, both Bader and Aaron were disturbed by the information contained in CIA files about journalists; they urged that further investigation be undertaken... Bader's investigation was conducted under unusually difficult conditions. His first request for specific information on the use of journalists was turned down by the CIA on grounds that there had been no abuse of authority and that current intelligence operation might be compromised. Senators Walter Huddleston, Howard Baker, Gary Hart, Walter Mondale and Charles Matthias ... shared Bader's distress at the CIA's reaction. In a series of phone calls and meetings with CIA director George Bush and other agency officials, the senators insisted that the committee staff be provided information about the scope of CIA-press activities. Finally, Bush agreed to a search of the files and have those records pulled which deal with operations where journalists had been used. But the raw files could not be made available to Bader or the committee, Bush insisted instead, the director decided, his deputies would condense the material into one paragraph summaries describing in the most general terms the activities of each individual journalist. Most important Bush, decreed the names of journalists and of the news organizations with which they were affiliated would be omitted from the summaries.

The discussion ... grew heated. The committee's representatives said they could not honor their mandate-to determine if the CIA had abused it authority – without further information. The CIA maintained it could not protect its legitimate intelligence operations or its employees if further disclosures were made to the committee. Many of the journalists were contract employees of the Agency, Bush said at one point, and the CIA was no less obligated to them than to any other agents.

Finally, a highly unusual agreement was hammered out: Bader and Miller would be permitted to examine "sanitized" versions of the full files of twenty-five journalists selected from the summaries; but the names of the journalists and the news organizations which employed them would be blanked out, as would the identities of other CIA employees mentioned in the files. Church and Tower would be permitted to examine the unsanitized version of five of the twenty-five... The whole deal was contingent on an agreement that Bader, Miller, Tower or Church would not reveal the contents of the files to other members of the committee or staff...

Exposure of the CIA's relationship with journalists and academics, the Agency feared, would close down two of the few avenues of agent recruitment still open...

"We weren't about to bring up guys to the committee and then have everybody say they've been traitors to the ideals of their profession," said a senator...

Had the CIA abused its authority? It had dealt with the press almost exactly as it had dealt with other institutions from which it sought cover – the diplomatic service, academics, corporations...

The files show that the CIA goes to the press for and just as often as the press comes to the CIA...

The findings of the Senate committee's inquiry into the use of journalists were deliberately buried from the full membership of the committee, from the Senate and from the public.... Bader's findings on the subject were never discussed with the full committee, even in executive session.... Colby's misleading public statements about the use of journalists were repeated without serious contradiction or elaboration...

Assembling the summaries was difficult, according to CIA officials who supervised the job. There were no "journalist files" per se and information had to be collected from divergent sources that reflect the highly compartmentalized character of the CIA.... After several weeks Bader began receiving summaries, which numbered over four hundred by the time they said it had completed searching its files.... We gave them a broad, representative picture, said one Agency official, "We never pretended it was a total description of the range of activities over 25 years, or of the number of journalists who have done things for us." A relatively small number of foreign journalists...

Bader and others to whom he described the contents of the summaries immediately reached some general conclusions: the sheer number of covert relationships with journalists was far greater than the CIA had ever hinted: and the Agency's use of reporters and news executives was an intelligence asset of the first magnitude. Reporters had been involved in almost every imaginable kind of operation. [41]

In 1977 ABC aired "The Trial of Lee Harvey Oswald" produced by Lawrence Schiller, FBI asset and Jack Ruby's business manager. The program was generally supportive of the Warren Commission findings, though some hints were given that Oswald could have been part of a conspiracy composed of the Mafia and some intelligence agents. Shiller had the full cooperation of the Dallas Police Department.

Only a few newspapers committed investigative resources to the assassination coverage during the HSCA tenure. Notable for their contributions were the *Washington Post*, the *Village Voice*, the *San Francisco Chronicle*, and the *Dallas Morning News*.

Jack Anderson's column, 12/1/77 revealed, "The DOD has unaccountably destroyed files on the assassination." Anderson shifted his contention in his 12/10/77 column. Army intelligence agents should be given credit for "being ahead of almost everyone else in establishing Oswald's background." The vital questions of how Army Intelligence knew so much, what was the role of Army Intelligence agents in Dealey Plaza, as well as why most of Oswald's military files were destroyed, remained unanswered. [42]

The *Washington Post*, 12/13/77, printed portions of an FBI memo, stating that in 1967 President Johnson told White House aide Marvin Watson that he "was convinced that there was a plot in connection with the assassination" and that the CIA was involved. The *San Francisco Chronicle*, 9/12/78, which ran a provocative piece by Warren Hinkle revealed a statement by CIA finance officer, Jim Wilcott, that "CIA people killed Kennedy." Wilcot testified to the House Select Committee on Assassinations:

> It was common knowledge in the Tokyo station that Oswald worked for the agency.... He testified that he overheard CIA agents say "agency people" had Kennedy murdered because the President had reneged on a "secret agreement" with former CIA director Allen Dulles to militarily support the CIA-backed 1961 invasion of Cuba.... "CIA people killed Kennedy." [43]

In December as the HSCA was searching for more funding, Priscilla Johnson McMillan, who was a witting CIA asset, worked the interview circuit to promote her book *Marina and Lee*, which she had been working on for years. On Tom Snyder's TV show she reiterated, "It's hard for people to accept the idea that one person who is not so different from themselves, went off and did a thing like that. It threatens people's sense of order about history ... when one man can step up there and nullify the will of an entire country, it makes life seem meaningless and without order, and I think conspiracy theorists want to give life an order and coherence that it lacks."

Gallery, 4/78, ran Willem Oltmans new assertion that General Donald Donaldson, a Bulgarian émigré, claimed that J. Edgar Hoover, Allen Dulles and Richard Nixon conspired in the assassination. Oltmans interviewed George de Mohrenschildt and his wife in 1967 for Dutch television station NOS, and CBS did the camera work. This 40-minute film mysteriously disappeared from NOS files in 1975. In 1977 a depressed de Mohrenschildt revealed that "he felt responsible for Oswald's role. He wanted to confess" but was receiving death threats. Recall that de Mohrenschildt supposedly committed suicide with a rifle just hours before a HSCA staffer, Gaeton Fonzi, was to interview him.

General Donaldson, who had written Senator Frank Church (D-ID), chair of the Senate Intelligence Committee, claimed important knowledge regarding the assassination of JFK. He told Oltmans that de Mohrenschildt was murdered. Donaldson (formerly Adamou Dimitrov) also asserted that

Jacqueline Kennedy had a top-secret report on the assassination. Former Kennedy aide Ted Sorenson knew details of the assassination. When President Carter nominated Sorenson as CIA Director, to clean out the agency, Sorenson was somehow immediately smeared and was not confirmed.

Donaldson advised Oltmans to meet with President Carter, and 8/29/77 he met with a presidential lawyer. Soon thereafter, Oltmans supposedly confronted Donaldson, who balked, and supposedly threatened to shoot him if he released any information. Oltmans recounted Donaldson's "assertions" on ABC TV's *Good Morning America* 9/8/77, but never again heard from Donaldson.

Colonel Fletcher Prouty posits that General Donaldson could have been a "cover story" for an intelligence operation. Perhaps "Donaldson" gave Oltmans a story which could be discredited after publication – a common ruse.

As public revelations of the CIA mounted, the *New York Times* ran a three-part series "Wordwide Propaganda Network Built by the CIA," 12/25/77 to 12/27/77, by John Crewdson and Joseph Treaster. They asserted fewer media-CIA connections than Carl Bernstein did in his *Rolling Stone* article but revealed new examples and tactics. They noted that, "The CIA had a formal operation known as KMFORGET in which stories planted by the agency in one country would be clipped and mailed to media in other countries, and such efforts enhanced the likelihood that the stories would be seen by an American correspondent and transmitted home" [blowback or domestic fallout] This "gray propaganda" was used to circumvent a government ban [from the 1970s-2013] on using published materials from U.S. government agencies created for foreign audiences being aimed at America.

Dick Russell's next report explored the career and connections of Antonio Veciana, a high level anti-Cuban activist who worked with U.S. intelligence agent "Maurice Bishop." Bishop and Veciana formed Alpha 66, the militant anti-Castro group, and once Veciana allegedly met with Bishop and Lee Harvey Oswald in Dallas. A year after the assassination Veciana asserted that Bishop offered him money if Veciana's cousin, a Cuban intelligence agent, would say that he had met with Oswald. Bishop later dropped the plan. Veciana continued to work with Bishop in Puerto Rico, Bolivia and Chile. Veciana was later shot in the head – but he survived. In 1971 Bishop had started a plot to assassinate Castro on a visit to Chile but the plan never materialized. Russell hoped that the HSCA could identify Bishop (who we now know is David Phillips).[44]

Reader's Digest managing editor William Charles Ouster decided to examine the enigmatic Oswald. *Digest* editors had long been close with J. Edgar Hoover and the CIA, and Nelson Rockefeller's brother Lawrence sat on their board. They asked Edward Epstein to write a book and provided him with two staffers. *Digest* editors were then contacted by "Jaime Jamieson" a "former" CIA officer who acted as a media consultant and arranged interviews with Soviet defectors. One defector, Yuri Nosenko, had maintained that Oswald had no ties to Soviet intelligence, but after a long and harsh interrogation by James Angleton (CIA Counter Intel) he changed his mind.

Epstein cited confidential, unnamed sources and classified materials stating that Nosenko was a double agent who assisted Oswald. Epstein later revealed that his source was CIA Counterintelligence Chief James Angleton. His book, *Legend: The Secret World of Lee Harvey Oswald*, which portrayed Oswald as a Soviet Agent, came out in 1978.[45]

Variety Magazine 10/25/78 interviewed CBS News President Richard Salant about the seventy plus hours of outtakes on the assassination. Salant stated that he had no intention of making them public, because nothing indicated that Oswald did not act alone.

In November of 1978 the *Dallas Morning News* ran a three-page lead story by Earl Golz, revealing that an amateur cameraman, Charles Bronson, had shot film of the Texas School Book Depository six minutes before the assassination. The FBI Dallas office viewed the film in 1963 and reported that it "was not sufficiently clear" and that it "failed to show the building from which the shots were fired," thus it languished in obscurity. When the footage was declassified through the FOIA, the *Dallas Morning News* obtained it.[46] HSCA Senior staff members thought they saw movement in more than one window on the sixth floor. The film footage was given to HSCA photographic research expert Robert Groden who observed, "The fact that there is movement in two windows that are separated by a good eight feet indicates beyond question that there was more than one person up there." Solid reporting on the declassified Bronson film also can be seen in the *Dallas Times Herald* 11/27/78. The FBI Dallas office suppressed the frames from being seen by the FBI headquarters, the Warren Commission, or as the Secret Service.[47]

The *Fort Worth Star-Telegram* continued its support for reporter Jim Marrs with his article, 10/22/78, about Earlene Roberts. Roberts had actually named two Dallas police officers that stopped in front of Oswald's rooming house and honked twice, while he was in his room after the assassination. Those policemen were never called to testify by the Warren Commission.

The small right-wing newspaper, *Spotlight,* carried a revelation from Victor Marchetti, the former Executive Assistant to the Deputy Director of the CIA. Marchetti said that he had seen an internal memo from James Angleton, head of CIA Counterintelligence, to CIA Director Richard Helms stating that CIA officer E. Howard Hunt was in Dallas the day President Kennedy was assassinated. Hunt sued for libel, but ultimately lost on appeal in 1984. More on this case later.

Clare Booth Luce, the activist wife of Henry Luce, resurfaced and this time told the HSCA that she was called late on the night of the assassination from an Anti-Castro Cuban who knew Oswald to be a communist who made several trips to Mexico City. Oswald was to have returned from Mexico City with an ample supply of money, and boasted that he was "a crack marksman and could shoot anybody – including the President or the Secretary of the Navy." Lastly, her alleged caller told her, "There is a Cuban Communist assassination team at large, and Oswald was their hired gun." The HSCA referred to this as "unsubstantiated allegations." This seems merely a new spin on old disinformation.[48]

Earl Golz tracked down TSBD employee Carolyn Arnold to clarify what she told the FBI regarding her seeing Oswald at 12:25, five minutes before the assassination. Golz reported in the *Dallas Morning News* 11/27/78 that Arnold was shocked the FBI had not reported her sighting.[49]

On 11/30/78 the *New York Times* ran an op-ed by Anthony Lewis which accused leading critic Mark Lane, recently returned from Jonestown, Guyana, of being a "ghoul … pitchman … creature … [who profited from] assassination bumper stickers…" Lewis called for "talk shows hosts and editors" to "refuse to permit Lane to be heard. It is time for the decent people of the United States to tune out Mark Lane." Lewis ironically, had taught at Columbia University School of Journalism, and since 1982 has held the James Madison chair in First Amendment Issues.

Earl Golz again unearthed new leads in "Witnesses Overlooked in JFK Probe," 12/19/78, *Dallas Morning News*:

> Johnny Powell, an inmate in the county jail at the time of the assassination of John F. Kennedy, recently told the *Dallas Morning News* he and others in his cell watched two men with a rifle in the 6th floor window of the TSBD across the street. When he looked the men were "fooling with" a scope on the rifle…. The authorities did not question Powell and his fellow inmates…

Golz noted the coercive grilling of Dealey Plaza witness Ronald Fischer.

> David Belin, an assistant counsel for the Warren Commission tried
> to intimidate him into testifying the one man he was able to see
> didn't have the light-colored hair he insisted he did have... 'Belin
> and I almost had a fight in the interview room over the color of, the
> man's hair.... He wanted me to tell him the man was dark-headed,
> and I wouldn't do it.[51]

Congressman Richardson Preyer expressed frustration to this author
that Ruby's calls to various crime figures in the weeks and days leading
up to the assassination were never thoroughly investigated. He said that
"the HSCA needed at least six more months to pursue the necessary leads
and that the CIA and the military did not cooperate fully," but Congress
denied them additional funding to fulfill their mandate to conduct a "full
and complete investigation." [52]

Meanwhile, unknown to Congressman Preyer and many others on
the HSCA, the investigators were being directed by HSCA Chief Counsel Blakey to restrict themselves to "issues we can answer.... Reality is
irrelevant here – this is Washington.... It will take too much time." HSCA
staffer Edwin Lopez provided some context:

> The HSCA ... had a fixed budget and a definite period of longevity.
> The CIA knew this. They only had to wait us out. The first stipula-
> tion was the super secrecy oath all who would have access to CIA
> files had to take ... who was working for whom?

Young HSCA staff investigators Dan Hardaway and Edwin Lopez repeatedly complained to Blakey that CIA liaison George Joannides was
hiding evidence of "a conspiracy involving the CIA in the assassination."
Meanwhile, in testimony to the HSCA David Phillips spread stories tying
Oswald to Castro. Phillips was so nervous that he had "three or four cigarettes going at once."[53]

Congressman Henry Gonzalez, the second chairman of the HSCA,
declared upon his departure that the committee was "a put up job and a
hideous farce that was never intended to work."

Regis Blahut, a liaison officer of the CIA, was arrested in June 1978 for
breaking into the safe of the House Assassination Committee and tamper-
ing with the autopsy photographs. Blahut admitted his involvement and
noted cryptically "There's other things involved that are detrimental to

other things." The CIA incredibly claimed that Blahut acted out of "mere curiosity." Although Blahut was fired, most HSCA committee staffers felt that "curiosity" was not consistent with the way the evidence should have been handled.

While the investigators from the FBI, CIA, Washington D.C. police, and Committee Chief Counsel Blakey knew about this break-in prior to the summer of 1979, the HSCA members and researchers did not. A more probing set of questions regarding the autopsy X-rays was not asked because by the time researchers could view these pictures the investigation was over. This incident was never adequately investigated.

Blakey focused on trying to prove Oswald acted alone, and only late in the investigation, based on audio evidence, shifted to conclude that the assassination was "probably the work of a conspiracy" This was met with media indifference and curious conjecture.

When the HSCA Report was being written Chief Counsel Robert Blakey hired Richard Billings of Time-Life to assist him. Notably, Billings was also the son-in-law of C.D. Jackson – "Henry Luce's personal emissary to the CIA" according to *Washington Post* investigative reporter Carl Bernstein. Recall that Billings had also been a member of the failed Bayo-Pawley Mission to Cuba in September of 1963 along with mafia and CIA-connected operatives, to smuggle Soviet colonels into the U.S. Although William Pawley committed suicide prior to being interviewed by HSCA staffer Gaeton Fonzi, nothing regarding the Bayo-Pawley mission was mentioned in the HSCA Report.

Blakey in his introduction to the HSCA Report noted, "Realizing that there would be an opportunity for others to fill in the details – that there might be indictments and trials as a result of future investigation – we decided to present an understated case." Let's ponder some of the sobering facts determined by the HSCA "understated" case as seen by reporter Jim Marrs:

> A conspiracy with at least two gunmen resulted in the death of President Kennedy. Jack Ruby's killing of Oswald was not spontaneous and Ruby likely entered the Dallas police station with assistance.
>
> The Dallas police withheld from the Warren Commission relevant information about Ruby's entry to the Police basement when Oswald was shot. The Secret Service was deficient in performing its duties in connection with the assassination. The FBI; performed with varying degrees of competency and failed to investigate adequately the possibility of conspiracy.

The CIA was deficient in its collection and sharing of assassination information. The Warren Commission failed to investigate the possibility of conspiracy adequately, partly because of the failures of government agencies to provide the commission with relevant information.

Investigation of conspiracy by the Secret Service was terminated early on by President Johnson's order that the FBI assume investigative responsibility.

Since the military 201 file on Oswald was destroyed before the committee could view it, the question of Oswald's connection with military intelligence could not be fully resolved.

Years later, at the AARC conference in 2014, Blakey strongly condemned the CIA.

The CIA lied to the Warren Commission, the HSCA, and the ARRB regarding Joannides connection to DRE. The CIA violated its own charter and ran a covert operation to subvert the HSCA – an outrageous breach of the agency's charter and the laws of our country." Staff attorneys Dan Hardaway and Edwin Lopez revealed that after Joannides assumed the role of CIA liaison to the HSCA that access to CIA documents was tightly controlled, the process was slowed down, they were not able to get access to as many people, and many of the CIA files were then expurgated.

After the HSCA report was released, former CIA asset Jeremiah O'Leary of the *Washington Post*, 1/6/79, (later of the *Washington Times*) creatively editorialized that two lone nuts were in Dealey Plaza firing at the same time.

Could it have been some other malcontent who Mr. Oswald met casually? Could not as much as three or four societal outcasts with no ties to any organization have developed in some spontaneous way a common determination to express their alienation in the killing of President Kennedy? Is it possible that two persons acting independently attempted to shoot the President at the same time?

FBI files show that "very friendly" journalists like O'Leary who had worked previously with the CIA, were seemingly used in a cover-up regarding the role of the FBI and CIA.

Newsweek claimed it was a "Rush to Judgment." No new evidence generated by the HSCA was discussed except for the acoustical evidence of a police Dictaphone belt. "But the trail from there was old and cold ... and neither speculation nor science nor the committee itself could point the way ahead.... The failure of the committee was precisely that it cried conspiracy with so much haste, so little deliberation – and so such scantly guidance for any new attempt to pick up the pieces." *Newsweek* carefully quoted the two HSCA committeemen who questioned the 5-2-majority opinion "if two robbers bursting through separate doors into the same bank at the same time they are probably in cahoots." Ranking Republican Sam Devine argued, "that connecting two gunmen in a crowd of 10,000 people was an assumption based upon an assumption."

Newsweek conceded that the 600-page report would be "the best drawn case yet against Oswald and Ray – and a surrounding cloud of rumor, circumstance and under-examined science proposing that they did not act alone."[54]

The *New York Times* initially buried their story on page 37 –"experts say that second gunman almost certainly shot at Kennedy." The editors similarly suggested a "coincidence theory" of history, that if there were a shot from the grassy knoll, perhaps "two independent assassins pulled their triggers in the self-same second." The HSCA was "more interested in inflaming than informing." The *New York Times* did print researcher Jim Lesar's letter, chiding that the evidence was stronger than the *New York Times* editorial, which had been written by "two lone nuts."

Time, 1/15/79, spent just three paragraphs on the "unexpected" and "bewildering" conclusions of the HSCA. The challenges of this brief, under-funded Congressional Committee were unmentioned, and few of its findings were revealed. No mention was made concerning fruitful lines of inquiry. "[The Report] said it did not know who might have conspired with Lee Harvey Oswald in the shooting, but it specifically excluded such familiar scapegoats as the FBI, the CIA, the Secret Service, the Soviet government, the Cuban government, all anti-Castro Cuban groups, and the Mafia."

After the HSCA report was released, *Time* 7/30/79, claimed that "The committee's conclusion appears to have outstripped its evidence." Although eight of twelve HSCA members urged the Justice Department to continue the investigation, the most vocal critic on the HSCA, Harold Sawyer, was the only Congressman quoted – "supposition upon supposition upon supposition.... I'd have put it in the circular file."

The *Saturday Evening Post*, a subsidiary of the Curtis Publishing Company, which was now owned and chaired by ex-OSS officer Beurt Ser Vaas, did not report the HSCR findings.

The *L.A. Times* 7/17/79, relied on an AP report "Panel Sees Plot in Kennedy's Death" subtitled "Probe Finds Possible Mob Involvement." Mafiosi Sam Giancana and Carlos Marcello were "cited by the panel as the most likely family bosses of organized crime to have participated in such a unilateral assassination plan." They noted that the panel said that the President "was probably assassinated as a result of a conspiracy.... The committee also was reported to have concluded that both the Warren Commission and the FBI performed inadequately in exploring the possibility of a conspiracy in Kennedy's death." The brief article concluded with HSCA Chief Commission Counsel G. Robert Blakey "has firmly supported the conspiracy theory.... There were two assassins there, I believe it is based on evidence and I think you would too if you saw the evidence I saw."

The following day, the *L.A. Times* story by Ronald Ostrow focused on the tenuous nature of the evidence, four of the twelve dissenting HSCA members, and possible mafia connections. HSCA Chief Carl Stokes "Admits conspiracy evidence is less than clear and convincing." Richardson Preyer, chairman of the HSCA, conceded that the report "left some major questions unanswered." He admonished, "But the more the nation knows about these assassinations, the better. Truth does make us free."

Republican Harold Sawyer (R-Michigan) was quoted to close the story. "He would file the committee's report in the wastebasket if it were given to him as a prosecutor." The *L.A. Times* editorial, "$5.5 million worth of holes" was similarly derisive.

> ...No credible evidence has come to light in the intervening years to support conspiracy theories.... The report is so full of speculation, so hedged about by qualifications and so lacking in relevant facts that its principal effect on the public will be one of confusion.

The editorial acknowledges the HSCA conclusions that it is possible that one organized crime leader or "a small combination" of leaders conspired to kill the President.

Yet the editorial concluded that the report was based on "supposition, upon supposition, upon supposition," and chose to neither follow nor speculate on any of the leads generated.

The New Republic, now published by neo-con Marty Perez, chose Tom Bethell, a CIA asset and a former Garrison volunteer, who illegally provided Garrison's trial brief to Clay Shaw's lawyers, to review the HSCA.

In "Conspiracies End" (9/22/79), he started by commending the HSCA for "an inquiry conducted with due thoroughness and skepticism," yet asserted that it has "some preposterous claims," and "in the end the same desperate grasping at the straws of conspiracy [as with the Martin Luther King case]." Bethell viewed Congressman Sawyer's rebuttal to the acoustical evidence as "devastating." He then pleaded for the press to bury the HSCA report.

> Then, heaven help us, we have the Lee Harvey Oswald-David Ferrie connection, dredged up from Garrison's investigation. There never was any credible evidence that Oswald even knew Ferrie... but the committee seems hypnotized by the fact that Ferrie knew Carlos Marcello, the Louisiana tomato salesman and reputed Mafia boss. Years ago, when Jim Garrison came out with his assorted linkages and called them a conspiracy, the heavy artillery of the press pounded away at the eccentric DA – with some justice, as I ruefully noted at the time from my precarious vantage point in his office. Where is that artillery today... ?[55]

The Nation responded (12/22/79) to the HSCA by mocking official, journalistic and citizen efforts. "Conspiracies Unlimited – The Assassination Circus" by Frank Donner was more psychological speculation of Oswald and James Earl Ray than a forensic update. Donner condemned some useless and misleading research, yet chose to view the new information as merely "wispy leads." He admonished – "Is it not time to abandon the escapism, media hustle and radical chic of political conspiraphobia and face the desperate challenge of organizing a left movement in this country?"

Earl Golz clarified the conundrum of researchers with his piece "Public once again in the dark on assassination," sixteen years after the assassination, in the *Dallas Morning News.*

> A 50-year secrecy lid on testimony, reports and other documents generated by the House Assassinations Committee has private researchers and historians fuming.... An estimated 800 boxes of files – much of it testimony in executive session – has been restricted from public access and are not accessible by the Freedom of Information Act.... G. Robert Blakey, who was Chief Counsel to the HSCA said he is "sure the critics are uptight ... this followed the normal rules of the house" The dean of assassination researchers, Harold Weisberg ... said "the only reason they chose to do it (re-

strict material) was so they could hide it." Also sealed for 50 years is a committee interview of Will Fritz, former head of Dallas Police homicide division who presided over the questioning of Oswald before he was killed. Very little of the contents of the Fritz interview by the committee was released ... Fritz told the Warren Commission he kept no notes during the interrogation of Oswald.... However, U.S. Postal inspector H.D. Holmes, present during some of the Oswald interrogation, told the Warren Commission he heard Oswald tell Fritz, "You took the notes, just read them, if you want to refresh your memory." John Kinas, legislative aide to Rep. Floyd Fithian, D-Ind., a committee member stated "I am really surprised at that (sealing of all committee files) ..."

Remarkably, the most extensive coverage of the House Select Committee Report (HSCR), as well as critique and conjecture regarding the role of the U.S. government, came from the *L.A. Free Press*. The independent weekly, published by Art Kunkin, devoted an entire issue to exploring conspiracies and cover-ups regarding the assassinations of President Kennedy, Robert Kennedy, and Dr. Martin Luther King. The mainstream media avoided any documentary overview similar to that which CBS aired to "illustrate" the Warren Report.

In sum, the brief post-Watergate phase of independent journalism barely changed the coverage of the assassination. The leaked copy of the Zapruder film afforded a cautious ABC in 1975 the chance to air it on *Goodnight America*. The death of the feared J. Edgar Hoover seemingly enabled some mainstream sources to explore the FBI connections to the assassination and cover-ups as well as a call for a new investigation. The Congressional investigation of CIA activities seemed to catalyze mass media cooperation to limit congress as well as media coverage of national security issues, in part to counter the "neo-McCarthyism" claims from some in the press. CBS cooperated with the CIA on their assassination series, and soon thereafter fired experienced reporter Daniel Schorr for leaking the classified Congressional Intelligence Report on CIA activities – the Pike Report.

The *New York Times*, the *Washington Post*, and to a lesser extent the *LA Times*, then viciously attacked the initial HSCA counsel Richard Sprague, who had started an aggressive investigation. The *San Francisco Chronicle* and the *Dallas Morning News* ran a few investigative pieces during the HSCA hearings but most of the media, alternative, and mainstream, waited for the final report. Despite debilitating constraints, the House Select

Committee Report still broke considerable new ground, yet the mass media generally elected not to pursue the numerous vital new leads. The *New York Times, Time, Newsweek,* the *Washington Post* and the *L.A. Times* denigrated even these cautious findings. They even suggested a "coincidence theory," with two independent assassins firing at the same time. Fifteen years after the assassination, questioning the legitimacy of the political institutions remained off limits during the Cold War.

Sociologist Pierre Bourdieu sees the influences of the market, political leaders, and the lack of time and information, as causing journalism to create "a vision [which] is at once dehistoricized and dehistoricizing, fragmented and fragmenting." Further, some media confusion is "struck in all innocence and all the more effective for being unconscious. ... There is a sense in which this can only be done because the people who practice this violence are themselves victims of the violence they practice, and this is where we get the false science of the half-educated that likes to give the appearance of scientific ratification to the institution of common sense."[56]

British journalist and author Anthony Summers observed:

> The American press, to it discredits, has generally played down the achievements of the Assassination Committee or brushed its conclusions aside. This lethargy may stem in part from the fact that sixteen years ago – there was no serious attempt at investigative reporting of the Kennedy assassination ...
>
> Two years after the HSCR Chief Counsel Robert Blakey wrote his perspective on the case which suggested organized crime. His book was generally ignored by the mass media.[57]

The alternative press, weaker than in the previous decade, seemingly wanted to build a new progressive movement rather than pursue the assassination. *The New Republic* called for the press to criticize even the cautious House Select Committee Report (HSCR.) The vigilant *Village Voice,* and to a lesser extent the *L.A. Free Press, Spotlight, Harper's* and *Gallery,* pushed to pursue the new leads. A few assassination researchers ran radio shows including George Michael Evica on WWUH in Connecticut, and Mae Brussell with "Dialogue: Conspiracy" on KAZU-FM in California. Mark Lane held regular press conferences during the span of the HSCA but there were few media outlets that attended. The vibrant fourth estate of Watergate had retreated to caution and complacency.

10

COMMEMORATIVE PROBES:
THEN DRIFTING INTO HISTORY

*It wasn't necessary to completely suppress the news; it was sufficient to
delay the news until it no longer mattered.*
— Napoleon

The truth crushed to earth will rise again.
— Martin Luther King Jr.

Every violation of the truth is a stab at the health of society.
— Ralph Waldo Emerson

The media coverage of the assassination of JFK as well as of intelligence agencies began to drift by 1980. Perhaps in part they reflected a national desire for a calmer time and an executive branch more resistant to declassification. Except for the 25th year commemorative coverage, the Reagan-Bush era helped the case drift quietly into history.

The CIA excesses revealed in the 1970's pushed Congress to enact the Foreign Intelligence Surveillance Act (FISA) and the Foreign Intelligence Surveillance Court (FISC). The Reagan-Bush administration resisted these reforms and appointed former spy, financier, and media mogul William Casey to head the CIA. Casey controlled Cap Cities, which owned ABC as well as a number of newspapers. Casey's OSS experience with propaganda and disinformation could be targeted against America despite Reagan's executive order #12333 which prohibited this.[1]

A few print journalists from major media outlets had steadily developed leads; maybe the most effective during this period was Earl Golz of the *Dallas Morning News*. Golz constantly fought with his editors to continue his investigation. In the early 1970s Golz published one of his stories in the *Village Voice* as leverage against his editors. "I kind of blackmailed them to run it." By 1979, however, his managing editor saw Golz's reporting as a crusade, which needed to be set aside.

> I am increasingly bothered by the amount of time and energy being devoted to further investigation of the JFK theories. The investigation of assassination theories, I fear, had become something of a personal crusade on your part. A crusade which consumes great amounts of your time but produced virtually nothing that this newspaper can or will use. If you please, I think it's time your energies will be more immediately productive.

Similarly, Peter Kihss of the *New York Times* wrote numerous critical articles on the Kennedy assassination, but usually they were not printed. Inside The *Times* Kihss was dubbed "Crazy Peter" and this mocking atmosphere contributed to his resignation. Jim Marrs, as a reporter for the *Fort Worth Star-Telegram* was told "not to write any more about the Kennedy assassination as it was upsetting people at the Petroleum Club."[2]

David Lee, a book reviewer for the *Washington Post*, wrote a supportive review of BBC journalist Anthony Summers' reporting on the role of CIA agent David Phillips in *Conspiracy* in 1981. This review however, was never published under the policies of publisher Ben Bradlee.

The *Washington Post* perspective on the role of the CIA and the assassination had not been modified even two years after the HSCR was released. Anthony Summers had completed a comprehensive book on the assassination, *Conspiracy*, which incorporated HSCA findings and developed some of the leads regarding the link between CIA officer David Phillips and Maurice Bishop. Summers called the *Washington Post* editor, Ben Bradlee to alert him to the Phillips-Bishop material. Bradlee lashed back with a litany of expletives and bellowed that he would not puff Summer's book. A few weeks later *Post* reporter David Lee was assigned to the Phillips-Bishop leads but was admonished by his editor that he should demolish the story. Lee proceeded to develop the story and actually confirmed what Summers had written. Lee's probe, however, was never printed.

Around this time Summers presented his findings to an eclectic social gathering hosted by Norman Mailer. Summers inadvertently critiqued the denigrating introduction to the new Bantam publication of the HSCR, by *New York Times* editor Tom Wicker. Unknown to Summers, Wicker was at the party, and confessed that he was under a deadline and didn't have the time to read all of the material he needed. Wicker then promised to read Summers' book on his vacation and then they would get together to talk about it. But he never called Summers, and never returned Summers' calls. After 18 months, Summers stopped calling.[3]

The *Gallery*, 3/81, printed another provocative piece by Dick Russell "The Man who had a Contract to Kill Lee Harvey Oswald before the Assassination of President John F. Kennedy." We learn of double agent Richard Case Nagell, who was trailing Oswald in late 1963 for the KGB to try and stop an assassination attempt on President Kennedy. Nagell, unclear as to whether the CIA or KGB had ordered him to shoot Oswald, and unwilling to live abroad away from his family, placed himself in federal custody in El Paso (He shot a gun into the ceiling of a bank and sat down to be arrested). While there, two FBI agents as well as Secret Service agents visited him. Nagell was released from Leavenworth Penitentiary April 1968, but was never questioned by the HSCA.[4]

President Ronald Reagan confronted the press with the most widespread effort to restrict information in our peace-time history. Presidential Executive Order 12356 on classification reversed a 25-year trend toward making government information more accessible. Agencies now classified at the highest level when "in doubt." The principle of declassification after 20 years was reversed, and FOIA requests were delayed. The American Society of Newspaper Editors characterized Reagan's orders as "peacetime censorship of a scope unparalleled in this country since the adoption of the Bill of Rights."[5]

Mass media and intellectual coverage of the assassination disappeared for a few years until it was explored by Christopher Lasch in his story "The Life of Kennedy's Death," *Harper's* 10/83. Lasch asserted that while many liberals have attributed the assassination to a "climate of hatred," and that the mainstream press likewise stayed in a "psychiatric mode," concentrating on what the assassin's action revealed about the American character, rather than reviewing the evidence.

> ...This pseudo-introspection did not address the still unanswered questions about the location of the shots that killed the President, the nature of his wounds, or the special circumstances that might have led to the shooting. Instead it addressed the pseudo-question, even if one accepted its dubious premise that Oswald acted alone, on the social meaning of his crime.
>
> ...It replied to a popular speculation about conspiracy with its own kind of speculation about conspiracy mentality, which reached a climax in the report of the National Commission on the Causes and Prevention of Violence, issued in October of 1969. Like the Warren Report, Assassination and Political Violence began by assuming Oswald's guilt and went on to build an elaborate

structure of speculation on this shaky premise. In the section one the "Psychology a presidential assassins" the commission found a common pattern of family disruption ... hostility toward mother and authority figures ... loners.

Lasch disputed a widespread belief by "liberal intellectuals" who "dismiss the conspiratorial view of history as an irrational view held only by a naïve and untutored minds." He included a Gallup poll which showed "opinion in the case of the Kennedy assassination is basically the same up and down the socioeconomic scale, with no more than one person in seven in any demographic group holding onto the belief that Oswald acted alone."[6]

He claimed, "The most remarkable feature surrounding the assassination is not the abundance of conspiracy theories, but the rejection of conspiracies by the 'best and brightest." While uncritical of President Johnson's role, he lambasted Garrison for his "rhetorical exaggerations and his unsubstantiated charges against Johnson." Lasch portrayed the left as spreading "wild and wishful theories ... the CIA, the FBI, Texas oilman, the radical right, Lyndon Johnson and international bankers."

He saw JFK as a "tragic hero," womanizer, and elitist, and the New Frontier as "backward, provincial and naïve." He concluded by suggesting the Cuban blowback theory.

> What we know of the assassination suggests that Kennedy was the victim of bungling intervention in this case by the misguided effort to get rid of Castro-encouraged by the dream of Imperial greatness and unlimited power. John F. Kennedy was killed, in all likelihood not by a sick society or some supposedly archetypal, resentful common man but a political conspiracy his own actions may have helped set in motion. The mythology of his death can no longer prop up the mythology of his life.

The *Wall Street Journal* covered the 20th anniversary (11/22/83) of the assassination with Edward Epstein's story, "Who Was Lee Harvey Oswald." Formerly a critic of the Warren Commission, who worked closely with CIA counterintelligence Chief James Angleton, he had became a purveyor of the Oswald-as-Communist dupe perspective. Epstein omitted almost all of Oswald's connections to the FBI, military intelligence, and the CIA in a manner that would have made Angleton proud. Critics were characterized as "excessively fascinated; if not entirely blinded ... buffs."

Oswald was linked to the Soviet downing of U-2 pilot Francis Gary Powers; however, Oswald's top-secret clearance at Atsugi, Japan, where he worked as a radar operator was unmentioned. The sole CIA officer Oswald was to have met was George de Mohrenschildt but only as a "friend" to debrief him. Epstein treated questions raised by the HSCA as irrelevant. *WSJ* even sketched Oswald with a hammer and sickle behind his head.[7]

In 1984 the populist conservative Liberty Lobby and their weekly newspaper, the *Spotlight*, won their appeal regarding the statement by CIA officer Victor Marchetti that a CIA memo indicated that CIA agent E. Howard Hunt was in Dallas the day of the assassination. During the appeal lawyer Mark Lane revealed testimony from CIA operative Marita Lorenz that Watergate burglar Hunt was working with Jack Ruby and Frank Sturgis in November 1963, and was allegedly the paymaster for the assassination.

For the first time a jury heard evidence presented by both sides with cross-examination. After the trial the foreman of the jury read her statement to the assembled media. She declared that the jury "unanimously concluded that the CIA assassinated President Kennedy."

Although these revelations could have opened up the Watergate trial as well as the assassination of President Kennedy, the mass media did not explore them.[8] Attorney Mark Lane could not even find a publisher for his book about the trial, *Plausible Denial*, until independent publisher Thunders Mouth Press agreed years later.

The relentless Penn Jones broadened his investigation with a piece "Disappearing Witnesses" published in the tiny alternative magazine *The Rebel* in January 1984. He noted more than 100 murders, suicides and mysterious deaths – the strange fate of those who saw or knew about the assassination of President Kennedy.

Reagan's Director of the CIA, William Casey, in May 1986 increased pressure on the media by reinterpreting the 1917 Espionage Act. National Security leaks to the press were now viewed as espionage and Casey threatened prosecution. Casey telephoned authors Bob Woodward and Seymour Hersh, both working on books dealing with the CIA, to warn them that they could be subject to prosecution if they divulge communications intelligence. *Washington Post* Executive Editor Ben Bradlee admitted that the Post had withheld information from more than a dozen stories so far this year "for reasons of national security."[9]

On the twenty-fifth anniversary of the assassination of John Kennedy the broadcast media aired several new programs which reached a wider share of the public than at any time since 1963. The new television documentaries included CBS's "Four Days in November," "The Kwitny Report" aired over selected PBS stations, "America Exposé: Who Murdered JFK?" (Narrated by Jack Anderson) over FOX Network, PBS's *NOVA* ran "Who Shot President Kennedy" narrated by Walter Cronkite, Viewpoint 88: "The Men who killed JFK" produced by Nigel Turner for British Central Television, and "The Killing of JFK: A Conspiracy of the Mob?" developed by Geraldo Rivera and aired on NBC. Significant new information was revealed, along with the recycling of several discredited theories.

Dan Rather hosted the two-hour documentary, "Four Days in November," and noted that this "hastily prepared biography ... make(s) no comment on the past, we only bring it back," without lamenting the lost opportunity to clarify festering concerns. This piece was part paean to the power of television as a national narcotic: "Hour after hour, day after day, from murder to burial, the flow of images and pictures calmed the panic. Someone has said that those four days marked the coming of the age of television." CBS never contrasted the precise care, custom, and reverence in the burial of President Kennedy with either his lack of protection in life, or the confused process of examining his assassination. CBS did show the Zapruder film, but chose not to analyze it regarding location or number of shots or wounds. Rather avowed that "(back in 1963) it [the Zapruder film] was not shown for 'legal reasons.'"

This documentary served to legitimate the reporters efforts based on past public discourse. Sociologists refer to this as rhetorical legitimation, whereby narratives beget authority, which begets memories, which beget more narratives, which beget more authority, and so on. In November 1988, PBS selectively recycled old arguments in a visually creative special "Who Shot President Kennedy" as part of its *NOVA* series. Former CBS producer Robert Richter produced and directed it and former CBS anchor Walter Cronkite narrated. This oft-shown program attempted to reconcile critical research with the HSCA version, yet clarity was sometimes sacrificed for brevity and bias.

Oswald's presence on the sixth floor at the time of the assassination was assumed since he worked there that morning. No mention was made of witnesses Eddie Piper and Carolyn Arnold who saw Oswald other places after noon, or of Bonnie Ray Williams, the TSBD employee who testified that Oswald left the sixth floor at about 12:20 and he saw no one there. Witnesses Ruby Henderson, Carolyn Walther, Arnold Rowland and prisoner John Powell have stated that either a person with a dark complexion was in the "sniper's nest" or two people were there.

No mention was made of the Dallas police reports of a German-Mauser rifle being found first. Cronkite said that Oswald's palm print was later found on the Manlicher-Carcano rifle, not mentioning that the palm print was actually found three days later – according to FBI agent Vincent Drain who had stated this to author Henry Hurt in 1984.[10] Cronkite asserted that "cartridges and fragments from the presidential limousine were all ballistically traced to Oswald's rifle." According to HSCA studies, Connally's' wrist fragment contained 850% more copper, 2400% more sodium and 1100% more chlorine than Bullet 399, the so-called magic bullet. *NOVA* neglected to note this. No mention was made of Oswald's testing negative in a paraffin test of his face – indicating he probably did not fire a rifle that day.

NOVA attempted to defend the single-bullet theory with a computer model of Dealey Plaza. The first shot, which missed according to the Warren Commission and the HSCA, somehow occurred earlier than Zapruder frame 169, but no rationale was given. *NOVA* speculated that if the President was leaning forward and Governor Connally was turning to his right, as he said he was, then the angle lines up with the sixth floor. This assumes that: 1) Kennedy and Connally were sitting further apart than pictures and the Zapruder film indicate; 2) that Connally turns and returns to facing forward in less than 1/8 of a second after he is hit; and 3) that Connally moves backwards in order to move to the right. Thus Cronkite declared that the "single-bullet theory can't be ruled out." *NOVA* failed to mention that more grains of the "magic bullet" were found in Connally's body than were lost from the bullet.

Next *NOVA* explored the hypothesis of David Lifton, that the wounds of the President were altered. Four of the doctors at Parkland – McClelland, Peters, Jenkins and Dulaney, went to the National Archives to view for the first time (off-camera) the autopsy pictures. Dr. Dulaney though worked only on Governor Connally. Although Dulaney's role was not clarified by *NOVA*, he commented that, "I don't see any evidence of any alteration of his wound in these pictures from what I saw in the Emergency Room."

Dr. McClelland was not asked to explain his Warren Commission testimony about the head wound exposing the cerebellum, which he noted at Parkland to be partially "blasted out." In a documentary developed by KRON-TV San Francisco, 11/18/88, McClelland stated, "a portion of the cerebellum fell onto the table as we were doing the tracheotomy." Curiously, on *NOVA*, McClelland commented that examining the head wound was "not the appropriate thing to do at the time."

Drs. Peters and Jenkins both stated that they could have been mistaken about the cerebellum during a time of urgency. Although McClelland, Peters, and Jenkins had all previously stated their belief that the wound in the back of the head was one of exit, *NOVA* chose not to ask the doctors whether the wound was one of entrance or exit.

Regarding eyewitness testimony, *NOVA* producer Richter told author David Lifton that it is the "earliest recollection, which is given the greatest weight," yet *NOVA* senior researcher Steve Lyons told Richter he would "go with a 1988 recollection." *NOVA* avoided a conclusion regarding the wounds.

NOVA then chose to use an old film clip in which Dr. John Lattimer fired at a skull filled with white paint that supposedly showed that a shot from the back could snap the head backwards. Critics have long contended that this research is useless since the skull was not attached to a human body wearing a rigid back brace, which President Kennedy was wearing. *NOVA* neglected to note these objections. Cronkite finally did concede that he understood why this case had become a "national obsession." He called for "a new rifle test, a new acoustics test, an examination of the brain if it is ever found, an analysis for traces of blood on the bullet ... but the ultimate solution to the mystery may lie outside the domain of science."[11]

"The Kennedy Report" special, by Jonathan Kwitny, viewed the Warren Commission as "hopelessly inconclusive" and briefly explored a range of theories, before focusing on organized crime boss Carlos Marcello. Kwitny rejected motives for the CIA or for Castro. HSCA investigator Edwin Lopez stated that after studying the CIA surveillance photographs purported to be of Oswald visiting the Cuban Embassy in Mexico City that they were not pictures of Oswald. This supported FBI director J. Edgar Hoover's memo that someone impersonated Oswald at the Russian Embassy in Mexico City. Kwitny observed that this pointed to a conspiracy, but he then drifted from the role of the CIA to a focus on Carlos Marcello.

He explored Marcello's links to Dallas mob boss Joseph Civello through the testimony of Joseph Nellis, a former assistant council from the Kefauver Senate Committee on organized crime. Kwitny also revealed a videotaped conversation between journalist Dan Moldea and Jimmy Hoffa Jr. in which Hoffa confirmed that his dad knew Jack Ruby and was close to Marcello.[12]

Jack Anderson repackaged his Castro-Mafia theory in his TV documentary *American Exposé: Who Murdered JFK*, but also explored new aspects of the case. Perhaps most revealing was a statement by Marina Oswald which expanded her true recollections in the November 1988 *Ladies Home Journal*:

> I could never buy an idea that Lee did not like or want to kill President Kennedy. Everything that I learned about President Kennedy was good through Lee. (Marina no longer claimed that the rifle shown for her by the Warren Commission was Oswald's) ... someone could plant the rifle ... I had been used by the Warren Commission ... that investigated so dishonestly sometimes to make Lee a guilty party ... I was very easy to mold at the time ... young, immature and naïve ... he [Oswald] was working for the government, and he was just simply infiltrating groups. He was doing what he was told to do.... He was implicated in the plot.

Anderson showed videotaped interviews with three witnesses who claimed to have seen Oswald with Ruby. Carousel Club waitress Esther Ann Marsh, Dallas attorney Carroll Jarnagin, and Madeline Brown, who claimed to be LBJ's longtime mistress, all said they saw Oswald and Ruby together, just weeks prior to the assassination.

Anderson interviewed Dallas Policeman Malcolm Summers, who testified that he ran up the grassy knoll after the assassination, the direction from where he thought at least one shot had been fired. He then encountered someone who appeared to be concealing a rifle under his coat. This person showed Secret Service credentials and told Summers to back off. Investigators were later informed by the Secret Service that none of their agents were assigned to Dealey Plaza 11/22.

Retired Dallas Policeman Billy Grammer stated that he received a telephone warning Saturday, that Oswald would be killed the next day. Grammer thought that the call came from Jack Ruby, although he was not certain. Grammer stated that the caller seemed to be aware of the plans to transfer Oswald to the Dallas County Jail, knew about the decoy vehicle, and the time of the transfer.

The program included re-enactments of CIA-Mafia-Cuban exiles attempts to assassinate Castro, the mysterious killings of Sam Giancana and Johnny Roselli, and the wild drinking party at Pat Kirkwood's Cellar Door nightclub the night prior to the assassination with nine Secret Service men present. Kirkwood suggested that Ruby might have sent some of his strippers over that night.

Anderson also showed a videotaped interview with Dr. Victor Weiss, head of Psychiatry at East Louisiana State Hospital, who examined Rose Cheramie, the injured prostitute who had warned that JFK would be killed 11/22/63. Weiss stated that Cheramie was certain and that "the word was out in the New Orleans underworld" about a contract on Kennedy.

Anderson continued to rely exclusively on Johnny Roselli's story that Castro retaliated for the U.S. attempts on his life by using Santos Traffi- cante to coordinate the assassination. Just one of Oswald's ties to Amer- ican intelligence was explored; however, since Oswald's uncle was the numbers runner for Carlos Marcello, Oswald was again portrayed a mob pawn.[13]

ABC examined the shooting of Oswald in a half-hour program "Crimes of the Century." Journalist Seth Kantor briefly mentioned Jack Ruby's connections to organized crime, whereas many others speculated that Ruby acted on impulse.

Mark Lane cast some doubts regarding Ruby's access to the transfer of Oswald and the complicity of the Dallas Police Department. Jim Leavelle, Dallas Police Captain, recalls numerous phone death threats for Oswald but viewed them merely as threats. Notably, Leavelle's fellow employee, Bill Grammer, again stated that one of the threats he heard was definitely Ruby's – since he knew Ruby, and claimed to have recognized the voice.

Seth Kantor described his encounter with Ruby in Parkland Hospital, just after JFK was shot, which contradicted the statements of Jerry Coley of the *Dallas Morning News*, who claimed that Ruby stayed at the newspa- per. A small clip of Ruby stating there was "a complete conspiracy against me" was shown, but no mention was made of Ruby's nine meetings with the FBI, his pleadings to Chief Justice Earl Warren to be transferred from Dallas to Washington because he feared for his life, his numerous Mafia connections or his televised prison statements asserting that "people in high places" were involved.

In November 1988 ABC's *Nightline* disregarded "Crimes of the Cen- tury" and instead focused on "Was Oswald Shooting at Connally?" No established critics of the Warren Commission or the HSCA were even interviewed.

KRON-TV in San Francisco aired probing of interviews by Sylvia Chase, which explored X-rays, autopsy pictures, and the President's cof- fin. Jerrol Custer, the man who took the X-rays at Bethesda was shown with the official copies and he stated that they were not what he had seen. Custer said "from the top of the head to the base of the skull. That part was gone. My job was to remove the brain. There was no brain to remove, the brain wasn't there."

Paul O'Connor, a Navy medical technician at Bethesda stated that he found the body in a body bag, and that was not the rubber sheet in which Kennedy left Dallas. O'Connor insisted that the body arrived 15 to 20 minutes prior to the ambulance carrying the bronze coffin from Andrews Air Force Base, and that it was in a cheap shipping casket. Dennis David said that the body arrived in a black ambulance "like a hearse," and the President's body was in "just a gray casket … a metal shipping casket … not the bronze casket."[14]

In 1988 *Washington Post* reporter George Lardner recycled a rationale echoed by many reporters, "We Evaded the Truth Then, And Now It Can't Be Found Out." The *NOVA* program "Who Shot President Kennedy" also concluded that we will probably never know the truth. This rationale justifies no further investigation, which leads to a self-fulfilling prophesy.

Newsweek, 11/28/88, in its one-page piece for the 25th anniversary of the assassination pondered in "The Kennedy Conundrum: Still too many questions – and too many answers." Mafia "conspiracy" theorists were mentioned and critiqued by asking simply: 1) Why would Oswald be used?; 2) Why would a $21.00 mail order rifle be used?; and 3) How could Ruby be induced to murder Oswald in full view of cops and cameras? The Zapruder film, they contended for the first time, "proved" that Oswald did not have time to fire the shots, which hit Kennedy and Connally.[15]

The controversial British Central Independent Television series, *The Men Who Killed Kennedy*, produced by Nigel Turner, was briefly mentioned in the American media. It aired in more than twenty countries, though it would be three years before a re-edited version was shown in America, on The History Channel and A&E. In one segment, reporter Steve Rivele relied on information from two convicted French drug smugglers, Christian David and Michel Nicoli, who claimed to have cooperated with U.S. Mafiosi. Despite this conjecture, the documentary revealed some significant interviews.

Beverly Oliver, a Dallas singer, stated that she used to visited Ruby's Carousel Club and that two weeks before the assassination she was introduced to Lee Oswald at that club by a stripper named Jada, who had worked for Carlos Marcello.

Former Dallas Police officer Don Ray Archer stated that Ruby constantly asked if Oswald was still alive, and became relaxed when told that Oswald was dead. This fits the pattern of a mafia hit.

Dealey Plaza witness Gordon Arnold, who was on the grassy knoll next to the picket fence at the time of the assassination, stated that shots came from behind him. Newsweek saw the documentary as "a miniscule corner of a puzzle that never seems to come together – and which, like any one of a hundred such details, can seduce the most rational observer into obsession."[16]

Geraldo Rivera's programs, 11/21 and 11/22, focused on organized crime and extended the previous interviews with LBJ's mistress Madeline Brown, Esther Ann Marsh, and Governor and Mrs. Connally. Rivera read a letter from LBJ's estate attorney, recently published in *People Magazine*, stating that the Johnson estate would continue to support Brown, as was LBJ's desire. Brown asserted that in addition to seeing Oswald and Ruby together in Dallas, she had a vague impression that Lyndon Johnson knew President Kennedy would be killed. In Geraldo's other interview Dallas waitress Esther Ann Marsh claimed that she saw Oswald and Ruby together numerous time at the Carousel Club. She believed that Ruby was involved with the mob. Governor Connally reconfirmed his belief that he was not hit by the shot that hit President Kennedy.[17]

The *New York Times* poll data was cited showing that, "only 13% of Americans believe the Warren Report... two thirds believe there was a conspiracy to kill the president ... 61% think there has been an official cover-up... (Yet) 59% oppose further investigation.

The article opined:

> There's nothing more American than an active distrust of institu-
> tions – it's in the Constitution – but the Kennedy assassination has
> bred a passive despair that is unhealthy in a democracy.

You have to wonder what the contribution of the *New York Times* was to that despair.

Life's December 1988 cover story, "Why We Still Care" by Lisa Grun-wald, characterized the assassination as an "American obsession" pro-longed by "buffs." The Warren Report and the actions of *Life* regarding the Zapruder film were again defended. Grunwald psychologized that "peo-ple want to give meaning to a random event even like the assassination."

Remarkably, *Life* merely reprinted its Dec. 6, 1963 edition for a twen-ty-fifth anniversary edition. This ode to rhetorical legitimation ran as:

> The first copies of this magazine, published two weeks after John
> F. Kennedy's killing, sold out immediately as a grieving America,

seeking a memoir of its sadness, turned to Life... We believe this account to be richer than any anniversary review could be. We have reprinted our original for the 100 million Americans who are too young to remember, and for those too old to forget – the assassination of a President.

This replay of mind-numbing sadness, which chose to ignore the HSCA and all of the new leads, was endorsed by Forbes "In the November *Life* some of the most vividly famous photographs of the instant and stunning aftermath..." (12/5/88) The validation of Time-Life was repeated in the CBS-*Washington Post* series on the assassination, which included a montage of some of the best-known photos of the assassination, most of them from *Life* magazine.

Nevertheless, in 1988 President Reagan abolished the Fairness Doctrine as a favor to broadcast media elites who supported his election. FCC Chairman Mark Fowler mocked critics' concerns about diminished democracy – "Television is just another appliance – a toaster with pictures." They rationalized that the rapid rise of cable TV satisfied the Supreme Court's apparent concern for diverse sources of information. Broadcasters recognized no obligation to air views other than their own.

The Reagan administration embraced some strategies to spin the media which they called "perception management." For example, CIA disinformation specialist Walter Raymond Jr. was shifted from the CIA to the NSC to coordinate "public diplomacy," targeting the foreign and U.S. press as well as Congress, to sell administration policies. When *Newsweek* reporter Robert Parry confronted one of Reagan's public diplomacy people about Iran-Contra, he was told to back down or "We will controversialize you."[18]

Journalist and author Andrew Kreig asserts that middle management worried about government retribution and costs. However, "the more insidious problem as media conglomerates and their debt grew in the 1980's was that the media's ownership increasingly overlapped with government leadership and the higher-ups who controlled the news organizations and government"[19]

Katherine Graham, Chairman of the Board at the *Post*, avowed in a speech to the CIA in 1988:

> We live in a dirty and dangerous world. There are some things the general public does not need to know and shouldn't know. I believe democracy flourishes when government can take legitimate steps to keep its secrets and when the press can decide whether to print what it knows.

301

Another unspoken dynamic may explain the behavior of journalists who had previously cooperated with the government on national security issues – fear of exposure. Author Deborah Davis noted that, "Many Mockingbirds (CIA-media) have been faced with this choice"[20]

Professor Jerry Rose published and edited *The Third Decade: A Journal of Research on the John F. Kennedy Assassination*. Researcher Mae Brussell cancelled her weekly radio show due to numerous death threats. After the brief round of solid reporting for the 25th commemoration academe, government, and the media appeared content to let the case drift into history, until Oliver Stone jolted the country with his film *JFK*.

11

JFK: Reactions and Responses

The people should fight for their law as for a wall.
— Heraclitus

Freedom of conscience, of education, of speech, of assembly is among the fundamentals of democracy and all of them would be nullified should freedom of the press ever be successfully challenged.
— Franklin Delano Roosevelt

Is a government worth preserving when it lies to the people, when it is no longer accountable to the people? It has become a dangerous country, sir I say; let justice be done though the heavens fall!
—Jim Garrison

While the mass media greeted the findings of the 1979 HSCR with indifference and disdain, the film *JFK* (1991) provoked some good reporting as well as vitriolic debate and hyperbole. The movie, and even the idea of the movie, was viciously attacked by much of the mainstream media, primarily by journalists active at the time of the assassination. Oliver Stone was mocked as a historian. However, many younger journalists and film critics disagreed, and more than 15 million Americans saw the movie. *JFK* generated a deep groundswell of political pressure to release the remaining classified documents. It became the first American movie to lead directly to a law, (Senate J.R 282 HJR 454) which created the Assassination Records and Review Board. The ARRB ultimately declassified close to five-million pages of government documents, which the public and Congress had not seen.

The *New York Times* devoted thirty articles, op-eds, letters, notes, addenda, editorials and columns to attacking the film. They even ran "news" from their Hollywood correspondent questioning why Warner Brothers permitted the movie to proceed, and suggested that the studio censor it.

In early May of 1991, Oliver Stone had just started filming *JFK* in Dallas, yet a litany of derisive mass media criticism had already been hurled against it. Jon Margolis, a syndicated columnist for the *Chicago Tribune*, warned that *JFK* would prove an insult to intelligence and "decency." In "*JFK* Movie and Book Attempt to Rewrite History," 5/14/91; Margolis claimed, "There is a point at which intellectual myopia becomes morally repugnant. Mr. Stone's new movie proves that he has passed that point. But then so has [producer] Time-Warner and so will anyone who pays American money to see the film." How Margolis could give this warning without seeing a screenplay remains unclear. Reporters from the *Boston Globe, Boston Herald, Washington Post, Chicago Tribune*, and *Time* magazine and several other outlets were known to have been prowling around the *JFK* set looking for angles.[1]

George Lardner's, 5/19/91, *Washington Post* review of Stone's movie, "On the Set: Dallas in Wonderland" viewed the Garrison investigation as "zany" and a "fraud." This lengthy and disingenuous review was published six months prior to the release of *JFK* and was based on a leaked or stolen first draft of the movie (ultimately there were six versions). Lardner wrote that HSCA "may have" heard testimony linking Oswald with Ferrie with the CIA, yet since he had covered the HSCA he should have known that they found this testimony convincing. Then he imaginatively asserted that the HSCA "may also have" heard no such thing.

Lardner discarded the Dallas Police treatment of the so-called "three tramps," who were arrested in the railroad yard just north of Dealey Plaza, (where more than one-third of the eyewitnesses believed shots came from) – but were not questioned at all. Lardner said that even if the police had taken their names, those who believe a conspiracy occurred "would just insist the men had lied about who they were."

He mocked the stolen first-draft version of the screenplay for arguing that as many as five or six shots were fired. "Is this the Kennedy assassination or the Charge of the Light Brigade?" However, the House Select Committee Report stated that, "Six sequences of impulses were initially identified as having been transmitted over channel 1 [of the police radio]. Thus they warrant further analysis." Lardner elected not to pursue this conundrum, but belatedly acknowledged "that a probable conspiracy took place."

Oliver Stone's response to the *Washington Post* was heavily edited.[2] In June 1991, ostensibly clarifying a major foreign policy contention in *JFK*, Lardner wrote in the *Washington Post* that after the assassination National Security Action Memorandum, NSAM 273 merely continued NSAM 263 and "ordered the withdrawal of 1000 troops [from Vietnam] to be carried out." It did not, since only a couple-hundred non-combat individuals were withdrawn by the end of the year.

Time's story By Richard Zoglin, 7/1/91, "More Shots in Dealey Plaza" portrays Stone's version of events as "near the far out fringe," which has "outraged" experts on the assassination. David Belin, former counsel to the Warren Commission and the Rockefeller Commission predictably called the partial script, "A bunch of hokum." Stone was accused of trying to block the production of a rival movie on the assassination, *Libra*, which Stone refuted in a letter to *Time*. Stone was quoted as trying to pay "homage" to President Kennedy, yet Zoglin claimed it "may wind up doing more harm than homage."

Esquire's "The Shooting of *JFK*" (12/91) by Robert Sam Anson presented a raw, lengthy, unflattering critique, to which Oliver Stone responded. Anson started by quoting Stone: "What is history, who the fuck knows," and "you call yourselves journalists? You have become Winston Smith [*1984*].... You just invent history ... learn honesty." Regarding the film *JFK*, "Stone has given as well as he has gotten," while Stone saw those who challenged the film with controversy as trying to "maximize negative advance impact ..."

Anson saw Stone as seduced by Garrison, while Stone claims Anson's old perspectives were inaccurate and were merely character assassination of Garrison. Anson discounted Colonel Fletcher Prouty as an "aide," whereas Stone used Prouty, chief of Special Operations for the Joint Chiefs, as a consultant. Stone asserted he was often misquoted, that he never tried to block *Libra*, that actor Kevin Costner helped with the script, that Madeline Brown was misquoted, and that he tried to understand history.

Anson revealed the on-set arguments between Major John Newman and Colonel Fletcher Prouty, (the two men providing the basis of Mr. X) yet seemed to gloss over their areas of agreement. Anson provided more context and insider access to researchers than other articles during the period, yet his clever piece cut some corners on evidence, perhaps in part due to CIA-friendly source Gus Russo.

The *L.A. Times* (12/15/91) story, "Opinion-The Political Rorschach Test" by Jefferson Morley, started, "How we make sense of the assassination of John F. Kennedy is directly related to how we make sense of public life." He reminded us that every poll taken "over the last quarter century has shown between 60%-80% of the public favoring conspiratorial explanation." This supportive overview concluded, "The crime of the century remains unresolved less because we don't know who fired the fatal shots than because there is no agreement whether the story of the Kennedy assassination should be invested with confidence in our national institutions or with fears of conspiratorial power."

James O'Byrne's piece in the *Times-Picayune* "The Garrison Probe: The Story Hollywood Won't Tell" lionized Clay Shaw and condemned Garrison as a "megalomaniac'" While Garrison's procedural challenges and mistakes got highlighted, none of Garrison's useful leads or evidence got mentioned. O'Byrne denied that Clay Bertrand was Clay Shaw, he omitted Shaw's ties to Oswald, as well as witness Perry Russo's claims about pressure and bribery. O'Byrne closed by quoting one of Shaw's friends claiming Garrison's "cynicism was appalling." (12/15/91)

The *New York Times* Tom Wicker slammed *JFK*, 12/15/91, "Does *JFK* Conspire Against Reason. Oliver Stone transforms a discredited theory into the sole explanation for the assassination." Wicker trotted out the discredited NBC broadcast, 6/19/67, by Walter Sheridan to claim Garrison threatened and bribed witnesses, and claimed "even by other conspiracy believers, [it was] a travesty of legal process." Wicker ridiculed the notion that Kennedy may have been seen as "soft on communism" by "anyone active in Washington at that time. *JFK* may prove persuasive to audiences with little knowledge of events presented." Wicker bristled at Stone's assertions that the media were "paid off journalistic hacks" but sidestepped any discussion of the media's performance. Stone's "wild assertions ... to propagate the one true faith – even though that faith ... would be contemptuous of the very constitutional government Mr. Stone's film purports to uphold."

The *New York Times* printed responses from Oliver Stone and Fletcher Prouty. Stone noted that NBC's documentary on Garrison was so one – sided that the FCC granted a one half hour rebuttal. "Never has an unfinished movie been so prejudged and precensored." Stone declared.

> Let me further suggest that the media itself is part of the problem and seems to resent it when an artist tries to interpret a history that Newsmen have failed to explain. From day one, the American media (in contrast to the foreign media) never looked for an honest motive in President Kennedy's killing and accepted the cover story of Lee Harvey Oswald as lone assassin put out by government officials and reinforced by the appointed Warren Commission, which allowed the intelligence agencies to disclose files and investigate leads at their discretion.

Mr. Wicker ignored the illegitimacy of Operation Mongoose, back-channel negotiations with Castro, and major defense cuts. Stone asserted that Wicker "ignores the fractious history of conflict with the Joint Chiefs over Laos and Vietnam, which is described in a new book by Major John Newman, *JFK and Vietnam*, and which was sent by my associates to Mr. Wicker in hopes that he would accept a fresh perspective."

Perhaps the nastiest and most contentious exchanges appeared in the *Washington Post* 12/24/91 piece by Gerald Ford and David Belin, which generated responses by Oliver Stone, Fletcher Prouty, Donald Squires, Jamie Aparisi, Cyril Wecht, and Harold Weisberg. Ford and Belin blame the media for sensationalism, and claim that the commercial production of *JFK* and *The Men Who Killed Kennedy* use Hitler's method of "the big lie." "False charges of this kind are a desecration of the memory of President Kennedy, a desecration to the memory of Earl Warren and a fraudulent misrepresentation of the truth to the American public. "They ironically closed, if the press were ever to approach this with the kind of diligence and with the kind of fairness that the American people have a right to expect, then the over whelming majority of Americans will not only eventually understand the truth but will also understand the techniques of perpetuation of the big lie so the kind of deceptive techniques used by the producer of *JFK* and the A&E series *The Men Who Killed Kennedy* will be exposed to all to see…"

Stone's robust retort contrasted assertions with evidence.

> **Belin and Ford:** Nineteen medical experts have examined the autopsy photographs and x-ray of President Kennedy and concluded that all the shots struck Kennedy from the rear.
>
> **Evidence:** While the "Official" autopsy photos and x-rays do show that all shots came from the rear, the 26 trained medical personnel – doctors, nurses, technicians – who treated the president at Parkland Hospital testified to the Warren Commission that they saw an exit type wound in the head, a wound that is inconsistent with the photos and x-rays. Neither the Warren Commission nor the HSCA showed the photos and x-rays to the Dallas doctors. Until that happens, the medical evidence proves absolutely nothing.
>
> **Belin and Ford:** Witness Howard Brennan saw the gunman fire out of the sixth floor window.
>
> **Evidence:** Warren Commission counsel Joseph A. Ball questioned Brennan and found several reasons to doubt his credibility. Bren-

nan's account had several glaring inaccuracies with respect to the gunman's clothing and his shooting position. Brennan could not identify Oswald as the gunman when he first viewed the police lineup. Two months later, Brennan repeated to the FBI that he wasn't able to identify Oswald at the lineup. But in March 1964 Brennan told the Warren Commission that he could have identified Oswald as the gunman but he lied to protect himself and his family.

Belin and Ford: Ballistics evidence proved that Oswald's revolver was the Tippit murder weapon.

Evidence: There is no chain of evidence for the four cartridge cases found at the scene. Both policemen who handled them marked them with their initials, but neither could identify the cases as the ones they turned in when they testified to the Warren Commission – they couldn't find their initials. Furthermore, the cartridge cases-two Western-Winchester and two Remington-Peters – don't match the bullets – three Western – Winchester, one Remington-Peters recovered from Tippit's body.

All of Ford and Belin's "evidence" comes from the Commission Volumes and Report – they ignored all the Commission Documents (not published in the volumes), all of the evidence turned up by the Garrison investigation, the 1975 Senate Intelligence Committee hearings, (the Church Committee) the House Select Committee on Assassinations investigation, and all of the evidence brought to light over the years by private researchers and scholars through the Freedom of Information Act.

Jonathan Kwitny's story in the *Wall Street Journal* "A Better Conspiracy Theory than Oliver Stone's" pointed toward the mafia. He focused on Carlos Marcello's connections to Banister and Ferrie and castigated Garrison for not meeting with Marcello. Kwitny neglects all links to the CIA, military, FBI and the Secret Service. He omitted Garrison's theory that the mafia was involved but, "at a lower level" in the assassination – probably through Ruby. Kwitny concluded that Stone has "sadly muddied the waters."

The *Chicago Sun-Times* claimed *JFK* was "widely inaccurate … propaganda" in its op-ed, "Stone's film Trashes Facts, dishonors *JFK*." The *L.A. Times* ran Warren Commission staffer Richard Mosk's screed "The Plot to Assassinate the Warren Commission." Mosk defended the Warren Commission as finding "overwhelming evidence" and proclaimed the movie moguls were "after a fast buck to portray fiction as fact." Stone responded a week later, 1/16/92, with a measured defense "*JFK* is not irresponsible – choosing to ignore the evidence is." Stone clarified the time frame for the shooting, the "neuromuscular reaction," the 26 witnesses in Parkland Hospital who saw an exit wound in the rear of the President's head, the inconclusive results of the Neutron activation analysis, the HSCA audio studies, as well as Kennedy's changing foreign policy.

Z magazine editor Michal Albert relented somewhat from his instrumentalist take on the JFK assassination a month earlier. In "*JFK* and U.S." he claimed that Kennedy was "not a good guy and would not have turned history on its head" but argued that *JFK* raises some useful questions. Kennedy was described as arguably "the best friend of the military industrial complex," and that efforts to coerce Kennedy were not used first by the establishment. Yet clarifying the "nonsense of the single bullet," the use of the Zapruder film, the "revealing portrait of the autopsy room and Donald Sutherland's (Mr. X) speech were seen as "rays of serious concern emerging from Hollywood."

A week before *JFK* opened in theaters on December 20th the film had been attacked by Dan Rather on CBS, the *Washington Post*, the *New York Times*, *Time*, the *Dallas Morning News*, the *New Orleans Times-Picayune* and the *Chicago Tribune*.

Frank Mankiewicz, former Kennedy confidant, and a publicist for *JFK* declared:

> That every American owes [Oliver Stone] a debt of gratitude ... he kicked open a door that had been closed too long ... the political writers, the Establishment writers, the editorialists, and the thumb suckers were almost unanimous in attacking *JFK*, because it challenged the work they did in the 1960's – which was very little.

When compelling new assassination research is developed in documentary form, it generally goes unreported by the mainstream and alternative media. British filmmaker Nigel Turner's documentary series, *The Men Who Killed Kennedy* (The History Channel and Arts and Entertainment) unearthed critical aspects of the case. Major American networks still have not aired this series, which ran interviews with a number of witnesses who had not been seen before on American television. These included:

> Beverly Oliver, who discussed seeing Oswald and Ruby together in Ruby's nightclub.

The Miami police audiotape of Minuteman Joseph Milteer's death threats, which sound like plans for the assassination of President Kennedy.

Dallas police communications officer Billy Grammer, who told of Ruby calling the switchboard, while Oswald was in custody. Ruby, who was known by Grammer, did not identify him, said, "The police needed to change their plans to move Oswald or we will kill him."

Paul O'Connor, the naval medical assistant who saw Kennedy's body in the autopsy room, stated that Kennedy's brain was blown out. He also observed that in the autopsy room Admiral Murphy prevented Commander Humes from tracing the trajectory of the wound in President Kennedy's back during the autopsy.

FBI agent James Hosty, who had been the agent in Dallas who communicated with Oswald, confirmed that he was told not to cooperate with the Dallas police by FBI Chief of Domestic Counterintelligence, Bill Sullivan. "Sullivan was the FBI link to the NSC." (National Security Council)

The statements from witnesses Ed Hoffman and Gordon Arnold regarding the location of a shooter behind the picket fence on the grassy knoll corroborated the testimony of witness Lee Bowers – All three stated that two men were behind the picket fence at the time of the assassination.[3]

ABC's *Nightline*, 11/22/91, took a look at Oswald's newly released KGB files and concluded that "the lone nut" assassin of President Kennedy "genuinely defected" to the Soviet Union. While dozens of Oswald's fellow Marines could have been interviewed, Mack Osborne alone was questioned. He stated as he had to the Warren Commission, "I'm totally convinced Oswald meant his defection." Witting CIA asset Priscilla Johnson McMillan was recycled as an expert reporter, and predictably noted that Oswald was an unstable misfit in the Soviet Union. Daniel Schorr psychologized, "He did it as a self-motivated individual – not as part of a conspiracy, but only as a conspiracy of a diseased mind."

WCAP radio reporter Woody Woodland in Lowell, Massachusetts, had interviewed top JFK aide Dave Powers. After the interview Woodland asked Powers what he thought of *JFK*. Powers said "[the movie] got it right … we were driving into an ambush … they were shooting from the front, from behind that fence." Woodland noted that Powers did not say that to the Warren Commission. Powers revealed that, "No, we were told not to by the FBI."[4]

The *New York Times* 1/5/92 ran Stefan Kanfer's sarcastic "Reflections from the Grassy Knoll" which spins his "Second Director Theory." "On the bases of research and innumerable interviews, I think I can prove that in the making of this lurid and shallow film Kevin Costner did not act alone."

Four days later the *New York Times* ran Leslie Gelb's piece "Kennedy and Vietnam" in which he claims that Stone "grossly distorts the record." Stone is "swaggering" and "foolish" in his theory of Kennedy pulling out of Vietnam.

Similarly, Arthur Schlesinger, Jr. in *WSJ*, 1/10/92, saw Oliver Stone's film as "indefensible, "paranoid" and "hopelessly loyal to ... fantasy – and their fantasies hopelessly abuse the truth." *WSJ*, 1/28/92 printed Joseph Califano Jr's letter to Rep. Louis Stokes " A Concoction of Lies and Distortions," the LBJ aide saw Stone's film as "disgraceful," and that Johnson thought Castro was responsible and that Oswald didn't act alone. He ended though by calling for a release of all HSCA files.

In early 1992, *JFK* became very popular at the box office, despite getting as many scathing reviews as Jim Garrison's investigation. Stone responded to the numerous attacks in the *New York Times* and the *Washington Post*, by declaring "History may be too important to leave to newsmen." In a speech to the National Press Club (1/15/92) in Washington, he objected passionately and lucidly to the settled version of history "...lest one call down the venom of leading journalists from around the country." Criticism of the film mainly came from older journalists on the right and left.

Roger Ebert provided some context – "Thank God for President Bush's stomach flu. It gave the op-ed pundits something to write about other than Oliver Stone's *JFK*. Never in my years as a newsperson have I seen one subject pummeled so mercilessly and hopelessly as this movie which questions the official wisdom on the assassination of Kennedy. Saddam Hussein did not receive half the vituperation the op-ed crowd has aimed at *JFK*..." Oliver Stone observed.

> Some journalists of the 60's are self-appointed Keepers of the Flame. They talk about this history and fight savagely those who would question it. But confronted with the Crime of the Century, with no motive and hardly any alleged perpetrators, they stand mute ... what I have tried to do with this movie is to open a stall in the marketplace of ideas and offer a version of what might have happened...

Ironically, Time-Warner produced the film, perhaps in part to begin to compensate for past reporting and suppression of the Zapruder film.

Also, the intense Time-Life ideology of the Luce era, as well as the cold war, had faded, and probably Time-Warner perceived a profitable and perhaps even worthy movie.

The *Village Voice* boldly ran "*JFK*: How the Media Assassinated the Real Story" "by Robert Hennely and Jerry Policoff. The article synthesized the role of Time-Life, the *New York Times*, and CBS, and explored "the media on the media." BBC reporter Anthony Summers noted, "In 1981, I went to Dallas ... knocking on doors of witnesses. My preamble would be "I'm sure you spoke to everyone back in 1963" and the response would be, "No. Where have you been all these years?" The media and, in some cases, law enforcement had not spoken to them. Helen Thomas, UPI correspondent, and the unofficial dean of the White House press corps lamented, "We were all remiss, period." Historian Arthur Schlesinger observed, "It does seem apparent that a lot of loose trails would have been picked up by a more alert press." Earl Golz, an investigative reporter for the *Dallas Morning News* recalled, "I had continuous fights with my editors. Many of them were reporters back in 1963, who were spoon-fed by the FBI." Bill O'Reilly, then anchor of *Inside Edition*, announced, 2/5/92, that sealed documents from the HSCA revealed that the CIA lied when they denied a link between Oswald and the CIA, and that the CIA had "agents infiltrating Jim Garrison's investigation." The *New York Times*, the *Washington Post* and the *Boston Globe* wouldn't even assign a reporter to look into this discovery. They said, "sorry, we'll pass."

Author Lisa Pease clarified some of the context for covering the assassinations. Ralph McGehee, a former CIA operative who eventually quit the Agency in disgust over the operations he had learned about during his 25 year career there, obtained a document from 1991 regarding the operations of the CIA's Public Affairs Office (PAO):

> PAO now has relationships with reporters from every major wire service, newspaper, news weekly, and television network in the nation. This helped turn some "intelligence failure" stories into "intelligence success" stories.... In many instances, we have persuaded reporters to postpone, change, hold or even scrap stories."

The dominant establishment voice defending the work of the Warren Commission became author Gerald Posner. His 1993 book, *Case Closed*, was riddled with dozens of errors; nonetheless, the mainstream media offered him dozens of interviews to promote his book. The *New York Times* and the *Washington Post* devoted 30 stories or references to *Case Closed*, often as "definitive" or the "gold standard."

CBS's *48 Hours* developed another "documentary," moderated by Dan Rather, coinciding with the release of *JFK*. The omission of established facts and data as well as the selection of experts interviewed was again remarkable. Oswald's connections to Shaw and de Mohrenschildt, and the connections of these men to the CIA, went unmentioned. The evidence concerning initially reporting the German Mauser rifle, as well as the timing of finding the palm print on the Mannlicher-Carcano (at the morgue) was omitted. The view from the TSBD was reported as unobstructed, forgetting the existence of a live-oak tree obscuring the line of sight until the last split second. Reporter Erin Moriarity asserted, "The answer as to why Oswald was on that sixth floor window is a secret he will take to his grave." But Oswald's location was an implied fact, which has never been proven. Guy Banister and David Ferrie were described as having ties to the Mafia and the anti-Castro movement; however, their ties to the FBI, CIA and the ONI were omitted. Oswald's alleged trip to Mexico City, supposedly to later visit Cuba, a trip which was never proven by the HSCA, was reported by Rather as fact.

Rather claimed that the "physical evidence is solid," while not mentioning the contradictory evidence involving Kennedy's back wound, the weight and shape of CE 399, or the quality of the rifle. No attempt was made to analyze the autopsy pictures or X-rays, or to interview witnesses to determine the number and location of the shots. Again, no mention was made of the fact that the bullets in Tippit's body did not match Oswald's pistol.

Moriarity asked Dallas D.A. Henry Wade why no notes were taken during the twelve-hour interrogation of Oswald. When Wade responded, "I didn't take any notes because Oswald didn't say anything," Moriarity, incredibly, chose not to pursue the point.

Moriarity mistakenly reported that Oswald "was also the only employee reported missing from the Texas School Book Depository – and that's when Lee Harvey Oswald became the first and only suspect in the assassination of John F. Kennedy." Actually a number of employees were missing from the Texas School Book Depository and Oswald was neither the first nor the only suspect arrested.

Although the stated CBS standard was that "facts, hard evidence must be the guide," even the Warren Commission Report evidence was neglected in declaring, "Oswald learned Russian on his own." (evidence showed that he was taught Russian during his Marine service) CBS continued to maintain that "no credible evidence ties Oswald to the FBI" and "no one firmly established the link between Oswald and Ruby."

CBS claimed that conspiracy theories fell into just three categories –CIA, Mafia, and Cuba. They omitted theories involving the FBI, Texas oilmen, rightwing militants, the military, and Lyndon Johnson. CBS then elected to ask two former Directors of the CIA, Richard Helms and Bill Colby, to give their opinions. Their responses were predictable denials of government involvement. Henry Wade, the Dallas D.A. at the time of the assassination and a former FBI operative, again flatly stated that there "was no question as to Oswald's guilt."

Oliver Stone took his few minutes to clarify his critique. He quickly attacked the press for not following up on the leads generated by the HSCA. Rather responded by stating that CBS had done a number of documentaries on this subject – predictably he never mentioned that they all supported the lone-gunman theory and the single-bullet theory of the Warren Commission. The program conveniently concluded:

> We do know a lot – and there is much to support the Warren Commission's conclusions. But unanswered questions also abound. Not all of the conspiracy theories are ridiculous. And, however disturbing, conspiracy theories are also comforting in a way – that is one reason they thrive. They explained the unexplainable, and neatly tied up the loose ends. But a reporter should not take refuge there; facts, hard evidence, these are the journalist's guide. For nearly thirty years now, we have independently looked for plotters and accomplices in the shadows behind Lee Harvey Oswald. So far we have not found them. What we do know is that uncertainty, all of the lingering doubts, may be as difficult for America to accept as the assassination itself... [5]

The movie stirred dialogue and bolstered the critics of the Warren Commission. *PBS News Hour* anchor Robin McNeil legitimized the critics in an interview for the documentary *Beyond JFK* (1992), when he observed, "There is a predisposition of the mainstream press still to believe that it all works, the system works, only the crazies on the fringes said it doesn't. These two views are converging, based on evidence, which has brought them together."[6]

On that documentary Tom Wicker, then an editor for the *New York Times* viewed *JFK* as "propaganda" which "weakens respect for institutions." This echoes his past statements in the *New York Times* and in the introduction of the Bantam version of the HSCA Final Report. He continued to claim that "chance and circumstance" conspired against Kennedy, and that Garrison engaged in "a frivolous prosecution." The iconic former CBS anchorman Walter Cronkite responded similarly. He reiterated his belief in the "lone gunman" and opined, "It's too Machiavellian to be a conspiracy."[7]

The Progressive Review's editor Sam Smith in "Why They Hate Oliver Stone," 2/92, supported Stone and castigated the mass media.

> In a hysterical stampede, even for the media herd, scores of journalists have taken time off from their regular occupation ... to launch an offensive against what is clearly perceived as a major threat to the republic: a movie maker named Oliver Stone.... Stone's crime was not that his movie presents a myth, but that he has the audacity and power to challenge the myths of his critics.... Stone has accomplished something truly remarkable that goes beyond the specific facts of the Kennedy killing ... his underlying story tells a grim truth ... a parable of the subsequent thirty years. By accepting the tyranny of the known, the media inevitably rely on official version of the truth, seldom asking the government to prove its case, while demanding the critics of the official version the most exacting tests of evidence, In the end, David Ferrie in the movie probably said it right, "The fucking shooters don't even know who killed JFK."

Erwin Knoll, editor of, *The Progressive*, (3/92) viewed *JFK* as "manipulative ... a mélange of fact and fiction." Knoll contended that the Warren Commission did a "hasty, slipshod job" but he also "despises" Stone for playing on the gullibility of the public. Author Michael Parenti had repeatedly tried to interest Knoll in new research but to no avail. Parenti noted that Knoll admitted that he had not read the new research, yet he continued to dismiss conspiracy charges.

In early 1992, Dr. Charles Crenshaw, a Parkland surgeon who had tried to revive President Kennedy, revealed in his book, *JFK: Conspiracy of Silence*, that the wounds clearly indicated shots from the front. Crenshaw had been given an edict of secrecy by the director of the emergency room and he feared for his job and his life.[8] The book quickly became a best seller. Broadcast and print media covered the story with the ABC-TV show *20/20* reaching 19 million homes. A few days after Dr. Crenshaw's initial interviews, the *Dallas Morning News* printed an interview with the Director of the Dallas-based FBI "Buck" Revell, a Hoover protégé, who had worked directly under FBI Director William Sessions in Washington as the third in command. Revell contended:

> The documentation does not show that the doctor [Crenshaw] was involved in any way. I'm very dubious as to his motivations and whether or not he has any factual information to add to the investigation.... Until the FBI can examine Dr. Crenshaw's theory as set out in his new book and national television appearances, the FBI will not interview him.

The prestigious *Journal of the American Medical Association* responded to Dr. Crenshaw's book by holding a national press conference, 5/19/92, to trumpet an article in its upcoming issue. The editor of *JAMA* Dr. Charles Lundberg, who stood behind a podium with an AMA seal, (although he later admitted he was speaking only for himself), claimed,

> The scientific evidence documented during the autopsy provides irrefutable proof that President Kennedy was struck by only two bullets that came from above and behind.

The press release asserted that the article had been peer-reviewed. Lundberg attacked Crenshaw and all "conspiracy theorists." He alleged, "Dr. Crenshaw's book is a sad fabrication based on unsubstantiated allegations."

The press conference was widely attended and uncritically reported by the mass media. A muted response came from the *New York Times* medical editor, Lawrence Altman, 5/20/92, and 5/26/92, who clarified that Dr. Crenshaw was indeed in Trauma Room 1 and tending to President Kennedy, according to Drs. Baxter and McClelland.

Only after Dr. Crenshaw legally sought to defend his reputation was it determined that Dr. George Lundberg was not an expert on the case, and he had not even read Dr. Crenshaw's book. Peer review, which was the norm at *JAMA*, did not occur for this article according to its author, Dennis Breo. Breo never even interviewed Crenshaw, and Lundberg was aware of this. Although numerous letters were written to *JAMA* to correct aspects of the article, few were printed and no retractions were made, "according to policy." Lundburg was later fired for politicizing *JAMA*.

In addition to errors of omission, there were errors of commission. A *New York Times* editorial again maintained that all of the discrepancies regarding the nature of President Kennedy's wounds had been ended. Reporters George Lardner and David Brown of the *Washington Post* wrote that the *JAMA* interviews clarified, "the loose ends that have perplexed and inspired conspiracies for years." Knight-Ridder columnist Sandy Grady described the pathologist's statements as definitive.

Bethesda autopsy doctors Humes and Boswell told *JAMA* that one bullet hit JFK in the back of the neck, exited the throat and then hit Governor Connally – the so-called "magic bullet." How could this be known if the pathologists did not dissect the neck or in any way trace its path through the body? The throat wound was not examined, since it was thought to be a tracheotomy (a surgical incision of the respiratory tract to create a breathing hole). The following morning, after learning from the doctors in Dallas that the tracheotomy had been done over a bullet wound, the Bethesda doctors decided that this was an exit wound.

Four areas of evidence contradict this supposition. Dr. Boswell's autopsy diagram, which was signed by Admiral Burkley, the President's private physician, shows the wound to be in the back, not the neck. Secondly, the death certificate signed by Admiral Burkley placed the entry wound to the right of the third thoracic vertebra about six inches lower than where Humes and Boswell now locate it. Dr. John Ebersole, the attending radiologist during the autopsy and other military medical personnel in the autopsy room confirmed that location. Further, the bullet hole in the president's coat and shirt is well below the shoulder! Critics have long argued that these changes enable the location of the wounds to be consistent with shots from the sixth floor of the Texas School Book Depository. Also perplexing is Dr. Humes' reversal on the single-bullet theory, which contradicts what he and Dr. Boswell originally told the Warren Commission.[9]

By June 1992, Dr. Crenshaw's book was no longer on the bestseller list. That month two Navy technicians, Jerrol Custer and Floyd Riebe, who had taken autopsy photos and X-rays at Bethesda Naval Hospital, held a press conference. They confirmed their earlier statements that the photos and X-rays sent to the Warren Commission were not the ones they had taken. Though the mass and alternative media were repeatedly contacted, the press conference received minimal coverage. The media also afforded scant coverage to the June 17, 1992, press conference where Dr. Cyril Wecht, the former Chairman of American Forensic Pathologists, and a former HSCA forensic pathologist, discredited the *JAMA* article word for word.

Later that year, PBS chose to highlight mafia hearsay rather than explore the forensic evidence. *Frontline*, 11/17/92, broadcast "*JFK*, Hoffa and the Mob," which focused on Frank Ragano, the former lawyer for Jimmy Hoffa and Santo Trafficante. Ragano, the intermediary between Hoffa and Trafficante, argued that his two clients, as well as Mafioso Carlos Marcello all hated and were threatened by the Kennedys. On the day of the assassination, Ragano alleged that Trafficante boasted of Kennedy's death over drinks, purportedly asserting "We got him today." Years later, on his deathbed, Trafficante supposedly told him that, "Carlos fucked up – he should have gotten rid of Bobby instead." HSCA Chief Counsel Robert Blakey concurred that Marcello and Trafficante were "likely behind the assassination." Ragano then alleged that he had a conversation with Jim Garrison in 1969 where Garrison spoke of Marcello being his man (ally). He claimed that Garrison's case was self-serving and that Garrison was trying to protect the mob. Only at the end of the program did viewers learn that Ragano, at 69, was facing three years in prison for his second tax evasion conviction.[10] Nonetheless, *Frontline* viewed his allegations as atonement rather than opportunism. The program made no effort to explain the roles of the CIA, FBI, and the military, Secret Service, Lyndon Johnson, Texas oilmen or the Warren Commission. The insinuation was that the mob completely controlled them all – as well as Congress, the mass media and the National Archives. This program was aired again on PBS, 3/22/94.

Edward Jay Epstein concocted a screed about Garrison's investigation "Shots in the Dark," for *The New Yorker*, 11/30/92. Garrison was portrayed as "McCarthyite" and "delusional." Garrison's mistakes with the mass media, pursuing evidence and open theorizing were all duly noted – yet no new information or promising leads found their way into the nine-page story. Epstein characterized the trial by quoting the *New York Times*, "one of the most disgraceful chapters in the history of American jurisprudence."

Perhaps the most significant story run by a major mass-media outlet on the 29th anniversary of the assassination was a front-page story in the *Houston Post* by Mary and Ray Lafontaine regarding Oswald's ID card. The card was military ID, form DD1175, found along with a phony Selective Service card, was discovered in Oswald's wallet. Loose ends still exist beyond the inconsistencies of the card having a picture of Oswald without a Marine-style haircut, and the card was not laminated.

The Marine Corps' response to an FOIA noted: the negative and one print of the photograph taken for the card should be retained in the permanent file of the recipient. However, Oswald's photo was not retained – at least not by the Marine Corps. On October 10, 1963, the CIA in Mexico City had cabled the Office of Navy Intelligence, requesting the Navy's most recent pictures of Lee Harvey Oswald. ONI never sent the picture, but after the assassination of President Kennedy, it produced an envelope addressed to the CIA and containing Oswald's 1956 induction photo.

Another loose end was the role of the FBI in the Oswald Defense card affair. FBI special agent Manning Clements had underestimated the significance of the Defense ID in his report to the Warren Commission by omitting not only the fact that it had the picture, but that is was the same Oswald picture as on the phony A.J. Hidell Selective Service card. But the Bureau also misled (or cooperated with) the Commission by mishandling another copy of the same Oswald photograph.

The letter appeared in the Warren Report and Evidence volumes as Exhibit 2892 and was labeled (from data provided by the FBI) "Photo taken in Minsk." This photo was identical to the "Hidell" and DOD photo, and even showed a white circular cutout in the lower right-hand corner corresponding to the overlapping postmarks on the Defense ID card.

The Minsk connection – the fact that Oswald's trip to Russia occurred after the issuance of the DOD card – was not evident to the Warren Commission, which felt confident enough to include the "Minsk" photo among its exhibits. The most benign explanation for the misstep on the part of the Warren Commission investigators is that the FBI withheld the Defense card from their direct examination.

The FBI went on to destroy the original, quite literally, as archivist Sue McDonough of the National Archives would report to the LaFontaines. In December 1966 the Bureau finally released the Oswald Defense card to the Archives, it arrived "nearly obliterated by FBI testing," McDonough said.[11]

This news never reached the public beyond the range of the *Houston Post*. Although the front-page article was well documented, the AP ignored it, as they had previously ignored both Lafontaine articles in the *Houston Post* on the assassination.

The surge of concern generated by the movie *JFK* led to the 1992 Congressional resolutions to release the remaining documents. Jim Garrison, as with Clarence Darrow at the Scopes Trial, lost the case but ultimately won the battle for hearts and minds. For the first time in our history, a movie caused Congress to pass a law requiring that government tell the truth.

The "Assassination Materials Disclosure Act," often referred to as the "JFK Records Act," mandated the collection of all records and generated remarkable revelations, though it was constrained from the outset. Tax records were exempted from declassification. The procedures to review evidence developed by citizen investigators were not specified. The Review Board was to have a life of only two years. It seems fair to question whether any commission or political body can be the proper forum for a homicide investigation, yet about four million pages were released which the public had not seen.

Three decades after the assassination, the coverage from some mass media outlets had changed more in form than content. *U.S. News & World Report* (6/6/93) sought to dispel the issue of a puff of smoke on the knoll as reported by railroad workers after the assassination. They printed portions of Gerald Posner's *Case Closed*, "because modern ammunition is smokeless, it seldom creates even a wisp of smoke." This can be disproved by observation at a rifle range, and years earlier HSCA noted "modern weapons do in fact emit smoke when fired."[12]

In July 1993, the *Washington Post*, CBS, and *Newsweek* embarked on a joint investigation of the JFK assassination. The reporters included: Walter Pincus (a history of CIA cooperation), George Lardner, and Anne Eisele of the *Washington Post*; the news staff at CBS; and Anne Underwood, Evan Thomas, Melinda Wu and Adam Wolfberg of *Newsweek*.

Lardner and Pincus relied on the questionable testimony of Oleg Nechiporenko, an ex-KGB agent stationed at the Russian Embassy in Mexico City. It is hard to reconcile the calm demeanor of Oswald (if it was Oswald) at the Cuban Embassy, as reported by HSCA researchers Ed Lopez and Dan Hardaway, with the "nervous," "trembling," "extremely agitated" Oswald depicted by Nechiporenko and his colleagues Kostikov and Pavel Yatskov. Recall that Oswald was calm in the Dallas police station.

The themes of the *Washington Post*, CBS, and *Newsweek* remained the same: major policy makers made honest mistakes under pressure that led to accusations of conspiracy and cover-up – but government got the guilty man anyway.

The *Newsweek* article, "The JFK Assassination: It is Not What You Think," argued that LBJ, Hoover and Katzenbach feared the outbreak of nuclear war as the reason for their memos that "the public must be convinced that Oswald was the lone assassin."

Historian Michael Bechloss' essay psychologized about an American public which has "rudely discovered that they had been taught ... a 'child's history' of government," and he lamented the cost.

> As psychologists know, when children discover vital flaws in their parents for the first time, they often begin searching frantically for other imperfections. Americans have now come to adopt the Old World proclivity to look for wheels within wheels, viewing government officials as guilty until proven innocent with a fervor that would have grieved Thomas Paine ... [however] even the staunchest supporters of the Warren Commission's lone-gunman verdict must concede that thousands of details we have learned about the murder seem to radiate conspiracy ... New and vital evidence shows that Lyndon Johnson, J Edgar Hoover, Robert Kennedy, Nicholas Katzenbach, and others, feared an unfettered investigation ... would lead in a dangerous direction.... The effect was to purchase short term political calm at the price of thirty years of doubt, not only about John Kennedy's murder, but about the integrity and purpose of American government. Thirty years later, if we can wring any moral out of John Kennedy's murder, it is that in the long reach of American history, the rewards of full disclosure tower over its immediate perils.

The lofty goal of full disclosure framed the truncated and misleading *Newsweek* piece. This seemed a new overview to promote another "limited hangout" – a partial release of information to give the illusion of full cooperation.

"The Real Cover-up," the article by Evan Thomas, admits agencies "safeguarded their own agendas." A "hysterical public" would demand revenge, so "with remarkable speed and unanimity, officials at the top levels of government decided that they must convince the public that the president's death was the work of a madman, not of some communist plot." Some specifics regarding the CIA-mafia assassination plots against Castro were revealed, while Castro's threats to retaliate were highlighted. Notably, Oswald's purported visit to the Soviet Embassy in September of 1963, including a purported visit with senior KGB agent Kostikov, was reported as fact – completely disregarding the HSCA findings.

In its strident attack on Warren Commission critics, Oswald was again portrayed as a tormented, violent, pro-Castro loser. And, yet again, Priscilla Johnson McMillan was utilized as the expert on Oswald in the article.

> Marina ridiculed Oswald in bed and made no secret of her attrac-
> tion to JFK; who reminded her of an old boyfriend in Minsk....
> But given Oswald's tormented psyche, even a small provocation
> could have been enough to send him into a murderous rage.

The single-bullet theory was again diagrammed and supported – and though there was no new credible evidence, Oswald was placed on the sixth floor of the TSBD.

While CIA covert operations were seen as a bastion of patriotic, responsible eccentrics, the connections of Oswald to the CIA remained unexamined. *Newsweek* concluded, "There is no solid evidence leading to the CIA or to the Cubans."

Medical evidence was unexplored and disingenuously dismissed, "the fact that Kennedy's physician failed to disclose his Addison's disease led to decades of conspiracy theories."

Newsweek still viewed Jack Ruby's murder of Oswald as an unplanned crime of passion. They continued to claim that Ruby, "left his beloved dog Sheba in his car on the 24th, something he would never have done if he were planning to kill Oswald, for he would have been separated from his beloved animal while in custody."

The results of the paraffin test were again misrepresented. The FBI lab identified traces of nitrate on Oswald's hands, as if the findings were indications of guilt.

The three-day *Washington Post* series, 11/14/93-11/16/93, although somewhat more comprehensive, still avoided many contradictions in physical and medical evidence. The Mexico City mystery was discussed without drawing upon the HSCA "Lopez Report" (on Oswald in Mexico City) or HSCA researcher Gaeton Fonzi's book *The Last Investigation*.

On the thirtieth anniversary of the assassination the Associated Press ran a number of pieces, all of which continued to faithfully support the Warren Commission's version. Reporter John Diamond contended "Facts haven't changed much in 30 years" and proclaimed that research has only, "...tended to support the single-gunman case by disproving various conspiracy allegations; or add tantalizing detail – but no solid scenario – to those pursuing the conspiracy case."

The AP ran a one-page pictorial description of the assassination including Dealey Plaza, wounds, the rifle, etc, which again totally defended the Warren Report. Polling data determining American attitudes toward a cover-up or conspiracy showed 78% of the American public thought a cover-up had occurred, and 55% thought the CIA was responsible. Reporter Howard Goldberg attributed this to a distrust of government, a sloppy Warren Commission investigation, a lack of hard evidence and "a desire to close the wound to the national psyche."

The CBS News program for the 30th anniversary of the assassination, "Who killed JFK?" uncritically focused on Oswald. Oswald visited Marina on weekends at a home owned by Michael Paine, for two months prior to the assassination. When Paine was interviewed by the FBI he stated "I went one afternoon to pick Oswald up, went upstairs, and I think the first thing he did, practically, was pick up this photograph of himself, 8 by 10, holding his rifle there and some papers.... I suppose he was looking for a big revolution..." As author Stewart Galanor recounts, Paine had kept this information to himself for thirty years. If he were telling the truth, then he lied under oath to the Warren Commission when he said, "I didn't know prior to the assassination that he had a rifle."

Michael Paine further undermined his credibility in the CBS interview by stating, "at the police station when I saw him (Oswald) later on that night (11/22) he was proud of what he had done, he thought he would be recognized as somebody who did something." However, Paine told the Warren Commission that he never saw or spoke to Oswald at the police station, and recalled that Oswald emphatically denied that he shot anyone. These new links to the Mannlicher-Carcano went unchallenged by CBS. Years later, privately, CBS anchorman Dan Rather admitted to HSCA Deputy Chief Counsel Bob Tannenbaum, "We really blew it on the Kennedy assassination."[13]

PBS ran a program, "Who was Lee Harvey Oswald?" which claimed that he was an emotionally unbalanced nut who shot the president. The findings of the HSCA were ignored in order to highlight Priscilla McMillan Johnson, Ruth and Michael Paine, Ed Epstein, Ed Butler (INCA), Dan Rather, Richard Helms, Rosemary James, Max Holland, Vincent Bugliosi, and portions of the 1967 CBS special. Recall the CIA connections of Johnson, the Paines, Epstein, Holland, Butler and Helms.

Short clips of critics Cyril Wecht, Mark Lane, Penn Jones and Jim Garrison were included but Jones and Garrison were mocked. The show concluded that conspiracy was just more comforting to believe than a deranged lone shooter – and critics caused the loss in public confidence in government.

In March 1995, Nigel Turner produced another program in *The Men Who Killed Kennedy* series, which aired on The History Channel. Promising new leads were generated in the areas of doctoring autopsy photos, Colonel Daniel Marvin's assertions of CIA-military complicity, as well as new documents on Project Freedom, the violent anti-Castro actions overseen by Robert Kennedy. In the *Wall Street Journal*, 4/1/95, television reviewer Dorothy Rabinowitz nonetheless derided the documentary as "anti-government drivel ... (from) the more deluded quarters of the lunatic fringe." Assassination researchers were referred to as an "army of retirees, students, assorted obsessives and similarly qualified sleuths." Rabinowitz never got around to refuting or exploring anything in the documentary, nor have any other mass media or alternative outlets.

In early April 1995, the *Washington Post*, after five months of vetting, printed a probing piece by editor Jefferson Morley, "The Oswald File: Tales of the Routing Slips," on the op-ed pages. He highlighted the research of historian Dr. John Newman, a 20-year veteran of U.S. Army Intelligence. Declassified CIA documents revealed that in 1963 senior officials at CIA headquarters in Langley elected to claim to their subordinates in Mexico City, including Chief of Station Winston Scott that they had not learned anything new about Oswald in the last year and a half. "Just days earlier though, two CIA counterintelligence offices had received an FBI report on Oswald's recent pro-Castro activities, according to the routing slips. The CIA had also received FBI reports on Oswald in September 1963 and in August 1962..." The CIA claimed that the cable 10/3/63 focused "only on the status of Oswald's citizenship." Yet retired CIA officer, Jane Roman, in an interview with Morley and Newman, saw no reason "...why, if the information was available, it would not have been forwarded to Mexico... I would think that there was definitely some operational reason to withhold [the information] ... when you see how many people signed off on this." Morley noted, "the combination of strong CIA interest in Oswald and a desire for internal secrecy suggests the agency may have had some relationship with Oswald that it was trying to protect." Morley sensed at the paper a "lack of comfort with the issue," and a good friend at the *Washington Post* admonished, "Jeff, this isn't good for your career."[14]

Amid the accelerating declassification of assassination-related documents as well as numerous scholarly conferences on political assassinations, novelist Norman Mailer chose to rework the lone-nut scenario in *Oswald's Tale: An American Mystery*. His book was widely embraced by the mass media. Mailer myopically explored "Why did Oswald Choose Kennedy?" in *Parade* magazine, 5/14/95, by focusing on "Would Oswald pushed to the extreme, have the soul of a killer?" Contradictory or new evidence in the case was seen as "impenetrable" or unable to "answer the mystery."

He imaginatively speculated as to what Oswald might have been thinking and surmised:

> As Oswald saw it, an explosion at the heart of the American establishments' complacency, would be exactly the shock therapy needed to awaken the world.... Like Hitler, Stalin, or Lenin, a trial and imprisonment would forge his agenda.

This was specious speculation since Oswald tried to escape and repeatedly stated that he was a patsy. Then Mailer remarkably recycled the "coincidence theory" of the assassination.

> One would not be surprised that there was indeed another shot; it was not necessarily fired by a conspirator of Oswald's. Such a gun could have belonged to a conspirator working for a group unattached to Lee Harvey. It is not inconceivable that two gunman with wholly separate purposes both fired in the same lacerated few seconds of time."
>
> He closed his fable with another flight of clairvoyance.
>
> Oswald may never have read Emerson, but the following passage from the essay "Heroism" gives us luminous insight into what had to be Oswald's opinion of himself as he sat on the sixth floor waiting for the Kennedy motorcade – he was committing himself to the most heroic deed he was capable.[15]

The *Washington Post* chose novelist Joseph Finder to review the book. The novel method of a novelist analyzing a novelist regarding a homicide led to a strongly supportive review. Finder noted that Mailer did unearth new evidence from KGB documents in the former Soviet Union, but that he also relied heavily on Warren Commission material as well as material from Priscilla Johnson McMillan. Once again, McMillan was not identified as a "witting" CIA asset.

Mailer was rightly credited with clarifying the source of material [J.J. Angleton] given to author Edward Epstein for Epstein's book *Legend* (1978) on Oswald – CIA sources back then suggested a KGB link to Oswald. Mailer's KGB documents show that Oswald was suspected of being a U.S. intelligence agent. Finder nonetheless viewed that "Oswald's life is a maddening warren of false leads, blind alleys, counterfeit identities... feeding the conspiracy theories that even now would deny him credit for his great claim to celebrity." He disregarded the documented information on Oswald, which was cogently discussed by Jefferson Morley in the *Post* just one week earlier.

The *New York Times* review, 4/30/95, by Thomas Powers, author of friendly biography of Richard Helms, strongly supported Mailer's conclusion. Only Mailer's notion of a kinder, more humanized lone nut was rejected, as Powers concluded, "It was an insect that brought Kennedy down..." *Oswald's Tale* made the "Top Ten Books of the Year" list in the *Dallas Morning News*.

Mailer appeared on CBS's *Sunday Morning*, 6/17/95, for a segment, "The man who changed us all" to discuss his new book. Reporter Charles Osgood reframed forensics and fantasy.

> The man who changed us all put a rifle to his shoulder that day in Dallas in November 1963, looked through the rifle's telescopic site, centered its crosshairs and squeezed the trigger. Most accounts agree on that much at least. Who killed John Kennedy? To say it was Lee Harvey Oswald begs the question. Who was Lee Harvey Oswald? You would have to be a great novelist to write that story. Well, a great novelist has.

Dan Rather began his interview with Mailer by asking how history would view the "four dark days in Dallas." Mailer saw it as a spiritual disaster, which created an American obsession. Rather noted "he spent part of his life and CBS's money trying to prove that Oswald was not the assassin of John Kennedy but came to the conclusion the evidence and best testimony points to him as the assassin. Mailer agreed. Rather asserted "nobody who hasn't been to the (TSBD) window can fully realize what a comparatively easy shot [it was] ... particularly from that angle and distance, Mailer again agreed. Neither the quality of the rifle nor the FBI or CBS's rifle tests would deter Mailer's tale.

Mailer, like the Warren Commission, abruptly refocused exclusively on Oswald, an "interesting ... and extraordinary fellow." He claimed that Oswald "thought he would be a future world leader." His "cunning" came from his mother, "a character worthy of Dickens."

Rather noted that Oswald's wife, Marina, seemed to change her story by the hour, and Mailer surmised that she probably feared being sent to an American gulag. Mailer spent five days with her and found her a "remarkably honest woman."

Instead of following up on the notable interview Jack Anderson had with Marina for his 1988 documentary, where she stated that she was used by the Warren Commission and that Lee was innocent, Mailer psychologized that what haunted Marina was her crumbling marriage and her rejection of Lee sexually. Marina had told Anderson that Lee was working for the government by infiltrating groups, that Lee liked President Kennedy, that the rifle was not his, and that he was doing what he was told to do. Mailer then claimed that Marina felt her rejection of Lee the night before left him thinking that there was nothing left of the marriage, and this led to the assassination. "If there was a great night of love – there was a great day of assassination." The Pulitzer Prize winner had drifted into incoherent pulp fiction. Mailer closed by proclaiming that Oswald "did more to change American inner life than any other individual."[16]

Oprah Winfrey's program on the 33rd anniversary of the assassination, (11/22/96), probed new dimensions of the case. She interviewed Marina Oswald Porter; author Mary Lafontaine, Oliver Stone, John Tunheim, the ARRB chairman, and former FBI clerk William Walter.

After a decade of trying, Oprah finally got Marina Oswald to appear for a lengthy interview. Marina changed her mind in 1983 regarding her former husband's guilt, based on "understanding the facts better" and repeated much of the statement she gave to Jack Anderson. Mary Lafontaine revealed the record on Oswald's Dallas cellmate John Elrod, based on the declassification of 1992 Dallas P.D. files. Though officially denied, Elrod seemingly ran guns with Jack Ruby, as did Oswald. LaFontaine contended:

> In a week prior to the assassination, on November 14, a National Guard Armory was burglarized in Texas. On November 16, just 2 days later, Lee Harvey Oswald met with the FBI in Dallas. The following day a Teletype went out warning that President Kennedy might be assassinated in Dallas later that week ... on November 18 ... two men were arrested with a carload of guns. One of them worked for Jack Ruby. It was one of those men that Oswald identified in his cell.
>
> I believe that Lee Harvey Oswald was an FBI informant who was reporting on a group that was suspect in the assassination.... I believe he was set up as a patsy to neutralize the FBI.

Despite legal constraints, the Assassination Records and Review Board made significant progress, but with only 27 researchers and a two-year life span, many agencies delayed the process and stalled until the Board was disbanded. By 1996, according to the ARRB "the FBI created considerable delays," and the Secret Service, "has yet to undertake a thorough search of all of its holdings." The DEA "seems to understand that they have no obligation to the ARRB," however, the "extent of cooperation may be unknowable because of some current record destruction." The U.S. Customs Service failed to initiate a search of records until June of 1995, and due to "their general record destruction policy and poorly labeled storage boxes "Customs officials are not optimistic." The CIA has released almost 300,000 pages of documents but 50,000 pages of documents and lengthy redactions remain. The Department of Defense had not complied with the JFK Records Act by the beginning of 1996. NSA compliance was minimal, merely transferring mainly unclassified press reports and requests for postponement. The ARRB publicly admitted that it couldn't finish its job, and that it had been difficult to get the press interested in their work.

The ARRB declassifications spurred releases of Cuban secret files on the assassination. In December 1995 a select group of Cuban officials and U.S. researchers, including a member of the ARRB, met in the Bahamas to review the documents. Cuban intelligence had penetrated a number of U.S.-based anti-Cuban groups. Cuban General Fabian Escalante, former Chief of the G-2 intelligence agency, had headed an official investigation of the JFK assassination since 1992 and determined that one of the objectives of the assassination was to blame Cuba. General Escalante had two informants that said "Maurice Bishop" was David Phillips.

Escalante revealed that a captured Cuban exile leader, Tony Cuesta, named two other exiles associated with the JFK assassination, Eladio Del Valle and Hermino Diaz Garcia. Recall that Del Valle was murdered the same night in 1967 that David Ferrie supposedly committed suicide. Cuban UN Ambassador David Lachuga argued that when word of the secret talks with Cuba leaked out, it sparked the assassination conspiracy. Reporter Dick Russell explored these revelations in *High Times* (8/96), as well as naming CIA-Oswald connections through Desmond FitzGerald, David Phillips, Henry Hecksher, Colonel William Bishop and Richard Case Nagell. Phillips was in charge of CIA anti-Castro operations in Mexico in 1963, as well as penetrating the Fair Play for Cuba Committee (FPPC) in the U.S. Oswald's activities were closely followed by Desmond FitzGerald's CIA Special Affairs staff. Richard Case Nagell, a CIA double agent, claimed that he warned FitzGerald, 8/27/63, about an assassination plot against Kennedy. Nagell worked with CIA agent Henry Hecksher, who was a special assistant to FitzGerald. Russell interviewed Colonel Bishop who said that he worked under CIA officer Desmond FitzGerald and that he was aware of a plot to assassinate President Kennedy. Bishop stated that he covertly raised funds for the Alpha 66 (anti-Castro Cubans) through mafia contacts including Jimmy Hoffa, and wealthy anti-Communist types in Dallas.

One anti-Castro Cuban, Felipe Vidal Santiago, told Cuban intelligence after his arrest that he had a relationship with Colonel Bishop. Santiago said that Bishop drove him to Dallas to spend four days raising money for re-taking the island. Vidal Santiago was also a close friend of CIA contact, and Miami mobster, John Marino.

As new documents regarding the Warren Commission's descriptive re-location of the bullet wound in President Kennedy's back surfaced in July of 1997, mass media coverage was mostly decontextualized. Gerald Ford suggested that the panel change its initial description "a bullet entered his back at a point slightly below the shoulder to the right of the spine" to read "a bullet had entered the back of his neck slightly to the right of the spine." The final report said "a bullet had entered the base of the back of his neck slightly to the right of the spine." Recall that these descriptions varied markedly with the location of the third thoracic vertebrae, 5 3/4 inches below the base of the neck, indicated by the signed death certificate, the autopsy report, and the holes in both Kennedy's shirt and coat. Critics have long contended that the change in location was necessary to accommodate a downward trajectory from the sixth floor of the TSBD and still have the throat wound be "presumably of exit."

The Associated Press report by Mike Feinsilber, 7/3/97, asserted that Gerald Ford "changed – ever so slightly – the Warren Commission's key sentence on where the bullet entered John Kennedy's body. The effect of Ford's change was to strengthen the Warren Commission's conclusion that a single bullet passed through Kennedy and severely wounded Governor Connally." Gerald Ford, the only remaining member of the Warren Commission, declared, "My changes had nothing to do with a conspiracy theory.… My changes were only an attempt to be more precise." No critics were quoted in some AP versions, in others, an obscure and unpublished assassination "researcher," Robert Morningstar, was quoted for one unsupported sentence, "This is the most significant lie in the whole Warren Commission report." No context was provided from the evidentiary record regarding the location of the back wound.

The *New York Times* buried the story, 7/3/97, on page A-19, and edited the already brief AP version down to four inches. While essential background evidence regarding the location of the wound in the back was unmentioned, the article opines that Ford's, "editing was seized upon by conspiracy theorists who reject the commission's conclusion that Mr. Oswald had acted alone."

The *Washington Post* piece by George Lardner, Jr. "Ford Editing Backed 'Single Bullet' Theory" was only somewhat more revealing. Lardner at least quoted a longtime critic of the Warren Report, Harold Weisberg:

> ...What Ford is doing is trying to make the single bullet theory more tenable. The official story is that the bullet hit no bone, but it did. They are trying to make it seem that the bullet traveled downward, but it didn't.

Lardner, though, neglected the evidence on the location of the wound, which made Weisberg's statement appear to be merely opinion. The article then changed the subject: "Weisberg and others have long maintained that the wound in the front of Kennedy's neck was an entry wound, not an exit wound." Lardner attacked the possibility of a shooter from the front by quoting from the HSCA, which held "by an 8 to 1 vote that Kennedy was struck by two and only two bullets, each of which entered the rear." This one-liner neglected to note that the HSCA also concluded that a shooter fired from the front of the president that the doctors at Parkland hospital thought the neck wound was a wound of entry, or the testimony of fifty-one witnesses that shots came from the grassy knoll.

One Hell of a Gamble (1997), a respected scholarly work on the Cuban Missile Crisis by Timothy Naftali and Alexander Fursenko, revealed a remarkable communication between Robert Kennedy and the Soviets after the assassination, based on secret documents from a number of Soviet agencies. RFK sent his trusted friend Bill Walton to the Soviet Union to meet with George Bolshakov, a Soviet agent formerly stationed in Washington. Walton told Bolshakov that Bobby and Jackie believed that the president was killed by a large political conspiracy coordinated by U.S, not foreign opponents, and that Johnson was perceived as more pro-business than JFK and "incapable of realizing Kennedy's unfinished plans."[17]

The book was widely reviewed in the media, yet none of the reviews mentioned Walton's mission or statements on behalf of the Kennedys. Robert Kennedy seems to have placed more trust in Soviet leaders than the American government.

When the ARRB issued its Final Report at the end of September 1998, the AP led its story with a quote from the Report that the U.S. government "needlessly and wastefully" withheld records on the JFK Assassination, "Causing Americans to mistrust their government." Contradictory quotes characterize the dispatch. Gerald Posner avowed that the Board provided "documents that help fill in the details of this horrible event," while James Lesar submitted that, "there is physical, medical, and ballistics evidence that leads you to conclude that one person could not have fired all the shots."

By the beginning of 1998 the ARRB had reviewed and released thousands of CIA documents on Lee Harvey Oswald and the assassination of President Kennedy, hundreds of HSCA records on Oswald in Mexico City, thousands of FBI assassination files, hundreds of private and local records and the records of Jim Garrison. Those declassifications included:

1. A transcript of a phone call between President Johnson and FBI Director Hoover from the morning after the assassination, where Hoover informed LBJ that Oswald was impersonated in Mexico City. Portions of the tape of this call were erased.

2. In response to a cable reporting Oswald's call to the Soviet Embassy in Mexico City, CIA HQ cabled back false information about Oswald to its own CIA station there. One of the cabling officers said in 1995: I'm signing off on something I know isn't there and said this indicated, "A keen interest in Oswald held very closely on the need to know basis."

3. Acknowledgement by the CIA that at least one defector to the Soviet Union was part of a false defector program.

4. Captain Will Fritz' contemporaneous notes of an interview with Oswald on Nov. 22, in which Oswald provided an alibi for his whereabouts at lunch.

5. A report from Dr. Burkley's lawyer to the HSCA, saying that his client (JFK's personal physician) had information that others besides Oswald must have participated.

6. Documents showing that the HSCA had tested the Navy camera, which was supposed to have, taken JFK's autopsy photographs and it, failed authenticity tests.

7. HSCA interviews of autopsy witnesses found that directly contradicted the depiction of wounds presented by the medical panel the interviews were suppressed and misrepresented by the HSCA.

8. A sworn interview with Sandra Kay Spencer, who developed the JFK autopsy pictures in which she declared that the photos in the

Archives are not the ones she developed. Autopsy photographer John Stringer disavowed the supplemental autopsy brain photographs.

9. Papers on "Operation Northwoods."

10. Plans for the complete withdrawal of U.S. forces from Vietnam drawn up in spring 1963.

Nonetheless, the *New York Times* led its story by creating conclusions, which the ARRB never drew, "There is no second gunman, no assassin skulking on the grassy knoll, no vast conspiracy." The Board was created to release records rather than draw conclusions. So even four decades later when some of the basic evidence was finally released, the *New York Times* still withheld "all the news that is fit to print."

The NBC *Today Show* pitted prominent Warren Commission apologist Gerald Posner against critic Harrison Livingstone. Posner stubbornly asserted that the ARRB Report,

> Doesn't show any mob involvement, it doesn't show Oswald having any link to the CIA ... [the Report said] exactly what I have said five years ago in my book, that the FBI and CIA had a massive cover up, not of an assassination, but trying to cover up their own bureaucratic reputations. And in doing so, they didn't serve the Warren Commission correctly, nor serve history, and they laid the groundwork for a lot of conspiracy speculation.
>
> Livingstone clarified that the mandate of the Board was not to draw conclusions and then noted:
>
> What the Board did that was stunning was to re-interview the doctors, and go down the chain of evidence and give us this raw material ... these new interviews and depositions show conclusively that the autopsy was faked, and that the photography was false ... Gerald Posner has never done his homework in this case; he doesn't understand the evidence.
>
> The photographer who took the photographs of the brain says those are not his pictures; the photographs of the body are stated by the person who developed them not to be the pictures that she developed; all of the doctors, all of the medical witnesses have insisted that the wounds are not in the correct place.

At the Coalition on Political Assassinations (COPA) annual commemoration, held at the grassy knoll on, 11/22/98, Mark Lane thundered,

There were a number of brave, courageous residents of the city, longtime residents of Texas , who had the courage to speak truth to power – in the face of threats and intimidation.... This is hallowed ground – and the people of the country know it.... That day in Dallas ... when their government of the United States executed its own President – when that happened we as a nation lost our code of honor – lost our sense of honor – that can only be restored when the government of the United States ... tells us the truth, including their role in the murder – when that day comes, for the first moment, honor will be restored to this nation.

The prophesy was enthusiastically received, yet the mass media was generally mute.

"Study Backs Theory of "Grassy Knoll," by *Washington Post* reporter George Lardner Jr., 3/26/01, led with, "The House Assassinations Committee may have been right after all. There was a shot from the grassy knoll."

A new peer-reviewed article in *Science and Justice*, a quarterly publication of Britain's Forensic Science Society, says the NAS panel's study was seriously flawed. It says the panel failed to take into account the words of a Dallas patrolman that show the gun like noises occurred "at the exact instant that John F. Kennedy was assassinated." The author of the article, D.B. Thomas, a government scientist and JFK assassination researcher, said it was more than 96% certain that there was a shot from the grassy knoll ... in addition to three sound bursts from the Book depository window... G. Robert Blakely, former chief counsel of the House Assassinations Committee, said the NAS panel's study always bothered him because it dismissed all four putative shots as random noise... we thought there was a 95% chance it was a shot. He puts it at 96.3%, either way that's "beyond reasonable doubt." The sounds of assassination were recorded at Dallas police headquarters when a motorcycle patrolman inadvertently left his microphone switch in the "on" position, deluging his transmitting channel with what seemed to be motorcycle noise. Using sophisticated techniques, a team of scientists enlisted by the HSCA filtered out the noise and came up with "audible events" within a ten second frame that it believed to be gunfire... the NAS panel assigned to conduct further studies after the committee closed down, said in 1982 that the noises on the tape previously identified as gunshots "were recorded about one minute after the president was shot..."

The NAS experts made several errors, Thomas said "…they ignored a much clearer instance of cross talk when police Sgt. A.Q. Bellah can be heard on both channels asking, "you want me to hold this traffic on Stemmons until we find out something or let it go?… when Bellah's words are used to line up the two channels, Thomas found the gunshot sounds occur at the exact instant that John F. Kennedy was assassinated…"

Other important evidence steadily emerged, mainly in the alternative media, and continued to confront stiff resistance. In April 2001, the weekly *Miami New Times* published an article by Jefferson Morley on CIA agent George Joannides, the agent in charge of DRE in Miami in the early 1960's, which actively portrayed Oswald as pro-Castro. Joannides then served as the CIA liaison to the HSCA (1977-1979) where he blocked significant portions of the investigation.

As the national newspaper of record the *New York Times* influences the agendas of most news outlets large and small. For the 40th year after the assassination, the *New York Times* merely reprinted its early assassination coverage in its book *Four Days in November*, with a laudatory introduction by Tom Wicker. Not one question critical of the Warren Report was raised.

The ABC 40th year special report declared that "In all these years there has not been a single piece of credible evidence to prove a conspiracy." Historian Robert Dalleck recycled a common mass media rationale by psychologizing to ABC anchor Peter Jennings that, "it's very difficult for them [the public] to accept the idea that someone as inconsequential as Oswald could have killed someone as consequential as Kennedy." Author William Manchester concurred in conclusion, "If you put the murdered president on one side of the scale and that wretched waif, Oswald on the other, it doesn't balance. You want to add some weight to Oswald. It would invest the president's death with meaning…. A conspiracy would do the job nicely." Critics, again, were not given a chance to respond.

In November 2003, The History Channel aired the ninth episode in *The Men Who Killed Kennedy* series, "The Guilty Men." This segment directly implicated former President Johnson, and generated protests from Lady Bird Johnson, Bill Moyers, ex-President Jimmy Carter, Jack Valenti (former LBJ aide) and ex-President and former Warren Commissioner, Gerald Ford. This group formally complained of libel to the History Channel. They then threatened to sue the A&E Company, the owner of The History Channel. The History Channel responded, 4/7/04, with a program entitled, "The Guilty Men: A Historical Review." The panelists, Robert Dalleck, Stanley Kutler, and Thomas Suzrue all argued that the documentary was not credible and should not have aired. Notably though, Barr McClelland, author and key interview in this controversial segment of "The Guilty Men," was not interviewed, and neither was the producer/director of the series, Nigel Turner.

The History Channel then issued a statement saying, in part, "that they recognize that 'The Guilty Men' failed to offer viewers context and perspective, and fell short of the high standards that the network sets for itself." The History Channel apologized to Mrs. Johnson and its viewers, and then permanently withdrew the three newest segments by Turner.

A letter to the editors of the *New York Review of Books*, 12/16/2003, revealed new CIA connections, as well as clear, continued CIA stonewalling on the JFK assassination in the face of logic and law.

JFK
DECEMBER 18, 2003

by Jim Lesar, Jim Hougan, John McAdams, John Newman, Robbyn Swan

To the Editors:

As published authors of divergent views on the assassination of President John F. Kennedy, we urge the Central Intelligence Agency and the Department of Defense to observe the spirit and letter of the 1992 JFK Assassination Records Act by releasing all relevant records on the activities of a career CIA operations officer named George E. Joannides, who died in 1990.

Joannides's service to the U.S. government is a matter of public record and is relevant to the Kennedy assassination story. In November 1963, Joannides served as the chief of the Psychological Warfare branch in the CIA's Miami station. In 1978, he served as the CIA's liaison to the House Select Committee on Assassinations (HSCA).

The records concerning George Joannides meet the legal definition of "assassination-related" JFK records that must be "immediately" released under the JFK Records Act. They are assassination-related because of contacts between accused assassin Lee Harvey Oswald and a CIA-sponsored Cuban student group that Joannides guided and monitored in August 1963.

Declassified portions of Joannides personnel file confirm his responsibility in August 1963 for reporting on the "propaganda" and "intelligence collection" activities of the Directorio Revolucionario

Estudantil (DRE), a prominent organization known in the North American press as the Cuban Student Directorate.

George Joannides activities were assassination-related in at least two ways.

1. In August 1963, Oswald attempted to infiltrate the New Orleans delegation of the DRE: The delegation – dependent on $25,000 a month in CIA funds provided by Joannides – publicly denounced Oswald as an unscrupulous sympathizer of Fidel Castro.

2. After Kennedy was killed three months later, on November 22, 1963, DRE members spoke to reporters from The New York Times and other news outlets, detailing Oswald's pro-Castro activities. Within days of the assassination, the DRE published allegations that Oswald had acted on Castro's behalf.

The imperative of disclosure is heightened by the fact that the CIA has in the past, failed to disclose George Joannides activities. In 1978, Joannides was called out of retirement to serve as the agency's liaison to the House Select Committee on Assassinations. The agency did not reveal to the Congress his role in the events of 1963, compromising the committee's investigation.

In 1998, the Agency again responded inaccurately to public inquiries about Joannides. The Agency's Historic Review Office informed the JFK Assassination Records Review Board (AARB) that it was unable to identify the case officer for the DRE in 1963. The ARRB staff, on its own, located records confirming that Joannides had been the case officer.

This is not a record that inspires public confidence or quells conspiracy-mongering. To overcome misunderstanding, the CIA and the Defense Department should make a diligent good-faith effort to identify and release any documents about George Joannides.

The government should make these records public in conjunction with the fortieth anniversary of the Kennedy assassination on November 22, 2003, so as to help restore public confidence and to demonstrate the agencies' commitment to compliance with the JFK Assassination Records Act.

The law requires immediate disclosure, nothing less.

G. Robert Blakey
Former General Counsel
House Select Committee on Assassination
Jefferson Morley
Also signed by:

Don DeLillo
Paul Hoch
Norman Mailer
Gerald Posner
Anthony Summers
Richard Whalen
And six others

Sometimes a new facet of the case will be explored by the media but it will lack evidentiary and political context, so that the public may misinterpret or underestimate its importance. The *Reader's Digest* article March 2005 by Jefferson Morley "The JFK Murder- Can New Technologies Finally Crack the Case?," illustrates this. He explained that new sound preservation techniques which if applied to the open police dictabelt could reveal the number of shots fired. U.S. DOE scientists Carl Harber and Vitaly Fadegev were encouraged by an archival panel to explore whether their confocal microscope could coax new findings from the old and cracking "Dictabelt No. 10," which the HSCA determined revealed four, not three shots. Morley probably knows the case better than any mainstream media reporter, yet no mention was made regarding the possible role of anti-Kennedy forces in the government – an area that Morley has been effectively writing about for years.

Mother Jones, December 2008, wistfully speculated on the Democrats' dilemma and in a list of "what ifs" included, "if only Oswald would have missed ... if only James Earl Ray and Sirhan Sirhan would have missed..." In February of 2006, *The Nation* published a piece by contributing editor Max Holland, "The JFK Lawyer's Conspiracy," which was also run on the official CIA website. Holland claimed that four lawyers, Mark Lane, Jim Garrison, Senator Gary Hart and Robert Blakey, conspired to put "the Warren Report into undeserved disrepute." Lane was smeared as dishonest and a KGB dupe, Garrison's trial was characterized as a "legal farce," and the allegation of a lawyer's conspiracy was unproven nonsense. An incensed Lane responded to *The Nation* with a lengthy, scathing letter.

Ms. Katrina vanden Heuvel
Editor and publisher
The Nation
33 Irving Place
New York, NY 10003

Ms. Katrina vanden Heuvel:

It began with a CIA document classified "Top Secret," How do I know that? A decade after the assassination of President Kennedy, with the assistance of the ACLU, I won a precedent – setting lawsuit in the United States District Court in Washington, D.C. brought pursuant to the Freedom of Information Act. The court ordered the police and spy organizations to provide to me many long-suppressed documents.

The CIA document stated that it was deeply troubled by my work in questioning the conclusions of the Warren Commission. The CIA had concluded that my book, *Rush to Judgment*, was difficult to answer; indeed, after a careful and thorough analysis of that work by CIA experts, the CIA complained that almost half of the American people agreed with me and that "Doubtless polls abroad would show similar, or possibly more adverse, results." This, "trend of opinion," the CIA stated, "is a matter of concern" to "our organization." Therefore, the CIA concluded, steps must be taken.

The CIA directed that methods of attacking me should be discussed with "liaison and friendly elite contacts (especially politicians and editors)," instructing them that "further speculative discussion only plays into the hands of the opposition." The CIA stressed that their assets in the media should "Point out also that parts of the conspiracy talk appear to be deliberately generated by Communist propagandists." Further, their media contacts should "use their influence to discourage" what the CIA referred to as "unfounded and irresponsible speculation," *Rush to Judgment*, then the *New York Times* number one best-selling book, contained no speculation.

The CIA in its report instructed book reviewers and magazines that contained feature articles how to deal with me and others who raised doubts about the validity of the Warren Report. Magazines should, the CIA stated, "employ propaganda assets to answer and refute the attacks of the critics," adding that "feature articles are particularly appropriate for this purpose." The CIA instructed its media assets that "because of the standing of the members of the Warren Commission, efforts to impugn their rectitude and wisdom tend to cast doubt on the whole leadership of American society." The CIA was referring to such distinguished gentlemen as Allen Dulles, the former director of the CIA; President Kennedy had fired Dulles from that position for having lied to him about the Bay of Pigs tragedy. Dulles was then appointed by Lyndon Johnson to the Warren Commission to tell the American people the truth about the assassination.

The purpose of the CIA was not in doubt. The CIA stated: "The aim of this dispatch is to provide material for countering and discrediting the claims" of those who doubted the Warren Report. The CIA stated that "background information" about me and others "is supplied in a classified section and in a number of unclassified attachments."

With this background we now turn to the article by Max Holland published by *The Nation* in its February 20, 2006 issue. It states that there was a "JFK Lawyers' Conspiracy" among four lawyers, Sen. Gary Hart, Professor Robert Blakey, Jim Garrison the former District Attorney of New Orleans and later a state judge in Louisiana, and me.

Before I wrote *Rush to Judgment* I had never met any of the other three "co-conspirators." I still have not had the pleasure of meeting Sen. Hart, and I know of no work that he has done in this area. I met Prof. Blakey only once; he had been appointed chief counsel for the House Select Committee on Assassinations and at that meeting I told him that I was disappointed in his approach and methods. Not much of a lawyer's conspiracy.

Each of the other statements as to alleged fact are false and defamatory. Mr. Holland states that I am not scrupulous, that I am dishonest and that I spread innuendo about the sinister delay on the Warren Commission investigation, an assertion not made by me but fabricated in its entirety by Mr. Holland. As a silent echo of his CIA associates, Mr. Holland does not point to one assertion as to fact, of the thousands I have made about the facts surrounding the death of our President that he claims is inaccurate.

Finally, Mr. Holland strikes pay dirt. He uncovers, are ready you for this, the fact that I had asserted that "the government was indifferent to the truth," I confess. Is that a crime under the "Patriot Act" isn't that what *The Nation* is supposed to be asserting and proving.

Mr. Holland states that the KGB was secretly funding my work with a payment of "$12,500 (in 2005 dollars)." It was a secret all right. It never happened. Mr. Holland's statement is an outright lie. Neither the KGB nor any person or organization associated with it ever made any contribution to my work. No one ever made a sizable contribution with the exception of Corliss Lamont who contributed enough for me to fly one time from New York to Dallas to interview eye-witnesses. The second largest contribution was $50,000 given to me by Woody Allen. Have Corliss and Woody now joined Mr. Holland's fanciful conspiracy?

Funds for the work of the Citizens Committee of Inquiry were raised by me. I lectured each night for more than a year in a Manhattan theatre. The *New York Times* referred to the very well-attended talks as one of the longest running performances off Broadway. That was not a secret. I am surprised that Mr. Holland never came across that information, especially since he refers to what he calls "The Speech" in his diatribe.

Apparently, Mr. Holland did not fabricate the KGB story; his associates at the CIA did. There is proof available for that assertion, but I fear that I have taken too much space already.

Am I being unfair when I suggest a connection between Mr. Holland and the CIA? Here is the "CIA?" here is the "CIA" game plan:" fabricate a disinformation story. Hand it to a reporter with some liberal credentials; for example, a contributing editor to *The Nation*. If the reporter cannot find a publication then have the CIA carry it on its own website under the byline of the reporter. Then the CIA can quote the reporter and state," according to..."

Mr. Holland writes regularly for the official CIA website. He publishes information there that he has been given by the CIA. The CIA, on its official website, then states "According to Holland..." If you would like to look into this matter of disinformation laundering enter into your computer – "CIA Gov. + Max Holland." You will find on the first page alone numerous articles by Mr. Holland supporting and defending the CIA and attacking those who dare to disagree as well as CIA statements attributing the information to Mr. Holland.

A question for *The Nation*. When Mr. Holland writes an article for you defending the CIA and attacking its critics, why do you describe him only as "a *Nation* contributing editor and author." Is it not relevant to inform your readers that he also is a contributor to the official CIA Website and then is quoted by the CIA regarding information that the agency gave to him?

An old associate of mine, Adlai Stevenson, once stated to his political opponent, a man known as a stranger to the truth; – "if you stop telling lies about me I will stop telling the truth about you." I was prepared to adopt that attitude here. But I cannot. Your publication has defamed a good friend, Jim Garrison, after he had died and could not defend himself against demonstrably false charges.

You have not served your readers by refusing to disclose Mr. Holland's CIA association. *The Nation* and Mr. Holland have engaged in the type of attack journalism that recalls the bad old days. If I fought McCarthyism in the 1950's as a young lawyer, how can

I avoid it now when it appears in a magazine that has sullied its own history? The article is filled with ad hominem attacks, name calling, fabrications and it has done much mischief. I will hold you and Mr. Holland accountable for your misconduct. I can honorably adopt no other course.

To mitigate damages I require that you repudiate the article and apologize for publishing it. That you publish this letter as an unedited article in your next issue. That you did not publish a reply by Mr. Holland in which he adds to the defamation and the damage he has done, a method you have employed in the past. That you provide to me the mailing addresses of your contributing editors and members of your editorial board so that I may send this letter to them. I am confident that Gore Vidal and Bob Borosage, Tom Hayden and Marcus Raskin, all of whom I know, and many others such as Molly Ivin's, John Leonard and Lani Guinier who I do not know but who I respect and admire, would be interested in the practices of *The Nation*. In addition, I suggest that ethical journalism requires that in the future you fully identify your writers so that your readers may make an informed judgment about their potential bias.

If you have a genuine interest in the facts regarding the assassination you should know that the House Select Committee on Assassinations (the United States Congress) concluded that probably a conspiracy was responsible for the murder and that, therefore, the Warren Report that Mr. Holland defends so aggressively, is probably wrong. In addition, the only jury to consider this question decided in a trial held in the United States District Court in a defamation case that the newspaper did not defame E. Howard Hunt when it suggested that Hunt and the CIA had killed the president. The forewoman of the jury stated that the evidence proved that the CIA had been responsible for the assassination.

I have earned many friends in this long effort. Those who have supported my work include Lord Bertrand Russell, Arnold Toynbee, Prof. Hugh Trevor-Roper, Dr. Linus Pauling, Sen. Richard Schweiker, Paul McCartney, Norman Mailer, Richard Sprague, Robert Tannenbaum,; also members of the House of Representatives, including Don Edwards, Henry B. Gonzalez., Andrew Young, Bella Abzug, Richardson Preyer, Christopher Dodd, Herman Badillo, Mervyn Dymally, Mario Biaggi and, above all, according to every national poll, the overwhelming majority of the American people. I have apparently earned a few adversaries along the way. Too bad that they operate from the shadows; that tends to remove the possibility of an open debate.[18]

Rolling Stone, 4/5/07, ran a provocative story, "The Last Confessions of E. Howard Hunt" by Erick Hedegard. In a deathbed confession to his oldest son Saint John, the old spy claimed to outline the chain of command for the JFK assassination.

> Under LBJ, connected by a line, he wrote the name Cord Meyer. Meyer was a CIA agent whose wife had an affair with JFK, later she was murdered, a case that has never been solved. Next his father connected to Meyer's name, the name of Bill Harvey, another CIA agent; also connected to Meyer's name was David Morales, yet another CIA man, and a well-known particularly vicious black–op specialist. And then his father connected to Morales name with a line, the framed words "French Gunman Grassy Knoll. "...By the time he handed me the paper I was in a state of shock, Saint says. "His whole life ... he always professed to not know anything about it."
>
> Later that week, E. Howard also gave Saint two sheets of paper that contained a fuller narrative. It starts out with LBJ again, connecting him to Cord Meyer, then goes on: "Cord Meyer discusses a plot with [David] Phillips who brings in William Harvey and Antonio Veciana. He meets with Oswald in Mexico City... Then Veciana meets with Frank Sturgis in Miami and enlists David Morales in anticipation of killing JFK there. But LBJ changes the itinerary to Dallas, citing personal reasons..." E. Howard goes on to describe his own involvement. It revolves around a meeting he claims he attended in 1963, with Morales and Sturgis. It takes place in a Miami hotel room ... Morales leaves the room, at which point Sturgis makes reference to the "Big Event" and asks E. Howard. E. Howard, "incredulous" says to Sturgis "you seem to have everything you need why do you need me?... "There is no way to confirm Hunt's allegation – all but one of the co-conspirators he named are long gone. Saint John, for his part, believes his father...

While the dying covert operative, propagandist, and fiction writer may have been spinning again, this story bolsters dozens of books making similar cases. The mainstream and alternative media refrained from responding.

In May 2007, Vincent Bugliosi's lengthy and staunch defense of the Warren Report, *Reclaiming History* met positive reviews. A strongly supportive piece came from the *Wall Street Journal*, 5/20/07, written by Max Holland, a long supporter of the Warren Commission, and in 2001 the first author working outside the government to receive a Studies in Intelligence Award from the CIA.[19] A supportive *Atlantic* review was written by Thomas Mallon, another supporter of the Warren Commission. The *L.A. Times* review by Jim Newton effused, "It is a book for the ages."

The PBS *American Experience* series aired "Oswald's Ghost," 1/14/08, which briefly explored the impact of the assassination on American culture, while reweaving the "lone nut" theory. Remarkably, after 44 years of citizen and government efforts, not one shred of contradictory evidence was examined. This piece stopped with the Church Committee and never even mentioned the HSCA or the AARB. Of the eleven interviews, four discussed the sociological and political context; five supported the Warren Commission, while two opposed it. The Warren Report advocates, who were given long stretches to narrate, included: Priscilla Johnson McMillan; Edward Epstein; Hugh Aynesworth; Dan Rather; and the late Norman Mailer.

Director Robert Stone's creative cinematography framed the case by opening with a shot of the so-called snipers' nest window, and ended with Norman Mailer's voice-over of *Oswald's Ghost*.

Recall that Priscilla Johnson McMillan was a "witting" CIA asset, Hugh Aynesworth had ties to both the FBI and CIA, and Edward Epstein had acknowledged that he has had extensive talks with CIA Counterintelligence Chief Angleton for his books on the assassination.

Epstein asserted, "Most of the public thought Oswald was guilty but there was a possibility he didn't do it alone ... the evidence even at the beginning was persuasive, if not overwhelming..." Dan Rather, whose views have evolved on the case, assessed the lack of media coverage of the Warren Commission hearings, "I think the attitude of the country was we need to know what happened but we need to move on. Unity is important in an event like this, so let's give the government the benefit of even very serious doubt." Two noted early critics of the Warren Report, Mark Lane and Josiah Thompson shared their perspectives, but were not given time to explore evidence. After *Oswald's Ghost* recreated a chronology of events similar to the Warren Report, it visually portrayed the early critical books as swirling down a black hole.

The magic bullet, CE 399, was not mentioned. No critics discussed the single-bullet theory. The Zapruder film was not enlarged and slowed down (as in *JFK*) Robert Stone actually stopped the Z-film prior to the head snap in frame #313 – then curiously cut to a shot of Oswald seemingly walking away.

Aynesworth and Epstein narrate a misleading rendition of the Garrison investigation. Aynesworth mentioned the Sodium Pentothal session, conducted by Dr. Esmond Fatter on Perry Russo, by again rearranging the time sequence to make it appear that Fatter was influencing Russo. This was used by Clay Shaw's defense team, of which Aynesworth was an active member; a relationship unmentioned in the film.

Garrison's major discovery along with Bill Turner of Oswald's links to right-winger and former FBI man, Guy Banister's, office in New Orleans was omitted. Recall at 544 Camp St. Oswald came in contact with Guy Banister, Clay Shaw, David Ferrie, Kerry Thorrnley, and others with CIA connections.

Epstein could have been asked why the CIA distributed his articles on Garrison. Why did you forward your research to Clay Shaw's defense team? And why were you in contact with other lawyers who were defending witnesses or suspects in the Garrison investigation?

Robert Stone could have explored:

-How did Oswald learn Russian?

-Why did the Warren Commission treat the allegations that Oswald was an FBI informant as a dirty rumor, "which must be wiped out"?

-Why did the Commission fail to interview Jack Ruby until the Report was already being written, and then leave its own Ruby experts out of the interview?

-Why did the woman who developed JFK's autopsy photographs disavow the official set in the sworn testimony?

-Why did these same photos fail a key autopsy test, which was then buried?

-Why did Kennedy's brain disappear, along with tissue, slides and the original autopsy report?

-Why was a portion of the Presidential phone recording from the morning after the assassination, when Hoover and Johnson discussed an imposter in Mexico City, who tied Oswald to a Soviet assassination expert, purposefully erased?

-Why do so many around Oswald outside of New Orleans also have CIA ties? – Priscilla Johnson-McMillan, George de Mohrenschildt, Marina's host Ruth Paine? – Why does the Chief Counsel of the HSCA, Robert Blakey, now believe that the CIA obstructed the investigation?

- If Oswald was a communist who were his comrades?

- What was Oswald doing with Clay Shaw in Clinton and Jackson, Louisiana?

- Why was Oswald being impersonated before the assassination?

- How can we reconcile the Bethesda autopsy with almost two dozen witnesses regarding the gaping wound in the back of the Presidents head?

Edward Epstein was undeterred in summarily proclaiming "not a shred of evidence has come out which would indicate what the conspiracy was. After forty years none of the theories pan out." Historian Robert Dalleck psychologized, "People are comforted by the idea, I think, that human affairs are not the product of random events – there's some larger force at work here." Novelist Norman Mailer divined that Oswald had the motive and capability. He seemed to have forgotten that Oswald claimed that he was a "patsy." Even the Warren Commission could not "ascribe any motive or group of motives." [20]

Kennedy's ghost still haunts our democracy. As with the previous PBS *Frontline* special on Oswald in 1993, "Oswald's Ghost" takes us back to 1970 – before the HSCA, the movie *JFK*, and the ARRB. The tired fable was reinvoked with gloss and panache. The "Noble Lie" morphed into the "Big Lie."

Bold reporters and editors have wanted to work this story, yet business and political pressures have increasingly stifled journalism. Jim Hougan, former Washington editor for *Harper's*, revealed some decision-making by the CBS show *60 Minutes*. Hougan had been under contract with CBS to pitch stories for Mike Wallace. He was convinced that the acoustical study by Dr. Don Thomas virtually proved that there had been a conspiracy in the Kennedy assassination, and went to New York to pitch the story. He openly pondered, "Whether this story is too important to cover at this late date."

Mike seemed convinced by it and thought the story was something we should pursue. But first it had to go through Phil Sheffler who was a senior editor at *60 Minutes*. I had worked with him in the past, he is a fine journalist and a very fine editor … but he is not much inclined to do any stories with a conspiracy angle. This had come up in the past. He said, "Hougan do you know any conspiracy stories which have not been adequately reported?" I thought about it, and said the Kennedy assassination. He said, "Funny you should bring that up because I probably know more about the Kennedy assassination than anyone else at CBS. I was astonished.... He said he was involved with the early efforts of CBS looking over the Zapruder film.... He said it was so obvious that at least two people firing in Dealey Plaza that day. I said oh – did I miss something? – Was that reported? He said you have to understand, that just because two people were firing in Dealey Plaza does not mean that it was a conspiracy. I didn't know what to say – then I said well that's true but its still kind of newsworthy and I don't recall it coming out...

In the end what did happen is Mike got back to me and said we're not going with this.... Essentially there were three objections. One was they felt that science was at the heart of Don Thomas's work. I said that wouldn't be a problem since CBS routinely dramatizes science stories. Mike agreed ... but he was concerned that the story might have an ambiguous result. I said that's possible ... but we know that there is a 96% certainly that the results will be less ambiguous [than now]. He said that's true.

Then he said, "But in the end there is a bigger problem.... Everyone knows the Warren Commission got it wrong. Everyone knows it's a conspiracy.... That's Phil's point – this is not news" [Also] there is such a heavy investment in the story by people in the past...

Mike Wallace said there is one way that this story could get on the air ... If [Senator] Howard Baker would front the piece then we'd do it.

What it meant is that *60 Minutes* have only their own credibility to sell basically and if they get a story like this wrong they are completely destroyed. But if someone such as Howard Baker were to pitch the story then they can report, without fear of contradiction, that Howard Baker said A-B-C and they won't get it wrong.[21]

Mass media mergers have heightened the importance of corporate profits, yet Wallace's fear of being "completely destroyed" by a story of conspiracy that "everyone knows," speaks volumes. Letting a scientist report findings on autopsy photos or x-rays would satisfy Wallace's third party method. Don Hewitt, longtime Executive Producer of *60 Minutes*, told Bill Moyers in the mid-1990s, "This is a bad year for journalism but a good year for journalists." A good year in terms of high salaries.

No mass media outlet has consistently followed up on citizen-generated developments in the investigation. After *JFK*, the *Houston Post,*

Washington Post, Oprah Winfrey, *Reader's Digest*, the A&E Channel, and the History Channel, among others, covered new aspects of the case. Reporters need time, money, and most importantly, owners, publishers, executive editors or news directors who will take risks. However, since 2000, newspaper revenues have fallen by about half, causing cuts in staff, shrinking the news hole, and closing bureaus. On-line divisions of legacy media are experimenting with models, as are new online outlets, but the transition remains uncertain for investigative reporting. Former *Washington Post* editor Ben Bagdikian sees core problems with journalism in America: 1) reliance on official sources; 2) fear of context; 3) a corporate bias concerning what is off-limits. Increasingly the corporate-owned media views Americans as consumers attracted by entertainment rather than citizens attracted by information.[22]

American journalism has adopted a one-sided notion of "objectivity" which emphasizes statements from people in power. Controversy is drained, so journalists are unlikely to antagonize the sources they are dependent upon. Context is often avoided since it risks partisanship, and in this case, the legitimacy of government and the media itself. Bill Moyers observed that "objective journalism means describing the object being reporting on ... as well as the big lie of people in power ... freedom and freedom of communication were birth twins in the United States ... neither has fared well in the absence of the other."[23] (*Selling the Story*) Carl Bernstein bluntly warned that the media "have abdicated our responsibility, and the consequence of our abdication is the spectacle and the triumph, of the idiot culture."[24]

If journalists raise an issue that no one in power is debating, they are often accused of being ideological and unprofessional, which can jeopardize careers. This "sphere of legitimate controversy" has long constrained the press. Most reporters enter journalism with noble intentions, yet corporate profits have eroded journalistic norms and increasingly highlighted info-tainment. The ratio of P.R. specialists to journalists has changed from five to four in 1980 to seven to two today.[25] Serious investigative journalism remains on the defensive in a media system which lacks clear standards of press accountability.

Following the existing leads in this case can be perceived as delegitimizing the past press performance, as well as government. The incestuous relationship between the mass media and government continues in new forms. To most this case has become history, best left to the historians, to others it is a time-consuming endeavor on a very complicated case where reputations are risked and the leads are cold.

Bill Moyers admonished that unprecedented secrecy and media co-operation with economic elites developed during the George W. Bush era. "Never has there been an administration so disciplined in secrecy, so precisely in lockstep in keeping information from people at large – in defiance of the Constitution.... Never has so powerful a media oligopoly ... been so unabashed in reaching like Caesar for still more wealth and power. Never have hand and glove fitted together so comfortably to manipulate free political debate, new contempt for the idea of government itself and to trivialize the people's need to know..."[26]

These attitudes were foreshadowed by Dick Cheney when he served as Secretary of Defense during the first Gulf War. "Frankly, I looked on it as a problem to be managed. The information function is extremely important. I did not have a lot of confidence that I could leave it to the press."[27]

Sometimes distortions are subtler – using misleading headlines, burying the lead, and shoveling fog and confusion. After the 2000 election a consortium of news organizations explored voting in Florida. It included the *New York Times*, the *Wall Street Journal*, the Tribune Company, the *Washington Post*, the Associated Press, the *St. Petersburg Times*, the *Palm Beach Post* and CNN. The story, which took almost a year and cost more than a million dollars, Concluded that Al Gore got more legal countable votes than George Bush.

Florida law was clear regarding the need for a recount in elections decided by one-half percent or less of the votes counted. So the Florida court ordered a recount – until the U.S. Supreme Court shut the recount down. The public wanted to know who actually got the most votes.

The consortium recount explored "over votes," where the voter both punches in and writes in the name of the candidate. This met the Florida law, affirmed by the courts, that a vote must be counted if there is "clear indication of the intent of the voter."

Headlines from the Consortium members:

> The *New York Times*: "Study of Disputed Florida Ballots Finds Justices Did Not Count the Deciding Vote."

> *Wall Street Journal*: "In Election Review, Bush Wins Without Supreme Court Help."

> *Los Angeles Times*: "Bush Still Had Votes to Win in Recount, Study Finds."

CNN.Com: "Florida Recount Study: Bush Still Wins."

St. Petersburg Times: "Bush."

The *New York Times* article supported the headline until the fourth paragraph. "If all the ballots had been reviewed under any of seven single standards, and combined with the results of an examination of over votes, Mr. Gore would have won, by a very narrow margin."

The rest of the article discussed other possible partial recounts in certain counties, that Gore and Bush lawyers had called for – but the Florida Court ordered a statewide recount.

Apparently national security concerns two months after 9/11 pre-empted straight-forward reporting about the legitimacy of the governmental system.

The rapid rise of FOX Network contributed to unprecedented cooperation between a network and the Republican administration. Rupert Murdoch loathed the Kennedys. FOX News was run by the long-time top Republican strategist Roger Ailes, who framed the news daily to FOX reporters with talking points memos. Hardly "fair and balanced," these memos are clearly partisan as well as very conservative.

Digital journalism uses fewer reporters and uses speed as a significant part of the appeal. Former *Washington Post* executive producer Katherine Zaleski sees budget constraints for digital journalists impacting their patience for great journalism. There aren't the resources to check everything, so transparency and trial and error have been seen as building trust. A change in culture and business needs is emerging which increasingly values truth. Some larger websites are transitioning to more copy editors, more fact checking, and building investigative units – after attracting resources and a following.

David Talbot's best-selling book, *Brothers*, about the relationship between RFK and JFK, was initially embraced by Hollywood. Lionsgate (producers of *Mad Men*) optioned the book and had "high hopes of making it into a mini-series ... [but] they went to every network in Hollywood, and every network in Hollywood turned us down." This confirmed Oliver Stone's admonition to Talbot about Hollywood.[28]

Even the well-respected *Columbia Journalism Review* (May/June 2009) printed a literary retrospective of William Manchester's *The Death of a President*, rather than wrestle with the evidence or the failures of the media. The author, Thomas Mallon, a self-described "implacable lone nutter," extolled Manchester's efforts which 40 years ago creatively supported Oswald's guilt. Mallon highlighted some of Manchester's vivid prose, which psychologized about Oswald motives, but he explored no new evidence. For him the Garrison investigation, the HSCA, the ARRB, new books, and dozens of conferences did not exist. Mallon shared his disdain for the "bilious bubbling up of scorn from the still feverish swamps of conspiracy theory." This cleverly worded echo of new journalism – valued form over content. An aging Manchester supposedly told Mallon in 2002 that Oswald's "Money Mad" mother had "defiantly uttered ... you can't say my son wasn't a good shot." *CJR* chose to reinforce "the sphere of legitimacy."

Time's commemorative issue "JFK, His Enduring Legacy" combined wonderful pictures with positive, and at times effusive, prose – but did not touch the assassination evidence.

NPR *Fresh Air* guest-host Dave Davies, 10/28/13, interviewed former *New York Times* investigative reporter Philip Shenon about his new book, *A Cruel and Shocking Act: The Secret History of the Kennedy Assassination.* Shenon reviewed the shortcomings of the Warren Commission, J Edgar Hoover's determination that Oswald was the assassin within two days after the assassination, the rushed autopsy, the FBI cover-up by agent Hosty, the lack of CIA effort to get to the truth, and the CIA's withholding of plots to assassinate Castro. Shenon claimed that the "big question [was] as to whether Oswald was talking openly [in Mexico City] about his plan to kill President Kennedy." He never got around to mentioning the findings of the HSCA, or the ARRB. Shenon asserted that the single-bullet theory was the most logical explanation of the wounds. He blamed RFK for withholding evidence rather than further question the cover-ups of the CIA, the Secret Service, the military, and LBJ.

About two weeks later, NPR interviewed ARRB member Jeremy Gunn who clarified the cover-up by Dr. James Humes, who headed the autopsy, his atypical procedures and his destruction of his original notes. Gunn spoke of autopsy photographer Sandra Spencer, never questioned by the Warren Commission, who said that she did not recognize nor develop the autopsy photos in the National Archives. Further, the paper of the autopsy prints did not match the paper of the photos that Spencer took at the White House a few days earlier. Gunn believed that a conspiracy and a cover-up occurred but he never had a chance to develop his ideas in the brief segment.

The lengthy *New York Times Sunday Book Review* by executive editor Jill Abramson vaguely concluded that there was some "kind of a void" at the center of the JFK mystery. "Many of the theories have been circulating for decades and have now found new life on the internet, in websites febrile with unfiltered and unhinged musings."(11/13)

The *Washington Post* review of professor Larry Sabato's book, *The Kennedy Half Century*,(2013) was also filled with ad hominem attacks. "While the book's first section is perfunctory, the second part, which deals with the assassination, is somewhat wearying and likely to interest only hardcore buffs – I realize there are many – who wallow in outraged speculation about who was behind Kennedy's murder."

The *New Yorker* ran Adam Gopnik's reflection on regicide and culture, while suggesting that "we will never know." PBS *Frontline* 11/19/13 choose to rerun "Who Was Lee Harvey Oswald" a creative defense of the Warren Report, which never explored the findings of the HSCA, nor the five-million pages of declassified documents released through the ARRB.

At the National Press Club forum on the JFK assassination 11/22/13, Dan Rather and his former CBS colleague Marvin Kalb still argued that Oswald alone was the assassin. Rather intoned "This is America. We love to doubt as well as to know. My belief is that beyond a reasonable doubt, there was one shooter and one gun."

The *Dallas Morning News*, despite the work of reporter Earl Golz, stated "Oswald was the killer in JFK conspiracy theories abound, despite a lack of evidence."

Mother Jones and OPED News ran David Corn's "The Real Conspiracy behind the Assassination." Oswald was the lone shooter, but like Zelig, he had a range of unusual connections.

The *Boston Globe* ran Bryan Bender's piece "Troves of files on the JFK assassination remain secret." 11/25/13. He quoted Judge John Tunheim who chaired the ARRB: "We only put a few pieces of the puzzle together. Lots of the jigsaw is missing."

George Orwell admonished that "thought corrupts language, [and] language can also corrupt thought." Words help construct frames and spin, granting normality to the surreal. Cold War historian Colonel Fletcher Prouty argues that "the Secret Team" has shattered our democracy. "One of the greatest casualties of the Cold War has been the truth. At no time in the history of mankind has the general public been so misled and so betrayed, as it has by the work of the propaganda merchants of this century and their historians." In this deception the CIA was violating its charter and targeting America with its propaganda operations.

The young John Kennedy wrote *Profiles in Courage* to clarify perspectives for dignity in public service. As president he increasingly practiced what he preached. Ironically, after his death, the mass media generally contributed profiles in confusion and cowardice to the public discourse regarding his assassination.

The response of the alternative press was varied. *The Nation* printed pieces by Alex Cockburn and Noam Chomsky, which viewed Kennedy as a Cold Warrior whose assassination did not change foreign policy. *The New Republic* continued to maintain that the new information was speculative and unconvincing. The journal *Z* viewed Kennedy as a Cold Warrior, who would not have Vietnamized the war. *The Progressive* strongly condemned *JFK* and Oliver Stone, and elected to avoid coverage of the ARRB and independent researchers. *Mother Jones* conceded that Oswald could have had confederates. The *Village Voice* along with online outlets Salon.com and *Huffington Post* sustained ongoing coverage. The lack of resources in the alternative media remains a major factor but this case also reveals the role of ideology in their decisions to not cover the new leads. As time dims the tragedy, continued media inaction mocks the aspirations of the First Amendment. Let's now recap the case in light of the massive declassifications, along with the work of some of the media and the citizenry.

12

SECRET SERVICE SECURITY?

The only thing necessary for the triumph of evil is for good men to do nothing.

– Edmund Burke 1775

Guard against the importance of pretended patriotism.
– George Washington
1796 Farewell Address

Experience should teach us to be most on our guard to protect liberty when the government purposes are beneficent.... The greatest danger to liberty lurks in insidious encroachment by men of zeal, well meaning, but without understanding.

– Justice Louis Brandeis 1915

The role of the Secret Service in protecting the president, and in the investigation afterward still raises perplexing and troubling questions. The president had received numerous death threats in late 1963 and the Presidential motorcade actually had been cancelled in Chicago on November 2nd. Secret Service judgments and breaches of procedure strongly suggest security stripping; their actions after the assassination indicate a cover-up. Secret Service connections to Allen Dulles and LBJ were strong.

The Secret Service was a branch of the Treasury Department, then run by establishment Republican banker C. Douglas Dillon, whose father joined with the Dulles brothers in banking and trading with the Nazis. Allen, Foster and C. Douglas were close friends and political allies. Dillon, like Dulles, served in the OSS and often disagreed with JFK on banking, trade, tax and foreign policy. He had been John Foster Dulles' ambassador to France from 1953-57, and Foster had convalesced at Dillon's home in 1959. Allen had vacationed with Dillon in France. Dillon's Chief Counsel, Acting Secretary of the Secret Service, Gaspard d'Andelot Belin, had responsibility for the Dallas trip. Belin's family had also long been friends with Allen Dulles.[1] Belin had also worked in military intelligence (OSS) with William Bundy and James Angleton, and later married Bundy's sister.[2] William Bundy was a senior Pentagon official and former CIA officer, who later edited the corporate elite Council on Foreign Relations journal Foreign Affairs; while his brother McGeorge served as a National Security advisor. William Bundy was married to the daughter of former Secretary of State Dean Acheson, and Secret Service Chief James Rowley was a close friend of Lyndon Johnson.[3]

The threat in Chicago to assassinate Kennedy seemingly involved four or five men, two were never caught and three were briefly detained. Thomas Vallee, a troubled ex-Marine, who like Oswald had worked with the U-2 program in Japan, and later trained anti-Castro Cubans, also had a job with a good view of the motorcade. Although Chicago police had followed Vallee for hours, he was arrested after the presidential motorcade was cancelled. He had an M-1 rifle and 3000 rounds of ammunition in his car. Chicago police Lieutenant Berkeley Moyland investigated Vallee and then informed the Secret Service about him. He was told that the Secret Service would take care of things. Moyland soon joined Vallee for lunch and engaged him in conversation – clarifying the serious consequences of talking as he had. Moyland then informed the Secret Service about Vallee and was told that the Secret Service would take care of things. The FBI had alerted the Chicago police but would not share information with them.[4]

One of the Chicago officers arresting Vallee was Daniel Groth, who six years later commanded the police squad that killed Black Panthers Fred Hampton and Mark Clark. Groth stated under oath that he followed an FBI request regarding the Panthers. Northern Illinois University Professor Dan Stern determined that Stern worked in counterintelligence, probably with the CIA.[5] Vallee, like Oswald, claimed that he was framed.[6]

Author James Douglass interviewed Secret Service agent Abraham Bolden and unearthed part of the process used to bury the information on this plot. "Secret Service agents were told to prepare no documents on their own. Following [SAIC] Martineau's orders the Chicago agents' dictated oral reports to the office's top secretary … then turned in their notebooks. Secret Service Chief James J. Rowley had phoned Martineau from Washington, asking that the Chicago office use a special COS (Central Office Secret) file number for the case – a process which sequestered the Chicago plot documents, making their subterranean existence deniable by the government. SAIC Maurice Martineau, who once had declared that "The bastard [JFK] should be killed", gave his agents orders about the Chicago threat, "Don't talk to anyone about it."[7]

Former Secret Service agent Abraham Bolden disregarded orders from Martineau to never talk about the Chicago threat. Months later he tried to talk to Warren Commission staffers, but he was arrested the next day by fellow agents. He was accused of trying to sell Secret Service files to a counterfeiter. One of Bolden's accusers worked for Sam DeStefano, an associate of Richard Cain, the chief investigator in the Cook County/Chicago Sheriff's office. Cain worked with Johnny Roselli and Santos Trafficante on the CIA-mafia plots. Bolden was sentenced to six years, although his primary accuser Joseph Spagnoli, later admitted to committing perjury.[8]

Bolden's judge actually told the jury before their deliberations that Bolden was guilty. Even after that misconduct resulted in a mistrial, the same judge was allowed to conduct Bolden's second trial. The result was another conviction, and Bolden has been fighting to clear his name ever since. Bolden has written and spoken about the racism he encountered in the Secret Service as well as about their pervasive lack of respect for President Kennedy.[9]

While Bolden was in prison, a shot was fired into his Chicago home, his wife was followed, a brick was thrown through her car window, and their garage was burned. Douglass speculated that "If Kennedy had been murdered in Chicago on the day after Diem's and Nhu's murder in Saigon, the juxtaposition of events would have created the perfect formula to be spoon-fed to the public: Kennedy murdered Diem, and got what he deserved."[10]

Twelve days after the assassination, article appeared in the *Chicago Daily News* and the *Chicago American* on Vallee's arrest which characterized him as gun-toting malcontent who expressed violent anti-Kennedy views. The anonymous police detectives and federal agents who informed the media after the assassination of Vallee's arrest in Chicago did not mention the Secret Service detention and questioning of the two suspected plotters.[11]

Recall the warnings from the Miami police regarding the threats from right-wing extremist Joseph Milteer, 11/9/63, proclaiming that Kennedy would be assassinated "from an office building with a high power rifle ... it's in the works. They will pick up somebody ... just to throw the public off." The taped threats were forwarded to the Secret Service and the FBI but the case was quickly closed, and Milteer was not arrested.[12] The Secret Service stated to the Warren Commission that Milteer was not put under surveillance because they lacked the manpower.[13]

Also, remember the assertion by FBI employee William Walter of threats to assassinate the President in Dallas, 11/7/63, where he notified five agents. This teletype was allegedly later removed from the FBI files, and there is no evidence that they alerted the Secret Service.

The Secret Service informed Tampa Police Chief J. P. Mullins of a plot to murder Kennedy during his trip to Tampa the next day. Mullins advised the President to cancel his visit but JFK decided to proceed anyway. The threat included at least two men; one was "a slender white male, 20" with a "high power rifle ... shooting from a window in a tall building." Tampa police were positioned "at every overpass with rifles on alert." Author Lamar Waldron notes that Secret Service agent Sam Kinney said that he heard that organized crime was behind the threat. This was the center of Mafioso Santos Trafficante's territory.

Chief Mullins and the Secret Service did not know anything about the connections of the two suspects. This attempt to assassinate the President in Tampa was withheld from the Warren Commission and the HSCA. Waldron alerted the ARRB, 11/24/94. "According to the Review Board's Final Report ... January 1995, the Secret Service destroyed Presidential survey reports for some of President Kennedy's trips in the fall of 1963, including Tampa."[14] Mullins stated that he gave the considerable information to the FBI, yet those documents have not appeared in the declassified files.

The day after the president was assassinated, the *Tampa Tribune* ran a short story that Tampa officers had been "warned about a young man who had threatened to kill the president during his trip." Note the similar scenarios with the plots in Chicago, Tampa, and Dallas. Incredibly, the Secret Service responded to the rising number of serious threats by reducing their protection in Dallas. Bobby Kennedy did not trust the Secret Service and had plans to take responsibility for presidential protection. The Secret Service action in Dallas violated numerous standard policies.

- Advance publication of an insecure route was in the Dallas newspapers.
- The motorcade route was re-directed to include a turn of 120 degrees.
- No protective military assistance was used.
- There was no coverage of open windows, manholes or sewers.
- There was no coverage of roofs.
- Motorcade vehicles were in an atypical sequence.

• The typical flatbed truck carrying press and photographers riding in front of the Presidential limousine was canceled. Photographers were put in cars # 9-11.

• Nearby hospitals were not on alert status.[15]

• Despite precedent, publication of the parade route was released to the media 11/21/63.

• Dallas Police Department Homcide detective car was removed fro the motorcade 11/21/63.

• Secret Service Chief Rowley and other did not convey recent threats to the Presidential advance team in Dallas.

• General Godfrey McHugh and Admiral Burkley (the president's physician) had their car moved, over their objections, to the back of the motorcade.

• Security was inadequate along the motorcade route from the airport to downtown Dallas.

• The overpass in Dealy Plaza was not cleared or properly protected.

• Nine agents on Kennedy's White House Detail were drinking heavily at "The Cellar" nightclub until 4 AM the night before. None were punished in any way.

• Agents were ordered off the riding platforms of the presidential limousine.

• Presidential limousine driver, Agent Bill Greer, almost slowed to a halt after shots were fired, disobeying orders from his superior agent, Roy Kellerman, seated next to him, who screamed "Get us out of the line."

• Other agents were unresponsive to the shots being fired.

• The motorcade security protocol is the Standard Wedge Formation around the Presidential limousine. In Dallas, five motorcycle police were uselessly placed in front of the lead car, no units were at the sides, and the Secret Service follow-up car was not close behind the Presidential limousine.

• Why for the first time in American history were the President and Vice-President together in the same motorcade?[16]

Dallas Police Chief Jesse Curry testified to the Warren Commission that he was instructed by Secret Service agent Winston Lawson not to station four motorcycle police on either side of the presidential limousine – but rather place two on either side but at the back fender. Lawson, an army reserve officer, denied this, yet numerous other reports from Dallas police confirmed that Lawson redeployed the side escorts.[17]

The HSCA cautiously observed:

> The Secret Service alteration of the original Dallas Police Department motorcycle deployment plan prevented the use of maximum possible security precautions.... Surprisingly, the security measure used in the prior motorcades during the same Texas visit [11/21/63] shows that the deployment of motorcycles in Dallas by the Secret Service may have been uniquely insecure ... [The Secret Service] defined and supervised the functions of the Dallas police during Kennedy's visit [to Dallas].[18]

The night before the assassination, many in the President's Secret Service entourage drank at The Cellar night club, owned by Pat Kirkwood, an acquaintance of Jack Ruby. Kirkwood's father was a close associate of Ruby and Lewis McWillie, who worked for Santos Trafficante. However, none of the Vice-President's Secret Service detail went to the Cellar that night.

As the presidential limousine started to leave the Dallas airport, Secret Service agent Don Lawton was ordered off the rear of the car by Shift Leader of the White House Service Detail, Emory Roberts. Footage aired on the History Channel in 2003, shows Lawton gesturing "What's going on?" After Kennedy was assassinated, Roberts remarkably ordered his superior SAIC Roy Kellerman "You stay with Kennedy. I'm going to Johnson."[19]

While the Warren Commission and the HSCA blamed JFK for cutting security, by law the President cannot tell the Secret Service what to do. Author Vince Palamara, who has interviewed more than 70 Secret Service agents, writes "President Kennedy understood about protection and never interfered with Secret Service protection protocols." Secret Service Agent Floyd Boring ASAIC White House Detail has written that President Kennedy "was very cooperative with the Secret Service."[20] Agent Clint Hill wrote that he had "never heard the president ever question procedural recommendations by his Secret Service Detail."[21]

Boring was in charge of the Dallas trip, although he stayed in Washington. Boring appears to have approved the Trade Mart site for the President's speech against the security advice of JFK's aides Jerry Bruno and Ken O'Donnell. He was aided by Dallas police and Winston Lawson, (a member of the Army Intelligence reserve), Advance Agent David Grant, and Forrest Sorrels, Special Agent in Charge Dallas. Boring also told agent Clint Hill to not ride on the rear of the presidential limousine.[22]

After 11/8/63, Advance Agent Grant was a key planner of changes in the motorcade route, when it was altered to turn off of Main Street. This included planning an unnecessary 120-degree turn in front of the Texas School Book Depository, although Secret Service regulations prohibit turns of more than 90 degrees.

Films taken at the time show that when the first shot rang out the brake on the presidential limousine came on. Sixty witnesses, including eight policemen, two presidential aides, and Governor Connally, have testified or publicly stated that the presidential limousine failed to accelerate until after the fatal shot. Former CIA agent Colonel John Stockwell recalled that when he received training in a "bang and burn" course, he was drilled to react to a situation with bullets flying, "You mash down on the gas and get the hell out of the area."

Secret Service actions, before and during the assassination, foreshadow their actions after the assassination regarding evidence, witnesses, and procedures. After the assassination several witnesses stated that they had seen or encountered Secret Service agents behind the stockade fence atop the grassy knoll. The Secret Service maintains that none of its agents were stationed in Dealey Plaza.[23]

Gordon Arnold, a young soldier, encountered a man who identified himself as Secret Service behind the stockade fence, before the assassination. When Arnold challenged his authority, he was shown a Secret Service badge and told "I don't want anybody up here."[24]

Sergeant Harkness testified that when he reached the rear of the TSBD before 12:36 p.m. "there were some Secret Service agents there. I didn't get them identified. They told me they were Secret Service agents."

Dallas officer J.M Smith followed up on a statement from a women that "they were shooting the President from the bushes." He pulled his pistol and along with a deputy sheriff, rushed toward the grassy knoll – where he encountered someone who identified themselves as Secret Service.[25]

Witness Jean Hill said that she ran up the grassy knoll and behind the stockade fence when she encountered men who identified themselves as Secret Service. Deputy Constable Seymour Weitzman also stated to the Warren Commission that he encountered Secret Service agents behind the short wall adjacent to the stockade fence.[26] Dallas Policeman Malcolm Summers also ran up the grassy knoll, and he too encountered someone who identified himself as Secret Service and told Summers to back off.

Colonel Robert Jones testified to the HSCA that "our people were under the control and supervision of the Secret Service. We never assumed responsibility for the President's protection.... We provided a small force ... I would estimate between eight and twelve during the President's visit to San Antonio, Texas and then on the following day, on his visit to Dallas, the regions also provided additional people to assist, that are additional people from Region 2... [James W. Powell] was a captain and also wore civilian clothes and was assigned to Region 2 of the 112 MI Group.... Yes he was [on duty that day]"

The HSCA tried to question these agents but the Department of Defense reported "no records ... indicating any Department of Defense Protective Services in Dallas. The committee [HSCA] was unable to resolve the contradiction."[27]

About an hour and a half after the assassination, recall that Secret Service agents forcibly took the president's body and casket to Bethesda. Dallas County Medical Examiner Dr. Earl Rose and Judge T. Ward argued that Texas law required an autopsy in Texas. Dr. Crenshaw the surgeon who struggled to save the President in trauma room 1, recalls Secret Service SAIC Roy Kellerman declaring "We are taking President Kennedy back to the capital." Dr. Rose argued, "You are not taking the body anywhere, there's a law here, we're going to enforce it." Another Secret Service agent screamed "Goddammit, get your ass out of the way before you get hurt" while another yelled "We're taking the body now."[28] They were pushed to the wall at gunpoint, and the Secret Service took Kennedy's body to Washington.

On orders from LBJ, the Secret Service flew the presidential limousine to Washington and assisted the FBI in inspecting it. Then the limousine was scrubbed, washing away traces of blood, bones and bullets, and the windshield was replaced. Deputy Secret Service Chief Paul Paterni and ASAIC Floyd Boring oversaw the limousine inspection at the White House garage where the vehicle damage was "noted." The windshield hole became a "crack" and the dented chrome was seen as insignificant. When the limousine was then driven from Dearborn to Cincinnati to replace the chrome molding strip which was damaged in the shooting, the driver Carl Renan noticed a "primary strike" on the molding strip. Renan, head of security for Ford Motor Company Dearborn, was told by the Secret Service to "keep his mouth shut."[29]

Secret Service agent David Grant and U.S. Marshall Robert Nash were present at the interrogation of Oswald, yet no report or testimony from either man can be found in the Hearings and Exhibits.[30]

Recall that Secret Service Agent Elmer Moore confessed in 1970 that he had "leaned on Dr. Perry" to cease describing the wound in Kennedy's throat as one of entrance. Moore told graduate student James Gochenaur that the Secret Service had to investigate the assassination in a predetermined way or face repercussions. Moore also mentioned that at times he saw JFK as a "traitor" regarding the Cold War.[31]

Recall the role of the Secret Service in supplying a second, edited version of the Zapruder film to the NPIC lab from the Hawkeye Works lab, after viewing the first version with NPIC Information Officer Dino Brugioni. It was Secret Service agent "Bill Smith," who along with NPIC Deputy Director USN Captain Pierre Sands, ordered NPIC employees to swear to secrecy what they had seen.

The Secret Service conducted twenty-four interviews with Parkland doctors, nurses and orderlies, yet none of these interviews appeared in the Warren Commission Hearings and Exhibits (Six FBI interviews were not included either). The Secret Service is also alleged to have confiscated original recordings of the Parkland Memorial press conference where Dr. Perry stated repeatedly that the throat wound was an entrance wound. Dallas KLIF news director, Joe Long, told this to Marvin Garson editor of the *S.F. Express Times*. Recall CIA asset Gordon McLendon owned KLIF.[32]

The Warren Commission Counsel generally gave witnesses a chance to review and correct FBI and Secret Service reports of interviews with them prior to testimony. This was not done with Parkland personnel.

Recall the superficial Secret Service investigation of Oswald's activities in New Orleans out of Guy Banister's office on Camp Street. The Secret Service claimed to the Warren Commission that their extensive investigation found no links between Oswald and the Fair Play for Cuba Committee and Banister's office. Banister's secretary, Delphine Roberts, was not interviewed, although she later admitted that Oswald used a room on the third floor and that Oswald met a number of times with Guy Banister. If the Secret Service had chosen to walk 50 feet from their New Orleans office to Banister's office they would have found "Fair Play for Cuba" leaflets in Banister's office.

Assistant to the Special Agent in charge (ATSAIC) Emory Roberts, who ordered agent Donald Lawson to not ride on the rear of the presidential limousine, was given a Special Service award by the Treasury Department in 1968, was made LBJ's receptionist, and in 1969 was promoted to the Inspector of Secret Service headquarters.[33]

Dallas Secret Service agent Robert A. Steuart told author Bill Sloan (*JFK; Breaking the Silence*) "There are so many things I could tell you, but I just can't … it was a very heavy deal, and they would know, someone would know. It's too dangerous, even now."[34]

Former Secret Service Chief U.E. Baughman observed in his book *Secret Service Chief*, "I only know that far too many men around our Presidents are quite willing, if it will benefit them, to let the Chief Executive put his life on the line. Some Secret Service agents were frustrated being relegated to "butlers" and "errand boys," while some on the White House Detail were upset with JFK's private life. Further, most of the core of southern born agents disliked the president's stands on civil rights and his rumored plans to merge the FBI with the Secret Service."[35]

Nixon aide Charles Colson asserted that the Secret Service was infiltrated by the CIA. Professor Philip Melanson noted that "The Secret Service has received training and equipment from the CIA … [36] although the precise nature and extent of Secret Service dependency upon the CIA remains top secret…"

Secret Service actions before the assassination constitute security stripping, while their actions afterward constitute a pattern of cover-up. These actions constitute "security stripping" the assassination, before and after, along with a creative pattern of cover-up. Secret Service imposters could have gotten identification from the CIA, which sometimes did this type of false credential printing. A CIA memorandum, 5/8/73, from Sidney Gottlieb of the Technical Service Division confirmed that TSD had "furnished" the Secret Services with a range of passes as well as a "secure ID photo system."[37]

Secret Service Chief James Rowley participated in the protection of the presidential limousine, the cleaning and reconstruction of it after the assassination, and the ordering of removal of Kennedy's body from Parkland Hospital before a possible autopsy. When President Johnson returned to Andrews Air Force Base from Dallas, Rowley was the first person he talked with.[38]

When Warren Commission junior counsel Arlen Specter asked the Secret Service for the video tapes and transcripts of the press conference with Dr. Malcolm Perry the day of the assassination, Rowley wrote back that "After a review … no video tape or transcript can be found of a television interview with Dr. Malcolm Perry." Years later the ARRB found a transcript of that press conference which was stamped "Received U.S. Secret Service 1963 Nov 26 AM 11:40, Officer of the Chief." Rowley had lied, he had Perry's statement that there was an entrance wound from the front of the neck, before the Warren Commission had started. This transcript was also not included in the five volumes FBI Report.[39]

As Colonel Fletcher Prouty observed in *Gallery* 9/75:

> No one has to direct an assassination – it happens, the active role is played secretly by permitting it to happen.... He was not murdered by some lone gunman, but by the breakdown of the protective system that should have made an assassination impossible.... Once insiders knew that he would not be protected, it was easy to pick the day and the place.... This is the greatest single clue to the assassination.[40]

In a HSCA interview SAIC John Marshall stated that "someone in the Secret Service could possibly be involved in the assassination." Many documents which could shed light on Secret Service procedures in 1963 were destroyed in 1995 during the tenure of the ARRB. The Secret Service claimed that it destroyed the presidential protection survey reports for twenty-three of President Kennedy's trips in fall of 1963, "by mistake" – four months after the ARRB had begun its work.[42] The JFK Act specifically forbids the destruction of any documents, and public hearings were considered.

The Warren Commission tried unsuccessfully to get some Secret Service records related to the assassination from Douglas Dillon. Dillon then appealed to his old Wall Street friend John McCloy, and even to President Johnson to not be grilled by the committee. When he did appear in the final weeks of the Committee, he was given a superficial examination, and allowed to advocate for a larger budget. Allen Dulles helped Dillon place the false story – that JFK preferred his Secret Service guards to ride behind him – into the Warren Commission Report.[43] Dillon even claimed that "it was not the practice of the Secret Service to make surveys or checks of buildings along the route of a Presidential motorcade."

Notably, the ARRB recorded that Secret Service agent James Mastrovito destroyed a vial holding a portion of JFK's brain as well as 5-6 cabinets of material sometime after the assassination. Mastrovito went on to work for the CIA.

President Johnson later turned to this trusted pillar of the Eastern Establishment, Dillon 11/22/64, to chair the Dillon Committee – to give recommendations about the Warren Report, it's release and distribution, monitoring the TV control room, and accommodations for the Secret Service reviewing the CIA and foreign press. Years later President Ford turned to Dillon to serve on the Rockefeller Commission to reexamine the Warren Commission; not surprisingly, they confirmed its findings.

13

THE PATSY:
WIDE-RANGING ASSOCIATIONS

No man chooses evil because it is evil; he only mistakes it for happiness, the good he seeks.
— Mary Wollstonecraft

Security is like liberty in that many are the crimes committed in its name.
— Supreme Court Justice Robert Jackson

Everywhere you look with him, there are fingerprints of intelligence.
— Senator Richard Schweiker (R-Pa),
Senate Intelligence Committee, 1975

Lee Harvey Oswald's life confronts us with the classic maze of mirrors. Portions of Oswald's career in military intelligence and his relationships with the CIA, FBI and INS have been systematically suppressed or destroyed by these agencies as well as the Justice Department. Foreshadowing the challenges, recall the memos from J. Edgar Hoover as well as Asst. Attorney General Nicolas Katzenbach, 11/25/63, that "the public must be convinced that Oswald was the assassin and that he did not have confederates.

When Oswald was arrested after the assassination, he was carrying an address book with the name of FBI Agent James Hosty of the Dallas Bureau office. When the FBI gave the Warren Commission a list of the contents of Oswald's address book, it had omitted Special Agent Hosty's number. The FBI rationalized that the omission had been made because the person who transcribed the list was only looking into "lead information," Oswald was also carrying a military I.D. card.[1]

FBI agents were ordered by William Sullivan of FBI Counterintelligence, to not cooperate with the Dallas Police and the investigation less than four hours after Oswald was arrested The FBI did not fully cooperate with the Warren Commission. Sullivan was also the FBI liaison to the National Security Council[2] and to the U.S. Intelligence Board, the top agency which supervises foreign intelligence.[3] Sullivan had been good friends with CIA Chief of Counterintelligence James Angleton and CIA Mexico City Chief Win Scott, whom he directed during WWII.

The HSCA investigation confronted minimal cooperation from the CIA, because the CIA liaison to the HSCA, George Joannides, had formerly coordinated many anti-Castro Cubans including the CIA sponsored DRE, a group that Oswald encountered in New Orleans.

In a secret session of the Warren Commission on January 22, 1964, Waggoner Carr, the Attorney General of Texas, stated that evidence he had acquired from Allan Sweatt, the chief of the criminal division of the Dallas Sheriff's office, indicated that Oswald had been employed by the FBI as a confidential agent, number S-172 or S-179, at $200 a month. The chief of the Dallas sheriff's division was never called to testify by the Warren Commission.[4] The Warren Commission special counsel given the assignment of investigating charges that Oswald was a government agent was Texas Attorney General Leon Jaworski. Subsequently, Jaworski served as a director of the M.D. Anderson Fund, a CIA front which had been exposed in 1967.[5] Jaworski found no links between Oswald and the government. Notably, a decade later, when President Nixon fired Watergate Special Prosecutor Archibald Cox, he appointed Jaworski to replace him.

Strong evidence shows that this was not Oswald's only connection to the U.S. intelligence community. On the day of the assassination, according to the HSCR, the FBI asked the CIA for "any information" it had on Oswald. The CIA's official response, according to the FBI was that "there is nothing in the CIA file regarding Oswald other than material furnished to the CIA by the FBI and the Department of State." This denial is part of a cover-up, as indicated by both the subsequently declassified and missing or destroyed documents.

Years after the Warren Commission inquiry, newspapers reported that a woman at the Dallas Bureau office had received a threat by Oswald to blow up the FBI office. FBI Agent Hosty explained that this message was merely a warning to him to stop questioning Oswald's wife. If the note was a threat, the FBI Dallas headquarters would normally place him immediately on the "dangerous character" list – but this was not done. What the note actually said will never be known for sure, since Hosty told the HSCA that his superior, Gordon Shanklin, ordered him to destroy the note after Oswald was shot, which he did.[6]

If the note indicated Oswald's guilt or erratic behavior, why would it have been destroyed immediately? According to Hosty, he was initially assigned to cooperate fully with Dallas police during Oswald's interrogation after the assassination, but within hours senior agents in FBI Counterintelligence instructed him to not cooperate with Dallas police regarding Oswald's background.[7]

In a significant revelation, the HSCA disclosed an internal CIA memorandum dated 4/27/79, concerning Oswald's 201 file, a routine file for persons considered to be of potential or counterintelligence significance. The memo notes that 37 documents, including 25 cables, were missing from Oswald's file. The HSCA, however, accepted the CIA claim that those documents just happened to be checked out of the file on the day the memorandum was prepared. These 37 documents were never found for examination by the HSCA and their contents remain a mystery today.[8] One CIA document viewed by HSCA referred to a "forged and backdated 201 file to be used in connection with political assassinations" – the ZR-Rifle Project.[9] The extent to which the CIA double-files its records is classified information.

Oswald's first overseas assignment as a Marine was to Japan's Atsugi Air Base, the CIA's most secret base, where U-2 intelligence flights over China originated. Oswald's anti-aircraft unit had the job of guarding the U-2 hanger, for which a highly classified security clearance was required. Oswald's possible intelligence role at Atsugi might be confirmed by two CIA documents mentioned in the Warren Commission Report: CD 931, "Oswald's access to information about the U-2," and CD 692, "Reproduction of CIA official dossier on Oswald"; however, these documents are still classified as national security secrets.[10]

Oswald returned to El Toro Marine Base in Southern California in 1959 to learn Russian, and five months later he was given an honorable discharge supposedly to help his ailing mother. After spending only three days with his mother he traveled to the Soviet Union and defected. While in route to Russia, he flew to Helsinki, Finland at a time when no commercial flights were scheduled. To Embassy Consul Robert Snyder at the U.S. Embassy in Moscow he claimed his allegiance to the Soviet Union, announced that he would give them radar information, and was allowed to defect. Oswald appears to have been part of the "fake defector" program which infiltrated nine operatives into the Soviet Union during this period. Senator Richard Schweiker, Co-Chairman of the Senate Intelligence Subcommittee to investigate the JFK assassination determined that

"The accused assassin was the product of a fake defector program run by the CIA." The False Defector Program was run by the CIA and ONI from a facility in Nags Head, N.C. Tosh Plumlee (a longtime CIA asset) accidentally met Oswald again in Dallas in 1962 at a Cuban "safe house" where they both participated in a government-sanctioned gun running operation. In an interview with Dick Russell, Plumlee stated that "Oswald was military intelligence."[11] In a sworn affidavit Plumlee states that he met Oswald at "Illusory Warfare" training at Nags Head, NC in 1957, where Oswald was taking language courses." Of the more than 50 letters he sent home during his time in the Soviet Union the CIA mail-intercept program contains only one. According to Victor Marchetti, staff officers in the Office of the Director, and an executive assistant to the Deputy Director "espionage missions were to be coordinated with the CIA...but the military often failed to do this...the tribalism that plagues the intelligence community is at its worst in the military intelligence agencies."[12] Recall that the Army "routinely" destroyed their files on Oswald in 1973.

Oswald married a Russian woman and returned to the U.S. in June 1962. Spas Raikin, a former secretary of the CIA-backed American Friends of Bolshevik Nations, greeted them upon their return. The State Department approved Oswald's return and authorized the American Embassy in Moscow to lend him $436. In 1978, James A. Wilcott, a former CIA finance officer, told the House Select Committee that Oswald had been recruited from the military by the CIA "with the express purpose of a double agent assignment in the USSR, and that he had received financial disbursements under an assigned cryptonym."[13] Wilcott's wife Elsie, who also worked for the CIA, concurred. After quietly clarifying Oswald's background, the Wilcotts received threatening calls, Jim was forced to resign from his job, and their tires were slashed. When Oswald returned to the U.S. he was debriefed by CIA officer Aldrin Anderson. The debriefing report was read by CIA officer Donald Deneselya and confirmed ... in the 1993 *Frontline* program, "Who was Lee Harvey Oswald?"[14]

A partial list of "unavailable documents" in the Warren Commission Report prior to the AARB in 1993 illustrates the difficulties in clarifying these relationships:

Commission Document No. Title / and Originating Agency

90 / Income tax returns of Lee Harvey Oswald and relatives (FBI)

278, 281, 285 / Reports of various assassination attempts throughout the world (State Department)

299 c-d / Tax returns of Jack Ruby and Earl Ruby (FBI)

384 / Activity of Lee Harvey Oswald in Mexico City (CIA)

540, 548 / George de Mohrenschildt file (FBI)

698 / Reports of travel and activities; Lee Harvey Oswald and Marina Oswald (CIA)

700a-d / Various social security records; Jack Ruby and associates g-i, k-p (HEW) / IRS information on those mentioned in CD 681 (Carroll, Ruby, Meyers, and Volper) (IRS)

902 / Criteria for giving information to Secret Service (CIA)

1171 / Lee Harvey Oswald; Internal Security; Cuba (FBI)

1378 / Various Moscow embassy conversations (State)

1424 / Earl Ruby letter to the Commission

The Oswalds moved to Fort Worth, Texas, where Russian-born oil geologist Baron George de Mohrenschildt of the powerful Dallas Petroleum Club befriended them. De Mohrenschildt convinced the Oswalds to move to Dallas where he introduced them to the Russian émigré community. De Mohrenschildt's good friend, J. Walton Moore, an agent in the CIA's Domestic Contacts Division, "encouraged" George to befriend Oswald,[15] and he did. He would never have contacted Oswald if Moore had not sanctioned it.

De Mohrenschildt had previously worked with the Office of Strategic Services, as well as in Yugoslavia, representing the International Cooperation Administration, a well-known CIA front. He was accused by the Yugoslavian government of sketching military facilities.[16] De Mohrenschildt had also been in Haiti where he was involved in a "government oriented" (Warren Commission language) business venture, where he hung out in an establishment frequented by intelligence agents.[17] De Mohrenschildt visited with Oswald regularly, leading many to speculate whether de Mohrenschildt committed suicide or was murdered hours before an arranged meeting with Gaeton Fonzi, an investigator from the House Select Committee on Assassinations, in March 1977.[18]

De Mohrenschildt's wife did not believe that her husband committed suicide, and she feared for her own life. She has confirmed that her husband worked in intelligence, that he was friendly with powerful oilmen like H.L. Hunt, Bob Kerr, Clint Murchison Sr., and D. Harold Byrd (owner of the Texas School Book Depository building), and that his closest friend was Dallas' top CIA man J. Walton Moore.[19] In 1977, author Edward Jay

Epstein interviewed de Mohrenschildt, and later reported in a 1983 *Wall Street Journal* story that de Mohrenschildt had stated that the CIA had asked him "to keep tabs on Oswald."

In de Mohrenschildt's address book the names of many prominent political and military leaders can be found, including George H.W. Bush, Col. Howard Burris (aide to LBJ), and Vice-President Lyndon Johnson.[20] The day after Kennedy was assassinated George H.W. Bush was briefed by the FBI on "the attitude of anti-Castro Cubans." Bush was not yet a member of Congress, and supposedly not in the CIA, although his name was listed with Zapata Petroleum, which was a known CIA front organization.

By November 1962, Oswald was also meeting with many of the wealthy and prominent "White" Russian community as well as retired Air Force Colonel Max Clark, who was chief security officer for General Dynamics in Fort Worth. It was around this time that de Mohrenschildt helped Oswald get a job at Jaggars-Chiles-Stovall, which was under Pentagon contract to produce charts and maps for military use. Author Henry Hurt observed in *Reasonable Doubt* that, "part of the work appeared to be related to the top-secret U-2 missions, some of which were making flights over Cuba." This job required a high security classification, to say the least, yet neither the Warren Commission nor the House Select Committee explored this area in depth.[21]

In Dallas, Texas Oswald had some very sophisticated photographic equipment, especially for a "stock boy" on a limited income. At his North Beckley Street apartment after the assassination the Dallas police found his expensive Minox camera, which has been referred to as a spy camera, two other cameras, two telescopes and a variety of film.

Police also found several rolls of pictures taken with a Minox camera. These were released in 1978 after a Freedom of Information Act suit against the FBI. Although most of the released photos show scenes of Europe, five are of military facilities thought to be in Asia or Latin America.[22] Police also found Oswald's address book, which contains these notations on one page:

Jaggars-Chiles-Stovall
TYPOGRAPHY
522 Browder
RIII550
Microdots

Microdots are used in espionage to transmit and store information. Oswald spoke of micro-dotting to a fellow employee, Dennis Ofstein, who had also served in the army and had also studied Russian.[23] He also spoke of Soviet military logistics, the Soviet MVD (roughly equivalent to the FBI) and the MVD headquarters at Minsk. [24]

Shortly after Oswald moved to New Orleans in April of 1963, he got a job at the William B. Reily Co, a coffee company two blocks from Guy Banister's office. Reily, an ardent anti-communist, supported Ed Butler's INCA and Arcacha Smith's Crusade for Free Cuba. A CIA memo indicates that the company had been of interest to the CIA since 1949, (CIA memo from M.D. Stevens dated 1/11/64).

In April 1963, de Mohrenschildt went to Haiti, stopping en route in Washington, D.C. to meet with a CIA agent and an Assistant Director of Army Intelligence. The HSCA learned that de Mohrenschildt had received a "substantial sum" of money shortly after the assassination, which was paid to his account in Haiti. Jacqueline Lancelot, who owned a Haitian restaurant frequented by intelligence types, reported that she learned from a source in a Haitian bank that $200,000 to $250,000 had been deposited into de Mohrenschildt's account.[25] Stockbroker Joseph Dyer told the HSCA that Haitian banker Clemard Charles met with de Mohrenschildt and the Assistant Director of the Office of Intelligence in the Army. Dorothy Matlock said that $200,000 was put into de Mohrenschildt's account at another bank as well.

De Mohrenschildt had written a stack of letters to Vice-President Johnson regarding his business in Haiti. One letter from LBJ's administrative assistant Walter Jenkins to de Mohrenschildt offered a meeting with Colonel Howard Burris, LBJ's military aide, or LBJ himself. Some researchers posit that this business provided an alibi to get Oswald's "babysitter" out of the country in November of 1963.

Oswald's actions with the Fair Play for Cuba Committee in New Orleans link him to various intelligence agencies. Warren Commission testimony exhibit #3120 demonstrates that Oswald was passing out pamphlets on the topic of "Crime against Cuba." This was the fourth printing of a pamphlet, which was purchased by the CIA in its first edition.[26] It appears that Oswald's work with Guy Banister in New Orleans was with an operation that had links to the FBI, CIA and Military Intelligence. Joe Oster, a friend and employee of Banister, recalled that Banister sometimes got calls from J. Edgar Hoover, (NODA memo 9/30/68, DiEugenio p.104). The Banister files which were seized by the FBI, but not integrated into the subsequent investigations, included the following topics: American Central Intelligence Agency, Ammunition and Arms, Anti-Soviet Underground, B-70 Manned Bomber Force, Civil Rights Program of JFK, Dismantling of Ballistic Missile System, Fair Play for Cuba Committee, and International Trade Mart, among others.

Jim Garrison's chess partner, Jack Martin, who worked for Banister, a former FBI Special Agent in Charge for Chicago, told him that Oswald and David Ferrie met regularly with Banister. According to Victor Marchetti, a former Executive Assistant to the Deputy Director of the CIA, Ferrie was a CIA operative who also worked for Mafia kingpin Carlos Marcello. Ferrie mysteriously died of a "brain hemorrhage" on February 22, 1967, prior to being called as a witness by Garrison. Further, Banister's office at 544 Camp Street in New Orleans was part of a military supply line along the Dallas-New Orleans-Miami corridor that provided arms and explosives for use against Castro's Cuba.[27]

On August 2, 1963, the FBI, upon the order of JFK in an effort to stop the unending violations of the Neutrality Act by the CIA, arrested eleven people and seized more than a ton of dynamite, napalm and other devices at a resort area near Lake Pontchartrain, Louisiana, in a house loaned to newly-arrived Cuban refugees. The actual raid uncovered not only the ammunition described, but also a nearby un-described training camp at which the nine Cuban exiles and two Americans were arrested. Garrison speculated that the FBI deliberately concealed portions of the story from the American public so the Banister operation could continue.

Garrison obtained more information in a supplementary report that the FBI had sent to U.S. Customs. One of the participants, a former CIA employee named Gorden Novel,[28] stated that the Banister operation was on a mission to acquire combat ammunition. Ferrie assisted Banister and one of the leaders of the local CIA-related Cuban Revolutionary Front, among others. Novel (who subsequently fled New Orleans) and Ferrie drove from Banister's office to the blimp air base at Houma, in southern Louisiana. They entered one of the explosives bunkers and removed the land mines and other ammunition. According to Novel, these were CIA weapons.[29] It seems safe to say that Oswald was working closely with American intelligence in some capacity and was hardly the Communist he was portrayed to be.

According to the Warren Commission Report, when Oswald was arrested on August 9, 1963, after a brief scuffle while leafleting on Canal Street and brought to the police station, he immediately asked to see an

FBI agent. Oswald was separated from the other arrested men and brought into a private room where he talked with Special Agent John Quigley of the local FBI office. Later, this same Special Agent Quigley – contrary to standard Bureau procedure – burned the notes he had taken during this interview. Special treatment for a communist organizer seems inexplicable unless Oswald was actually working with Guy Banister, former FBI agent in charge in Chicago, who could have easily arranged it.[30] Oswald also met with FBI agent Warren de Brueys in New Orleans, according to the HSCA testimony of FBI asset Orestes Pena. The FBI was so concerned about Oswald's relationship with de Brueys, that they destroyed Pena's FBI files prior to the formation of the HSCA, (FBI teletype 1/15/76). A week later, Oswald was again leafleting in front of the International Trade Mart of New Orleans when a camera crew from NBC-affiliated television station WDSU arrived to film this inconsequential action.

The next day someone arranged for him to participate in a radio debate on a WDSU in New Orleans on the subject of capitalism versus communism. Oswald portrayed himself as a Marxist debating Carlos Bringuier and George Butler, both of whom were linked to the OSS and CIA through INCA (Information Council of the Americas).[31] Butler at times spoke of INCA contacts with CIA Deputy Director General Charles Cabell. A copy of the debate was forwarded to CIA headquarters.[32] Bringuier was clearly more than an anti-communist activist. After Garrison interviewed him 2/1/67, Bringuier immediately requested an interview with Hunter Leake of the New Orleans office of the CIA.[33] Bringuier was active in DRE, which was supported and overseen by CIA agent George Joannides (more about him later). Suspiciously, less than a day after Oswald was murdered, copies of this taped debate were sent to members of Congress and the Associated Press as "proof" that a communist had killed the president.

Oswald was also seen by a number of witnesses with New Orleans corporate businessman and CIA contact Clay Shaw in Clinton, Louisiana, along with David Ferrie in September 1963.[34] Clay Shaw also met regularly with Guy Banister. It was Clay Shaw, AKA Clay Bertrand, who called attorney Dean Andrews to assist Oswald after his arrest in Dallas, according to New Orleans District Attorney Garrison. Shaw was close to the Stern family, which owned station WDSU, as well as Ed Butler, his associate in launching INCA. Former CIA Director Richard Helms finally revealed in 1977 that Clay Shaw, like George de Mohrenschildt, was a CIA operative in the Domestic Contract Division.[35]

A CIA memo 4/26/67, originally released slightly redacted in the late 1970s, was released almost intact in 1992. After indicating Shaw's numerous contacts with DCS it noted:

> A memorandum marked only for file, 16 March 1967, signed Marguerite D. Stevens, says that J. Monroe Sullivan #280207 was granted a covert security approval on 10 December 1962 so he could be used in Project QKENCHANT. Shaw had #402897-A.

CIA officer Victor Marchetti, former Executive Secretary to DCI Richard Helms, surmises that the security clearance given to Shaw would indicate possible links to the Department of Domestic Services run by Tracy Barnes.

HSCA team 3 reported:

> We have reason to believe Shaw was heavily involved in the anti-Castro efforts in New Orleans in the 1960s and (was) possibly one of the high level planners or "cut out" to the planners of the assassination.

This line of inquiry was deliberately not pursued by the HSCA. Perhaps the reason was that George Joannides, the CIA appointed liaison to the HSCA, had actually coordinated DRE and other anti-Castro activities in New Orleans in 1963, and had to be aware of Lee Harvey Oswald.

Later in autumn of 1963, a leader of Alpha 66, (CIA-funded militant anti-Castro organization) Antonio Veciana, saw Oswald with a CIA officer he knew as "Maurice Bishop." A number of sources have long claimed that "Bishop" was David Atlee Phillips, the Chief of CIA Western Hemisphere. Veciana has no doubts, and neither did HSCA researcher Gaeton Fonzi, who researched this for over a year. Former CIA officer Frank Terpil admits knowing that Phillips was Bishop as well.[36] Phillip's role remains unclear, but after the assassination Phillips was given a major promotion. Terpil commented to former HSCA staffer Kelvin Walsh: "My private opinion is that JFK was done in by a conspiracy, likely including rogue American intelligence people."

Further, Oswald and Ferrie both worked out of Banister's New Orleans detective office. When Banister was agent-in-charge of the Chicago FBI in the 1940s he employed an agent named Robert Maheu, (later to become a front man for Howard Hughes). Maheu, in the early 1960's enlisted Sam Giancana, John Roselli and Santos Trafficante in the CIA-Mafia plots to kill Castro. According to the Senate Intelligence Report on Foreign Assassinations, Maheu's firm, Robert Maheu and Associates, was used for domestic covert operations, jobs with which the CIA did not want their own personnel associated.[37]

In 1975, when Representative Don Edwards' FBI Oversight Committee had held its hearing focusing on the FBI's relationship to both Oswald and Jack Ruby, it made eight specific demands on the Bureau for information. The next day the FBI was let off of the hook when the Justice Department decided not to press charges for the destruction of the Oswald note to FBI agent Hosty. Former Attorney General under President George H.W. Bush, Richard Thornburgh, who was then chief of the Justice Department's Criminal Division, had decided not to prosecute. He later became an Attorney General under George H.W. Bush.

> The FBI conducted its investigation in an atmosphere of concern among senior Bureau officials that it would be criticized and its reputation tarnished. Rather than addressing its investigation to all significant circumstances, including all possibilities of conspiracy, the FBI investigation focused narrowly on Lee Harvey Oswald.
> – Final Report U.S. Senate Church Committee, Book II, 1976.

Oswald's uncle, Charles "Dutz" Murret was a former boxer and "bookie" with ties to Marcello. Oswald's mother was a good friend with mob politician Clem Sehrt. Sehrt was determined by the HSCA to be a business associate of Marcello. Blakey chose to omit information supplied to him that Sehrt was also chairman of the Democratic regulars in New Orleans. [38]

After Oswald's "arrest" in New Orleans he was bailed out by Emile Bruneau, who was an associate of two of Marcello's syndicate operatives. One of the two, Nofio Pecora ,also received a telephone call from Ruby on October 30, 1963, according to the HSCA report.[39]

Disagreement continues regarding the funding sources for Guy Banister's New Orleans office at 544 Camp Street. Most have argued intelligence sources, some have mentioned the Mafia, while it seemed possible to the HSCA that both forces were jointly at work.

A declassified CIA document confirmed that Sergio Arcacha Smith, who was organizer of the CIA-funded Cuban Revolutionary Council, "maintained extensive relations with the New Orleans FBI.... Two of his regular contacts were (name deleted) and Guy Banister."[40] Peter Dale

Scott's notion of a "gray alliance" between mafia and intelligence sources, police departments and elements of corporate America provides a useful hypothesis. Banister, according to his former secretary, was working with David Ferrie to block the deportation of Marcello to Guatemala. In 1961 Marcello had offered anti-Castro Cuban Sergio Arcacha Smith financial support to overthrow Castro.[41]

The HSCA reiterated the Warren Commission's conclusions regarding Oswald's lack of links to intelligence agencies. The background of HSCA Chief Counsel G. Robert Blakey may be pertinent. Blakey had spent four years in the organized crime and racketeering section of the Kennedy Justice Department and was the principal consultant to Johnson's Commission on Law Enforcement and Administration of Justice. Inexplicably, when Rancho La Costa sued *Penthouse* magazine for libel, it was Blakey who provided an affidavit condemning the magazine's charges of mob ownership, while conceding ignorance of the truth of the charges. Any questions concerning this support of a resort built by Teamster pension fund money were referred to Blakey's attorney, Louis Nizer.[42] Nizer, coincidentally, was the attorney who wrote the introduction to the Warren Commission Report and passionately defended its findings. Also, Blakey and Nizer were both attorneys for mobster Moe Dalitz.

Blakey told HSCA investigator Ed Lopez, "We are not an investigative body. ... We are a Congressional Committee." Lopez has stated that "he did not have time to even skim the CIA files … he needed five more years to review the CIA files."[43]

In the summer of 1996 Lopez spoke out after the release of his 1978 HSCR on Oswald in Mexico City.

> You cannot see the scoffing expression on the CIA technician's face when questioned about cameras not working at the times of the alleged visits of Oswald to the embassies. You cannot see the smile that came on his face when he affirmed that he always had more than one working camera. You cannot see the sureness with when CIA personnel in Mexico told us they knew the Cuban embassy staff believed that Oswald was not the person who had approached them. You cannot see the increasing nervousness with which David Atlee Phillips lit up cigarettes as he was grilled on obvious lies told to the committee...
>
> The CIA refused to allow us [Dan Hardaway and Ed Lopez] to see the results of the photographic surveillance of the Soviet embassy in Mexico City during the periods that Oswald allegedly vis-

ited the embassy. [Are they still hiding methods and sources?] ...
The CIA had some double agents planted in the Cuban embassy
but the CIA would not permit us to interview these double agents.[44]

Oswald, or an impersonator, was seemingly accompanied to Mexico
City by William Gaudet, a CIA asset, who had worked with David Phillips in 1963. Phillips was CIA for Mexico City Chief of covert operations.
The FBI suspected that he was "baby sitting" Oswald just before he left
Mexico City. CIA documents released in 1997 show that the CIA thought
it possible that an Oswald imposter was in Mexico City. The CIA Special
Affairs staff (SAS) set up to direct a covert campaign to topple Castro,
had an operational interest in Oswald weeks before the assassination. SAS
executive officer Desmond FitzGerald and a few SAS officers kept their
interest in Oswald from CIA Mexico City Chief of station Win Scott, and
John Whitten, the experienced and respected CIA officer tasked to conduct the CIA internal investigation of Oswald. Whitten's removal and replacement with Angleton reveals some of the factional fights and template
for further investigation.[45]

When Oswald returned to Dallas, Ruth Paine, whose husband Michael
was closely related to the Forbes and Cabot families, hosted him. One
of Michael's cousins, Thomas Dudley Cabot, had served as president of
United Fruit. Michael's mother, Ruth Forbes Paine Young, had a friend-
ship with Allen Dulles' lover, Mary Bancroft. Although Michael and Ruth
were separated, Ruth stayed close to the Forbes family. Ruth's sister Sylvia
worked for the CIA and her father worked for the Agency for International Development (AID), which worked closely with the CIA. Recall that
Marina Oswald lived with Ruth, and Ruth helped Lee get the job at the
Texas School Book Depository.

Oswald appears to have started his intelligence career with ONI, and
then worked as an asset with the CIA and FBI on a range of operations.
Just who gave him his marching orders in 1963 remains a mystery. HSCA
Chief Counsel Robert Blakey safely stated on *Frontline* in 1993, "He is
not, to put it in simple words, an easy man to explain."

14

MAFIA CONNECTIONS

Nothing is easier than self-deceit. For what each man wishes, that he also believes to be true.

— Demosthenes

We are not afraid to follow truth wherever it may lead, nor tolerate any error so long as reason is left free to combat it.

— T. Jefferson

There's not much question that both the FBI and CIA are somewhere behind this cover-up. I hate to think what it is that they are covering up or who they are covering for.

— Congressman Don Edwards,
Chair of the Constitutional Rights Subcommittee, 1975.

Elements of the Mafia, anti-Castro Cubans, and the CIA had mutual interests in overthrowing Castro, and they worked together in this regard. Havana was the Las Vegas of the 1940s and 1950s in part, from mafia investments. When the Bay of Pigs operation failed in 1961, and Kennedy cut back on anti-Castro operations, many of these factions saw him as a traitor to their cause. The Mafia had cooperated with the CIA and OSS in times past, and attempted to assassinate Castro in the early 1960s. Many authors have separated the roles of the Central Intelligence Agency, the FBI, the Department of Defense, and the Dallas Police Department from the Mafia. This separation can be arbitrary and misleading since Oswald, Ruby, Roselli, Giancana, Banister, Trafficante, Helms, Harvey, Phillips, Hunt, Sturgis, Artime, Ferrie, Clay Shaw, Robert Maheu and a number of others were often working with two or more of these organizations. Perhaps the concept of a gray alliance is useful.

Warren Commission member Allen Dulles had been closely involved with the CIA-Mafia plots to assassinate Castro – plots which broke both national and international laws. CIA cooperation with the Mafia had existed with the CIA's forerunner, the OSS, as early as 1942. The Mafia served as a junior partner with the United States government in operations including:

> The Navy ONI "Operation Underworld," in 1942 where Mafia protection was bought against Nazi sabotage on the East Coast docks in exchange for favors involving Lucky Luciano;
>
> The Army's alliance with the Mafia in General Patton's Sicilian Campaign in WWII;
>
> The CIA-Mafia efforts to destroy Communist dominated unions in Marseilles, France in 1947 and 1950;
>
> CIA-Mafia political campaign to support the Christian Democrats against the Italian Communist Party in 1948. [1]

Warren Commission member and Louisiana Congressman Hale Boggs was allegedly indebted to Marcello, at least according to former FBI agent Aaron Cohn, an assistant to Hoover. (Recall that Boggs died in a plane crash not long after declaring to congress that the FBI used "Gestapo" tactics).

Chairman Earl Warren conceivably had another reason to divert the investigation. His campaign manager in his race for Governor of California, Murray Chotiner, handled the legal defense in 221 Mafia prosecutions from 1949-1952.[2] Chotiner was close to mob front-man D'Alton Smith, and brother-in-law of Marcello's top associate, Nofio Pecora.[3] (Chotiner was also Richard Nixon's Senate Campaign manager).

FBI Director Hoover was probably so compromised by the Mafia due to his heavy gambling, socializing with Mafia and Mafia-related people, as well as his alleged homosexuality, that he denied the existence of the Mafia until 1957. Even after Senator Kefauver's Commission on Organized Crime convincingly concluded that a powerful and dangerous organized crime network existed, Hoover continued to deny their existence, and actually cut funds for investigations involving the "top hoodlums program."[4] Since the FBI controlled the Warren Commission investigation, Hoover appears to have been protecting his career, the reputation of the FBI, his friend Lyndon Johnson, elements of the Mafia, the CIA, Clint Murchison, and Allen Dulles, among others.

The Warren Commission avoided pursuing Jack Ruby's obvious ties to organized crime, and ignored his insistence to Chief Justice Warren that he be removed from Dallas, so he could speak more freely. Ruby's early ties to Al Capone, Lewis McWillie, Santos Trafficante, Carlos Marcello, Joe Civello and Jimmy Hoffa have been well documented. Warren Commission attorney Burt Griffin, assigned to examine Jack Ruby, has expressed frustration that relevant documents on Ruby were withheld.

Recall that the night before the assassination the President's Secret Service partied until 4 AM at The Cellar nightclub owned by Ruby acquaintance Pat Kirkwood. Kirkwood's father was a close associate of Ruby and Lewis McWillie, who worked for Santos Trafficante.

Ruby's phone calls prior to the assassination, in September 1963, reveal that the he was in touch with his old associate Lewis McWillie, Santos Trafficante's casino contact from the Havana days. In early October, Ruby called a number listed to the ex-wife of Russell Matthews, another Trafficante associate from the same period. Late in October Ruby called Irwin Weiner, a Mafia bondsman who worked closely with Jimmy Hoffa, Sam Giancana and Santos Trafficante. In early November, Ruby received a call from "Barney" Baker, Hoffa's strong-arm man. The next day Ruby called Hoffa lieutenants "Dusty" Miller and "Barney" Baker. Then Ruby called Nofio Pecora, a lieutenant for Carlos Marcello.[5] Jack Ruby was about $40,000 in debt to the IRS, yet on November 19, 1963, Ruby told his tax lawyer he had a "connection" who could settle his debts.[6] Three hours after President Kennedy's death Ruby brought $7,000 to his bank. The HSCA concluded that in Jack Ruby, those with the motive and means to commit the murder, "had knowledge of a man who had exhibited a violent nature and who was in serious financial trouble."[7]

Ruby's ongoing courtship of the Dallas Police afforded him access into the police station, and enabled him to be present for the press conference at 10 PM on the night of the assassination. Although Ruby tried to pass himself off as a translator for the Israeli press, no one believed him or seemed to care. Just prior to the presenting of Oswald to the press, Ruby persuaded the Dallas Police to page KLIF radio reporter Joe Delong. At the press conference Ruby helped Dallas D.A. Henry Wade (a former FBI agent) on a question regarding Oswald's background. When Wade was asked, "Do you have anything to indicate why the man killed the President, if he did so? He replied, "Well, he was a member of the movement – the Free Cuba Movement." Ruby somehow knowledgeably corrected him and chimed in by saying it was the "Fair Play for Cuba Movement."

Jack Ruby knew Lee Harvey Oswald. Four of Ruby's nightclub dancers risked their safety and stated that they saw Oswald in Ruby's club – Melba Marcades (Rose Cheramie), Beverly Oliver, "Jada" Conforto and Marilyn Walle. Also, Carousel waitress Esther Ann Marsh, Dallas attorney Carroll

Jarnagin, entertainer Bill DeMar and Madeline Brown all say they saw them together the week before the assassination. Jack Ruby's mechanic Bill Chester stated that he saw Oswald in Ruby's car. Jesse Ventura writes about Oswald's friend Judyth Vary Baker: "Jack Ruby visited David Ferrie's apartment on the day when Judyth and Lee were there. Ferrie introduced him to Judyth as Sparky Rubenstein. Ruby recognized Lee, and said that he used to see him at parties."[8]

David Ferrie, CIA operative and pilot for Carlos Marcello, who worked out of Guy Banister's office in 1963, knew Oswald from his youth. Oswald had been in David Ferrie's Civil Air Patrol (CAP) as a teenager in 1954-1955 according to CAP instructor Jerry Paradis in testimony to the HSCA.[9]

After the press conference Ruby called station KLIF and offered to bring over some sandwiches. Before delivering food to KLIF he set up two interviews for KLIF reporters with Henry Wade. Notably, Gordon McLendon then owned KLIF, and his media network cooperated regularly with the CIA. By 1 AM, Ruby left to go to the *Dallas Times Herald*, ostensibly to revise his club ads.[10] When Ruby was arrested after shooting Oswald, he shouted that he wanted McLendon's help.

Lyndon Johnson stood to be embarrassed because of the actions of his top Senate aide, "one of my most trusted friends," Bobby Baker. Baker, who was convicted of tax evasion, fraud, and theft, had done considerable business with Carlos Marcello. Johnson once told House Speaker John McCormack, in the presence of Washington lobbyist Robert Winterberger, that he believed Baker had it in his power to ruin him.[11] The Kennedy Justice Department and the IRS were examining the skim from Las Vegas casinos which impacted Bobby Baker's investment partners Ed Levinson, an old Meyer Lansky ally, and Ben Siegelbaum (Bugsy Siegal), a Hoffa ally.[12] When Johnson was Senate Majority Leader he had appeared as one of Cleveland mobster Moe Dalitz's guests of honor at the opening of the Stardust Hotel in Las Vegas.

Johnson had also allegedly siphoned a percentage of Marcello's gambling profits in Texas in the 1950s, states *Ramparts* reporter Michael Dorman in his book *Payoff*. According to Dorman, Johnson, because of his dependence on Halfen-Marcello money, had helped kill all anti-racketeering legislation proposals that could have affected Marcello's businesses.[13] A former Justice Department official told author John Davis that at the time of the assassination of President Kennedy there was a thick investigative file on Robert Kennedy's desk detailing the Marcello-Halfen-Johnson connection. The Attorney General was debating whether to pursue these leads. This would have helped the Kennedy brothers' behind-the-scene efforts to discredit Johnson and contribute to Johnson not seeking re-election. This file also seems to have disappeared. Author Gus Russo asserts that RFK helped supply information to Dorman.[14]

Another example of the difficulties in clarifying this gray alliance is analysis of the events surrounding Oswald's arrest in New Orleans. David Schiem, in *Contract on America*, concludes that the Mafia killed Kennedy. He notes that when Oswald was arrested for a scuffle on the streets of New Orleans on August 9, 1963, he was bailed out of jail by Emil Bruneau, who was an associate of Nofia Pecora, one of Godfather Carlos Marcello's most trusted aides. The night after he was released, Oswald was visited by his uncle, "Dutz" Murret, a Mafia numbers runner. Schiem, however, omits the role of Special Agent John Quigley of the FBI who met with Oswald while in jail. Oswald asked to see Quigley, and was separated from the others who were arrested; he talked with Quigley, who later burned the notes he took during this interview. Schiem's views have evolved to include CIA-mafia cooperation. Garrison, on the other hand, fails to mention Oswald's dealings with Bruneau and Murret. Garrison determined that when the Mafia has worked with the U.S. intelligence agencies, they have done so as a junior partner; and the Mafia could not have controlled the cover-up.

Carlos Marcello claimed to two associates while in prison that "yeah I had the son of a bitch killed. I'm glad I did it." The HSCA concluded that Marcello and Trafficante had the "motive, means, and opportunity to assassinate President Kennedy." The Kennedys' war on crime infuriated Marcello, who had been deported to Guatemala, and then illegally reentered the country; he faced: an $850,000 tax assessment; indictment for illegal reentry; new McClellan committee hearings; and an indictment for conspiracy and perjury.

Marcello worked closely with Jimmy Hoffa and Santos Trafficante, two key Kennedy DOJ targets. In the fall of 1962 Marcello held a meeting with close associates and declared an Old Italian proverb "If you want to kill a dog, you don't cut off the tail, you cut off the head." Ed Becker, who attended the meeting, interpreted this as "if the president were killed Bobby would lose his bite." Marcello added that he had a plan where a "nut" would take the fall. Marcello's associate Santos Trafficante told businessman Jose Aleman that "Kennedy's not going to make it to the election … he's going to be hit." Aleman was fearful in testifying before the HSCA, and now lives in virtual seclusion. The HSCA found Aleman credible, and that "Trafficante's stature in national organized crime ... and his role as the mobs chief liaison to criminal figures within the Cuban exile community, provided him with the capability of formulating an assassination conspiracy against President Kennedy."[15]

Jack Ruby's trips to Cuba in August 1959, according to the HSCA, "were an important, but minor, part of an organized crime operation, which may have had to do with Trafficante's detention." This is bolstered by statements from British journalist John Wilson, who was also in the Cuban immigration detention center Triscornia with Trafficante, who said Ruby frequently visited "an American gangster type named Santos."

The Kennedys threatened the secure Mafia niche. Prosecution of the Mafia dropped by about 83% after President Kennedy was assassinated. Even the cautious Chief Counsel for the HSCA, Robert Blakey, observed that the murder of Oswald by Jack Ruby "had all of the earmarks of an organized crime hit." After the HSCA Report, the mass media has often inferred or blamed the Mafia for the assassination without noting its ties to the FBI, the CIA, and leading politicians and justices. Media coverage, which generally separated the Mafia from the "gray alliances" they often work with, obscured the need for deeper investigation. The Mafia conveniently seems to be the third level of scapegoat – after Castro and Oswald.

15

"COMPANY" BUSINESS

I believe there are more instances of the abridgement of the freedom of people by gradual and silent encroachments of those in power than by violent and sudden usurpations.

– James Madison

The Truth Will Set you Free.
– Carved over the entrance of the
CIA Langley Building.

The CIA's growth was likened to a malignancy, "which the very high official was not sure even the White House could control … any longer…. If the U.S. experiences (an attempt at a coup) it will come from the CIA and not the Pentagon…. The agency represents a tremendous power and total unaccountability to anyone.

– Arthur Krock, N.Y. Times, 10/3/63.

Power corrupts, absolute power corrupts absolutely.
– Lord Acton

The origins of the CIA and its autonomy foreshadowed major threats to democracy. The CIA had often acted independently from the Chief Executive prior to and during JFK's presidency. Although he still strongly supported covert actions after the Bay of Pigs failure, CIA veterans were frustrated and fearful about Kennedy's increasing restraints on their missions, his National Security Action Memorandums 55 and 57, as well as his liberal push in foreign policy. These perceptions, along with Oswald's links to the CIA and its contract agents, the concerted and ongoing efforts by the CIA to conceal information from numerous committees, as well as the agency's policies to influence the mass media, indicate a significant role played by portions of the CIA in the assassination and its cover-up. The CIA connections to corporate America, the mass media, the Defense Department, and elements of the mafia, suggest a wide range of potentially cooperative elite factions.

The OSS, (Office of Strategic Services), forerunner of the CIA, was headed by corporate lawyer "Wild Bill" Donovan, who had worked for the Morgan banking group early in his career. The standard joke was the OSS stood for Oh So Social, referring to the leading roles played by the Ivy League elites. OSS officers (such as industrialist Andrew Mellon's son Paul and both sons of J.P. Morgan Jr.) worked creatively and effectively with leaders in industry, academe, and the military, without much oversight.[1] After WWII, the OSS was transferred to the War Dept., renamed OSO, and worked with Army G-2 intelligence.

By 1946 President Truman regretted the dismantling of the OSS, since numerous intelligence agencies gave conflicting reports, so he set about forming a Central Intelligence Agency. The War-Peace Studies Project of the Council on Foreign Relations had promoted a new intelligence agency, based on the OSS. This was bolstered by a report written for Navy Secretary James Forrestal by Wall Street banker Ferdinand Eberstadt. Both worked for the investment bank Dillon Read. The CIA had been shaped by Allen Dulles (CFR chair) along with the advisory group he formed, five of the six being Wall Street bankers or lawyers. In 1948 Forrestal appointed Dulles to chair a CIA oversight committee.

The CIA was to report to the National Security Council (NSC), and within a year the NSC was authorizing covert operations through the Office of Policy Coordination (OPC), a secret group within the CIA. In June 1948 the NSC secretly started the OPC through the State Department without congressional authorization, based on CIA successes in the April 1948 Italian election.

That Italian election is worth briefly reviewing. The NSC, on 12/14/47, gave its first top secret orders to the CIA, to use "covert psychological operations to counter Soviet and Soviet inspired activities." Before the Dulles-Jackson-Correa Committee had finished, Dulles and Forrestal met with Dulles' ally James Angleton, the CIA's Rome Station Chief. Angleton estimated that $10 million would be needed. Corporate leaders in Italy feared revenge if the Communists won, so to help, Forrestal and Dulles raised money from their friends on Wall St. More was needed, so Forrestal convinced Secretary of the Treasury John Snyder to access the Exchange Stabilization Fund, which held money for European reconstruction. It dispersed money to bank accounts of wealthy Americans, who sent it to Italian political groups set up by the CIA. Millions were given to Italian politicians, Catholic Action (a political arm of the Vatican) and the Christian Democrats. It worked, and Dulles pushed for the NSC to broaden the OPC powers.[2]

NSC Directive 10/2 permitted the overthrow of governments. The Director was selected by the State Department, the officers wore military uniforms, and they were paid by the CIA, while programming came from the State Department and the NSC. The OPC was headed by Wall Street lawyer Frank Wisner (formerly OSS), a man committed to "rollback" of communism rather than containment. He cooperated with John and Allen Dulles to protect favored Nazi generals, in order to recreate the SS underground networks in Eastern Europe, Byelorussia and Ukraine to agitate for anti-communist rebellion.

Without informing President Truman or other intelligence agencies, OPC brought leading Nazi collaborators into the U.S. Wisner and General Lewis Clay looked to Thomas Dewey's election, which would sanction this extension of OPC operations. The Dulles brothers, key figures in the Dewey campaign, were powerful supporters of OPC's political action programs.

OPC merged with the CIA in 1951 to form the Directorate of Plans. Ironically, a Secret Army Intelligence report noted that one branch of the CIA (apparently OSO) was hunting Ukrainian Nazis, while another branch (OPC) was recruiting them.[3]

The Ford Foundation worked closely with Marshall Plan and CIA officials during the early years of the Cold War. Richard Bissell served as a Ford Foundation staff member in 1953, before he become a special assistant to the director of the CIA, Allen Dulles. The Ford Foundation joined with the Carnegie and Rockefeller Foundation and the Air Force to set up RAND Corporation, the institute most involved in classified research. In the 1950s, the Ford, Rockefeller, and Carnegie Foundations gave a $2.5 million grant to the Council on Foreign Relations, which made it the dominant private agency in foreign relations. McGeorge Bundy, special assistant to the President for national security from 1961-1966, had worked for the CFR while at Harvard, before joining JFK's administration. He retired to become president of the Ford Foundation from 1966-1979, and then later became President of the Carnegie Foundation. His brother William Bundy worked for the CIA from 1951-1961.

Former CIA agent Philip Agee maintained that, "Everything the CIA does in the areas of psychological warfare and covert actions benefits multinational corporations."[4] Funding for many CIA programs, from public and private sources, has been laundered through major foundations (Carnegie, Rockefeller, Whitney, and Ford) since the late 1940s. Insiders joke that CIA stands for Corporate Interests of America, or refer to it as the "Company."

Allen Dulles' grandfather John Foster, as well as his uncle Robert Lansing, had served as Secretary of State, as did his older brother John during the Eisenhower years. Allen and John had earlier worked for the preeminent law firm Sullivan and Cromwell, which served the leading banks and corporations. Sullivan and Cromwell engineered the Panamanian independence movement to break away from Colombia in order to assist their French construction clients building the Panama Canal. Sullivan and Cromwell merged politics and global business. The Dulles brothers were instrumental in starting the Council on Foreign Relations – an elite corporate club designed to guide a growing America with the wisdom of bankers, businessmen and international lawyers. The Dulles' actively arranged large loans and investments with the growing Nazi regime, a source of profits and perceived as a bulwark against communism. Sullivan and Cromwell floated the first American bonds issued by German arms manufacturers Krupp A.G., extended I.G. Farben's global reach, and opened Canadian trade to German arms manufactures.[5]

Dulles' patrician style, along with his education, business, and OSS experience, generated confidence in the mainstream media, and in Congress. Dulles' penchant for rogue operations can be seen with his OSS actions to disregard Roosevelt's policy of unconditional surrender. He secretly negotiated with Nazi generals "Operation Sunrise" to co-opt their intelligence system and turn it against the Soviets. In late 1945 James Angleton arranged an unauthorized meeting between his mentor, Dulles, and then continued to develop safe escapes, "ratlines," for some Nazi war criminals to relocate in Latin America or the U.S., while other U.S. intelligence agencies hunted them. Meanwhile Dulles pressed for a global network of CIA stations and that "covert operations be increased in intensity and number." "The Great White Case Officer" as he came to be called, valued zeal in his subordinates. Dulles wrote, 'We are not really at peace with them, [the Soviet bloc] and we have not been since Communism declared its own war on our system of government and life." CIA officers spoke of waging a Cold War, with the emphasis on war.[6]

Allen Dulles' work to get Eisenhower elected aided his advancement to Director of the CIA in 1953. No longer would intelligence just support military action, run propaganda and influence elections – they would overthrow governments, plot the assassination of foreign leaders, prepare death lists, expand propaganda (Operation Mockingbird), and advance the agents implementing these programs.

By 1956, President Eisenhower suspected that the CIA was out of control and established a review led by David Bruce and Robert Lovett, pillars of the Eastern Establishment. They were concerned that the CIA had become engaged in unaccountable covert actions where sometimes the U.S. Ambassador in a country was unaware of CIA actions. This led to the President's Board of Consultants on Foreign Intelligence Activities which echoed the deep concerns of the Bruce-Lovett Report. Their review of clandestine services concluded that they were "operating for the most part on an autonomous and free-wheeling basis in highly critical areas." It recommended that Eisenhower either fire Allen Dulles or force him to accept an assistant. Eisenhower confided to his national security advisor Gordon Gray that "I'm not going to change Allen," so he chose to learn to live with him.[7]

The CIA by the 1950s was often making foreign policy rather than merely enacting it. Former CIA officer Joseph Burkholder Smith revealed in *Portrait of a Cold Warrior* a strategy similar to that used to sell the Iraq War.

> Before any direct action against Sukarno (President of Indonesia) could be taken, we would have to have the approval of the Special Group – that small group of top National Security Council officials who approved covert action plans. Premature mention of such an idea might get it shot down...
>
> So we began to feed the State Department and Defense Department's intelligence.... When they had read enough alarming reports, we planned to spring the suggestion we should support the colonels' plan to reduce Sukarno's power. This was a method of operation, which became the basis of many of the political action adventures of the 1960s and 1970s in many instances; we made the action programs up ourselves after we had collected enough intelligence to make them appear required by circumstance. Our activity in Indonesia in 1957-1958 was one such instance.... The most efficient way to handle ambassadors who demanded their rights as heads of U.S. missions abroad to be informed of CIA operational activities was to tell them plausible lies."[8]

President Kennedy inherited a CIA that had widely interpreted its 1947 National Security Act clause to perform "such other functions and duties related to intelligence affecting the national security as the National Security Council may from time to time direct." This clause had become the wedge for covert actions which included: running counterinsurgency wars in China, Greece, The Philippines, Albania, Korea, Laos, Peru, and Vietnam; organizing coup d'états in Iran, Iraq, Guatemala, Dominican Republic, Syria, and the Congo; influencing elections in Italy, Costa Rica,

British Guiana, Cambodia, and Ecuador, along with hundreds of propaganda operations and assassinations; as well as making foreign policy.

The CIA under Dulles strengthened the network of national security at the expense of democracy. Journalist David Halberstam noted, "...This was not just an isolated phenomenon but part of something larger going on in Washington – the transition from an isolationist America to imperial colossus. A true democracy had no need for a vast, secret security apparatus, but an imperial state did... what was evolving was a closed state within an open state."

Nelson Rockefeller, along with Hoover's FBI, ran U.S. intelligence in Latin America during WWII. Rockefeller's associate in Brazil, Colonel J.C. King, became CIA Chief of Clandestine activities in the Western Hemisphere. As author David Talbot writes, "The Rockefellers served as private bankers for the Dulles empire ... Tom Braden one of Dulles' top propaganda men ... briefed David semi-officially with Allen's permission..."[9] The Rockefeller Foundation supported early efforts to legitimize Diem as the leader of South Vietnam. Cold Warrior, World Bank President, and Warren Commission member John McCloy was a Rockefeller trustee. Dean Rusk went from the State Department to the presidency of the Rockefeller Foundation 1952-1960, and then became Secretary of State for Kennedy and Johnson. John Foster Dulles was a trustee at the Rockefeller Foundation at the same time he was chairman at the Carnegie Foundation, just before he became Eisenhower's secretary of state, ("Philanthropists at War").

CIA programs often targeted democratic socialists in partisan politics, and even church social reformers and union organizing. U.S. multinationals helped support the CIA-funded American Institute for Free Labor Development (AIFLD) which organized against socialist, liberal, and communist unions in Latin America in the 1960s and 1970s.

President Kennedy inherited other networks of interests. In 1949 the Shah of Iran brought in "Overseas Consultants" to give technical and economic advice; the legal spokesman was Allen Dulles. Dulles had long worked with the London-based Schroder bank, which had large holdings in the Anglo-American Oil Company as well as major U.S. oil companies. The Shah moved slowly to implement changes and was defeated in a free election by a democratic socialist Dr. Mossedegh, who moved to nationalize the oil industry.[10] In 1953 the CIA along with British intelligence overthrew Mossedegh, and they returned Shah Palevi to power, a leader who would not threaten the U.S. and British oil interests.

The Dulles brothers convinced a reluctant Eisenhower to intervene by arguing that Iran was part of a Cold War struggle rather than one of nationalism. Allen Dulles warned the NSC that if Iran fell into Communism, that 60% of the free world's oil would be in the hands of the Soviet Union. Mossedegh was portrayed as a Soviet pawn rather than the educated, wealthy, proud nationalist that he was.

In 1954, the CIA overthrew the democratically elected liberal leader of Guatemala, Jacob Arbenz, thereby protecting the interests of the United Fruit Company. The Dulles brothers also worked for Sullivan and Cromwell after doing legal work for the Schroder Bank, and were the key financial advisors for the rail lines in Guatemala. In 1936, John Foster Dulles, as counsel for Schroder Bank, negotiated a deal with United Fruit Company. Allen Dulles, who often helped his brother with Schroder Bank matters, soon was appointed to the Board of Directors. The Schroder Bank was a depository of secret CIA funds for covert operations.[11] John Moors Cabot, Assistant Secretary of State for Inter-America Affairs owned stock in United Fruit, and his brother had served as president of the corporation. UN Ambassador Henry Cabot Lodge was a stockholder too.

State Department policies during 1954 complemented that of the CIA. In Guatemala these policies were preceded by a two-year P.R. campaign by Edward Bernays, a propaganda expert hired by the United Fruit Company, who systematically influenced the major U.S. media on the dangers of President Arbenz. Junkets to Guatemala seemingly influenced reports from *Time, Newsweek,* Scripps-Howard, *U.S. News,* the *New York Times,* the *Miami Herald* and others. United Fruit's director referred to "a public relations coup" which promoted the pretense that the U.S. was not involved. Bernays commented, "It is difficult to make a convincing case for manipulation of the press when the victims proved so eager for the experience."[12]

The project officer for the CIA on the Guatemalan Coup (codenamed PBSUCESS) was Tracey Barnes. Barnes worked with David Phillips and Howard Hunt and other CIA field staff on a range of projects including assassinations of Arbenz supporters which would be blamed on surrogates. The CIA had an assassination manual developed for the coup. By 1954, CIA General Counsel Larry Houston had developed an arrangement with the Justice Dept. so that CIA crimes of murder would not be prosecuted.[13] At a PBSUCESS staff meeting in 1954 discussions included a list of 15-20 Guatemalan leaders who could be killed by gunmen sent by Trujillo (Dominican Republic). Subsequent assassination plans were not recorded in writing,[14] thus broadening a culture of deniability.

The Schroder Banking Corporation and the Schroder Trust functioned as prime depositories for CIA monies through the 1950s and 1960s, similar to B.C.C.I. in the 1980s. These German firms also facilitated Hitler's rise to power. Clients of Sullivan and Cromwell, served by Allen Dulles, sat on both Boards of Directors.[15] Former CIA director Richard Helms later noted, "Hell, the agency sloshed money all over the world." The Schroder Bank became the major funding source for PERMINDEX, one of whose initial directors was Clay Shaw. PERMINDEX was modeled after the New Orleans International Trade Mart directed by Clay Shaw. A State Department cable of 11/7/58:

> It appears that PERMINDEX has formed an affiliate called the Rome World Trade Center (Centro Mondale Commerciale de Roma).... An American, Mr. Clay Shaw Managing Director of the International Trade Mart has been named to the Board of Directors of the Roman affiliate which the news reporter said, has been incorporated with a capital stock of 100 million lire.... The Trade Mart is said to have furnished the model on which PERMINDEX bases itself. [The last 3 ½ lines of the above paragraph are still redacted.[16]

The principal speaker for the opening of Shaw's International Trade Mart in 1948 was William MacChesney Martin, then a supervisor for the Rockefeller Trust Fund, who later became the Chair of the Federal Reserve Board. During the Kennedy Administration he actively opposed Kennedy's low interest rate polices.

Clay Shaw and CIA asset David Ferrie were both involved with the Jock Whitney-controlled Freeport Sulphur Corporation. HSCA testimony from CIA Chief of Western Hemispheric Division David Phillips indicates his involvement as well.

> Mr. Phillips stated that he probably did have some contacts with someone or some persons associated with the Moa Bay Mining Company (a subsidiary of Freeport Sulphur), but he did not recall any names. He also "must have" had some contact with Freeport Sulphur people.

Freeport Sulphur's $75 million nickel mining operation in Cuba, which opened in 1957, was facing nationalization under Castro. This led to pressure from Freeport on CIA Chief of Clandestine Services in the Western Hemisphere J.C. King to eliminate Castro. King "recommended:"

Thorough consideration (should) be given to the elimination of Fidel Castro. None of those close to Fidel, such as his brother Raul or his companion Che Guevara, has the same appeal to the masses...

Johnny Roselli, (one of the CIA's mobsters involved in the Castro assassination plots), according to Peter Wyden in his book *Bay of Pigs: the Untold Story* told his Cuban contacts, "he represented Wall Street financiers who had nickel interests and properties in Cuba."[17]

Allen Dulles responded to a memo by Colonel J. C. King to set up Operation 40, a Cuban Task Force to remove Castro, headed by Richard Nixon and senior CIA officers Ted Shakley, David Phillips, E. Howard Hunt, Henry Hecksher, Tom Clines, William Harvey, Carl Jenkins, David Morales, Admiral Arleigh Burke and others. The committee also consisted of a number of CIA assets including Frank Sturgis, Felix Rodriquez, Gerry Hemming, Edwin Wilson, William Pawley, Antonio Veciana, Tony Cuesta, Eladio Del Valle, Carlos Bringuier, Rolando Mansfer, Luis Sanjenis, ChiChi Quintero, Eugenio Martinez, Rip Robertson, Hermino Diaz Garcia, Virgilio Gonzalez, and John Martino among others.

The CIA had developed policies of compartmentalization and deniability, which could essentially be "hijacked" or redirected by a handful of senior officers.

A number of sources have asserted that Operation 40 was redirected at President Kennedy. John Martino told *Miami Newsday* reporter John Cummings that two members of Operation 40, Hermino Diaz Garcia and Virgilio Gonzalez, were gunman in the conspiracy to assassinate President Kennedy. Martino claimed that his role was delivering money and facilitating things. HSCA staffer Fred Classen suggested that Oswald did not know who he was working for – "the anti-Castro people put him together." Author and reporter Anthony Summers interviewed Martino's wife, Florence, who reluctantly revealed that her husband said, "They are going to kill him [JFK] when he gets to Texas."[18]

Another key CIA officer in Operation 40, David Morales, died of a heart attack before he was to be interviewed by HSCA staffer Gaeton Fonzi. Fonzi then interviewed Morales' business partner, Bob Walton, who said Morales feared being killed by the CIA because he knew too much.

Military intelligence operative (Air Force OSI and Army CID) Gene Wheaton, who also worked with CIA on Cuban projects, revealed statements to the ARRB Chief Investigator Anne Buttimer, 7/12/95. Wheaton stated that senior CIA officer Carl Jenkins was involved in paramilitary activities for the Bay of Pigs and AM/WORLD (a covert anti-Castro insurgency), and along with Chi Chi Quintero (trained by David Morales) was involved in Operation 40. Jenkins claimed that he trained the Cubans that killed Kennedy. Author Larry Hancock noted in Someone Would Have Talked that Wheaton told Buttimer that Cuban exiles killed Kennedy because he was a "traitor" and that "people above the Cubans wanted Kennedy killed for different reasons." Further ARRB meetings with Wheaton were somehow not pursued.

According to Fabian Escalante, a senior officer in the Cuban Department of State Security (G-2) businessmen George H.W. Bush and Jack Crichton were recruited to raise money for Operation 40. Escalante pointed to Operation 40 as being responsible for the assassination.[19] George H.W. Bush would later head the CIA, from 1976 to 1977.

On a major matter of intelligence gathering by national technical means, elements of the CIA and Defense Department disobeyed orders from the Commander in Chief. Eisenhower had explicitly ordered the U-2 spy flights to be suspended by May 1, 1960, so as not to interfere with the upcoming summit meeting with Khrushchev, de Gaulle and Macmillan. Yet the U-2 flights continued. CIA Deputy Director Richard Bissell had developed and run the U-2 program for the CIA, and almost certainly ordered the Gary Powers flight. "Powers came down because his aircraft was fixed to fail," according to retired Air Force Colonel Fletcher Prouty, who was in charge of providing military support for the clandestine services. He argues that Powers had a shortage of proper fuel, he was laden with identification including a DOD I.D. card, and the U-2 bore identifying marks, violating NSC edicts. This catastrophe seemed timed to scuttle the May 16th summit that Eisenhower had hoped would thaw the Cold War.[20]

Prouty wrote that the U-2 incident evolved from a "tremendous underground struggle [between] the peacemakers led by Eisenhower and the cold warriors led by the Dulles "inner elite."[21]

During the presidential campaign in 1960 Kennedy repeatedly declared his commitment to nationalism in Africa. Notably, just prior to his inauguration, CIA station chief in Leopoldville, Congo, Lawrence Devlin spoke of the "need to take drastic steps before it was too late." The CIA arranged for the charismatic nationalist Patrice Lumumba to be quickly assassinated by Belgian collaborators just three days before JFK took office. When Kennedy was informed by phone of Lumumba's assassination, a photo shows him deeply distraught.[22]

Soon after becoming president, Kennedy confronted a confusing situation in Laos. Laotian communists were temporarily aligned with neutralist forces in a struggle against conservative elements, led by General Phoumi Nosavan, actively supported by the CIA. North Vietnam had a small force fighting with the Pathet Lao, the Soviets had given economic assistance, and Chinese involvement was considered a possibility. The Joint Chiefs of Staff and elements of the CIA and State Department supported military intervention. The Joint Chiefs even argued that the U.S. had to be willing to use nuclear weapons if necessary.

Kennedy rejected these recommendations to commit forces to Laos in order to preserve the existing right-wing government, and chose to develop a neutralist coalition. At his first press conference in January of 1961, Kennedy stated that Laos should be an independent country, free of domination of either side.[23]

In the early 1960s, a close friend of PERMINDEX director Ference Nagy, Albert Soustelle, the former Governor General of Algeria in the 1950s, met with CIA officials including Richard Bissell, then Deputy Director of Plans. According to the *New York Times*, Soustelle convinced the CIA that "Algeria would become, through de Gaulle's blundering, a Soviet base." In June 1975, the *Chicago Tribune* revealed portions of the Church Committee findings: "Congressional leaders have been told of the CIA involvement in a plot by French dissidents to assassinate the late French President Charles de Gaulle."[24]

Early in his administration Kennedy also confronted the Bay of Pigs invasion plan. Eisenhower's Secretary of Defense Thomas Gates, CIA Director Allen Dulles, and General Richard Bissel, Deputy Director of Plans at the CIA, had created the project. Kennedy, like Eisenhower, was largely kept in the dark about this operation. Recent research indicates that Bissell altered the amphibious assault plans of Marine Corps Col. Jack Hawkins. Hawkins told Bissell that without strong air support approved in advance the invasion should not proceed. The other main planner for the amphibious assault, CIA officer, Jake Easterline, was banned from all high-level meetings. Both Hawkins and Easterline threatened to resign if the air attacks were not guaranteed.[25]

After the failed invasion, Kennedy cited the following arguments made by his briefers to get his approval: that there was widespread discontent in Cuba, that the anti-Castro Cubans were well-trained and ready, that both seasonal concerns and increasing military aid to Cuba made it a now-or-never proposition; that the anti-Castro force would be hard to handle if it was not allowed to proceed, that the force could escape to fight a guerrilla war if the invasion did not go well initially.[26] These evaluations were wrong, and debate no longer exists as to whether these intelligence failures were honest mistakes or a strategy. An attempt was made to manipulate the president into a situation where he needed either to use military force in Cuba, or lose. Kennedy, however, refused to commit U.S. forces despite the pleas of the CIA, the Pentagon, and most of his top advisors, such as McGeorge Bundy and Dean Rusk. Notably, Bundy was a former student and later a colleague of Bissell at Yale and had worked with Dulles since the Dewey campaign in 1948.

JFK was furious with the CIA and Joint Chiefs of Staff and threatened to "shatter the CIA into a thousand pieces." After an investigation into the failure, Kennedy waited a few months before firing Dulles, Bissell, and Cabell. He appointed an outsider, a corporate Republican, John McCone, to run the CIA. Realizing the challenges McCone would confront, he tasked his brother Bobby to help McCone control the agency. Some sources now show that top CIA officers continued to regularly visit Dulles at his home in Georgetown after he was fired.[27]

Kennedy confronted a CIA hierarchy accustomed to autonomy and filled with the hubris of power. Born to privilege, nurtured by the Ivy League and WWII intelligence, they rationalized that the necessities of the Cold War required often making rather than following laws. These zealots were emboldened by significant elements of the military and intelligence leadership. They sometimes referred to themselves as "Bold Easterners," while critics like Director of Central Intelligence executive assistant Victor Marchetti saw them as a "Cult of Intelligence." William Colby, DCI in the early 1970's, called the early CIA "an order of Knights Templar, out to save western freedom from Communist darkness"[28]

DCI Allen Dulles had long been used to developing foreign policy with his brother John Foster Dulles, Secretary of State for Eisenhower. At a dinner party in Walter Lippmann's house Dulles boasted that he was still carrying out the foreign policy of his brother. When informed the next day by Kennedy confidante Bill Walton, the president was furious.[29]

The ambitious spy in line to succeed Dulles was Richard Bissell, who planned the CIA "monkey business" to overthrow democratically elected reformer, Arbenz, in Guatemala in 1954. The former Yale professor, who worked closely with Dulles, was a principal architect of the Bay of Pigs disaster.

James Jesus Angleton, longtime director of CIA Counterintelligence, was similarly raised to privilege and power. An Ivy League poet who served in the OSS, his connections and attitudes helped create the cluster of "Bold Easterners." He was the "Gray Ghost" to his colleagues – thin, clever, dedicated and suspicious. With Allen Dulles as his mentor, he quickly carved out his own autonomous agency within an autonomous agency. In 1954 Angleton convinced Eisenhower and Army General James Doolittle that the CIA needed a counterintelligence staff knowledgeable about the KGB methods to oversee CIA covert operations and resist Soviet penetration of the U.S. government.

Angleton saw Kennedy as faltering during the Bay of Pigs and the Cuban Missile Crisis. "Kennedy should have forced Castro from Cuba for having conspired with the Kremlin to bring Soviet missile power into the western hemisphere." Angleton then tried to shape Cuba policy with his "Cuban Control and Action Capabilities," which he distributed to the Joint Chiefs of Staff and 15 other agencies.

Years later he remained a legend in his own mind as seen by his responses to Senator Church's Intelligence Committee (1975). Angleton, who had drifted into alcohol, admitted to not informing President Kennedy of some CIA actions and misinforming him of others. Notably, he declared that, "it's inconceivable that a secret intelligence arm of the government has to comply with all of the overt orders of the government."[30] Years later, retired and in failing health Angleton divulged to reporter Joe Trento:

> Fundamentally, the founding fathers of U.S. intelligence were liars. The better you lied and the more you betrayed, the more likely you were to be promoted.... Outside of their duplicity, the only thing they had in common was a desire for absolute power.... [Trento asked how Angleton got appointed to run counterintelligence.] I agreed not to polygraph or require detailed background checks on Allen Dulles and 60 of his closest friends, they were afraid that their own business dealings with Hitler's pals would come out. They were too arrogant to believe that the Russians would discover it all.... There was no accountability, and without real accountability everything turned to shit.[31]

Allen Dulles gave a remarkable range of powers to his close friend James Angleton, who served as the CIA liaison to the FBI. As chief of counter-intelligence he spied on the CIA, he ran assets in other agencies. His close bond with Dulles lasted long after Dulles was fired by Kennedy. Angleton included Dulles in his will and he carried Dulles' ashes after he died.

In 1963 Angleton traveled to London with CIA Officer Bill Harvey (Executive Action) to ask MI6 for assassination advice. Back in 1961, Harvey's notes on assassination are revealing:

1. Never mention assassination.

2. Put nothing on paper.

3. If an operation blows up blame the Soviets or the Czechs.

4. Develop a phony 201 file – forged and backdated to look like a CIA file.

5. Run singletons – (one operations)

Angleton did not open a 201 file on Oswald after he defected to the Soviet Union, nor after he told the U.S. Embassy in Moscow that he was going to give up radar secrets. Only after the State Department started asking questions did Angleton finally open a 201 file.

Angleton chose to create an Office of Security file (OS file) rather than a 201 file, so that he could more closely control it. Perhaps Angleton was determining if a Soviet mole in the CIA was interested in him. He made his close associate Ray Rocco the official CIA liaison to the Warren Commission and he knew what to cover up after the Warren Commission ended.[32] Recall that Angleton ran a completely "independent group of journalist-operatives who performed sensitive and frequently dangerous assignments; little is known of this group for the simple reason that Angleton kept only the vaguest of files." One media asset was former Nazi war criminal Paul Hoffman, who got his job with The Rome Bureau of the *New York Times* through help from the Angleton family.[33]

Angleton's close friend and colleague, Richard Helms, directed the covert action arm of the CIA before becoming DCI. Born of affluence, Helms was educated in Switzerland with the future Shah of Iran. A former UPI correspondent, he viewed McCone as a front man "straight from central casting." Helms bitterly resented RFK's oversight and their distrust was deep and mutual.[34]

RFK's administrative aide John Siegenthaler Jr. "… thought the CIA was a rogue agency – it did wet (murder) work on its own … they were way too in thrall to 007 … the administration was particularly vulnerable with someone like McCone in charge – he was in over his head … and

Bob [Kennedy] shared that feeling – he didn't have any confidence that McCone had the slightest idea of what the CIA was doing."

After Kennedy dismissed Dulles, debates raged regarding his successor. McCone a Republican industrialist and former AEC chairman, was not the CIA's first choice – yet he remained more in line with the CIA old guard than with the New Frontier. Dulles indeed, continued to meet regularly with retired and active CIA officers at his Washington home. Those meetings included Frank Wisner, Charles Cabell, James Angleton, Richard Helms, Cord Meyer, Desmond FitzGerald, Howard Hunt, James Hunt, and Thomas Karamersines as well as John McCone.[35]

In the newly independent Congo in 1960, CIA surrogates assassinated the charismatic nationalist Prime Minister Patrice Lumumba, who had often expressed a passion for neutralism, a week before Kennedy took office. Eisenhower declared that Lumumba was a Soviet accomplice who should "fall into a river of crocodiles." Dulles directed the Congo's CIA station Chief Lawrence Devlin to make it happen. To reassert control of the Belgian-supported province, the CIA station chief in Congo, Lawrence Devlin, had "direct influence over the events that led to Lumumba's death," according to Stephen Weismann in *Foreign Affairs*, "What Really Happened in Congo."[36] (Based on recently declassified files from the Church Committee, a Belgian parliamentary investigation and U.S. State Department research, Newman, John p.266-269).

A secessionist faction, led by Moesha Tshombe, president of mineral rich Katanga province, had the support of financial and mining interests in Belgium, France, Great Britain, and factions in the U.S. In the struggle between "nationalism and colonialism" according to Kennedy advisor Chester Bowles, the Joint Chiefs, the Defense Department and the European Bureau of the State Department favored "spheres of influence (for) former colonial rulers," the largest CIA covert actions in their history, supported Britain, France and Belgium when Kennedy took office. In 1961, in the Congo, President Kennedy inherited a contradictory policy wherein U. S. Air Force C-130s were flying Congolese troops and supplies against the Katanganese rebels. At the same time, the CIA, along with elements of the Pentagon put together an air armada and mercenary units to aid the Katanganese rebels. Kennedy, however, supported the anti-colonial U.N. efforts, including the use of military forces to prevent the break-up of the Congo.[37]

UN General Secretary Dag Hammarskjold was mysteriously killed in a plane crash on September 17, 1961, attempting to negotiate a truce in the

Congolese civil war. Forman President Truman declared to the *N.Y. Times* 9/20/61 that "Dag Hammarskjold was on the point of getting something done when they killed him." CIA operative Roland Culligan admitted involvement in the assassination to the Church Commission. Confusion lingers regarding CIA involvement. Years later, the South African Truth Commission chairman, Desmond Tutu, released letters from the South African Institute for Maritime Research (SAIMR), said to be a front for the South African military,which include references to the CIA and British MI5. "In a meeting between MI5, special ops executive and the SAIMR, the following emerged, reads one document marked Top Secret, "it is felt that Hammarskjold should be removed ... I want his removal to be handled more efficiently than was Patrice." Another letter headed "Operation Celeste" detailed orders to plant in the wheel bay of an aircraft, explosives primed to go off as the wheels were retracted on takeoff. The Reuters report, 8/20/98, included the predictable CIA denial of involvement.[38]

This power struggle is indicative of a pattern of CIA defiance of the chain of command. The CIA had bypassed the State Department in nation after nation. Kennedy tried to change this by sending Chester Bowles on a trip around the world to clarify the supremacy of ambassadors in their embassies; however, a 1963 Senate report concluded that the Kennedy order had become "a shadow." It also noted, "To a degree the primacy of the ambassador is a polite fiction."[39] Frustration with the CIA in Vietnam led to press leaks. Scripps-Howard reporter Richard Starnes, 10/2/63, wrote "Spooks make life miserable for Ambassador Lodge." According to a highly placed source, the CIA "twice flatly refused to carry out instructions from Ambassador Henry Cabot Lodge. An American field officer declared that a Colonel at headquarters is a CIA agent and his role is unclear "unless he is spying on Americans." Military officers "scream over the way the spooks dabble in military operations." The source then speculated on the possibility of a coup and the CIA being involved

By 1962 JFK had directed his brother Robert to manage the CIA's Cuban policies, as well as oversee the agency. "Operation Mongoose" started in late 1961, used terror, crop burnings, destruction of Cuban power and water systems, and attacks on Soviet ships. The ambitious and uncoordinated plan spun off assassination plots with the mafia as well as major military exercises, simulating an attack on an island, "Operation Swift Strike II," and "Ortsac" (Castro backwards). RFK's point man, General Edward Geary Lansdale, attempted to circumvent the CIA elite, as seen by a memo to RFK suggesting they go around Bissell and "the CIA palace guard," and work with a mid-level CIA official. CIA elites loathed Lansdale's influence on Cuban policy. CIA agent Bill Harvey, who headed the Miami-based Cuba operations, viewed "Operation Mongoose as mostly for show,"[40] and saw the Kennedys as cowards. Harvey hated RFK and saw Lansdale as "a screwball." Respected CIA officer John Whitten saw Harvey as a "thug," in part because one of Harvey's best friends was Mafioso Johnny Roselli. HSCA staffers found Harvey to be heavily involved with mafia figures, and out of control, although some historians argue that Helms ordered Harvey to resume assassination plans with the mafia against Castro. CIA contract agent Joe Shimon viewed Harvey as always working for James Angleton.[41] Back in 1959, Harvey was one of three CIA officers privy to plans to send false defectors into the Soviet Union, and almost certainly knew of Oswald. Lansdale and Helms contributed to Soviet fears in Cuba. When the HSCA general counsel asked Whitten how he interpreted Harvey's wife burning his private papers after his death, Whitten retorted, "He was too young to have assassinated McKinley and Lincoln. It could have been anything."[42]

CIA defiance and mixed signals emerged after the Cuban Missile Crisis as well. Kennedy aide Ted Sorenson asserted that the President told his brother to stop the anti-Cuban operations after the Cuban missile crisis, and was assured that this would occur. Historian Thomas Patterson, however, argued that after October 1962, "raids by (Cuban) exiles, some of them no doubt perpetrated with CIA collaboration, and most of them monitored but not stopped by American authorities, remained a menace." Kennedy pursued a dual-track policy of "The plan for a coup in Cuba," as well as diplomacy; however, CIA covert actions had grown beyond the control of the chief executive, Director of Central Intelligence (DCI) McCone, and the Attorney General. According to the CIA inspector general in a report in 1967, Richard Helms gave Desmond FitzGerald the approval for AMLASH, the plan to assassinate Castro. He stated "it was not necessary to seek approval from Robert Kennedy for FitzGerald to speak in his name."[43]

Former President Harry Truman felt compelled to publicly question the direction of the CIA one month after the assassination. Declassified documents show that Allen Dulles visited Truman to persuade him to retract his op-ed piece in the *Washington Post* 12/22/63.

I think it has become necessary to take another look at the purpose and operations of our CIA…. For some time I have been disturbed by the way the CIA has been diverted from its original assignment. It has become an operational and at times a policy making arm of the government. This has led to trouble and may have compounded our difficulties in several explosive areas. I never had any thought that when I set up the CIA it would be injected into peacetime cloak and dagger operations... I would like to see the CIA be restored to its original assignment as the intelligence arm of the President...

CIA links with Lee Harvey Oswald appear ubiquitous. Oswald was: 1) stationed at Atsugi, Japan, from which the CIA made its U-2 flights, he had a "Crypto" clearance – higher than "Top Secret." Sergeant Gerry Patrick Hemming, who served in Japan with Oswald, and was later recruited by the CIA for action's with anti-Castro Cubans, says he believed that Oswald was recruited then by the CIA based on conversations with him. 2) Recruited by the CIA, according to CIA finance Officer James Wilcott, for his assignment in the USSR – in 1959 CIA Counterintelligence opened a 201 file on him. Senator Richard Schweiker, a member of the Senate Intelligence committee flatly stated in 2007 that Oswald "was the product of a fake defector program run by the CIA." Oswald's "defection" was approved by Richard Snyder, a Foreign Service Officer, who was probably working for the CIA at the American Embassy in Moscow;[44] 3) He was met upon return to the U.S. by Spas Raikin and representatives of the CIA-funded American Friends of Anti-Bolshevik Bloc Nations; 4) befriended by CIA Contract Division Agent George de Mohrenschildt in Dallas and Ft. Worth; 5) in contact with highly-paid CIA Contract Agent Clay Shaw as well as Contract Agent David Ferrie and CIA asset Jack Martin in New Orleans; 6) worked at the William Reily Coffee Co. – Reily was assigned CIA number EE-334.[45] 7) In contact with CIA Contract Agent Marita Lorenz in Miami; 8) met once with CIA and military intelligence asset Antonio Veciana and CIA agent David Phillips; and 9) encountered agents or operatives with the Cuban Student Directorate (DRE), which was supported by CIA officers George Joannides, and David Phillips.

The CIA followed Oswald closely the last month of his life, particularly from the offices of James Angleton and David Phillips. Former CIA Director Allen Dulles, fired by President Kennedy after the Bay of Pigs failure, was the most active member of the Warren Commission, and found no links between Oswald and any intelligence agency.

Recall that after the Bay of Pigs, Kennedy also fired CIA Director of Plans General Charles Cabell, whose brother Earle was then the Mayor of Dallas, and assisted in the rerouting of the Presidential motorcade. According to Dallas Deputy Sheriff Carson, Mayor Cabell, who we now know was a CIA asset, ordered the unusual transfer of Oswald to county facilities. Their father also had been the Dallas Chief of Police. Charles Cabell had been Dulles' deputy for nine years. He had also been E. Howard Hunt's coordinating superior on the CIA Guatemalan operation. When Charles Cabell spoke to the New Orleans Foreign Policy Association in May 1961, he was introduced by Clay Shaw.[46] The Warren Commission, however, never interviewed General Cabell. Richard Bissell, who directed the "Executive Action" branch of the CIA, which had the capacity to assassinate foreign leaders, was also fired. Kennedy cut the CIA budget in 1962 and 1963 and was aiming to cut 20% by 1966.[47]

Oswald's best friend in Dallas, George de Mohrenschildt, was a CIA contract agent working with J. Walton Moore. De Mohrenschildt's, the scion of a powerful oil family in Russia, worked with the OSS as had his brother Dmitri. George helped Oswald get a job at Jaggers Childs and Stovall, a photographic company with secret military security clearance to process maps and photos.

Oswald worked with Guy Banister ex-ONI, in New Orleans. Banister's office was frequented by CIA and mafia-connected David Ferrie as well as Clay Shaw. Banister's files, which were either "routinely destroyed" by the Louisiana State Police, or taken by the FBI, remains a mystery. Banister's index, which survived, included files categories of on the CIA, Ammunition and Arms, Anti-Soviet Underground, B-70 Manned Bomber Force, U.S. Civil Rights, Dismantling of Ballistic Missile System, Dismantling of U.S. Defenses, Fair Play for Cuba Committee and Clay Shaw's International Trade Mart.[48]

Aspects of the CIA role with the Warren Commission can be seen regarding Marina Oswald. Seemingly, the CIA coached Marina Oswald prior to her first testimony before the Warren Commission. A Warren Commission counsel wrote in a memo, 2/28/64, "Marina has repeatedly lied ... on matters which are of vital concern." After the assassination Jack Crichton, former OSS man, Army Intelligence operative and wealthy Dallas oilman, voluntarily worked with Marina Oswald.[49] Crichton also contacted the Dallas Police to bring in Ilya Mamantov as a translator for Marina Oswald. Mamantov, a vocal anti-communist, tried to establish that Oswald had ties to Cuba and that "leftist" Oswald had acted alone.

Crichton's connections warrant investigation. His company directors included Clint Murchison Sr. and D. Harold Byrd, owner of the Texas

School Book Depository building. Crichton started and commanded the 488th Military Intelligence Detachment, with forty or fifty of the approximately 100-man force being members of the Dallas Police Department. Crichton, the Texas GOP candidate for governor in 1964, was close friends with George de Mohrenschildt and George H.W. Bush.[50]

Former CIA employee Isaac Don Levine spent an intensive week with Marina just prior to her first testimony before the Warren Commission, under the pretext of writing a book about her. Levine in 1951 had served on the CIA-directed board of American Liberation Committee and was its European director, where he worked closely with Allen Dulles, C.D. Jackson, and John McCloy.[51]

Levine emphasized the claim that Marina and Marguerite Oswald willfully destroyed a copy of "the backyard photo" (the purported picture of Oswald with the alleged murder weapon Mannlicher-Carcano) that would have clinched the case against Oswald as the assassin. What emerged before the Warren Commission was a contrived story of Marina concealing the picture in her shoe while visiting Lee in jail and, later that night, destroying it at Marguerite's insistence.[52]

Levine may have played a role in Marina's late recalling of the "Nixon incident" – Oswald's alleged announced intentions to assassinate Nixon in the spring of 1963. Marina supposedly locked Lee in the bathroom to prevent him from carrying out the assault. When Chief Counsel Rankin asked Levine how, he creatively claimed, "You take a broomstick and put it through the handle and lock the door. Russians know how to do this better than anyone else." Levine later claimed Oswald also planned to go to Russia to assassinate Khrushchev.[53]

Another possible purpose for Levine's role was to gain information about Marina. Levine met more than once with Allen Dulles for private conversations as well as with William Sullivan, head of the FBI's Domestic Operations Division.[54]

Attorney William A. McKenzie, who had previously represented George de Mohrenschildt as well as Clint Murchison's Great Southwest Corporation, also advised Marina. The Warren Commission failed to pursue unsolicited sworn testimony that McKenzie had improperly coached Marina on what to tell the FBI, even though an FBI memo corroborated that Marina had in fact said just what McKenzie was supposed to have told her to say.[55] Murchison, a close friend of LBJ and J. Edgar Hoover, had hosted his friend and business partner, banker, and Warren Commission member John McCloy, on a visit to Texas during the summer of 1963.

The Warren Commission did not pursue investigations of Oswald's connections to intelligence agencies. The respected John Whitten initially ran the CIA investigation of the assassination, but Helms replaced him with Angleton when he complained that the CIA had omitted Oswald's pro-Castro activities from his files.[56] Angleton had close ties to Hoover, and quickly determined that Oswald's Pro-Castro connections were not important. Whitten told HSCA staffers that if he had been given FBI and CIA pre-assassination files on Oswald, he would have investigated the CIA's JM/WAVE station in Miami to explore what George Joannides, the station chief and SG and SAS, knew about Oswald.[57]

When public criticism of the Warren Report became widespread in late 1966, the CIA mobilized its assets to protect it. Through a lawsuit, attorney and author Mark Lane was able to obtain a top-secret CIA document, dated April 1, 1967, which explicitly outlined how to counter and discredit conspiracy theorists. Recall that certain writers, producers, and publishers who were intelligence assets doggedly defended the Report.

Former DCI Richard Helms has stated that the CIA was "very helpful to Johnson [on the JFK Assassination] and met the new president's request for an independent CIA study. Motion pictures of the Dallas motorcade and autopsy pictures were sent to the agency."[58] Although this report is still classified, hearsay evidence suggests that the new president seemingly did not find it compelling. An internal FBI memorandum, 4/4/67, notes that FBI informant Jack Anderson was told by Johnson aide Marvin Watson that "the President told him, in an off moment, that he was now convinced that there was a plot in connection with the assassination. Watson stated the President felt that the CIA had something to do with this plot..."[59]

True magazine, April 1975, ran a revelatory piece by former Executive Assistant to the Deputy Director of the CIA, Victor Marchetti, regarding CIA aid during the Garrison investigation. Marchetti got explicit about attitudes and actions at the morning meetings of DCI Richard Helms, attended by 12 to 14 leading deputies and 3-4 top staffers.

> During the Clay Shaw trial I remember the Director on several occasions asking questions like, you know, Are we giving them all of the help that they need? I didn't know who they or them were. I knew they didn't like Garrison because there were a lot of snotty remarks about him. They would talk in half sentences like "is everything going all right down there ... yea ... but talk with me

about it after the meeting. ..." I began to ask myself what's going on, what's the big concern ... one of the other people who attended the meeting ... at one time said, "well Shaw a long time ago had been a contact of the agency – the Domestic Contact Service – its been cut off a long time ago... of course the agency doesn't want this to come out because Garrison will distort it. The public will misconstrue it." [60]

Questions linger about the coverage of HSCA Chief Counsel Richard Sprague, the aggressive Assistant D.A. from Philadelphia, who wanted a thorough investigation. After his goal became known, Sprague was hit with a journalistic hatchet-job by David Burnham of the *New York Times* and Jeremiah O'Leary of the *Washington Star,* who had both previously worked with the CIA.[61] The ensuing internal dissent within the HSCA was only partly resolved by Sprague's resignation just a few months later.

Sprague noted in retrospect that if he could start over he would begin by probing "Oswald's ties to the CIA."[62] Sprague's deputy counsel, Robert Tannenbaum, was told by Senator Richard Schweiker (R-Pa) "in my judgment the CIA was involved in the murder of the President." Sprague had called David Phillips to testify regarding Oswald in Mexico City. He was probing how the FBI agents could have listened to a tape recording of Oswald talking with the Soviet Embassy in Mexico City in November, when Phillips said it had been destroyed in October. Sprague was pressured by the CIA to sign a secrecy oath to pursue the information but he refused, stating it was in conflict with the House Resolution.

The CIA or Angleton alone, withheld files on the alleged September 1963 Oswald-Kostikov meeting (a Russian officer in covert actions in Mexico) from the Warren Commission and the HSCA. Partially declassified CIA memos indicate that a member of the CIA's Mexico City station reported, 10/16/63, that this officer determined that Oswald had talked with Kostikov, yet the person alleged to be Oswald, who was photographed walking into the Cuban and Soviet embassies, was heavy set, balding and middle-aged.[63] The author of the memo was probably CIA Officer David Phillips. According to career CIA officer Joe B. Smith, J.C. King's CIA men recruited David Phillips. "Dave's not only a good writer; he's a great snake oil salesman."[64]

CIA station chief in Mexico City, Win Scott, a CIA loyalist, wrote an unpublished memoir asserting that the Warren Commission findings were false – because Scott had been following Oswald. When Scott died, the CIA stole his manuscript and kept it for a quarter of a century.[65]

A revealing internal CIA memo from Phillips to Deputy Director Helms noted: "Unless you feel otherwise, Jim Angleton CIA Chief of Counter Intelligence would prefer to wait out the [HSCA] committee on this matter."[66] Former HSCA Counsel Sprague contends that his pursuit of CIA documents was the beginning of his fall.

The next HSCA Chief Counsel, Robert Blakey, saw things quite differently; he even sought FBI and CIA clearance for hiring new employees. Chief researcher Robert Tannenbaum then quit and protested. "We're supposed to be investigating them, instead they're investigating us. Blakey met with CIA officer Larry Strawderman on 7/27/77, set the parameters for the HSCA; that certain areas of the investigation should be disregarded if they lack merit or corroboration; that the CIA could scrutinize the notes of HSCA investigators, who were only permitted to look at CIA documents in a closed room." HSCA Researcher Donovan Gay, the keeper of the records, asked about access to CIA classified files and was fired by Blakey. Blakey told Gay, "It would be easier for the CIA if you left."[67]

While the HSCA substantially clarified the role of the Mafia, the final report written by Chief Counsel Blakey and Dick Billings is remarkable for what it fails to cover regarding intelligence agencies and the military. Independent investigators presented significant information regarding the role played by the intelligence agencies to the HSCA in 1977; however, the price of being a Congressional research investigator was to sign a "nondisclosure agreement." This meant that all evidence was handed over to the HSCA and could not be disclosed elsewhere. Much, if not most, of the-new information was not pursued, according to Congressional researchers and staffers Gaeton Fonzi, Robert Groden, Cliff Fenton, and Ed Lopez. Most of that information was sealed for fifty years in the National Archives, until the movie *JFK* forced much of its release.[68]

HSCA Chief Investigator Gaeton Fonzi was convinced that Oswald met with CIA case officer "Maurice Bishop," a pseudonym for David Phillips. Fonzi based this on his extensive interviews with Antonio Veciana, an active anti-Castro Cuban, who repeatedly stated that he had once met with Oswald and Phillips. Veciana, an articulate accountant and leader of the terrorist anti-Castro group Alpha 66, had worked for years with "Bishop," including a four year stint in Bolivia for the Agency for International Development (oftentimes a CIA front). Veciana spent almost all of his time there working on anti-Communist and anti-Castro activities, including, allegedly, an attempt to assassinate Castro in Chile in early 1971. Phillips even asked Veciana if his cousin Ruiz, who worked for Cuban intelligence and was stationed in Mexico City could be "offered a huge amount of money" to testify regarding Oswald's Mexico visit.[69] In 1995 Cuban General Fabian Escalante, who was in charge of Cuban units that infiltrated CIA controlled anti-Castro groups in the U.S., asserted that Phillips was "Bishop" and that Phillips recruited Veciana.[70] After the assassination Phillips received a major promotion within the CIA.

Robert Tannenbaum, the initial HSCA deputy counsel, agreed with Fonzi that "Bishop" was in fact David Phillips. Tannenbaum's interrogation of Phillips regarding the FBI memo about Oswald being impersonated, as well as the pictures purportedly of Oswald entering the Cuban and Soviet Embassies in Mexico City, trapped Phillips in lies. When Tannenbaum confronted Phillips with FBI memos about the Oswald photos not being recycled, "Phillips just folded the memos and walked out of the room." Tannenbaum told the HSCA, "He's in contempt and he committed perjury. Let him know it," but the committee would not back him up. The assassination investigation then became tainted in the mainstream media, when false contentions led Tannenbaum and Chief Counsel Richard Sprague to resign.[71] Congress responded by cutting the HSCA budget.

HSCA staffer Gaeton Fonzi also planned to investigate William Pawley (Bayo-Pawley mission). However, the week after he sent his target list to the HSCA, Pawley allegedly committed suicide.

Fonzi also interviewed Sylvia Odio, an anti-Castro activist who stated that she had a meeting with Lee Oswald and two anti-Castro Cubans in late fall of 1963. The anti-Castro Cubans used the noms de guerre "Leopoldo" and "Angel," stating that they were members of Junta Revolutionary (JURE) as well as the Cuban Revolutionary Council. Two days after the meeting "Leopoldo" called Odio and said Oswald was "an ex-marine an excellent marksman ... tremendous asset, except you never know how to take him ... he's kind of loco ... the American says we Cubans don't have any guts ... he says we should have shot Kennedy after the Bay of Pigs..." The Warren Commission Chief Council Lee Rankin saw the matter as important but elected not to explore it.

Fonzi found Odio to be credible. It appeared that Oswald had confederates who were setting him up. Further, Oswald was supposedly in Mexico City at this time. Recall that CIA support for anti-Castro Cubans was extensive, even after it was supposedly reduced.

Although Sprague's replacement, Notre Dame professor Robert Blakey, claimed to have received everything of significance from the CIA, an internal CIA memorandum stated that Blakey "spent only twenty or thirty minutes discussing and examining the contents of some fifteen safes of Agency materials."[72] The CIA memo further stated, "Oswald's 201 file was not completely reviewed by HSCA staff members. One HSCA Staff member claimed that they did not review sixteen CIA file drawers, and noted that given the lack of access to the CIA file system it was not possible for the HSCA to tell if the CIA was responding fully. Blakey responded, "You don't think they'd lie to me, do you? I've been working with those people for 20 years."[73]

HSCA investigator Ed Lopez noted that the CIA knew that it could wait out a two-year HSCA investigation. The final HSCA report had to be approved by the CIA, which fought for 6 hours over the first 14 lines. The so-called Lopez report was finally released in 1997.

Fonzi later reflected that, "There is not one investigator – not one – who served on the Kennedy task force of the Assassinations Committee who honestly feels he took part in an adequate investigation, let alone a full and complete one."[74]

CIA involvement of E. Howard Hunt resurfaced in 1978. Victor Marchetti, former Executive Assistant to the Deputy Director of the CIA, wrote an article in a small right-wing newspaper, *Spotlight*, run by Liberty Lobby, stating that he had seen an internal CIA memo from James Angleton, head of CIA Counterintelligence to CIA Director Richard Helms stating that E. Howard Hunt was in Dallas the day Kennedy was killed. Hunt sued and initially won $650,000 in a 1981 libel suit against Liberty Lobby; however, in 1984 Liberty Lobby appealed the case to the Eleventh Circuit Court of Appeals and they proved that Hunt was in Dallas the day Kennedy was killed, and that indeed the memo did exist. Veteran CNN reporter, and quite reluctant witness, Joe Trento, had seen it. Attorney Mark Lane determined that James Angleton and former Marine officer William Corson were Marchetti's sources. Further, CIA operative Marita Lorenz testified that Hunt was the paymaster of the operation that killed Kennedy.[75] Lorenz had been part of a CIA mission to assassinate Fidel Castro, and had worked with various state and federal police organizations.

According to Marchetti, the CIA was furious with Hunt for his role in Watergate. He was to be part of what is called a "limited hangout" during the HSCA hearings; that is, they would tell part of the story while protecting most of it. E. Howard Hunt was part of the CIA planning staff for the Guatemalan coup in 1954 along with General Cabell and Frank Wisner, later Chief of Covert Operations. Hunt was in the CIA Asian command until 1959 and then assisted in the Bay of Pigs planning, where he worked with General Cabell and CIA Deputy Director of Plans Richard Bissell. When the invasion failed, Hunt was named to outgoing CIA Director Dulles's personal staff. A year later, after Dulles was fired, Tracy Barnes appointed Hunt to be the CIA's first Chief of Covert Operations for Domestic Operations Division.[76] This was a division designed for projects unwanted elsewhere in the CIA.[77] By his own admission Hunt was active in recruiting and training anti-Castro Cubans in the Cuban Revolutionary Council (CRC). The second most important CRC base was in the same building where Guy Banister had his "detective agency" in New Orleans.[78]

When Mark Lane and CIA attorney Kevin Dunne in the *Spotlight* newspaper lawsuit deposed Marita Lorenz, who had been working as a contract agent with the CIA since 1959, she declared that she had known both Frank Sturgis (a CIA and Army Intelligence asset),[79] and E. Howard Hunt, since then. While portions of her story have changed over the years, some of her testimony may be useful:

Lane: Did you ever witness anyone make payments to him (Sturgis) for the CIA work which you and Sturgis were involved in?

Lorenz: Yes.

Lane: Who did you witness make payments to Mr. Sturgis?

Lorenz: E. Howard Hunt.

Lane: Did Mr. Hunt pay Mr. Sturgis sums of money for the activity related to the transportation of weapons (Nov. 1963)?

Lorenz: Yes.

Lane: Was there anyone else that you met (at the motel) other than Mr. Hunt?

Lorenz: Jack Ruby.

Lane: Is it your testimony that the meeting, which you just describe with Mr. Hunt making the payment to Mr. Sturgis took place on November 21, 1963?

Lorenz: Yes.

Lane: The last paragraph states that you stated that Sturgis was the so-called man on the grassy knoll. Had you ever said that to anyone?

Lorenz: I think he himself said that, too, whatever; yes.

Lane: Had you ever told anyone that Frank Sturgis was the man on the grassy knoll?

Lorenz: The House Assassination Committee.

Lane: How did you know that?

Lorenz: He told me.

Lane: Did he say that he shot President Kennedy?

Lorenz: He said that he was there. [80]

In 1975, Frank Sturgis, one of Hunt's fellow Watergate burglars, told Gaeton Fonzi that he felt others were pressuring Marita Lorenz to say things. Fonzi spoke with Sturgis' wife, Jan, who played a taped conversation of Lorenz speaking to Sturgis wherein she claimed that two government agents spoke with her. It remains unclear as to how Lorenz could have afforded her fashionable Manhattan Upper East Side apartment.

Let's briefly backtrack to Jack Anderson's 1971 columns on the CIA-mafia plots of 1960, involving Nixon but not JFK, which he asserted could have "backfired against JFK." These columns caused a series of memos within the Nixon White House. Attorney General John Mitchell quickly relieved CIA-mafia liaison Robert Maheu from testifying in exchange for his silence on the Castro story. Two Senate Watergate Committee staffers stated that White House concern about Anderson's article could have been a possible motivation for the Watergate break-in.[81] Anderson was invited to lunch by Richard Helms (DCI) to convince him to omit some sensitive material in his next book. Anderson remained steadfast, and then got targeted by the "Plumbers" Unit. G. Gordon Liddy and E. Howard Hunt, Jr. confessed during the Watergate hearings that they met with a CIA operative Dr. Edward Gunn, in 1972, to consider poisoning, drugging, or killing Anderson.[82]

Just prior to the break-in at the office of Daniel Ellsberg's psychiatrist, the CIA called Nixon aide John Ehrlichman to claim that their assistance had ended. Ehrlichman said that the CIA was assisting Hunt. Soon thereafter, Nixon renewed his pursuit of CIA records. He directed Ehrlichman to tell Helms to hand over "full file [on Bay of Pigs] or else."

After two meetings with Helms, Ehrlichman briefed Nixon on Helms' rationale for not sharing the documents. [Helms] said that his relationship with past presidents had been such that he would not feel comfortable about releasing some of the very, very dirty linen to anyone without talking it through with you, because he was sure that when you become a former president you would want to feel that whoever was at the agency was protecting your interest in a similar fashion. This is incredibly dirty linen ... Helms is scared to death of this guy Hunt that we got working for us because he knows where a lot of the bodies are buried, and Helms is a bureaucrat first and he's protecting that bureau."

When Helms arrived, Nixon pounded his desk and shouted: "the president needs to know everything! The real thing you need from me is this assurance: I am not going to embarrass the CIA, because it's important. I believe in dirty tricks." Ehrlichman notes quote Nixon as saying to Helms: "Purpose of request for documents must be fully advised in order to know what to duck; won't hurt Agency, or attack predecessor," Helms responded: "I regard myself as you know, really, as working entirely for you and everything I've got is yours.... Should I turn this [file] over to John? " It was, however, just a slim report by a Marine colonel who had been assisting the CIA during the Bay of Pigs. In his memoirs Nixon lamented that what Helms gave him was "incomplete ... the CIA protects itself even from presidents."

According to top White House advisors during the Nixon Administration, the Watergate tapes contain clear references to the role of the CIA, and Hunt specifically, regarding the assassination. The taped Nixon conversation, 6/23/72, with his Chief of Staff Bob Haldeman is revealing. Nixon: "Very bad to have this fellow Hunt ... If it gets out that this is all involved the Cuba thing would become a fiasco. It would make the CIA look bad, and it's likely to blow the whole Bay of Pigs thing, which we think would be unfortunate." Since the Bay of Pigs had occurred more than a decade before, how could it "become" a fiasco? The tape continues: "It tracks back to the Bay of Pigs, other leads run out to people who had no involvement ... except by contacts and connections, but it gets into areas that are liable to be raised." In Haldeman's book, *Ends of Power*, he asserts that the Bay of Pigs was a code word for the JFK assassination.

Nixon in his memoirs suggested that Hunt could have been a double agent, and he was perplexed as to why Hunt would deposit a $25,000 cashier's check into Watergate burglar Bernard Barker's bank account. Nixon feared this revelation would open the "Bay of Pigs" thing again, and directed Haldeman to pressure Helms that Watergate "might be connected to the Bay of Pigs, and if it opens up the Bay of Pigs could be blown.Helms and his deputy were quickly directed to the White House. Haldeman wrote of "Turmoil in the room, Helms gripping the arms of his chair, leaning forward and shouting, and The Bay of Pigs had nothing. I have no concern for the Bay of Pigs. Silence…" I was absolutely shocked by Helm's violent reaction. Haldeman reported back to Nixon that there was "no problem" any leads "that would be harmful to the government would be ignored."[83]

James McCord's actions during the Watergate break-in suggest intentional mistakes. McCord re-taped a garage-level door, which tipped off the police. Although McCord claimed to have removed the tape from the doors, actually several had been taped to stay unlocked. A few days later, all of McCord's papers were destroyed in a fire at his home, while a CIA contract agent watched. James McCord had known E. Howard Hunt since the 1950s and worked with David Phillips in a domestic operation in 1961 against the FPCC, (Fair Play for Cuba Committee), the organization Oswald joined in 1962.[84] McCord had a CIA clearance to work with the State Department, a Cryptographer clearance and a "Q" clearance with the Pentagon since 1948.[85]

In August 1972 CIA Director Helms instructed McCord to send a letter to his friend Jack Caulfield, a N.Y. detective who worked with the Plumbers, and who had looked into Oswald's Cuban connections for the FBI. McCord wrote, "If Helms goes, and if the Watergate operation is laid at the CIA's feet, where it does not belong, every tree in the forest will fall. It will be a scorched earth. The whole matter is at the precipice right now. Just pass the message that if they want it to blow, they are on exactly the right course."[86] McCord's letter to Judge John Sirica revealed portions of the Watergate cover-up which led to Nixon's resignation.

Later Nixon explained why he thought the CIA would cooperate in his plan to block the FBI from investigating Watergate. "We protected Helms from one hell of a lot of things."[87]

Haldeman argued that "After Kennedy was killed, the CIA launched a fantastic cover-up…. The CIA literally erased any connection between Kennedy's assassination and the CIA … in fact Counter Intelligence Chief James Angleton of the CIA called Bill Sullivan of the FBI, head of Bureau Division Five in charge of domestic counterintelligence, the number three man under Hoover, and rehearsed the questions and answers they would have to give the Warren Commission."[88] Sullivan was the FBI liaison to the U. S. Information Board, which was chaired by the DCI, (Director of the Central Intelligence) and had as its participants high level agency chiefs from the intelligence community. Recall that it was Sullivan who directed FBI Agent Hosty not to cooperate with the Dallas Police at 4:06 P.M. the day of the assassination.[89]

Incredibly, Sullivan was shot to death while hunting in Northern New Hampshire, November 9, 1977 – two days before he was scheduled to testify to the HSCA. Robert Daniels, a New Hampshire trooper with a .30/06 with a scope, shot him in the neck while he was in an open field. Other high-level FBI officers and former officers also died during this period.[90]

Hunt's possible position in the assassination plot could explain the considerable leverage he had over President Nixon during the Watergate Scandal. It could also explain his blackmail threats, and the receipt of at least $154,000 in "hush money." Nixon apparently was prepared to offer as much as $2 million, promises of executive clemency, and even efforts to "stonewall" the investigation. Questions linger about the airplane crash that killed Hunt's wife Dorothy, after she picked up an installment of the "hush money." It may also explain why Nixon's Presidential Counsel John Dean, by June 21, 1972, had E. Howard Hunt's safe opened, as well as why Dean destroyed portions of Hunt's notebooks on projects unrelated to Watergate. Nixon aide Ehrlichman told Dean to "deep six" certain of Hunt's materials. Ehrlichman and Dean then communicated their intention to acting FBI director L. Patrick Gray to destroy some of Hunt's files, which he did.[91] Gray recalls that Dean said that these files were "political dynamite" that "should not see the light of day." In December 2012, Dean told the *Guardian* that Hunt once told him that he gave the Watergate burglars a "sham...excuse" that they were searching for Cuban government support for the Democratic Party campaign.[92]

Many persons connected with the Warren Commission were hired by Nixon and his closest aides during Watergate. Former Warren Commissioner Gerald Ford, later as-President Ford, pardoned Nixon of any crimes.

Finally in 1975, the Senate Intelligence Committee Report on Foreign Assassinations established that "In August 1960, the CIA took steps to enlist members of the criminal underworld with gambling syndicate contacts to aid in the assassination of Castro.... Allen Dulles personally approved the plots, the two top planners for which were Richard Bissell and Colonel Sheffield Edwards." The CIA Director of Security assigned his Operational Support Chief, General James O'Connell, a former FBI man, who contacted Robert Maheu. Robert Maheu, the top aide to Howard Hughes, later the employer of General Cabell, was the initial intermediary who went to Mafia leader John Roselli to begin setting up the murder plots. Roselli used Sam Giancana, the Chicago mob boss, and Santos Trafficante, mob boss of Tampa, to help plan the attempts.

After the revelations of the Watergate hearings, Congress demanded further investigations of CIA activities. President Ford then assigned his newly appointed Vice-President Nelson Rockefeller to head an investigation into the roles of the FBI and CIA in the assassination of President Kennedy. With David Belin as Chief Counsel, one of the most imaginative of the Warren Commission counsel in ignoring information, this 1975 investigation attempted a strategic retreat. Then-Governor Ronald Reagan quietly sat on that Commission, which essentially reiterated the Warren Commission's findings. The Rockefeller Commission was then followed in late 1975 by a more assertive Senate Intelligence Subcommittee of the Church Committee on the CIA and FBI, conducted by Senators Gary Hart and Richard Schweiker. George H.W. Bush was then appointed Director of the CIA to replace William Colby, who was vulnerable to Senate questioning from the Watergate revelations. The media-CIA information that Bush withheld from that Senate Intelligence Subcommittee still warrants investigation.

George H.W. Bush was apparently working with the CIA back in 1963. An FBI memo quoted in a June 16, 1988, issue of *The Nation* showed that Bush, along with Captain William Edwards of the DIA, was briefed on "the attitudes of anti-Castro Cubans" by the FBI's W.T. Forsyth on November 23, 1963. This memo from J. Edgar Hoover notes that information was orally furnished to Mr. George Bush of the CIA.[93] Forsyth, now dead, ran the investigation of Martin Luther King in the Bureau's subversive control section. Some sources posit that Bush worked in the area of recruiting anti-Castro Cubans.

The initial reaction of Senator Church, chair of the Senate Select Committee on Intelligence, to the firing of William Colby and the naming of Bush as Director of the CIA, was to complain that it was part of a pattern of attempts by President Ford to impede the committee's investigation into assassination plots. This was an investigation with which Colby had been cooperating but which Ford seemed to be trying to suppress.

The notion of CIA-controlled anti-Castro Cuban shooters could be consistent with the testimony of witnesses in Dealey Plaza who stated that they saw people on the sixth floor with a Latino look or with dark complexions. Witness Arnold Rowland's testimony to this effect was not only disregarded, he was also discredited as a witness, due to an unusual investigation by the FBI. Witness Ruby Henderson gave a similar eyewitness account to the FBI, yet was never questioned by the Warren Commission. Further, a number of inmates on the sixth floor of the nearby Dallas County Jail, including John Powell, also saw two men with dark complexions on the sixth floor of the Dallas School Book Depository. Yet these witnesses went unexamined.

While evidence regarding the assassins, or "mechanics" as the intelligence agencies would refer to them, is uncorroborated, the ongoing role of the CIA relationship with Oswald and the anti-Castro Cubans is becoming more clear. Both current and former top CIA officials had motives, means and opportunity to generate and cover up the assassination. They were experienced in these matters. CIA media assets, along with FBI Director Hoover and Assistant Attorney General Katzenbach initiated a cover-up. This was greatly assisted by the CIA Deputy-Director Richard Helms and former CIA Director Allen Dulles on the Warren Commission. According to George Lardner's 1992 *Washington Post* interview with CIA Director Robert Gates, "the CIA has 250,000 - 300,000 pages of files pertaining to the assassination, including 33,000 on Oswald – most of them received from other agencies."

Following the assassination of President Kennedy, the CIA rapidly expanded its scope and methods. From 1964-1967 the CIA budget almost doubled. CIA agent Ralph McGehee, in *Deadly Deceits: My Twenty-five Years at the CIA* noted, "the period from 1964-1967 was the most active era for covert operations." By 1974 the CIA had spent over $1 billion for propaganda activities, according to Victor Marchetti.[94]

John McCone, former CIA Director and at the time a member of the board of ITT, told a Senate committee in 1977 that he had discussed getting rid of Allende in Chile when ITT's properties were at risk of nationalization. In Latin America in the 1960s, CIA programs were used to teach Latin American police and military officers torture, surveillance methods, bomb making, and counterinsurgency to be used against liberals as well as communists. CIA officers even ran background checks on employees of U.S.-based multinationals.

Aspects of CIA-military cooperation surfaced in the 1970s, which indicated building upon the close psychological warfare cooperation developed during WW II and expanded during the Cold War, Jack Anderson observed in his column, 4/21/71, that the "CIA never makes a move without the DIA keeping close surveillance. Colonel Fletcher Prouty described extensive CIA – DOD cooperation in *The Secret Team*, and in a story for *Gallery*, 12/15, "The Fourth Force."[95]

In the 1940's Washington came up with a war plan that called for the creation of mobile, airlifted forces with global capability that could be dispatched immediately to areas in the Soviet Union where damage and radioactivity would be minimal following nuclear war. These forces would have the ability to form a military government and establish a communications system in the devastated areas.

At that time the CIA was assisting with the administration and questioning of tens of thousands of defectors from Eastern Europe. The Agency had countless leads into Eastern Europe and some, if exploited properly, would even stretch into Russia. Thus the CIA came to take an active part in this super secret war planning. The Agency established a presence in the Pentagon and in the major United States military headquarters all over the world. The Agency had available hundreds of skilled former military men. Most retained their reserve status while others were given equivalent rank. Some CIA personnel carried letters of authority that gave them rank above that of any three-star general or admiral. The CIA was moving in.

The CIA, under Allen Dulles, put exceptionally able operatives into each military headquarters. The over-worked planning staffs found these extra hands ready and eager to help with any odd task. Such offices as subsidiary plans, special operation, psychological warfare, and unconventional warfare, began to spring up and they were all loaded with "helpful" CIA men.

The law that created the CIA specifically prohibited the agency from building up forces for clandestine operations. The Secretary of Defense in the late 1940's, Louis Johnson, had informed the Director of Central Intelligence that if the Agency needed military equipment it would have to pay cash for whatever it ordered. In those days the CIA budget was small, so this order effectively controlled any undue clandestine use of military equipment in foreign countries by the CIA.

President Eisenhower continued the policy. One of the old clandestine operations documents known as NSCID 10/2 was updated to NSC 5412/2 and it set forth limitations concerning the role the CIA could play in clandestine operations. In the margin of one of the master copies of NSC 5412/2 Eisenhower had noted in his own handwriting that nothing was to be given to the CIA; that would enable it to create a force that would permit it to operate over any lengthy period of time, or to be able to operate in such a manner that the operation would not remain "covert." In other words, clandestine operations were to be small and "one time" – so said Eisenhower.

But the CIA was gathering power as the Fourth Force. It began in Europe, where military maneuvers were to be held in Germany. All the armed forces, including the Fourth Force were to take part. Each service had its own equipment, established by the war plan.

As the exercise took shape and the military forces began to prepare for their roles, the CIA asked for weapons, trucks, radios, jeeps, and other items it would need to "play" Fourth Force. This was a problem. The military couldn't fund the CIA and the CIA could not go to Congress itself and ask for military equipment on a permanent basis. The military forces came up with a solution. The Army, Navy, and Air Force all created phony CIA cover units. Then they let the CIA "equip" these units according to the war plan and in time the CIA acquired a huge stockpile of military equipment, even aircraft, ostensibly for its formal Fourth Force mission.

Over the next few years the CIA amassed more and more equipment. Its phony Army, Navy, and Air Force units did not have the usual "equipment lists" or "tables of equipment" that other United States military organizations had; so the Agency had in effect an open-ended horn of plenty. Warehouses in England, Germany, Libya, Okinawa, and the Philippines, among others, were bulging with CIA-owned military hardware.

By the mid-1950s the CIA was ready to exploit its new capability. It turned its back on hard-core Soviet and East European targets and began to operate secretly in the realm of the Third World. (When it wanted to equip a rebel cabal to overthrow some government the CIA did not have to ask anyone for weaponry. It could ask the Air Force for planes to fly "training equipment" into some country; and the next thing anyone knew a well-equipped and well-financed rebel force would be rising up against an "enemy" government)

The United States armed forces, meanwhile, had no idea how much equipment the CIA had gleaned from them. I recall in 1962 telling Gen. Lyman L. Lemnitzer, the Chairman of the Joint Chiefs of Staff that the CIA had 'hundreds of military units and that they were all well armed and equipped." He said he didn't know it had become as extensive as that.

The CIA has the world's largest private airline. It is generally known as Air America and it is part of the Pacific Corporation. But Air America itself has on occasion had more than one hundred subordinate affiliates all over the world. At one time Air America had more than four thousand men each on two separate bases. Of course, these bases appeared to be U.S. military bases and needed protection, which in turn involved the assignment of regular military forces.

CIA cooperation with the Secret Service seems significant as well. The CIA Technical Services Division furnished the Secret Service with "gate passes, security passes, passes for presidential campaign emblems for presidential vehicles, and a secure 10 photo system." A 1963 CIA memo written by Technical Services Director Stanley Gottlieb was declassified after a lengthy FOIA lawsuit.[96] This could be the source of I.D. for those in Dealey Plaza who presented Secret Service I.D. to Dallas law enforcement. Research by Anna Marie Kuhns Walko and Larry Hancock indicates that anti-Castro Cuban and CIA asset, Roy Hargraves, had Secret Service credentials and was in Dallas in November of 1963.[97]

Joe Shimon, a CIA liaison to the mafia to develop a plot for the Castro assassination, had at one time shown his daughter Tony five or six different I.D. badges: The D.C. Police Department, U.S. Secret Service, U.S. Department of Justice, White House I.D. badge and a CIA badge.[98]

The fearful reactions of CIA asset Garret Underhill after the assassination raise still more questions. Underhill, an expert on weapons and covert warfare, had long worked on special assignments consulting for Henry Luce of Time-Life, as well as *Esquire, Colliers, Fortune* and the *Washington Post*. In the 1950's Underhill was associated with CIA asset Samuel Cummings, who supplied weapons to resistance groups in Eastern Europe through INTERARMCO, (Hancock, 320-321). Underhill confided to his close friends Bob and Charlene Fitzsimmons that "Oswald was a patsy … I've been hearing things…. They've killed the President…. A violent group within the CIA … they knew that he had learned…. The CIA is under enough pressure already without that bunch in Southeast Asia…"

Underhill also shared his fears with Asher Brynes, a contributing editor for *The New Republic*. He fled Washington DC, and quietly investigated the assassination. When Brynes visited Underhill in May 1964 she found him in bed, dead from a shot behind his left ear. The coroner ruled the death a suicide but Brynes disagreed. Underhill's wife would not talk with anyone, and refused to share his writings on the assassination.[99] *Ramparts'* reporting on Underhill, in June 1967, brought this to Jim Garrison's attention.

The extensive cooperation between banks and corporations with the CIA also clouds causality. Did elements of the CIA operationalize an agenda in America that they had used overseas? The Western Hemispheric Operations Division 3 of the CIA appears to have the strongest need of any regional desk to redact and continue to classify documents. The ARRB estimates that "about 50,000 pages" related to JFK's murder have not been released. The continued classification of documents regarding CIA officer George Joannides highlights the ongoing cover-up. Joannides coordinated DRE, a CIA-backed group that Oswald encountered as a Castro sympathizer. During the HSCA investigation, Joannides was conveniently selected by the CIA to be the liaison to the committee. Years later, HSCA chief counsel Robert Blakey declared, "I no longer believe anything the Agency [CIA] told the committee any further than I can obtain substantial corroboration for it outside of the Agency for its veracity.... We also now know that the Agency set up a process that could only be designed to frustrate the ability of the committee in 1976-79 to obtain any information that might adversely affect the Agency. Many people have told me that the culture of the Agency is one of prevarication and dissimulation and that you cannot trust its people, Period ... I am now in that camp."[100] In 2014 at the AARC conference Blakey called the CIA treatment of the HSCA "treacherous."

Newly declassified records show that Angleton and Helms covered up their roles regarding Oswald and misled the Warren Commission and the HSCA through memos: 1) CIA efforts to assassinate Castro in 1962-1963; 2) the date that the CIA first opened a file on Oswald; 3) what they knew about Oswald's contacts with the FPCC and DRE in New Orleans and; 4) what the CIA knew about Oswald's supposed "visit" to the Cuban Consulate in Mexico City. CIA routing memos indicate that early intelligence on Oswald (December 1959) went to Angleton and his aide Ann Egerter. Egerter opened a public file on Oswald (a 201 file) only after Oswald appeared on a State Department list of defectors to the Soviet Union. Why did Angleton withhold his knowledge of Oswald, from 1959 until after the assassination, and then lie about what he knew about Oswald?

Jane Roman, a senior CIA Counter-Intelligence officer whose husband was a personal assistant to Allan Dulles, was asked to respond to a routine inquiry, the first week of October 1963, from the Mexico City Station on Lee Oswald. Although she had worked recently with the file, she signed off on a report that she knew was inaccurate. When confronted with documents 31 years later by Jefferson Morley and Dr. John Newman she admitted "I'm signing off on something that's not true." When pushed by Newman, she also admitted that "to me it indicates a keen interest [in Oswald], held very closely on a need-to-know basis."

George Joannides' patron within the CIA was Greek-American Tom Karamassines, who was the trusted assistant to DDP Richard Helms. Karamassines was the most senior officer to sign off on a cable 10/10/63 regarding Oswald in Mexico City, which omitted the September 1963 FBI report on Oswald's encounters with DRE in New Orleans.

Much fog remains surrounding Oswald's movements in Mexico City. After the assassination of President Kennedy, CIA Mexico Station Chief Win Scott aggressively moved to have Sylvia Duran, a receptionist at the Cuban Consulate in Mexico City, interrogated by Mexican authorities. She was the Cuban Consulate in Mexico City, who met with someone claiming to be Lee Oswald, who wanted to get a transit visa for Cuba. Karamassines instructed Scott:

> Arrest of Sylvia Duran is extremely serious matter which could prejudice [U.S.] freedom of action on entire question of [Cuba] responsibility. (Morley, Jefferson. *The Ghost*. St. Martins Press, 2017 page 147).

Duran told Mexican authorities that the man who visited the Cuban consulate was blond with blue or green eyes, which could not have been Lee Oswald. Years later Duran was interviewed by the HSCA but that testimony remains classified. She told author Anthony Summers that she told the HSC that the man who visited the Cuban Consulate was about her size, five foot one and one half inches. Duran also stated that the pictures of Oswald after the assassination were "not like the man she saw here in Mexico City."

Did Karamessine's order to Win Scott, within a day of the assassination, show a strategy to protect their "freedom of action" to blame the assassination on Cuba? Since the CIA is heavily compartmentalized, and their decision-making process is generally as opaque as their cryptonyms, good researchers move slowly. Many CIA files are "soft files," in essence, files kept in a desk and possibly not documented in any documentary record. Some files, like Win Scott's legendary "P" files, were destroyed, while some files, like Angleton's got dispersed throughout the agency. Further, when DCI's Gates and later Tenet issued directives for Office of Security files to be surfaced, they did not surface. Only when the ARRB found an earlier citing of Oswald's files from the HSCA did most of the "missing" files surface.

Allen Dulles spent the evening of the assassination of President Kennedy at a top secret CIA facility near Williamsburg, Camp Peary, or "The Farm." According to former CIA agents, training at "The Farm" included assassinations. HSCA investigator Dan Hardaway stated that "The Farm was basically an alternative CIA headquarters where Dulles could direct ops."

Win Scott received the CIA's highest honor, the Distinguished Intelligence Medal, and he was planning to publish his memoir before his untimely death in 1971. Angleton knew that Scott's account of Oswald's visit to Mexico City would contradict the CIA's version in the Warren Report regarding Oswald's Cuban contacts. It was Angleton who visited Scott's widow two days after his death to express condolences and retrieve the unpublished manuscript.

In James Angleton's deathbed confessions to reporter Joe Trento about the founders of U.S. intelligence he said, "Outside of their duplicity, the only thing they had in common was an absolute desire for power... that you had to believe [they] would deservedly end up in hell."[101]

George Kennan, the architect of containment policy during the Cold War, lamented his sponsorship of CIA expansion in NSC 10/2. He told a Senate committee that it was "the greatest mistake I ever made." President Eisenhower characterized the CIA as a "legacy of ashes."

Historian Arthur Schlesinger Jr., a Kennedy advisor, remarked to Jim Garrison's old classmate Wilmer Thomas "that the CIA exacted its revenge on Kennedy has been an open secret since 1963."[102] Means, motive, and opportunity plus the mass media assets for a cover-up, existed for that CIA faction, probably led by Dulles, not McCone, along with the business, military, political, security, and mafia factions they seemingly cooperated with. This network may become clearer as we explore possible military cooperation as well as who gained (*cui bono*) in the rapid and extensive policy changes after the assassination of President Kennedy.

16

MILITARY COOPERATION?

Overgrown military establishments are under any form of government inauspicious to liberty, and are to be regarded as particularly hostile to Republican liberty.
— George Washington, 1796 Farewell Address

In the councils of government, we must guard against the acquisition of unwarranted influence, whether sought or unsought, by the military industrial complex. The potential for the disastrous rise of misplaced power exists and will persist. We must never let the weight of this combination endanger our liberties and democratic processes.
— Dwight Eisenhower, 1961, Farewell Address

Paint us with all our blemishes and warts.... We compete with... those who are our adversaries who tell only the good stories. But the things that go bad in America you must tell that also.... We are not afraid to entrust the American people with unpleasant facts.
— John Kennedy 1962, Voice of America

As John Kennedy took his presidential oath, the government had long been bitterly divided over the Cold War. By 1949 Secretary of Defense James Forrestal had endured "constant attack from the admirals and generals he supposedly commanded." Forrestal was "ground down by the bickering and backstabbing of the Pentagon" and suffered a nervous breakdown. President Eisenhower later stridently warned of a military industrial complex after eight years of battling with them. "Any person who doesn't clearly understand that national security and national solvency are mutually dependent, and that permanent maintenance of a crushing weight of military power would eventually produce dictatorship should not be entrusted with any kind of responsibility in our country."[1] Cold war zealots viewed themselves as practical patriots. Leading Republican Senator Barry Goldwater warned "Neutralism, coexistence, appeasement, pacifism, unilateral disarmament and the suspension of nuclear testing are all products of the enervating fog of fear that smothers the Free World." General Edwin Walker declared Eisenhower to be a dedicated communist, and General Lyman Lemnitzer supported Walker's efforts to politicize military culture.

General Curtis LeMay, Chief of Staff of the U.S. Air Force declared, "It boils down to this: Are we going to continue to permit areas of the Free World to be dragged behind the Iron Curtain and have the Free World get smaller and smaller and the communist controlled areas get larger and larger?" The military was indoctrinating the troops with anti-communist propaganda, the Defense Department was not backing the State Department, and dissident military leaders were giving stridently anti-communist speeches to the public. Kennedy responded by ordering that all public speeches by military officers be limited to military subjects, as well as to be non-political and consistent with the State Department. Henceforth, DOD reviewed military speeches. Kennedy then relieved General Walker of his command in Europe for accusing former President Truman of being "pink." The furious Pentagon reaction led to hearings by a Senate Select Committee.

The military closely cooperated with the CIA by the late 1950s. DCI Allen Dulles directed Colonel Fletcher Prouty to create a network of subordinate focal point offices in the armed services and throughout the entire U.S. government.[2]

Kennedy's conflicts with the military in philosophy and strategy accelerated after the Bay of Pigs debacle in 1961. The CIA and the Joint Chiefs of Staff, led by trusted Dulles ally General Lemnitzer, supported the failed invasion by anti-Castro Cubans. Castro's troops were waiting for them, no spontaneous internal uprisings occurred, and the invaders ran out of ammunition on the beach. The Joint Chiefs bellowed for air support but Kennedy refused.

When the invasion forces became trapped on the Cuban beaches, Kennedy convened an extraordinary meeting of civilian and military leaders. Admiral Arleigh Burke and General Lemnitzer joined Richard Bissell (CIA Covert Action Chief) in pushing Kennedy hard to provide air cover. Bissell and Burke saw the operation as so vital to national security that they had already broken the chain of command. Bissell instructed the Bay of Pigs brigade in Guatemala to mutiny against their U.S. advisors if the administration tried to block the invasion. Burke sent the U.S. aircraft carrier Essex and helicopter ship Boxer close to the Cuban coast. He disregarded Kennedy's order to keep U.S. ships fifty miles offshore.[3] Burke roared at Kennedy to engage a destroyer to "knock the hell out of Castro's tanks" but Kennedy stood his ground. Internal CIA memos indicate that the invasion was "unachievable, except as a joint Agency/ DOD (CIA/ Pentagon) action." There is no evidence that the CIA informed Kennedy of these analyses.

Charles Bartlett, the Washington correspondent for the *Chattanooga Times*, informed Allen Dulles that the Cubans knew of the invasion plans. Dulles was content to use the Cuban exiles as political fodder to catalyze a military invasion, and manipulate JFK into calling in U.S. forces.

The enraged Lemnitzer deplored Kennedy's caution as "pulling out the rug. It's absolutely reprehensible and almost criminal." General Lauris Norstad, Supreme Commander Allied Forces in Europe, told a friend that this was the worst American defeat "since the war of 1812." Admiral Burke viewed Kennedy as "inexperienced ... a very bad president ... who jeopardized the nation."[4]

Supreme Court Justice William O. Douglas thought that the event "seared Kennedy ... I think it raised in his mind the specter: Can the president of the United States ever be strong enough to really rule these two powerful agencies?"

General LeMay viewed Kennedy's administration as "the most egotistical people he had seen in his life ... they had no respect for the military at all." Years later, LeMay, in an oral history for the LBJ library, referred to the Kennedy crowd as "ruthless, vindictive ... cockroaches." General LeMay, "Old Iron Ass," was a gifted pilot and organizer, and had rapidly expanded the Strategic Air Command after assuming power in 1948. By the mid-1950s he oversaw 200,000 personnel from 55 bases, "an air force within an air force," and a "cocked gun." Eisenhower's strategy of massive retaliation "catalyzed" the massive modernization program, which as an economic stimulus made LeMay a welcome speaker in Congress.[5]

Time viewed LeMay as "the indispensable man in the Air Force's top field command," Life described him as "the toughest cop in the western world." *U.S. News & World Report* saw SAC as "the bastion of the West," while *Harper's* claimed the "SAC bomber crews have assumed the burden of America's international commitments ... LeMay ran SAC like Dulles ran the CIA, and both were dedicated cold warriors." Many in the press and Congress saw LeMay as ultimate judge for the readiness of American air power, and LeMay had absolute control over SAC war plans. He pushed one conviction at SAC, "we are at war."[6]

Many times Kennedy walked out on LeMay. Once JFK remarked "I don't want that man near me again.[7] After the Bay of Pigs Kennedy declared, "Those sons of bitches with all of the fruit salad sat there nodding, saying it would work."[8]

At the National Security Council meeting June 20th, 1961 General Lemnitzer and Allen Dulles proposed an official plan for a surprise nuclear attack on the Soviet Union. According to historian Arthur Schlesinger, Dean Rusk and McGeorge Bundy, Kennedy walked out in disgust in the middle of the meeting.[9]

JFK's conversation with his old friend Paul Fay, then Undersecretary of the Navy revealed:

> Now in retrospect, I know damn well that they didn't have any intention of giving me the straight word on this.... Looking back at the whole Cuban mess, one of the things that appalled me was the lack of broad judgment by some of the heads of the military services. They wanted to fight and probably calculated that if we committed ourselves part way and started to lose, I would probably give the OK to pour in whatever else was needed. I found out... that when it comes to making decisions I want facts more than advice.[10]

Perhaps the relationship between Kennedy and the Joint Chiefs "reached a new low," according to the *New York Times* military correspondent Hanson Baldwin, when Kennedy ordered the FBI to search the Pentagon offices to clarify the origin of press leaks on the Berlin Crisis. Kennedy was challenged by his top military envoy to Berlin, General Lucius Clay. According to David Talbot:

> Valentin Fallon, Soviet ambassador to West Germany, said Moscow later learned that Clay had ordered his tank commanders to knock down the Berlin Wall – As he had instructed them to practice doing it in a nearby forest, without informing the White House. If that had happened, Soviet troops would have returned fire ... and slid closer to the third world war. Clay responded to a call from Kennedy, "We're not worried about our nerves. We're worrying about those of you people in Washington."[11]

After one meeting with the Joint Chiefs during the Berlin crisis, a furious JFK left the room stating, "These people are crazy."[12] Kennedy used a Khrushchev-initiated back channel, KGB agent Georgi Bolshakov, to smuggle letters to press secretary Pierre Salinger. Clay's unauthorized provocation led to a standoff with Soviet tanks at "Checkpoint Charlie." Robert Kennedy Jr. recounted, "JFK promised that if Khrushchev withdrew his tanks within 24 hours, the U.S. would pull back twenty minutes later." Khrushchev did and so did Kennedy. Two weeks later, with tensions still running high, Khrushchev sent a second letter to JFK, "I have no ground to retreat further, there is a precipice behind [me]." Khrushchev was also powerfully pushed by his military and intelligence complex.[13] It is not clear if Kennedy ever trusted the CIA and Joint Chiefs of Staff again, and he formed his own private National Security Council.

Retired General Maxwell Taylor's investigation of the Bay of Pigs led to Kennedy appointing him as a special assistant. Taylor was given four aides, one from the Army, Navy, Air Force, and one from the civilian sector, and was asked to concentrate on Laos, Berlin and overall intelligence. Taylor and General Chester Clifton, the President's Army aide, would give him daily briefings on global events.

Taylor then developed a "little national security council" consisting of himself, Defense Secretary Robert McNamara, Secretary of State Rusk, Treasury Secretary Douglas Dillon, and White House Advisor McGeorge Bundy. Kennedy's restructuring had insulated him from the Joint Chiefs, and the National Security Council, which included the intelligence agencies. McNamara's restructuring at the Department of Defense to develop efficiency based on a corporate model served to further the isolation, distrust, and anger of the Joint Chiefs.

In March 1962 the Chairman of the Joint Chiefs, General Lemnitzer, proposed "Operation Northwoods," a covert strategy of false-flag operations to justify a U.S. invasion of Cuba. The plan recommended:

> 1. Harassment plus deceptive actions to convince the Cubans of imminent invasion
>
> 2. A series of well-coordinated incidents will be planned to take place in and around Guantanamo to give the appearance of being done by hostile Cuban force…
>
> 3. A 'Remember the Maine' incident could be arranged in several forms: We could blow up a U.S. ship in Guantanamo Bay and blame Cuba…
>
> 4. We could develop a Communist Cuban Terror campaign in the Miami area, in other Florida cities and even in Washington. Exploding a few plastic bombs in carefully closed spots, the arrest of Cuban agents and the release of prepared documents substantiating Cuban involvement also would be helpful in projecting the idea of an irresponsible government.[14]

Lemnitzer recommended that the Joint Chiefs run the program. President Kennedy rejected the plan. Less than a month later Lemnitzer and the Joint Chiefs pushed for a preemptive invasion of Cuba (4/10/62). Kennedy refused. By September 1962 he replaced Lemnitzer.

The widespread military dissent seeped into the mainstream media in the 4/23/62 issue of *U.S. News & World Report*.

> Military men no longer call the tunes, make strategy decisions and choose weapons. In years past, mainly military men ran defense of the U.S. – suddenly all that has changed, in the Pentagon, military men say they are being forced to the sidelines by civilians, their advice, either ignored or not given proper hearing in many vital military matters...

President Kennedy's restructuring of the military, the muzzling of military brass, the installation of a civilian authority, his policies in Berlin, Laos, Cuba and Vietnam, his rejection of Operation Northwoods, and his rethinking tactical nuclear weapons strategies in Europe, deepened dissent, distrust, and fear throughout the military brass. The Cuban Missile Crisis strengthened these sentiments.

By October 1962 hard evidence indicated that the Soviets were building missile sites in Cuba. The Joint Chiefs adamantly asserted that invasion was essential to America's security. Kennedy's decision to run a naval quarantine prevailed and succeeded, yet widening factions of the military now viewed him as a dangerous threat to national security. As popularized in the movie *Thirteen Days*, during the crisis Generals LeMay and Thomas Powers (SAC Commander) along with other in the top brass and the CIA pushed provocative behaviors and rules of engagement. These actions heightened tensions, seemingly seeking to promote a military confrontation with the Soviets.

Without the president's orders, the Air Force launched an unarmed ICBM, 10/28/62, from Vandenberg AFB. Meanwhile, SAC bombers were flying toward the Soviet Union and passing the established "turn around points," leaving the misperception of a first strike.

CIA officer William "Two Gun Bill" Harvey was coordinating three commando teams of sixty men each, sending them into Cuba for destabilization purposes, despite a presidential order to stop.[15]

General Powers raised the readiness of SAC to DEFCON-2, one step away from war, without the president's authorization.[16] Instead of issuing this order in code; he sent it in the clear to ensure that the Soviets could pick it up.[17] Powers argued at an Ex-Com meeting, "Restraint? Why are you so concerned with saving their lives? The whole idea is to kill the bastards..."

Even though the Joint Chiefs were actively engaged in contingency planning throughout the crises, they were not directly privy to Ex-Com (Executive Committee). In his memoirs General Maxwell Taylor acknowledged that some of the Chiefs distrusted him. Over the course of the crises he repeatedly volunteered to arrange more meetings with the President, but none of the Service Chiefs showed any interest. The Joint Chiefs were never consulted, nor were they given an opportunity to comment on the strategic implications of the settlement.[18]

Khrushchev recounted that during the Cuban Missile Crisis Robert Kennedy told Soviet Ambassador Dobrynin, "The President is in a grave situation. We are under very severe stress. In fact, we are under pressure from our military to use force against Cuba.... That is why the President is appealing directly to Chairman Khrushchev for his help in liquidating the conflict. If the situation continues much longer, the President is not sure that the military will not overthrow him and seize power. The American army could get out of control."[19] We will never know to what extent this statement was a bargaining ploy. Recall that less than two years later, October 14, 1964,. Soviet Premier Khrushchev was overthrown by a bloodless military coup d'état in the Soviet Union.

Kennedy confidante and Navy Undersecretary, Paul Fay, recalled in *The Pleasure of his Company* that JFK calmly spoke of the possibility of a military takeover if a third "Bay of Pigs" type of failure occurred to a young President. "The military would almost feel that it was their patriotic obligation to stand ready to preserve the integrity of the democracy, and only God knows what segment of democracy they would be defending if they overthrew the elected establishment."[20]

Daniel Ellsberg (Pentagon Papers) was then consulting with Air Force generals and colonels on nuclear strategy and recalled "fury" after the Kennedy – Khrushchev settlement. "There was virtually a coup atmosphere in Pentagon circles...hatred and rage..."[21] Tensions with the JCS were at an all-time high – the compromises and concessions were seen as excessive and unnecessary."

The unnerving trauma of the Cuban Missile Crisis accelerated Kennedy's push for a Nuclear Test Ban Treaty; however, none of the Joint Chiefs were consulted or taken to Moscow for the negotiations.

The bureaucratic debate regarding detection of nuclear tests was so contentious that the Air Force deliberately hid one of its experts. Carl

Kayser, a deputy national security advisor for Kennedy, recounted to author David Talbot that the Air Force hid Carl Romney, the man in charge of the Air Force operation monitoring Russian underground testing from Iran and Pakistan, from him.[22] The prestige and power of the JCS had never been lower than at the close of the Test Ban debate.[23] Nonetheless, the JCS again proposed in May 1963 that "the engineering of a series of provocations to justify military intervention [in Cuba] is feasible and could be accomplished with the resources available."

The president then confronted the JCS and the military industrial complex on the TFX contract. In the big battle for the $6.5 billion to produce a new tactical fighter jet between Boeing and General Dynamics, the multi-agency Source Selection Board had chosen Boeing. The Kennedy team, led by McNamara, instead awarded General Dynamics the contract on grounds of efficiency and politics (jobs in Democratic districts). Colonel Fletcher Prouty notes, "The decision sent tremors throughout the entire aeronautical industry and business world." McNamara told Congress that the services would no longer be allowed to develop their own weapons systems.[24]

The president's seminal speech at American University in June 1963, reflecting *Pacem in Terris* of Pope John XXIII, further widened the chasm with the Joint Chiefs.

> By defining our goal more clearly, by seeking to make it seem more manageable and less remote, we can help all peoples to see it, and to move irresistibly toward it. Our primary long range interest in Geneva, however, is general and complete disarmament desired to take place in stages … one major area of these negotiations where the end is in sight, yet where a fresh start is needed is in a treaty to outlaw nuclear weapons…
>
> I am taking this opportunity, therefore, to announce two important decisions in this regard.
>
> First: Chairman Khrushchev, Prime Minister Macmillan, and I have agreed with Moscow looking toward an early agreement on a comprehensive test ban treaty…
>
> Second: To make clear our good faith and solemn convictions on the matter, I now declare that the United States does not propose to conduct nuclear tests in the atmosphere so long as other states do not do so. We will not be the first to resume. Such a declaration is no substitute for a formal binding treaty, but I hope it will achieve one, nor would such a treaty be a substitute for disarmament, but I hope it will help us achieve it…

Genuine peace must be the product of many nations, the sum of many acts. It must be dynamic, not static, changing to meet the challenge of each generation. For peace is a process – a way of solving problems.... "When a man's ways please the Lord" the scriptures tell us, "He maketh even his enemies to be at peace with him," and are not peace, in the last analysis basically a matter of human rights.... While we proceed to safeguard our national interests, let us also safeguard human interests, and the elimination of nuclear arms is clearly in the interest of both.

But surely the acquisition of such idle stockpiles – which can only destroy and never create – is not the only, much less the most efficient, means of peace...

The United States, as the world knows, will never start a war. We do not want a war; we do not now expect a war. This generation of Americans has already had enough, more than enough of war, and hate and oppression. We shall be prepared if others will it. We shall be alert to try and stop it. But we shall also do our part to build a world of peace, where the weak are safe and the strong are just. We are not helpless before the task or hopeless to its success. Confident and unafraid we labor on – not toward a strategy of annihilation, but toward a strategy of peace.

Meanwhile, Kennedy reaffirmed his Cold War pragmatism in his soaring oratory and steadfast commitments to beleaguered West Berlin late in June 1963.

There are many people in the world who really don't understand, or say they don't, what is the great issue between the Free World and the Communist world. Let them come to Berlin. There are some who say that Communism is the wave of the future. Let them come to Berlin. And there are even a few who say that it is true that Communism is an evil system, but it permits us to make economic progress. Let them come to Berlin. Freedom has many difficulties, and democracy is not perfect, but we never had to put up a wall to keep our people in to prevent them from leaving us. All free men, wherever they may live are citizens of Berlin, and, therefore, as a free man, I take pride in the words 'Ich bin ein Berliner.'

Nonetheless, many Cold Warriors somehow perceived a dangerous lack of resolve.

U.S. News & World Report, 7/15/63 warned:

High officers in the Armed Forces are deeply concerned over what they say is an apparent trend in U.S. Defense policy to "disarm by example." They insist the present policies are weakening the U.S. position relative to Russia and will go on weakening it until a shift in the balance of power will threaten.

By August 5, 1963, an alarmed *U.S. News & World Report* declared:

It was over unanimous opposition of the Joint Chiefs of the country's military services, reported but withdrawn at the last moment, that the U.S. negotiated with Russia on a nuclear test ban treaty... the Joint Chiefs of Staff, on at least two occasions, filed written formal dissents to the administration's proposals for such a ban... Last spring the Chiefs of the Air Force, Army, Navy, and Marines told the Senate Armed Services Committee that testing in the atmosphere was absolutely vital. ... A major upheaval in U.S. defense is now taking place. A vast arsenal is being cancelled or dismantled. The Kennedy Administration is not responsible. The military establishment feels that the new strategy adds up to a type of intentional, one-sided disarmament ... the Joint Chiefs of Staff, often with unanimity, have opposed almost all of the cutbacks now being considered.

1. B-58 bomber – carries 15 megaton bomb at supersonic speed-scrapped.

2. RS-70 bomber – Air Force plan for the 1970's scrapped.

3. Thor missile – medium range – ordered dismantled after Soviet Union withdrew its missiles from Cuba.

4. Jupiter missile – bases in Turkey and Italy, 45 missiles ordered abandoned.

5. Skybolt eliminated – Britain complained.

6. Nike Zeus – "missile killer" Army requested to put this anti-missile around U.S. Cities. Requests refused over strong protest of General Maxwell Taylor, Chair Joint Chiefs of Staff.

7. Midas sky satellite killed.

8. Signposts indicating a cut of 1/3 of the Navy's 15 attack carriers.

9. Overseas bases, flying bases in England, Morocco, Spain, France, and Guam – shut down.

10. Atomic production – shut down 14 major plants manufacturing nuclear materials for weapons. The administration feels that the present stockpile is bigger than any demand can foresee.

11. Nuclear Test Ban Treaty. Military request to continue testing were set aside.

Kennedy built on his American University address with his 9/20/63. speech to the United Nations.

> Peace is a daily, a weekly, a monthly process, gradually changing opinions, slowly eroding old barriers, quietly building new structures... If this pause in the cold war merely leads to its renewal not its end – then the indictment of posterity will rightly point its finger at us all ... if we can now be as bold and farsighted in the control of deadly weapons as we have been in their creation – then surely this first small step can be the start of a long and fruitful journey... a desire not to bury ones adversary, but to compete in a host of peaceful arenas in ideas, in production and ultimately in service to all mankind.

Kennedy's plans to withdraw from Vietnam in late 1963 were perceived by the JCS as "an ominous repetition of the stalemate in Korea – A remote war, offering no sign of early resolution, consuming previous resources, and diverting attention from larger threats. Hence their support for a more aggressive, immediate strategy to confront the enemy directly with strong, decisive force."[25]

These actions, combined with clear signals from JFK to consider normalizing relations with Cuba, the development of the Alliance for Progress, as well as a draw-down in Vietnam, further confirmed to the Joint Chiefs and many in the top brass that Kennedy was a major threat to national security. Former JFK Special Advisor Arthur Schlesinger bluntly stated, "We were at war with the national security people."[26]

After the assassination of President Kennedy, the immediate reversals in foreign policy regarding Vietnam, Indonesia, and Cuba, the major cuts in the Alliance for Progress, the increased CIA covert actions, the increased reliance on his private NSC, the increased defense spending and the termination of negotiations for a Comprehensive Test Ban Treaty raise real circumstantial questions. The military's withholding, destruction, and loss of evidence related to the assassination; their use of questionable methods and procedures, before and after the assassination, open other perspectives regarding their role.

Just hours after the assassination the White House Situation Room, "Crown," contacted both Air Force One and Air Force 2 by radio to inform the many cabinet members aboard that "there was not a conspiracy... and that someone named Oswald who had been to the Soviet Union had done this." Recall that Oswald was not charged with the murder of the president until about seven hours later. Doug Horne, who served as chief counsel for the ARRB, wrote that the first version of these tapes released in the 1970s was edited and condensed. In 2011 a longer version (27 minutes longer) was found in the effects of Army Brigadier General Chester Clifton. Notably, the second version reveals evidence of General LeMay being urgently contacted by his aide Colonel Dorman, which allowed LeMay to break orders and attend the autopsy at Bethesda. A discussion unfolded regarding autopsy procedure as well as which caskets should be used. Further, since three wave-lengths were utilized in communication, and the Clifton tapes are only two hours and 22 minutes – where are the other 5 1/2 hours of tapes? Was Oswald framed from the outset? Radio communication for Air Force 1, the Strategic Air Command, and for the plane carrying the Kennedy Cabinet was through Collins Radio – whose founder, Art Collins, was a friend of General Curtis LeMay.[27]

Presidential historian Theodore White described the announcement in *The Making of the President 1964*, "on the flight the party learned that there was no conspiracy, learned of the identity of Oswald and his arrest." This was confirmed by a state department official, Robert Manning, who was on board the Air Force Boeing 707 with cabinet members returning to Washington.[28] White and reporter William Manchester seem to have had access to the unedited tapes, since they quote passages which are not on the existing tapes.

Recall that Dallas Mayor Earle Cabell's brother, CIA Deputy Director General Charles Cabell, was fired by Kennedy after the Bay of Pigs. General Cabell was Dulles's close ally and top assistant. His brother Earle collaborated on the Dallas motorcade route and was perhaps the first public official to assert that the assassination was "an irrational act ... of a deranged mind." (*Dallas Morning News* 11/23/63). Documents finally declassified in 2017 confirm that Earle Cabell was a CIA asset.

Oswald was trained to speak Russian at El Toro Marine base and appears to have been involved with Naval Intelligence. (ONI) He worked as a radar operator at Cubi Point in the Philippines, and then at the Marine Air Base in Atsugi, Japan, where the CIA ran a squadron of super-secret U-2 spy planes. He had a "Crypto" clearance – higher than "Top Secret." When Oswald was arrested in Dallas, he was carrying a military ID issued for those injured on active duty to insure medical coverage or for civilian employees overseas who needed military I.D. Similar I.D. was carried by U-2 pilot Gary Powers. This card was finally released by the FBI in December 1966 and was noted in former Dallas Police Chief Jesse Curry's book, *Assassination File*.[29] Oswald's card DD1173-N4 was issued 9/11/59, before his "defection" to the Soviet Union. Oswald's "defection" was immediately described as an "intelligence" matter by ONI, and over the years Marine G-2 (intelligence) sustained interest in Oswald. ONI, G-2, and the FBI have long collaborated, yet they failed to share files with JFK's head of the DIA, Air Force General Joseph Carroll as well as the Warren Commission.

Upon Oswald return to America he continued his contacts with retired military men and worked for high-level military contractors, when he could have been charged with treason and had his clearances revoked.

In late 1962 Oswald got work at Jaggars-Chiles-Stovall, a photo-lithographic firm in Dallas that did classified work for the U.S. Army Map Service (developed by Army Intelligence during WWII. Oswald had access to the Army Map Service, which also required a security clearance from the FBI.[30]

Oswald's friend George de Mohrenschildt had CIA and military connections. De Mohrenschildt's wife and daughter both said that George got Oswald the job at Jaggars. This job, like the job at Atsugi Base, required a "top secret" clearance. Some of the work appeared to be related to U-2 missions, some of which were over Cuba. During this period de Mohrenschildt introduced Oswald and his wife to the chief of industrial security for General Dynamics in Fort Worth, retired Air Force Colonel Max Clark, as well as Colonel Lawrence Orlov, and Admiral Chester Bruton, among others. De Mohrenschildt was a member of the Dallas Petroleum Club, which included George H.W. Bush, George Bauhe and D. H. Byrd – owner of the TSBD building. Byrd was an owner of LTV, a major Air Force contractor, which produced aircraft as well as electronic guidance systems for reconnaissance planes and missile systems. Byrd was friends with Generals Doolittle and LeMay as well as LBJ. In May 1963 LeMay awarded Byrd an Air Force award for his founding of the Civil Air Patrol, a volunteer military group that Oswald had joined as a teen.[31] De Mohrenschildt also introduced the Oswalds to Michael and Ruth Paine. In April 1963 de Mohrenschildt wrote a letter to LBJ, which contained the suggestion to meet with LBJ's security advisor Colonel Howard Burris. They did meet Burris, a Texas oilman, who was friends with General Charles Cabell and CIA officer Richard Helms. Burris retained his position as LBJ's top military aide after the assassination and rapidly made a fortune in the oil business. Later, Burris' son married the niece of the Shah of Iran, a close friend of Helms.

Burris' close friend, Colonel O'Wighton Delk Simpson, had worked with him politically for LBJ and in intelligence matters. Colonel Simpson's son, Delk Jr., testified to the HSCA, 7/18/78, that his dad was a "bagman" for the assassination. He recounted that he saw his father counting money that he had brought back from Haiti in the summer of 1963 that his father admitted was to be used in the assassination. Delk Jr's girlfriend, Didi Hess, stated that Colonel Simpson told her he became involved "because it was necessary." The HSCA did not investigate the story.[32] Delk Simpson was also close to the CIA, since he later served on the board of the Association of Retired Intelligence Officers, founded by David Phillips and Gordon McLendon.

Oswald worked in New Orleans for Guy Banister, who had been in the Office of Naval Intelligence before working with the FBI. Oswald also worked with David Ferrie and Clay Shaw, both with CIA connections, out of Banister's office surrounded by ONI, CIA and FBI offices in New Orleans. He later worked briefly in New Orleans for the William Reilly Coffee Company. Reilly was a CIA asset, and three of his employees moved on to NASA after Oswald departed.

Military connections to the motorcade, the investigation, and the autopsy also seem significant, yet they are still shrouded in mystery. The Fourth Army Group and its 112th Military Intelligence Group (MIG) headquartered at Fort Sam Houston in San Antonio worked with the 316th counter-intelligence unit. The 112th worked closely with the FBI and local police departments, police "red squads," the ATF and the Secret Service.

The HSCA, in Executive Session 4/20/78, formally questioned only Lt. Colonel Robert Jones, the operations officer, and Captain James Powell of the 112th. The unit commander and the commanders of the 316th, however, were not questioned.

Jones stated that, "We provided a small force – I do not recall how many but I would estimate between eight and twelve – during the presidential trip to San Antonio, Texas and then the following day, on his visit to Dallas. The Regions also provided additional people to assist ... James Powell was one of those liaison personnel ... he was a Captain and also wore civilian clothes and was assigned to Region 2 of the 112th MIG. He was on duty the day of the assassination."

Colonel Maximillian Reich and his deputy Major Jose Cabaya Sr. were never questioned but have publicly contradicted portions of Jones' testimony. They assert that the morning of the assassination, the 316th Counter-Intelligence Group at 4th Army Headquarters at Fort Sam Houston in San Antonio was told to "stand down" rather than report for duty in Dallas. This order superseded the "violent" protests of the unit commander Colonel Maximillian Reich, and Major Jose Cabaya Sr. CIA-Pentagon liaison Colonel Fletcher Prouty wrote, "Who has the power to make this kind of call? Only someone with [military code] knowledge can make the call and use such code words that are needed to 'stand down' an entire army unit."

The morning of the assassination, an army intelligence agent, Edward Coyle, met with FBI agent James Hosty and ATF agent Frank Ellsworth. Hosty, whose name appeared in Oswald's notebook, reportedly described Oswald as "a member of the Communist Party ... capable of committing the assassination"[33]

Was it a coincidence that Secret Service agent Winston Lawson, who was partially responsible for changing the parade route in Dallas, had been an Army counterintelligence agent as well as Special Agent in Charge (SAIC) of the Liaison Division? Lawson met with the Dallas Citizen's Council to plan the trip and insisted on a motorcade. Lawson also met with Dallas Police Captain W.P. Gannaway, head of the Dallas Police Special Service Bureau, who was a member of the Army Intelligence Reserve. Gannaway's secretary was reported by an out of town police chief to be "closely connected" to Jack Ruby.[34] Gannaway's subordinate, Lt. Jack Revill, worked on "espionage and subversive activities" in Dallas in conjunction with the FBI and military intelligence, the Law Enforcement Intelligence Unit (LEIU) being one conduit. The pilot car of the motorcade was driven by Deputy Police Chief George Lumpkin, also a member of the local Army Intelligence Reserve Unit. Lumpkin, a friend of Jack Crichton, later told the HSCA that he had been consulted by the Secret Service regarding motorcade security, and that his input had ruled out another route.[35] Also in the pilot car was Lieutenant Colonel George Whitmeyer, the commander of all Army Reserve units in East Texas, although Whitmeyer was not on the approved police list to ride in that car. Chronically short-handed, the Secret Service routinely worked with Army intelligence.

SA Lawson also met with the Dallas Fire Department, the Trade Center employees, the Sheriff's Deptartment and the Texas Department of Safety, yet nowhere in the "after action" reports of these agencies is there any mention of the 112th or the 316th.

Lt. Colonel Jones "believed" he opened a file on Oswald in mid-1963 after Oswald's arrest in New Orleans. The HSCA investigation determined that the 112th Military Intelligence Group office in Dallas had possessed a file on "Harvey Lee Oswald," who was "procommunist," had traveled to Russia, and had been involved in pro-Castro activities. This military file gave Oswald's address as 605 Elsbeth, the same error found on Dallas Police Lt. Jack Revill's list.

After the assassination, Jones called FBI SAIC (Dallas) Gordon Shanklin and summarized the military documents on file for A.J. Hidell (Oswald's alias). The "after action" reports from military intelligence agents who performed liaison functions with the Secret Service in Dallas were maintained in Oswald's file. To Jones' knowledge neither the FBI nor any law enforcement agency ever requested a copy of the military intelligence file on Oswald. Remarkably, neither the FBI, Secret Service, CIA, nor the Warren Commission ever interviewed him. Jones told the HSCA that no one ordered him to withhold information. The Department of Defense never gave Oswald's military intelligence file to the Warren Commission despite repeated requests. They could not share it with the HSCA since it was "routinely destroyed" in 1973.

Captain James Powell initially maintained that he was "off" the day of the assassination, and that he just decided to view the motorcade and take pictures. Powell, a trained army intelligence photographer, just happened to take several photos of Dealey Plaza at the time of the assassination and of the TSBD seconds after the shooting.[36] He claims to have rushed up to the sixth floor with Dallas sheriffs. Powell told researcher Penn Jones that he "worked with the sheriff's deputies at the TSBD for about six or eight minutes." None of his other photos have been published and the government did not interview him in depth.[37]

After the assassination, Dallas Police Lieutenant Jack Revill drove an "Army intelligence man" or OSI (Air Force Intelligence) agent back to his office from the TSBD,[38] shortly before he met FBI agent James Hosty. This was shortly after Revill had organized the search of the TSBD, which discovered the Mannlicher-Carcano, where Powell and Deputy Chief George Lumpkin were located.[39]

On the evening of the assassination Lieutenant Revill's assistant, a detective from Dallas criminal intelligence, Don Stringfellow, falsely notified 112th Military Intelligence Group that Oswald revealed he had defected to Cuba in 1959 and that he was a card-carrying Communist. Jack Crichton, Commander of the 488th Military Intelligence Detachment, called Ilya Mamantov, from a CIA-subsidized "church," to head "a local Army Intelligence Unit"[40] to translate for Marina Oswald. Coincidentally two minutes later, Deputy Chief Lumpkin, a member of the Army Intelligence reserve, also called Mamantov with the same request.

FBI agent and former Marine officer, Oliver "Buck" Revell, assisted the FBI investigation of Oswald's military connections after the assassination. He conducted a detailed inquiry into Oswald's military background at the Marine Corps facility in New River, N.C., although there is no record of Oswald being there. Then after advancing to the number three man in the FBI, Revell became in charge of criminal investigations and to follow up on the findings and recommendations of the HSCA. By 1991, he became SAIC of the FBI's Dallas Division with the responsibility to conduct further investigation into the Kennedy case as warranted. He was a reliable guardian.

The HSCA however, concluded that the military's "routine' destruction of the Oswald's military files "extremely troublesome," especially when viewed in light of the Department of Defense's failure to make the file available to the Warren Commission. Despite the credibility of Jones's testimony, without access to this file, the question of Oswald's possible affiliation with military intelligence could not be fully resolved. Congressman Richardson Preyer, Chair of the HSCA, expressed profound frustration at the destruction of these files when I interviewed him in 1990.

Some FBI files from 1959-1964 were somehow held at the U.S. Army Investigative Records Repository, until the HSCA requested files (classified Secret) on Loran Hall. Hall was an associate of General Walker (fired by JFK) and oilman H.L. Hunt in a range of radical right causes. General Walker was also closely associated with Guy Banister, Joseph Milteer, Lt. General Pedro Del Valle (ret.) and Colonel William Gale (ret.).

The ARRB experienced similar frustrations. The ONI twice informed the ARRB that they had no relevant files. The third attempt by the ARRB staff seemed promising. They met with an ONI team directed by Lieutenant Commander Terri Pike, who was somehow belatedly informed on March 7, 1997, that they were tasked to turn over relevant files. Pike dove into the job and had identified where the record collections were held. She reported to the ARRB within 2 months that her team had already located about 125 cubic feet of documents related to the ARRB requests and that ONI had identified about 950 cubic feet of records which might be related. Pike told ARRB staffers 4/21/97, that most of the relevant records were discovered "by accident" since they were misfiled in boxes they should not have been in. When the ARRB next contacted Pike, she informed them that she had been "relieved of her leadership on the project." Pike then faced court-martial charges over "fraudulent" travel expenses. The final certification of compliance to the ARRB stated that the ONI was unable to find any relevant file for the Director of ONI from 1959-1964. ONI also acknowledged that there were additional ONI records which were not reviewed for assassination records, but that they would be reviewed under Executive Order 12958.

Deputy Chief of the Secret Service, Paul Paterni served in the OSS during WW II in Milan, Italy, with James Angleton, CIA Counter Intelligence Chief, and Ray Rocco, his loyal assistant at CIA-CIC. Paterni was active behind the scenes with evidence after the assassination. Paterni's good friend, Chief Inspector Michael Torina, noted that "Paterni [also] served in the military reserve from the late 1930's through the mid-1960s.[41] Paterni's assistant, and later his replacement, N. Jackson Krill, was also a former member of the OSS. There is no report of the Secret Service calling for support in Dallas.

Within this context, military actions surrounding the autopsy seem more problematic. Why was the regular autopsy doctor at Bethesda Naval Hospital, Dr. Karnei, told by Admiral Gallaway that he would not perform the autopsy? Why two days afterward did Dr. Karnei sign a pledge to not talk about the autopsy for 10 years? Why after 10 years was the time limit extended for another 15 years? Why was Dr. Karnei not questioned by the Warren Commission? Why did Commander James Humes burn his notes on Kennedy's autopsy on November 24, 1963? Why were Admiral Kenney and Admiral Galloway, General White and possibly General LeMay, and the Secret Service in the autopsy room at Bethesda Naval Hospital? Does this account for the variance of the Bethesda medical reports, with those descriptions of doctors from Parkland Hospital? Why were qualified civilian experts excluded from examining the body? Why was the location of the back wound relocated to the lower neck region? Why are the two reports regarding the removal of an additional bullet from the body not integrated into the final reports? Why, contrary to standard medical practice, wasn't the brain sectioned during supplemental examination two weeks later? Why did Colonel Pierre Finck testify to New Orleans D.A. Jim Garrison in 1969 that he was told by Admiral Galloway not to examine the neck wound during the autopsy? Why did they deny Colonel Finck the opportunity to examine the clothing? Why hasn't Admiral Burkley, the President's private physician, who was present at the autopsy, ever been called to testify?

Similarly, the role of Colonel William C. Bishop, a Military Intelligence aide to Generals MacArthur and Willoughby, who worked with the

CIA Executive Action Operation 40, remains perplexing. By 1963 Bishop worked under CIA officers Desmond FitzGerald and David Phillips organizing anti-Castro groups in Miami. Colonel Bishop admitted to reporter Dick Russell that they were aware of the assassination plot to kill the president. Bishop claimed that Jimmy Hoffa arranged the assassination through CIA operative, and anti-Castro Cuban, Rolando Masferrer[42] "or that's what he was to say, or that was what he was told to say."

Another anti-Castro Cuban, Felipe Vidal Santiago, who claimed that he worked with Bishop, recounts events differently. When Vidal Santiago was arrested by Cuba for acts of sabotage in 1964, he recalled Bishop's actions in November of 1963.[1] Santiago remembered Bishop inviting him to Dallas to meet wealthy people financing anti-Castro actions. Santiago said that he had been informed of Kennedy's effort to open dialogue with Castro in December of 1962, and he alerted his cohorts of this betrayal.[43]

Dick Russell said that Bishop claimed that he was involved with Operation 40 in Mexico City assassinations and propaganda, and that he had visited Mexico City "two or three times in 1963." [44]

Recall that Gene Wheaton, military intelligence operative (OSI and Army CID) told ARRB investigator Anne Buttimer that senior CIA office Carl Jenkins had told him that Jenkins had trained the Cubans that killed Kennedy. Jenkins was a paramilitary organizer for the Bay of Pigs and AM/WORLD, and, along with Wheaton, another CIA-military nexus. Unfortunately, the ARRB somehow did not fully investigate Wheaton's assertions.

Also, recall that Antonio Veciana, co-founder of the violent anti-Castro Alpha 66, had been an asset of both the CIA and U.S. Army counter-intelligence starting in October 1962. Veciana was assigned code number DUP 748 on 1/30/63. In September of 1963, in Dallas, Veciana saw Oswald meeting with CIA officer Maurice Bishop, a man that he and others have identified as David Phillips. Phillips was in charge of psychological warfare – an expert on propaganda operations.

Why has Paul O'Connor, the medical assistant in Bethesda during the autopsy, stated that Admiral Burkley gave the order to Lt. Colonel Finck not to probe the back wound? Four days after the autopsy, why did Admiral Kenney, the Surgeon of the Navy, warn those involved in the autopsy not to discuss the proceedings with anyone, lest they be subject to court-martial? Why did Colonel Finck receive directives by telephone, from the White House and through the Naval Medical School in Bethesda, not to discuss the subject beyond the Warren Report, in September

1964?[45] Why did Colonel Finck's autopsy notes go missing? Why was Dallas FBI agent James Hosty ordered by Bill Sullivan, the FBI liaison to the National Security Council, not to cooperate with the Dallas police in their questioning of Oswald, less than three hours after Oswald's arrest? Why did the Army "routinely" destroy many of their files on Oswald in 1973, a matter the HSCA found "extremely troublesome?"

Photographic evidence suggests that General Ed Lansdale might have been in Dealey Plaza during the assassination. Col. Fletcher Prouty and General Victor Krulak, who both worked with Lansdale, identify him as being there. Krulak wrote Prouty, "The haircut, the stoop, the twisted left hand, the large class ring, it's Lansdale. What in the world was he doing there?" Lansdale, an expert in psychological warfare, worked closely for almost a decade with Allen Dulles, and headed Operation Mongoose. His military title was largely a cover.[46]

Why was Lt. Commander William Pitzer, head of the Navy Audio Visual Unit at Bethesda Hospital, who took the autopsy photographs, and had a 16 mm videotape of the autopsy, visited periodically by military personnel and told never to discuss what he had seen during the examination – for reasons of national security? Bethesda X-ray technician Jerol Custer, who was present at the autopsy while Pitzer was filming it, has stated that military men "flipped out" upon seeing him filming.[47] In 1966 Lt. Commander Pitzer was due to retire after 28 years in the service, to start a $45,000 a year job with network television, and write a book about his experiences. Strangely, on October 29, 1966, Pitzer was found dead from what authorities said was a self-inflicted wound to the head with a .45 caliber pistol. FBI tests indicated that: 1) no powder burns were found on Pitzer's head; 2) the paraffin test "reflected no substance characteristic of, or which could be associated with, gunpowder or gunpowder residue"; 3) the latent finger prints in the room where Pitzer's body was found did not match either the Navy investigators or Pitzer.[48] Mrs. Pitzer was refused access to the autopsy of her husband by the Navy. She was told by several captains and an admiral not to talk about it.

ARRB releases in 1998 included documents showing that the HSCA had tested the Navy camera, which was supposed to have taken JFK's autopsy photographs, and it failed the authenticity tests. In a sworn interview with Sandra Kay Spencer, who developed the JFK autopsy photos in the archives, she stated that the photos are not the ones she developed. Autopsy photographer John Stringer similarly disavowed the authenticity of the supplemental autopsy brain photographs[49] that he was supposed to have taken. Autopsy witness Dr. Karnes stated to the ARRB that he was sure he remembered an autopsy photograph taken with a probe in President Kennedy's body. Robert Knudsen, the White House photographer involved with the processing of the autopsy pictures, was frustrated that no pictures with probes were in the Archives. His interview with the HSCA was suppressed, and released by the ARRB. Also, an internal CBS memorandum published by the ARRB noted that Dr. Humes told a CBS employee that a photo was taken of the body with a probe in it.

Regarding photography, recall the cooperation between the Secret Service, the NPIC CIA lab, and USN Captain Pierre Sands with the treatment of the Zapruder film. The CIA-Military nexus with the NPIC lab, as well as the Hawkeye Works lab was used in the cover-up of critical evidence.

Lt. Colonel Daniel Marvin asserts that in 1965, as a Green Beret captain trained for assassinations, he was assigned by Colonel Clarence Patton to meet a "Company" man for a mission to assassinate a Naval Officer before his retirement – a Lieutenant Commander William Bruce Pitzer. Marvin refused the mission and states that Captain David Vanek spoke next with the "Company" man. Lt. Colonel Marvin has never been able to get in touch with Captain Vanek, and the Navy denies that Vanek ever served.[50] Marvin, however, saved old military orders which indicated that he and Vanek did indeed serve together.

In December 1963 Marvin was a specialist training on assassinations at Fort Bragg where he claims the assassination of President Kennedy was discussed to exemplify a classic program of assassination. Maps of Dealey Plaza were used to show crossfire, and a cover-up plan was discussed. Marvin's book, *Expendable Elite*, reveals his CIA assignment to assassinate Prince Sihanouk, the Crown Prince of Cambodia in 1966. When Marvin aborted the mission, the CIA sent an ARVN force to destroy Marvin's Special Forces camps for standing up to the CIA.

The evening of November 23rd a desperate Oswald seemingly tried to call John Hurt in Raleigh, N.C, formerly of Army Counterintelligence in WWII. Hurt didn't answer. Two telephone operators working the switchboard, which controlled, among other Dallas city offices, the jail, perhaps point to another piece of the puzzle. Mrs. Alveeta Treon was told by co-worker Mrs. Louise Swinney that their supervisor told them to assist law enforcement officials in listening to a call that Lee Oswald would be making soon. Two men that Ms. Treon thinks may have been Secret Service agents entered the switchboard area. At about 10:45 p.m. the call came through and Mrs. Swinney handled it and wrote down the number Oswald was calling.

Mrs. Treon said that Mrs. Swinney disconnected Oswald without trying to put the call through. Mrs. Swinney left work at 11:00 pm and Mrs. Treon retrieved the paper notation of Oswald's call. Two John Hurts resided in Raleigh; John D. Hurt was possibly the intended recipient, according to HSCA chair Robert Blakey. Former Secret Service agent Abraham Bolden, then duty officer for the Secret Service in Chicago that weekend, recalls being asked to do a run down on Hurt or "Heard" the evening of 11/23/63. Was Oswald calling a "cut out" for assistance?[51]

Chairman Earl Warren consulted with the Defense Department to secure some historians to write the final Warren Report. Dr. Alfred Goldberg from the Air Force and Mr. Cokery with the Army were recommended by Dr. Rudolph Winnacker, a former analyst for the OSS and then Chief of the Historical Division of the Pentagon. Goldberg and Cokely were major authors of the final report – a report that clearly does not reflect the 26 volumes of Warren Commission Hearings.

Rogue factions of the military and CIA, in both Cuba and Vietnam, undercut some presidential policies. By 1963 Kennedy had both ordered anti-Castro Cubans in Alpha 66 to cease their attacks on Cuba and he had secretly appealed to Henry Luce, who was a major financial backer, yet the attacks were stepped up. Indeed the raids were being tolerated by mid-level ranks of the Navy, and the U.S. Army was using Alpha 66 and DRE (Cuban Student Directorate) operationally.

Oswald appears to have been a shared asset of Marine G-2, ONI, the CIA (Counter-Intelligence) as well as the FBI. Oswald probably had little idea of who ran him and why. A shared asset could provide additional insurance for a thorough cover-up.

Kennedy got an early copy of the book *Seven Days in May,* which portrayed a military coup in America and he encouraged Hollywood director John Frankenheimer to turn the book into a movie. According to Arthur Schlesinger, "The president said the first thing I'm going to tell my successor is "Don't trust the military men – even on military matters."[52] The Defense Department requested a copy of the script for "consideration," as military censors called their process. Frankenheimer refused. Kennedy then cooperated with the filming, which included scenes at the White House and staged riots on Pennsylvania Ave.

President Nixon also confronted deeply distrustful anti-communist Joint Chiefs, who disagreed with the ABM and SALT Treaties, opposed his withdrawal from Vietnam, and his openings to the Soviet Union and China. National Security Advisor Henry Kissinger was viewed as soft on communism, and they opposed the risky support for Pakistan against India which involved nuclear weapons. Admiral Elmo Zumwalt, former Chief of Naval Operations, wrote that the Nixon Administration was "inimical to the security of the United States. The Administration "reflected Henry Kissinger's world view: that the dynamics of history are on the side of the Soviet Union ... (In Watch PXIV) Zumwalt also feared their "deliberate, systematic efforts to conceal their real policies about the most critical matters of national security."

One response from the Joint Chiefs was to spy on Kissinger. Admiral Moorer, the Chair of the Joint Chiefs of Staff, directed Rear Admiral Robert Welander and Rear Admiral Rembrant Robinson to spy on the NSC. Navy Yeoman, Charles Radford, the liaison between the NSC and Joint Chiefs, stole more than five thousand pages of highly classified documents from late 1970 through 1971. Radford stated that his "superiors" believed that Kissinger's foreign policy was "catastrophic ... a conspiracy of the CFR and the Rockefeller family to win Soviet cooperation in creating Rockefeller domination over the world's currency."[53]

When columnist Jack Anderson revealed "Nixon's Tilt toward Pakistan," the White House knew that the leak must have come from an NSC meeting of the Washington Special Action Group (12/3/71). Pakistan was being used as a pathway for secret negotiations with China. Revisionist scholarship clarified the context for the deepening of distrust. The Pakistani relief to East Pakistan after the devastating cyclone of 1970 proved far from adequate, and the East Pakistani candidate won the national election weeks later. When West Pakistanis would not accept the results, the East Pakistanis generated a national strike. West Pakistan invaded and killed some 200,000, while around 6 million fled to India. Nixon remained silent to what the U.S. consulate saw as "Selective Genocide." India prepared for war to stop the refugee crisis but Pakistan attacked pre-emptively.[54] Nixon secretly sent weapons to Pakistan after it invaded India. He circumvented Congress and law by using intermediary countries. Nixon then moved the 7th fleet into the Bay of Bengal, which provoked the Soviets to move their fleet to protect their ally India – rapidly escalating a regional crisis.

The White House investigation of the NSC leak led to uncovering the JCS spy operation. Admiral Robert Welander later admitted to Nixon aide John Ehrlichman that he had used Radford and had delivered the documents to the Chairman of the Joint Chiefs Admiral Thomas Moorer. Welander also implicated General Al Haig. The so-called Pentagon's man in the White House, Haig, then Kissinger's deputy, worked with Welander and Robinson but said nothing.[55] Nixon shrewdly decided to forego an election year public investigation of this espionage, which would have been embarrassing and impolitic.

Admiral Elmo Zumwalt wrote that Nixon and Kissinger were almost treasonous and that Kissinger was a Soviet sympathizer. Retired Admiral Chester Ward claimed that Kissinger was a Soviet agent. Nixon also angered many in the CIA when he fired DCI Richard Helms during Watergate, and charged his appointee James Schlesinger to "clean house." Schlesinger fired more than 1000 members of the clandestine service.[56]

Military connections also surfaced during the Watergate scandal as well. Watergate burglars Frank Sturgis and James McCord had previously worked with Army Intelligence as well as for the CIA. *Washington Post* reporter Bob Woodward learned that McCord in 1971 was a member of an Army Reserve unit in Washington attached to the office of Emergency Preparedness. A fellow reservist said McCord was tasked to compile lists of "radicals" and develop contingency plans for censorship of the news media and the U.S. mail in time of war.[57] McCord, recruited to the Plumbers by his old CIA colleague E. Howard Hunt, had worked with the Pentagon since 1948 with a top secret "Q" clearance (When a C-117 cargo plane was shot down over Azerbaijan in 1958 for spying, McCord was tasked to debrief the passengers).[58] Recall that McCord headed security for the "Plumbers," yet somehow taped a door horizontally in the Watergate hotel, which directly led to the police discovery of the operation. During the trial McCord was outspoken regarding the innocence of the CIA. Watergate burglar and CIA asset Eugenio Martinez has written that he thought their arrest in the Watergate Hotel was a set-up.

Bob Woodward's military background and connections are noteworthy. He was first commissioned as an ensign on the USS *Wright*, "the floating Pentagon," the National Security ship, where the Cabinet and the President could meet in the event of a nuclear war. Woodward had a "crypto" clearance. Admiral Welander, the leader of the JCS liaison office at the NSC, had been Woodward's commanding officer on the USS *Fox*. Admiral Moorer, chair of the JCS, was Woodward's commander at the Pentagon where Woodward worked as the Communications Duty Officer, directing messages to the NSC and the White House. Later, while working at the White House, Woodward briefed General Haig on the developments at the Pentagon. Woodward never revealed these relationships to his readers.[59]

General Al Haig, Nixon's domineering chief of staff, consistently misled Nixon. Haig's aide, Alexander Butterfield, who alerted the Congress to the existence of the White House tapes, was a former high-level briefing officer for Naval Intelligence. Bob Woodward was also an old military friend of Butterfield and White House lawyer Fred Buzhardt.[60] According to Nixon special assistant Steven Bull, Haig once declared, "If you think that the president can run the country without Al Haig ... you are mistaken."[61] Tony Ulasewicz, who provided private security for Nixon wrote, "Haig was turning against the President in the final days before Nixon resigned ... Haig ordered the U.S. Army's Criminal Investigation Command (CIC) to conduct a high priority investigation" to determine if Nixon accepted cash gifts from Asian leaders or from organized crime.[62]

Haig told Nixon's aide Charles Colson, "If the President's going to be impeached, better he go down himself, than take the whole intelligence apparatus with him." Perhaps it was no coincidence that General Haig pressured Nixon to resign, after threatening Vice President Spiro Agnew to "Go quietly or else."[63]

Many authors think Haig was one of the sources of "Deep Throat," along with FBI associate director Mark Felt, and CIA asset Bob Bennett. Bennett's PR firm (Robert Mullen Company) was a CIA front which employed E. Howard Hunt. Bennett's CIA case officer, Martin Lukoskie, wrote a Memorandum for the Record to the House Armed Services Committee's 1973, "Inquiring into the Alleged Involvement of the CIA in the Watergate and Ellsberg Matters," which admitted tasking Bennett to "kill off any revelation" of CIA involvement in the Mullen Company. The rest of the Memorandum attempted to convince reporters to not pursue a "Seven Days in May" scenario that included the CIA. CIA officer Lukoskie's boss, Eric Eisenstat, wrote in a memo to CIA DDP that Bennett "has been feeding stories to Bob Woodward of the *Washington Post* with the understanding that there is no attribution to Bennett'... [64] The release of remaining Watergate documents might still clarify which factions generated what was probably a palace coup.

Similarly, the remarkable number of missing military and CIA files could still clarify the assassination of President Kennedy. Not only did Army Intelligence "routinely" destroy their files, but the NSA claims that none of their intelligence documents contain anything significant to the JFK assassination. The Office of Naval Intelligence claims that they have no records for the ONI Director from 1959-1964. Eighteen staff "D" CIA dispatches to the NSA are not retrievable, because supposedly they lack a file number. The ONI Defection File, identified as an assassination record by Navy Commander T. Pike, was never turned over to the National Archives. The Office of Special Investigations (OSI) military intelligence review of Oswald's State Department file is missing. Records of the Dallas-based 488th Military (Strategic) Intelligence Detachment unit histories and rosters are missing, as are those records for the 349th Military Intelligence Detachment (Counterintelligence). Eisenhower era reports on assassinations of foreign leaders, previously available, are now missing from the National Archives. Also, now missing is Oswald's CIA Office of Security file, volume 5, which was last seen by the HSCA.

Researcher Rex Bradford posed a reflection to probe the nature of beliefs. Imagine that it is 1963, and Nikita Khrushchev, recently humiliated by the U.S. during the Cuban Missile Crisis, has been assassinated:

> Khrushchev received a military autopsy, which ran counter to the civilian doctors who first treated him. Imagine that later one of the autopsy doctors admitted that a Soviet general ran the autopsy, and that this doctor said he was ordered not to track the path of the bullet. That crucial autopsy known to be taken went missing, that trained medical witnesses disputed what was shown in those that remained, that the official autopsy camera went missing after an investigation failed to match it to the photographs. Imagine it was Russia where the security services destroyed evidence linking themselves with the purported killer, who was declared to be a "rabid capitalist," but who seemed to be surrounded for the last year of his life by KGB operatives. That secret evidence finally revealed that the purported killer had been impersonated in a supposed conversation with CIA agents. But Khrushchev's successor, without revealing the impersonation, had led those investigating the crime to think that the alleged assassin had indeed made the disturbing calls, and that there might be a nuclear war with America if this got out… Take the single bullet theory, the killing of the alleged assassin while in police custody… including that the murder was followed by a major expansion of a war that secret documents later showed Khrushchev had ordered to be wound down.

It would be obvious that his political enemies, including the KGB, killed Khrushchev. The basic facts reflect the reality of the Kennedy assassination, but imagining that the U.S. military and the CIA may have been complicit created cognitive dissonance for most Americans – especially with the mainstream media burying the lead. In Federalist Papers #25 Alexander Hamilton wrote, "For it is a truth, which the experience of all ages has attested, for the people are commonly most in danger when the means of inspiring their rights are in possession of those whom they entertain the least suspicion." If a coup d'état occurred in America, could it ever get reported?

17

LBJ

Cui bono? - Latin for who gains.
           - the standard question in Roman trials

Power always thinks it has a great soul.
           – John Adams

A long habit of not thinking a thing wrong, gives it a superficial appearance of being right, and raises at first a formidable outcry in the defense of custom.
           – *Thomas Paine*

L yndon Johnson had such a burning ambition to be president that he took a step down from Senate Majority leader to serve as Vice-President for a man he did not like. But by 1963, Johnson's public scandals presented the very real possibility that he might be dumped from the Democratic ticket in the 1964 election and even imprisoned. While these motives were strong, the evidence linking Johnson at the planning stages of the assassination seems circumstantial, yet his role as an accomplice to the cover-up is clear. Johnson ordered the seizure of all evidence after the assassination. His rapid order to clean the presidential limousine and to launder Connally's clothes constitutes destruction of evidence. He created the Warren Commission to head off independent Texas and Congressional investigations, and directed it to report to him. He tried to influence the Commission and called certain Commissioners regularly during the hearings. Johnson supported the "national security" classification for more than two million pages of the Warren Commission and related documents until 2029.

By mid-1963 Johnson was seriously concerned about two senate investigations of his top aide Bobby Baker. The Senate Rules Committee, in November of 1963, was investigating Baker's role in the award of a $7 billion contract for the TFX fighter plane to General Dynamics. Baker's business associate, Don Reynolds, had testified about a big lobbyists' sex party in New York, and a $100,000 payoff to Johnson for his role in securing the Fort Worth TFX contract. Baker was financially connected with Carlos Marcello as well as Fred Black, one of mobster Johnny Roselli's close friends and the next-door neighbor to LBJ. This and numerous bribery allegations seriously threatened Johnson's political career. Johnson's benefactors in oil, banking and defense spending feared the implications if LBJ resigned. Recall the Justice Department and IRS were examining Baker's Las Vegas connections to Meyer Lansky associate Ed Levison as well as Ben Siegelbaum, a Hoffa ally. Meanwhile RFK was examining Johnson's reputed dependence on Marcello's support, which helped push Johnson to kill anti-racketeering legislation. Not surprisingly, Baker's testimony was ended by the news that Kennedy had been shot.

Johnson's long-time mistress, Madeline Brown, has claimed in interviews and in her book, *Texas in the Morning*, that Johnson knew of the assassination attempt more than a week before it occurred, and that he approved of it. Brown maintained that Johnson met with J. Edgar Hoover, Texas oilman Clint Murchison, and others at Murchison's house the evening prior to the assassination. When LBJ arrived, the assembled then reconvened in a private room. After the meeting, Johnson supposedly said "the Kennedys won't bother me anymore." Although Brown's story has changed over the years regarding who attended this gathering, the essence of her assertions has been constant.

Barr McClellan, a Johnson attorney working with Edward Clark's law firm, has stated and written that two of his associates had told him that Clark had Kennedy assassinated. McClellan was told this story by both attorney Jon Coats as well as by Johnson's long-time business attorney Don Thomas.[1] (McClellan's son was the press spokesperson for President G. W. Bush). Perhaps foreknowledge and some level of complicity somehow evolved into hyperbole in the minds of McClellan's partners that Clark was responsible.

Johnson's top political aide, Billy Sol Estes, testified in a Texas court in 1984 after release from prison that Johnson was involved in eight political murders, including President Kennedy. Briefly, the first of these alleged murders was Henry Marshall, a U.S. Department of Agriculture inspector exploring Estes' business. Marshall supposedly died by shooting himself five times in the chest with a .22 bolt action rifle, on his farm. No blood samples or fingerprints were taken from the truck or murder weapon. Carbon monoxide was found in Marshall's body. Marshall's family knew of no motive. When the case was reopened in May 1962 the doctor who examined the exhumed body, Joseph Jachimczyk, said "I believe this was not a suicide."[2] While this portion of con-man Estes' testimony may be plausible, the rest seems speculative or vindictive.

In 1963 John Connally, LBJ's protégé, convinced JFK of the need to campaign in Texas. Kennedy placed the Dallas trip, which was announced April 23, 1963, in Johnson's hands. Less than 45 days later, Kennedy, Johnson, and Governor Connally confirmed the trip at the Cortez Hotel in Texas. Kennedy advanceman Jerry Bruno disagreed with the Texas planners over the proposed motorcade route, since it created risks for President Kennedy. In late October, Bruno flew to Dallas to discuss more details of the trip. Before meeting Connally, Bruno met with Texas Senator Yarborough who warned him that, "Johnson and Connally would be ... after John Kennedy in a minute if they thought they could get away with it."[3]

Bruno and Connally got into a heated dispute regarding the proposed route, which caused Connally to call the White House in Bruno's presence. It appeared to Bruno that the White House had sided with Connally, so Bruno relented. Only after the assassination did Bruno learn that the White House staff did not agree with Connally. Bruno claimed that in his three years as an advanceman he had never encountered any other group that refused to alter plans related to the safety of the president.[4]

Curiously, on the evening of November 21, 1963, Johnson entered Kennedy's hotel suite to try to change the seating positions in the motorcade. A fiery argument ensued, and Johnson left the presidential suite "like a pistol," looking furious.[5] Kennedy had stayed with previous plans, which had Johnson riding with his enemy, Senator Yarborough, rather than his former close aide, Governor Connally.

Johnson's motorcade seatmate Senator Ralph Yarborough reported that he smelled gunpowder near the grassy knoll. He also stated that at the time of the assassination Johnson had his ear up to a small walkie-talkie with the sound "turned down real low." Johnson refused to supply a sworn affidavit of what he had seen. He signed an unsworn statement, which explained little about what he saw, heard, or smelled.[6]

Before Kennedy was even buried, Johnson ordered the presidential limousine, which had already been shipped from Dallas to Washington, to be shipped to Detroit for complete refurbishing. This destruction of evidence is a crime – yet it was never investigated.

We know that LBJ spoke with J. Edgar Hoover that day after the assassination regarding Oswald's actions. Recall:

LBJ: Have you established any more about the Oswald visit to the Soviet Embassy in Mexico in September?

Hoover: No, that's one angle that's very confusing for this reason. We have up here the tape and photograph of the man who was at the Soviet Embassy, using Oswald's name. That picture and tape do not correspond to this man's voice or appearance. In other words, it appears that there is a second person who was at the Soviet Embassy.

The next fourteen minutes of this tape were somehow deleted. Were Johnson and Hoover driven to cover-up a complicitous and venal CIA, or a dangerously penetrated one?

Authors Penn Jones, *Forgive My Grief*, and Gary Shaw, *Cover-up*, report that less than 24 hours after the assassination Johnson called Dallas police Homicide Chief Will Fritz and said, "You have got your man." Johnson directed his aide Cliff Carter to call Dallas D.A. Henry Wade and ordered him not to allege a conspiracy. Wade said Carter called three or four times and said that it "would hurt foreign relations if I alleged a conspiracy … and whether I could prove it or not … I was to charge Oswald with plain murder."[7] Police Chief Jesse Curry, State Attorney General Wagoner Carr and Captain Will Fritz also received similar calls from Cliff Carter.[8] Fritz recalled receiving a number of calls Friday evening and Saturday morning. Further, Johnson called Parkland Hospital to obtain a deathbed confession from Lee Harvey Oswald.

According to Dr. Charles Crenshaw, one of the surgeons working on Oswald, LBJ stated "I want a deathbed confession from the accused assassin. There's a man in the operating room who will take the statement. I will expect full cooperation on this matter."[9] Parkland Hospital switchboard operation Phyllis Bartlett confirmed Johnson's call to Crenshaw.

Three days after the assassination, President Johnson's Deputy Attorney General Nicholas Katzenbach, filling in for a grieving Robert Kennedy, wrote to press secretary Bill Moyers that:

> The public must be satisfied that Oswald was the assassin; that he did not have confederates who are still at large; and that the evidence was such that he would have been convicted at trial. Speculation about Oswald's motivation should be cut off, and we should have some basics for rebutting the thought that this was a Communist conspiracy or a right-wing conspiracy to blame it on the Communists.… We need something to head off public speculation or congressional hearings of the wrong sort.

Johnson's good friend and political crony for twenty years, J. Edgar Hoover, was the major source of investigation for the Warren Commission. Johnson regularly called and met with Hoover during the life of the Commission. Hoover had been helpful in deflecting investigations regarding Johnson's ties with Mafioso Carlos Marcello as well as the ties Johnson's top aide, Bobby Baker, also had with Marcello and other Mafiosi.[10] The day after the President was assassinated, the Justice Department stopped getting information from the FBI on the Bobby Baker investigation.[11]

CIA contract agent George de Mohrenschildt's letters to Johnson while he was Vice-President, as well as Johnson's relationships with Clint Murchison and other Texas oilmen, both warrant further research. Recall that George and his wife Jeanne befriended the Oswald's; making introductions, driving them around, and helping Lee get jobs and apartments. George was friends with the CIA man in Dallas, J. Walton Moore, who worked with the Domestic Contacts Service (DCS), which debriefed Americans returning from abroad.

De Mohrenschildt met in April 1963 with CIA operative WUBRINY/, at the Knickerbocker Club in New York to ostensibly discuss Haiti. WUBRINY/, was Thomas Devine, a former business partner of George H.W. Bush in his oil company Zapata Offshore.

De Mohrenschildt and Devine also met with C. Frank Stone III, chief of operations for the European section of the CIA's clandestine wing along with M.C. Joseph Charles, the manager of Bangui Commercialese D' Haiti. This meeting was supposedly about "sisal" (rope), and a subsequent meeting was supposedly to get U.S. support to overthrow "Papa Doc" Duvalier.

A letter dated 4/18/63 shows de Mohrenschildt and Charles had met with Colonel Howard Burris, LBJ's top military advisor and friend of Richard Helms, and possibly also met with LBJ.

> Dear, Mr. de Mohrenschildt,
>
> Your letter has come in the Vice-President's absence from the office... I would like to suggest that you see Colonel Howard Burris, Air Force Aide to the Vice President, when you come to Washington. Should Mr. Johnson happen to have any office hours here during your stay, We will be happy to see if a mutually convenient time can be found for you to meet... with warm wishes.
>
> Sincerely, Walter Jenkins,
> Administrative Assistant[12]

Johnson's role might have been clarified by the first draft of William Manchester's *The Death of a President*, which mentioned the fight between Kennedy and Johnson over the fateful trip to Texas, the dispute between them in Texas, and Kennedy staff suspicions about Johnson; however, the Kennedy clan filed a lawsuit to stop the publication of the book. Perhaps this version was seen as harmful to Robert Kennedy's political future or to the future of the Democratic Party. The lawsuit was settled with all parties agreeing to an "approved" version of the book.[13]

Recall that Johnson crony D.H. Byrd owned the TSBD, and had started the national Civil Air Patrol that David Ferrie and Oswald had worked with. The military contractor Byrd had worked closely with General LeMay, as well as Texas oilmen and businessmen who had generously funded Johnson. Byrd's membership with the Dallas Petroleum Club and the "Suite F" group also made him cronies with H. L. Hunt, Sid Richardson, Jack Crichton, Gordon McLendon, William Pawley, Herman Brown (of Brown and Root) and Robert Kerr (Kerr-McGee Oil Industries).

Johnson regularly met and called Warren Commission members Russell, Dulles, and Ford, while the Commission was still gathering evidence, as well as with Texas Attorney General Waggoner Carr, who still strongly supports the Warren Commission findings. Johnson's other actions raise suspicions regarding these calls and meetings as well.

Johnson's appointment of fellow Texan, Ramsey Clark, as Attorney General, and Clark's efforts to withhold basic evidence regarding this assassination, including autopsy x-rays and photographs, was clarified by the AARB. During the Garrison investigation in New Orleans, the Clark Commission (1968) not only echoed the Warren Commission, but it also remarkably cleared Clay Shaw of any involvement in the assassination, even though Shaw's name did not even appear in the Warren Commission Report.

Evelyn Lincoln, the trusted personal secretary of President Kennedy, has stated that Hoover blackmailed Kennedy to offer the VP position to Johnson. She says that she was in the hotel room during the 1960 convention when John and Robert Kennedy were agonizing over how to deal with Hoover's call on behalf of Johnson, as well as Hoover's knowledge of JFK's compromising extramarital affairs.[14]

Noted Johnson biographer Robert Caro recounted the embarrassments and humiliation of his vice presidency. He concluded that LBJ developed "an utter ruthlessness in destroying obstacles in his path, and a seemingly bottomless capacity for deceit, deception and betrayal" in part to overcome his childhood suffering.[15] Caro remains silent regarding any role LBJ could have had in the assassination of JFK.

Johnson's notions of reporters remain noteworthy:

> Reporters are puppets.... They simply respond to the pull of the most powerful strings.... Every story is always slanted to win the favor of someone who sits higher up.... There is only one sure way of getting favorable stories from reporters and that is to keep their daily bread – the information, the stories, the plans and details they need for their work in your hands, so that you can give it out when and to whom you want.[16]

We seem left with a crisis period after the assassination of either a co-nundrum of presidential pragmatism, or complicity masked by pragma-tism. Johnson's actions before and after the assassination suggest the later.

18

DÉTENTE DELAYED –
FOREIGN POLICY CHANGES

As a nation we think not of war but of peace; not of crusades of conflict but covenants of cooperation; not of pageantry of imperialism but of the pride of new states freshly risen to independence.
— Senator Kennedy 1959

If we cannot end now our differences, at least we can make the world safe for diversity. For in the final analysis, our most basic common link is that we all inhabit this planet. We all breathe the same air. We all cherish our children's future. We are all mortal…
— President John F. Kennedy, June 1963
at American University

I decided that having put our hand to the plough, we would not turn back.
— Dean Acheson 1954 On Vietnam

Amid the tense international setting in 1960, candidate John Kennedy campaigned as a cold warrior, hammering the Eisenhower Administration for allowing a "missile gap" and for being overly tolerant of Castro. As president he appeared as hawk and dove, idealist and pragmatist. He sponsored the Peace Corps as well as the Green Berets. He called for respect for Third World nationalism, yet he intervened in Vietnam and Cuba. He appealed for liberalized trade, yet he supported many protectionist measures. He proclaimed that "America should never fear to negotiate," yet he often used military rather than diplomatic options. He generally opposed neo-colonialism and after the Cuban Missile Crisis he took major risks to end the Cold War.

Chester Bowles, one of Kennedy's top foreign policy advisors, noted numerous decisions Kennedy made against a majority of his advisors: refusing to invade Cuba during the Bay of Pigs disaster; initiating an Alliance for Progress; refusing to intervene in the Dominican Republic fol-

lowing the assassination of Trujillo; refusing to introduce ground troops
into Laos; refusing to escalate in Vietnam; backing U.N. policy in the
Congo; not attacking the Soviets during the Cuban Missile crisis, and
backing India in its disputes with China and Pakistan.[1]

Some of JFK's congressional speeches foreshadowed his foreign policy independence and his direct challenge to the American status quo. In
1951, Congressman Kennedy toured the Middle East and Asia and reported by radio a critical perspective.

> The fires of nationalism are ablaze.... A Middle East Command op-
> erating without the cooperation and support of the Middle Eastern
> countries ... would intensify every anti-western force now active
> in the area, [and] from a military standpoint would be doomed to
> failure. The very sands of the desert rise to oppose the imposition
> of outside control on the destinies of these proud people...
>
> Our intervention on behalf of England's oil interests in Iran,
> directed more at the preservation of interests outside of Iran than
> at Iran's own development.... Our failure to deal effectively after
> three years with the terrible tragedy of more than 700,000 Arab
> refugees [Palestinians], these are things that have failed to sit well
> with Arab desires, and make empty the promises of the Voice of
> America."

Kennedy's key mentor on Vietnam was State Department official Edmund Gullion, who clarified the futility in the French colonial war. JFK
thought so highly of Gullion that he brought him into the White House
upon his election to the presidency.

In 1956 Senator Kennedy declared:

> The Afro-Asian revolution of nationalism, the revolt against colo-
> nialism, the determination of people to control their national des-
> tinies...in my opinion the tragic failure of both Republican and
> Democratic Administrations since WWII to comprehend the na-
> ture of this revolution, and its potentialities for good and evil, has
> reaped a bitter harvest today – and it is... a major foreign policy
> campaign issue that has nothing to do with anti-communism.

Senator Kennedy's speech on Algeria in July 1957, which attacked the
Eisenhower administration and France, generated protest and concern
from Eisenhower, John Foster Dulles, Nixon, Acheson, Adlai Stevenson
and more than 100 newspapers:

The most powerful force in the world today ... is man's eternal desire to be free and independent.... We did not learn in Indochina.... Did that tragic episode not teach us that whether France likes it or not, or has our support or not, their overseas territories are sooner or later, one by one, inevitably going to break free and look with suspicion on the Western nations who impeded their steps to independence...The time has come to face the harsh realities of the situation and to fulfill its responsibilities as leader of the free world.[2]

In 1959 Kennedy declared to the Senate:

Call it nationalism. Call it anti-colonialism.... Africa is going through a revolution.... The word is out – and spreading like wild fire in nearly a thousand languages and dialects – that it is no longer necessary to remain forever poor or forever in bondage.

During the presidential campaign he declared, "We have lost ground in Africa because we have neglected and ignored the needs and aspirations of Africa."[3]

As Kennedy critically evaluated the wisdom of the CIA and the Joint Chiefs after the failed Bay of Pigs invasion, Premier Khrushchev critically evaluated Kennedy at the Vienna Summit in June 1961. When Kennedy decided to flaunt the massive U.S. nuclear superiority in number of nuclear weapons and delivery systems through the speech of an aide in October, the Soviets responded by detonating a 30-megaton bomb followed by a 50-megaton bomb – far larger than anything in the U.S. arsenal.

The rising Cold War tensions reinforced the American need to respond to Cuba. The Kennedys launched Operation Mongoose, a campaign of terror to wreck the Cuban economy and possibly assassinate Castro. Robert Kennedy planned a "policy of sabotage, general disorder, run and operated by the Cubans themselves." The CIA program called JMWAVE, located in South Florida, included 600 CIA officers, nearly 5000 contractors, and the third largest navy in the Caribbean, led by counterinsurgency expert General Ed Lansdale. By March 1962 Lansdale was asking the Joint Chiefs for pretexts to invade Cuba. General Lyman Lemnitzer directed Brigadier General William Craig to generate a list of possible provocations, which was code-named Operation Northwoods. The list included: a "Remember the Maine" type of incident, hijacking attempts against American aircraft to be pinned on the Cuban government, a "terror" campaign against Cuban refugees, including sinking a boat-load of refugees headed to Florida, a series of well-coordinated incidents around Guantanamo to give the appearance of having been carried out by hostile Cuban forces; staging a Cuban government shoot down of a civilian airliner.

These actions, along with U.S. efforts to suspend Cuba's membership in the OAS, as well as three military exercises in the Caribbean, contributed to the Soviet perception that action was needed to defend Cuba. Khrushchev gambled that placing middle-range ballistic missiles MRBMs and warheads into Cuba would deter an attack on themselves and Cuba. He blundered by not revealing that the missiles and the nuclear warheads had been placed in Cuba, which undercut the deterrent effect.

In response. most of Kennedy's military leaders and advisors advocated a military strike followed by an invasion. General LeMay pushed, "The Russian bear has always been eager to stick his paw in Latin American waters, let's take his leg off up to his testicles. On second thought, let's take off his testicles too." Confiding to aide Kenny O'Donnell, JFK wryly observed, "These brass hats have one great advantage, if we listened to them, and what they want to do, none of us will be alive to tell them that they were wrong."

JFK agreed with McNamara that the Soviet missiles did not change the balance of power, but the new status quo risked security in Latin America. Further; he believed that if he did not take strong action, he could be impeached.

Kennedy opted for a blockade, which was called a quarantine, to de-emphasize that it was an act of war. On October 22nd the president informed the American public, "we will not prematurely or unnecessarily risk the course of worldwide nuclear war in which the fruits of victory would be ashes in our mouths, but neither will we shrink from that risk any time it must be faced." As noted, the military were furious with this course of action.

Years later McNamara discovered that the reconnaissance flights missed some of the S-4 missiles, and that SS-5 intermediate missiles had also been shipped. And critically, we did not know that the Soviets had already positioned about 100 battlefield nuclear weapons in Cuba. Nor were we aware that we would be facing 43,000 Soviet military personnel and 270,000 armed Cubans. In 1992 McNamara declared that 100,000 Americans would have died in an invasion and that the U.S. would have wiped out Cuba with a "high risk" of nuclear war between the U.S. and the Soviet Union.[4]

The crisis proved to be a political epiphany for both Kennedy and Khrushchev. Khrushchev wrote Kennedy a long letter on October 30, 1962, outlining a series of far-reaching proposals to eliminate, "everything in our relations capable of generating a new crisis." He proposed: disbanding all nuclear blocs, formal acceptance of two Germanys based on existing borders, he urged the U.S. to recognize China and let it join the UN, and quickly concluding a treaty to stop all nuclear testing everywhere. Kennedy largely agreed, and started promoting a test ban treaty.

Saturday Review editor and anti-nuclear activist Norman Cousins worked as an intermediary between Kennedy and Khrushchev. In April he met with Khrushchev, who described the pressure he faced from Kremlin hardliners. When Cousins briefed Kennedy on Khrushchev's situation Kennedy lamented, "He would like to prevent a nuclear war but is under severe pressure from his hardliner crowd, which interprets every move in that direction as appeasement. I've got similar problems."

Kennedy inherited a powerful, semi-independent CIA, which ignored Executive branch policies in country after country. Eisenhower lamented the power of the military-industrial complex, and saw the CIA as "a legacy of ashes." CIA policies in the Far East challenged him as much as the Bay of Pigs. At home Kennedy confronted a coalition of cold warriors, bankers, and corporate leaders as he attempted to revise U.S. policy towards Indonesia. When he took office U.S.-Indonesian relations were severely strained after a CIA attempt to overthrow non-aligned nationalist leader President Achmed Sukarno.

In 1960 the Netherlands still controlled West New Guinea, and President Sukarno began a campaign to gain control of the colony. Domestically, Sukarno was balancing the military against a strong indigenous communist movement. There was also Soviet and Chinese interest in the Indonesian-Dutch conflict. Within the CIA and the State Department there was strong support for the Netherlands, yet Kennedy supported Sukarno, and helped pressure the Dutch to transfer New Guinea to Indonesia.[5]

In 1962 JFK sent Robert Kennedy to Indonesia to speak against imperialism, and then to Holland to demand that the Dutch remove their military from the mineral rich Indonesian island of New Guinea.

Kennedy bluntly reiterated his opposition to colonialism, to India's Prime Minister Jawaharlal Nehru, January of 1962.

> I grew up in a community where the people were hardly a generation away from colonial rule … the colonialism to which my imme-

diate ancestors were subject was more sterile, impressive and even cruel than that of India.

In the Middle East Kennedy moved to reopen support for Egypt's Pan Arabist and socialist Prime Minister Nasser as the best route to moving Arab nationalism toward development and democracy. This opposition to the policies of John Foster Dulles extended to supporting Egypt against Saudi Arabia in the civil war in Yemen. Kennedy did not support the Dulles/Eisenhower intervention in Lebanon in 1958, and he opposed Israel acquiring nuclear weapons – which he thought would further destabilize the region. Further, he opposed the monarchies in Saudi Arabia and Iran, and advocated commissioning a study to explore the costs of returning Mossedeq to power in Iran.[6]

In Vietnam, Kennedy inherited an ill-conceived policy, which was wracked with bureaucratic infighting. He often was deprived of information and unable to control factions of the CIA and DOD. Some debate continues as to whether he was pulling out of Vietnam, although recent scholarship, as well as documents that were released through the ARRB, significantly strengthens the case that he was withdrawing.

Early policy concerns can be seen in a 1952 NSC memo, which stated "Communist control of all of Southeast Asia would render the U.S. position in the Pacific offshore island chain precarious and would seriously jeopardize fundamental U.S. security interests in the Far East." America supplied the French with almost 80% of their arms in the failed effort to recapture Vietnam. After the French surrendered to Ho Chi Minh in 1954, the Geneva Accords were signed, temporarily separating Vietnam until elections could be held in 1956. At this point Secretary of State Dulles, Admiral Radford and General Twining initiated a plan to invade Vietnam, but Eisenhower blocked it. In 1954, NSC 5429/2 set in motion a CIA policy, led by Allen Dulles and directed by General Lansdale, which installed a puppet dictatorship under Diem, opposing Ho Chi Minh and the Viet Cong. Lansdale had previously crushed rebellious forces in the Philippines through counter-insurgency, and was able to dethrone Boa Dai and place the U.S.-educated Diem in office. In 1956 Eisenhower chose to cancel the planned U.N.-sponsored elections, realizing that Ho Chi Minh would get around 80% of the vote. A separate government was then created and supported by the U.S. in South Vietnam. Eisenhower then steadily widened the war and furthered the U.S. commitment to counter-insurgency.

By June of 1961 Kennedy confronted proposals from his top civilian and military aides to send 60,000 troops to neighboring Laos. Some historians argue that a SEATO invasion plan called for more than twice that many. He rejected these proposals based on the intelligence failure with the Bay of Pigs. JFK told Arthur Schlesinger, "If it hadn't been for Cuba, we might be about to intervene in Laos." Waving cables from General Lemnitzer he noted, "we might have taken this advice seriously." Five months later, he was confronted by his personal military advisor General Maxwell Taylor, and his deputy National Security Advisor, Walt Rostow with the "Taylor Report" to "save" Vietnam with at least 8,000 troops. According to John Galbraith, the U.S. Ambassador to India, the lobbying was intense. Secretary of Defense McNamara was pushing for 200,000 troops immediately. Galbraith, who had surreptitiously picked up a copy of the "Taylor Report" from Rostow's office, counseled caution. Unnamed "senior White House officials" leaked word that, as one *New York Times* headline noted, "Kennedy Remains Opposed to Sending Forces after Hearing Report." McNamara, Rusk, and Maxwell Taylor pushed to convene an NSC meeting but Kennedy delayed for a week. During that time no visible support arose in Congress, the press or the public.[7]

Harvard Professor Richard Parker shed light on this period with recovered notes about the NSC meeting.

> ... After listening to the arguments for intervention, an impassioned Bobby Kennedy kept insisting 'We are not sending combat troops. Not committing ourselves to combat troops' They also show that when Rusk proposed making "saving Vietnam" a formal national policy goal, the President – who'd been largely silent until then-briskly refused. Telling the group coolly that "troops are the last resort"; he said that if they were ever to be sent, he would let them go only as part of a multilateral force, under the sanctions of the UN Security Council.[8]

Then in NSAM (National Security Action Memorandum) 111 President Kennedy withstood wide-ranging and coordinated military and CIA pressure and decided against committing armed infantry divisions. Kennedy shared General MacArthur's fears regarding a large land war in Asia, yet he did not want to run for reelection as the president who "lost Vietnam." A middle path was chosen:

1. "Advisers" were increased from 900 to nearly 17,000.

2. Eased instructions of U.S. military, authorizing "advisors" to engage in combat and combat support, such as spraying defoliants like Agent Orange.

3. More than doubled the material support to the ARVN, including heavy artillery and 300 aircraft.

Intense infighting on many foreign policy fronts continued through the Cuban Missile Crisis, where Kennedy chose the least militant option. His attempts to dismantle Operation Mongoose, and the CIA effort to overthrow Castro, were often disregarded. Ironically, in Europe, as Kennedy was assuring French President de Gaulle that the U. S. was not involved with the plot against him, CIA and NATO generals were actually encouraging the would-be assassins.

In Laos, after the 1962 agreement, the CIA regrouped in Thailand to initiate a covert war against the Kennedy-supported neutralist government. NSAM 263 (Kennedy's plan to withdraw troops) and NSAM 273 (Johnson's plan to continue support for South Vietnam) indicate intense American bureaucratic infighting between one faction which gave priority to "winning" the war and another faction which also hoped to win, but would withdraw regardless of the outcome.

Many analysts and government officials have observed a significant change in Kennedy's Vietnam policy from NSAM 263, just prior to 11/20/63, to NSAM 273, written immediately after the assassination. They include among others: Army Intelligence Major Dr. John Newman; Colonel John Stockwell; former Executive Assistant to the Deputy Director of the CIA Victor Marchetti; Congressman Henry Gonzalez; temporary Chairman of the HSCA; Roger Hilsman Assistant Secretary of State for Far Eastern Affairs, the officer responsible for Vietnam; Daniel Ellsberg, co-author of the Pentagon Papers; Colonel Fletcher Prouty, who in 1962-3 was the Chief of Special Operations in the Office of the Joint Chiefs of Staff; and Peter Dale Scott, a former Canadian diplomat.

John Newman, in *JFK and Vietnam*, reviewed about 15,000 pages of military documents and concluded Kennedy was withdrawing from Vietnam. Following President Kennedy's rejection of the Joint Chiefs' proposal for 8,000 armed infantry troops in November 1961, in NSAM 111, no agency asked for combat troops in Vietnam.

Kennedy declared to an audience in Seattle, 11/16/61, "We must face the fact that the United States is neither omnipotent nor omniscient – that we cannot impose our will upon the other 94% of mankind – that we cannot right every wrong or reverse every adversity – and that therefore there cannot be an American solution to every world problem."

Subsequently, Kennedy and his Secretary of Defense McNamara were given sanitized NSC reports falsely showing the effectiveness of the Vietnam policy, including the story that the enemy's size and areas of control were manageable, and that the South Vietnamese Army was winning on the battlefield, a story that was supported by faked body counts, pacification rates, and captured weapons totals. Meanwhile, Vice-President Johnson, the Joint Chiefs of Staff and a select circle of military officers were given different reports through privileged back channels – reports which indicated the need for more men and materials for success.[9] By March of 1962 it was clear that the reports from the Military Assistance Command Vietnam (MACV) given to McNamara were markedly different from those of the U. S. Army Pacific (USARPAC) given to the Joint Chief of Staff and the National Security Council. It appeared that Kennedy was being encouraged to at least remain in Vietnam since he was not moving to widen the war, whereas Johnson, a longtime advocate for widening the war, was being encouraged to develop policies to widen the war.

U.S. Ambassador to India, John Galbraith, reported on Vietnam in early 1962 and questioned U.S. involvement. The president instructed Averill Harriman and NSC staffer Michael Forrestal to "seize upon any favorable moment to reduce our commitment."[10]

The release of the last of the eight SECDEF meetings held, 5/8/63 shows that McNamara supported Kennedy's plans for a phased withdrawal.

> In connection with this presentation.... The Secretary of Defense stated that the phase-out appears too slow. He directed that training plans be developed for the GVN [Government of Vietnam] by CINCPAC [Commander in Chief, Pacific] which will permit a more rapid phase out of U.S. forces, stating specifically that we should review our plans for pilot training with the view of accelerating it materially. He made a particular point of speeding up training of helicopter pilots, so that we may give the Vietnamese our copters and thus be able to move our own forces out.... [The] VNAF was programmed for 50 hours per aircraft but were getting approximately 80 hours per aircraft. Flying hour authorization would be increased. SECDEF stated the percentage of VNAF [Vietnamese Air Force] effort was no greater then a year ago. Our sights should be higher and he wanted to get U.S. pilots out of combat and transport operations.[11]

Colonel Fletcher Prouty (Mr. X in the movie *JFK*) served in the Pentagon for nine years supporting clandestine operations with Generals Erskine and Lansdale in the Office of the Secretary of Defense. By 1963 he was one of the primary authors of NSAM 263, the "Report by Taylor and McNamara." Prouty was given daily information from Taylor and McNamara, who were in constant touch with JFK and RFK. Prouty argues that Kennedy ordered a complete withdrawal, "Kennedy was for having the Vietnamese handle their own internal affairs and certainly was not for an escalation of the covert activities he had inherited from his predecessors."[12]

Prouty contends that during Kennedy's time in the White House the CIA was running the war in Vietnam ... not the military, and certainly not the ambassador. He noted that the Pentagon and the CIA responded to NSAM 263 with outrage.

In September of 1963 Secretary McNamara and General Taylor were dispatched for an "on-the-spot appraisal of the military and paramilitary effort."[13] This report led to National Security Action Memorandum (NSAM) 263, with parts dictated by JFK. This was the first document printed by the *New York Times* in 1971 when it began the publication of the Pentagon Papers. The President read this report on October 2, 1963. Prouty notes, "it contained two important recommendations that were basic to Kennedy's plans for Vietnam. They were that: a) The Department of Defense should announce plans ... to withdraw 1000 military personnel by the end of December 1963; b) We believe the U.S. part of the task (i.e. the security of South Vietnam) can be completed by the end of 1965."[14]

McNamara asserts in his book *In Retrospect* that "America was limiting its role to providing training and logistical support. We actually began planning for the phased withdrawal of U.S. forces in 1963."[15] This position was further confirmed by the release of Pentagon documents, through the work of the ARRB, in late 1997. As noted by author Jim DiEugenio:

> On page after page of these documents, at every upper level of the Pentagon, everyone seems aware that Kennedy's withdrawal program will begin in December of 1963 with a pull out of 1,000 men and that this would be the beginning of an eventual and complete withdrawal by 1965... on one of the documents, a 5/6/63 meeting of the Pacific command, General Earle Wheeler stated 'that proposals for overt action invited a negative PRESIDENTIAL decision' [Capitalization in the original].... It seems clear, that as John

Newman has written, Kennedy was trying to 'Vietnamize' the war just as he told Walter Cronkite in their famous 9/2/63 interview.[16]

The *New York Times* headlined its story "Kennedy Had a Plan for Early Exit in Vietnam." The *Philadelphia Inquirer* article was titled "Papers support theory that Kennedy had plans for a Vietnam pullout." The AP version mitigated the new findings as "New Documents Hint That JFK Wanted U.S. Out of Vietnam." No mass media account of these declassified documents mentioned that this foreign policy change had been part of the thesis in Oliver Stone's *JFK*.

The military journal *Stars and Stripes* ran a clear headline, 10/4/63: "President Says – All Americans Out by 1965." Kennedy's public statement was consistent with conversations he had had with General James Gavin, Navy Undersecretary Paul Fay, Congressman Tip O'Neil (D-Mass.), Senator Wayne Morse (D-Ore.),[17] Senator Mike Mansfield (D-Mont), aide Ken O'Donnell, NSC staffer Michael Forrestal, and reporter Charles Bartlett. Pentagon Papers analyst Daniel Ellsberg noted in an interview, "the major decision Kennedy made was to reject the recommendation made to him by virtually everyone (in 1961) that he send combat troops to Vietnam."[18] General Gavin stated in 1968, "I know he was totally opposed to the introduction of combat troops in Southeast Asia."

General Bruce Palmer wrote in 1984 that he did not think President Kennedy would have committed major U.S. combat forces to Vietnam. In 1963 Palmer served as the number two man for the Army's deputy Chief of Staff of Operations.

Historian Arthur Schlesinger, Jr. a top Kennedy advisor, states "From the beginning to the end of his administration, he steadily opposed repeated military recommendations that he introduce an American expeditionary force." General Maxwell Taylor stated, "The last thing he wanted was to put in our ground forces."

Roger Hilsman, Kennedy's Assistant Secretary of State for Far Eastern Affairs wrote a lengthy letter to the *New York Times* (1/20/92) stating that in 1963 "President Kennedy was determined not to let Vietnam become an American War – that is, he was determined not to send U.S. combat troops (as opposed to advisors) to fight in Vietnam nor to bomb North Vietnam." Assistant Press Secretary Malcolm Kilduff has stated, "There is no question that he was taking us out of Vietnam. I was in his office just before we went to Dallas and he said that Vietnam was not worth another American life."[19]

On November 11, 1963, Kennedy informed Marine Corps Chief of Staff General David Shoup that he was "getting out of Vietnam." The next day he told Senator Wayne Morse that he was finishing an intensive study on Vietnam and that "I've decided to get out. Definitely!"[20] Shortly before his death he told Senate Majority Leader Mike Mansfield that he agreed with a U.S. withdrawal, "but I can't do it until 1965 – after I'm re-elected."

Journalist Charles Bartlett, a friend of Kennedy, recalled that JFK often worried about the 1964 election. "We don't have a prayer of staying in Vietnam. We don't have a prayer of prevailing there.... But I can't give up a piece of territory like that to the Communists and get the American public to re-elect me." President Kennedy told his aide Ken O'Donnell in the spring of 1963 that he could not pull out of Vietnam until he was reelected "So one had better make damn sure that I am elected."

On October 5, 1963, Kennedy made his formal decision and clearly did not want to pressure Diem. The JCS minutes of the meeting-

> The President also said that our decision to remove 1,000 U.S. advisors by December of this year should not be raised formally with Diem.

NSAM 263 implemented the October 5 order, and subsequent CIA reporting reflected "comparatively realistic pessimism." At a press conference November 12, Kennedy publicly restated his goals "to intensify the struggle" and to "bring Americans out of there." The murders of Diem and his brother on 11/1/63, show a divided and disorganized foreign policy. Historian Howard Jones indicates that a faction consisting of Averell Harriman, Roger Hilsman and Michael Forrestal fomented the coup without a follow-up plan. Ironically the ineffective, unpopular and erratic Diem had sent his brother Nhu to meet with intermediaries of Ho Chi Minh, about a possible deal between the North and the South, (*Death of a Generation*).

Only two days after President Kennedy's assassination, the authorized and secret NSAM 273 shows a reversal of policy toward Vietnam. Professor Peter Dale Scott's research in this area has been supported by the further declassification of NSAM 273, which represented a change of the policy in at least six areas:

> 1. An assertion that the "central objective" of the U.S. was to assist South Vietnam "to win" rather than to "help" South Vietnam;
>
> 2. A deletion of aid restriction to the GVN (Saigon Government);

3. A quiet cancellation of the November 20th plans to withdraw troops, disguised by a public reaffirmation of a previously announced "objective" with respect to withdrawal;

4. Authorization of planning for a coherent program of covert activities in 1964 and for exploring the feasibility of initiating a wider war against North Vietnam;

5. An order to "all senior officers" to avoid any criticism of U.S. Vietnam policy;

6. A directive to the State Department to develop a "case" which would demonstrate Hanoi's control of the Vietcong.

Shifts in language indicate a change in policy – the U.S. was to begin to carry the war north. Perhaps the best proof is that the planned withdrawal of units advising combat troops was not implemented. Despite statements to the contrary, only a few hundred individuals were withdrawn and those were from non-combat elements. NSAM 273 appears to have been designed to give the illusion of continuity with Kennedy's policies by reaffirming the objectives, while it directed that the military and economic assistance programs should not appear to be lower than they had been under the Diem government.

The ARRB declassification of military documents in 1997 clarified that on November 26, 1963, President Johnson ordered through NSAM 273 CINCPAC OPLAN 34A, which "intensified operations against North Vietnam ... covering the full spectrum of sabotage, psychological and raiding activity." Laos and Cambodia were specifically mentioned as staging sites though they appear to have been off-limits under Kennedy.

Two months after President Kennedy was assassinated, General Taylor, under the influence of George Ball, wrote to Secretary McNamara, "The Joint Chiefs of Staff consider that the U.S. must: commit additional U.S. forces, as necessary, in support of the combat action within South Vietnam, and commit U.S. forces as necessary in direct actions against North Vietnam." These two top-level officials had changed their recommendations under President Johnson. A full declassification of NSAM 263 and 273 may prove as difficult as the full declassification of the HSCA files.

General Lansdale envisioned a distinctly different policy direction for the U.S. in Vietnam. He had worked in the Saigon Military Mission during the Eisenhower Administration and owed his promotion to Brigadier General to CIA Director Allen Dulles. Lansdale advised General McGarr when McGarr and then Vice-President Johnson visited Vietnam and advocated widening the use of U.S. troops under the guise of training in 1961. Former DCIA William Colby has noted that at that time, "LBJ might have been freewheeling out there (in Vietnam)."[21]

At a White House reception on Christmas Eve, a month after he succeeded to the presidency, Lyndon Johnson reportedly told the Joint Chiefs: "Just get me elected, then you can have your war."[22]

In early 1964 Johnson's National Security Advisor decided that something was needed to overcome the U.S. public's apathy toward the war. This seemly led to U.S. provocations in the Gulf of Tonkin, which elicited a light North Vietnamese counterattack on two U.S. destroyers. The Vietnamese response was intentionally misrepresented as an attack on U.S. ships in international waters. Congress reacted immediately by passing the Tonkin Gulf Resolution to support American sovereignty, arouse the public, and widen the war powers of the presidency in Vietnam.

To further bolster the case to widen American involvement, the State Department developed a White Paper (a major policy research backgrounder) based on contrived CIA intelligence. One CIA operation, concocted to prove the paper's thesis, involved a scheme to print large numbers of postage stamps showing the Viet Cong shooting down a U.S. helicopter. The professional production technique was meant to indicate that the stamp was printed in North Vietnam but the Viet Cong lacked the capability to print stamps. An enlarged "North Vietnamese Stamp" appeared on the cover of *Life*, 2/26/65, just two days before the publication of the White Paper.[23]

President Kennedy also set policies for international economic development that placed him in conflict with many factions of the corporate and banking communities. A Senate speech in 1959 foreshadowed this.

> We can finally make it clear to ourselves that international economic development is not, somehow, a nagging responsibility, to be faced each year in the context of giveaways and taxes – but a vast international effort, an enterprise of positive association, which is close to the heart of our relating with the whole Free World and which requires active American leadership.

In 1959 Senator Kennedy criticized the loan policies of the Export-Import and World Bank. In 1960 he condemned the policies of private banks by arguing that the United States must assist development "in a spirit of generosity motivated by a desire to help our fellow citizens of the world – not as narrow bankers or self-seeking politicians."[24]

The Alliance for Progress reflected broader goals than anti-communism, just as JFK's confrontation with U.S. Steel reflected broader goals than corporate profits. Even though the U.S. economy expanded robustly during his administration, significant banking, and corporate interests, some aligned with elements of the mass media, could see their power challenged. They leveled a scathing rebuke.

Fortune magazine (Time-Life), viewed Kennedy's notion of foreign nationalism as "insane" to bypass those in Latin America who favor "sound money, higher productivity in exportable goods and internal free enterprise."[25] Kennedy's attempts to use the tax credits to guide investments was characterized as an "elaborate gimmick" to "manipulate the economy" from a "reactionary... who belongs to a cult as old as Diocletian."

Fortune editor Charles Murphy, a close friend of Allen Dulles, asserted that economic assistance should be accompanied by "a combined effort to organize the capacity of the underdeveloped countries to produce more and more primary commodities for export, the only path for those countries toward true self-sustaining growth and social stability." Kennedy's failure to attach tough conditions to loans was repeatedly criticized. "Would it not have been wise to seek a cure for Latin America's economic woes through an international apparatus that included the major European nations, loan bankers to that region and its first market?"

John McCloy, one of the leaders of the Eastern Establishment, saw an inexperienced president who "makes no effort to institute any connections to the Council on Foreign Relations or other establishment institutions." *Time, Life, Fortune, Newsweek* and the *Wall Street Journal* attacked Kennedy's budget, tax, banking and deficit spending policies, which the *WSJ* saw as a "potential threat to the national interest." Milton Friedman saw JFK's role in the steel crisis as "how much power for a police state resides in Washington."

The *Wall Street Journal* accused the Kennedy administration of giving "lip service to economic freedom," while pursuing a foreign aid program that favored socialism and a domestic program that led to bureaucratic control of the economy." It criticized Kennedy's policy of providing soft loans (long-term with little or no interest) and advised adherence to World Bank policies. Kennedy's budget deficits and low interest rates were characterized as "the most restrictive and reactionary economic policy" in U.S. history. Domestically, Kennedy's deficit spending was seen as a "deep and damaging delusion," while *Life* viewed this as "reckless."[26]

Kennedy opposed the powerful Bank for International Settlements by keeping interest rates low. This bank reflected the goals of the central banks of the major non-communist countries. Their members believed financial policies should not be left to politicians. Kennedy also opposed the largely non-financial corporate Committee for Economic Development (CED) advice regarding taxes, government spending and monetary policy. JFK's concern about capital flight led him to try to limit overseas tax shelters. Wall Street bankers viewed this as a threat to their profits and the flow of capital.[27]

Life criticized President Kennedy and the Department of Justice for confronting mergers in the airline and railroad sectors. They also castigated Kennedy for proposing increased taxes on American purchases of foreign securities, as well as betraying European allies in opposing colonialism.

Kennedy's movement towards "a managed economy" according to the *Wall Street Journal* was leading "towards an all-encompassing government." Moreover, "Mr. Kennedy has come increasingly to believe that large and global banking problems are too important to be left entirely to bankers."

Life printed a landmark exchange of letters between Kennedy and David Rockefeller 7/6/62, which highlighted their differences. Rockefeller wrote that the president's proposed exchange controls over capital movements "would destroy the effective functioning of the dollar." And that his requiring a "25 [percent] gold reserve against the Federal Reserve notes and deposits should be suspended." Kennedy met with Rockefeller a week later and they pushed through the Trade Expansion Act of 1962, which widened trade and reduced tariffs – but their differences far outweighed their agreements.[28]

JFK steadfastly focused on the balance of payment deficit "to the chagrin of bankers."

To confront the outflow into Eurodollar accounts, Kennedy proposed a temporary 15% tax on loans made by American banks to foreign borrowers – which angered the banking community. Walter Wriston, executive vice-president of First National City Bank declared, "Who is this upstart President interfering with the free flow of capital?"[29]

Newsweek frequently raised similar criticisms. Editor Henry Hazlitt railed against budget deficits, easy money, low interest rates and foreign aid, which promote national planning and socialism.[30]

The Kennedy Act, 10/16/62, confronted the oil industry by removing the distinction between repatriated profits and profits reinvested abroad.

Both became subject to U.S. taxes. This prevented taxable income from being hidden in foreign subsidiaries and tax havens. In 1963 Kennedy proposed closing corporate tax loopholes, including the oil depletion allowance.[31]

After the assassination, *The National Review*, published by former CIA officer William F. Buckley, revealed a deep fear of Kennedy's policies among cold warriors and elements of the corporate establishment. "His programs and policies – we judged to be, for the most part, dangerous to the nation's well-being and security, and to the survival of perilously threatened Western civilization."[32]

In addition to Wall Street fears over stronger government, lower interest rates, deficit spending and the Alliance for Progress, there was a split within Kennedy's administration over banking policy. The Kennedy crowd was opposed by the Douglas Dillon and the Federal Reserve group which represented the major banks. Dillon was a close associate of David Rockefeller and former director of the Chase Manhattan Bank. Generations of elite control of the U.S. and the global economy was challenged by a popular president. Trillions of dollars were at stake.

President Kennedy's Latin American policy, the Alliance for Progress, based on the Marshall Plan, tried to "modernize" and "democratize." In his speech to launch La Allianza in March 1961, he declared that "those who made democracy impossible make violent revolution inevitable." This lofty rhetoric, coupled with a commitment of $20 billion over 10 years, was enthusiastically greeted in Latin America. JFK saw La Allianza as countering corporate interests as well as Castro's charisma.[33] New Frontiersman Richard Goodwin initially advised the program. He pushed for, among other projects, providing equipment for nationalized mines in Bolivia, as well as U.S. government financing to state-run oil companies. The Rockefeller family, corporate elites and the Republican Party staunchly resisted – and Goodwin was reassigned. More moderate central planning generally failed to excite Latin American civil society and it was fought by Latin American oligarchs. Further, most of the countries then lacked experienced economists and agronomists to develop long range plans. Few observers dispute that the Alliance lost its way, yet the reasons remain controversial.

The Alliance for Progress generated a large infusion of aid and investment which funded the construction of housing, schools, airports, clinics, water systems, agricultural loans as well as textbooks. To placate Latin American elites, military and police aid increased rapidly as well as funding for military courses in riot control, counterinsurgency, psychological operations and "civic action" programs to counter perceived internal threats. Significant reforms were often not attempted due to lack of expertise as well as skepticism toward central planning, especially toward a largely American run program. By October 1963, the State Department concluded that the Alliance's goal of development within the framework of democracy was not attainable in the near future, because "in most of Latin America there is so little experience with the benefits of political legitimacy." Kennedy, according to advisor Ted Sorenson, recognized "the Latin American military often represented more competence in administration and more sympathy with the U.S. than any other group in the country."

This meant that the military could maintain the status quo for the oligarchs. In many cases civilian conservatives urged the military to act before elections brought undesirable liberals to power, which threatened their interests. Regular meetings produced tensions over complicated political and economic reforms. Meanwhile a impatient and resistant congress cut funding in 1962. Congress viewed it as not popular enough in many countries as well as The Alliance was seen as less influential than U.S. military missions and the School of the Americas.

Nonetheless, a U.N. analysis in 1963 stated that the Latin American middle class was turning restless and radical. CIA reports in early 1964 warned of increased "statist" support, and that as any appearance of success in Cuba could have an extensive impact on the statist trend elsewhere in the area. The revolution of rising expectations also posed threats to elite interests at home and abroad:

> ...political and popular demands for accomplishments in short periods of time are irrational and unrealistic. Political parties and candidates who attain power extra-legally have stimulated popular aspirations, which are impossible of attainment...[34]

Despite the limitations of the Alliance for Progress, Kennedy was supportive of most progressive Latin American institutions and leaders. Under Johnson, however, the programs quickly reverted to a neocolonialism which gave free rein to bankers and businesses, and accelerated military sales.

The pace and scope of foreign policy changes in Latin America under President Johnson were extraordinary. Upon taking office, Johnson appointed his old friend, conservative Texan Thomas Mann to three posts: Director of the Alliance, Special Assistant to the President, and Assistant Secretary of State for Inter-American affairs. Richard Goodwin viewed Mann as a "colonialist who believes that the natives need to be shown who is boss." One of Mann's first official acts in his new posts was to give official recognition to the Somoza-United Fruit Coup in Honduras.[35] He then helped plan for the invasion of the Dominican Republic. Johnson wrote David Rockefeller to underscore his "grateful private sector leadership" in this "great undertaking."[35] Mann carried out David Rockefeller's request that the economic portion of the Alliance be quickly dismantled, and that the aims of democracy and structural change, such as modest land reform and income redistribution, be dropped as goals. -Mann had been a former assistant to John Foster Dulles at the State Department, an organizer for the Bay of Pigs, as well as the U.S. Ambassador to Mexico during Oswald's visit. After the assassination, CIA cables indicate that Mann promoted the CIA assertion to LBJ that Oswald was a Cuban agent.[36]

Former Supreme Court Justice William Douglas observed: "When Johnson took over the Alliance for Progress the emphasis of that program shifted from external threats to internal security. We not only built up the Latin American military, we set up police schools in the Canal Zone.... We also spent large sums of money through the Alliance to equip local police and gendarmes. Soon the clubs used to crack the skulls were all marked 'made in USA.'"[37] Meanwhile, U.S. aid to Latin America rapidly dropped from .57% GDP from 1961-1964 to .44% GDP from 1965-1968.[38]

Cuban policy uniquely plagued Kennedy's presidency. After the Missile Crisis a controversial reassessment led to the destabilization campaign, "Operation Mongoose." In March 1963, after a Cuban exile group attacked a Soviet ship in Cuban waters, Kennedy ordered restrictions on unauthorized exile activities; however, with over 500 anti-Castro groups of raiders trained to sabotage and kill in Cuba (many of them armed and trained by the CIA), the Administration seemingly scaled back on its own restriction.

By spring 1963, relations between Time-Life and Kennedy needed mending. At a White House lunch the Luces browbeat Kennedy about the need to invade Cuba, until JFK suggested that Luce was a "warmonger." The Luces immediately marched out of the White House,[39] and back to Time-Life headquarters to convene an editors meeting. "Luce told his editors that if the Kennedy administration could not be counted on to confront the communist bastion in the Caribbean, Time-Life Inc. would." Time-Life's funding for anti-Castro Cubans and the Bayo-Pawley raid could be called "paramilitary journalism."

Kennedy's Cuban policy was moving in two directions: he was probing for talks but sustaining multi-track pressures. Documents show that Kennedy placed high priority on a normal relationship with Cuba. The White House rejected a State Department recommendation that Cuba loosen its ties with the Soviet Union and China as the price for normal relations. A White House memo, 4/4/63, said, "We don't want to present Castro with a condition that he obviously can't fulfill. We should start thinking along more flexible lines. The President himself is very interested in this one." To some ideologues, this represented a dangerous reassessment of foreign and intelligence policies. U.S.-Cuban diplomacy in 1962 through spring of 1963 worked through a sole direct channel, James Donovan, a "volunteer" attorney, overseen by the CIA and Robert Kennedy. Donovan negotiated a number of prisoner swaps, built trust with Castro, and effectively shared a vision of normalized relations.[40] In 1963 President Kennedy had opened a "back channel" to Castro through TV reporter Lisa Howard and UN Special Advisor, former *Look* editor, William Attwood, and the Cuban UN Ambassador Carlos Lachuga. Republican and former business leader CIA Director John McCone opposed the policy shift toward Cuba.

Attwood found Castro quite receptive: "Castro would very much like to talk to the U.S. official anytime and appreciated the discretion.... The final effort undertaken through back channels was by President Kennedy through French journalist Jean Daniel, who was sent to Kennedy by Attwood. Castro responded well to Daniel's mission and told him that "JFK would become the greatest president of the United States; the leader may at last understand that there can be coexistence between capitalists and socialists, even in the Americas."[41]

Although Castro had been receptive, after the assassination, National Security Advisor McGeorge Bundy told Attwood that, "the Cuban exercise would probably be put on ice for a while."[42] It was. Castro's concerns can be seen in his startling message to LBJ, through reporter Lisa Howard, on February 12, 1964. Castro proposed that if "there is anything I can do to [help] his (Johnson's) majority ... if LBJ needs to take some hostile action [against Cuba] because of domestic considerations, he would understand." He only asked to be informed before the fact. Still receiving no response, Castro tried to use a Spanish mediator, an interview with the *New York Times*, and a private meeting with Howard, Senator Gene McCarthy, and Che Guevara. But to no avail; Cuban-American relations were now indeed on ice.

CIA covert operations chief, Richard Helms, controlled American intelligence reports out of Cuba. He had taken over the Castro murder plots in 1962 and kept JFK uninformed. It was Helms' top aide Thomas Karamassines, who signed off on the false Mexico City reports about Oswald, and it was Helms who arranged the Warren Commission's non-investigatory trip to Mexico.

In the Dominican Republic, U.S. policy sometimes obstructed reformist President Juan Bosch from accomplishing land reform and labor mobilization. In November 1962 U.S. Ambassador John Martin sent directives to repress opposition leaders. This was reiterated in 1963 with Robert Kennedy advocating U.S. training and Dominican police use of riot control techniques. President Kennedy did not support all of the Bosch government's reforms, which were seen as too extensive. In September 1963 the democratically elected Bosch was overthrown by a military and civilian coup. Immediately afterward, Kennedy suspended diplomatic relations and ended economic aid. It seems highly unlikely that Kennedy would have intervened with 20,000 troops in 1965, as Johnson did, to keep Bosch from retaking office.

The reverberations from the Cuban Missile Crisis provoked Kennedy to shift policy on the space race in September of 1963. At the UN JFK proclaimed,

> Finally, in a field where the United States and the Soviet Union have a special capacity – in the field of space – there is room for a new cooperation, for further joint efforts in the regulation and exploration of space. I include among these possibilities a joint expedition to the moon... Why, therefore should man's first flight to the moon be a matter of national competition? Surely we should explore whether the scientists and astronauts of our two countries – indeed all of the world – cannot work together in the conquest of space, sending someday in this decade to the moon not representation of a single nation, but representatives of all of our countries.

In October, Kennedy confronted the Soviet food shortages with the policy of selling them U.S. surplus grain, although LBJ and other conservatives opposed it. Publicly Kennedy declared that our nation had a grain surplus, that the Soviets would pay in cash, that it would help our balance of payments, and that it would be transported on American ships. In a letter to Congress JFK argued that it "was one more sign that a peaceful world is possible and beneficial to us all."

In Brazil, President Kennedy directed his brother to slow the drift to the left of Brazilian President Joao Goulart. Unable to convince Goulart to denounce either domestic communists or Castro, a special task force then tried to use the Brazilian military to "urge" Goulart to resign. Achieving no success, the task force recommended in October 1963 "the most favorable succession."[43] Military assistance and riot control equipment were given to elements of the Brazilian military and the CIA also distributed slush funds to right-wing groups along with weapons stockpiles. Whether the 1964 coup would have been promoted by Kennedy, or so brutally consolidated in its aftermath, also appears highly unlikely. Five months after Kennedy's death, his foreign policy adversary John J. McCloy supervised the coup d'état named "Operation Brother Sam." After the coup, President Johnson and Assistant Secretary of State Thomas Mann openly de-emphasized land reform, democracy, and income distribution, and encouraged General Branco to use intimidation to get the Brazilian Congress to accept the IMF (International Monetary Fund) austerity programs. Johnson characterized these actions as "courageous."[44]

President Kennedy continued to oppose the CIA and his military advisors on Indonesia as well. President Sukarno was to be supported with expanded civic action, military aid, economic stabilization programs, and development programs, as well as diplomatic initiatives (NSAM 179).

By November 4, 1963 Sukarno informed the U.S. Ambassador, Howard Jones, that he had been given evidence of a CIA plan to topple him and his government. Sukarno knew of JFK's support and invited him to Indonesia the following spring. On November 19 Kennedy had accepted the invitation – dramatically supporting third world nationalism, as opposed to corporate profits and Cold War ideology.[45]

LBJ completely changed U.S. policy toward Indonesia in his first month in office by cutting economic aid and then backing the British policy of isolating and punishing Indonesia. U.S. support for the British dominance in the newly formed Malaysian Federation was opposed by Sukarno, a leader of the Non-Aligned Movement. This contributed in 1965 to the Sukarno government withdrawing from the International Monetary Fund and World Bank and seizing properties of major U.S., British and Dutch companies. This triggered a CIA- directed coup, led by junior officers, which placed the corporate-minded and repressive

General Suharto in power. Estimates of slaughtered Indonesian Communists range from 300,000 to 1,000,000. In April 1965, Freeport Sulphur reached a preliminary arrangement with Indonesian officials for what would later become a $500 million investment in copper in West Papua, New Guinea.[46]

Shifts in policy and style by LBJ can also be seen regarding Greek democracy. President Johnson told the Greek ambassador, "Mr. Ambassador, fuck your Parliament and your Constitution. America is an elephant.... If your Prime Minister gives me talk about Democracy, Parliament and Constitution, he, his Parliament, and his Constitution may not last very long."[47] In 1967, after the Greek coup mostly led by CIA trained and funded colonels, Johnson gave his support.

The Joint Chiefs of Staff and a number of military leaders had vehemently opposed Kennedy's Limited Test Ban Treaty. Would the CIA have overthrown the governments of Bolivia, Ghana, and Greece under Kennedy? Would the Alliance for Progress have been gutted by the Assistant Secretary of State for Inter-American Affairs and White House Special Assistant, Thomas Mann? Would the CIA have rapidly expanded its operations? Dr. Loch Johnson, former aide to Senator Church, has estimated that CIA spending for covert actions almost doubled during the Johnson presidency.[48] Kennedy's economic programs promoting low taxes, low interest, rates of government spending, banking regulations and corporate taxes on oil, all changed quickly under LBJ.

President Kennedy was anti-communist, often anti-colonialist, and pro-capitalist regarding development. Increasingly, he charted a moderate and less confrontational path. He proposed increased cooperation among nations and bankers to facilitate economic development within limits, and foreign aid and lending programs often served that goal. He was tolerant of, and at times supportive of considerable government economic planning within and among nations. After the Cuban Missile Crisis, a strong commitment to coexistence emerged toward the Soviet Union, Cuba, and Vietnam; however, this détente was delayed for decades. His anti-colonial policies threatened many elements of banking and corporate America, the military industrial complex, as well as many of the old cold warriors within government and the mass media, as well as the mafia. The Kennedys were challenging the Eastern Establishment led by the Dulles brothers.

His foreign policy principles can be seen in portions of the speech he never delivered in Dallas:

We in this country, in this generation, are – by destiny rather than choice – the watchmen on the walls of the world of freedom. We ask, therefore, that we may be worthy of our power and responsibility – that we may exercise our strength with wisdom and restraint – and that we may achieve in our time and for all time the ancient vision of peace on earth, good will toward men. That must always be our goal - and the righteousness of our cause must always underlie our strength. For it is written long ago: "Except the Lord keep the city, the watchmen waketh but in vain."

19

REFLECTIONS

Tragedy moves from pity--to terror--to cleansing catharsis.
  – Aristotle

How many ages hence
Shall this lofty scene be acted o'er
In states unborn and accents yet unknown
  – Shakespeare
  Julius Caesar

No nation could preserve its freedom in the midst of continual warfare.
  – James Madison, 1793

We seek a nation at peace with its own conscience.
  - Martin Luther King, Jr.

The CIA-elite-media connections of the 1960s and 1970s had a significant impact on framing Oswald, supporting the FBI investigation and the Warren Commission, marginalizing critics, blunting the Garrison investigation, weakening the HSCA, diminishing the impact of *JFK*, and generally ignoring the findings of the ARRB. Elite factions, often reflecting blocks of capital as well as ideology, constantly vie for power. The Dulles family and their supporters were challenged by the Kennedys. In this case, bitter political and economic fights led to a coup d'état. Preserving systemic legitimacy and perceived self-interest contributed to the establishment factions supporting the government institutions. The independence of the media to report on powerful illegitimate factions remains problematic regarding major abuses of power. Some examples of the failed mass media include: the counting of national election votes in Florida in 2000; the assassination of progressive leaders, Dr. King and Robert Kennedy; the lead-up to the war in Iraq, the 9/11 attack, the banking crisis of 2008, the Trans-Pacific Partnership, or coverage of inequality, fracking, climate change, or international institutions.

The media more fully explores how wars should be fought, rather than whether they should be fought – or how failed wars should be ended. Investigations of the legitimacy of government, even decades ago, remain beyond real coverage. Proximity to power clouds perceptions. George Washington warned:

> Government is not reason, it is not eloquence – it is force. Like fire it is a dangerous servant and a fearful master; never for a moment should it be left to irresponsible action.

Genuine investigative reporting now would expose the inept and compromised reporting of the past. The reputation and power of reporters, news directors, publishers, editors, and their organizations would be tarnished or discredited. The model of a "Prisoner's Dilemma" seems in effect, because more is gained by mutual silence and defensiveness than through pursuit of the truth. Elizabeth Nowell-Newman, in *The Spiral of Silence,* saw silence as reflecting the profound power of social control. Fear of being socially isolated for supporting an unpopular idea leads to a downward spiral of fewer people supporting it. Acceptance within the ruling elite, of which the mass media are a major part, weighs heavily on pursuing questions of systemic legitimacy.[1] Reporter Jefferson Morley's conversation with a senior editor at the *Washington Post* about revealing new facts about JFK's murder is apt.

> This is a messy, complex slippery subject with nothing analogous in journalism. To take on the task of saying something new and definitive at this late date, to sell the story today, the bar is very high. The political implications are huge. People don't like to talk about this consideration in the newsroom. Credibility is on the line. To say there was a conspiracy in the assassination of President Kennedy would be a remarkably bold and political statement. The story is old but the CIA budget is upwards of $20 billion a year. The political implications are very alive.[2]

The perceived threat to national security after the assassination appears to have been crafted by factions within the CIA in advance, built upon Oswald's persona as a communist sympathizer and his visit to Mexico. CIA Counter-Intelligence, CIA DDP, and elements of military intelligence, sought to portray Oswald visiting the Cuban and Russian Embassies as an attempt to return to Russia. This could generate national pressure to retaliate, perhaps an invasion of Cuba – or to force a cover-up story characterizing Oswald as a lone nut. LBJ argued to Chief Justice Warren and government elites that the public demand for revenge could risk world war, thus neutralizing pressure for independent inquiry. Recall that LBJ and Hoover knew the day after the assassination that the supposed pictures of Oswald visiting the Cuban and Russian Embassies were not pictures of him, and the recordings supposedly of Oswald talking with those embassies in Mexico City were not his voice.

If national security was seen as a legitimate reason to cover up the assassination by the mass media at first, why was it still necessary by late 1964? 1967? 1992? Today? John Dewey noted, "it is not easy to interest the public in the public interest," yet this assassination still stirs interest and controversy. Clearly ratings, a key element in the bureaucratic model determining what is written or aired, cannot account for the lack of media coverage.

When JFK's close friend Ben Bradlee became the managing editor at the *Washington Post* in the fall of 1965 he noted: "I think I probably felt that since I had been a friend of Kennedy that – you know, this is just [two] years later, and the first thing he [Bradlee] does is come over to the paper that he's hopefully going to run for a while – and he concentrates on that [the JFK assassination] ..." Author David Talbot thought Bradlee was afraid that he would "be discredited for taking the efforts [of the *Post* newsroom] down that path."[3]

The Cold War cooperation of mass media elites with government and business elites developed in formal and informal networks. Considering the leadership roles of John and Allen Dulles and John McCloy in the Council on Foreign Relations, the CFR served as a significant network to strengthen the "lone nut" scenario. Later the CFR, which includes media executives and editors, would protect the Warren Report, as well as sustain the perception of legitimacy in government.

Coverage of this assassination is woven into the abrupt and unsettling reshaping of American journalism – now owned by huge corporations. Mergers in the mass media since the assassination have rapidly increased in size and scope. Five conglomerates now control the majority of the American mass media – and are owned or financially linked to much of corporate America. For example, the Associated Press now has 242 bureaus, reporters in 121 countries, and reaches more than one billion daily through 8,500 subscribers. The AP Board of Directors consists of 22 newspaper and media executives including the Presidents/CEOs of ABC, Cox News, McClatchy, Gannet, Scripps, Tribune, Hearst, *Washington Post*, and several smaller newspaper chains. Two directors are members of conservative policy councils, including the Hoover Institute and the Business Round Table, three are on the board of Mutual Insurance and one is on the board of defense contractor Lockheed Martin.[4]

Currently the New York Times Co. has interlocking directorships (those sitting on one corporate board who also sit on other corporate boards) with 360 Degree Communication, Alcoa, Avon, Bristol-Myers Squibb, Campbell Soup, Carlyle Group, Chase Manhattan, Cummins Engine Corp, Ford, Grace & Co., Hallmark Cards, Hanson PLC, Johnson & Johnson, Knoll, Lehman Bros., Lucas Digital, Lucas Arts, Lucent Technologies, Metropolitan Life, PepsiCo, Principal Financial Group, Schering-Plough, Sears, Springs Industries, Starwood Hotels & Resorts, State Street Research and Management, Texaco, U.S. Industries, Warburg Pincus & Co. and Zurich Insurance.

Amazon.com founder Jeff Bezos owns the *Washington Post*, while the CIA has a $6 million dollar contract with Amazon.com. Rupert Murdoch's global media empire includes FOX network and the *Wall Street Journal*.

Sometimes national security pressures on the mass media are thinly veiled yet unmentioned. President George W. Bush's communications director was Catherine Martin, whose husband Keven chaired the FCC. President Obama's deputy national security advisor for strategic communications was Ben Rhodes, whose brother David is president of CBS News.[5]

The *Columbia Journalism Review* article "Money Lust" posited that increased "pressure for profit is perverting journalism," by increasing its reliance on news services and infotainment, while cutting reporters.[6] The Project for Excellence in Journalism (Harvard) determined that from 1977 to 1997, coverage of celebrity, scandal gossip, and "human interest" increased from 15% to 43% of the coverage. Front-page stories about government dropped from 1 in 3 to 1 in 5 by 1997. a rapid erosion of investigative journalism.

As David Simon testified to the Senate, "When the newspaper chains began cutting personnel and content, the industry was one of the most profitable yet discovered on Wall St. ... The *Baltimore Sun* was eliminating its afternoon edition in an era when the paper was achieving 37% profit ... "In short, my industry butchered itself, and we did so at the behest of Wall Street."[7]

The rise of the Internet, the loss of advertising revenue to online sites, and the great recession, further weakened the legacy mass media. Journalism professor Philip Meyer unsuccessfully tried to "convince the owners and managers of newspapers of the futility of cutting the quality of their products in an attempt to gain monopoly profits after the monopoly was gone."[8]

Bill Moyers recalls the challenges of investigative reporting under complicit editors and government officials:

> Trying to tell the truth about people whose job it is to hide the truth is almost as complicated and difficult as trying to hide it in the first place. Unless you're willing to fight and refight the same battles until you go blue in the face, to drive the people you work with nuts going over every last detail to make certain you are right, and then take hit after unfair hit accusing you of having a bias, or these days a point of view, there is no use in even trying…[9]

When Moyers served as President Johnson's aide, he was tasked by Assistant Attorney General Nicholas Katzenbach, through a memo, to "convince the public that Oswald was the lone assassin and that he did not have confederates." This early shielding of information may account for Moyers not reporting as vigorously on this assassination as on other issues.

Playwright Bertolt Brecht wrote in 1935:

> Nowadays, anyone who wishes to combat lies and ignorance and to write the truth must overcome at least five difficulties. He must have the courage to write the truth when truth is everywhere opposed; the keenness to recognize it although it is everywhere concealed; the skill to manipulate it as a weapon; the judgment to select those in whose hands it will be effective; and the cunning to spread the truth among such persons.

Interviews with media owners, publishers, producers, editors, and reporters could clarify media coverage of this assassination, but precious few have gone on the record. They would still risk much in order to question the political legitimacy of government, their profession, their bosses, their friends and associates. How legitimate would the government and the mass media appear, if even five decades later, it could be proven that a coordinated effort covered up the assassination?

When powerful officials refuse to contend with government claims, there appear to be few catalysts to engage news coverage. Journalist Kristina Borjesson explored this conundrum when she interviewed former *Nightline* anchor Ted Koppel about the justification for the Iraq war1.

> No, I don't just take their [the government] word for it. But when they tell me why they're going to war, I certainly have to give proper deference to … if the president says I'm going to war for reasons A, B and C, I can't very well stand there and say, "The president is not telling you the truth, the actual reason that he's going to war is some reason he has not mentioned." I as a reporter have to say, "Here is what the president is saying. Here's what the secretary of defense is saying. Here's what the director of the CIA is saying." And indeed, when everyone at that point who has access to the classified information is with more or less one voice agreeing that, yes, there appears to be evidence that Saddam Hussein still has weapons of mass destruction – maybe not nuclear, but certainly chemical and biological – are you suggesting that the entire American press corps then say, "Well horse manure."[10]

Numerous senators, congressmen, and foreign policy experts offered opposing perspectives, yet they were rarely interviewed during the build-up to the Iraq War. The sphere of legitimate controversy narrows and self-censorship increases markedly when notions of national security collide with systemic legitimacy. The context of seventy years of U.S. and British policies to control the oil in the Middle East remained almost invisible – as has the politicization of intelligence to justify the Iraq war.

It is impossible to know how frequently the media suppress stories for national security reasons, or how this is done after requests are made. *New York Times* ombud Margaret Sullivan bluntly declared, "The real threat to national security is a government operating in secret and accountable to no one, with watchdogs too willing to muzzle themselves."[11]

Respected reporters experience visceral social and organizational constraints. Citizens' critiques of the 9/11 Commission are as extensive as the criticisms of the Warren Report, yet they rarely reach the mainstream news. Dan Rather, no longer with CBS, offered a vivid explanation on *BBC News Night* (11/25/01)

> There was a time in South Africa when people would put flaming tires around people's necks if they dissented. And in some ways, the fear is that you will be necklaced here. You will have a flaming tire

of lack of patriotism put around your neck. Now it is that fear that keeps journalists from asking the toughest of the tough questions. Fear of loss of respect, job assignment, job security, friends and status were all heightened after 9/11.[12]

Rebecca Abrahams, an assignment editor with ABC News, concurred,

I think news reporting has drastically changed since 9/11. The reporting now always has the use of caution in how we cover a story. We are every day kicking and screaming to get stories out, but it may not make air. You have someone from the corporation making the editorial decisions.[13]

Jefferson Morley suggests that belief and fact are not separate entities but on a continuum, with tension between them. He recalls finishing a piece about CIA officer John Whitten, "The Good Spy," for the *Washington Monthly*.

...I was talking with the editor, a very good editor, about the last line. 'Whitten was interested in pursuing the investigation of Oswald's Cuba related activities'. I noted that his thinking along this line paralleled Lyndon Johnson, Richard Nixon, Robert Kennedy and, Fidel Castro. The editor replied, 'No, I believe you – I just want to cut the line. I said 'It's true'. [The editor responded] 'But this line about an interesting man at an interesting time tips the piece into being a conspiracy piece' [Morley noted] 'well, the line is true, and you think it is persuasive, so we have to take it out because it is true and persuasive'. So I took it out, because I wanted the piece published.

Journalism remains more art than science. American journalism is a loosely organized profession, ill-equipped to report on anatomy, radiology, ballistics, forensic science, trajectories, forged x-rays, and neutron activation analysis, let alone a coup d'état. Codes of journalistic ethics remain unclear, most journalists reject licensing procedures, and most journalists are indifferent to professional associations. The press system, which has been adrift, still lacks a clear standard of accountability.

Within a very complicated case, some inaccurate reporting has the appearance of propaganda when, in fact, complexity is the cause. Mass media pressures for profit limit the resources of investigative reporters. The assassination was a successful covert operation, cleverly covered-up and tough to investigate – yet the work of the HSCA and the ARRB released millions of pages of critical documents which could be explored in the National Archives.

Again, the citizenry continues to develop new leads and unearth critical documents, sharing them on websites such as the Mary Ferrell Foundation, Kennedy and King, JFK Facts, Education Forum, and AARC, among others. This suggests that limited media resources are less a factor than self-censorship.

The conflict-theory concept of corporate control of the mainstream media provides a more useful framework than pluralist or bureaucratic models. Media-elite-intelligence networks overlap and often merge into cooperation. This protection became aggressive to support the Warren Commission findings due to Oswald's supposed Russian and Cuban connections within the context of the Cold War. Challenges to the Warren Commission findings, thus challenges to government, prodded by citizen critics, were sporadically printed in the mainstream media particularly throughout 1966 and 1967. Elements of government, protecting themselves and the legitimacy of a corporate dominated society, aggressively mobilized media assets to bolster the lone-nut scenarios to counter the conspiracy-related findings during the Garrison investigation. Years later, the movie *JFK* generated a threat to government as well as media legitimacy. It was met with a wide range of responses, including unprecedented mainstream media vitriol poured on a Hollywood movie.

New mainstream journalistic norms tend to conform to older ones – that they should avoid examining systemic threats to democracy in order to save profits, power, their jobs, and status. The forces of ambition are still stronger than the forces of truth and law. The temptation of access to power for reporters, editors, publishers, and owners, comes at the expense of truth. Secular mass media priesthood has defined political parameters that fit with their corporate and social pragmatism. American media has drifted on many national security issues toward Joseph Goebbels' goal, "What you want in a media system is ostensible diversity that conceals actual conformity." Philosopher Herbert Marcuse referred to this condition as "oppressive tolerance."

The mass media tendency to frame science vs. opinion as partisan disputes, as with climate change, continues to confuse the public. The push for profits along with digital technology has widened the role of entertainment, spectacle and celebrity. We have a range of bread and circuses undreamed of at the founding of our republic – or even during the Reagan years. The digital revolution increases freedom of expression and access to information but decreases the power and legitimacy of the mainstream media. A Pew Research Center poll in 2011 found that 77% of Americans believe that news stories tend to favor one side," and 80% believe that "powerful people and organizations unduly influence the news."

The Pentagon and the CIA have also covertly impacted public attitudes on national security by influencing some movies and television series. The Pentagon liaison to Hollywood, Phil Strub, for decades controlled movie industry access to military equipment and weapons – with power to censor scenes or scripts. By 1996 the CIA appointed Chase Brandon, a veteran of Clandestine Services, as the first CIA Entertainment Liaison. The CIA has influenced films – *The Sum of All Fears*, *The Recruit*, *Argo*, *Zero Dark Thirty Company of Spies*, and *Mission Impossible*, and TV series – *The Agency*, *Alias*, *24*, *Covert Affairs*, *Homeland* and *The Americans*.[14]

Academe can sometimes move major ideas from the margins to the mainstream, yet assassination research remains marginalized in the disciplines of Political Science and History. Rigorous research threatens a paradigm shift – to accepting that a coup d'état occurred. Academe would be obliged to admit that they have confused, rather than clarified, that American political legitimacy has long been lost, and that officialdom and the mainstream media have generally acted as witting or unwitting accomplices.

Ironically, based on numerous polls, the public more effectively sorted through the Warren Report and its coverage than did academe. To some extent academic "groupthink" paralleled that in the mass media. The notion that some of their life work had actually confused their students and the citizenry is painful to confront. Philosopher Thomas Kuhn observed that "the proponents of competing paradigms practice their trades in different worlds." Careers, reputations, access to resources, anxiety, and self-deception preclude paradigmatic change – particularly when no middle ground exists for reformist views. Kuhn saw new scientific truth triumphing not so much by convincing its opponents, but rather because its opponents eventually pass away.

Future scholars may compare the U.S. assassinations of the 1960s with the era of assassinations in Japan, Italy and Germany in the 1920s and 1930s. The investigation of foreign assassinations parallels cases of U.S. "show trials" in the assassinations of Reverend Martin Luther King, Jr. and Senator Robert Kennedy, as well as the scandals of Watergate, Iran-Contra, B.C.C.I. (the contemporary PERMINDEX), the October Surprise, the invasion of Panama, the CIA involvement in the drug trade, the 2000 election recount in Florida, the 9/11 Commission, the rush to war in Iraq, Abu Ghraib, Guantanamo, the 2008 banking crisis, the covert role of the Joint Special Operations Command, and the Trans Pacific Partnership. Although all of these cases have steadily unraveled, mass media coverage has been erratic. Despite the CIA efforts of "The Mighty Wurlitzer" to manage news in the 1950s and the 1960s, polls show that confidence in government dropped quickly after November 1963. The mainstream media has faltered on all of these challenges, and consistently supported systemic political/economic legitimacy, and the status quo, rather that the truth.

Educator John Dewey viewed the press of his day as "a class of experts inevitably so removed from common interests as to become a class with private interests and private knowledge." Political organizer Antonio Gramaci viewed journalists, academics and public relations specialists as "efforts in legitimation." Writer Michael Parenti argues that propaganda is a constant defense of the ruling class, which always denies the existence of propaganda. Similarly, Karl Marx and Noam Chomsky see journalists as an instrument in a superstructure to maintain the ruling class. The assassination coverage shows the responses to a split ruling class in crisis – which included, as George Orwell saw political speech, "the defense of the indefensible." Sociologist Ralph Miliband sees the pluralist diversity in the media as misleading and creating a "mobilization of bias" toward an ideology supporting free enterprise, anti-communism, the Cold War, and the role of hegemony of the U.S. in the world. Most powerful reporters willingly accept a "long leash." The venerable former CBS anchor Walter Cronkite noted in 2007 that there is a ruling class, and that it is better to be part of it.[15] If a coup occurs, when can the mass media cover it?

In a similar case, it seems hardly surprising that the HSCA, which viewed the Martin Luther King assassination as a conspiracy of racist nuts, FBI incompetence, and perhaps the Mafia, was also denied additional funding to investigate King's death. Nor is it surprising that the FBI, the CIA, Military intelligence, the Memphis Police department, and the Tennessee judicial system still have numerous unresolved areas of involvement in the case. The HSCA files on the Martin Luther King investigation remain sealed from the American public for fifty years, supposedly to protect "national security." The mass media, with few exceptions, has failed to follow major new leads in this case, even after involvement from the King family in 1996, who believed in James Earl Ray's innocence..

The Tennessee District Court concluded in a civil suit, brought about by King's death, in Memphis in December 1999, that Lloyd Jowers was guilty of involvement in a wide-ranging assassination plot including the FBI, Army Intelligence and Mafia elements. Trial testimony included; that the key witness was dead drunk at the time of the assassination; four witnesses thought that the shots came from the embankment in front of Bessie Brewer's flophouse; the supposed murder weapon was dropped in a bundle minutes before the assassination; and the day of the assassination two army officers told Fire Department captain Carthell Weeden that they needed to use the Firehouse roof for surveillance of the adjacent Lorraine Motel – which they did. The mass media and alternative press coverage was almost non-existent, except for Court TV. The *New York Times* (10/12/99) buried its brief mention on page 25. The only way to believe the government's position on the assassination of Martin Luther King is to not read it. Neglect of the 1999 MLK assassination trial by the mainstream and alternative media raises sobering parallels with the coverage of the JFK assassination.

The conscious and unconscious public denial of threatening news regarding everything from global warming to foreign policy contributes to the lack of coverage. The U.S. public has despaired over, but largely denied the implications of even the HSCA findings, and thus has been unable and unwilling to recognize the implications and aftershocks from this assassination. George Orwell called this phenomenon "crimestop," essentially "stopping short, as if by instinct, at the threshold of a dangerous thought … failing to perceive logical errors … misunderstanding the simplest arguments." Although the vast majority of the public believes there was a government conspiracy and a cover-up, they don't *know* it. To move from belief to knowledge is to move from irresponsibility to responsibility – a very threatening change. The public seems gripped in psychic and political paralysis – a contemporary political "purgatory."

Carl Bernstein on CNN's *Reliable Sources* (3/2/14) warned of a recent and related phenomenon, "that more and more people are not open in the country to the best obtainable version of the truth."

> Instead they are looking to cable news; they're looking to the web, to find information that girds … their already preconceived notions, ideologies and prejudices. … That's different than at the time of Watergate. We no longer have kind of a two way process, in we have these media outlets. Online and in cable news, feeding these

prejudices, feeding these ideologies, without interest in the truth. And we don't know the extent that citizens are responsible, that the media is responsible and that the political system is responsible – but they are all irresponsible. [16]

James Madison warned of treasonous factions being the natural off-spring of free government in Federalist Paper #43. In John Kennedy's assassination a network of factions inside and outside of government planned and coordinated the conspiracy and the cover-up. The finger-prints of factions involved at the operational level have become clearer and more extensive with ARRB declassifications, while further declassification will clarify the case. Much was not written or has been destroyed. Nonetheless, the partial records releases in 2017 and 2018 in turn will generate some new leads along with work such as Russ Baker's on the connections of the oil, and industrial and banking interests to LBJ, Army Intelligence, George H.W. Bush, Allen Dulles and J. Edgar Hoover, Dallas Police, the Texas School Book Depository, and a range of anti-communist cohorts. Authors David Talbot and Jefferson Morley explored the extensive corporate and banking connections to Allen Dulles. Even after his firing, Dulles continued to meet regularly with high-level CIA officers, and wielded considerable power to mobilize political, economic and elite CFR media factions, critical to a cover-up. They also needed the cooperation of the desperate and ambitious LBJ as well as the powerful and vulnerable J. Edgar Hoover to insure the cover-up.

The conference on the 50th anniversary of the Warren Report, run by the Assassination Archives Research Center (AARC), deepened our understanding of CIA involvement in the assassination. Robert Blakey, former Chief Counsel of the HSCA, characterized the CIA obstructions as "treacherous" to his committee and to other committees. This was echoed by HSCA staffer Edwin Lopez, who detailed the daily obstructions to access of CIA files. Further, CIA asset Antonio Veciana publicly asserted that when he met with his case officer Maurice Bishop, Bishop was CIA officer David Phillips, and that he also saw Phillips meeting with Oswald.

A wide-ranging group of people and factions including LBJ, the FBI, the CIA, retired DCI Allan Dulles, DDP Helms and Counter Intelligence Chief Angleton, the Secret Service hierarchy, some of the top brass at DOD, elements of the Dallas sheriffs and police departments, portions of the mass media, along with elements of corporate America, the Mafia, and Warren Commission and HSCA insiders; have for various reasons effectively avoided, crushed, classified, or obfuscated enough of the truth for long enough that the conspirators have succeeded. Our Cold War strategies generated some attitudes and actions as brutal as our adversaries. Khrushchev and Kennedy were both removed less than two years after the Cuban Missile Crisis. Kennedy's assassination accelerated the growth of our National Security State, while mass media freedom was further co-opted.

Part of our tragic and ironic legacy is that President Kennedy built trust in government by promoting the public interest. When most of the public perceived a cover-up and a government role in the assassination, trust in government plummeted. As in 1963, America confronts a crossroads – the path of a military-industrial-intelligence-corporate path or the path of a republic, the path of an empire or the path of a democracy, the path of a national security state or the path of human rights.

With such a wide-ranging conspiracy, why hasn't it unraveled? It seems plausible that the shooters were well paid, and later were eliminated, to prevent them from talking. Those who knew of the assassination and gained from it had no reason to divulge information. Factions with partial knowledge and suspicions weighed the costs and benefits of pushing for the truth, mindful of media coverage as well as the fate of cooperative trusting witnesses. English writer John Harrington noted, "If treason doth prosper – none dare call it treason." Oswald's clear ties to the FBI forced the powerful J. Edgar Hoover to protect his agency and himself. Oswald's ties to the CIA and military intelligence forced their aggressive non-cooperation with investigation.

The intelligence agencies had long practiced "plausible deniability" to protect covert operations. Imagine if sensitive and problematic covert operations were co-opted and redirected, while multiple layers of operations served as a shield. This could include: the CIA-mafia operations to assassinate Castro, Nixon's Plumbers unit seemingly co-opted by McCord and Hunt, and the national security anti-terrorist exercises on the day of 9/11.

On national security issues the mass media remains faithful to officialdom, so public involvement is essential. It took a few years for the public to organize and analyze the 26 un-indexed volumes of Warren Commission Hearings and Evidence, and determine some of what was omitted from the Warren Report. The involved agencies still protect themselves. Most of the agencies and elected officials who ran investigations (i.e. HSCA) will appear incompetent or treasonous by the declassification of the files, and until recently, they have lobbied against or resisted full disclosure. It was primarily citizen investigators who generated public pressure for the formation of the HSCA. Many in Congress believed that a new investigation was necessary, but they were concerned that citizen advocacy increased the chances of being targeted in future elections. Consider the challenges faced by aggressive investigators like Senators Church and Hart in their presidential runs. By contrast, Gerald Ford of the Warren Commission, George H.W. Bush of the CIA, and Ronald Reagan of the Rockefeller Commission, all became Presidents. In a sophisticated news management system, the release of national security documents is usually painfully slow. Thousands of documents on World War II remain classified. On the JFK assassination the CIA, FBI, State Department, Secret Service, DOD and INS have all withheld many files from the ARRB.

Former U.S. Solicitor General Edwin Griswold, who had worked for the Nixon Administration to prevent the continued publication of the Pentagon Papers, recanted in a *Washington Post* op-ed 1989.

> There is massive over-classification and that the principal concern of the classifiers is not national security, but rather with governmental embarrassment of one sort or another. There may be some basis for short term classifications while plans are being made, or negotiations are going on, but apart from details of weapons systems, there is rarely any real risk to national security from the publication of facts related to transactions in the past, even the fairly recent past.[17]

The most powerful tool to gain access to this material had previously been the 1966 Freedom of Information Act, which was enacted in response to citizen requests for documents regarding the assassination of President Kennedy. FOIA has been severely damaged by the 1984 amendments eliminating access to CIA operational files, the 1986 amendments limiting access to law enforcement records, as well as numerous court decisions. FOIA cases remain expensive and lengthy. Harold Weisberg's FOIA lawsuit for documents on the Martin Luther King assassination took 15 years.

The Defense Intelligence Agency claims it has released everything – but recall that, in 1973, Army Intelligence "routinely" destroyed its files. Archivists estimate that more than 50,000 pages are still withheld by the CIA on this case alone. In 1978, after the HSCA ended hearings, it determined that its vast records should be classified "Congressional materials," a category that cannot be touched by the Freedom of Information Act and that keeps them from the public for 50 years.

Watergate hearings examined thousands of hours of White House tapes, yet only 63 hours had been released by February 1996. Nine boxes of documents detailing the role of the "Plumbers" were somehow "lost." The final 340 tapes were released in 2013.

Attorney General John Ashcroft significantly restricted the FOIA policies of former Attorney General Janet Reno. After the 9/11 attack, Ashcroft issued a memo directing DOJ to be mindful of "institutional, commercial, and personal privacy interests, when considering FOIA requests. Senate Judiciary member Patrick Leahy (D-VT) remarked, "These steps are contrary to the spirit of the FOIA confidentiality over all records." Open record laws were rolled back more than three hundred times during the Bush administration, while the pace of classification for federal documents increased markedly.

Reporter Jefferson Morley filed a FOIA lawsuit against the CIA for failing to disclose records about a CIA officer named George Joannides. Joannides was responsible for running DRE, an anti-Castro CIA front group that had numerous interactions with Lee Harvey Oswald in the months leading up to the assassination. The CIA has been legally required by the 1992 JFK Assassination Record Act to release these files. Yet they have consistently refused and neither President Obama nor President Trump have forced the issue.

An article which ran in the *Huffington Post* and Consortiumnews.com 10/20/07, clarified Joannides' role as CIA liaison to the HSCA, as well as DRE's involvement with Oswald.

> Oswald approached the DRE's delegation in New Orleans and offered to train guerrillas to fight the Castro government. He was rebuffed. When DRE members saw Oswald handing out pro-Castro leaflets a few days later an altercation ensured that ended with the arrest of all the participants.
>
> A week after that, the DRE's spokesman in New Orleans debated the Cuba issue with Oswald on a radio program. After these encounters, the DRE issued a press release calling for a congressional investigation of the pro-Castro activities of the then-obscure Oswald.... The secret CIA files on Joannides may shed new light on what, if anything, Joannides and other CIA officers in anti-Castro operations knew about Oswald's activities and contacts before Kennedy was killed.[18]

In 1977-1978, the CIA conveniently chose for agent George Joannides to come out of retirement to serve as their liaison to the HSCA. When two staffers of the HSCA, who had been set up with full access to CIA records pertaining to that period, dug up possible CIA involvement in a plot to kill Kennedy, Joannides had the two staffers removed.

Joannides kept his 1963 activities secret from the HSCA, violating the CIA agreement with the HSCA that no operational officer from the time of Kennedy's assassination would work with the HSCA Chief Counsel Robert Blakely. In 2003 Blakey publicly declared, "I now no longer believe anything the Agency told the committee any further than I can obtain substantial corroboration for it from outside the Agency for its veracity." Blakey later characterized the CIA conduct as a criminal violation of 18 USC 1505 by "impeding the due and proper exercise of power of inquiry... of any committee of either house..." Morley tried to interest the *Washington Post* in the Joannides story but was told that it was "not news."

Morley then joined with FOIA attorney Jim Lesar to sue the CIA for the release of the Joannides records. The limited response revealed that in April and May of 1964, Joannides traveled to New Orleans – the same day that the Warren Commission notified DRE leader Carlos Bringuier that the Commission wanted his testimony. The CIA refused to release 33 other documents on Joannides and planned to keep secret 1,100 JFK assassination records until at least 2017. The Secret Service destroyed records after the ARRB ruled that they were related to the assassination. Overall, of the 318,886 documents in the JFK Act database, 11% have partial redactions, and 3,603 documents are withheld in full, (AARC website).

The ARRB ordered that many records that were initially withheld be disclosed by 2018; however, they were still withheld. Many records containing third-agency information were referred to those agencies for action, which in many cases failed to process the materials. Many Church Committee records that should be in the JFK Records Collection are not. The CIA's file on Eladio Del Valle, a Cuban exile activist leader long suspected of involvement in the assassination, is missing. The collection does not have the audiotapes of communications between the White House and Air Force One after the assassination. The ARRB failed to obtain the records of President Kennedy's personal physician Admiral Burkley, the only doctor present both at Parkland Hospital and Bethesda Hospital. CBS television argreed to donate film outtakes of Kennedy assassination materials, yet no part of its collection has been deposited. NBC has not turned over papers from Walter Sheridan's family. Sheridan worked for

NBC for their special on Jim Garrison and NBC claims ownership. Also, Mexican intelligence on Oswald's visit to Mexico City, which Mexican television reported was shared with the CIA, is still withheld.[19]

CIA officer William Harvey, who created assassination teams through the ZR-RIFLE program, has a 123-page file withheld by the CIA. Regarding David A. Phillips, Chief of CIA operations in Latin America, involved in pre-assassination surveillance of Oswald, and seen with Oswald by Antonio Veciana in September 1963, the CIA retains four files totaling 606 pages. The CIA still holds six files containing 332 pages on E. Howard Hunt. David Morales, a CIA officer who worked with Hunt and Phillips, who reportedly said about the Kennedy assassination, "we took care of that son of a bitch, didn't we" – has a 61-page file which has not been released. CIA officer Anne Goodpastor, who worked closely with David Phillips in Mexico City, and admitted under oath her role in disseminating the tapes supposedly of Oswald's Mexico City calls, has a 286-page file unreleased by the CIA. The CIA holds three files of 222 pages on Birch O'Neal, the CIA officer who ran the counterintelligence keeping closest track of Oswald from 1959 to 1963. About Yuri Nosenko, the KGB officer who defected to the U.S. and claimed to have seen Oswald's KGB flies – the CIA is withholding 2,234 pages of materials.

In July 2013, the Smith-Mundt Act of 1948, which prohibited U.S. propaganda from being aired domestically, was quietly overturned by the 2013 National Defense Authorization Act. New U.S. programming for Voice of America, RFE/Radio Liberty and the Middle East Broadcasting Networks (viewed in more than 100 countries) will be available to the American media. How will this additional national security spin impact ongoing national security reporting? Further, 71% of national security reporters believe that the government is spying on them, based on a 2015 Pew Research Center poll. "As the government stores more and more data, it will become next to impossible for journalists to keep their sources confidential," wrote Geoffrey King of the Committee to Protect Journalists.[20]

In October 2017, the long-awaited release of all of the remaining files, as mandated by the JFK Records Act, showed the government's contempt for the law. The 1992 JFK Records Act states that "each assassination record shall be publicly disclosed in full, and available in the Collection no later than 25 years after the date of this act." Exemptions are allowed only if the President "certifies" that the release of each document will cause identifiable harm to either 1) military defense; 2) intelligence operations.; 3) law enforcement; or 4) the conduct of foreign relations, and the "identifiable harm is of such gravity that it outweighs the public interest in disclosure."

The ARRB Chair, Judge John Tunheim, declared that this material should be released in full. The recommendations from the Mary Ferrell Foundation, the leading JFK assassination archives, seem reasonable: 1) Release all files in their entirety; 2) Require all agencies to provide and publish in the Federal Register explanations for each and every postponed document (or portion of a document) before you certify that all JFK records have been released; 3) Full disclosure of all JFK documents, in particular those 375 which appeared in the 2016 listing but are no longer referenced; 4) The database be updated with the latest information from all government agencies to ensure accountability and public confidence in the disclosure process.

The government declassification of April 26, 2018 still withheld in part 15,834 assassination files, most of them from the CIA and the military, which will not be released until 2021, if then. Nonetheless, from July 2017 to April 2018 more than 35,000 assassination records were released, and for the first time they were made available online. Many cryptonyms were revealed including LIOSAGE for CIA asset Carl Migdail, a journalist for *U.S. News & World Report*, and AMCARBON-3 for Don Bohning, CIA asset and journalist with the *Miami Herald*. Critics rightly note the excessive and undocumented redactions, errors and anomalies with online data, files still "withheld in full," and no system of accountability for releases and the full collection. Jefferson Morley has declared that the JFK Records Act "is being slowly repealed by CIA fiat. In defiance of law and common sense, the Agency continues to spend taxpayers' money for the suppression of history around JFK's assassination…" Even anti-conspiracy authors Gerald Posner and Vincent Bugliosi have sided with the law, calling for the CIA documents to be released.[21]

President Truman's admonition about the political truth versus real truth still resonates. In a time when public trust in government is low, the support within the mass media for political truth increasingly outweighs actual truth. Notions of political truth are facilitated by the social, political, and economic connections of the mass media elites with government and corporate elites. News regarding government incompetence or venality on this case, and by implication mass media cooperation or incompetence, is unlikely to get much mainstream coverage, since it would embolden critics and delegitimize elite power. This loosely defined government-mass media-elite acts in their interest, not the public interest, and is subject to the same social pressures as any group. The drive for power and prestige as well as the fear of social isolation, creates and reinforces elite norms.

Some alternative outlets, like *The Nation*, have highlighted Andrew Cockburn and Noam Chomsky, who viewed President Kennedy as a Cold Warrior, similar to LBJ. Their structural analysis contends that the military-industrial complex has always been in control, thus not much changed after the assassination. *The Nation* editor Max Holland maintains that Jim Garrison was a KGB dupe, even though he has attended political assassination conferences, which have compellingly countered these notions. His work is still found on the CIA website, as well as a cover story for *Newsweek* 11/28/14.

The New Republic rejected its formerly critical approach with a change of publishers in 1968. Other alternative journals are probably picking their battles, considering their limited resources, and particularly after 9/11, the fact that national security issues have changed.

The liberal monthly *Mother Jones* has steadily increased circulation, yet has shown little interest in the case. Oswald was the lone assassin, according to David Corn in an article published November 2013, yet he had confederates.

The alternative journal *Z* is independent left, and generally views conspiracy cases as a distraction from structural analysis of the ruling class. Structuralists view the Republican and Democratic parties as factions in the ruling class, yet the possibility of other significant covert violent splits in the ruling class seem less newsworthy.

Rolling Stone has taken risks to explore the CIA and national security issues. In November 2013 they ran pieces by both Oliver Stone and Robert Kennedy Jr. underscoring JFK's continuous struggle with our military and intelligence agencies. Robert Kennedy Jr. believes President Kennedy's "greatest ambition was to break the militaristic ideology that has dominated our county since WWII."[22]

Since 2000, on-line publishers, such as Salon.com, Consortiumnews.com, and the *Huffington Post*, have printed critical assassination research.

Alternative media organizations, like all organizations, fall prey to what sociologists call "an iron law of oligarchy." All institutions deteriorate into rule by a few of the most ambitious, who consolidate power and information, while justifying it with the supposed norms and values of the institution. Owners, publishers, and senior editors chart the priorities, outside of the view of subscribers and reporters. The alternative media remains weak and divided over what happened in November 1963. Notably, when the upstart journal *Ramparts* (in the mid-1960s) covered political assassination and CIA abuses, its circulation rapidly surpassed the combined circulation of *The Nation* and *The New Republic*. Arguably, the *Village Voice* remained the most intrepid, and increased sentiment for formation of the HSCA.

Mass media caution outweighed the commitment to transparency and accountability regarding the "October Surprise" and Iran-Contra. NSC strategist Gary Sick helped expose the "October Surprise" scandal, where Reagan's top aides secretly negotiated with the Iranians to delay the hostage release until after the 1980 election. Sick was hopeful that this political treachery would be widely explored by the media. He observed, "When confronted with evidence of a systemic attempt to undermine the political system, we recoil in a general failure of imagination and nerve."

Former AP and *Newsweek* reporter Robert Parry, who broke the Iran-Contra story in 1985 only to see the mass media back off of it for a while, observed, "It is as if the final price for winning the Cold War is our confinement to a permanent childhood where reassuring fantasies and endless diversions protect us from the hard truth of our own recent history." This contributes to an American public who, like an adult-child afraid to confront its abusive parents, languishes in cherished myths of the past.

On the 40th year commemoration of the assassination of President Kennedy, Duquesne Law School held a two-day symposium on the assassinations of JFK and MLK, attended by more than a thousand people. The remarkable range of topics and perspectives was exceeded only by the quality of the presenters-physicians, scientists, lawyers, judges, historians, forensic experts, teachers, authors, as well as former HSCA and ARRB members and staff. Senator Arlen Specter, the author of the single-bullet theory, participated on a panel exploring his theory. After twenty minutes of a floundering defense, his aides "notified" him that he had to leave. Although the media were again handed an award-winning series on a platter, they did not cover the conference with any depth. The media did not extend their coverage much for the conference on the 50th commemoration of the Warren Commission Report, either.

The *Boston Globe*, 10/24/14, notably ran coverage by Bryan Bender, "Answers sought on CIA role in '78 JFK probe: Investigators say files could prove interference." HSCA investigator Eddie Lopez asked if still classified records could reveal, as he and some other staffers have alleged, that the CIA interferred and placed committee staff under surveillance. CSPAN 2 distinguished itself by airing the 2014 AARC conference.

The *Washington Post* marked a 50th anniversary of the Warren Report with Philip Shenon's presumptive column "Meet the Respectable JFK Conspiracy Theorists." He found minor errors in the report but agreed that Oswald alone fired three shots. Shenon noted that Warren Commission staffer Charles Shaffer suspects that organized crime might have been involved with Oswald. No HSCA staffers nor assassination researchers were deemed respectable enough to be included.

The American mass media were also handed a "smoking gun" story on the build-up to the Iraq war, "The Downing Street memo," and showed little interest. A British investigative reporter revealed secret memos of discussions involving British intelligence aides with members of Prime Minister Tony Blair's inner circle when the Bush Administration was pushing Britain to support the invasion. Blair's aides were skeptical that they could convince the British public to go to war, but Sir Richard Dearlove, the Chief of MI-6 intelligence unit, assured them that the Bush Administration was busy "fixing the intelligence and facts" in order to develop the rationale for war. Although European journalists ran with the story in the spring of 2005, the American mass media ignored it until Americans who learned of it from the Internet pressured them. It was generally dismissed as "old news." Between May and June 20, 2005, ABC did 121 segments on Michael Jackson, 42 on Natalie Holloway (a missing teenager) and none on the "Downing Street memo." CBS News did 235 segments on Jackson, 70 on Holloway and none on the "Downing Street memo." NBC News ran 109 segments on Jackson, 62 on Holloway and six on the memo. The *Washington Post* editorial page asserted that the memo doesn't prove anything. Coverage of Congressman Conyers' hearing on the "Downing Street memo" was cursory or derogatory, but mainly it was ignored.[23]

In 2008, James Douglass finished arguably the definitive revisionist book on President Kennedy, his foreign policy and the assassination. *JFK and the Unspeakable* was carefully researched and revealed significant new information regarding Kennedy's conflicts with the military and the CIA, as well as his extensive communication in 1963 with the Pope and Khrushchev in pursuing détente. Neither the mass media nor the alternative media reviewed the book. This brings to mind Albert Camus' notion, "Truth is mysterious, elusive, ever to be won anew. Liberty is dangerous, as hard to get along with as it is exciting."

A secular fundamentalism continues to protect the appearance of legitimacy of the government – with sins of omission. The media refrain; "we will never know" has become a self-fulfilling prophesy, which serves to justify their failure to investigate high treason. If high treason is proven, the public would demand a real change in the distribution of power, as well a reinvestigation of the assassinations of Martin Luther King, Jr., Robert Kennedy, the Watergate scandal, the October Surprise, Iran-Contra, the CIA and the drug trade, the 2000 election, 9/11, the wars in Iraq and Afghanistan, Abu Ghraib, the 2008 banking debacle, and the expanding role of the Joint Special Operations Command (JSOC). Cold War cooperation, time-tested news management, concentrated corporate ownership of the mass media, government concerns of political illegitimacy, along with the fear of government repression, and loss of government sources and social status, has fed the sins of greed, and journalistic pride. A lonely Cold War challenge to protect the first amendment in 1953 could be prophetic. The *New York Times* Chief of Staff, John Swinton, castigated the New York Press Club by quoting from Upton Sinclair.

> The business of the journalist is to destroy the truth; to be outright; to pervert; to vilify; to fawn at the feet of mammon, and to sell the country for his daily bread. We are the tools and vassals of the rich men behind the scenes. We are the jumping jacks, they pull the strings and we dance ... we are intellectual prostitutes...

Corporate media has succumbed to the service of American Empire, along with the quest for quarterly profits. Wittingly and unwittingly, the media has in essence rewritten our collective memory on national security. This case is ripe for reexamination, yet the media cooperation from the Cold War continues in the seemingly endless "War on Terrorism." As courtiers for the faltering New Rome they sanction imperial hubris as well as historical amnesia. How long can they bury the leads before they bury democracy? There can be no redemption without political atonement.

The Greeks viewed the goddess Nemesis as giving divine retribution for hubris. Empires reap what their elites and courtiers sow – now shrouded in mass media myth. Shadow elites flourish – being the source of Madison's fears of violent factions in the Federalist Papers #57. Empires fall from within. Decades of unparalled greed, coupled with mass media lies and indifference, contributed to the worst inequality since 1928, endless wars, a dysfunctional government, a broken healthcare system, unprecedented environmental challenges, loss of trust in government and the mass media, and a confused and angry public.. Fertile ground for a demagogue.

In the current fractured media landscape, the bombastic Donald Trump played the populist by fighting the Republican and the Democratic party establishments as well as the mass media. He relied on FOX network, rallies, talk radio, Twitter and social media – aided at times by Vladimir Putin. The "perception management" of the Reagan Administration morphed; "fake news," which had been called "black propaganda," drifted beyond AM radio to FOX News, and reverberated online. Trump constantly condemned the mass media and his opponents as liars, and "The enemy of the people" – while he regularly lies, exaggerates, rapidly changes positions, distracts, threatens and disregards federal agencies, threatens our allies and international agreements, threatens nuclear war, and threatens the constitution. As the noose of the Special Prosecutor began to tighten, Trump proclaimed, "Don't believe the crap you see from these people, the fake news," and "What you're seeing and what you're reading is not what is happening." Dan Rather saw Trump's attacks as "straight out of Orwell."

This stiffened the resolve of the establishment to mobilize the fourth estate to confront a dangerous demagogue. In a seemingly "post-truth era," sourcing and fact checking become even more critical. In an increasingly polarized media landscape, the mainstream media, other than FOX, has belatedly found their critical voice to report Trump's clear and present danger to national security. The FBI and the CIA, weaker and less politicized than in the 1960s, are pressing for accountability and the rule of law to investigate and expose a tyrant – a threat to established factions and democracy. Many active and retired military leaders are also raising blunt criticisms. Again, leaks from intelligence agencies have fueled the mainstream media coverage of Russian collusion in the 2016 election, Russian cyberattacks and the Trump administrations extreme recklessness, unilateralism, and disdain for the rule of law. Again, Bob Woodward tapped his military and intelligence sources to deepen the dialogue on the widening threat to national security.

Let's work to change the media landscape so that the past will not be prologue regarding the brief duration of a vibrant mainstream media after the Trump administration. Trumpism is embedded in the Republican Party, as well as Fox, talk radio, and social media--unlike Nixon's power. Into this unfolding crisis of polarization there is danger and opportunity. In the spectacle of Trump, reality often surpasses satire. Our angry, confused, distrustful, and dispirited public seems distracted by sports, entertainment, social media, and shopping – seeking affirmation more than information – and drifting toward deeper division.

Independent media, local TV, newspapers, and radio, as well as the Internet remain somewhat open to new research. The "legacy media" gatekeepers have lost their monopoly to bury the new fact-pattern on this case. A number of websites provide rich archives with vibrant discussions, including the Mary Ferrell Foundation, JFK Facts, Assassination Archive Resource Center (AARC), Kennedys and King, The Assassination Web, JFK Lancer, Spartacus Education, Black Op Radio, JFK Countercoup, the Real History Archive, and the Mae Brussell Archive. The Poage Legislative Library at Baylor University has an extensive collection and the Mary Ferrell Foundation now has far more documents online than the National Archives. The JFK research community seems to be a citizens' counterintelligence collaboration – which can regain momentum with the recent declassifications amid the political turmoil.

There are a number of steps citizens could take: Congress can be pressed to enforce their previously agreed upon unanimous mandate that disclosure be given urgent attention. Congress can be pushed to follow up the ARRB model for declassification, and to finally declassify the documents regarding the assassination of Martin Luther King, Jr. An amnesty could be declared by the Justice Department in these cases to relieve governmental agents from their oaths of secrecy as well as to free the remaining documents. A congressional investigation into subversion of the HSCA and the JFK Act can be undertaken by the House Committee on Oversight and Government Reform. The most promising movement in these areas is the new Truth and Reconciliation Committee.

Legal action may still be required to release hundreds of thousands of NSA, Secret Service, and military intelligence files which were never submitted to the National Archives. Lingering scientific contention could be clarified by the Lawrence Livermore Lab, which has refused to research the acoustical aspects of this case. And finally, the Kennedy family and other private collections should completely open the remaining papers under their control.

The pursuit of this case is infuriatingly complicated and slow, but to abandon it is to break our faith with the dream of democracy. The Declaration of Independence called on us to pledge "our lives, our fortunes and our sacred honor" to form our nation. This same commitment is needed to re-form our nation.

Thomas Jefferson declared: "I know of no safe depository of the ultimate powers of society but the people themselves; and if we think them not enlightened enough to exercise their control with a wholesome discretion, the remedy is not to take it from them, but to inform their discretion by education."

President John Kennedy's admonition for Eastern Europe through Voice of America in 1962 remains as vital for the American government and mass media today, "We seek a free flow of information.... For a nation that is afraid to let its people judge the truth and falsehood in an open market is a nation that is afraid of its people."

Carved into Robert Kennedy's gravestone at Arlington National Cemetery is an admonition from his favorite playwright, Aeschylus. "He who learns must suffer. And even in our sleep, pain that cannot forget falls drop by drop upon the heart. And in our own despair, against our will, comes wisdom to us by the awful grace of God."

ACKNOWLEDGMENTS

This book began as a dissertation in political science at the University of South Carolina under Dr. Jerel Rosati – but life intervened. I am deeply grateful to Congressman Richardson Preyer for our frank two-hour discussion about the work of the HSCA. I thank my family for their patience and support in this two decades-long effort. Many in the JFK research community have been generous with their time and insights. In particular, I appreciate the encouragement and input from David Starks, Jerry Policoff, Jim Lesar, Jim DiEugenio, Alan Dale, and John Judge. David Starks was very patient in reviewing earlier versions of this manuscript.

I am indebted to colleagues and friends who critiqued my research and focused my organization: Dr. Jerel Rosati, Dr. Leara Rhodes, Bill Heitzman, Rabbi Jeff Ronald, Dan Shanks, Patrick McGaugh, Dr. Jen Heusel, Paul Skolnick, Jackie Kirven, Monte Jackson, and Prof. Dick Puffer.. I am thankful for the rare courage of my publisher Kris Millegan, for his commitment to democracy and the first amendment. Kris introduced me to a careful and encouraging editor, Marian Bussey, who coaxed new clarity to this unexpectedly lengthy book. I am grateful to former students Dorothy McVay and Darlene Del Verde for their patience, typing and editing, to Kelly Ray for proofreading, and my wife, Carole Holloway, for her encouragement.

None of this would have been possible without the efforts of thousands of citizens over decades, as well as many reporters, who painstakingly developed this case – often at great risk. Countless times I referred to remarkable websites – literally online libraries, which are labors of love for democracy – Assassination Archives Resource Center, Mary Ferrell Foundation, Kennedys and King, JFKFacts.org, Spartacus Education, Countercoup2, JFK Lancer, Black Ops Radio, and the Harold Weisberg Archive.

SOURCES & NOTES

1. CRISIS COVERAGE; CONFUSION, COOPERATION AND COVER-UPS

1. MacNeil, Robert. *The Right Place at the Right Time*. (Canada: Little, Brown and Company, 1982), pp. 207-215.
2. Marrs, Jim *Crossfire: The Plot that Killed Kennedy* (NY: Basic Books, 2013) p 9.
3. Hlavach, Laura and Payne Darwin. *Reporting the Kennedy Assassination*. (Dallas: Three Forks Press, 1996) p.97.
4. *Broadcasting* 12/2/63.
5. Trost, Cathy and Bennett, Susan. Newseum. *President Kennedy Has Been Shot*. (Indiana: Sourcebooks, 2003) p. XIV. SA. Herskovitz, Jon. "How the John F Kennedy Assassination Changed Media Coverage Forever" Reuters 1/21/13.
6. Bernstein, Carl. *Rolling Stone*. 10/20/77.
7. Stockwell, John. *Praetorian Guard* p. 123-4.
8. "David, Atlee Phillip, Clay Shaw and Freeport Sulphur." HSCR 221.
9. Stone, Oliver and Sklar, Zachary. *JFK: The Film of the Book*. (NY: Applause Books, 1992). p. 107.
10. Kelly, Bill, Mary Ferrell Foundation website.
11. MacNeil, Robert. *The Right Place at the Right Time*. (Canada: Little, Brown and Company, 1982), p. 208.
12. Newseum. *President Kennedy Has Been Shot*. p. 26.
13. Kelly, Bill 7/11 Committee for Truth about the Kennedy Assassination (CTKA). CIA # 104-10124-10182.
14. 3AH 476; Schwicker-Hart Report p. 34-35.
15. Zelizer, Barbie. *Covering the Body*. (Chicago: University of Chicago Press, 1992) p. 54. Quote of Wilbur Schramm.
16. Newseum *President Kennedy Has Been Shot*. p. 103.
17. *New Republic* 12/21/63.
18. Noyes, Peter. *Legacy of Doubt* (NY Pinnacle Books, 1983). p. 191.
19. Scott, P.D. *Deep Politics and the Death of JFK*. (London, U.C. Press, 1993).
20. Newseum *Coverage of the Assassination of JFK* p. 159-160.
21. *Policoff, Jerry. Village Voice*. 3/31/92.
22. P.D. Scott, *Deep Politics and the Death of J.F.K* p. 270.
23. Jefferson, Morley. Salon.Com 12/17/03.
24. Kritzberg, Connie. *Secrets from the Sixth Floor*. (Tulsa: Undercover Press 1994).
25. Ibid. p 25-26.
26. Ibid. p 25-26.
27. Palamara, Vincent. *Survivors Guilt: The Secret Service and the Failure to Protect President Kennedy*. (Trine Day 2013) p.201.
28. McKnight, Gerald. *Breach of Trust: How the Warren Commission Failed the Nation and Why*. (Kansas: U. of Kansas Press 2005) p 350.
29. Hancock, Larry. *Someone Would Have Talked*. (JFK , Lancer Productions and Publication, 2011.) p. 17.

30. Kritzberg, Connie *Secrets from the Sixth Floor* p. 26-28.
31. Hancock, Larry Ibid. p. 225-226.
32. Curry, Jesse. *JFK Assassination File* 1967.
33. Newseum. *The President Has Been Shot.* p 108.
34. Kantor, Seth. *The Jack Ruby Cover-up.* (NY Zebra Books, 1978)
35. Noyes, Peter. Ibid, p.192.
36. Rather, Dan. *The Camera Never Blinks.* (NY:Marrow Pub. 1977) p 123.
37. Turner, William. *Hoover's FBI.* (Thundersmouth Press, 1993) p. 116, 118.
38. Rather, Dan. The Camera Never Blinks. p.308.
39. Ibid.
40. Horne, Doug. ARRB Interview with Dino Bruglioni (NPIC) 2009, youtube.
41. Janney, Peter. *Mary's Mosaic: The CIA Conspiracy to Murder John F. Kennedy, Mary Pinchot Meyer, and their Vision for World Peace.* (NY: Skyhouse Pub., 2012) p 307-308.
42. CIA Segregated files. Press Coverage, Box 153.
43. Turner, William. *Hoover's FBI.* (Thunder Press, 1993) p. 116.
44. *The Nation* 1/18/10.

2. Cold War Cooperation

1. Olmsted, Katherine. *Challenging the Secret Government.* (N.C. UNC Press 1996) p. 20-22.
2. Lee, Martin and Soloman, Norman *Unreliable Sources* (NY Lyle Stewart, 1991) p105; Knightley, Philip. *The First Casualty - From Crimea to Vietnam: War Correspondent as Hero, Propagandist and Mythmaker.* p. 315.
3. Memorandum of "Establishment of Service of Strategic Information" 6/10/41 William Donovan to President F.D. Roosevelt.
4. Smith, Sally. *In All His Glory The Life and Times of William S. Paley.* (NY: Touchstone, 1990) p. 209-213.
5. Evica, George, *We Are All Mortal.* (Hartford .Com. Press, 1978) p. 206-207.
6. Mitchell, Greg. "Atomic Cover-Up" EXTRA 4/13.
7. Evica, George Ibid.
8. Saunders, Francis S. *The Cultural Cold War: The CIA and the World of Arts and Letters* (NY: The New Press, 2000) p. 41.
9. Mickelson, Sig. *America's Other Voice The Story of Radio Free Europe and Radio Liberty.* (NY: Praeger, 1983) p. 26.
10. Troupbour, John. *Who Rules Harvard.* (Boston: South End Press, 1989), pp. 63- 66.
11. Davis, Deborah. *Katherine the Great* (NY: Harcourt Brace Jovanovich, 1979), p. 138.
12. Ibid. p. 138.
13. Wilford, Hugh. *The Mighty Wurlitzer: How the CIA Played America.* (Cambridge: Harvard Press, 2008) p. 227-228.
14. Ibid. p. 231.
15. Aronson, James. *The Press and the Cold War.* (NY: Bobbs Merrill, 1970) p. 114.
16. Ibid. p 120.
17. Bernstein, Carl. *Rolling Stone* 10/20/77 "The CIA and the Media."
18. Parry, Robert. Consortium News,/ 6/30/97.
19. Jefferies-Jones, Rhondi. *The CIA and American Democracy.* (New Haven: Yale University Press, 1989). pp. 90-95.
20. *Washington Post,* 4/6/73.
21. Senate Intelligence Report, 12/18/75, p. 16.
22. Ibid. p. 138.
23. Johnson, Loch and Wirtz, James. *Strategic Intelligence.* (LA: Roxbury Publishing Co., 2004) p. 255.
24. McBride, Joseph. *The Nation* "Where Was George?" 6/16/88.

25. *New York Times* 12/25/77-12/27/77.

26. *San Francisco Chronicle.* 12/28/77; Probe 3-4/96 Lisa Pease.

27. Wise, David and Ross, Thomas. *The Invisible Government.* (NY: Bantam, 1965) pp. 134-5, 267; Columbia Journalism.

28. *Columbia Journalism Review* July-August 1976. p. 39.

29. Permanent Select Committee on Intelligence, House, 1978 "The CIA and the Media" p. 391-403. Bernstein, Carl. *Rolling Stone* 10/20/77.

30. *Probe.* March/April 1996 Lisa Pease "Manufacturing Reality."

31. Bernstein, Carl. "The CIA and the Media" *Rolling Stone,* October 20, 1977.

32. Ibid.

33. Kreig, Andrew. *Presidential Puppetry.* (DC: Eagle View Books, 2013) p. 48.

34. Gentry, Curt. *J. Edgar Hoover: The Man and the Secrets.* P. 388-389.

35. Kluger, Richard. *The Paper: The Life and Death of the New York Herald Tribune.* p.115.

36. *Probe.* March/April Lisa Pease, 1996 .

37. Merry, Robert. *Joseph and Stewart Alsop; Guardians of the American Century.* (NY: Viking press, 1996) p. 355.

38. Davis, Deborah. *Katherine the Great.* p. 139-150.

39. Halberstam, David. *The Powers That Be.* (NY: Dell, 1979) p. 91, III; Swanberg, W.A. *Luce and His Empire.* (NY: Scribner and Sons, 1972) pp. 181-182.

40. Alterman, Eric. *Sound and Fury.* (Hica, NY Cornell Press, 1999) p. 31-34.

41. Talbot, David. *Brothers.* p. 189.

42. *Penthouse* "The Spies Who Came in From the Newsroom." Joe Trento and Dave Roman 7/19/76.

43. Gans, Herbert. *Deciding What's News.* (NY: Vintage, 1979) p. 272.

44. *Penthouse* 7/19/76. Ibid.

45. Tannenbaum, Robert. *Without Fear or Favor.* (NY: Times Books, 1980) p. 584-5.

46. Catledge, Turner. *My Life and the Times* (N.Y. Harper and Row, 1971) p. 248.

47. DiEugenio, J. and Pease, Lisa. *The Assassinations* p. 337.

48. Ibid.

49. Domhoff, W.A. Jr *The Power Elite and the State.* (NY: Aldinede Gruyter, 1990) pp. 147-148 and Dye, Thomas *Who's Running America.* (NY: Prentice Hall, 1976). p. 88.

50. Mickelson, Sig. *America's Other Voice* p. 124. GAO Report 173239 5/15/72.

51. Bernstein, Carl. Ibid.

52. Smith, Sally. *In All His Glory The Life and Times of William S. Paley and the Birth of Modern Broadcasting.* (NY: Touchstone, 1990) pp. 209-213.

53. Groden, Robert. *The Killing of the President.* p. 202.

54. Friendly, Fred. *Due to Circumstances Beyond Our Control.* (N.Y. Random House, 1967) pp. 216-217.

55. Smith, Sally. op cit. p. 306

56. Horrock, Nicholas. *New York Times* "CIA Ties to Journalists," 1/28/76.

57. Schiller, Herbert. *Mass Communications and American Empire.* (N.Y. Augustus Kelley Publishing, 1969) p. 58.

58. Kelly, Bill. Citizens for Truth about the Kennedy Assassination (CTKA) website 7/11.

59. Choate, Pat. *Agents of Influence.* (NY: Knopf 1990) p. 163.

60. Senate Select Committee on Intelligence Activities, Book II; *CJR* July/August 1976, pp. 39-41.

61. Wise, David. *The Politics of Lying.* (NY: Vintage Books, 1973). p. 200-203.

62. Halberstam, David. *The Powers That Be.* (NY: Dell, 1979) p. 622-626.

63. Ibid., p. 526.

64. Bernstein, Victor and Gordon, Jesse. "The Press and the Bay of Pigs" The Columbia University Forum. Fall 1967.

65. Bradlee, Benjamin. *Conversations with Kennedy* (NY: Pocket Books, 1975).

66. Holbrooks, Richard. Maximsnews.org 5/2/07.
67. Miller, Merle. "Washington , The World and Joseph Alsop," *Harper's*, June 1968.
68. *Time*, 9/30/63; Emory, Michael. *On the Front Lines* (DC: American University Press, 1995), p. 151-152.
69. Ibid., pp. 627-8.
70. Scott, Peter Dale. *Deep Politics and the Death of JFK*. (London: U.C. Press, 1993) p.113.
71. Ibid., p. 114-116.
72. 11 AH 65.
73. Acoca, Miguel and Brown, Robert. "A Plot to Destroy JFK and Invade Cuba." *Soldier of Fortune*, 1975/June.
74. The Joint Chiefs of Staff. 3/13/62. Memorandum for the Secretary of Defense.

3. LBJ's Damage Control

1. President Johnson's phone conversations 11/20/63 - 1/64.
2. Wilford, Hugh. *The Mighty Wurlitzer: How the CIA Played America*. (Hartford Press, 2005) p. 129.

4. While Waiting For The Warren Report

1. Summers, Anthony. *Conspiracy* p.318.
2. Summers, Anthony and Dorrill, Steven. *Honeytrap*. p.269.
3. Palamara, Vince *Survivor's Guilt*. p. 200.
4. Lee, Martin and Soloman, Norman. *Unreliable Sources* p. 119.
5. Scott, Peter Dale. *Politics and the Assassination of JFK* p. 45; FBI Oversight Hearings p. 36-59 and p.124-125.
6. *Editor and Publisher*. 14 December 1963; Zelizer, Barbie. Covering the Body p. 95.
7. Associated Press *The Torch is Passed* (Wester Printing & Lithography Co. 1963)
8. UPI and American Heritage *Four Days*. 1964.
9. Zelizer, Barbie. *Covering the Body*. p. 92.
10. Lane, Mark *A Citizens Inquiry* p. 139.
11. Lynd, S. & Mimms, J. "Seeds of Doubt" *New Republic* 12/21/63.
12. Norden, Eric. *The Minority of One*. Jan. 1964, "The Death of a President.
13. Schonfeld, Maurice. "The Shadow of a Gunman." *Columbia Journalism Review*. July/August 1975.
14. Ibid.
15. Simkin, John. Educational Forum. 3/28/08.
16. WR 127.
17. XXI p. 449-458.
18. XXI p. 456.
19. WCR 647.
20. Kilgallen, Dorothy. *New York Journal-American*. 2/21/64.
21. Ibid.
22. Talbot, David. *Brothers* p. 262-263.
23. Ibid. p.263.
24. Zelizer, Barbie. *Covering the Body*, p. 94.
25. Epstein, Ed, *Inquest* (NY: Bantam Books,1966) p. 19.
26. Winchester, James. "TV's Four Days of History" *Reader's Digest*, April 1964.
27 Emory, Michael. *Time* 9/30/64; *On the Front Lines* p. 151-152
28 Brucker, Herbert. *Saturday Review*. 1/64. "When the Press Shapes the News."
29. Policoff, Jerry. Ibid. *Village Voice*, 3/31/92.
30. *Washington Post* 5/2/64.
31. Lewis, Anthony. *NYT* 6/1/64, "Panel to Reject Theories of Plot in Kennedy's Death"

32 Weisberg, Harold. *Never Again* p. 371.

33. Lane, Mark. *A Citizen's Inquiry* 1966.

34. Noyes, Peter. *Legacy of Doubt*. (N.Y.: Pinnacle, 1973) p. 117-120. Cooper, Marc. *The Nation*. 8/28/96.

35. Kilgallen, Dorothy. *New York Journal-American*. 9/17/64.

36. Kilgallen, Dorothy. *New York Journal-American* 9/30/64.

37. Kilgallen, Dorothy. *New York Journal-American* 9/24/64.

38. Cook, Fred. *The Nation*. 6/22/64.

39. Russell, Bertram. *A Minority of One*. 9/6/64.

5 The Warren Commission-The Noble Lie

1. Gibson, Donald. *Battling Wall Street*. p. 100-101.

2. McKnight, Gerald, *Breach of Trust*. p. 120-121.

3. Ibid. p. 146.

4. Brinkley, Alan. "Minister Without Portfolio," *Harper's* F'1983.

5. Marrs. *Crossfire*. p. 470.

6. "The Secret File of J. Edgar Hoover." *Frontline* PBS, Feb. 1993, written by William Cramer.

7. Bird, Kai. *The Chairman*. (NY: Anson and Shuster, 1992) p. 562.

9. Scott, Peter; Hoch, Paul; Rauftel, Robert. Unpublished *The Dallas Conspiracy*.

10. Gibson, Donald. *Battling Wall Street*. p. 100-101.

11. Wise, David. *The American Police State*. (N.Y. Random House, 1976) p. 244.

12. McKnight, Gerald. *Breach of Trust*. p. 11.

13. *The Men Who Killed Kennedy*. Nigel Turner.(#4) The History Channel. A&E.

14. WCR 645.

15. Meagher, Sylvia *Accessories After the Fact* p. 9-21.

16. 113 WC p. 407.

17. Ibid.

18. Hurt, Henry, *Reasonable Doubt* p.233.

19. Fensterwald, Bernard. *Assassination of JFK*. p. 133.

20. Lane, Mark, *Probable Cause*. p. 68.

21. 8 HSCA 212.

22. WR 180.

23. Summers, Anthony. *Conspiracy* p. 173.

24. Marrs, Jim. *Crossfire: The Plot that Killed Kennedy* (NY Carrol and Graf Pub 1988) p. 478-480.

25. Ibid.

26. Fensterwald, Bernard, *Assassination of JFK*. p. 134.

27. FBI Memo to R. Mohr from C.D. DeLoach file # 62-19060-453.

28. McKnight, Gerald. *Breach of Trust*. p. 17-18.

29. IV p. 51.

30. XIX 507; Vll 105-109.

31. XIX p.524.

32. XIX 524, 526, 541, 528.

33. XIX 530.

34. XIX 516.

35. XIX 543, 505-506, 522.

36. XIX 502.

37. Vll 544-546.

38. Vll n294-295.

39. Vl 297-299.

40. Vll 533-536.

41. Ibid.

42.93 WCH 440-445.

43. Trask, Richard. *Pictures of the Pain* p. 80.

44. McKnight, Gerald. *Breach of Trust* p. 4.

45. Shenon, Phillip. *A Cruel and Shocking Act*. p. 315.

46. Meagher, Sylvia *Accessories After the Fact* p. 107-108.

47. FBI Memo 10/2/63 Jevons to Conrad.

48. Kurtz, Michael. *Crime of the Century*. p. 50-54.

49. Lane, Mark Rush to Judgment. p. 194. The Barry Gray Show radio, 7/19/64.

50. Palamara, Vince, "Boring is Interesting". The Third Decade Jan/March 1992. 7H 107; 6H 312; 7H 535.

51. Ibid.

52. Palamara, Vincent. Survivor's Guilt. p.116-122.

53. Summers, Anthony. *Conspiracy* p.8.

54. Garrison, Jim. *On the Trial of the Assassins*. p.25.

55. Vll HSCA 3m 25.

56. Xll HSCA 60.

57. Summers, Anthony. *Conspiracy* p.357.

58. V HSCA p.206.

59. HSCR pp 369-370.

60. Navasky, Victor. *Kennedy Justice*. p. 53-55.

61. Scott, Peter Dale. *Crime and Cover-Up, the CIA, the Mafia, and the Dallas-Watergate Connection*. Westworks 1977.

62. Douglass, James. *JFK and the Unspeakable*. 6H 7-139

63. Marrs, Jim. *Crossfire* p. 469-471.

64. Crenshaw, Charles. *JFK: Conspiracy of Silence*. p.9. WC 64 p.33.

65. McKnight, Gerald. *Breach of Trust*. p. 137.

66. Ibid. p. 359

67. Hurt, Henry. *Reasonable Doubt*. p. 350 Ibid. 70-71.

68. The History Channel. "The Warren Commission." Roger Mudd. 1999.

69. Senate Select Committee- Report on Intelligence V p. 59.

70. *New York Times*. 2/5/64.

71. Shenon, Philip. *A Cruel and Shocking Act*. p. 22.

72. Ibid p. 328.

73. McKnight, *Breach of Trust*. p. 2-3.

74. Lane, Mark. *Probable Cause*. p. 90.

6. Warren Report Coverage: Mainstream Spin vs. Journalism

1. CIA Propaganda Notes Series A Bulletins 9/22/64. Agency file #000187.

2. Midgely, Leslie. *The Making of the Broadcasts*. p. 201.

3.. Packwood, Herbert. *The Nation*. 11/2/64.

4.. Lane, Mark. *A Citizen's Inquiry* 1969. p. 76.

5.. Orwell, George. *1984*.

6.. Marrs, Jim. *Crossfire*. p. 576. Lane, Mark. *A Citizen's Inquiry*. 1969. p. 76.

7. Kilgallen, Dorothy. *New York Journal-American*. 10/08/64.

8. Craig, Roger. "When They Kill a President" (Manuscript)

9. Meagher, Sylvia. *Accessories After the Fact*. p. 458-459.

10. *The State* (SC) 11/15/64.

11. 11 H 93.

12. XV11. H. 48.

13. Schotz, Martin E. *History Will Not Absolve Us*. (Brookline, Masa.: Kurty, Ulmer DeLuccia,

1996) p. 220-226.

14. Rosati, Jerel. *The Politics of United States Foreign Policy.* 1999 p. 512-513.

15. Kelin, John. *Praise from a Future Generation.* (San Antonio, Wing Press) p. 216.

16. NACA 541 misc 3.

17. Shaw, Mark. *The Reporter Who Knew Too Much.* p. 90.

18. Ibid. p. 114.

19. Ibid. p. 117.

20. Hancock, Larry. *Someone Would Have Talked.* p. 326-327.

21. Talbot, David. *Brothers.* p. 285.

7. Citizens Prod the Press

1. Salandria, Vincent. *A Minority of One.* "A Separate Connally Shot".

2. FBI memo, 6/1/66, generated background on Weisberg and Epstein, Rec. #124 10034-10056.

3. CIA document # 1035-960.

4. *N.Y. Times Book Review,* 7/03/66, by Fred Graham "Whitewash" and "Inquest."

5. Moyers, Bill, *Moyers on America* (NY: Random, 2005) p. 157.

6. Kelin, John. *Praise from a Future Generation.* p.293.

7. Cook, Fred. *The Nation* 6/13/66, 6/20/66.

8. Cohen, Jacob. *The Nation,* 7/11/66, "The Vital Documents."

9. Kelin, John. *Praise from a Future Generation.* p.278.

10. Ibid. p. 320.

11. Schonfeld, Maurice "The Shadow of a Gunman" *Columbia Journalism Review.* July/August 1975.

12. Ibid.

13. Talbot, David. *Brothers.* p. 598.

14. Billings, Dick, Chandler, David, Aynesworth, Hugh and McCombs, Holland "A Matter of Doubt," *Life,* 11/25/66.

15. FBI document #124-10051-10216.

16. Policoff, Jerry. Interview with author, 2016.

17. Policoff, Jerry and Hennely, John. *Village Voice* 1975.

18. Schonfeld, Maurice. *Columbia Journalism Review.* July/August 1975.

19. Ibid.

20. Talbot, David. *Brothers.* p. 308.

21. FBI memorandum 11/18/66 Sullivan to DeLoach Agency file #62-109060-4339

22. Bickle, Alexander. "Reexamining the Warren Report" *The New Republic* 1/767.

23. Lifton, David and Welsh, David. "The Case for Three Assassins" *Ramparts,* 1/67.

24. Lane, Mark. *Rush to Judgment* p. 68-70.

25. Twain, Mark. *A Connecticut Yankee in King Arthur's Court.* p.87.

8. The Garrison Investigation: Confronting Psychological Warfare

1. Garrison, Jim. *On the Trail of Assassins..* p. 114.

2. DiEugenio, Jim. *Destiny Betrayed.* p. 222.

3. *New York Times.* 6/3/67.

4. FBI document 124-10101-10005. 4/4/67.

5. Turner, William. *Hoover's FBI.* p.229.

6. CD 990.

7. Davy, Bill. *Let Justice Be Done.* p. 122.

8. Blum, William. *Killing Hope.* p. 105.

9. Joesten, Joachim. *The Garrison Enquiry: Truth and Consequences.* 1967. p. 100-101.

10. DiEugenio, Jim. *Destiny Betrayed,* p. 164; and Barbour, Jim. "The Garrison Tapes." (Blue Moon 1992).

11. Ibid p. 26.

12. Charles, Roberts. *The Truth About the Assassination* (N.Y. Grosset and Dunlap 1967). p.53.

13. Warren Report p.71.

14. Warren Commission, Decker Exhibit #5323.

15. Roberts, Charles, *The Truth About the Assassination.* p. 57.

16. Garrison, Jim. *On the Trail of the Assassins.* p. 245

17. CIA memo from Lansdale 5/11/62.

18. Barbour Jim. "The Garrison Tapes" . video Blue Moon 1992.

19. DiEugenio, Jim. *Destiny Betrayed* p. 166.

20. Davy, William. *Let Justice Be Done.* (Reston, VA: Jordan Publishing 1999) p. 135.

21. Ibid., p. 247.

22. Schiller, Herbert. *Mass Communication and American Empire.* (N.Y. Augustus Kelley, 1969) p. 56.

23. DiEugenio, Jim. *Destiny Betrayed.* p. 255.

24. Frewin, Anthony. *The Assassination of John F. Kennedy An annotated Film, TV and Videography*, 1963-1992. (Westport, Conn: Greenwood Press 1993). p. 2.

25. Gibson, Donald. *The Kennedy Assassination Cover-up.* p. 165.

26. *Columbia Journalism Review.* 1975.

27. *N.Y. Post* 6/25/67; CBS Press Release 6/29/67, cited in Lane, Mark. *A Citizen's Dissent* p. 98.

28. Kelin, John. *Praise From a Future Generation.* p. 331.

29. Sprague, Richard. *The Taking of America.* pp. 92-93.

30. Lane, Mark. *A Citizen's Inquiry* 1968. p. 89.

31. Pollicoff and Hennelly. *Village Voice* 3/31/92. Lane, M. *A Citizen's Inquiry.*

32. *CBS News Inquiry*, "The Warren Report." Part one. June 25, 1967.

33. Lane, Mark. *A Citizen's Inquiry* 1968. p. 85.

34. Barbour, Jim *The Jim Garrison Tapes.* video Blue Moon 1992..

35 *CBS News Inquiry.* "The Warren Report." 1967.

36. Galanor, Stewart. *Cover-up New York*: Kestral Books 1998 pp. 54-55.

37. WR 97.

38. Sprague, Richard. *The Taking of America.* p. 93.

39. DiEugenio, Jim. *Destiny Betrayed.* 2nd edition. p. 267-269.

40. Livingston, Harrison. *High Treason 2.* (N.Y.: Caroland Graf, 1992) pp. 508-9.; also *St. Petersburg Times* and *Chicago Times* 12/26/91.

41. Associated Press, *The Torch is Passed*, 1967.

42. Mellon, Joan. *A Farewell to Justice.* p. 257.

43. Garrison, Jim. *On the Trail of the Assassins.* p..217.

44. DiEugenio, Jim and Pease, Lisa. *Assassinations.* p. 41.

45. Russell, Dick. *On the Trail of the JFK Assassins.* p. 33.

46. Sprague, Richard. *The Taking of America.* 1-2-3. p. 107.

47. DiEugenio, Jim. *Destiny Betrayed.* p. 186.

48. Schweiker Report p. 80. Evica, George. *We Are All Mortal.* p. 212-213.

49. DiEugenio, Jim. *Destiny Betrayed.* p. 381.

50. Weisberg, Harold. *Whitewash IV.* p. 8.

51. Talbot, David. *Brothers* p. 330.

52. DiEugenio, Jim. *Destiny Betrayed* p. 397.

53. Davy, William. *Let Justice Be Done.* p. 147. Ibid p. 138; CIA memo for file from Lloyd Ray 5/28/68.

54. Ibid. p. 142.CIA document # 1127-987. 7/19/68.

55. Policoff, Jerry. *Village Voice.* 3/31/92.

56. Ibid.

57. Summers, Anthony, *Arrogance of Power.* p. 187.

58. Dye, Thomas. *Who's Running America*. p. 83-84.
59. Scott, Peter Dale. Presentation at COPA Conference Dallas, Texas 11/22/72.
60. Ventura, Jesse. *American Conspiracies* (Skyhouse Press:NY, NY 2010) p. 80-81.
621. Ray, Ellen & Preston, William. *Covert Action* Spring-Summer 1983. "Disinformation and Mass Deception: Democracy as a Cover Story"
62. Ventura, Jesse. *American Conspiracies* p. 82.
63. Weisberg, Harold. *Whitewash IV*. p. 9-10.
64. Orwell, George. "Politics and the English Language" 1946.

9. Post Watergate: Media Retreat and Congressional Investigations

1. Fulbright, J.W. "Fulbright on the Press". *Columbia Journalism Review*. November/December.1975.
2. Greider, W. *Who Will Tell the People?* (NY: Simon and Schuster), p. 297. Olmsted, Kathryn. *Challenging the Secret Government*. p. 27.
3. Policoff, Jerry. *NewTimes*, 8/8/75, "The Media and the Murder of Kennedy".
4. *Ramparts* November 1975.
5. *National Tattler*, November 24, 1974
6. Shenon. Phillip. *A Cruel and Shocking Act*. p. 538.
7. Sprague, Richard. *The Taking of America. 1-2-3*. p. 126. Hersh, Burton. *The Old Boys: The American Elite and the Origins of the CIA*. p. 299, 318.
8. *New York Review* Fensterwald, Bernard, O'Toole, George. 4/3/75. "The Man Who was not Oswald."
9. Debra, Davis. *Katherine the Great*. P.148.
10. Powers, Thomas. P. *The Man Who Kept the Secrets. Richard Helms and the CIA*. 1978. p. 293.
11. *U.S. News & World Report*. 6/2/75.
12. CIA memo 9/19/75. Rogovin to DCI Colby.
13. *New York Times Magazine*. Sept, 1973. James Phalen "The Assassination That Will Not Die."
14. Prouty, Fletcher. *Gallery* 10/75 "The Guns of Dallas."
15. CIA Record #104-10322-10028.
16. Ibid.
17. CBS "The American Assassins" 11/22/75.
18. Anson, Robert. *Washington Post* 11/23/75 "JFK and the CIA: Dallas Revisited."
19. Policoff, Jerry. *New York Times* 12/8/75. "A Critic's View of the Warren Commission Report."
20. Russell, Dick. *Village Voice* 12/8/75. "JFK Assassination Probe: CBS Leaves a Skeptic Skeptical."
21. Meagher, Sylvia. *Accessories After the Fact*. Preface.
22. Prouty, Fletcher. *Gallery* 12/75. "The Fourth Force."
23. Russell, Dick. *Argosy* 4/17.
24. Russell, Dick. *Village Voice*. 4/26/76.
25. CBS *Face the Nation* 9/27/76. Richard Schweiker statement.
26. Mohamed, Frank and Griffin, Ryan. *Huffington Post* 11/20/13. "Senator Who Investigated JFK Assassination: American Journalism News never followed up on that story."
27. PBS *Robert MacNeil Report*- Jim Lehrer 6/24/76.
28. Branch, Taylor. *The New York Times Magazine* "The Trial of the CIA" 9/12/76.
29. Scott, Peter Dale. *The Assassination-Dallas and Beyond*. 1977
30. Morris, Donald. *Houston Post* 12/2/76. "No Cover-up and Oswald's Mexico Visit."
31. Burnham, David. *New York Times* 1/6/77.
32. *Los Angeles Times* 11/7/77.
33. *CBS Evening News* 2/20/77.

34. *Fort-Worth Star-Telegram* 5/11/78.
35. CIA Document 104-10030-10011.
36. Russell, Dick. *On the Trial of the JFK Assassins.* p.51-55.
37. *Washington Post.* 6/21/77.
38. Tannenbaum, Robert. Speech. Duquesne Law School. 11/22/2003.
39. Herman, George. *Face the Nation* 6/27/76.
40. Fonzi, Gaeton. Speech at ASK Conference. Chicago 6/18/93.
41. Bernstein, Carl. *Rolling Stone* 10/20/77. "The CIA and the Media."
42. Anderson, Jack. Merry Go Round column 12/1/77 and 12/10/77.
43. Hinkle, Warren. *San Francisco Chronicle.* 9/12/78.
44. Russell, Dick. *Village Voice* 8/14/78.
45. Baker, Russ. *Family of Secrets* p. 264-266.
46. Marrs, Jim. *Crossfire.* p.22.
47. McKnight, Gerald. *Breach of Trust: How the Warren Commission Failed and Why.* p.379.
48. 1 HSCR p. 528-533.
49. Golz, Earl. *Dallas Morning News.* 11/22/78.
50. Golz, Earl. *Dallas Morning News* 12/19/78. "Witnesses Over Looked. in the JFK Probe."
51. Author's interview with Congressman Richardson Preyer. July 30, 1989.
52. Talbot, David. *Brothers* p.387.
53. *Newsweek* "Rush to Judgment." 1/15/79.
54. Bethell, Tom. "Conspiracies End. *The New Republic.* 9/22/79.
55. Bourdieu, Pierre. *Sociology is a Martial Art.* p.79.
56. Summers, Anthony. *Conspiracy.* p. 153.

10. Commemorative Probe: Then Drifting into History

1. Kreig, Andrew. *Presidential Puppetry* p. 45.
2. Marrs, Jim. *Crossfire* p. 547.
3. Summers, Anthony. COPA Conference 2005.
4. Russell, Dick. *Gallery* 3/81.
5. Nader, Ralph. Multinational Monitor 8/86.. "Reagan's Reign of Secrecy."
6. Lasch, Christopher. *Harper's* 10/83 "The Life of Kennedy's Death."
7. *WSJ* 11/22/83 Ed Epstein. "Who Was Lee Harvey Oswald.7
8. *The Spotlight.* 2/18/85.
9. Nemeth, Lois. *Multinational Monitor.* "Suppressing the Press" 1989.
10. Hurt, Henry. *Reasonable Doubt.* p. 418
11. *Nova* "Who Shot President Kennedy" 11/22/88.
12. *The Kwitny Report* "The Kennedy Report" 11/1/88.
13. Anderson, Jack. American Exposé. Who Murdered JFK?" 11/2/88.
14. KRON-TV San Fransico 11/22/88.
15. *Newsweek,* 11/28/88 "The Kennedy Conundrum.
16. "The Men Who Killed Kennedy" Nigel Turner. 1988. The History Channel. A&E
17. Davis, John. *Mafia Kingfish.* p. 601-606.
18. Parry, Robert. "How the U.S. Press Lost Its Way." Consortium News. 5/15/12.
19. Kreig, Andrew. *Presidential Puppetry.* p. 47.
20. Davis, Deborah. *Katherine the Great.* p. 38.

11. *JFK*: Reactions and Responses

1. Ogelsby, Carl. "Who Killed JFK? The Media Whitewash." *Lies of Our Times.* September 1991.
2. *Washington Post* 5/19/91.
3. "The Men Who Killed Kennedy". Nigel Turner. The History Channel. A&E.
4. Janney, Peter, *Mary's Mosaic: the CIA Conspiracy to Murder JFK.* (NY Skyhorse Press, 2012)

p. 284-285.

5. CBS *48 Hours* 1991.

6. *Beyond JFK - The Question of Conspiracy*. Gobalvision film 1992. Directed by Danny Shecter and Barbara Kopple.

7. Ibid.

8. Crenshaw, Charles. *Conspiracy of Silence* p. 10-17. Parenti Michael. Dirty Truths p. 172-181.

9. *Journal of the American Medical Association*. June, 1992.

10. *Frontline* PBS. 11/17/92. "JFK, Hoffa and the Mob." Produced by Charles Stuart. Written by Charles Stuarrt and Jack Newsfield.

11. LaFontaine, Ray and Mary. *Oswald Talked*. (Gretna, La. Pelican Publishing Company, 1996). p. 78-79

12. HSCR p 606.

13. Tannenbaum, Robert. Political Assassination Conference at Duquesne Law School 2003..

14. Morley, Jefferson. "The Oswald File. Tales of Routing Slips." *Washington Post*. April 1995. DeBrosse, Jim. *See No Evil: The JFK Assassination and the U.S. Media*. (Oregon: Trineday, 2018) p.162.

15. Mailer, Norman. "Why Did Oswald Choose Kennedy."

16. *CBS Sunday Morning*. 9/17/95.

17. Assassination Archives and Research Center Conference 2004.

18. Talbot, David. *Brothers* p. 7.

19. Lane, Mark. *The CIA and the JFK Assassination*. P. 103-113.

20. DiEugenio, Jim. *Reclaiming Parkland*. p. 17.

21. PBS *American Experience* "Oswalds Ghost. 2008."

22. Hougan, Jim. AARC Conference 2004.

23. Bagdikian, Ben. *Media Monopoly* p. 47.

24. *New York Times*, Selling the Story. 7/29/94.

25. Bernstein, Carl. *The New Republic*. 6/8/92.

26. Nichols, John and McChesney, Robert. *Tragedy and Farce*. p. 36.

27. *War Made Easy* 2007 documentary.

28. *Censored 2009* p. 127-129.

29. DeBrosse, Jim. *See No Evil: The JFK Assassination and the U.S. Media*. p. 66-67.

12. Secret Service Security?

1. Talbot, David. *Brothers*. p. 170.

2. Wink, Robin. *Cloak and Gowns* p.289.

3. Stone, Roger. *The Man Who Killed Kennedy: The Case Against LBJ* p 226

4. Douglass, James. *JFK and the Unspeakable*. p. 207.

5. Ibid. p.204.

6. Palamara, Vincent. *Survivor's Guilt*. p. 417-421.

7. Ibid.

8 Waldron, Lamar. *Ultimate Sacrifice*. p. 11.

9 Ibid p. 321.

10. Ibid p.322.

11. Douglass, James. *JFK and the Unspeakable*. p. 217.

12. Palamara, Vincent, *Survivor's Guilt*. p. 140-158.

13. Ibid. p.351; 3 HSCA 357-359, 390-391.

14. Waldron183-185., Lamar. *Ultimate Sacrifice* p. 11.

15. 2H 121; 18 H 711.

16. Palamara, *Vincent. Survivor's Guilt*. p. 237; 7H 521; 3 WH 244; 18 WH 809; 21 WH 571.

17. Palamara, *Vincent. Survivor's Guilt* p.

18. HSCR p. 184.

19. Palamara, Vincent. *Survivor's Guilt* p. 9.
20. Ibid. p. 6.
21. Ibid p.14.
22. 6H 312.
23. 7H 535.
24. Douglass, James. *JFK and the Unspeakable*. p. 250.
25. Ibid.
26. Ibid. 262.
27. HSCR p. 184.
28. Douglass, James. *JFK and the Unspeakable*. p. 263.
29. Palamara, Vincent. *Survivor's Guilt*. p. 201.
30. Palamara, Vincent. *Survivor's Guilt*. p. 136-137..
31. Crenshaw, Charles. *JFK Conspiracy of Silence*. p. 119.
32. Palamara, Vincent. *Survivor's Guilt*. p. 201.
33. Ibid.
34. Sloan, Bill. *JFK; Breaking the Silence*. p. 188.
35. Palamara, Vincent. *Survivior's Guilt*. p. 136-137.
36. Douglass, James. *JFK and the Unspeakable*. p. 266.
37. Ibid. p. 262-264.
38. Palamara, Vincent. *The Not So Secret Service*. p. 168-169.
39. DiEugenio, Jim. *Reclaiming Parkland*. p. 307. Horne, Doug V. 2 p. 649.
40 Prouty, Fletcher, *Gallery* 9/75.
41. HSCA interview with Secret Service AIC John Marshall 2/22/78 RIF #1801007410393.
42. Palamara, Vincent. *Survivor's Guilt*. p. 146.
43 Ibid.

13. The Patsy: Wide Ranging Associations

1. Hurt, Henry. *Reasonable Doubt*. p. 126.
2. Donner, Frank. *The Age of Surveillance* (N.Y. Vintage Press, 1980) p. 188.
3. Johnson, Loch. *America's Secret Power* (Oxford Press 1989) p. 41.
4. Garrison. *On the Trail of the Assassins*. p. 225.
5. Weisberg, Harold. *Whitewash IV* (1967 Self-Published) p. 146.
6. U.S. Congress. HSCA. Vol. 8 p. 143.
7. "The Men Who Killed Kennedy" Nigel Turner "The Forces of Darkness". 1988. The History Channel. A&E..
8. IV HSCA, p. 208.
9. IV HSCA, p. 189-91.
10. Ibid., p. 47.
11. Ventura, Jesse. *They Killed Our President*. p. 69-72.
12. Marchetti, Victor and Marks, John. *The CIA and the Cult of Intelligence* (N.Y.: Alfred A. Knobb 1974).
13. HSCA Final Report p. 249.
14. Janney, Peter. *Mary's Mosaic*. p. 430. Douglas, James. *JFK and the Unspeakable*. p.148.
15. *Dallas Morning News*, 3/30/78. Earl Golz.
16. CD777a.
17. HSCA XIII p. 60.
18. Groden, Robert and Livingstone, Edward. *High Treason*. (Baltimore: The Conservatory Press, 1988.) p. 113.
19. Scott, Peter Dale; Hoch, Paul; Rauftel, Robert. Unpublished *The Dallas Conspiracy*.
20. FBI Document #001193.
21. Hurt, *Reasonable Doubt*. p. 225.

22. HSCA XII, p. 390.

23. Epstein, Edward. *Legend: The Secret World of Lee Oswald*, (NY: McGraw-Hill, 1978) p.121.

24. Melanson, Philip. *Spy Saga*, (NY: Sheridan Square Press, 1990.) p. 86.

25. HSCA XII, p. 60.

26. DiEugenio, Jim. *Destiny Betrayed*. (NY: Sheridan Square Press, 1992) p. 218-219, 104.

27. Garrison. *On the Trail of Assassins*. p. 39.

28. CIA Memorandum 5/1/67, "Memo to Deputy Director for Support".

29. Garrison. Jim . *On the Trail of Assassins*. p. 57.

30. Ibid., p. 43.

31. DiEugenio, Jim. *Destiny Betrayed*. p. 207-8.

32. CIA Memo. # 411-168.

33. Davy, Bill. *Through the Looking Glass*. CIA memo from Chief New Orleans Office to Director DCS 2/6/67 believed to be document #1236-520-A.

34. HSCR pp. 142-145.

35. Lane, Mark. *Plausible Denial* 1991 p. 223.

36. Summers, A. *Conspiracy*. pp. 515-517.

37. Senate Committee on Intelligence Report p. 75.

38. 1 WH 197; Blakey, Robert and Billings, Richard. *The Pilot to Kill the President* (N.Y.: NYT Books, 1981) p.344.

39. HSCR 170.

40. CIA Document #501; 11 WH 348, 357.

41. 10 HSCA Hearings 110.

42. 10 HSCA Hearings 171-2; 5 HSCA Hearings 314, 360-361.

43. Lopez, Ed. Speech at 1993 Midwest Symposium on Assassinations, 4/93.

44. Lopez, Ed. *AARC Quarterly*. "The Mexico City Report" Spring/Summer 1996.

45. McKnight, Gerald. *Breach of Trust*. p. 347.

14. Mafia Connections

1. Scheim, David. *Contract on America*. (New York: Shapolsky Publisher's, 1988) p. 195.

2. Garrison. *On the Trail of Assassins*. p. 224.

3. Hougan. *Secret Agenda*. p. 303.

4. "The Secret File of J. Edgar Hoover." *Frontline* 2/93, written by William Cram.

5. HSCA IX p. 192-194.

6. Warren Report, p. 797.

7. Kantor, Seth. *Dallas Morning News*. 10/12/78.

8. Ventura, Jesse. *They Killed Our President*. p. 143-144.

9. DiEugenio, Jim. *Destiny Betrayed*. 2nd ed. p. 85.

10. Bishop, Jim. *The Day Kennedy Was Shot*. (NY: Harper Perennial, 1968) pp. 591, 627, 631.

11. Davis, John. *Mafia Kingfish*. (N.Y.: Signet Books 1989). pp. 300-1.

12. Navasky, Victor. *Kennedy Justice*. (NY: Antheneum, 1971). pp. 79-81.

13. Stone, Roger. *The Man Who Killed the President*. p. 122.

14. Russo, Gus. *Live By the Sword* p. 414-415.

15. Waldron, Lamar and Hartman, Thom. *Ultimate Sacrifice*. p. 160-161.

15. "Company" Business

1. Loftus, John. *America's Nazi Secret*. (Or.: Trineday, 2011)).

2. Weiner, John. *Legacy of Ashes* (NY: First Anchor, 2008) p. 29-31. Scott, P.D. *Deep Politics and the Assassination of JFK* (London V.C. Press, 1993) p. 12-13.

3. Loftus, John. *Americas Nazi Secret*. p. 170.

4. *Inside the CIA. On Company Business*. Video. Writer and Director Allen Francovich 1979. MPI.

5. Kinzer, Steven. *The Brothers.* (N.Y. Post Books 2013) p. 51. Loftus, John. *Americas Nazi Secret.* (OR Trineday, 2011 p. 170.

6. Bracevich, Andrew. *The Limits of Power.* (Henry Holt, 2009) p. 39-41.

7. Talbot, David. *Brothers.* (Free Press, 2007) p. 44, 97.

8. Smith, Joseph B. *Portrait of a Cold Warrior.* (Putnam, 1976) p. 229.

9. Talbot, David. *The Devils Chessboard.* p. 203, 555. Halberstam, David. *The Fifties.* p. 205 & 553.

10. Hersh, Burton. *The Old Boys.* (NY Charles Scribners Sons, 1992) p. 330.

11. Schlesinger, Steven and Kinzer, Steven. *Bitter Fruit.* (NY Archer Doubleday, 1982) p. 386. Talbot, David. *The Devil's Chessboard* .p.232.

12. Hersh, Burton. *The Old Boys.* p. 386.

13. Hancock, Larry. *Someone Would Have Talked.* p. 17.

14. Ibid p. 34-35.

15. Hersh, Burton. *The Old Boys.* p. 386-387.

16. State Department Cable 11/7/58. Davy, Bill. *Through the Looking Glass.* (Self- published 1995) p. 12. Wyden, Peter. *Bay of Pigs, The Untold Story.* p 1-11.

17. *Probe.* March/April 1996 Lisa Pease "David Atlee Phillips, Clay Shaw and Freeport Sulphur," HSCA notes 8/24/78.

18. Summers, Anthony. *Not in Your Lifetime.*

19. Furiati, Claudia. *ZR-Rifle: The Plot to Kill Kennedy and Castro.* p 73-77.

20. Mellon, Joan. *Farewell to Justice- Jim Garrison, JFK's Assassination, and The Case that Should Have Changed History.* (Potomac Books, 2005) p. 163.

21. Talbot, David. *The Devil's Chessboard.* p. 366.

22. Douglas, James. *JFK and The Unspeakable.* p.212.

23. Newman, John. *JFK and Vietnam* (NY Warner, 1992) p. 9.

24. Chicago Tribune, 6/15/75, as noted by Bill Davy. *Through the Looking Glass.*

25. Hancock, Larry. *Someone Would Have Talked.* (JFK Lancer Productions and Publications, 2010) p. 53-54.

26. Wyden, Peter. *Bay of Pigs: The Untold Story.* p. 10-11.

27. Talbot, David. *The Devils Chessboard.* p. 613.

28. Bracevich, Andrew. *The Limits of Power.* p. 39.

29. Talbot, David. *The Devil's Chessboard.* p. 378.

30. Wise, David, Thomas, Ross. *The Invisible Government.* 208-209. Morley, Jefferson. *Ghost* p. 130.

31. Janney, Peter. *Mary's Mosiac: The CIA's Conspiracy to Murder JFK, Mary Pinchot Meyer and Their Vision for Peace* (NY Skyhorse Press, 2012) p. 372.

32. Pease, Lisa. Presentation at AARC 2014.

33. Talbot, David. *The Devil's Chessboard.* p. 383.

34. Talbot, David. *Brothers.* p. 102-103.

35. Ibid. p. 88.

36. Weismann, Stephen, *Foreign Affairs.* July/August 2014. "What Really Happened in Congo?"

37. Ibid.

38. South African Truth Commission; Williams, Susan. *Who Killed Dag Hammarskjold.* 2001.

39. Wise, David and Ross Thomas. *The Invisible Government;* Cook, Fred. *The Nation.* 6/22/64

40. Talbot, David. *Brothers.* P. 97-99.

41. Janney, Peter. *Mary's Mosiac.* p. 389

42. McKnight, Gerald. *Breach of Faith.* p. 349.

43. Ibid. p. 340.

44. Summers, Anthony. *Conspiracy* p. 149.

45. Davy, Bill. *Through the Looking Glass.* p. 36.

46. Ibid. p. 78.

47. Talbot, David. *Brothers*. p. 237.

48. Garrison, Jim. *On the Trail of Assassins*. p. 37 -38.

49. Scott, Peter D. *Crime and Cover-Ups*. p. 36.

50. Baker, Russ. *Family of Secrets*. p. 120-122.

51. Mickelson, Sig. *America's Other Voice*. p. 62-63.

52. W.C. Interview p. 6-8; Rose, Jerry. *The Third Decade* 1/95. "Plain Talk about Isaac Don Levine."

53. Warren Commission Interviews p. 18-25.

54. HSCA Record # 1801004810108, Agency File # 105-126032 10th NR 92 Sullivan to Belmont, 5/11/64.

55. 2-H 321 and 22H 785.

56. Morley, Jefferson. *Washington Monthly* "The Good Spy," 12/03.

57. McKnight, Gerald. *Breach of Faith*. p. 359.

58. Beschloss, Michael. *The Crisis Years*. P. 682.

59. FBI Memorandum 4/4/67. C.D. DeLoach to Mr. Tolson, # 124-10101-100005. *True Magazine*. April 1975.

60. Johnston, Oswald. *Washington Star News* 10/30/93.

61. Fonzi, Gaeton. *The Last Investigation*. p. 195.

62. WR 364, 20 WH 691.

63. Morley, Jefferson. *Our Man in Mexico*. p. 155.

64. Smith, Joseph. *Portrait of a Cold Warrior*. p. 237.

65. Fonzi, Gaeton. *The Last Investigation*. p. 210.

66. Fonzi, Gaeton. *Gold Coast Magazine*. 11/80.

67. Fonzi, Gaeton. *The Last Investigation*. p. 146-147.

68. Ibid. p. 147.

69. Furiate, Claudia, *ZR Rifle. The Plot to Kill Kennedy and Castro*. (Ocean Press, 1994) p. 130-131.

70. Talbot, David. *Brothers*. p. 385.

71. Hurt, Henry. *Reasonable Doubt*. p. 537.

72. Groden, Robert and Livingston, Harry. *High Treason*. p. 320.

73. Ibid. p. 538.

74. Lane, Mark. *Plausible Denial*.p.202.

75. Hougan, Jim. *Secret Agenda*. p. 3-7.

76. Morrow, Robert. *The Senator Must Die*. (LA Roundtable Pub, 1988) p. 60.

77. HSCR p. 57; Hunt, E.H. *Give Us this Day*. p. 40-51.

78. Kelly, Bill. "Frank Sturgis-Run By U.S. Military not CIA." JFK Countercoup 2. 4/15/13; Calhoun, Jack. *Gangsterisms. vs. Cuba and the Mafia. 1933-1966*. (OR Books, 2013) p. 226.

79. Lane, Mark. *Plausible Denial*. p. 147.

80. Summers, Anthony. *Arrogance of Power*. p. 198.

81. Feldstien, Mark. *Poisoning the Press*. p. 280-286.

82. Haldeman, Robert. *Ends of Power*. p. 38-39.

83. Ventura, Jesse. *They Killed Our President*. p. 85-86; Nixon, Richard. *Nixon Memoirs*. p. 634.

84. CIA Documents # 104-10124-10012; 104-10124-10057; 104-10124-10008.

85. Ventura, Jesse. *They Killed Our President*. p. 88-89.

86. Haldeman, Robert. *Ends of Power*. p. 40-43.

87. Ibid. p. 66-67.

88. Turner, Nigel. *The Men Who Killed Kennedy*. Video #4.

89. Groden, Robert. *High Treason*. p. 290.

90. Colodny, Len and Gettlin, Robert. *Silent Coup*. (NY: St. Martins Press, 1991) p. 211-212.

91. Talbot, David. *Brothers* p. 403.

92. McBride, Joseph. *The Nation*. "Where was George?" 6/16/88.

93. McGehee, Ralph. *Deadly Deceits*. p. 87.

94. Prouty, Fletcher. *Gallery*, 12/15/75, "The Fourth Force."

95. Douglass, James. *JFK and The Unspeakable*, p.266.

96. Hancock, Larry. *Someone Would Have Talked*. p. 196.

97. Janney, Peter. *Mary's Mosaic*. p. 382.

98. Di Eugenio, Jim. *Destiny Betrayed* 2 ed. p. 98-100. Hancock, Larry *Some Would Have Talked*. p. 320-321.

99. Blakey, Robert. In an addendum to the web page for the Frontline episode "Who was Lee Harvey Oswald?"

100. Talbot, David. *The Devil's Chessboard*. p. 620. Morley, Jefferson. *The Ghost*. p. 124. Summers, Anthony. *Conspiracy* . p.266. Blunt, Malcolm & Dale, Alan. JFK Lancer NID 2017.

101. Mellon, Joan. *A Farewell to Justice*. (Wash: Potomac Books 2005) p. 162.

16. Military Cooperation?

1. Beschloss, Michael. *May-Day: Eisenhower, Khrushchev and the U-2 Affair* (Harper Collins, 1986) p. 153.

2. Douglass, James. *JFK and the Unspeakable*. p.86.

3. Talbot, David. *Brothers-The Hidden History of the Kennedy Years*. p. 45-46.

4. Ibid. p. 150.

5. Bracevich, Andrew. *The Limits of Power*. (Henry Holt, 2009) p. 49.

6. Ibid. p. 50.

7. Reeves, Richard. *Portrait of Camelot*. (Abrahams 2010) p. 182.

8. Ibid. p. 103.

9. Talbot, David. *Brothers*. p. 69.

10. Reeves, Richard. *Portrait of Camelot*. p. 104.

11. Talbot, David. *Brothers*. p. 70.

12. Reeves, Richard. *President Kennedy: Pride of Power*. p. 222.

13. Kennedy, Robert Jr. *Rolling Stone* 11/20/13.

14. Bamford, James. *Body of Secrets*. p. 67.

15. Janney, Peter. *Mary's Mosaic*. p. 246.

16. Reeves, Richard. p. 401-402.

17. Stone, Oliver and Kuznick, Peter. *The Untold Story of the U.S.* (Gallery Press, 2012) p. 309.

18. Reardon, Steven. *Council of War*. p. 229.

19. Khrushchev, Nikita *Khrushchev Remembers*. p. 551-552.

20. Fay, Paul. *The Pleasure of His Company*. (Popular Library, 1966)

21. Talbot, David. *Brothers*. p. 172.

22. Ibid. p. 211.

23. Reardon, Steven. *Council of War*. p. 229.

24. Prouty, Fletcher. *Gallery*, "Secret Team." p. 146-147.

25. Reardon, Steve. *Council of War*. p. 281.

26. Mellon, Joan. *A Farewell to Justice*. p.162.

27. Salandria, Vincent. Kelly, Bill and Horne, Doug. MFF.

28. Nelson, Phillip. *LBJ the Mastermind of the JFK Assassination*. (Skyhorse Pub, 2013) p. 432.

29. Curry, Jesse. *Assassination File*. 1967.

30. Scott, P.D. *Deep Politics* p. 245. ; EWR 246.

31. Baker, Russ. *Family of Secrets*. p. 410. Talbot, David. *The Devil's Chessboard*. p. 540.

32. Mellon, Joan. *Our Man in Haiti*. 142-143.

33. 17 WH 495; 17 WH 780-784.

34. WCD # 354.

35. Baker, Russ. *Family of Secrets*. p. 410.

36. WCD 329 57-58.

37. Conway, Debra. JFK Lancer 2001.

38. 5 WH 57.

39. WCD 329 57-58.

40. WCD 386 SS 1058.

41. Palamara, Vince. "The Third Alternative". Kelly, Bill. JFK Countercoup.blogspot.com 2013. COPA 2/12/13 "Oswald's ONI Records Revisted".

42. Russell, Dick. *The Man Who Knew Too Much*. 1992.

43. Russell, Dick. *High Times* August 1996; Escalante, Fabian. JFK and the Cuba Files p. 114.

44. Hopsicker, *Daniel Barry and the Boys: The CIA the Mob and America's Secret History*. p. 170-171.

45. Weisberg, Harold. *Never Again*. p. 286. Affidavit of Leonard Saslaw, PhD. 5/15/96 AARB MD 74.

46. Ventura, Jesse, *They Killed Our President*. p. 303.

47. Marvin, Daniel, Rose, Jerry, *The Third Decade*. January 1998.

48. Palamara, Vince. *The Third Decade*. May 1998.

49. Mary Ferrell Foundation.website. ARRB MD 178; HSCA p. 21 and 33; AARB MD 230. (An internal CBS memo published by the ARRB Humes told a CBS employee that a photo was taken of the body with a probe in it. ARRB MB 16; CBS memo 1/10/67 Richter to Midgeley. Rex Bradford. COPA conference 2004.

50. Turner, Nigel. *The Men Who Killed Kennedy*. The History Channel. part 6, 1994. Marvin, Daniel. *Expendable Elite* p. 314-317.

51. Douglass, James. *JFK and the Unspeakable*. (Orbis, 2008).

52. Talbot, David. *Brothers*. p. 148.

53. Hougan, Jim. *Secret Agenda*. p. 75.

54. Saunders, Harold. *Foreign Affairs*. July/August 2014. "What Really Happened in Bangladesh?"

55. Feldstein, Mark. *Poisoning the Press*. p. 187-189.

56. Weiner, Tim. *Legacy of Ashes*. p. 374-376.

57. Woodward, Bob, Bernstein, Carl. *All the President's Men* p.23.

58. CIA files.

59. Colody, Len and Locker, Ray Bob Woodward's Secret-Shouldn't He Have Disclosed It? HNN 6/12. Pease, Lisa *Probe* 1996.

60. Colody, *Silent Coup*. Gettlin 1991. p.163.

61. Ibid.

62. Ulasewicz, Anthony, *The President's Private Eye*. 1990.

63. Agnew, Spiro. *Go Quietly-Or Else*. (Morrow 1980) p. 189-190.

64. CIA Memo 3/1/73.

17. LBJ:

1. McClelland, Barr. *Blood, Money and Power: How LBJ Killed JFK* (Hannover House, 2003).

2. Stone, Roger. *The Man Who Killed Kennedy*. p. 206.

3. Bruno, Jerry, and Greenfield, Jeff. *The Advance of Man*, (NY: William Morrow and Company, 1971) p. 82.

4. Ibid., p. 83.

5. Zirbel, Craig. *The Texas Connection*, (Scottsdale, Arizona: The Texas Connection Pub. 1991) p. 193.

6. Ibid., 254.

7. Nelson, Phillip *LBJ: The Mastermind of the JFK Assassination* (NY: Skyhorse Pub. 2013) p. 412.

8. Hancock, Larry. *Someone Would Have Talked*. (Lancer Pub . 2010) p. 3/6.

9. "The Men Who Killed Kennedy". Nigel Turner. "The Guilty Men" History Channel. A&E. 2003.

10. North, Mark. *Act of Treason*, (NY: Carroll and Graf, 1991), p. 400.

11. Rowe, Robert. Bobby Baker Story, (NY: Parallax Pub. 1967), p. 87; North, Mark. *Act of Treason* p. 417.

12. Baker, Russ. *Family of Secrets*. p. 215.

13. Zirbel, Craig. *The Texas Connection,* p. 256. Abe Fortas coordinated the investigation from the White House.
14. *The Men Who Killed Kennedy.* Nigel Turner. #7 The History Channel. 1997 (Comment by Walt Brown); Cram, William. "The Secret File of J.E. Hoover. Video. Frontline. 2/93. Cram, William. "The Secret File of J. E. Hoover". Video, Frontline, 2/93.
15. Brands, H.W. *Foreign Affairs,* Sept/Oct 2012. "Robert Caro and LBJ."
16. Kearns, Doris. *Lyndon Johnson and the American Dream.* (New York: Signet, 1976) p. 108.

18. Foreign Policy Changes - Detente Delayed

1. Bowles, Chester. *Promises to Keep: My Years in Public Life* (N.Y.: Harper & Row, 1971) p. 439.
2. DiEugenio, James. *Destiny Betrayed* 2nd edition. p. 159.
3. Douglass, James. *JFK and the Unspeakable* p 212.
4. Stone, Oliver and Kuznick, Peter. *The Untold History of the United States.*
5. Blum, William. *CIA Killing Hope*(N.Y.: Zed Books, 1990) p. 164-170.
6. Mahoney, David. *Ordeal in Africa* 1983., DiEugenio, James *Destiny Betrayal* 2nd ed; Rakove, Robert.
7. Newman, John *JFK and Vietnam.* 2008 p. 381.
8. *The Nation* 3/14/05.
9. Prados, John. *President's Secret Wars.* (NY: William Morrow, 1986) p. 171-2.
10. Newman, John. *JFK and Vietnam.* p. 228.
11. Stone, Oliver and Kuznick, Peter. *The Untold History of the United States.*p. 315.
12. Newman, John. *JFK and Vietnam.* p. 228.
13. Prouty, Fletcher. *Secret Team* 1973. p. 274.
14. Ibid. p. 280.
15. McNamara, Robert. *In Retrospect,* (N.Y.: Random House, 1995).
16. *Probe.* March/April 1998. Jim DiEugenio.
17. Oglesby, Carl. *The JFK Assassination.* p. 67.
18. Ellsberg, Daniel. *Rolling Stone* 12/6/83.
19. DiEugenio, Jim. *Destiny Betrayed.* p. 253; Blumenthal, Sidney and Yazijian, Harvey *Government by Gunplay* (N.Y.: New American Library, 1976) p. 166.
20. Douglass, James *JFK and the Unspeakable.* p. 305.
21. Scott, Peter, Dale, Hoch; Paul and Stetler, Russell. *The Assassinations: Dallas and Beyond* (N.Y.: Vintage Books, 1976) p. 406-415.
22. Newman, John. *JFK and Vietnam.* (N.Y.: Warner, 1992) p. 67.
23. McGehee, Ralph. *Deadly Deceits.* p. 140.
24. Gibson, Donald *Battling Wall Street.* p.36; "Foreign Aid" House Documents 87th Congress 1st session doc. #117.
25. Fortune. March 1963.
26. Gibson, Donald. *Battling Wall Street.* p. 261; Wall Street Journal 10/5/63.
27. Gibson, Donald. *Battling Wall Street.* p. 264. 10/03/63 Talbot, David *The Devil's Chessboard.* P. 556.
28. Ibid, p. 264.
29. *Wall Street Journal* 10/31/63. Prins, Nomi *All the Presidents Bankers.*
30. Ibid. Prins, Naomi. *All the President's Bankers* p. 245.
31. Ibid, p.246.
32. *National Review.* "R.I.P." 12/10/63.
33. Cochrane, James. *Journal of Latin American Studies* 4. 11/72 "U.S. Policy towards Recognition of Governments". Talbot, David *The Devil's Chessboard.* P. 557.
34. LaFabre, Walter. Inevitable Revolutions. p. 157; CIA Survey of Latin America 4/1/64 enclosed in Cline to Bundy 4/17/64 NSC Country file Latin America, Container, Lyndon

Johnson Library.

35. Scott, Peter. *Deep Politics*. p. 124.

36. Prins, Nomi. *All the President's Bankers* p. 264, Gibson, Donald. *Battling Wall Street*. p. 78

37. Talbot, David. *Brothers* p. 181.

38. World Book Group: Tends in Developing Countries (Washington D.C. 1973.

39. Talbot, David. *Brothers* p. 189.

40. Kornbluh, Peter. *The Nation* 4/29/13. "U.S.-Cuban Diplomacy".

41. LaFabre, Walter. *Inevitable Revolutions*. p. 158-9.

42. Patterson. Thomas. *Kennedy's Quest for Victory*. p.228.

43. Standing Group on Brazil, "Proposed Short-Term Policy for Meeting of Standing Group on Brazil, Folder 10/1-1/15/63. In Patterson *Kennedys Quest for Victory* p. 120.

44. Gibson, Donald. *Battling Wall St*. p. 89.

45. Douglas, James. *JFK and the Unspeakable* p. 258-259.

46. Gibson, Donald. *Battling Wall St*. p 81.

47. Blum, William. *CIA Killing Hope* p. 244.

48. Interview with Dr. Loch Johnson 1991.

19. Reflections

1. Nowell-Newman, *The Spirit of Silence*. p. 42.

2. Morley, Jefferson. Speech at COPA Conference 2009.

3. Talbot, David. *Brothers* p. 393.

4. *Project Censored. 2007* p. 345.

5. Kreig, Andrew. Justice Integrity Project. 3/14/15.

6. *Columbia Journalism Review* "Money Lust" July 1998.

7. McChesney, Robert and Nichols, John *Tragedy and Farce*. p 36-37.

8. Ibid.

9. Moyers, Bill *Moyers on America: A Journalist and his Times* p. 147.

10. Bennett, Lance W. *News The Politics of Illusion* (University of Chicago 2007) 8th ed.

11. Sullivan, Margaret. *New York Times*. 2/6/13.

12. Rather, Dan. *BBC News Night* 11/25/01.

13. Abrams, Rebecca. *Press for the Truth: The Media and 9/11*. Video. 2006.

14. DiEugenio, Jim. *Reclaiming Parkland*. p. 332-360.

15. "The American Ruling Class. 2007 director John Kirby Koch Entertainment.

16. CNN *Reliable Sources* interview with Carl Bernstein, 3/2/14.

17. Sanford, Unger. *Columbia Journalism Review*. "Unnecessary Secrets" March/April 2011.

18. Jefferson, Morley. *Huffington Post* and Consortiumnews.com 19/2007.

19. Lesar, Jim. Assassination Archive Resource Center Conference, Washington, DC. 2014..

20. Common Dreams. 2/5/15.

21. Pease, Lisa. Consortuimnews.com 10/02/07.

22. Stone, Oliver and Kennedy, Robert Jr. *Rolling Stone* 11/13.

23. McChesney, John and Nichols, Jon. *Tragedy and Farce*. 2007. p.78-84.

BIBLIOGRAPHY

Books

Agnew, Spiro. *Go Quietly--Or Else*. (N.Y. Morrow, 1980).

Alterman, Eric. *Sound and Fury The Making of the Punditocracy* (Ithica: Cornell Univ. Press, 1999).

Anson, Sam. *They've Killed the President*. (N.Y. Bantam 1975).

Aronson, James. *The Press and the Cold War*. (NY: Bobbs Merrill, 1970).

Associated Press. *The Torch is Passed*. (Western Printing & Lithography Company, 1963.)

Baker, Russ. *Family of Secrets*. (NY: Bloomsbury Press, 2005).

Bamford, James. *Body of Secrets: Anatomy of the Ultra-Secret National Security Agency* (N.Y. Doubleday, 2001).

Belin, David. *Final Disclosure*. (Macmillan Publishing).

Bennett, W. *Lance: The Politics of Illusion*. 6th ed. (Chicago: U of Chicago Press 2004).

Bennett, Lance, Lawrence, Regina, Livingstone, Steven. *When the Press Fails* (Chicago: U. of Chicago Press)

Beschloss, Michael. *May-Day: Eisenhower, Krushchev and the U-2 Affair* (N.Y. Harper Collins, 1986).

Bird, Kai. *The Chairman*. (NY: Anson and Shuster, 1992).

Bishop, Jim. *The Day Kennedy Was Shot*. (NY: Harper Perennial, 1968).

Blakey, Robert and Richard Billings. *The Pilot to Kill the President*. (N.Y.: NYT Books 1981).

Blum, William. *The CIA: A Forgotten History*. (London: Zed Books, Ltd., 1986).

Blum, William. *Killing the Hope*. (Monroe, Maine. Common Courage Press, 1995).

Blumenthal, Sidney and Harvey Yazijian. *Government by Gunplay*. (N.Y.: New American Library, 1976).

Bourdieu, Pierre. *Sociology is a Martial Art* (NY: The New Press, 2010)

Bowles, Chester. *Promises to Keep: My Years in Public Life*. (N.Y.: Harper & Row, 1971).

Bracevitch, Andrew. *The Limits of Power*. (NY: Holt, 2009)

Bruno, Jerry, and Jeff Greenfield. *The Advance Man*. (NY: William Morrow and Company, 1971).

Byden, Peter. *Bay of Pigs: The Untold Story*.

Calder, Michael. *JFK vs. CIA* (L.A. : West L.A. Publishers, 1998).

Catledge, Turner. *My Life and the Times*. (N.Y. Harper and Row, 1971).

Chernow, Ron. *The House of Morgan*. (N.Y.: Touchstone Simon and Schuster, 1990).

Choate, Pat. *Agents of Influence*. (NY: Knopf, 1990).

Clark, Thurston. *JFK's Last Hundred Days*. (NY: Penguin, 2013)

Colodny, Len and Robert Gettlin. *Silent Coup*. (NY: St. Martins Press, 1991).

Crenshaw, Charles. *JFK Conspiracy of Silence*. (NY: Signet, 1992).

Curry, Jesse. *JFK Assassination File*. (self published, 1969.)

Davis, Deborah. *Katherine the Great*. (NY: Harcourt Brace Jovanovich, 1979).

Davis, John. *Mafia Kingfish*. (N.Y.: Signet Books, 1989).

Davy, Bill. *Through the Looking Glass*. (self published 1995).

Davy, William. *Let Justice Be Done*. (Reston VA: Jordan Publishing, 1999).

DeBrosse, Jim. *See No Evil: The JFK Assassination and the U.S. Media.* (Oregon: Trineday, 2018).

DiEugenio, Jim. *Destiny Betrayed.* (NY: Sheridan Square Press, 1992).

DiEugenio, Jim. *Destiny Betrayed 2nd Edition.* (NY: Sheridan Press, 2012).

DiEugenio, Jim. *Reclaiming Parkland* (N.Y. Skyhorse Publishing, 2013).

Domhoff, W.A. *The Power Elite and the State.* (NY: Aldine De Gruyter, 1990).

Donner, Frank. *The Age of Surveillance.* (NY: Vintage Press, 1980).

Douglas, James W. *JFK and the Unspeakable.* (NY: Orbis, 2008).

Douglas, William. *Holocaust or Hemispheric Co-op.* (NY: Vintage, 1971).

Dye, Thomas. *Who's Running America.* (NY: Prentice Hall, 1976).

Escalante, Fabian, *JFK The Cuba Files-The Untold Story of the Plot to Kill Kennedy,* 2006.

Emory, Michael. *On the Front Lines.* (Washington DC: American University Press, 1995).

Epstein, Edward. *Inquest.* (N.Y.: Bantam, 1966).

Epstein, Edward. *Legend: The Secret World of Lee Oswald.* (NY: McGraw-Hill, 1978).

Epstein, Edward. *News From Nowhere.* (NY: Random House, 1973).

Evica, George Michael. *We Are All Mortal.* (Hartford: U. Conn. Press, 1978).

Feldstin, Mark. *Poisoning the Press* (NY: FSG, 2010).

Fensterwald, Bernard, Jr. *Assassination of JFK by Coincidence or Conspiracy?* (N.Y. Kensington Pub., 1977).

Flammonde, Paris. *The Kennedy Conspiracy.* (NY: Meredith Press, 1969).

Fonzi, Gaeton. *The Last Investigation.* (N.Y.: Thunder Mouth Press, 1993).

Frewin, Anthony. *The Assassination of John F. Kennedy. An Annotated Film, TV and Videography – 1963-1992.* Westport, Connecticut: Greenwood Press 1993).

Friendly, Fred. *Due to Circumstances Beyond Our Control.* (N.Y.: Random House, 1967).

Furiati, Claudia. *ZR Rifle: The Plot to Kill Kennedy & Castro.* (Melborne, Australia: Ocean Press, 1994).

Galanor, Stewart. *Cover-up.* (New York: Kestral Books, 1998).

Gans, Herbert. *Deciding What's News.* (NY: Vintage Press, 1979).

Garrison, Jim. *On the Trail of Assassins.* (N.Y.: Sheridan Square Press, 1988).

Gates, Gary P. *Air Time The Inside Story of CBS News.* (N.Y.: Harper and Row, 1978).

Gentry, Curt. J. Edgar Hoover: *The Man and the Secrets.* (NY: Norton, 2001).

Gibson, Donald. *Battling Wall Street.* (NY: Sheridan Square Press, 1995).

Gibson, Donald. *The Kennedy Assassination Cover-up.* (San Diego Progressive Press, 2014).

Goodman, Amy & Goodman, David. *Static* (N.Y. Hyperion, 2006).

Greenberg, Bradley and Parker, Edwin (eds.). *The Kennedy Assassination and the American Public.* (Palo Alto, Stanford, 1965).

Groden, Robert and Edward Livingstone. *High Treason.* (Baltimore: The Conservatory Press, 1988).

Groden, Robert. *The Killing of the President.* (Penguin Pub. 1993).

Groden, Robert and F. Peter Model, *JFK: The Case for Conspiracy.* (Manor Books, 1975).

Halberstam, David. *The Powers That Be.* (NE: Dell Publishing, 1979).

Haldeman, Robert. *Ends of Power.*

Hancock, Larry. *Nexus the CIA and Political Assassination* (JFK LancerProductions and Publications, 2011).

Hancock, Larry. *Someone Would Have Talked.* (JFK LancerProductions and Publications, 2010).

Hersh, Burton. *The Old Boys.* (NY: Charles Scribner's Sons, 1992).

Hilsman, Roger. *To Move a Nation.* (N.Y. Dell Publishing, 1964).

Hlavach, Laura and Payne, Darwin. *Reporting the Kennedy Assassination.*

Hogan, Michal. *A Cross of Iron* (Camgridge UK: Cambridge U. Press, 1998) (Dallas: Three Forks Press, 1996).

Hopsicker,David. *Barry and the Boys: the CIA, The Mob and America's Secret History* (Eugene, Oregon, Mad Cow Press, 2001).

Hougan, James. *Secret Agenda*. (New York: Random House, 1984).

Hunt, E. H. *American Spy My Secret History in the CIA, Watergate and Beyond*. (NJ: John Wiley and Sons, 2007).

Hurt, Henry. *Reasonable Doubt*. (N.Y.: Henry Holt and Company, 1985).

Issacs, Jeremy and Downing, Taylor *Cold War: An Illustrated History 1945-1991* (NY: Little & Brown & Co. 1998)

Janney, Peter. *Mary's Mosaic. The CIA Conspiracy to Murder JFK, Mary Pinchot Meyer, and Their Vision for World Peace*. (NY: Skyhorse Press, 2012)

Jefferies-Jones, Rhondi. *The CIA and American Democracy*. (New Haven: Yale Press, 1989).

Joestin, Joachim. *The Garrison Inquiry*. (Peter Downay ,1967).

Johnson, Loch. *America's Secret Power*. (NY: Oxford Press, 1989).

Johnson, Loch and Wirty, James. *Strategic Intelligence: Windows Into a Secret World*. (LA: Roxbury Publishing Co., 2004).

Jones, Penn. *Forgive My Grief. Vol 1-4* self-published.

Kantor, Seth *Who was Jack Ruby* (Everest House, 1978).

Karnow, Stanley. *Vietnam: A History.*(Viking Press, 1983)

Kearns, Doris. *Lyndon Johnson and the American Dream*. (New York: Signet, 1976).

Kelin, John. *Praise from a Future Generation- The Assassinations of John F. Kennedy and First Generation Critics of the Warren Report*. (San Antonio: Wings Press, 1964).

Kinzer, Stephen. *The Brothers* (N.Y. Post Books, 2013).

Kitano, Harry. *Race Relations*. (N.Y. Prentice-Hall, 1986).

Knightley, Philip *The First Casualty - From Crimea to Vietnam: War Correspondent as Hero, Propagandist and Mythmaker*. (NY: Harcourt, Brace, Javonich, 1975).

Kreig, Andrew. *Presidential Puppetry*. (Washington D.C.: Eagle View Books, 2013).

Kritzberg, Connie. *Secrets from the Sixth Floor Window*. (Tulsa: Undercover Press, 1994).

Khrushchev, Nitika. *Khrushchev Remembers*. (Little Brown and Co., 1970).

Kurtz, Michael. *Crime of the Century*. (Knoxville: University of Tennessee Press, 1982).

LaFabre, Walter. *Inevitable Revolutions. LaFontaine, Ray and Mary. Oswald Talked The News Evidence in the JFK Assassination*. (Gretra, La: Pelican Publishing Co., 1996).

Lane, Mark. *A Citizen's Dissent*. (NY: Holt, Rinehoart , Winston, 1968)

Lane, Mark. *Plausible Denial*. (NY: Skyhorse Pres, 2011).

Lane, Mark. *Last Word: My Indictment of the CIA in the Murder of JFK*. (NY:Skyhorse Pub. 2011).

Lee, Martin and Norman Soloman. *Unreliable Sources*. (NY: Lyle Stewart Publishing , 1991).

Levine, D. I. *Eyewitness to History*. (NY: Hawthorne, 1973).

Livingston, Harrison. *High Treason II*. (N.Y.: Caroland Graf, 1992).

Loftus, John. *America's Nazi Secret*. (Ore: Trineday, 2011).

Lundberg, Ferdinand. *America's 60 Families*. (N.Y.: Vanguard Press, 1951).

Luskin, John. *Lippmann, Liberty and the Press*. (Alabama: University of Alabama, 1972).

Macneil, Robert. *The Right Place at the Right Time*. (Canada: Little Brown and Company, 1982).

Marchetti, Victor and John Marks. *The CIA and the Cult of Intelligence*. (N.Y.: Alfred A. Knobb, 1974).

Marrs, Jim. *Crossfire – The Plot that Killed Kennedy*. (New York: Carrol and Graf Publishers, 1990.).

Marvin, Daniel. *Expendable Elite: One Soldiers Journey Into Covert Warfare*. (Ore. Trine Day, 2006)

Matthews, Chris. *Jack Kennedy Elusive Hero* (NY Simon and Schuster, 2011).

McCoy, A. *The Politics of Heroin in Southeast Asia*. 1972.

McGaffin and Knoll. *Scandal in the Pentagon*.

McGehee, Ralph. *Deadly Deceits*. (NY: Basic Books, 1993).

McKnight, Gerald. *Breach of Trust: How the Warren Commission Failed the Nation and Why*. (Uof Kansas Press, 2013)

McNamara, Robert. *In Retrospect*. (N.Y.: Random House, 1995).

Meagher, Sylvia. *Accessories After the Fact*. (N.Y.: Bobbs Merrill, 1967).

Melanson, Philip. *Spy Saga*. (NY: Sheridan Square Press, 1990).

Mellon, Joan. *A Farewell to Justice.* (Potomac Books, 2005)

Mellon, Joan. *Our Man in Haiti. George de Mohrenschildt and the CIA in the Nightmare Republic* (Or.:TrineDay, 2013)

Mickelson, Sig. *America's Other Voice. GAO Report 173239 5/15/72.* (NY: Praeger, 1983).

Morley, Jefferson. *The Ghost The Secret Life of CIA Spymaster James Jesus Angleton.* (NY: St. Martin's Press 2017).

Morrow, Robert D. *The Senator Must Die* (L.A.: Roundtable Pub. 1988).

Mosley, Leonard. *Dulles: A Biography of Eleanor, Allen and John Foster Dulles and their Family Network.* (N.Y.: Dell Publishing,1978).

Moyers, Bill. *Moyers on America* (NY Random House, 2005).

Navasky, Victor. *Kennedy Justice.* (NY: Antheneum, 1971).

Nelson, Phillip. *LBJ: The Mastermind of the JFK Assassination.* (NY Skyhorse Pub 2013).

Newman, John. *JFK and Vietnam.* (N.Y.: Warner, 1992).

Newman, John. *Count Down to Darkness. The Assassination of President Kennedy. Vol. 2.* (N. Charleston: Independent Publishing. 2017)

Newman, John. *Oswald and the CIA.* (Skyhorse, 2008)

Newseum with Trost, Cathy and Bennett, Susan. (Indiana: Sourcebooks, 2003).

Nichols, John & McChesney, Robert. *Tragedy and Farce.* (NY: The New Press, 2005)

Nowell Newman, Elizabeth. *The Spiral of Silence 2nd Ed.* (Chicago: v, of Chicago Press,1993)

North, Mark. *Act of Treason.* (NY: Carroll and Graf, 1991).

Noyes, Peter. *Legacy of Doubt.* (NY: Pinnacle Books, 1973).

Oglesby, Carl. *The JFK Assassination - The Facts and the Theories.* (NY: Pengiun 1992)

Olmsted, Kathryn. *Challenging the Secret Government.* (N.C.: UNC Press, 1996)

Palamara, Vincent. *Survivors Guilt. The Secret Service and the Failure to Protect President Kennedy.* (Trine Day, 2013)

Parenti, Michael. *Dirty Truths.* (SF: City Lights, 1996).

Patterson, Thomas. *Kennedy's Quest for Victory-American Foreign Policy 1961-1963.* (Oxford Press, 1990).

Prados, John. *President's Secret Wars.* (NY: William Morrow, 1986).

Prins, Nomi. *All the President's Bankers.* (NY: Nation Books, 2014).

Prouty, Fletcher. *Secret Team.* (Elizabeth Prouty, 2008).

Prouty, Fletcher. *JFK- The CIA, Vietnam, and the Plot to Assassinate John F. Kennedy.* (N.Y. Skyhorse Pub. 2009).

Rather, Dan. *The Camera Never Blinks.* (N.Y.: Morrow, 1977).

Reardon, Steven. *Council of War. A History of the Joint Chiefs of Staff 1942-1991.* (Military Bookshop 2012).

Reeves, Richard. *President Kennedy: Profile of Power.* (NY: Simon and Schuster, 1993)

Richard Reeves. *Portrait of Camelot* (Abrams, 2010).

Roberts, Charles. *The Truth About the Assassination* (N.Y. Grosset and Dunlap 1967).

Rosati, Jerel. *The Politics of United States Foreign Policy* (NY: Harcourt, Brace, Jovanovich, 2003).

Rowe, Robert. *Bobby Baker Story.* (NY: Parallax Pub. 1967).

Russell, Dick. *On the Trail of the Assassins. A Ground Breaking Look at America's Most famous Conspiracy.* (N.Y. Skyhorse Publishing, 2008).

Russo, Gus. *Live By the Sword: The Secret War Against Castro and the Death of JFK.* (Bancroft Press 1998)

Salandria, Vincent. *Survivors Guilt- The Secret Service and the Failure to Protect President Kennedy.* (Oregon: Trineday Pub 2013)

Scheim, David. *Contract on America.* (New York: Shapolsky Publisher's, 1988).

Schiller, Herbert. *Mass Communications and American Empire.* (NY: Augustus Kelley Publishing, 1969).

Schlesinger, Stephen and Stephen Kinzer. *Bitter Fruit.* (Garden City, NY: Archer/Doubleday 1982).

Schotz, Martin E. *History Will Not Absolve Us* (Brooklin, Mass.: Kurtz, Ulmer & DeLuccia, 1996).

Scott, Peter, Paul Hoch, and Robert Rauftel. Unpublished. *The Dallas Conspiracy.*

Scott, Peter Dale, Paul Hoch and Russell Stetler. *The Assassinations: Dallas and Beyond* (N.Y.: Vintage Books, 1976)

Scott, Peter Dale. *Deep Politics and the Death of JFK.* (London: U.C. Press, 1993).

Scott, Peter Dale. *Crime and Cover-up, the CIA, the Mafia, and the Dallas-Watergate Connection.* Westworks 1977.

Seldes, George. *Lords of the Press.* (NY: Julian Mussner, Inc., 1938).

Shaw, J. Gary. *Cover-up.* Self-published, 1976.

Shaw, Mark. *The Reporter Who Knew Too Much.* (Port Hill Press, 2016)

Shenon, Phillip. *A Cruel and Shocking Act: The Secret History of the Kennedy Assassination.* (NY: Henry Halt, 2013).

Smith, R. Harris. *OSS. The Secret History of America's First CIA* (London: V of Cal Press, 1972).

Smith, Sally B. *In All His Glory The Life of William S. Paley.* (NY: Touchstone, 1990).

Sprague, Richard E. *The Taking of America 1-2-3.* (Self-Published, 1976).

Steinberg, Alfred. *Sam Johnson's Boy.* (NY: McMillan, 1968).

Stockwell, John. *The Praetorian Guard.* (Boston: South End Press, 1991).

Stone, Oliver and Zachary Sklar. *JFK: The Book of the Movie.* (NY: Applause Books, 1991).

Stone, Oliver and Kuznick, Peter. *The Untold History of the United States.* (NY Gallery Books, 2012)

Stone, Roger. *The Man Who Killed Kennedy: The Case Against LBJ.* (NY Skyhorse Publishing, 2013)

Summers, Anthony. *Conspiracy.* (New York: McGraw-Hill, 1981).

Summers, Anthony, and Dorrill, Steven. *Honeytrap.* (London: Hodder and Stoughton, 1988).

Summers, Anthony. *Not in Your Lifetime.* (NY Open Road. 1998).

Swanberg, W.A. *Luce and His Empire.* (NY: Scribner and Sons, 1972).

Talbot, David. *Brothers The Hidden History of the Kennedy Years.* (NY: Free Press, 2007)

Talbot, David *The Devil's Chesslboard: Allen Dulles, the CIA, and the Rise of America's Secret Government* (NY: Harper Collins, 2015).

Theoharis, Athan and John Stuart Cox. *The Boss.* (NY: Bantam Books, 1990).

Thompson, Josiah. *Six Seconds in Dallas.* (Bernard Geis Associates,1967).

Trask, Richard. *Pictures of the Pain.* (Mass: Yeoman Press, 1994).

Trento, Joseph. *The Secret History of the CIA.* (Roseville, Ca: Prima Publishing 2001)

Troupbour, John. *Who Rules Harvard.* (Boston: South End Press, 1989).

Turner, William. *Hoover's FBI.* (N.Y.: Thunders Mouth Press, 1993).

Ventura, Jesse. *American Conspiracies* (NY: Skyhorse Publishing, 2010).

Ventura, Jesse. *They Killed Our President. 63 Reasons to Believe There was a Conspiracy to Assassinate JFK* (NY: Skyhorse Publishing, 2013).

Waldron, Lamar & Hartman, Thom. *Ultimate Sacrifice* (NY Carroll & Graf, 2006).

Weiner, Tim. *Legacy of Ashes.* (NY First Anchor, 2008).

Weisberg, Harold. *Post Mortem.* (MA: Mary Ferrell Foundation, 2007).

Weisberg, Harold. *Whitewash IV.* (1967 Self-Published).

Wilford, Hugh. *The Mighty Wurlitzer How the CIA Played America.* (Cambridge: Harvard Press, 2008)

Wise, David. *The American Police State.* (N.Y. Random House, 1976).

Wise, David. *The Politics of Lying: Government Deception, Secrecy and Power.* (NY: Vintage Books, 1973).

Wise, David and Thomas Ross. *The Invisible Government.*

Wofford, Harris. *Of Kennedy's & Kings: Making Sense of the Sixties.* (N.Y.: Farrar, Strauss, Gorovy, 1980).

World Book Group. *Trends in Developing Countries.* (Washington D.C., 1973).

Wyden, Peter. *Bay of Pigs: The Untold Story.* (NY: Simon and Schuster, 1979).

Zelizer, Barbie. *Covering the Body.* (Chicago: University of Chicago Press, 1992).

Zirbel, Craig. *The Texas Connection.* (Scottsdale, Arizona: The Texas Connection Pub. 1991).

Documents

WH and WR refer to the Hearings and Report of the Warren Commission (1964), HSCH and HSCR refer to Hearings and Reports of the House Select Committee on Assassinations (1979), and WCE to Warren Commission Exhibits and WCD to Warren Commission Documents.

Videos

"American Assassins, The" CBS Evening News, CBS News 25-26 November 1975.

Barbour, Jim. "The Garrison Tapes", video (Blue Moon - 1992) Interview with Mark Lane.

"Beyond JFK - The Question of Conspiracy", Gobalvision film 1992. Directed by Danny Shecter and Barbara Kopple.

CBS News Inquiry. "The Warren Report, Part one". June 25, 1967.

CBS *48 Hours*, 1991.

Cramer, William. "The Secret File of J. Edgar Hoover", *Frontline*. PBS. February 1993.

NOVA 1988, "Who Shot JFK?".

Inside the CIA: On Company Business. Writer and Director Allan Francovich, 1979. MPI.

Turner, Nigel. "The Men Who Killed Kennedy". The History Channel; A & E Network 1993.

Turner, Nigel. "The Men Who Killed Kennedy - The Truth Will Set You Free". A & E Network 1995.

Charles, Stuart and Newfield, Jack "JFK, Hoffa and the Mob". 11/17/92 and 3/22/94. Produced by Charles Stuart.

CBS Reports "Who Killed JFK? The Final Chapter", 1/22/93.

PBS *American Experience* "Oswald's Ghost" 2008.

Press For The Truth: 9/11. Paul Thompson. 2006.

The History Channel "The Warren Report" Roger Mudd 1999.

Speeches

Feinman, Roger "40th Anniversary of the Warren Report." Duquesne Law School, 2004.

Fonzi, Gaeton, HSCA investigator. Speech, 4/93, Chicago at the Midwest Assassination Symposium.

Fonzi, Gaeton. Speech at The Second Research Conference of the Third Decade, 6/18/93.

Hougan, Jim."40th Anniversary of The Warren Report" Duquesne Law School, 2004.

Morley, Jefferson. ."40th Anniversary of The Warren Report" Duquesne Law School, 2004.

Lopez, Ed. "Speech at 1993 Midwest Symposium on Assassinations". 4/93.

Websites

History Matters JFK

Mary Ferrell Foundation

Lancer JFK

Assassination Archives Resource Center (AARC)

JFK Facts

Kennedys and King

Black Op Radio

Spartacus Education WhoWhatWhy JFK

Index

O